W9-BMF-119

Laboratory Manual

Computer Service and Repair

A Guide to Upgrading, Configuring, Troubleshooting, and Networking Personal Computers

Richard M. Roberts

Publisher
The Goodheart-Willcox Company, Inc.
Tinley Park, Illinois
www.g-w.com

Copyright © 2008

by

The Goodheart-Willcox Company, Inc.

Previous editions copyright 2005, 2003

All rights reserved. No part of this work may be reproduced, stored, or transmitted in any
form or by any electronic or mechanical means, including information storage and retrieval
systems, without the prior written permission of
The Goodheart-Willcox Company, Inc.

Manufactured in the United States of America.

ISBN 978-1-59070-858-3

1 2 3 4 5 6 7 8 9 – 09 – 13 12 11 10 09 08

The Goodheart-Willcox Company, Inc. Brand Disclaimer: Brand names, company names, and illustrations for products
and services included in this text are provided for educational purposes only and do not represent or imply endorsement
or recommendation by the author or the publisher.

The Goodheart-Willcox Company, Inc. Safety Notice: The reader is expressly advised to carefully read, understand,
and apply all safety precautions and warnings described in this book or that might also be indicated in undertaking the
activities and exercises described herein to minimize risk of personal injury or injury to others. Common sense and good
judgment should also be exercised and applied to help avoid all potential hazards. The reader should always refer to the
appropriate manufacturer's technical information, directions, and recommendations; then proceed with care to follow
specific equipment operating instructions. The reader should understand these notices and cautions are not exhaustive.

The publisher makes no warranty or representation whatsoever, either expressed or implied, including but not limited to
equipment, procedures, and applications described or referred to herein, their quality, performance, merchantability, or
fitness for a particular purpose. The publisher assumes no responsibility for any changes, errors, or omissions in this
book. The publisher specifically disclaims any liability whatsoever, including any direct, indirect, incidental, consequential,
special, or exemplary damages resulting, in whole or in part, from the reader's use or reliance upon the information,
instructions, procedures, warnings, cautions, applications, or other matter contained in this book. The publisher assumes
no responsibility for the activities of the reader.

Copyright by Goodheart-Willcox Co., Inc.

Table of Contents

Copyright by Goodheart-Willcox Co., Inc.

Chapter 4

Chapter 5

Chapter 6

Chapter 7

Chapter 8

Chapter 9

Chapter 10

Chapter 11

Chapter 12

Copyright by Goodheart-Willcox Co., Inc.

Copyright by Goodheart-Willcox Co., Inc.

Introduction

This lab manual is designed to give you the basic skills necessary for success in PC repair, upgrade, and support. The order of the labs matches the chapter sequence of the textbook, *Computer Service and Repair*. It is important to complete each lab to the best of your ability. Illustrations and screen captures have been added as necessary to assist you throughout the series of lab activities.

The A+ Certification exams developed by CompTIA are designed to test persons with PC support and repair experience. The object of this lab manual is to teach you those skills necessary for the exams and more. The exams are written to test people with approximately six or more months of experience with PCs. Those individuals must also prepare for the examination by classroom instruction in PC theory and operation. These lab activities simulate real-life jobs, and will provide you with the hands-on experience needed to pass the A+ Certification exams.

Let's go over some conventions that will help you understand the information presented in this lab-textbook. There are certain screen images that you will be referred to, such as dialog boxes, menus, radio buttons, and check boxes. Look at the illustrations that follow as the information about each type of interface element is covered. This terminology is the same for all of Microsoft's software products, and most of Microsoft's products are similar in design. In other words, many times it will be difficult to distinguish between a Windows 98, XP, or Vista edition of the software. Even other operating systems have the look and feel of the classic Windows design.

A menu is a displayed list of commands that you choose from. Look at the following figure. This is the **View** menu from the Explorer window. Notice that the commands are grouped according to function and are separated by faint gray lines, called command separators.

View	Favorites	Tools	Help

Toolbars ▶
✔ Status Bar
Explorer Bar ▶

Thumbnails
Tiles
● Icons
List
Details

Arrange Icons by ▶

Choose Details...
Customize This Folder...

Go To ▶
Refresh

✔ Standard Buttons
✔ Address Bar
Links

✔ Lock the Toolbars
Customize...

Copyright by Goodheart-Willcox Co., Inc.

Sometimes you will see a bullet in front of a command. The bullet indicates a default setting. You can select a different default setting by clicking another command within the same command separators. For example, to change the default Explorer window display from list to details, click **Details**. The bullet will now be in front of the **Details** command. When bullets are used to indicate a default setting, only one command within the command separators can be selected. Sometimes, a default setting is indicated by a check mark. When check marks are used to indicate a default setting, more than one command within the command separators can be selected. An arrowhead to the right of a command indicates that pointing to the command will reveal a submenu.

A dialog box requires some type of input. The following dialog box is used to properly shut down Windows. This is the **Shut Down** dialog box, which is similar in design in all Windows products starting with Windows 95, except for Windows Vista.

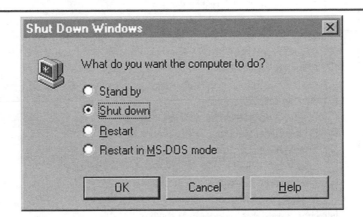

The Windows Vista shut down options are presented as commands in the **Start** menu as shown in the following figure. Notice that Windows Vista offers several different options compared to those in previous versions of Windows.

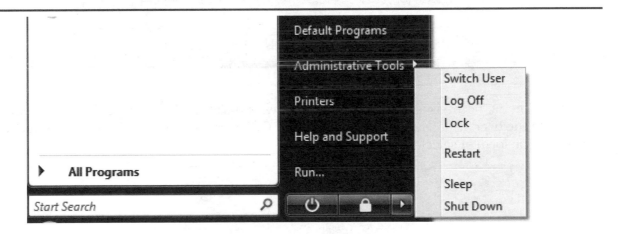

Dialog boxes display options with radio buttons or check boxes to the left of the option. Radio buttons are used when only one option is allowed. You cannot pick two items. If two or more items can be chosen, a check box is used. With check boxes, multiple items can be selected. See the following figure.

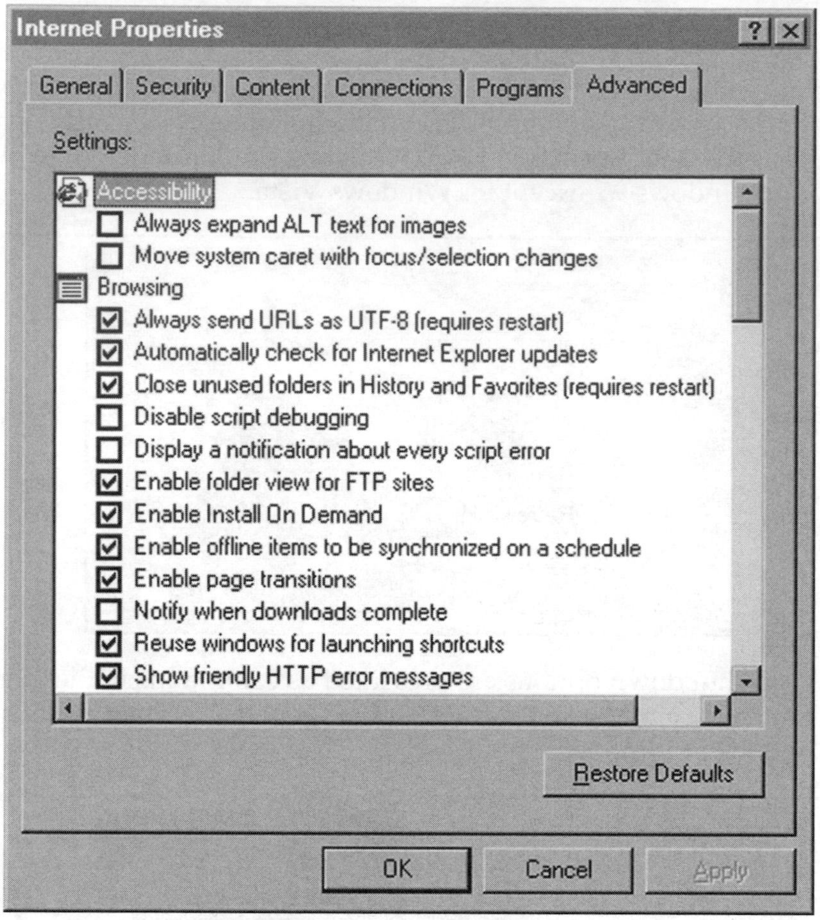

The following figure is an example of a Windows message box. A message box communicates a message to the user, usually when an error occurs. Often a message box will offer the user various options in the form of selectable buttons.

Copyright by Goodheart-Willcox Co., Inc.

Some dialog boxes contain various types of control buttons and text boxes. Look at the Windows **Date/Time Properties** dialog box in the following illustration.

At times you will be instructed to open a certain file or program. Rather than fill the pages with pictures of menus and dialog boxes, a simple notation will be given. For example, when you are requested to open the accessories file and activate the Paint program, you will see **Start | Programs | Accessories | Paint**. This serves as an abbreviated set of instructions of how the task can be accomplished. You can use other methods, such as clicking icons and folders until you reach the program and run it, but the previous notation style is used throughout this lab manual and the accompanying textbook. Microsoft and most professional journals also use it.

Windows XP and Windows Vista operating systems are used for the lab activities in this Laboratory Manual. If time permits and both operating systems are available, the lab should be performed in both operating systems. When a feature is unique to either Windows XP or Windows Vista, then only that operating system is used in the lab. For these labs, "Windows XP" or "Windows Vista" is part of the title of the lab to indicate the specific operating system the lab was written for. Also, the operating systems appropriate for each lab activity are mentioned in the Equipment and Materials section.

Again, I must emphasize the importance of completing each of the lab activities.

Using This Manual

Each lab activity begins with a number of learning objectives. These are the goals you should accomplish while working through the activity. In addition to the objectives, each lab activity contains an Introduction section, which presents a brief description of the lab and, in some cases, an overview of the required theory.

Following the Introduction, you will find an Equipment and Materials list. This list provides a general guideline for the material requirements of the activity. Most of the activities in this manual can be completed with Microsoft Windows XP and Windows Vista. If a lab activity requires a particular operating system, the name of that operating system appears in the title of the lab. Lab

Copyright by Goodheart-Willcox Co., Inc.

activities that do not include an operating system name in the title can be completed with Windows XP, Windows Vista, or both.

The Procedure sections of the lab activities provide step-by-step instructions for completing the labs. You should read through the entire lab activity, including the Procedure section, before beginning a lab. If you have any questions about the requirements or procedures involved with the lab, ask your instructor for help. Some lab activities require you to enter information in the Procedure section. These are not test questions, but simply opportunities to record information about the computer you are using. Often, this information will be required in later steps in the activity.

The final part of each lab activity is the Review Questions. These questions were written to make you think about the material presented in the activity. Not all questions can be answered simply by reading through the lab. Some questions require you to deduce the answer using the knowledge you have gained from working through the exercise. Other questions require you to consult outside sources. Such questions force you to use your new knowledge, reinforcing it.

As you read this text, you will also notice that certain words or phrases stand out. Filenames, such as notepad.exe, student.txt, and io.sys, appear in a Roman sans-serif typeface. Internet addresses also appear in Roman sans-serif, such as www.g-w.com. In this manual, any time you direct the computer to perform a function, whether by entering a line of text at the command prompt or clicking an element in the GUI, it is considered a command. Commands, such as **dir C:** or **Start | Programs | Accessories | System Tools**, are set in bold sans-serif typeface.

Be sure to read any Notes or Warnings that you encounter. Such features may alert you to an act that may damage your computer or cause you injury. Losing all of your data is the most common danger you will encounter with computers. You may also encounter some dangerous voltages, especially when dealing with monitors. Those repairs should be left to special technicians.

The lab activities that appeared in the *Computer Service and Repair* textbook are reprinted in this manual in write-in form. These lab activities are nearly identical to their counterparts in the textbook. The following is a list of the end-of-chapter labs in the textbook and the corresponding lab activity in this manual.

Lab Name	Textbook	Lab Manual
Part Identification	Chapter 1	Lab Activity 1
Installing Windows Vista	Chapter 2	Lab Activity 4
Identifying PC BIOS and Operating Systems	Chapter 3	Lab Activity 21
Installing a Pentium 4 Processor	Chapter 4	Lab Activity 25
Exploring and Replacing the Power Supply	Chapter 5	Lab Activity 28
Viewing RAM and Virtual Memory Information	Chapter 6	Lab Activity 29
Windows Vista Keyboard Properties	Chapter 7	Lab Activity 34
Display Properties	Chapter 8	Lab Activity 36
Typical ATA (EIDE) Hard Drive Installation	Chapter 9	Lab Activity 37
CD/DVD Drive Installation	Chapter 10	Lab Activity 45
Installing a Printer	Chapter 11	Lab Activity 46
Wireless Ad-Hoc Installation and Configuration	Chapter 12	Lab Activity 50
Modem Installation	Chapter 13	Lab Activity 53
Virus Test Software	Chapter 14	Lab Activity 57
Advanced Boot Options	Chapter 15	Lab Activity 61
Installing and Configuring a PCI Network Adapter	Chapter 16	Lab Activity 71
Creating a Network Share in Windows XP	Chapter 17	Lab Activity 74
IP Address Verification with IPCONFIG	Chapter 18	Lab Activity 77
Using the Windows XP Network Setup Wizard	Chapter 19	Lab Activity 81

Copyright by Goodheart-Willcox Co., Inc.

General Safety Procedures

1. Before opening a computer's case, turn off all power to the PC and accessories and unplug the power cord from the outlet.

2. Before working on the computer, discharge static electricity by touching an unpainted, metallic surface. Paint is an insulator, and may prevent a static discharge from the body.

3. Do not touch pin connectors on chips or other components. Pins can be easily bent. Also, when a person touches something, the oils in the person's skin leave a residue, which can hinder a low-voltage electrical connection.

4. Leave parts in their anti-static bags until the parts are needed. When you are done with the parts, return them to the anti-static bags. Do not leave parts on work surfaces or on the PC case.

5. Handle all board-mounted components, such as DIMMs, by the edges. Do not touch bare edge connectors or electrical leads on the board.

6. Never unplug or connect any device while power is applied to the PC. Unplugging a component, such as the hard drive, while power is applied can seriously damage the component.

7. Never open a monitor. A typical monitor can hold an electrical charge in excess of 20,000 volts, even long after the power to the unit has been cut off. In general, a PC technician does not service any parts found inside a computer monitor.

Copyright by Goodheart-Willcox Co., Inc.

Copyright by Goodheart-Willcox Co., Inc.

Name _____ Date _____

Class/Instructor _____

Part Identification

After completing this laboratory activity, you will be able to:
- Identify major motherboard components.
- Identify common motherboard ports.

Introduction

In this lab activity, you will learn to identify the major components inside a typical PC. You will be asked questions throughout the lab activity that will later be reviewed in your classroom as an instructor-lead activity. Answer all questions to the best of your ability. Short answers are acceptable. Do *not* remove any of the major components or disconnect any of the wiring connections during this activity. This is strictly a visual identification exercise. You may use your textbook to help you identify the components.

Equipment and Materials

- Anti-static wrist strap.
- Pen or pencil and notebook paper.
- Basic PC tool kit.

Procedure

1. ____ Report to your assigned PC for this activity.

2. ____ Answer the following question:

   Is the assigned PC a desktop model or a tower? _____

3. ____ Note if each of the following components are in your computer.

   ____ Floppy disk drive.

   ____ CD drive.

   ____ DVD drive.

4. ____ Look at the back of the case and identify the types of port access for the computer. You may use the following figure to help you identify common ports.

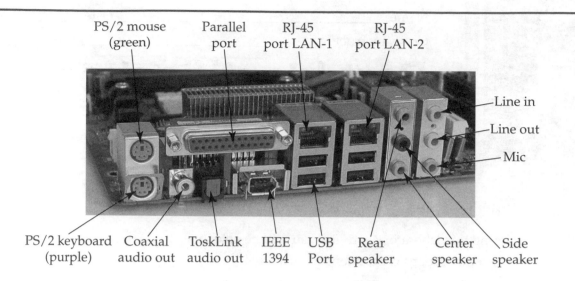

PS/2 mouse (green)   Parallel port   RJ-45 port LAN-1   RJ-45 port LAN-2   Line in   Line out   Mic

PS/2 keyboard (purple)   Coaxial audio out   ToskLink audio out   IEEE 1394   USB Port   Rear speaker   Center speaker   Side speaker

5. ____ Sketch and identify, in the space provided or on a separate sheet of paper, each of the following ports:

- VGA, DVI, or S-Video connection port to the monitor.
- RJ-11 telephone modem connection.
- RJ-45 network connection.
- PS/2 mouse.
- PS/2 keyboard.
- Parallel port.
- Serial port.
- Audio ports.
- Game port.
- Others.

Copyright by Goodheart-Willcox Co., Inc.

6. ____ Observe your instructor closely as to the proper procedure for removing the computer case enclosure. There are many different variations of case styles, and it can be very difficult to properly remove a computer case enclosure. You may inadvertently damage the case if you apply force or remove an enclosure improperly.

7. ____ After removing the case enclosure, identify the power supply location. The power supply is very obvious. Look at the exterior power cord connection coming from the 120-volt wall outlet. It will connect directly to the power supply unit. You will also see a bundle of various colored wires and power connectors leading to various components inside the computer case. Answer the following questions:

Does the power supply have a cooling fan? _____

If yes, where is it located? _____

Approximately how many connectors are associated with the power supply unit? _____

8. ____ Look at the power supply for information such as the voltage and wattage of the unit. Record the wattage rating of the power supply unit. _____

_____

9. ____ Identify the CPU unit. It should be mounted directly on the motherboard with a heat sink and a fan assembly mounted on top.

10. ____ Look for the RAM modules and their location in the corresponding slots. For example, if there are four RAM slots and only two are filled, which two are filled? _____

_____

11. ____ Identify the main motherboard and the type of expansion slots located on the board. Many times the expansion slot is identified by placing its name or acronym at the slot location like that shown in the following illustration.

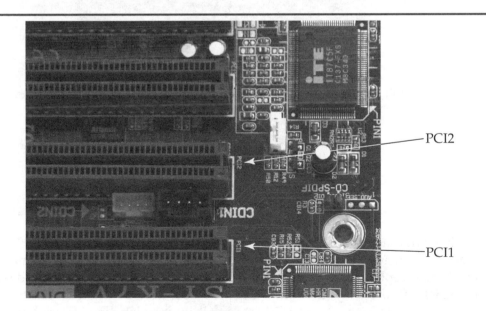

Look closely and you will see PCI1 and PCI2 printed on the motherboard beside the corresponding PCI slots. Note that not all motherboards identify the type of slot.

12. ____ If a floppy drive is not installed, skip to the next step. If a floppy disk drive is installed, look at the back of the drive and identify the data cable. Identify the location on the motherboard where it connects. See if you can locate pin 1 or if there is a colored stripe running down

Copyright by Goodheart-Willcox Co., Inc.

one side of the cable. If yes, record the color of the stripe and its orientation to the motherboard connector. Identify the power cable connection on the floppy disk drive. How many wires does it use? _____

_____

_____

13. ____ Identify the hard disk drive. Determine if it is connected to an IDE-type of connector on the motherboard or a SATA-type connection. Again, these types of connectors usually have an ID printed on the motherboard beside the connection. Look for the letters SATA and IDE, and then answer the following questions:

Does the hard disk drive use a flat ribbon type of data cable? _____

If so, does the cable have a red or blue stripe along one edge? _____

Do you see a power cable from the power supply to the hard disk drive? _____

How many wires are used for the power cable? _____

14. ____ Look at the various chips mounted on the motherboard. Are they soldered in place, or are they inserted into sockets? _____

_____

15. ____ Locate the CMOS battery. Look for a circular silver disk approximately 1″ in diameter. The battery normally has the voltage labeled on it or a positive plus sign like that shown in the following illustration. Look at the BAT1 printed on the motherboard below the battery location.

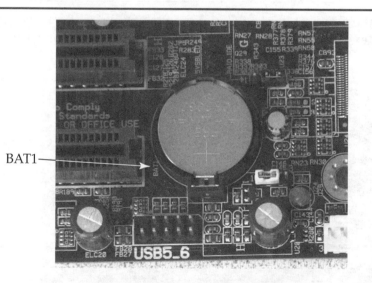

17. ____ Lastly, it is often necessary to make a sketch of the PC components' layout. The sketch is used as a guide for reassembly after certain PC components have been disassembled. For example, if you must replace the motherboard, every wire connection point should be identified. Make a sketch of the PC layout in the space provided. It should look similar to that in the following figure. The one in the example is very small, and the labeling is very limited. Make yours larger. Use a separate sheet of paper if needed. Be sure to identify the fan, LED, and switch connections. Draw the sketch with as much detail as reasonably possible, as it will help during reassembly. Pay particular attention to how the flat ribbon cable connects to devices. Be sure to draw the orientation of the colored stripe along the cable in respect to the connection points.

Copyright by Goodheart-Willcox Co., Inc.

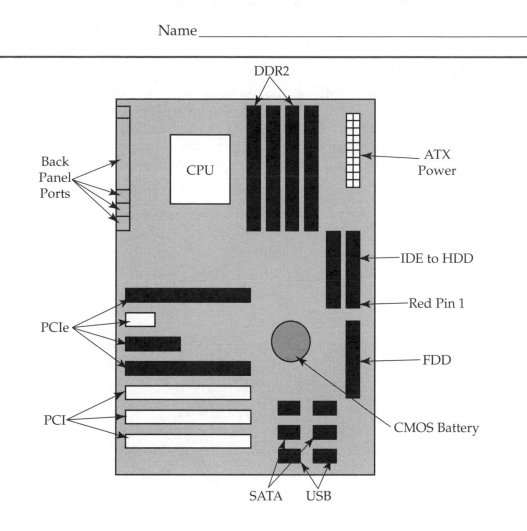

Internet Assignment

1. Locate the motherboard layout for the PC you are using in this lab activity. Go to the manufacturer's Web site and see if you can locate the motherboard schematic showing the location of all major components. Also, see if you can locate the manual that comes with the motherboard. This should provide detailed information about such items as how to access the BIOS Setup program, what type of memory can be installed on the motherboard, and which CPU can be used with this motherboard.

Copyright by Goodheart-Willcox Co., Inc.

Name _____ Date _____

Class/Instructor _____

Windows XP Clean Installation

After completing this laboratory activity, you will be able to:

■ Explain how to determine if the computer hardware will support Windows XP.

■ Select the correct version of Windows XP (Home or Professional) for use on a network domain.

■ Select the proper file system for a clean installation.

■ Identify how to automatically create, delete, or modify partitions during the installation process.

■ Explain the difference between a "clean install" and a "system upgrade."

■ Identify hardware minimum and recommended requirements.

■ Identify possible causes of installation problems.

Introduction

In this lab activity, you will perform a "clean install" of Windows XP. A clean install completely wipes out any existing files from the hard disk drive. This is in sharp contrast to performing a system upgrade, which installs over the existing operating system and preserves files, documents, and settings.

A clean installation is performed for several reasons:

■ To install an operating system on a new computer that has never had an operating system installed before.

■ To replace the non-Microsoft operating system that is currently installed.

■ To change the file system structure, such as the partition characteristics.

■ To change the type of file system, such as FAT16, FAT32, or NTFS.

Note:
There are third-party tools available for converting one file system to another.

When performing a clean installation, Microsoft recommends using NTFS as the file system. NTFS allows for enhanced security features such as disk encryption. You can also install Windows XP over FAT32 and FAT16. FAT16 is not a practical choice for Windows XP because FAT16 is limited to hard disk partitions of 2 GB. FAT16 does not leave sufficient room for additional software packages on the same partition.

FAT32 is typically used for hard disk drives that run from 512 MB to 32 GB. NTFS is the choice used for hard disk drives larger than 32 GB. NTFS supports drives as large as 2 TB (Terabytes). Microsoft recommends using NTFS for hard disk drives larger than 32 GB and recommends using FAT32 for drives smaller than 32 GB.

Copyright by Goodheart-Willcox Co., Inc.

Performing a clean install is a relatively easy task if the computer hardware will support the operating system. A Windows XP installation requires the following:

- 233 MHz Pentium (or higher) microprocessor.
- 64 MB RAM (128 MB recommended, 4 GB maximum).
- 2 GB of unused hard drive space. (*Note: The recommended amount of hard disk space will vary from 1.5 GB to 2 GB according to various Microsoft sources. The first release notes stated 1.5 MB required.*)
- VGA monitor (SVGA recommended).
- Keyboard and mouse.
- CD-ROM drive (required for CD installation).

Note the difference in the list for recommended and required specifications. For example, 64 MB of RAM is required, but 128 MB of RAM is recommended. This means that the operating system can be installed on a computer with only 64 MB of RAM, but the performance will be poor. There will not be sufficient memory for the computer to operate in an efficient manner. The system performance will appear sluggish and be impractical to use. In general, the more memory that can be installed, the better the performance. Also, be aware that certification test questions often include the terms *required* and *recommended*. Be very careful when answering questions that contain either of these two words.

The list of hardware does not include a network adapter or a device such as a modem for connecting to the Internet. These two items can cause a problem in successfully installing a clean operating system. Neither of these items is required for performing a clean installation. It is best you install them after installing the operating system.

Performing a clean install on a PC that is not connected to the network is an easy task. You will simply boot the computer to the Windows XP CD. When the Windows XP CD is used with a system that can boot to the CD drive, the Setup Wizard automatically starts up and you simply follow the screen prompts.

If the CD drive does not support self-booting, you can go to the Microsoft Web site and download a software image to make a set of six floppy disks to start an installation process. The six-disk set contains all the basic files required to start the Windows XP installation. You should download the image and make a set of Windows XP startup disks for your own personal use as a technician. The disk images are different for Windows Home Edition and Professional Edition. You will need a total of 12 disks to make a set of disks for each system.

Note:
You may also use a Windows 98 startup disk to start the installation process. It contains the generic drivers required for supporting most CD-ROM drives.

When installing a Windows XP operating system on a PC that is connected to a network, you will need network information such as how the IP address is to be assigned and what workgroup or domain name to use. Joining a workgroup does not require any special administrative permission. You simply provide the workgroup name when prompted. To join a domain, you must have an account set up on the existing client/server network. This requires the assistance of the network administrator.

If you are not sure about joining a workgroup or domain, you can use the default settings, which automatically configures the computer for a workgroup. You can later reconfigure the computer to join a domain.

If you have problems with the installation, use the following lists of possible problems and solutions. You can refer to Help and Support.

CD-Related Problems:
- Check the CD for scratches; clean if necessary.
- Make sure the CD drive is on the Hardware Compatibility List (HCL).
- Check the boot sequence in the BIOS Setup program.

Copyright by Goodheart-Willcox Co., Inc.

■ Try using a Windows 98 startup disk to start the installation. The Windows 98 startup disk contains the generic drivers for CD drives.

Blue Screen and Stop Errors:

■ Check the Microsoft Support Web site for information on the specific stop error. Write down all related information from the display before going to the Microsoft Web site.

■ If specific hardware devices are identified in the stop error, remove or replace the hardware item.

■ Remove unnecessary hardware items that may prevent a successful installation, such as network adapters, sound cards, and video cards.

■ Check for system BIOS updates. This may resolve some hardware problems.

■ You may need to reformat an existing hard drive before attempting to install the operating system. This is especially true of hard disk drives used in previous lab activities.

■ Try starting the computer using the Advanced Startup feature. Reboot the computer and press [F8]. The **Advanced Startup** menu will appear and you can then select options such as **Safe mode** or **Startup without network adapter**.

Network Connection Problems:

■ Check if the Caps Lock light is on.

■ Make sure you correctly typed in the password. Remember, passwords are case sensitive.

■ Make sure the correct domain name or workgroup name is used. Check each letter carefully.

■ Make sure the administrator has set up a user account on the domain you are attempting to access.

■ Check if there is a complete physical path to the network server. Try using the **ping** command to check for connectivity with the server.

■ Verify that the network server and DNS server are running.

Equipment and Materials

■ PC that meets these minimum requirements:
233 MHz (or better) processor.
64 MB RAM (128 MB preferred.)
Hard disk drive with at least 1.5 GB of unused disk space.
Windows 98, 2000, Me, NT 4.0 service pack 6, or XP operating system (either Home Edition or Professional).

■ Windows XP installation CD.

■ Product Key: _____ _____ _____ _____ _____.

■ The following information provided by your instructor:
Computer name: _____

User name: _____

Organization: _____

Password: _____

Domain name _____ or Workgroup name _____

IP Address _____ or DHCP server _____

Note:

In this lab activity, you will be installing Windows XP on a stand-alone computer. You will not need a domain name or an IP address. This lab can be repeated on a PC that is or will be connected to a network. Then you will need to know about IP addressing and domain or workgroup names. Remember that Windows XP Home Edition does not support connecting to a domain.

Procedure

Note:
Because your computer may already have an operating system or be connected to a network, the exact sequence of steps in this lab activity may vary somewhat.

Note:
Read each screen presentation carefully. Many times students have difficulty installing an operating system simply because they did not read the information presented in the screens. Critical screens often present several key press selections. Failure to read the screen information may result in an incorrectly configured system.

1. ____ Gather the required information and materials and report to your assigned workstation.

2. ____ Boot the PC and verify that it is in working order.

Note:
If there is no previous operating system, you should only see the POST.

3. ____ Place the Windows XP CD into the CD drive tray. The PC should automatically boot to the CD.

   If the computer does not boot to the CD, you may need to change the boot order in the BIOS Setup program so that the CD drive will be the first boot device. Also, be aware that not all early-model CD drives were self-booting. You may not have a self-booting CD drive.

   If the CD drive is capable of booting to a CD and is set to be the first bootable device, check the CD for scratches and clean if necessary. Also, make sure the CD drive is on the Hardware Compatibility List (HCL).

   If you are still having problems booting, you can use a Windows 98 startup disk to start the installation. The Windows 98 startup disk contains the generic drivers for CD drives.

4. ____ After the CD boots, Windows will copy all required preliminary setup files.

5. ____ A screen similar to the following will appear. You will be asked if you wish to perform a new installation or repair an existing installation. Choose to perform new installation.

Copyright by Goodheart-Willcox Co., Inc.

6. ____ Press [F8] to accept the licensing agreement.

7. ____ The next screen asks about the partition on which you wish to install Windows XP. Read this screen very carefully. At this step of the install process, you have the opportunity to create or delete partitions and to use the entire disk drive space. Do *not* use the entire disk. Create a 2 GB partition for practice. Using a small partition will speed up the installation process. Choosing to use the entire disk can cause the installation process to take more time than is available in your class period.

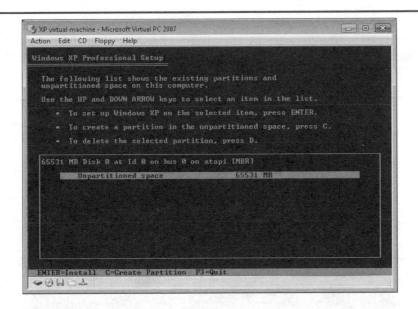

8. ____ Next, select the type of file system for the partition. Your choices will be FAT or NTFS. Choose FAT for this installation. This will allow you to practice converting FAT to NTFS later with your instructor's permission.

Note:

To convert the partition to NTFS at a later time, simply type and enter **CONVERT C: /FS:NTFS** at the command prompt. In the example, the partition is assumed to be drive C. You would use the letter for the volume you wish to convert to NTFS.

Note:

The term *volume* is used in place of partition in Windows XP when describing partitions formatted in NTFS.

Setup automatically progresses with the installation process after the partition is formatted. During the format, you should see a progress bar displayed on the screen of the monitor.

When the format is complete, the computer will reboot. The GUI Setup Wizard will appear and the remaining portion of the installation will consist of a series of dialog boxes asking you to make choices and providing you with progress information.

9. ____ The Windows XP Setup Wizard will gather information from you for configuring the installation. Such information will be region, language, name, and organization. Use the name and organization supplied by your instructor. You should have written this information down at the start of the lab activity.

Copyright by Goodheart-Willcox Co., Inc.

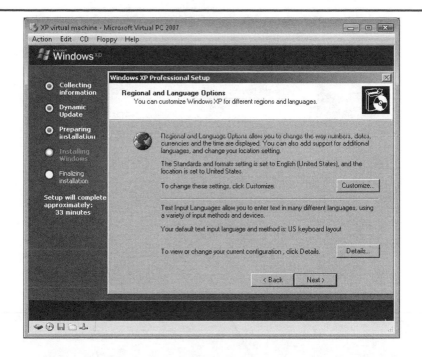

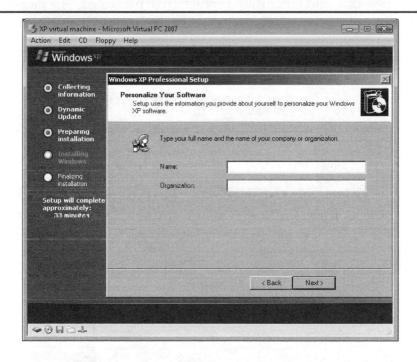

10. ____ Enter the 25-digit product key. This step may not be necessary if you are using a corporate edition of the Windows XP CD.

Copyright by Goodheart-Willcox Co., Inc. Laboratory Activity 2   25

11. ____ Name the computer and enter the administrative password. The password information was provided by your instructor at the beginning of the lab activity.

12. ____ Enter the correct date and time.

13. ____ Choose either a workgroup name or domain name. You should have this information provided by your instructor. You can always use a workgroup name and later change to a domain name.

Copyright by Goodheart-Willcox Co., Inc.

Note:

The domain name option is not featured in Windows XP Home Edition.

14. ____ You are given the option to register Windows XP. Do not register the Windows XP system at this time. Registering Windows XP is not the same as activation. Registering Windows XP is used to allow Microsoft to send information to the user through e-mail notifications. Activation is required for the operating system to prevent it from timing out.

15. ____ You are given the option to add additional users for this PC. Do not add any additional users at this time.

16. ____ The system is ready to reboot. Reboot the system and log on. If you have problems logging on to the system, call your instructor.

17. ____ After you have completed the Windows XP installation, go on to answer the review questions at the end of this laboratory activity.

Review Questions

1. What is the recommended amount of RAM for a Windows XP installation? _____

2. Why might the CD drive fail to automatically start the installation process? _____

_____

_____

3. Give three reasons for performing a clean install. _____

_____

_____

_____

_____

_____

4. What are the two common file systems used for a Windows XP installation? _____

_____

5. Why is FAT16 not a practical choice for Windows XP? _____

_____

_____

6. Which is the computer automatically configured for by default, a workgroup or a domain?

_____

7. Which requires the assistance of a network administrator, a workgroup or a domain? _____

_____

8. Can a Windows 98 startup disk be used to start a Windows XP installation? _____

9. What command is used to change an existing FAT partition to an NTFS partition?_____

_____

10. What is another name for partition in Windows XP? _____

Copyright by Goodheart-Willcox Co., Inc.

Name _____ Date _____

Class/Instructor _____

Windows XP Upgrade Installation

After completing this laboratory activity, you will be able to:

- Upgrade a PC with an existing Windows 98 (or later) operating system to a Windows XP operating system.
- Determine the minimum requirements for a Windows XP installation.
- Identify information required for a typical installation.
- Explain the Windows XP installation process in general terms.

Introduction

In this lab activity, you will install Windows XP as an upgrade for an existing Windows operating system previously installed on a computer system. Windows XP (eXPerience) operating system was released in October of 2001. Windows XP comes in two versions: Windows XP Professional and Windows XP Home Edition. The Windows XP Professional version is designed to replace the Windows NT and Windows 2000 family of desktop operating systems while the Windows Home Edition is designed to replace the Windows 9x and Windows Me editions. The Windows XP operating system is built on the Windows NT technology, which is more stable than the Windows 9x series.

The minimum requirements for installing the Windows XP operating system are as follows:

- 233 MHz Pentium (or higher) microprocessor.
- 64 MB of RAM (128 MB recommended, 4 GB maximum).
- 2 GB of unused hard drive space. (*Note: The recommended amount of hard disk space will vary from 1.5 GB to 2 GB according to various Microsoft sources.*)
- VGA monitor.
- Keyboard and mouse.
- CD-ROM or DVD drive.
- A network adapter card (when networking the PC).

Before you begin installing Windows XP, you should check the hardware compatibility list located at Microsoft's Web site (www.microsoft.com/hcl/). Don't assume that because a previous version of Windows is already installed on the PC that the hardware used in the PC is compatible with the Windows XP operating system. Check the listing of hardware for potential problems. Note that Windows XP does perform a hardware check as part of the installation procedure. However, the automatic hardware detection program is not completely reliable. Always check the Microsoft Web site for the latest information.

Near the beginning of the installation process, the Windows XP installation wizard will present a screen giving you an option to connect to the Microsoft Web site to check the hardware compatibility list and also look for updates to the operating system.

Copyright by Goodheart-Willcox Co., Inc.

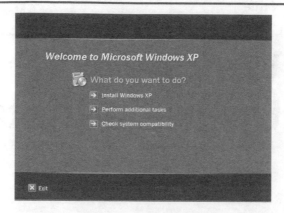

If you select the option to **Visit the compatibility Web site**, a screen image similar to the one that follows will appear.

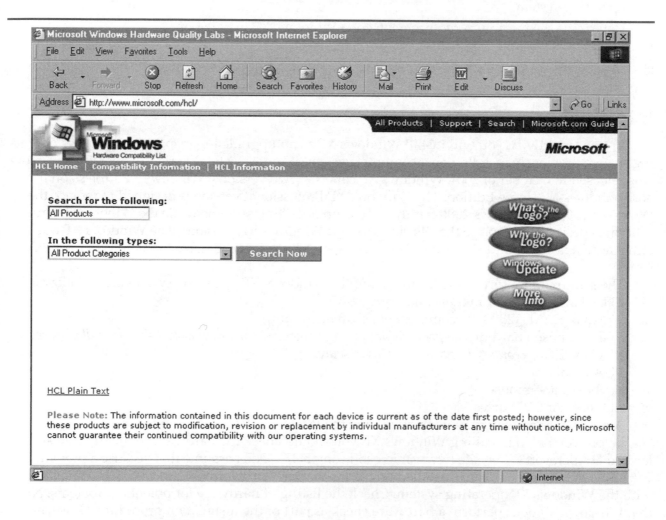

The hardware compatibility Web site allows you to search for compatible equipment by operating system and by type of product such as chipset, RAM, displays, and more. The following image is a screen capture of the hardware compatibility list taken from the Microsoft Web site. This is a partial list of displays that are compatible with various Windows operating systems. The circle with "Compatible" inside is used to identify the compatible displays by operating system.

Copyright by Goodheart-Willcox Co., Inc.

If your specific equipment is not on the compatibility list, you will need to go to the manufacture's Web site and download an updated version of the hardware driver that is compatible with Windows XP.

Certain information may be required for your installation of Windows XP. The exact order and specific information can vary depending on whether the PC is part of a network, and if so, what type of network system. Below is a list of typical information you will need before you begin the installation wizard. The following information will be supplied by your instructor.

■ Computer name.
■ Domain name.
■ Workgroup.
■ User name.
■ Organization.
■ Password.
■ IP address.
■ Name of DHCP server.

During a typical system upgrade, much of the information will be transferred to the new operating system from the old, but not necessarily all of the information listed.

When you start the actual system upgrade installation process, you will insert the CD into the CD-ROM or DVD drive after the PC has been booted. The installation wizard will direct you through the entire installation process. When in doubt about a screen prompt, check with your instructor. Usually choosing the default option will be fine. Because you may be installing the new operating system on a computer in a network arrangement, your instructor will brief you on any particular changes that may be required for the installation.

When the installation is complete, you will be prompted to create a user account. The user account uniquely identifies each user of the PC and allows each user to load their specific settings and files when they log on to the PC.

When performing a Windows XP operating system upgrade, you must perform the upgrade over an existing compatible operating system. The only compatible operating systems for upgrades are Windows 98 (any edition), Windows Me, Windows NT 4.0 (with service pack 6 installed), or Windows 2000. Other operating systems are not compatible for a successful upgrade. Some such systems, which are not compatible, are Windows 95, DOS, and various Linux versions.

Equipment and Materials

- PC that meets these minimum requirements:
  233 MHz (or better) processor.

  64 MB RAM (128 MB preferred.)

  Hard disk drive with at least 1.5 GB of unused disk space.

  Windows 98, 2000, Me, NT 4.0 service pack 6, or XP operating system (either Home Edition or Professional).

- Windows XP upgrade CD.
- Product Key: _____ _____ _____ _____ _____.
- The following information provided by your instructor:
  Computer name: _____

  User name:_____

  Organization: _____

  Password: _____

  Domain name _____ or Workgroup name _____

  IP Address _____ or DHCP server _____

Procedure

1. ____ Before you begin the installation process, gather all required materials and then report to your assigned station.

2. ____ Boot the PC and check that it has the minimum installation requirements. If the PC has the minimum requirements, you may proceed to step 3. If it does not have the minimum hardware requirements, notify your instructor.

3. ____ Access the Read1st.txt file on the CD-ROM. Read the information carefully.

Copyright by Goodheart-Willcox Co., Inc.

4. ____ With the PC booted to its operating system, insert the CD-ROM containing the Windows XP operating system. The CD-ROM may automatically start the installation process. The automatic startup of the installation will depend on the PC system equipment and BIOS. Wait approximately two minutes. If the installation has not automatically begun, start the installation process manually. You can manually start the program by typing and running **D:setup.exe** from the **Run** option located on the **Start** menu. See the screen captures that follow.

Note:

It is assumed here that D is the CD-ROM or DVD device. If this is not the case, substitute the correct drive letter in the command. If you are having difficulty, you can also **Browse** until you locate the program.

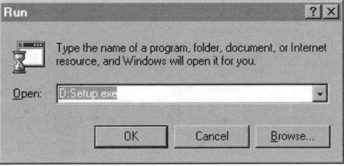

Copyright by Goodheart-Willcox Co., Inc.

5. ____ Select **Install Windows XP** from the menu selections by clicking the item.

6. ____ Next, a screen similar to the one that follows should appear. Select the default **Upgrade (Recommended)** from the dialog box.

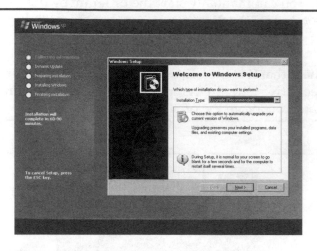

7. ____ Take note of the list on the left side of the screen display. This is a list of the installation activities as they occur during the system upgrade process. The amount of time for the total installation process is also listed. Observe the listing on the left as the installation wizard takes you through the installation upgrade process. You will be prompted for information throughout the installation process. This information will include asking you to accept the licensing agreement and to choose a file system, as well as inquiring about other details such as your regional settings, location, choice of language, name, organization, computer name, and administrator password.

8. ____ After the Windows XP operating system is installed, the computer should reboot and you will be prompted to log on for the first time. It is during this time you will have the option to activate your installed copy of Windows XP. You will also be prompted to set up user accounts for the PC. Check with your instructor about the specific requirements of these two prompts. The instructor may not want you to activate the Windows XP operating system. Activation requires using a modem to contact the Microsoft Web site and activate the software operating system. This is Microsoft's solution to prevent the pirating of their operating systems. When the system is activated, Microsoft creates a database describing the hardware of the PC system on which the original copy of the Windows XP operating system has been installed. If the specific hardware does not match when activating a second installation on another PC, the installation is disabled.

9. ____ Before ending this lab activity, ask the instructor if you will be leaving the upgraded operating system on the PC or uninstalling it.

10. ____ Complete the review questions at the end of this laboratory activity. You may use the Read1st.txt file located on the Windows XP installation CD to answer some of the questions.

Copyright by Goodheart-Willcox Co., Inc.

Name_____

Review Questions

1. What is the minimum CPU speed for Windows XP? _____

2. What is the recommended amount of RAM and the minimum amount of RAM required for a typical Windows XP installation? _____

3. What is the maximum amount of RAM that Windows XP can support? _____

4. What is the amount of free hard drive space required for a Windows XP installation? _____

5. What is the minimum monitor resolution required for Windows XP? _____

6. What does the acronym HCL represent? _____

7. From the list that follows, select the items that are recommended you complete before performing a Windows XP upgrade.

   A. Be sure that an anti-virus program is installed and running during the installation process.
   B. Perform a virus scan.
   C. Back up all important files.
   D. Contact your ISP and notify them that you are installing a new operating system.
   E. Format the hard drive.
   F. Access and read the Read1st.txt file located on the CD-ROM.

8. Which of the following operating systems can Windows XP perform a satisfactory upgrade on? Choose all that apply.

   A. Windows 95
   B. Windows 98
   C. Windows 2000
   D. Windows NT 4.0 with Service pack 6
   E. DOS 6.0
   F. Linux

9. What command is used to manually start the installation process of the Windows XP operating system CD? _____

Copyright by Goodheart-Willcox Co., Inc.

Name _____ Date _____

Class/Instructor _____

Installing Windows Vista

After completing this laboratory activity, you will be able to:

- Install or upgrade to Windows Vista.
- Determine the minimal and recommended system Windows Vista requirements.
- Describe how to use the Windows Upgrade Advisor.
- Describe the tasks to complete before performing a Windows Vista upgrade or installation.
- Describe the tasks to complete after performing a successful Windows Vista upgrade or installation.

Introduction

There are two ways to install Windows Vista: as a clean install or a system upgrade. A system upgrade allows the computer to retain all existing user files, such as documents, images, sounds, and similar collections of information. In addition, all user configurations are retained, such as user name and password. A clean install erases all previous files created by the user. For example, all document files will no longer exist after a clean install. Do not perform a clean install unless specifically told to do so by your instructor. A clean install will destroy all previously installed software applications as well as user files on your workstation.

The Windows Vista required and recommended hardware are listed below. The difference between recommended and required hardware is that Windows Vista will function properly using the required hardware; however, the performance will be poor. It is best to meet or exceed the Windows Vista recommended hardware specifications to have a system performance level equal to or exceeding the previous operating system. For example, if you upgraded from Windows XP and met the required hardware specifications for Windows Vista, Windows Vista would perform slower than Windows XP.

Minimum Hardware Requirements for all Windows Vista Editions:
- 800 MHz CPU.
- 512 MB RAM.
- 20 GB hard drive (At least 15 GB available space).
- Graphics processor DirectX 9 capable.
- CD-ROM drive.

Recommended Hardware Requirements for Windows Vista Home Basic Edition:
- 1 GHz processor.
- 512 MB RAM.
- 20 GB hard drive (At least 15 GB available space).
- Graphics processor with 32 MB graphics RAM and DirectX 9 capable.
- DVD-ROM drive.
- Audio output capability.

Copyright by Goodheart-Willcox Co., Inc.

- Internet access capability.

Recommended Hardware Requirements for Windows Vista Home Premium, Business, and Ultimate Editions:

- 1 GHz CPU.
- 1 GB RAM.
- 40 GB hard drive (At least 15 GB available space).
- Graphics processor with DirectX 9, Windows Display Driver Model (WDDM), 128 MB RAM, Pixel shader 2.0, and 32 bits-per-pixel capability.
- DVD-ROM drive.
- Audio output capability.
- Internet access capability.

Note:

Computers identified as Windows Vista Capable meet minimal system requirements, and computers identified as Windows Vista Premium meet recommended hardware requirements.

Windows Vista will run on either 32-bit or 64-bit processors. Visit the Microsoft TechNet Web site at www.microsoft.com/technet/windowsvista to find more information about Windows Vista. You can see detailed information about installing Windows Vista and common problems at the Microsoft Web site link http://support.microsoft.com/kb/918884.

There are many known issues that can cause a problem when performing an upgrade or clean install. For example, many software drivers, software applications, and hardware items will not successfully respond to a Windows Vista upgrade and may not be available for a clean install.

Microsoft provides a software program called Windows Vista Upgrade Advisor that will perform a pre-installation test to determine if the existing hardware and software are compatible for an upgrade to Windows Vista. The following shows the first screen of the Windows Vista Upgrade Advisor.

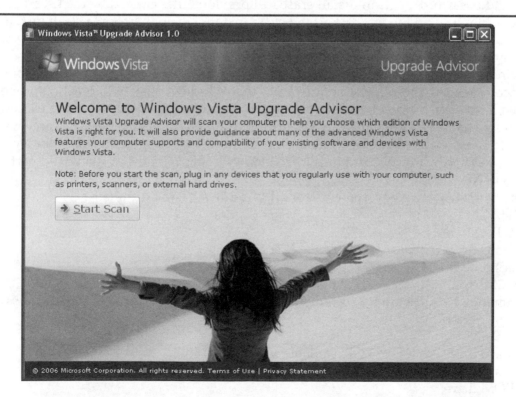

Copyright by Goodheart-Willcox Co., Inc.

Name_____

The Windows Vista Upgrade Advisor will identify known issues and display information about compatibility problems in report form. You can either download a copy of the Windows Vista Upgrade Advisor from the Microsoft Web site, or you can install and run the Windows Vista Upgrade Advisor as one of the first steps during a system upgrade.

The following shows a series of Windows Vista Upgrade Advisor screens, which provide information about Windows Vista compatibility and the computer system to be upgraded. A brief comparison of Windows Vista editions is displayed on the screen to help the user decide which edition is right for them.

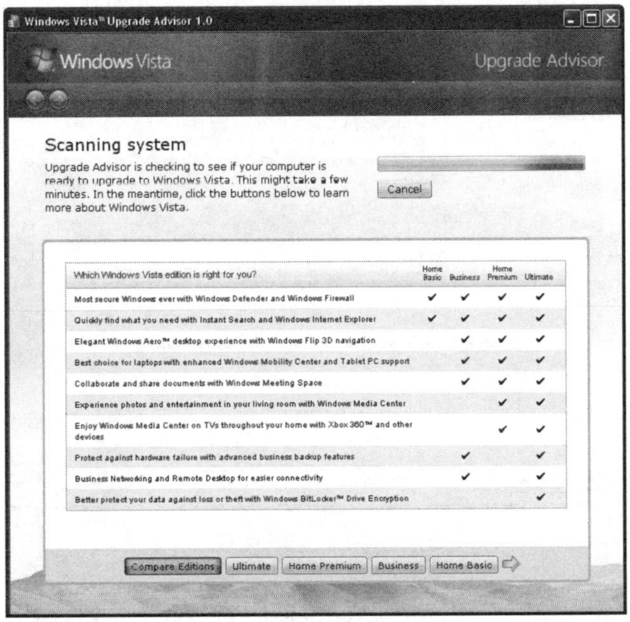

When the Windows Vista Upgrade Advisor has finished scanning the hardware and software on the computer to be upgraded, a **See Details** button will appear in the upper-right corner. You can use this button to access a detailed description of the scan.

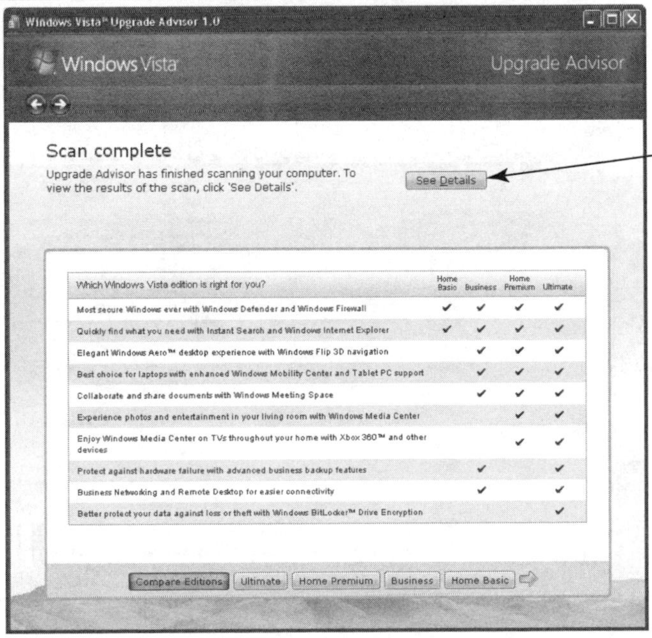

See Details button

If there are no known issues, the screen capture will state that the computer can be successfully upgraded to Windows Vista.

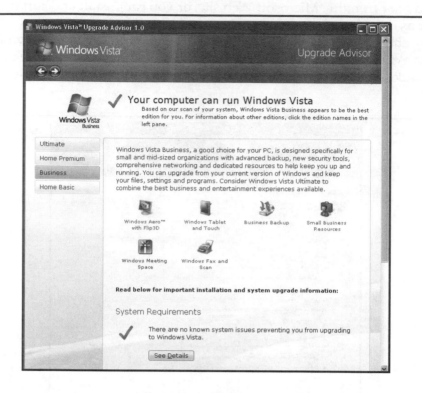

If the Windows Vista Upgrade Advisor detects known issues, it reports problems found with hardware or software and provides suggested remedies. Look at the next two screens to see how problems are identified.

Copyright by Goodheart-Willcox Co., Inc.

The Windows Vista Upgrade Advisor may perform a detailed analysis of the system prior to an upgrade operation and report that the system will upgrade without a problem. This analysis may not be true. Sometimes, there will be a potential problem that has not been identified by Microsoft. For example, early releases of Windows Vista installed on an improperly installed Windows XP system may result in a failed upgrade. Windows XP had a problem identifying hard disk drives over 137 GB, SATA hard drive controllers, and some RAID systems. The Windows Vista Upgrade Advisor would indicate that there were no problems for an upgrade, but the upgrade would result in a catastrophic failure during the first reboot of the system. This is why you should always do a complete backup of all important files and possibly the entire disk before performing an upgrade.

Note:

When an upgrade installation fails, you can typically recover and revert to the original system. You simply restart the computer and watch the display carefully. An option to revert to the original operating system will appear briefly. In some cases, the option will be displayed very quickly and you must use the keyboard to quickly select the option to run the original operating system. It may take some practice before you are successful. Be aware that many times you will need a set of recovery discs to reinstall the previous operating system.

The following are lists of tasks to perform before and after a Windows Vista upgrade or clean install. To ensure a successful upgrade or installation, be sure you complete these tasks.

Before Performing an Upgrade/Clean Install:
- Check if the computer meets the Windows Vista hardware requirements.
- Check hardware and software compatibility lists.
- Back up all personal files for an upgrade.
- Create a system recovery disk for an upgrade.
- Check if your computer has the latest BIOS version.
- Disconnect all unnecessary peripherals, such as printers, scanners, and cameras, during upgrade. Leave only the keyboard, mouse, monitor, and speakers attached.
- Disable any antivirus, antispyware, and firewall programs for an upgrade.

- Find the 25-character product key.
- Write down the computer name if connected to a network.
- Collect the latest driver software.
  After Completing an Upgrade/Clean Install:
- Reactivate or install antivirus, antispyware, and firewall programs.
- Check for the latest updates for your software programs.

Equipment and Materials

- Windows XP SP2 computer meeting at least the minimum requirements for Windows Vista.
- Record the following information provided by your instructor.
  Computer name: _____

  Computer workgroup/domain: _____

  User name:_____

  User password: _____

  Run the Windows Vista Upgrade Advisor during the lab activity: _____ (Yes or No.)

Note:

    A Windows Vista upgrade can only be installed on an existing NTFS format partition. If the partition is not NTFS, then it must be converted to NTFS before attempting to upgrade to Windows Vista. Access the following link for information about how to convert an existing FAT or FAT32 partition to NTFS: http://support.microsoft.com/kb/307881. Do not attempt a file system conversion without your instructor's permission.

Note:

    Lab activity time is typically limited. For this lab activity, you will perform a simple Windows Vista Upgrade or clean install. Other options, such as checking for hardware compatibility and transferring files, are covered in other lab activities.

Copyright by Goodheart-Willcox Co., Inc.

Procedure

1. ____ Report to your assigned workstation. Boot the computer and check if it is in working order.

2. ____ Run the Windows Vista Upgrade Advisor if directed by your instructor. Otherwise, proceed to the next step.

3. ____ Insert the Windows Vista installation DVD. There are several versions of Windows Vista. This lab activity is based on Windows Vista Business Upgrade version. After booting the DVD, you will see a dialog box similar to the following.

Notice that you have several possible selections: **Check compatibility online, Install now, What to know before installing Windows,** and **Transfer files and settings from another computer.**

4. ____ Review the contents of **What to know before installing Windows** before proceeding. Do not spend more than a few minutes reviewing this material.

5. ____ Select the **Install now** option. You do not need to run the **Check compatibility online** option at this time, unless you are directed to do so by your instructor.

The installation program will begin collecting information about the hardware and software. At the same time, a dialog box will appear asking you if you would like to go online for the latest updates. Do not select the latest updates unless you are required to do so by your instructor. You can obtain the latest updates at a later time from the Microsoft Web site.

6. ____ Next, you are prompted for the 25-character product key. Enter the product key and select the **Automatically activate Windows when I'm online** option. It should be checked by default. You have 30 days to activate the copy of Windows online or by telephone. Unless activated, the system will stop working in 30 days. When you select the **Automatically activate Windows when I'm online** option, the system will automatically activate Windows Vista three days after you perform your first logon.

Copyright by Goodheart-Willcox Co., Inc.

7. _____ Next, the terms of the license agreement appears on the screen. You must select the **I accept the license terms** option to proceed with the installation.

8. _____ You are now presented with two installation options: **Upgrade** and **Custom**. Select the appropriate option.

Copyright by Goodheart-Willcox Co., Inc.

If you selected the **Upgrade** option, a compatibility report will appear if there is a known compatibility issue with the hardware or software. If the issue is not determined to be serious, you will be able to proceed with the installation.

A dialog box will appear informing you that the upgrade process has begun and that it may take several hours to complete. The actual time will depend mainly on the computer hardware. If you are installing on a computer that exceeds the hardware specifications, the actual time will be much shorter. The following screen capture lists the five major steps in the upgrade process.

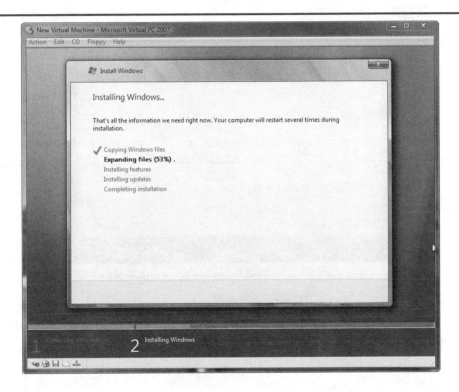

The percentage of the installation completed will appear on the screen during the upgrade process. Be aware that the computer may restart several times during this process. You should see a screen message "Please wait a moment while Windows prepares to run for the first time." After a short period or several minutes, the screen will display the "Completing upgrade" stage.

If you are performing an upgrade, proceed to step 9.

If you are performing a clean (custom) install, proceed to step 13.

9. _____ After a successful upgrade, you should see the **Help protect Windows automatically** dialog box. Select the **Ask me later** option.

Copyright by Goodheart-Willcox Co., Inc.

10. ____ When the dialog box for setting the date and time appears, make adjustments if necessary. Also, if you live in an appropriate area that observes daylight saving time such as Arizona and parts of Ohio, select the **Automatically adjust clock for Daylight Saving Time** option.

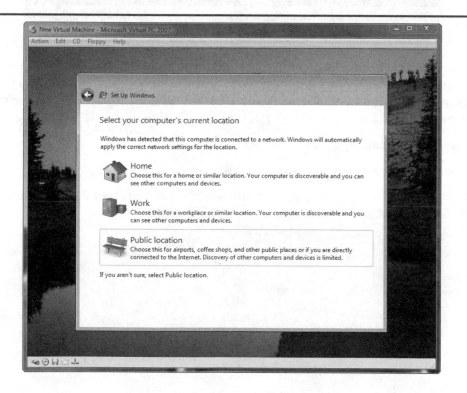

11. ____ Next, you are prompted to select your present location. The choices are **Home**, **Work**, and **Public location**. Select **Work** for this lab activity.

Copyright by Goodheart-Willcox Co., Inc.

12. _____ The **Set Up Windows** dialog box will display and look similar to that in the following screen capture.

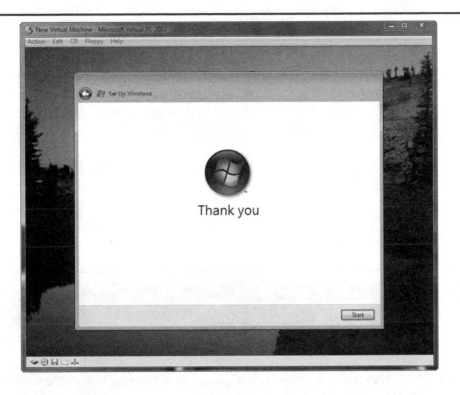

Click the **Start** button. The system will automatically check the system performance, which will take a few minutes. After it finishes, it will prepare the desktop.

You have now completed the Windows Vista upgrade. Call your instructor for inspection of the lab activity and then go on to answer the review questions. Return all materials to their proper storage area.

* * * *

13. _____ If you selected the **Custom** option, a dialog box like that in the following screen capture will display asking where you would like to install Window Vista.

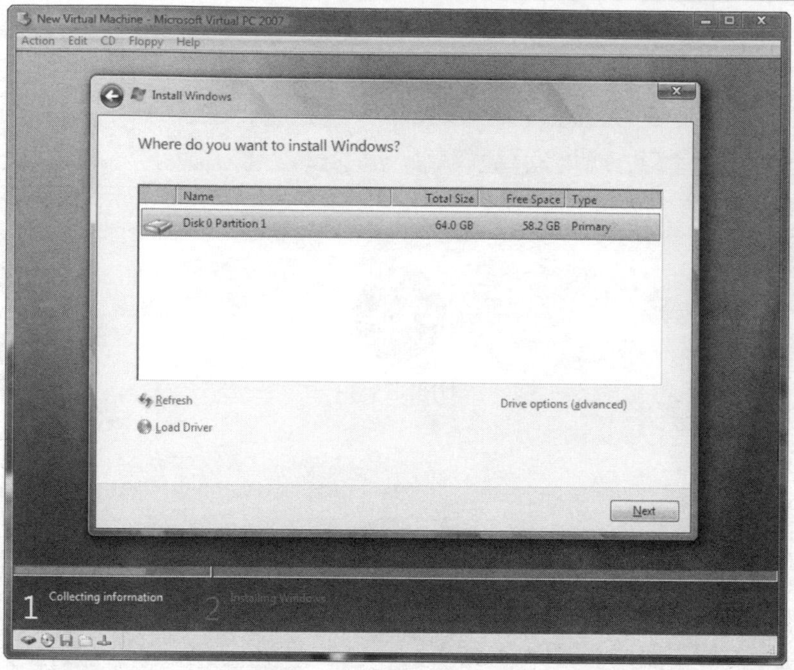

You can install it to an existing partition or to unallocated space. You can use all of the unallocated space, or a part of it after partitioning it into one or more partitions. You can also delete an existing partition and create a new partition. After you chose a location, Windows Vista will begin installing. When Windows Vista is finished installing, the computer will reboot.

14. _____ Enter a user name, password, and password hint. While it is not necessary to have a user name and password, it is always recommended. Only configure a user name and password if your instructor has provided them.

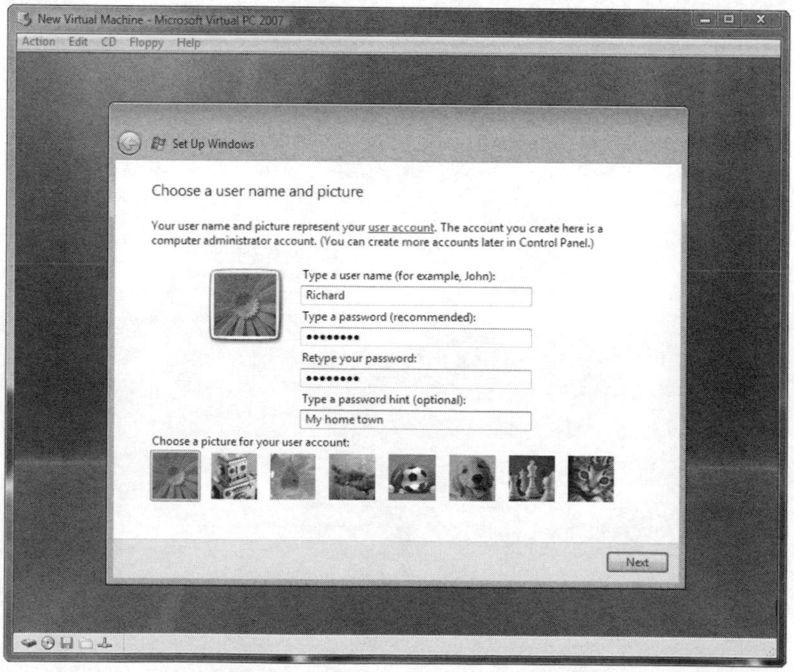

Copyright by Goodheart-Willcox Co., Inc.

15. ____ Select an icon, such as a fish or a flower.

16. ____ Next, the default computer name appears. It is a combination of the user name and PC, for example, Richard-PC. Change the computer name if directed to do so by your instructor.

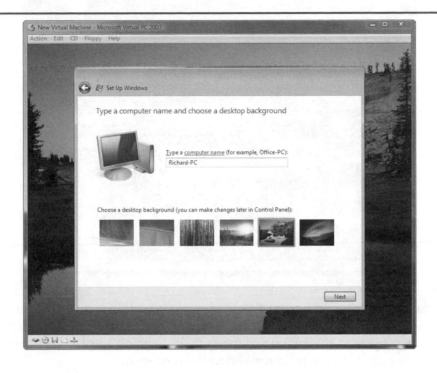

17. ____ Select a desktop picture when prompted.

18. ____ When prompted to set up Windows protection, choose one of the following options: **Use recommended settings, Install updates only**, or **Ask me later.** The **Install updates only** option is selected by default.

19. ____ Set the time zone, date, and time.

20. ____ Next, you are prompted to select your present location. The choices are **Home**, **Work**, and **Public location**. Select **Work** for this lab activity. The **Set Up Windows** dialog box will display.

21. ____ Click the **Start** button. The system will automatically check the system performance, which will take a few minutes. Your name and icon will display, and you will be prompted for your password.

20. ____ Enter your password.

21. _____ The default desktop appears on the display. If an antivirus program has not been installed for the previous operating system version, you will be prompted to install one now. Microsoft will direct you to their Web site through an existing Internet connection if one exist. You may ignore this dialog box and move on to the next step.

22. _____ The **Welcome Center** displays. Take a few moments to inspect the various items at this time.

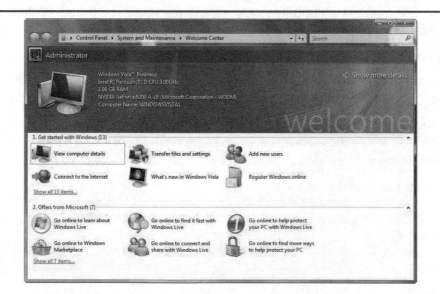

23. _____ Call your instructor to inspect your installation.

24. _____ Shut down the computer, and then reboot it once more to see the default desktop.

25. _____ Shut down the workstation and then answer the review questions. Return all materials to their proper storage area.

Copyright by Goodheart-Willcox Co., Inc.

Review Questions

1. What is the recommended CPU speed for Windows Vista? _____

2. What is the minimum required CPU speed for Windows Vista? _____

3. What should you do before upgrading to Windows Vista? _____

_____

_____

_____

_____

_____

_____

_____

_____

_____

_____

4. What are the five major steps in the Windows Vista upgrade process?_____

_____

_____

_____

_____

5. What file system must Windows Vista be installed on?_____

6. What is the difference between a clean install and a system upgrade? _____

_____

_____

Copyright by Goodheart-Willcox Co., Inc.

Copyright by Goodheart-Willcox Co., Inc.

Name _____ Date _____

Class/Instructor _____

Setting Up
a Dual-Boot System

After completing this laboratory activity, you will be able to:

- Install and configure a dual-boot system.
- Explain the dual-boot requirement for separate partitions/volumes.
- Create a partition during the operating system installation.
- Format a partition as FAT or NTFS.

Introduction

In this lab activity, you will configure a computer as a dual-boot system. A dual-boot system is also known as a *multi-boot system*. A dual-boot system allows you to select from two different operating systems during the boot process. For example, you can choose to boot to Windows XP or Windows Vista.

A dual-boot system is often used during the transition period of one operating system to another. For example, it is used when a user or company wants to gradually convert to the newest operating system while still maintaining their present operating system and software applications. Often when a new operating system is released, many versions of existing software applications will not function properly on the new operating system. A dual-boot system allows a user to run either operating system from the same computer until the software application manufacturer develops a version of software that is compatible with the new operating system.

Normally when installing an operating system, a single partition/volume is created using the entire hard disk drive. When you create a dual-boot system you must use two separate partitions/volumes—one partition/volume for each operating system. If you are creating a multi-boot system using three different operating systems, you would need three separate partitions/volumes.

In the first half of this lab activity, you will install Windows XP on a partition while leaving room for a second partition on the same physical drive. If you have already installed Windows XP on a hard disk drive and have used the entire hard drive as one large partition, you cannot install Windows Vista. You will need to install a second hard disk drive to accommodate Windows Vista.

The following screen capture show the Windows XP installation screen that allows you to allocate a portion of a hard disk drive to the Windows XP operating system.

Copyright by Goodheart-Willcox Co., Inc.

Notice that you are presented with three choices. If you press [Enter], you will install Windows XP on the entire hard disk drive. However, if you press [C], you can create a partition using only a portion of the hard disk drive, leaving sufficient space for the installation of Windows Vista. You must be sure to make this your choice during the installation process of Windows XP when performing this laboratory activity.

The last choice is to delete the existing partition(s) by pressing [D]. Since you will be using equipment in a computer lab that other students have used, it is not unusual to have a hard disk drive with existing partitions on it. If this is the case, you can delete the partition to remove unwanted existing partitions from the hard disk drive and then press [C] to create a partition using only a portion of the hard disk drive.

There are some unique problems you may encounter when using a classroom lab computer and lab hard disk drives. In classroom labs, the hard disk drives are used many times by different students and different classes for many different purposes. Some students may not follow their instructor's instructions to remove all existing files or partitions/volumes when they are finished with an operating system installation lab. Operating system partitions/volumes can be found on the hard disk drive after it is returned to the instructor.

Problems can arise from using a hard disk drive that contains previous versions of operating systems, especially Linux operating systems. Linux uses a partition/volume file system known as the Ext. Windows operating systems do not recognize the Ext file system. If a disk has been used in a previous class for installing a Linux operating system, you will most likely not be able to successfully boot into the Windows operating system, even though no problem occurred during the installation process of the dual-boot system. Often, the symptoms encountered are similar to an operating system being corrupt or to an operating system that fails to successfully install. When this occurs, you must reformat the entire hard disk drive. If you are familiar with Linux, you can start the Linux installation procedure, delete all partitions from the hard disk drive, and then abort the Linux installation.

Another option is to download from the disk drive manufacturer's Web site a utility to perform a low-level format on the hard disk drive. You may also find a number of different tools located at the disk manufacturer's Web site that will identify the existing Linux partitions/volumes and provide a means to remove the partitions. After the Linux partitions have been removed, you can install the Windows operating system in a dual-boot configuration.

Copyright by Goodheart-Willcox Co., Inc.

In the second half of this lab activity, you will install Windows Vista on a separate partition. The following are the Windows Vista recommended hardware requirements:

Recommended hardware requirements for Windows Vista Home Basic edition:

- 1 GHz processor.
- 512 MB RAM.
- 20 GB hard drive (at least 15 GB available space).
- Graphics processor with 32 MB graphics RAM and DirectX 9 capable.
- DVD-ROM drive.
- Audio output capability.
- Internet access capability.

Recommended Hardware Requirements for Windows Vista Home Premium, Business, and Ultimate editions:

- 1 GHz CPU.
- 1 GB RAM.
- 40 GB hard drive (at least 15 GB available space).
- Graphics processor with DirectX 9, Windows Display Driver Model (WDDM), 128 MB RAM, Pixel Shader 2.0, and 32 bits-per-pixel capability.
- DVD-ROM drive.
- Audio output capability.
- Internet access capability.

The computer used for this lab activity must be able to support the recommended requirements for the edition of Windows Vista you will be installing. You can download the Windows Vista Upgrade Advisor from the Microsoft Web site to determine if the system hardware will support Windows Vista.

Equipment and Materials

- PC that meets the recommended requirements for the Windows Vista edition you will be installing and also allows for the recommended hard drive requirements of Windows XP.
- Windows XP installation CD/DVD.
- Windows Vista installation DVD.
- The following information for the Windows XP installation:

Full user name: _____

Organization: _____

User name: _____

Password: _____

Windows XP 26-character product key: ____ ____ ____ ____ ____

Computer name: _____

Administrative password: _____

Workgroup name: _____, *or* Domain name: _____

- The following information for the Windows Vista installation:

User name: _____

Password: _____

Product ID: _____ - _____ - _____ - _____ - _____

Computer name: _____

Location type—Public, Private, or Work: _____

Part I—Windows XP

Procedure

1. ____ Report to your assigned workstation. The computer at your workstation may or may not have an operating system presently installed. If the computer does have an operating system already installed, you can still install Windows XP.

2. ____ Place the Windows XP installation disc into the CD/DVD drive and then reboot the computer. The Windows XP installation process should automatically begin. If the computer fails to start the Windows XP installation process, you will need to reconfigure the system BIOS. The system BIOS boot device sequence needs to be changed so that the first boot device is the CD/DVD drive. If you need assistance reconfiguring the BIOS, ask your instructor for assistance.

3. ____ After the Windows XP installation CD starts, you should see a screen that looks similar to the following.

Notice that you are presented with three options: **To setup Windows XP now, press ENTER, To repair a Windows XP installation using Recovery Console, press R**, and **To quit Setup without installing Windows XP, press F3**. Select **To setup Windows XP now, press ENTER** by pressing the [Enter] key.

Copyright by Goodheart-Willcox Co., Inc.

4. ____ The Microsoft Windows XP license agreement will appear and look similar to the following. Press the [F8] key to accept the license agreement.

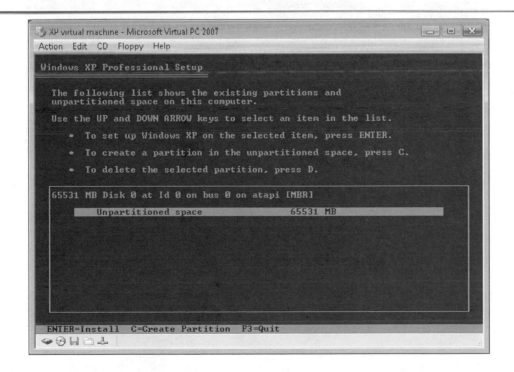

5. ____ Now, the most critical screen of the dual-boot process will appear. There are three options: **To set up Windows XP on the selected item, press ENTER**, **To create a partition in the unpartitioned space, press C**, and **To delete the selected partition, press D**. Press [C] to create a partition on the hard disk drive.

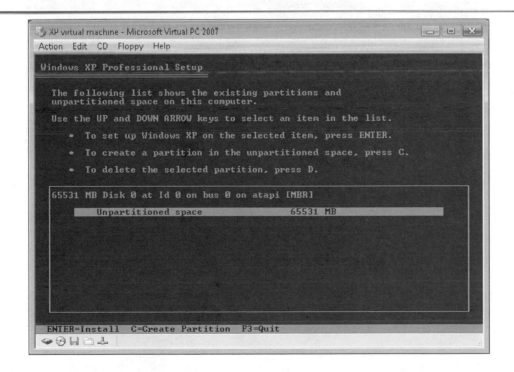

6. ____ The next screen to appear prompts you to choose the size of partition you will create. Create a partition of 20000 MB for the Windows XP operating system. This should still leave adequate space for Windows Vista.

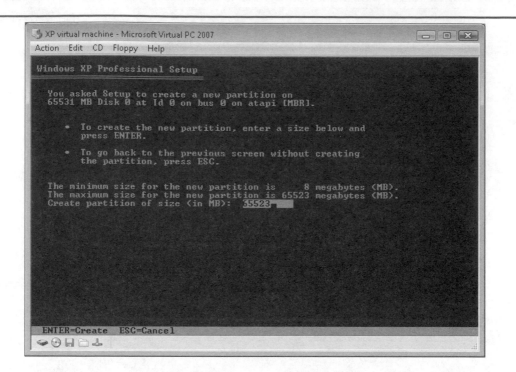

7. ____ The next screen prompts you to verify the creation of the new partition and will look similar to the following. Press the [Enter] key to install Windows XP on the selected partition.

Copyright by Goodheart-Willcox Co., Inc.

8. ____ The next screen will provide you with four file format options: NTFS (Quick), FAT (Quick), NTFS, and FAT. The difference between performing a regular format and a quick format is a quick format does not check for bad sectors. Also, a quick format can only be performed on a previously formatted partition.

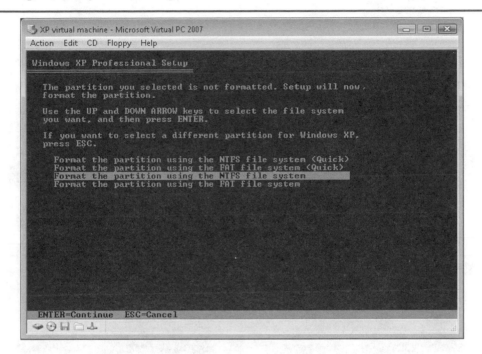

The Windows default choice is NTFS file system. However, for this lab activity, you will select the FAT file system, not the FAT (Quick) option. Choosing FAT (FAT32) for Windows XP and later choosing NTFS for the Windows Vista installation will provide you with an opportunity to compare each file format. You will be able to compare security features and user permissions. You will also be able to perform a file conversion from FAT32 to NTFS.

9. ____ The next screen to appear verifies your choice of the FAT file format.

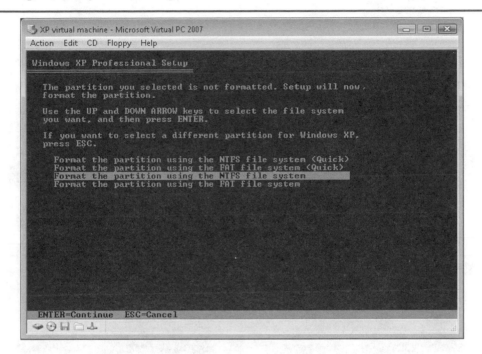

Notice the message that appears informing you that the partition is larger than 2048 MB and that setup will format it with the FAT32 file system. This is because the largest FAT16 partition is 2 GB. Anything larger requires FAT32. Press the [Enter] key to verify your choice of FAT32 for the Windows XP partition. You will see the format process being displayed similar to that in the following screen capture.

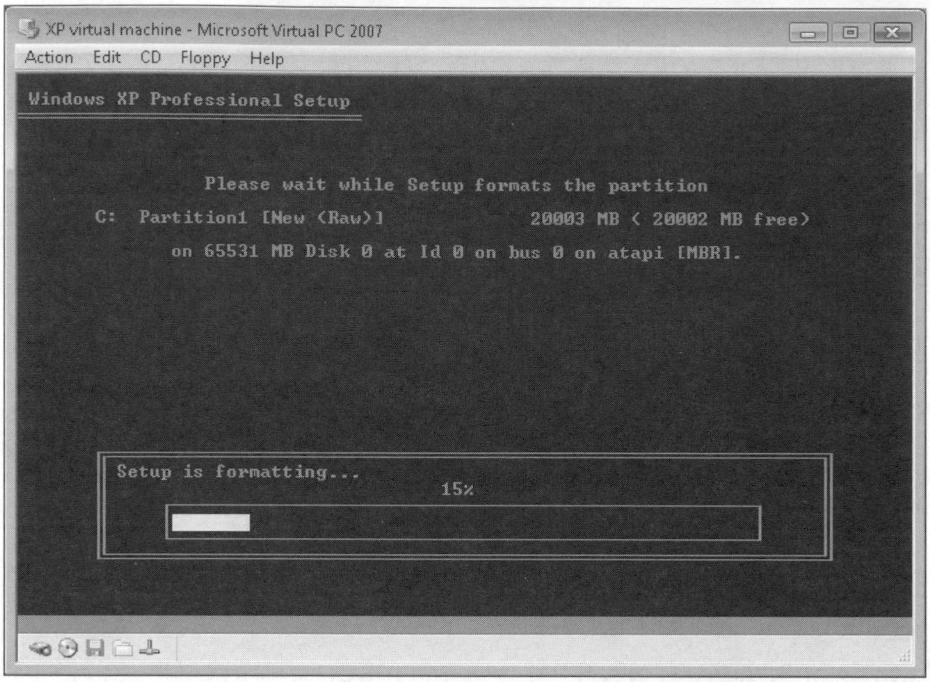

As you can see, the format progress is displayed as a bar graph and percentage. The larger the partition, the longer the format will take. After the format process is complete, the next screen to appear notifies you that the installation files are being copied from the installation CD. The display will look similar to that in the following screen capture.

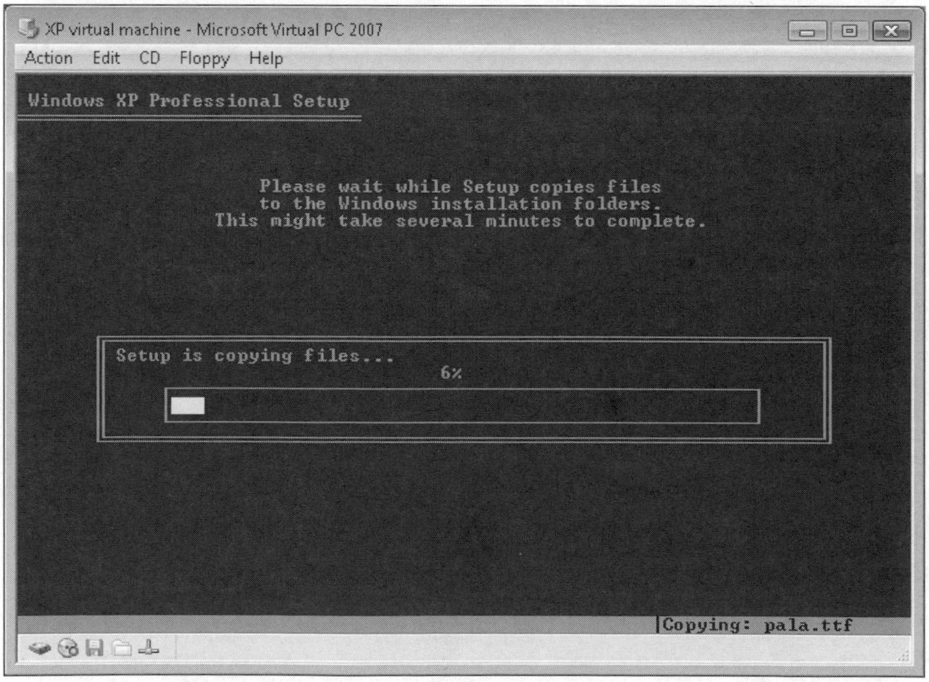

Copyright by Goodheart-Willcox Co., Inc.

The next screen to appear warns you that the computer is about to reboot and to remove any floppy disk from drive A. You also have the option to reboot the computer without the delay by pressing the [Enter] key.

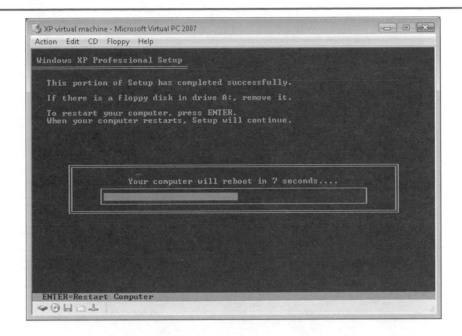

After the computer reboots, the command line input portion of the installation ends and the graphical user input portion begins. Look at the following screen capture of the graphical user installation.

You can view the progress of the installation by viewing the progress bar or watching the major installation portion indicated by the radial buttons on the left. In the previous screen capture, the "Preparing installation" portion of the installation process has ended and the "Installing Window" portion has begun.

The next series of dialog boxes to appear requests user information to complete the installation process. You may experience a system reboot several times during this portion of the installation.

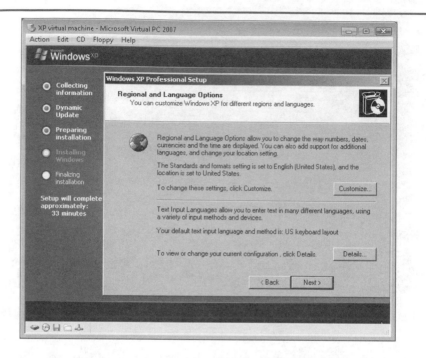

10. ____ The next dialog box informs you of the default region and language selection. You can choose different languages and regional settings at this point if you desire. In most instances, you will simply select the default English (United States) configuration.

11. ____ Next you are prompted for your full user name and organization. These are actually optional, but filling them in will provide information used in many Microsoft Windows software applications, such as Microsoft Office. Input the user name and organization provided in the required materials section.

Copyright by Goodheart-Willcox Co., Inc.

12. ____ Next you are prompted for the 25-character product key. As stated in the dialog box, the product key is typically on the back of the Windows CD case. You may also receive the product key from your instructor. Enter the product key now.

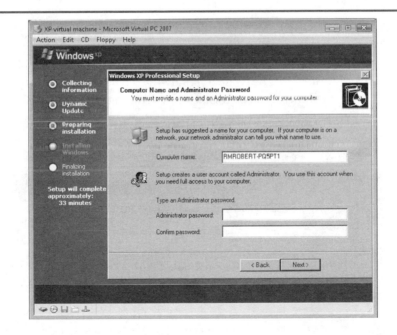

13. ____ The next dialog box to appear prompts you for the computer name and administrator password.

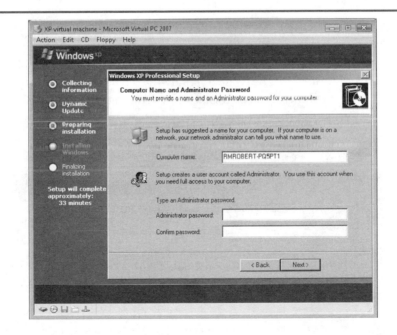

As you can see in the screen capture, Windows XP automatically generates a suggested computer name based on previously input information. Appended to this is a randomly generated set of characters. Each computer name should be unique to ensure proper networking communications and workstation identification. Computers identified with the same name will prove to be confusing.

The administrator password is entered twice to ensure that the first password entered does not contain a typo. Use the administrator password provided by your instructor.

14. ____ The next dialog box to appear prompts you for the date and time as well as the time zone.

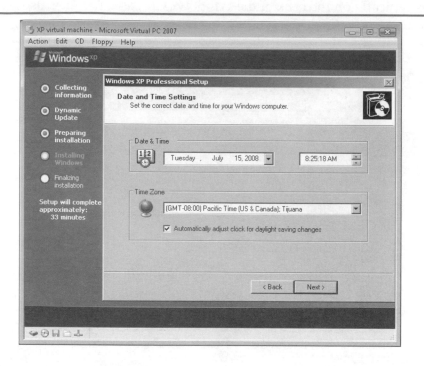

The correct time is typically already entered. It is based on the system BIOS. You will most likely need to identify the correct time zone.

15. ____ The next dialog box to appear prompts you for the network settings. In most instances, you will accept the default **Typical settings** option. The **Custom settings** option allows you to configure the network settings manually. For example, you can assign a static IP address for the computer rather than accept the default DHCP setting. The **Typical settings** option configures the computer to receive an IP address automatically from a network DHCP server or service provider. Accept the **Typical settings** option now.

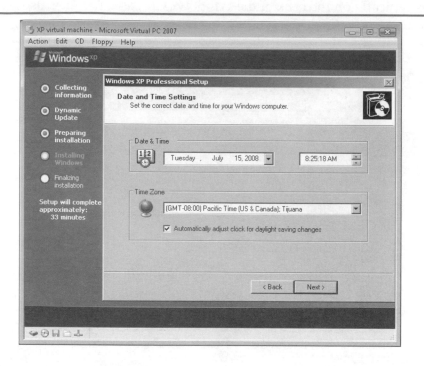

Copyright by Goodheart-Willcox Co., Inc.

16. ____ The next dialog box to appear also concerns the network configuration. Leave the default selection, which identifies the computer as part of a network not controlled by a domain administrator and server. The default name for this configuration is "Workgroup." Do not change this name unless otherwise instructed by your instructor. If you are going to make this computer part of a domain, you must refer to the required materials list to see the domain name issued by the instructor.

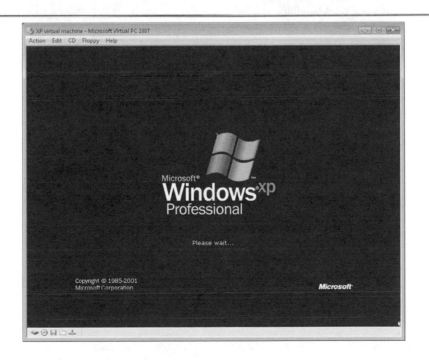

17. ____ The next screen to appear automatically is the Windows XP splash screen similar to the one in the following screen capture.

18. ____ After a few seconds the **Welcome to Microsoft Windows** screen appears. Click **Next** to proceed.

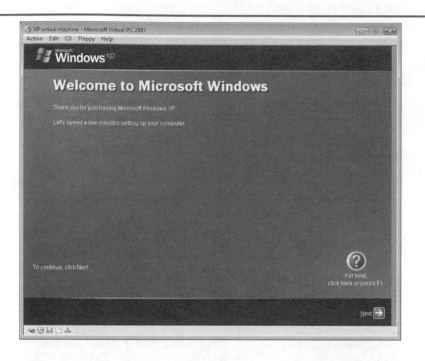

19. ____ The next screen to appear asks if the computer will connect to the Internet directly or through a network. Select **No, this computer will connect directly to the Internet**. You can also click the **Skip** button and configure the Internet connection at a later time.

Copyright by Goodheart-Willcox Co., Inc.

20. ____ Now, you will be prompted to activate Windows XP. You do not need to activate Windows XP at this time. You have 30 days to activate Windows XP. You can activate Windows XP at some future date. Select **No, remind me every few days** and then click **Next**.

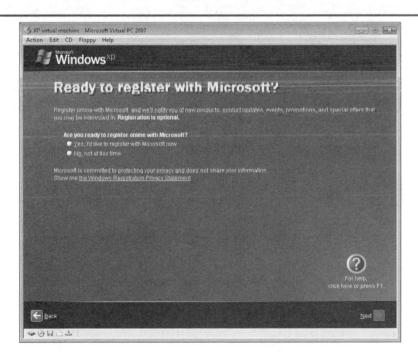

21. ____ You will be prompted to register with Microsoft at this time. Do not register with Microsoft. Select **No, not at this time** and then click **Next**.

22. ____ Now, you will be prompted to add an additional user who will use the computer. Do not add any additional users at this time. Click **Next** to proceed.

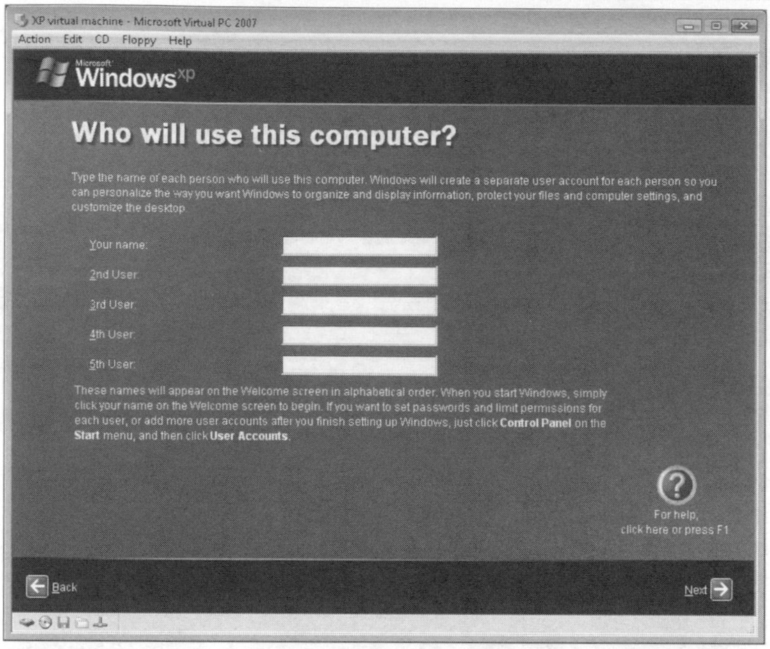

23. ____ The next screen to appear looks similar to that in the following screen capture. Click **Finish** to complete the installation of Windows XP.

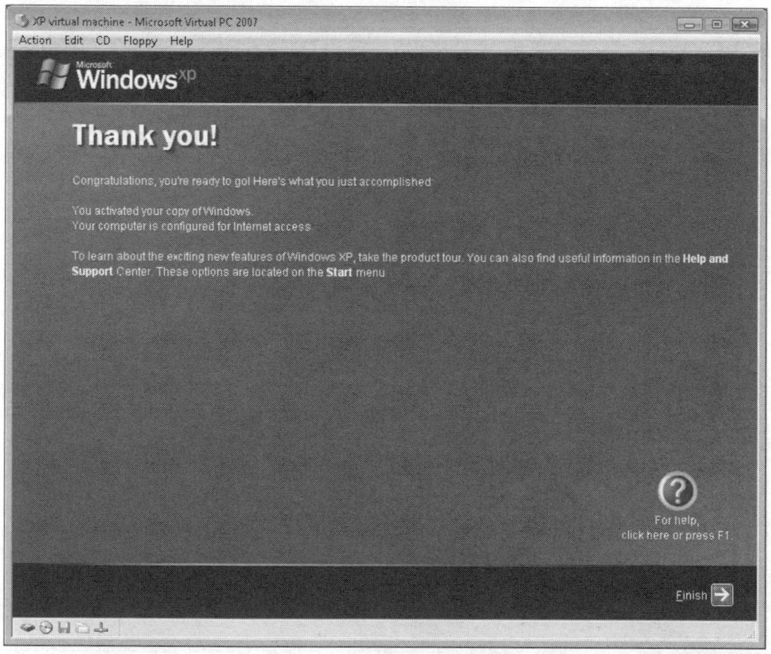

Copyright by Goodheart-Willcox Co., Inc.

24. ____ The system logon screen will appear and look similar to the following screen capture. Log on and verify that Windows XP has been successfully installed and is running properly.

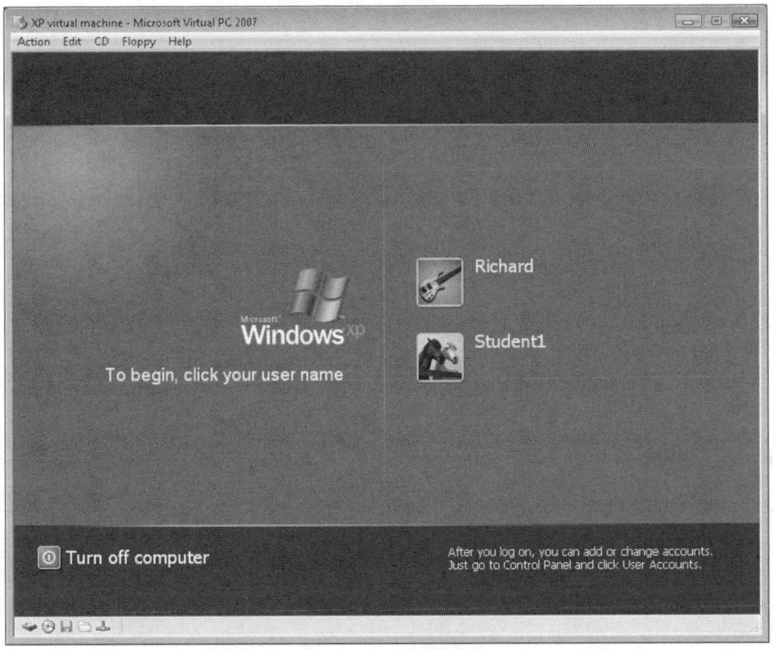

25. ____ Shut down the computer and then boot the computer to verify the Windows XP system is working.

26. ____ Have your instructor inspect your computer now.

Part II—Windows Vista

Procedure

1. _____ Boot the computer on which you have installed Windows XP. Insert the Windows Vista installation DVD in the CD/DVD drive and then restart the computer. When the computer boots, it will automatically start the Windows Vista installation.

2. _____ The first screen to appear is similar to that in the following screen capture. Notice that Windows Vista is set by default to **English** for the language to install, **English (United States)** for the time and currency format, and **US** for the keyboard or input format. You will accept the defaults in most cases.

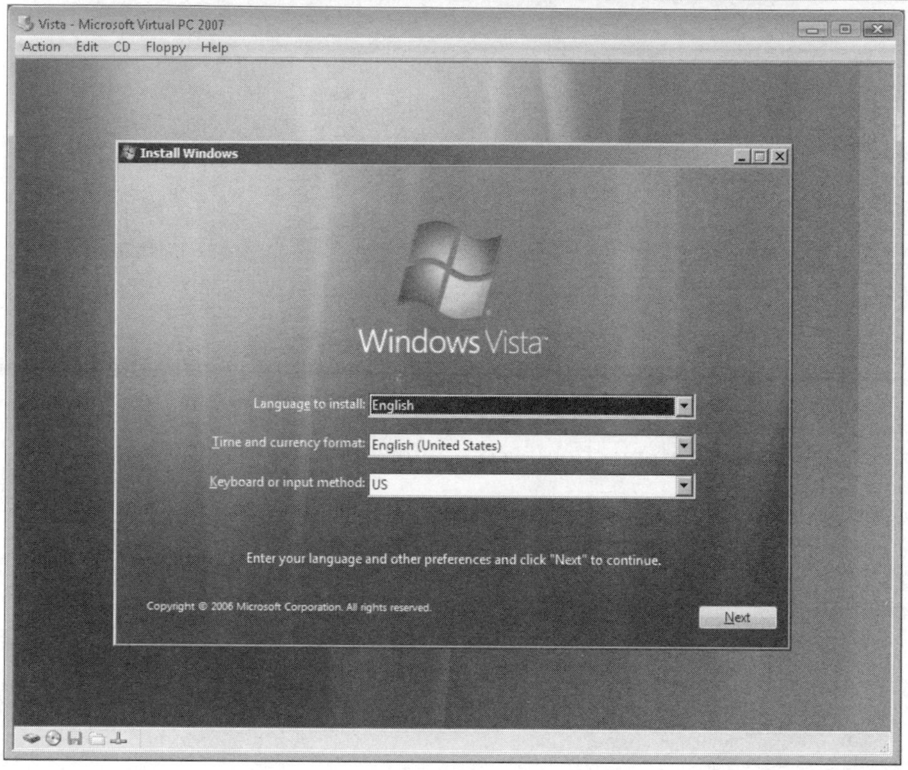

Copyright by Goodheart-Willcox Co., Inc.

3. ____ The next screen to appear prompts you to either install or repair an existing system. You also have an option to view material about what you should know before installing Windows. Simply click **Install now**.

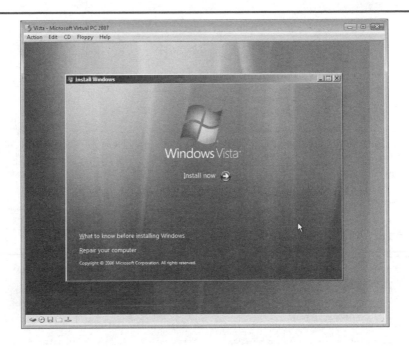

4. ____ The next screen prompts you for the 25-character product key. Enter the product key carefully. Some characters are often incorrectly read such as the uppercase letter *B* and number *8* and the uppercase letter *Q* and uppercase letter *O*.

Deselect the **Automatically activate Windows when I'm online** option and then click **Next**. You can activate Windows Vista anytime in the next 30 days. You should not activate at this time because you may experience a problem that will force you to reinstall after changing some hardware device. When Windows Vista is set to activate, it typically waits three days before performing the actual activation. You may have a problem reinstalling the operating system during this time.

Copyright by Goodheart-Willcox Co., Inc.

5. ____ You are prompted to accept the license agreement. Select **I accept the license terms** option and then click **Next**.

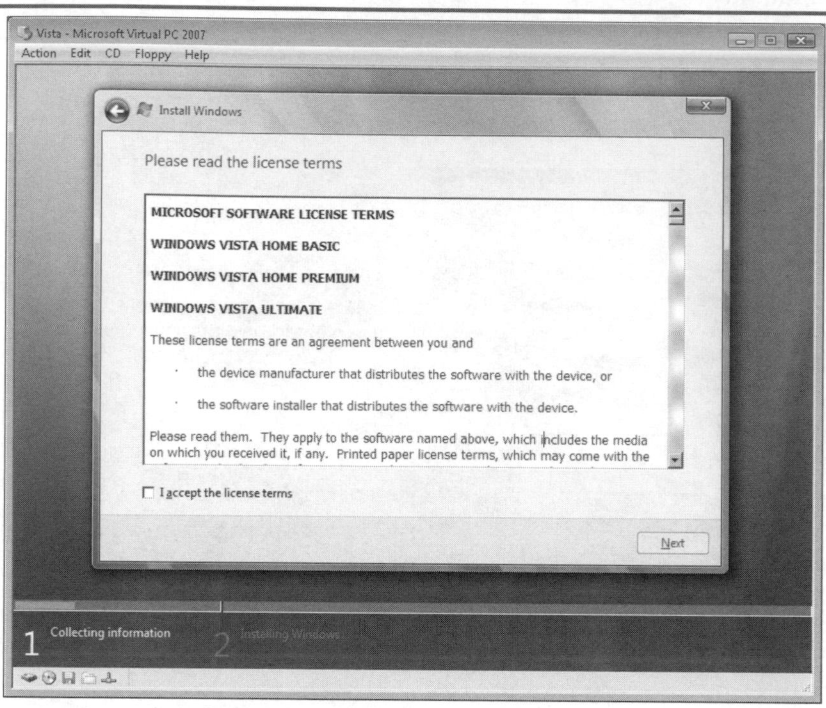

6. ____ The next screen asks if you want to perform an upgrade or a custom install. You must select the **Custom (Advanced)** option to install a clean copy of Windows Vista on its own partition. Click **Custom (Advanced)** now.

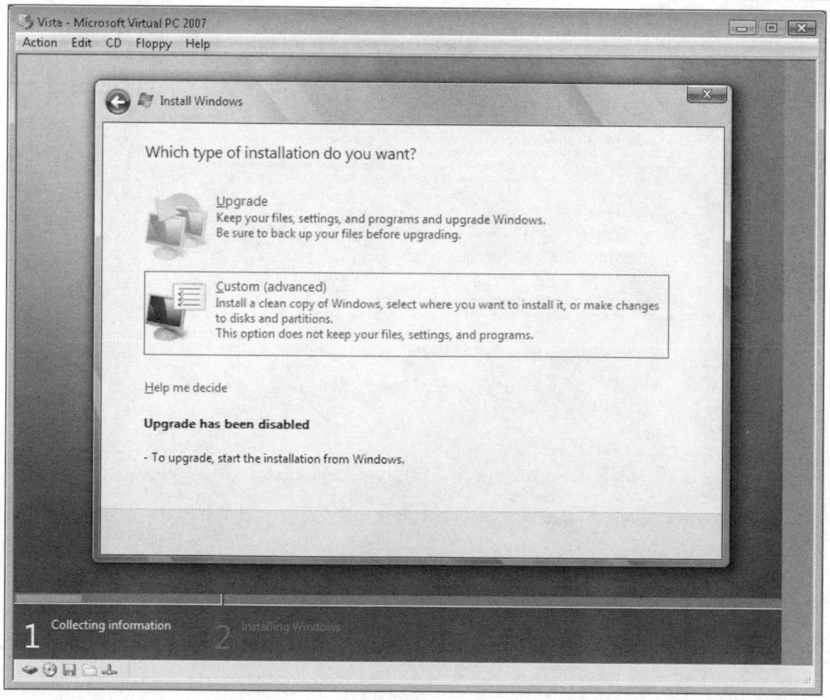

Copyright by Goodheart-Willcox Co., Inc.

Name____

7. ____ The next screen to appear presents the layout of any existing partitions and unused disk space. The following screen capture was taken from a Microsoft Virtual PC system and does not reflect a true screen capture of what you might see in a real dual-boot scenario.

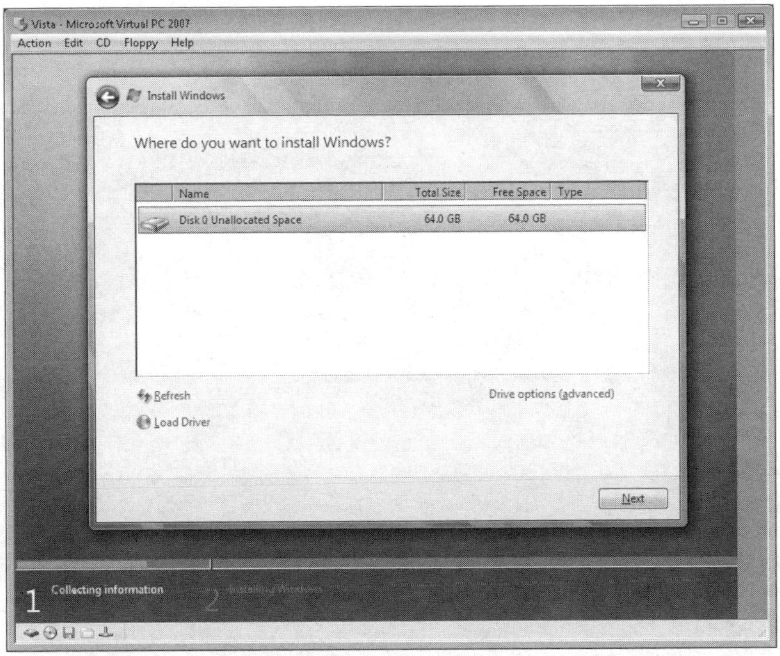

Your view should show the previously installed Windows XP partition as well as the unused portion of the hard disk drive. Clicking **Drive options (advanced)** will provide you with the tools necessary to create a partition in the unused space of the hard disk drive. You will install Windows Vista in the unused section of the hard disk drive. You will also limit the size for the Windows Vista partition to 40 GB. A large partition will take significantly longer to format. Your lab time is most likely very limited and formatting a very large drive could take hours.

8. ____ The next screen presents the progress of the installation. The series starts with "Copying Windows files" and ends with "Completing installation."

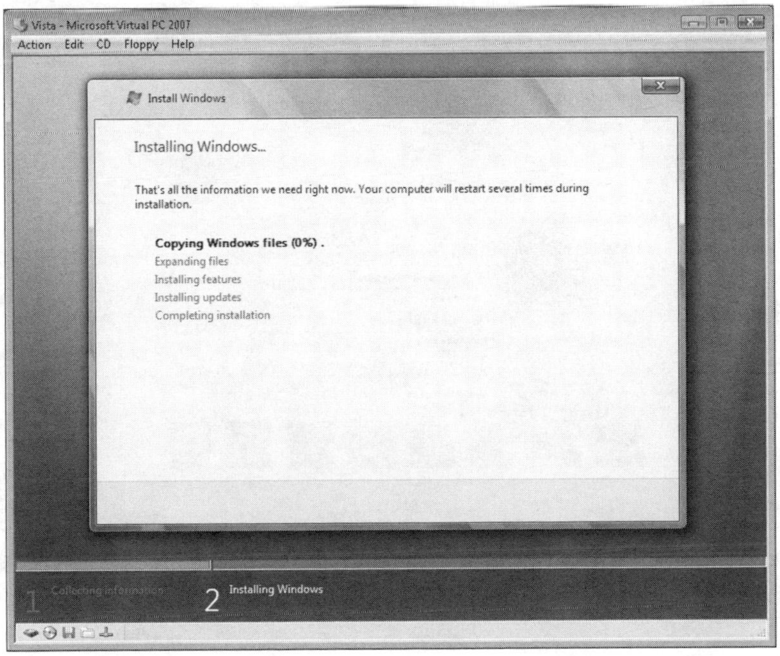

Copyright by Goodheart-Willcox Co., Inc.

You may see the computer reboot during this section of the installation process. When the computer reboots, you will see a screen similar to the following, prompting you to wait while Windows prepares to start for the first time. This portion can take quite awhile, much more than a few seconds. Please be patient.

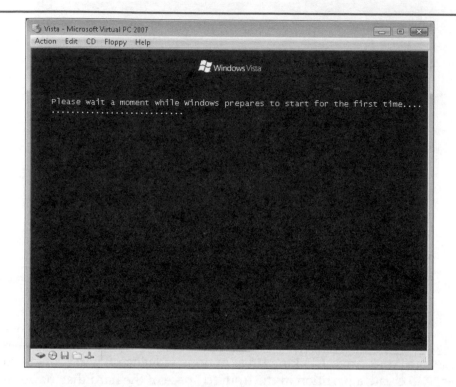

9. _____ The next screen to appear after Windows Vista starts for the first time will prompt you for a user name and password. You will need to enter the password twice. The option to enter a password hint is optional and generally not used. You may also pick an icon for the user account at this time.

Copyright by Goodheart-Willcox Co., Inc.

10. ____ Next, you are prompted to choose a computer name and a desktop image.

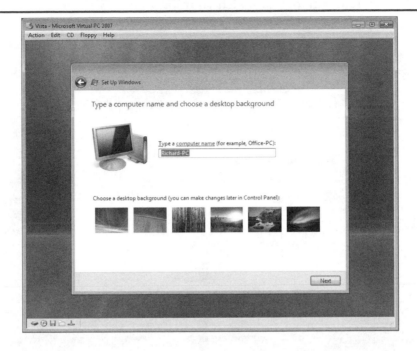

When choosing a computer name, you should use a name that does not match the previous Windows XP name. Using the same name for the same computer in a dual-boot scenario can cause some security problems. The security system detects the same name used for two different operating systems and may interpret this as an attempt to hack into a network. Many times a computer will have a difficult time connecting to a network share when the same computer name is used for both dual-boot operating systems. In the case of Windows Vista, you will notice that it does not generate a random set of characters the way Windows XP does. You should use the computer name issued by your instructor for the lab; otherwise, accepting the default name should be all right for this lab activity.

11. ____ The next dialog box prompts you for information about automatic updates. To save lab time, click **Ask me later.**

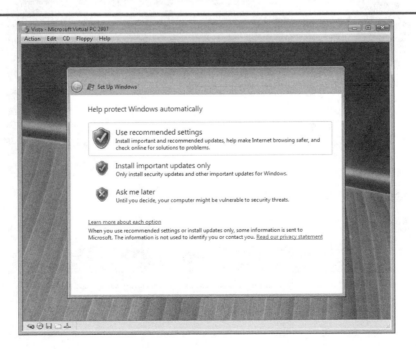

12. ____ The next screen prompts you for information concerning the date, time, and time zone. Complete or verify the information to match your location.

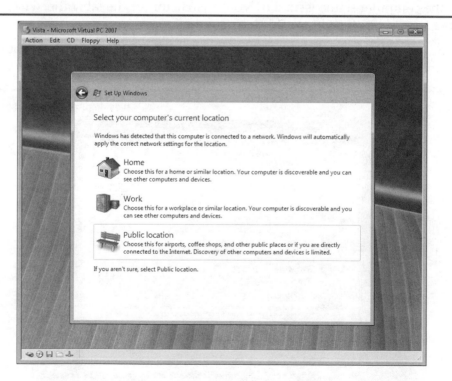

13. ____ Now you must select the type of setting your computer is used in. The three choices will determine how to configure network discovery and the Microsoft firewall. For this lab activity, simply click **Public location**, unless otherwise indicated by your instructor.

Copyright by Goodheart-Willcox Co., Inc.

14. ____ Next, the Windows Vista **Thank you** screen will appear followed by the logon screen.

You have now completed the Windows Vista installation. When you restart the computer, you will see the **Windows Boot Manager** screen.

Copyright by Goodheart-Willcox Co., Inc.

```
┌─────────────────────────────────────────────────────────────┐
│                     Windows Boot Manager                      │
│  ─────────────────────────────────────────────────────────   │
│                                                               │
│   Choose an operating system to start, or press TAB to        │
│   select a tool:                                              │
│   (Use the arrow key to highlight you choice, then press      │
│   ENTER.)                                                      │
│                                                               │
│           Earlier version of Windows                          │
│           Microsoft Windows Vista                             │
│           ┌───────────────────────────────────────────┐      │
│           └───────────────────────────────────────────┘      │
│                                                               │
│   To specify an advanced option for this choice, press F8.    │
│   Seconds until the highlighted choice will be started        │
│   automatically: 30                                           │
│                                                               │
│   Tools:                                                      │
│                                                               │
│           Windows Memory Diagnostics                          │
│                                                               │
│                                                               │
└─────────────────────────────────────────────────────────────┘
```

Notice that the boot manager refers to the Windows XP operating system as "Earlier version of Windows." You will have 30 seconds maximum time to select the operating system to which to boot. Otherwise, the boot manager will automatically select the Windows Vista operating system.

15. ____ You have completed the lab activity and created a dual-boot system. Go on to answer the review questions at this time.

Copyright by Goodheart-Willcox Co., Inc.

Name _____

Review Questions

1. How many partitions are required for a dual-boot installation? _____

2. What is the largest FAT16 partition? _____

3. What is the default partition format for Windows XP? _____

4. What is the default partition format for Windows Vista? _____

5. How long do you have before you must activate Windows Vista? _____

6. What is the recommended partition size for Windows Vista Home Basic edition? _____

7. What is the recommended partition size for Windows Vista Home Premium, Business, and Ultimate editions? _____

8. What is the recommended RAM for Vista Home Basic edition? _____

9. What is the recommended RAM for Vista Home Premium, Business, and Ultimate editions?

   _____

10. What is the name of the program that controls which operating system is selected during the boot operation? _____

Copyright by Goodheart-Willcox Co., Inc.

Name _____ Date _____

Class/Instructor _____

Configuring Start Menu Options

After completing this laboratory activity, you will be able to:

■ Locate the **Taskbar and Start Menu Properties** dialog box.

■ Configure the **Start** menu as classic style or default.

■ Pin a program to the **Start** menu.

■ Explain the various log off and turn off options associated with the **Start** menu.

■ Access the **Start** menu using shortcut keys.

Introduction

The laboratory activities in this manual are designed to expand your knowledge of the Windows XP and Windows Vista operating systems as well as earlier Microsoft operating systems. It is imperative that you complete each laboratory activity. Many of the labs contain information not found in your textbook and can only be fully comprehended by completing the entire activity. If you plan to pass the CompTIA A+ Certification exams at the end of your course of study, you need to complete all laboratory activities in this manual. Do not skip material, even if you feel you are familiar with the activity. Many times you will discover obvious features that you were not aware of before. Most laboratory activities can be completed on either a Windows XP or a Windows Vista computer. Sometimes the activity may be unique to a particular operating system and thus must be completed on that particular operating system.

Start Menu

You are most likely very familiar with the Windows operating system **Start** menu, but there are several items you may not be familiar with. It is therefore important that you complete this laboratory activity in its entirety before moving on in the lab manual.

Microsoft Windows operating systems try to maintain some user interface standards so that a user can intuitively adapt to a new version of the operating system. However, there are always some differences. For example, there are several differences in the design of the **Start** menu between Windows XP and Windows Vista as well as with previous Microsoft Windows operating systems. Look at the following screen captures of Windows XP and Windows Vista.

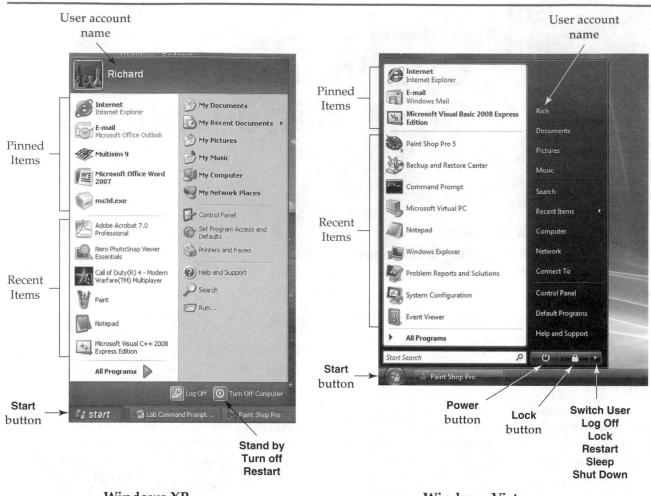

User account name

User account name

Pinned Items

Pinned Items

Recent Items

Recent Items

Start button

Start button

Stand by
Turn off
Restart

Power button

Lock button

Switch User
Log Off
Lock
Restart
Sleep
Shut Down

Windows XP

Windows Vista

In both Windows XP and Windows Vista, the account name appears at the top of the **Start** menu. This identifies the user account of who is logged on to the computer at this time. There is a section of "pinned" items located at the top left of the **Start** menu which appears each time the computer is started. You can add or remove items from the pinned items list.

Beneath the pinned items list is a section of recently accessed programs. This list of programs will change based on which programs are most commonly accessed during the normal use of the computer.

The right side of the **Start** menu has a list of standard default programs and folders most commonly used with the operating system. There are some slight differences in the right-hand side when the two systems are compared. Notice how the names of some items have changed. For example, **My Documents** in Windows XP is now simply **Documents** in Windows Vista.

The **Start** menu can be modified or customized to match the wishes of the individual user. To customize the **Start** menu, right-click the **Start** button or an empty section of the taskbar, which is located at the bottom of the screen. The **Taskbar and Start Menu Properties** dialog box will appear similar to those in the following screen captures.

    Copyright by Goodheart-Willcox Co., Inc.

Name_____

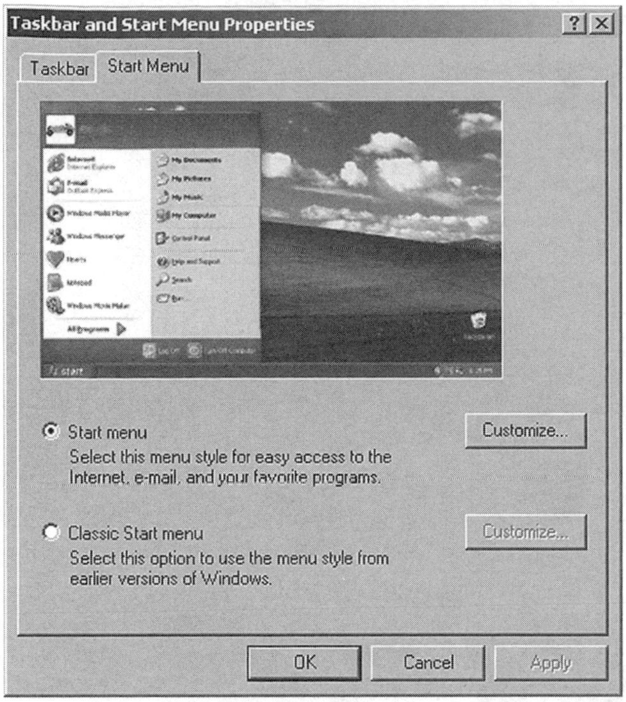

Windows XP 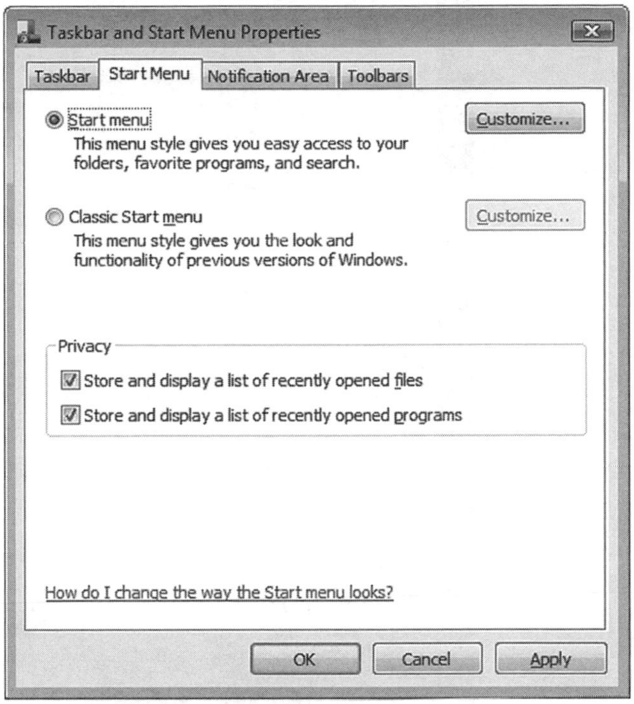   **Windows Vista**

The **Start** menu configuration options are very similar in Windows XP and Windows Vista. The major differences are the two new tabs in Windows Vista: **Notification Area** and **Toolbars**. There will be more about these two tabs in later laboratory activities.

Look at the option **Classic Start menu** which changes the **Start** menu to the classic style. The classic style has the look and feel of previous Windows operating systems dating back to Windows 95 and 98. The classic style is often requested by long time users of the operating system who are used to using the previous version of Windows. Many users prefer the original GUI and are not comfortable with the latest or newer version.

Note:
As a computer technician, you should become familiar with both menu styles. You may be employed as a help desk technician, which would require you to communicate with users and be familiar with both menu styles: default and classic.

Look at the following screen capture of the classic style of Windows XP and Windows Vista. In the classic style, the operating system is identified on the left side of the menu. Also, notice that the classic style has a single column of program options.

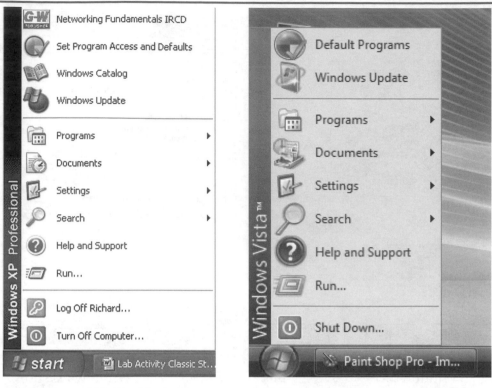

Windows XP Classic Style　　　　**Windows Vista Classic Style**

When more than one user account exists on a computer, changes to the **Start** menu will only affect the user who initiated the change. In other words, each user can have his or her customized **Start** menu.

Paths

The laboratory manual presents paths to programs and to dialog boxes by using a series of locations separated by a vertical line. For example, the following path to the Notepad program is indicated as **Start | All Programs | Accessories | Notepad**.

Look at the following Windows XP screen capture of the indicated path beginning at the **Start** button and ending at the Notepad program. Compare this to how the path is indicated in the previous paragraph.

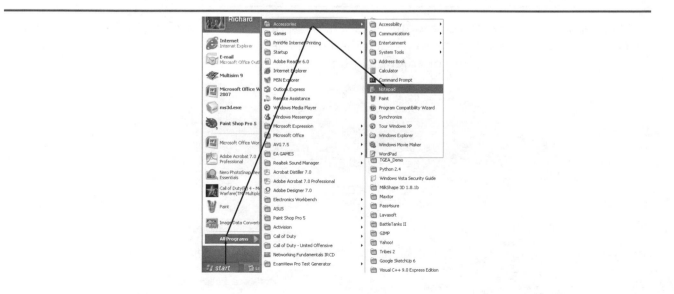

Copyright by Goodheart-Willcox Co., Inc.

Name_____

This path convention will be used throughout the beginning of the laboratory manual. As you become more familiar with the location of commonly accessed programs, the exact path will no longer be provided. You should become familiar with all common program locations as you progress through the laboratory activities.

Shutdown and Power-Saving Features

There are several ways to shut down, log off, or suspend a computer session on the Windows computer system. You can simply shut down the power to the system using the **Start** menu options, or you can temporarily suspend the current session and preserve the open programs that the current user is using. During suspending the current session, the computer operating system goes into power-saving mode by shutting down the monitor and suspending hard disk drive activity and the RAM refresh. On some systems, the activity of the CPU is slowed. All these methods are designed to save electrical energy.

Note:

Some shutdown features mentioned in the lab activity may not be available on your computer. This is most likely caused by the way the power options are configured on your computer system. For example, you may not have an option to place the computer into hibernation or sleep when shutting down the computer. Two other factors that may affect hibernation and sleep are the computer BIOS and the video card capabilities. If your computer is not configured for hibernation and or sleep mode, then skip these steps in the lab activity. They will be covered again in a later lab activity.

Equipment and Materials

■ Computer with Windows XP or Window Vista, or both, installed.

Part I—Windows XP

Procedure

1. _____ Report to your assigned workstation.

2. _____ Boot the computer and verify it is in working order.

3. _____ Look at the keyboard and see if a Windows logo key is part of the keyboard. It should be located in the lower left-hand side of the keyboard between the [Ctrl] and [Alt] keys.

If your keyboard does not have the Windows logo, move on to the next step. If your keyboard does have this key, press it now and note that the Windows XP **Start** menu automatically opens.

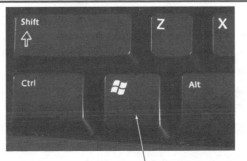
Windows logo key

4. ____ Another method to access the **Start** menu is by selecting the [Ctrl] and [Esc] keys simultaneously. This is a shortcut key combination that automatically opens the **Start** menu. Try it now.

5. ____ Click the **Turn Off Computer** button and then view the three options available to you: **Stand by**, **Turn off**, and **Restart**. The **Stand by** option places the computer in low-power mode. In low-power mode, the monitor and other power-consuming features of the computer are turned off. Only a bare minimum of power is consumed by the computer in standby mode. The computer can be brought out of standby mode by pressing any key, such as the spacebar. If a program like Microsoft Word is open at the time **Stand by** is selected, the Microsoft Word program will reappear when the computer comes out of standby.

The other two options are as implied by their names. **Turn off** completely turns off the computer after closing all programs. The **Restart** option shuts down the computer and then restarts it. This is commonly used as a first attempt to fix a program problem or required after installing some software programs. Take a few minutes and try each option.

6. ____ You can pin a program to the **Start** menu so that it appears in the top-left list of **Start** menu programs. Simply open the **Start** menu to the desired program, and then right-click the program. A shortcut menu will appear similar to the following.

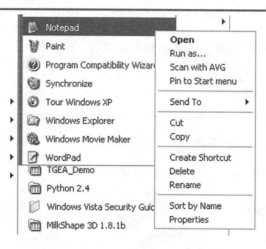

The shortcut menu in the screen capture is from Windows XP. A similar shortcut menu is used in Windows Vista. Notice the **Pin to Start menu** item. When selected, the Notepad program is added to the **Start** menu list. Select it now and observe the results.

7. ____ Open the **Start** menu at this time and see if the Notepad program has been added to the list of pinned programs. If it does not appear in the list of pinned programs, call your instructor for assistance.

8. ____ Now, unpin the Notepad program by right-clicking the Notepad program in the pinned items list and then selecting **Unpin from Start menu** from the shortcut menu. Unpin the Notepad program now. If you have difficultly, call your instructor for assistance.

9. ____ Right-click the **Start** button and then select **Properties** from the shortcut menu. The **Taskbar and Start Menu Properties** dialog box should appear with the **Start Menu** tab selected. Select the **Classic Start menu** option and then click **Apply**. Close the dialog box and then open the **Start** menu. It should have changed to the classic style. The name of the operating system should appear on the left side.

10. ____ Now, open the **Taskbar and Start Menu Properties** dialog box and return the **Start** menu to the default style.

Copyright by Goodheart-Willcox Co., Inc.

11. ____ When ending a computer session, you may log off, switch user, shut down, or place the computer in standby. The **Switch User** option is revealed after **Log Off** has been selected. The **Switch User** option is handy when a different user wishes to use the computer temporarily, such as to check his or her e-mail while another user is using the computer. After the user checks his or her e-mail, he or she logs off or switches users, thus giving control back to the other user. The **Stand by** option is revealed after selecting the **Turn Off Computer** option. When the Windows XP computer is placed in standby mode, the computer goes into power-saving mode. It shuts down the monitor, stops hard disk drive activity, and saves the current computer session in memory (RAM).

It is also possible to place the computer into hibernation, which saves even more energy by shutting down power to RAM. The computer is revived from standby or hibernation mode by keyboard activity, such as pressing the spacebar and, in some cases, pressing the physical power button.

Note:
Not all computer hardware systems or BIOS are the same, and there is not one uniform method for bringing a computer out of standby, sleep, or hibernation mode.

Any program open at the time the computer was placed into standby or hibernation mode should reappear on the desktop when revived. Beware that the computer will recover faster from standby than from hibernation. The reason for the faster recovery from standby mode is the current computer session is saved in RAM. Hibernation saves the current session to the hard disk drive. It takes longer to restart when the current session is saved to hard disk drive.

Also, be aware that if the computer experiences a complete power failure during standby, the current session is lost and will not be displayed on the desktop.

Take a few minutes and explore the various shutdown and logoff features. Open Notepad and leave it open on the desktop while you experiment with shutdown and logoff options.

12. ____ This concludes Part I of the laboratory activity. Do not answer the review questions until you complete Part II—Windows Vista.

Part II—Windows Vista

Procedure

1. ____ Report to your assigned workstation.

2. ____ Boot the computer and verify it is in working order.

3. ____ Pin the Notepad program to the pinned items list section of the **Start** menu. To do this, access the Notepad program using the path **Start | All Programs | Accessories | Notepad**. Right-click **Notepad** and select the **Pin to Start Menu** item from shortcut menu. The Notepad program should now be pinned to the pinned items list. If not, call your instructor for assistance.

4. ____ Now, remove the Notepad program from the pinned items list by right-clicking **Notepad** and clicking the **Unpin from Start Menu** item. The Notepad program should be automatically unpinned from the menu.

5. ____ Right-click the **Start** button and select **Properties** from the shortcut menu. The **Taskbar and Start Menu Properties** dialog box should appear. Select the **Classic Start menu** option in the dialog box and then click **Apply** and then **OK** to close the dialog box. The **Start** menu should

now appear as classic style when opened. This is indicated by the operating system name appearing on the left-hand side when the **Start** menu is opened.

6. ____ Return the **Start** menu to its default.

7. ____ Open Notepad once more and leave it open on the desktop.

8. ____ Use the Windows **Start** menu **Power** button [⏻] to turn off the computer while Notepad is still open on the desktop. Do not close Notepad.

9. ____ After one or two minutes, press the spacebar and give the desktop a chance to appear. You may need to log on once more to access the desktop. The Notepad program should appear on the desktop just like it was when you pressed the Windows Vista **Power** button.

10. ____ Now, leave the Notepad program open on the desktop, but this time select the **Shut Down** option from the **Start** menu, not from the Windows Vista **Power** button.

11. ____ After the computer has shut down, restart the computer. Is Notepad still open on the desktop?

_____

12. Repeat the experiment using the **Hibernate** and the **Sleep** options to shut down the operating system and observe the effect on the open Notepad program. If sleep mode is not available on your computer, it is most likely because the video card does not support sleep mode.

Note:
Most video cards do support hibernation.

Program still open? Yes or No? _____

Hibernation Yes or No? _____

Sleep Yes or No? _____

Both hibernation and sleep modes are designed to save power but not to completely power down the computer system. Sleep is typically used on laptop computers with graphic cards that support the sleep function. The **Sleep** option may not appear as an option if the graphics card does not support it. Hibernation is similar to sleep except that a copy of all open programs is saved to the hard disk drive. If the electrical power goes off while in sleep mode, the open program information would be lost. In hibernation, if the electrical power is lost, the open program data is still available on the hard disk drive and is not lost.

Note:
There is a hybrid **Sleep** option that is supported by some programs that not only put the computer into sleep mode but also back up to hard disk all open program information.

Note:
The **Power** button located on the Windows Vista **Start** menu places the computer in sleep mode.

---

13. ____ Experiment with the **Log Off** and the **Lock** options to see the effect on the computer system. Be sure to leave Notepad open on the desktop to see how the current desktop session is affected.

Copyright by Goodheart-Willcox Co., Inc.

14. ____ Go on to complete the review questions at this time. Be sure to return the computer to its original configuration before shutting it down. This is especially important if other students use the computer. You may use the Windows Help and Support program, which is located on the **Start** menu, to assist you with the review questions.

Review Questions

1. What will happen when you press the Windows logo key? _____
_____

2. Which keyboard combination of keys opens the **Start** menu?_____
_____

3. How do you access the **Taskbar and Start Menu Properties** dialog box? _____
_____

4. What three options are available in Windows XP when the **Turn Off Computer** button is selected? _____

5. What does the standby feature do in Windows XP? _____
_____
_____
_____
_____
_____
_____
_____

6. Two users share a computer and each have their own user account. When one of the two users customizes the **Start** menu, will it change for both users or only for the user who made the changes?_____
_____

7. Which Windows Vista power-saving feature (hibernate or sleep) is most like Windows XP standby? _____

8. Which Windows Vista power-saving feature saves the open session to the hard disk drive? ____

9. Which Windows Vista power-saving option recovers to the desktop the fastest? _____

10. What is the difference between Windows Vista **Log Off** and **Lock** options?
_____
_____
_____
_____
_____
_____

11. A user complains that they do not have the Vista **Sleep** option on their computer. What is *most likely* the reason not having this option? _____

_____

Copyright by Goodheart-Willcox Co., Inc.

Name _____ Date _____

Class/Instructor _____

Windows Taskbar

After completing this laboratory activity, you will be able to:

- Access and configure taskbar options.
- Add or remove items on the taskbar.
- Reposition the taskbar.
- Hide the taskbar.
- Use Windows Vista Help and Support.

Introduction

In this laboratory activity, you will explore the configuration options of the Windows taskbar. The taskbar is located by default along the bottom edge of the Windows desktop. Look at the following screen capture of a Windows Vista taskbar. It is very similar to a Windows XP taskbar.

Quick Launch bar   Running program   Notification area

The **Quick Launch** bar allows several common programs to be started easily by clicking the program icon once. The middle area of the taskbar shows all currently opened programs. In the example, you see the Paint Shop Pro program icon, indicating that it is currently loaded and running. On the right side of the taskbar, you see the notification area. The notification area is used to indicate the status of certain programs and computer settings. For example, an e-mail icon may appear when you receive an e-mail. You will also notice the clock at the extreme right, which is always configured to show by default. After a short period of time, inactive icons in the notification area are hidden.

Any icon in the taskbar will launch to the desktop the corresponding program when it is clicked or double-clicked. Right-clicking a taskbar icon will often reveal a short menu of additional program choices or modifications related to that particular icon. A menu that appears by right-clicking is called a shortcut menu.

The taskbar features, also known as properties, can be easily modified. You will explore and modify the taskbar properties in this laboratory activity. Changes made to the taskbar will only affect the current user and not other computer users.

Copyright by Goodheart-Willcox Co., Inc.

Equipment and Materials

■ Computer with Windows XP or Window Vista, or both, installed.

Part I—Windows XP

Procedure

1. ____ Report to your assigned workstation.

2. ____ Boot the computer and verify it is in working order.

3. ____ Right-click the Windows XP taskbar and look at the options available in the menu list. Select the **Lock the Taskbar** option in the menu. This option, when checked, will lock the taskbar in its present location. When the **Lock the Taskbar** option is unchecked, you can drag the taskbar to a new location at the top of the desktop or to the left or right side of the desktop. Simply click the taskbar and drag the taskbar to the new location. Move the taskbar to the top and to each side of the desktop now.

4. ____ Return the taskbar to the default location at the bottom of the desktop. Reselect the **Lock the Taskbar** option to lock the taskbar at the bottom of the desktop.

5. ____ Right-click the taskbar and select the **Properties** item from the menu. You should see the Windows XP **Taskbar and Start Menu Properties** dialog box similar to the one in the following screen capture.

Notice the options available such as **Lock the taskbar, Auto-hide the taskbar,** and **Keep the taskbar on top of other windows**.

6. ____ Experiment with the **Auto-hide the taskbar** option at this time. Simply select and deselect the option. Be sure to either click the **OK** or the **Apply** button to see the effect of the change. Clicking **Apply** makes the change without closing the dialog box. Selecting **OK** applies the change and closes the dialog box. Move the mouse pointer over the taskbar location and observe the result.

Copyright by Goodheart-Willcox Co., Inc.

7. ____ Now, experiment with the **Keep the taskbar on top of other windows** option. You will need to open the Notepad program to see how the option affects the taskbar. Be sure that Notepad is maximized to fill the entire desktop; otherwise, you will not observe the effect of the **Keep the taskbar on top of other windows** option.

8. ____ Look at the following screen capture to see the results of selecting the **Group similar taskbar buttons** option and opening several programs and files in the same session. The **Group similar taskbar buttons** option is useful when there are too many programs and files open to display properly in the taskbar area.

Notice how five different documents have been opened at the same time but are contained under one **Microsoft Office** icon in the taskbar. You can see the number 5 in the icon indicating that five files are opened. When the icon is selected with the mouse, the names of the five files appear on the desktop as in the screen capture.

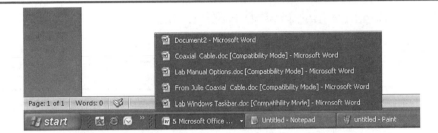

9. ____ Now, experiment with the **Quick Launch** bar located on the left side of the taskbar. If you have an Internet connection, you should see the Internet Explorer icon present in the **Quick Launch** bar. If there are no programs located in the **Quick Launch** bar, go on to the next step.

10. ____ Open the **Taskbar and Start Menu Properties** dialog box and click the **Customize** button. You will see a new dialog box titled **Customize Notifications** similar to the one in the following screen capture.

This dialog box allows you to select or deselect items for the notification area of the taskbar. You may take a minute to experiment with this feature. Be sure to return the notification area to its default values by clicking the **Restore Defaults** button before moving on to the next step.

Copyright by Goodheart-Willcox Co., Inc.

11. ____ Close the **Taskbar and Start Menu Properties** dialog box.

12. ____ Close the Windows XP operating system at this time and then go on to Part II—Windows Vista before completing the review questions.

Part II—Windows Vista

Procedure

1. ____ Report to your assigned workstation.

2. ____ Boot the computer and verify it is in working order.

3. ____ Right-click the Windows Vista taskbar and look at the options available in the shortcut menu. This shortcut menu is very similar to that in Windows XP. Take a minute to see that the **Lock the Taskbar** option in Windows Vista is exactly like that in Windows XP.

4. ____ Right-click the taskbar and select **Properties** from the shortcut menu. The **Taskbar and Start Menu Properties** dialog box will display and look similar to the one in the screen capture.

Notice that the Windows Vista version of this dialog box has two additional tabs when compared to the Windows XP version. These tabs are **Notification Area** and **Toolbars**. Both features are available in Windows XP, but there are no tabs for these.

5. ____ Look at the link near the bottom of the **Taskbar and Start Menu Properties** dialog box identified as <u>How do I customize the taskbar?</u> This is a new feature in Windows Vista, which helps users to learn about the taskbar properties. Click the link and view the contents now.

6. ____ Take several minutes to experiment with the Windows Vista taskbar properties to verify that they work in a similar fashion to the Windows XP taskbar properties.

7. ____ Locate the clock on the right side of the taskbar. Right-click the date and time, and then select **Adjust Date/Time** from the shortcut menu. A dialog box similar to the one following should appear.

Copyright by Goodheart-Willcox Co., Inc.

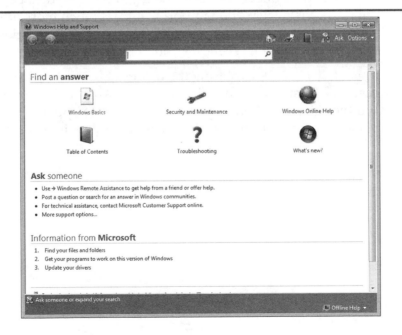

You can make changes to the date, time, and time zone; create a reminder for daylight savings time; and more. Look at the **Additional Clocks** tab, which allows you to display clocks from various time zones. This is a very handy worldwide business tool. Notice the **Internet Time** tab. When selected, this tab synchronizes the computer display clock with Internet time to keep it accurate. Without synchronization, the display clock will slowly lose time and accuracy.

8. ____ The Help and Support program located off the **Start** menu has been greatly improved in Windows Vista. Open the Help and Support program now. You should see the Help and Support window similar to the following.

Notice the six main areas identified as **Windows Basics**; **Security and Maintenance**; **Windows Online Help**; **Table of Contents**; **Troubleshooting**; and **What's new?**. Take a few minutes to explore these areas. You will find these areas very useful in the future.

9. ____ To see how the Help and Support search feature works, type the word *taskbar* into the search textbox. A list of search results corresponding to taskbar will display, similar to that in the following screen capture.

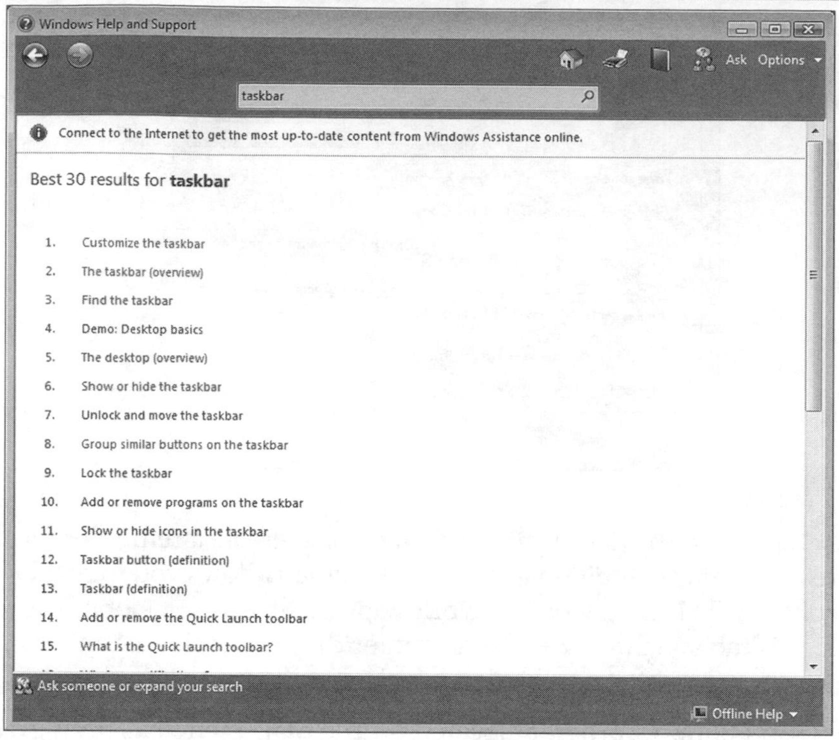

You can now simply click on any of the results in the list to learn more about the taskbar. As stated earlier, the Windows Vista Help and Support feature is much more advanced than the Windows XP Help and Support feature and provides much more information about various aspects of the operating system. Use it whenever you need additional help.

10. ____ After spending a few minutes exploring the results of the taskbar search, go on to complete the review questions. Be sure to return the desktop taskbar to its original configuration before shutting down the computer. You may use the Help and Support feature to assist you with the review questions and for all future laboratory activity review questions.

Copyright by Goodheart-Willcox Co., Inc.

Review Questions

1. Where is the notification area on the taskbar?_____

   _____

2. Where is the **Quick Launch** bar located on the taskbar?_____

   _____

3. What is the purpose of the notification area on the taskbar?_____

   _____

   _____

4. How do you access the **Taskbar and Start Menu Properties** dialog box for the taskbar?_____

   _____

   _____

5. What two new tabs are in the Windows Vista **Taskbar and Start Menu Properties** dialog box?

   _____

6. A user calls tech support and complains that she can no longer find the taskbar at the bottom of the screen. When she moves the mouse to the bottom of the screen, the taskbar suddenly reappears. It disappears once more when she moves the mouse away from the bottom of the screen. What will correct the user's problem?_____

   _____

   _____

Copyright by Goodheart-Willcox Co., Inc.

Name _____ Date _____

Class/Instructor _____

Windows Explorer

After completing this laboratory activity, you will be able to:

- Open Windows Explorer.
- Navigate the Windows Explorer directory structure.
- Customize Windows Explorer.
- Access the Help and Support program in Windows XP and Windows Vista.

Introduction

Windows Explorer displays a hierarchical structure of files, folders, drives, and even network connections when they exist. The term *hierarchical* means that the file structure is designed in levels. Files are contained inside folders, and folders can be contained inside other folders. Folders are also referred to as directories. The term *directory* originates back with older DOS and UNIX operating systems. The directory structure could only be viewed in text mode, not as an image. Later, when the graphical user interface (GUI) was developed, a folder icon was used to symbolize a directory. The term *folder* became synonymous with directory and is now used interchangeably. When a folder or directory is contained inside another folder or directory, it is referred to as a subfolder or subdirectory.

Look at the following screen capture. Notice that the My Documents directory is represented by an open folder icon. (This folder is located in the folder list.) The A+ Obj directory has been selected, thus revealing its contents in the right pane as a series of PDF type files and one word document file. The path is displayed at the top of Windows Explorer in the Address bar. Notice that C:\ Documents and Settings\Richard\My Documents\A+Obj is displayed. This is the complete path starting from drive C to the folder labeled A+ Obj.

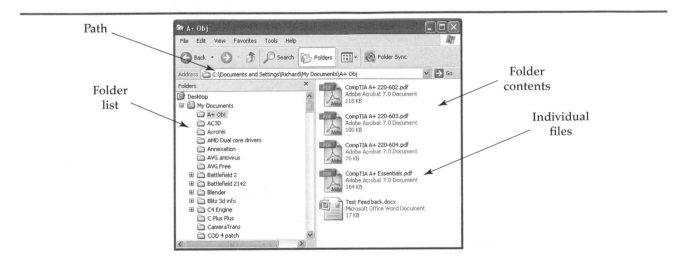

The following screen capture shows the Windows Vista directory structure. Windows XP and Windows Vista display file and directory information similarly. Yet there are a few differences. For example, the familiar icons are still available in Windows Vista representing files and directories, but the structure of the user directory and the way the views are organized has changed. This has lead to some confusion when changing from Windows XP to Windows Vista Explorer. For example, the Windows XP Explorer structure uses a single folder tree view in the left navigation pane of Windows Explorer. The left navigation pane in Windows Vista has more options. You still have a **Folders** list, but in addition there are now Documents, Pictures, Music, and more listed in the left pane.

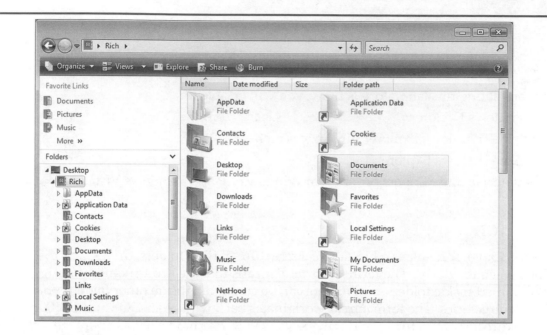

View options from the **Views** (located in the toolbar) menu are listed slightly differently. The following screen captures show the differences between the Windows XP and Windows Vista **Views** menu.

Windows XP   **Windows Vista**

Computer Service and Repair Lab Manual   Copyright by Goodheart-Willcox Co., Inc.

Since sharing information has become such a common function of computers, Microsoft redesigned the directory structure to make it easier to share information with other users. Windows XP contained only one simple shared folder labeled Shared Documents. Windows Vista was redesigned to expand the categories and type of information that could be shared. The directory structure in Windows Vista includes a directory folder labeled Public. Inside the Public folder are several other folders: Music, Documents, Pictures, Videos, Downloads, and Desktop. These folders contain commonly shared categories of data.

Windows Explorer will be used many times in future laboratory activities. It is imperative that you familiarize yourself with the basics of Windows Explorer.

Equipment and Materials

■ Computer with Windows XP or Window Vista, or both, installed.

Part I—Windows XP

Procedure

1. ____ Report to your assigned workstation.

2. ____ Boot the computer and verify it is in working order.

3. ____ Open the Windows Explorer by using the following path: **Start | All Programs | Accessories | Windows Explorer**.

4. ____ Close the Windows Explorer program, and then open Windows Explorer by pressing the Windows logo key and the [E] key simultaneously. Then, close Windows Explorer.

5. ____ Now, open Windows Explorer by right-clicking the **My Computer** option in the **Start** menu and selecting **Explore** from the shortcut menu. Then, close Windows Explorer.

6. ____ In the **Run** dialog box located off the **Start** menu, type **explorer** and then press [Enter]. Close Windows Explorer.

7. ____ Press the Windows logo key and [R] key simultaneously. The **Run** dialog box will appear. Type **explorer** and then press [Enter]. Windows Explorer should appear on the desktop once more. Close Windows Explorer.

8. ____ You can also access Windows Explorer by opening the **Start** menu, right-clicking **My Documents, My Recent Documents, My Pictures, My Music**, or **My Network Places**, and then selecting **Explore** from the shortcut menu. The Windows Explorer starting point and path name will vary according to the selection. Try opening Windows Explorer for each now, and then close Windows Explorer when finished.

9. ____ Now, open Windows Explorer by right-clicking **My Computer** in the **Start** menu and then selecting **Explore** from the shortcut menu.

10. ____ With Windows Explorer open, select Local Disk (C:) in the left pane. Watch closely how the Windows Explorer Address bar path changes as you select different files and directories in the left and right Windows Explorer pane. An example of the Address bar appears below in the partial screen capture.

Address bar

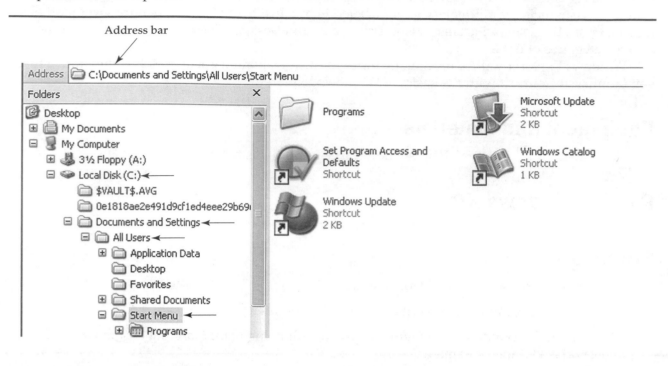

Look closely at the **Folders** list in the screen capture and at the selected folders indicated by the arrows. Open folders are indicated by the minus sign (–) inside the box in front of the folder names and drives. The contents are viewed in the right-hand pane of Windows Explorer. Folders proceeded with a plus sign (+) have not yet been opened.

11. ____ Select each of the folders in the order as indicated below. Watch the effect on the path in Explorer Address bar. First select the default drive C and then Documents and Settings, then All Users, and finally **Start Menu**. Notice how the path changes and correlates directly to the exact position you have selected in the directory structure using the mouse.

12. ____ Close Windows Explorer and then open **Help and Support** located on the **Start** menu. Type the word *files* into the Help and Support **Search** box. Look at the various topics displayed and review the information provided, such as how to move a file or folder, create a file or folder, and other related topics.

13. ____ Now, using Help and Support **Search** box, conduct a search using the term *directory* and then the term *Explorer*. You can always use the Help and Support program in Windows XP to find more about basic features of Windows XP.

14. ____ You can also automatically access Help and Support by pressing the Windows logo key and the [F1] key simultaneously. Try accessing Help and Support now using this key combination.

15. ____ ____ Close Windows XP and then go on to Part II—Windows Vista before completing the review questions.

Copyright by Goodheart-Willcox Co., Inc.

Part II—Windows Vista

Procedure

1. ____ Report to your assigned workstation.

2. ____ Boot the computer and verify it is in working order.

3. ____ Open the Windows Explorer by using the following path **Start | All Programs | Accessories | Windows Explorer**. Then, close Windows Explorer.

4. ____ Open Windows Explorer by pressing the Windows logo key and the [E] key simultaneously. Then, close Windows Explorer.

5. ____ Now, open Windows Explorer by right-clicking the **Computer** option in the **Start** menu and selecting **Explore** from the shortcut menu. Close Windows Explorer.

6. ____ In the **Search** dialog box located off the **Start** menu, type **explorer** and then press [Enter]. The Windows Explorer should appear. Then, close Windows Explorer.

7. Now, press the Windows logo key and the [R] key simultaneously. This will open the **Run** dialog box which was part of the **Start** menu in previous versions of Windows. Type **explorer** into the **Run** dialog box. Window Explorer will display. Close Windows Explorer.

8. ____ You can open Windows Explorer by right-clicking your name at the top of the **Start** menu as well as **Documents, Pictures,** and **Music** and selecting **Explore** from the shortcut menu. Open Windows Explorer now by right-clicking your name in the **Start** menu and selecting **Explore** from the shortcut menu.

9. ____ Select the **Folders** option located in the left-hand pane of Windows Explorer and observe the change that takes place.

10. ____ Select one of the folders or files located in the right-hand pane and observe the change in the path displayed in the Address bar.

11. ____ In the Windows Explorer toolbar, locate the **Views** button. The **Views** button can be selected clicking on the arrow beside it or by simply clicking the button itself. This will reveal a list of viewing options. Try both now. Notice how the display changes each time you click on the **Views** button.

12. ____ Take a few minutes to explore Windows Explorer. It is imperative that you become thoroughly familiar with Windows Explorer and the various options available for viewing and organizing files, folders, and drives.

13. ____ Using Windows Explorer, locate and open the folder labeled Public and then list in the space provided the names of all the folders that use the word *Public* as part of the name.

_____

_____

_____

14. ____ To learn more about the basics of Windows Vista files and folders, open the **Start** menu and then select the **Help and Support** option. Locate **Windows Basics** under the **Find an Answer** section of Windows Help and Support. Select **Working with files and folders** in the **Windows Basics: all topics list**. You can also open Help and Support and then type the word *files* into the search box. Working with files and folders should appear at the top of the search list. By reviewing the contents of **Working with files and folders**, you will learn more about basic file and

folder options not covered in this laboratory activity. Review the information thoroughly before answering the review questions.

15. ____ You can also automatically access Windows Help and Support by pressing the Windows logo key and the [F1] key simultaneously. Try it now.

16. ____ After completing the review questions, return the computer to its original condition.

Review Questions

1. What does the term *hierarchal* mean?_____

   _____

2. What Microsoft Windows term means the same as directory? _____

3. In which folder are software programs installed?_____

4. In which folder would you find the root directory for each local user?_____

   _____

5. Which folder is used by default to share user information in Windows Vista? _____

   _____

6. Name six default folders found under the user Public directory in Windows Vista._____

   _____

   _____

7. Which folder is used by default as a shared folder in Windows XP? _____

   _____

8. What keyboard letter do you press with the Windows logo key to open the Windows Explorer program? _____

   _____

9. Write the path used to access the Windows Explorer program in Windows XP and Windows Vista starting at the **Start** menu._____

   _____

10. Which folder option view is the most informative about a folder?_____

11. What does a plus sign in front of a folder name in the Windows Explorer Folder list indicate? __

    _____

12. What does a minus sign in front of a folder name in the Windows Explorer directory structure indicate? _____

    _____

13. Where is the Help and Support program located in Windows XP? _____

    _____

14. Where is the Help and Support feature located in Windows Vista?_____

    _____

15. What keyboard combination of keys will allow you to automatically open Help and Support in either Windows XP or Windows Vista?_____

Copyright by Goodheart-Willcox Co., Inc.

Name _____ Date _____

Class/Instructor _____

Command Prompt

After completing this laboratory activity, you will be able to:

- Open the Command Prompt window in Windows XP and Windows Vista.
- Close the Command Prompt window using the **Exit** command.
- Access the command prompt Help feature.
- Explain the term *syntax* as related to the command prompt.

Introduction

This laboratory activity will familiarize you with the command prompt in Windows XP and Windows Vista. The Windows command prompt is a DOS emulator. DOS was an earlier operating system. The term *emulator* means the command prompt will look and feel like the original DOS command prompt. The command prompt is also referred to as the command interpreter because it interprets commands. The path to the command prompt is the same for Windows XP and Windows Vista. The path is **Start | All Programs | Accessories | Command Prompt**.

There are two different programs that will generate a command prompt in Windows XP and Windows Vista: command.com and cmd.exe. Command.com is an early version of the original DOS program used to run the DOS prompt. It is identified by the Windows operating system as a DOS program. Cmd.exe is the DOS emulator program. It runs a more modern version of the command prompt and is identified by Windows as a program application.

When you start the command prompt from the Accessories folder, you are running cmd.exe not command.com. Cmd.exe is the NT version of the command prompt emulator and is the default emulator for Windows 2000, Windows XP and Windows Vista. Command.com is the default command prompt emulator for Windows Me, Windows 98, and earlier operating system versions, which are not based on the Windows NT operating system.

You access the command prompt by typing **cmd** or **command** into the **Run** dialog box in Windows XP or the **Search** dialog box in Windows Vista.

Copyright by Goodheart-Willcox Co., Inc.

Command Syntax

All letters, number, and special characters must be typed and entered as a stream of characters in a specific order, including spaces. The rules for inputting the commands at the command prompt are referred to as syntax. The command will not be recognized by the computer unless it adheres to the proper syntax. For example, the command for displaying and changing the time is shown in the partial screen capture below.

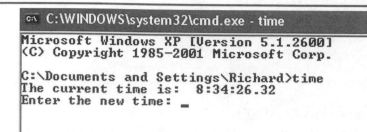

When the command **time** is issued at the command prompt, the time is displayed and an option to change the current time is displayed. You must enter the new time in the exact manner as indicated. The hour, minutes, and seconds must be entered as in the example, separated by colons. Otherwise, the new time will not be accepted by the computer. For most commands, the syntax will be much more complicated as in the following example of the **copy** command.

```
C:\WINDOWS\system32\cmd.exe                                    _ □ x
C:\Documents and Settings\Richard>help copy
Copies one or more files to another location.

COPY [/D] [/V] [/N] [/Y : /-Y] [/Z] [/A : /B ] source [/A : /B]
     [+ source [/A : /B] [+ ...]] [destination [/A : /B]]

  source       Specifies the file or files to be copied.
  /A           Indicates an ASCII text file.
  /B           Indicates a binary file.
  /D           Allow the destination file to be created decrypted
  destination  Specifies the directory and/or filename for the new file(s).
  /V           Verifies that new files are written correctly.
  /N           Uses short filename, if available, when copying a file with a
               non-8dot3 name.
  /Y           Suppresses prompting to confirm you want to overwrite an
               existing destination file.
  /-Y          Causes prompting to confirm you want to overwrite an
               existing destination file.
  /Z           Copies networked files in restartable mode.

The switch /Y may be preset in the COPYCMD environment variable.
This may be overridden with /-Y on the command line.  Default is
to prompt on overwrites unless COPY command is being executed from
within a batch script.

To append files, specify a single file for destination, but multiple files
for source (using wildcards or file1+file2+file3 format).
```

The **copy** command must be issued in proper order, identifying the source and destination of the file being copied. There are also many different switches available that can be used with the command to modify the results. A switch used with the command is represented by the slash symbol (/) and must be entered in a specific location. Look at the syntax for the **copy** command in the screen capture. Notice that the switch used to verify that the file has been copied is a slash followed

Copyright by Goodheart-Willcox Co., Inc.

by the letter *V*. It should be inserted into the command after the command **copy** and before the source location has been entered. Command syntax is very overwhelming to a new student at first, but the lab manual will introduce the important switches and the exact syntax as the commands are introduced.

You can always access limited help for a command by using the **help** command. When the **help** command is issued at the command prompt, a list of commands will appear. Look at the following screen capture of the results of issuing the **help** command at the command prompt.

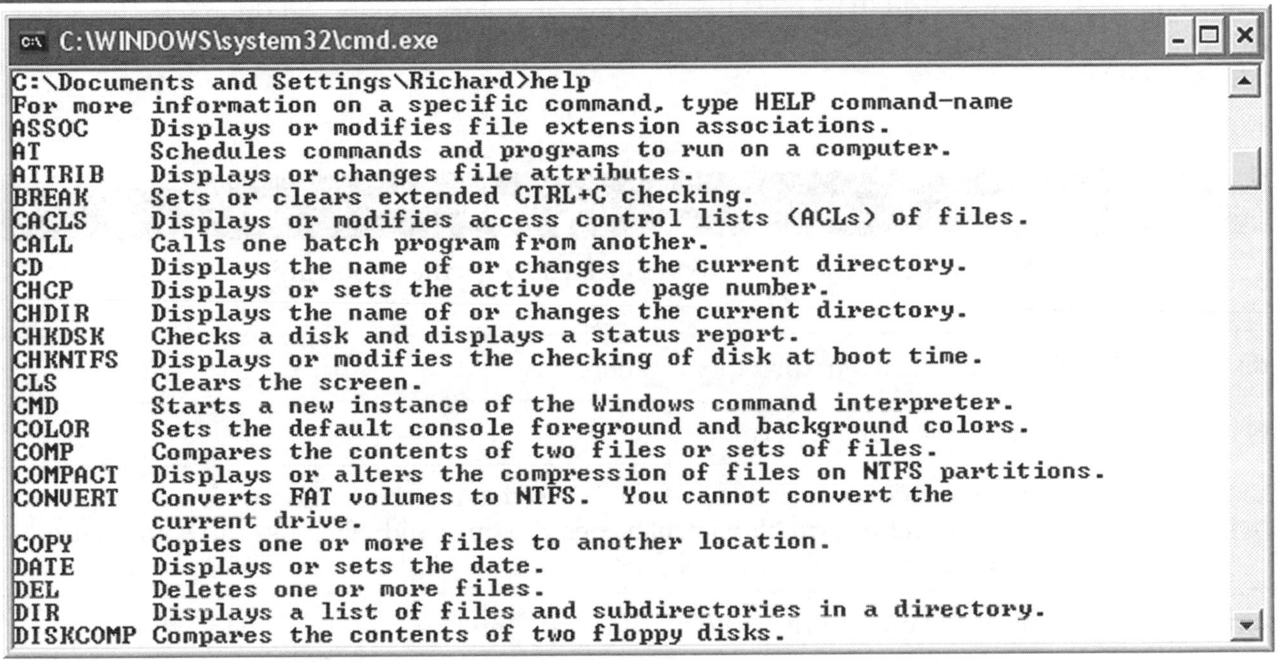

```
C:\WINDOWS\system32\cmd.exe                                    _ □ ×

C:\Documents and Settings\Richard>help
For more information on a specific command, type HELP command-name
ASSOC      Displays or modifies file extension associations.
AT         Schedules commands and programs to run on a computer.
ATTRIB     Displays or changes file attributes.
BREAK      Sets or clears extended CTRL+C checking.
CACLS      Displays or modifies access control lists (ACLs) of files.
CALL       Calls one batch program from another.
CD         Displays the name of or changes the current directory.
CHCP       Displays or sets the active code page number.
CHDIR      Displays the name of or changes the current directory.
CHKDSK     Checks a disk and displays a status report.
CHKNTFS    Displays or modifies the checking of disk at boot time.
CLS        Clears the screen.
CMD        Starts a new instance of the Windows command interpreter.
COLOR      Sets the default console foreground and background colors.
COMP       Compares the contents of two files or sets of files.
COMPACT    Displays or alters the compression of files on NTFS partitions.
CONVERT    Converts FAT volumes to NTFS.  You cannot convert the
           current drive.
COPY       Copies one or more files to another location.
DATE       Displays or sets the date.
DEL        Deletes one or more files.
DIR        Displays a list of files and subdirectories in a directory.
DISKCOMP   Compares the contents of two floppy disks.
```

Limited information about each command is displayed. Reading the description of the **copy** command, you can see that Help states that this command is used to copy one or more files to another location.

To find more specific but still limited information about a command, you will enter the **help** command followed by the command you wish more information about. An alternative method is to use the **?** switch after a command. For example, **dir /?** reveals help about the command **dir**. Look at the two examples of entering the command for help on the **copy** command below.

> **help copy**
> **copy /?**

Internal and External Commands

There are two types of commands that can be issued from the command prompt: internal and external. Internal commands are part of the command prompt emulator program and external commands are independent programs written to enhance the command interpreter's functions. For example, the command **date** is part of the emulator program. If you copy the cmd.exe program, the date function will be a part of it and can be run from the cmd.exe file. If you attempt to run an external command such as **format**, **chkdsk**, or **attrib**, from the cmd.exe program, it will fail. The files for these commands must be copied to the same location as the cmd.exe file. For example, if you copy the cmd.exe file to a USB drive, then you must also copy the external command to the same USB drive in order to execute the external command.

Copyright by Goodheart-Willcox Co., Inc.

A complete list of Microsoft DOS 5.0 internal and external commands are located at Microsoft support: http://support.microsoft.com/kb/71986. Another great location for information on all command prompt commands is at the Microsoft TechNet location: http://technet.microsoft.com/en-us/library/bb490890.aspx.

Note:
Basic knowledge of the command prompt is required for the CompTIA A+ 220-603 (remote support technician) exam.

Several basic commands will be introduced in this laboratory activity. Additional lab activities will cover additional commands. Commands introduced in this laboratory activity are listed in the following table.

Command	Description
date	Displays the current date and provides you with the opportunity to change the date.
dir	Displays the current directory contents.
exit	Closes the command prompt.
help	Displays a list of commands that can be used at the command prompt. It can also be used to find information about a specific command when used in combination with the command. For example, **help copy**.
time	Displays the current time and provides you the opportunity to change the time.
ver	Displays the current version of the operating system.

Equipment and Materials

■ Computer with Windows XP or Window Vista, or both, installed.
■ USB Flash drive.

Procedure

1. ____ Report to your assigned workstation.

2. ____ Boot the computer and verify it is in working order.

3. ____ Click the **Start** button and follow the path **All Programs | Accessories | Command Prompt**. (The **Start** button is located at the bottom left of the screen.) You should see a **Command Prompt** window similar to the one in the following figure.

Copyright by Goodheart-Willcox Co., Inc.

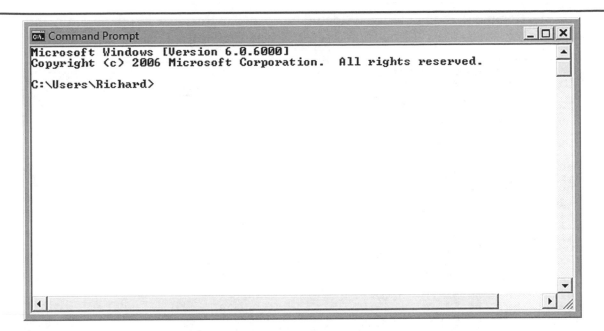

The **Command Prompt** window in the previous screen capture has been modified to display black lettering on a white background so it can be viewed easier in the lab manual. The actual default properties of the command prompt are gray letters on a black background.

Pay particular attention to the information displayed at the command prompt. Notice that you can see the version of the Microsoft Windows operating system and the copyright date.

The default Windows Vista command prompt is the name of the user account and the group the user belongs to. For example, in C:\Users\Richard>, the user account is Richard and the user group he belongs to is Users. The Windows XP default command prompt displays the directory Documents and Settings followed by the user account name. For example, C:\Documents and Settings\Richard>.

Record what your command prompt display looks like in the space provided.

_____

4. ____ Type the command **exit** at the command prompt. The **Command Prompt** window should close. If you need assistance, call your instructor.

5. ____ Open the command prompt again following the path described in step 2.

6. ____ Close the command prompt windows clicking the **Close** button. This button is located in the upper-right corner and is represented by an X inside of a box.

7. ____ The command prompt program file is cmd.exe. It can be started by entering **cmd.exe** in the **Run** dialog box located off the **Start** menu of Windows XP or the **Search** box of Windows Vista. Try accessing the command prompt now by typing **cmd** in the Windows XP **Run** dialog box or Windows Vista **Search** box. If you need assistance, call your instructor.

8. _____ The **Command Prompt** window should be opened at this time. Type the command **dir** and watch the screen closely. You should see a display similar to the following screen capture.

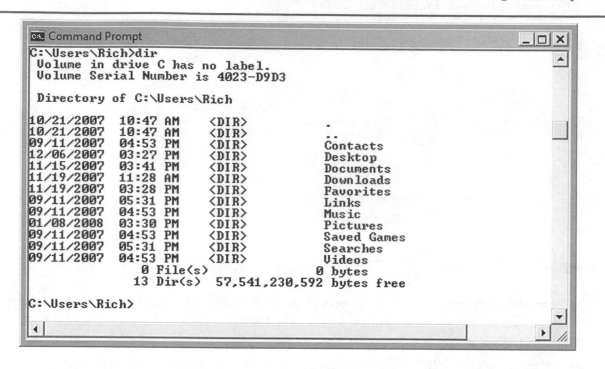

The **dir** command displays a list of directories as well as identifies the drive letter, the drive label (drive name), and the volume serial number. The volume serial number is created automatically at the time the hard disk drive partition is first created. The exact date and time in hours and seconds is expressed as a hexadecimal number. Since the exact date and time is used to create the volume serial number, each hard disk drive or each partition will be unique.

9. _____ Close the **Command Prompt** window and open Windows Explorer by right-clicking **My Computer** or **Computer** located on the **Start** menu and selecting **Explore** from the shortcut menu. You should see a view of all drives, such as the Local Disk (C:) and any DVD or CD drives installed.

10. _____ Plug in the USB driver and watch it appear in the Windows Explorer. Record the letter used to represent the USB drive. For example, a computer might have the default local hard disk drive represented as C, a new volume as D, and a DVD drive as E. The USB drive will typically automatically become F or G. The exact assignment of the drive letter for a USB drive will vary according to circumstances. Sometimes, a computer used in a lab setting that has had an external backup drive or a path set to a network drive will retain a letter for that location, thus causing the USB drive to skip the next logically assigned drive letter.

Look at the following screen capture. Notice that the USB drive is identified as a "Removable Disk" followed by the assigned drive letter in both Windows XP and Windows Vista. Your view may not match the screen capture as presented here. Remember that you can change the way the folders and directories are displayed by selecting the **Views** menu in Windows Explorer for Windows Vista and Windows XP. Call your instructor for assistance if you cannot determine the USB drive letter.

Copyright by Goodheart-Willcox Co., Inc.

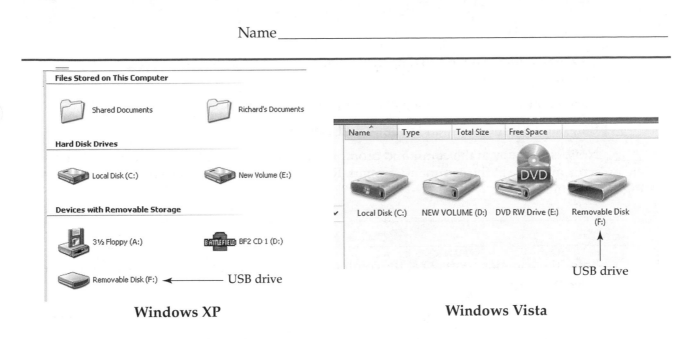

Windows XP   **Windows Vista**

Note:

During the laboratory activity, the USB drive will be referred to as drive **E** and presented as drive E: in the command syntax. You will substitute the correct drive letter that corresponds to the computer you are using.

---

11. ____ Open the command prompt.

12. ____ Enter the following command to reveal the contents of the USB drive:

dir e:

where *E* represents the drive letter of the USB Flash drive.

Use all lowercase letters for the command and be sure to leave one space between the command and the drive letter. The command will display the contents of the directory. Information such as a list of any files or directories contained on the USB Flash drive will be presented. You will also see the USB Flash drive referred to as a "volume." The volume drive letter will be identified as well as any label assigned to the volume. For example, the Gigabank brand will identify the USB Flash drive as volume GIGABANK. Also, note that the USB Flash drive will have a volume serial number assigned such as 0427-18AC. The serial number of the volume is unique and helps the computer operating system identify each available volume on the computer as well as any network volumes available.

13. ____ Enter the command **DIR E:** using all uppercase letters to see if there is any effect on the command.

14. ____ Enter the command **dir z:** and then record the screen message that appears when there is no drive Z.

_____

_____

15. ____ Now, enter the **help** command at the command prompt and view the results. A list of commands should appear in the **Command Prompt** window.

16. ____ Type the command **ver** to display the version of the operating system that is running.

17. ____ Enter the command **time** to display the time. After the time is displayed, press the [Enter] key once more without changing the time.

Copyright by Goodheart-Willcox Co., Inc.

18. ____ Enter the **date** command to display the date. After the date appears, press the [Enter] key without changing the date.

19. ____ Now, enter the command **help dir** and view the results.

20. ____ Enter **dir /?** at the command prompt and view the results.

21. ____ Now, enter **copy** at the command prompt. The **copy** command used by itself will generate an error message at the command prompt. Record the message displayed as a result of issuing the command.

_____

_____

22. ____ Enter the command **xyz123** at the command prompt and record the message generated in the space provided.

_____

_____

_____

Compare the two error messages that you created in this step and the last step. You will notice that the **copy** command is a recognized command and generated an error message because of the way it was entered. The second error message states that the input at the command prompt is not a recognized command. In other words, the first was a syntax error and the second is not a recognized or legal command.

23. ____ Take a few minutes to review or practice the commands covered before answering the review questions.

Copyright by Goodheart-Willcox Co., Inc.

Name_____

Review Questions

1. Which two commands will start the command prompt in Windows Vista or Windows XP? _____
   _____

2. What is the difference between command.com and cmd.exe? _____
   _____
   _____

3. True *or* False? Commands must be issued in lowercase. _____

4. True *or* False? There must be a space between a command and the drive letter?_____

5. What message is displayed when a drive cannot be located or does not exist? _____
   _____

6. What command would you use to display the current time? _____

7. What command would you use to display the current date? _____

8. What command would you use to see a list of common command prompt commands?_____
   _____

9. What command do you use to close the current command prompt session?_____

10. What command would you use to view a list of directories contained on drive C? _____

11. How is the USB Flash drive labeled in the Windows Explorer view? _____
    _____

12. Give two examples of how to obtain help about the **copy** command from the command prompt?
    _____

13. What will produce a syntax error?_____
    _____
    _____

14. What information is revealed when using the **dir** command with the USB Flash drive? _____
    _____
    _____

15. What is the path to the command prompt located off the **Start** menu in Windows XP and
    Windows Vista? _____
    _____

Computer Service and Repair Lab Manual

Copyright by Goodheart-Willcox Co., Inc.

Laboratory Activity

10

Name _____ Date _____

Class/Instructor _____

Copy Command

After completing this laboratory activity, you will be able to:

- Copy files using the **copy** command.
- Use the **Save as** command in Notepad.
- Explain what an ASCII file is.
- Explain the use of wild card symbols.
- Copy files using wild card symbols.
- Use the **del** and **erase** commands to delete a file.

Introduction

In this laboratory activity, you will use Microsoft Notepad to create a short memo and save it to your My Documents or Documents folder. You will then copy the memo file to a USB Flash drive using the **copy** command.

Notepad, as well as many other word processing applications, has a feature available that allows you to save a file in different file formats. When you simply "save" a document, you automatically save the document in a default format. The default format of word processing applications, such as Microsoft Word, use many enrichment features when it saves a document. For this laboratory activity, you will be saving the document you create as an ASCII text file. An ASCII text file contains no special enhancements, such as special fonts, highlight areas, drawings, or special icons. An ASCII text file contains only standard ASCII symbols and minimal punctuation.

Look at the following screen captures of Windows XP and Windows Vista Notepad program to see the **Save As** dialog box used for this laboratory activity.

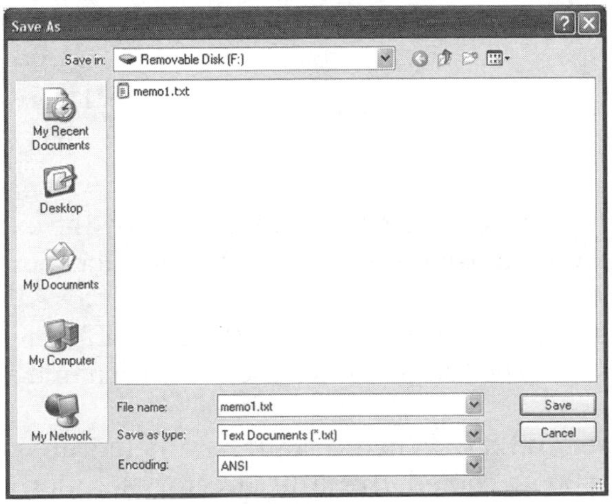

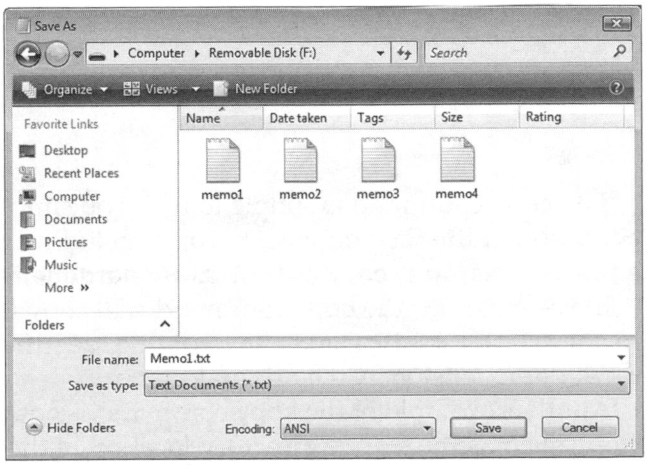

You must be sure to identify the removable USB Flash drive when saving the memos that you will create and copy in this laboratory activity. You will create four simple memo files that will be used in this and the next laboratory activity. The memo files will contain a single line of text, and each will be saved with a unique name. The four files will be named memo1, memo2, memo3, and memo4. The contents of each will be as follows:

File name = Memo1
Contents of file = This is memo 1.

File name = Memo2
Contents of file = This is memo 2.

File name = Memo3
Contents of file = This is memo 3.

File name = Memo4
Contents of file = This is memo 4.

Each of the four memos will be saved to the USB Flash drive. Then, you will explore how the **copy** command is used to copy files from one location to another.

The default location of the home directory when the command prompt is used will be different depending on which operating system you are using. In Windows XP, the default home directory for command prompt is C:\Documents and Settings\User Account Name> and for Windows Vista it is C:\Users\ User Account Name>. You will need to pay close attention to the default home directory. The exact default directory will be critical to this laboratory activity.

```
C:\WINDOWS\system32\cmd.exe                                        _ □ ×

Microsoft Windows XP [Version 5.1.2600]
(C) Copyright 1985-2001 Microsoft Corp.

C:\Documents and Settings\Richard>
```

The **copy** command is simple to use. You simply type the **copy** command followed by the exact file location of the file you wish to copy, including the file extension followed by the new location for the file. For example, **copy c:\USERS\Richard\memo1.txt f:.**

In the example, the **copy** command will copy the file called memo1.txt from the default home directory C:\USERS\Richard to any volume identified as F:. The file will have the same filename and three-letter extension as the original file.

Another example of the **copy** command is **copy memo1.txt f:.** When certain parameters are left out, such as the source directory location of the file being copied, then the directory location is

Copyright by Goodheart-Willcox Co., Inc.

Name_____

assumed to be the default directory. So, the command in the example looks for the memo1.txt file in the default directory and then copies it to the new location at F:.

Now when you copy from the USB Flash drive, you can also leave out the default directory. For example, **copy f:memo1.txt**. The memo1.txt file is copied from the source location of drive F to the destination location of the default command prompt directory location. Typing the **dir** command will confirm the existence of the memo1.txt file being successfully copied from drive F to drive C.

One of the most common mistakes made by new users and some experienced users is failure to use the three-letter file extension. In this exercise, the file extension is .txt. The three-letter file extension is left from the early DOS system way of naming files. The early DOS system used an eight dot three (8.3) file naming convention. This means the file name was a maximum of eight letters in length followed with a dot and then a three-letter extension that identified the file type. A file with the .txt extension is an ASCII text file.

To delete a file, you use the **del** or **erase** command in the same manner that you use the **copy** command. For example, **del c:memo1.txt** will delete the file named memo1.txt on volume C. The **del** command and the **erase** command will produce the same results.

Another concept used with copying and deleting files are the wildcard characters asterisk (*) and question mark (?). The asterisk is used to substitute for a file name or a file extension. For example, the command **copy f:*.*** will copy all files on volume F. The question mark can be used to substitute for one or more characters. For example to copy all memo files that have a name ending in any character, you could use the command **copy f:memo?.txt**, which would copy all text files with the name *memo* and any last character. In this laboratory activity, the last character of the memo files is a number.

Equipment and Materials

- Computer with Windows XP or Window Vista, or both, installed.
- USB Flash drive.

Note:
If you are using your own personal USB Flash drive for this lab activity, you will want to use Windows Explorer to copy all files from the USB drive to another location such as the My Documents folder when using Windows XP. All files contained on the USB Flash drive will be erased during this lab activity.

Procedure

1. ____ Report to your assigned workstation.

2. ____ Boot the computer and verify it is in working order.

3. ____ Insert the USB Flash drive and note which volume or drive letter is assigned to it. Record its drive letter assignment. _____

4. ____ Access the command prompt through **Start | Accessories | Command Prompt**.

5. ____ After the command prompt appears, record the exact default directory for the command prompt. Include spaces if necessary.

---

6. ____ Now, open the Notepad program through **Start | All Programs | Accessories | Notepad**.

7. ____ With Notepad opened, create the four files as indicated in the laboratory activity introduction. The four memos will be saved as memo1.txt, memo2.txt, memo3.txt, and memo4.txt.

8. ____ After the four memos are created and saved to the USB Flash drive, open Windows Explorer and verify they are located on the USB Flash drive.

9. ____ Now, verify that the four memos are located on the USB Flash drive by using the **dir** command. Example, **dir f:**. All four memos should appear.

10. ____ At the command prompt, type **help copy** and look at the information about the **copy** command syntax.

11. ____ Copy memo1.txt from the USB Flash drive to your default directory on drive C. To do so, simply type the following at the command prompt: **copy f:memo1.txt c:**.

12. ____ Verify the file has been copied by typing **dir c:** at the command prompt.

13. ____ Repeat step 11 for the remaining three memos copying each one at a time from the USB Flash drive to the default drive C. Verify that each one has been copied.

14. ____ Now, you will use the **del** command to delete the memo1.txt file on the USB Flash drive. Simply enter the command **del f:memo1.txt**. Verify the memo1.txt file has been deleted by using the **dir** command. For example, **dir f:**.

15. ____ Delete the memo2.txt file using the **erase** command. Simply enter **erase f:memo2.txt**. Verify that the memo2.txt file has been erased.

16. ____ Now, delete the remaining two files on the volume F using the command **del memo?.txt**. Verify that all files have been erased using the **dir** command.

17. ____ Copy all four memo files back to the USB Flash drive using the **copy** command. Simply enter **copy memo?.txt f:**. Verify all four have been copied back to the USB Flash drive.

18. ____ Now, erase all files on the USB Flash drive using the command **del f:*.*** and then verify their deletion using the **dir** command.

19. ____ Copy all files with a .txt extension from drive C back to the USB Flash drive using the asterisk as the file name. For example, **copy *.txt f:**.

20. ____ Now, you will use the **copy** command to copy the memo1.txt file and rename it simply MyMemo. For example, **copy f: memo1.txt MyMemo**. Verify the **copy** command and the renaming of the memo1.txt to MyMemo. Then, answer the two following questions.

Has the memo1.txt file been copied? Yes or No? _____

Has the file name been changed and is now without the three letter file extension? Yes or No? _____

If you answered "No" to any of these questions, call your instructor for assistance.

21. ____ Practice using the **copy**, **del**, and **erase** commands until you feel comfortable. Save a copy of the four practice files on the USB Flash drive for the next lab activity.

22. ____ Complete the review questions. After completing the review questions, return the computer to its original condition.

Copyright by Goodheart-Willcox Co., Inc.

Name_____

Review Questions

1. What command is equal to **del**? _____

2. Write an example of the command that you would use to copy a file called MyMemo.txt from a default command prompt of C:\USERS\James to a USB Flash drive identified as volume H, renaming the file MyMemo. Write this command after the following command prompt: C:\USERS\James> _____

_____

3. Which operating system would *most likely* have a command prompt similar to the following: C:\Documents and Settings\James>? _____

4. Which operating system would *most likely* have a command prompt similar to the following: C:\USERS\James>? _____

5. Write an example of using the **copy** command to copy all .txt files from a USB Flash drive identified as volume E to the default directory of the computer. _____

_____

6. What special character or symbol is used to substitute single characters in a file name?_____

_____

7. What special character or symbol is used to represent an entire file name or the file extension?

_____

Copyright by Goodheart-Willcox Co., Inc.

Name _____ Date _____

Class/Instructor _____

Directory Commands

After completing this laboratory activity, you will be able to:

- Navigate a directory structure from the command prompt.
- Issue the following commands at the command prompt: **md**, **mkdir**, **dir**, **cd**, **tree**, **del**, **rmdir**, **rd**, **format**, and **type**.
- Determine the active or default directory.
- Explain the difference between relative and absolute locations.

Introduction

In this laboratory activity, you will learn some basic directory commands and how to run **cmd. exe** as the system administrator. Some of the **cmd.exe** commands can only be used by the system administrator, not a typical user. These special commands are restricted to ensure system security. For example, you cannot change to the system directory or access special applications and files if you are not the system administrator. To access an application as the system administrator, you would simply right-click the application and then select **Run as Administrator** from the shortcut menu. The "Run as administrator" feature was first introduced in Windows Vista and is not a requirement for Windows XP or earlier versions of Windows.

Also in this laboratory activity, you will become familiar with several basic command prompt commands used to navigate, create, and delete directories. The command prompt can be a very powerful troubleshooting tool when used by a knowledgeable technician. There are many times when troubleshooting a computer that the graphic user interface (GUI) is not available because of a system hardware or software failure. Also, be aware that some Microsoft repair procedures require that you use the command prompt to perform the repair.

The **md** or **mkdir** command is used to create a directory, and the **rd** or **rmdir** command is used to remove a directory. For example, entering **md f:books** at the command prompt will create a directory labeled books on volume F.

The **del** command is used to delete a file but cannot be used to delete a directory. Students are often confused on this point, and it often appears as a trick question on many certification exams.

The **tree** command will display the arrangement of all directories. The **tree** command with the /f switch, **tree /f**, will display all directories and the file names contained within each directory.

Naming conventions used today have many restrictions that date back to the original DOS file system. Originally when you saved a file or created a directory in DOS, you had to conform to the DOS eight dot three (8.3) file naming convention. In the 8.3 naming convention, all files and directories must have a name that is composed of two parts. The first part can be up to eight characters long, and the second part can be up to three characters long. The two portions of the name must be separated by a period. There are certain characters that cannot be used in a DOS file or directory name, such as the back slash (\), which has a special meaning not only to DOS, but also for today's operating systems.

Copyright by Goodheart-Willcox Co., Inc.

For now, use the names as directed in the laboratory activity. The extensions usually indicate the type of file. For example, .txt usually indicates a text file. When using the command prompt in Windows XP or Windows Vista, you still must use a file name extension to manipulate a file from the command prompt. Otherwise, the file name will appear without the extension. When using Windows Explorer or most word processing applications, such as Microsoft Word or Notepad, you do not need to use a file extension.

Many of the commands require that the command prompt be run as the system administrator. When you select the command prompt program from the **Start** menu, simply right-click **Command Prompt** and then select the **Run as** or the **Run as Administrator** option from the shortcut menu. You may need to provide the administrator password. Once you have opened the command prompt as the administrator, you will have full access to all the supported commands that are capable of being run from the command prompt. If you do not run the command prompt as the system administrator, some commands will not be available to you. This is part of the built-in Windows Vista operating system security features.

Relative and absolute directories are determined by the default location you are at in the directory tree structure. In other words, you can change your location in the directory tree structure by using the **cd** or **chdir** commands. The **cd** followed by two dots, for example **cd..**, will move you one position up the directory structure. This would be a relative change. The term *relative* means the change is directly related to your present position in the directory structure. An absolute change in the directory structure would require a complete path to your new location in the directory structure. For example, **cd f:\level1a\level2a\level3a** would change the location of the command prompt to the directory at level3a. In other words, you gave the complete path to the new location in the directory structure and moved more than one level. To change to another drive letter, you would simply type that drive letter. For example, move to the F: prompt from the C: prompt, simply type **f:** and the default drive will be F.

Equipment and Materials

■ Computer with Windows XP or Windows Vista, or both, installed.
■ USB Flash drive containing no files.

Note:
   The USB Flash drive will be assumed as volume F for this lab activity. Your USB Flash drive volume may be different.

Procedure

1. ____ Report to your assigned workstation.

2. ____ Boot the computer and verify it is in working order.

3. ____ Launch the command prompt. You may review previous laboratory activities if you have difficulty remembering how to access the command prompt.

4. ____ Using the **Start** menu, open the program Notepad located at **Start | All Programs | Accessories | Notepad**.

5. ____ Type a short line of text as follows: This is memo1.

6. ____ Save the file as memo1.txt on the USB Flash drive.

7. ____ Type the name of the file, memo1, into the **File name** text box. The file must be saved to the USB Flash drive. Look at the **Save in** text box to see if the drive letter F is displayed. If it is

Copyright by Goodheart-Willcox Co., Inc.

not, change the drive letter to F or to the appropriate drive letter representing the USB Flash drive before saving the file.

8. ____ Close Notepad and launch the DOS prompt as you did in the last laboratory activity.

9. ____ Type the command **dir f:** followed by [Enter] and observe the screen. The **dir** command will display the directory of files. The **f:** is an option to the **dir** command. It displays all files located in volume F.

10. ____ Record the following data for memo1.txt, which is displayed on the screen.

Complete file name, including the extension: _____

The size of the file in bytes:_____

Date of the file creation:_____

Time of the file creation: _____

Amount of free disk space in bytes:_____

Note:
Do *not* continue in this lab activity until all information is filled in. Data on the disk will be destroyed in the next sequence of lab steps.

---

11. ____ At the command prompt, type the command **format f:** followed by [Enter]. The **format f:** instructs the **format** command to prepare the USB Flash drive for storage. This is assuming the USB Flash drive is represented by F. Be sure there are no files you need on the USB Flash drive, as all of its data will be erased.

When the **format f:** command is first issued, a command prompt window similar to the following will appear.

```
Command Prompt - format F:                                    _ □ X
C:\Users\Rich>format F:
Insert new disk for drive F:
and press ENTER when ready...
The type of the file system is FAT.
Verifying 1017M
Cannot open volume for direct access.
85 percent completed.
```

The following is a typical sequence of messages that appear when formatting a USB Flash drive using the command prompt.

The display first instructs you to "Insert new disk for drive F: and press ENTER when ready..."

Next, the type of file format being used to format the drive will appear as well as the size. For example, it might say the file system is FAT and that it is verifying 1017M. The 1017M represents 1017 megabytes (MB) of disk space. You will also see the percentage of the process completed. For example, "27 percent completed." Then finally, the screen will prompt you for a volume label with a screen prompt similar to the following: "Volume label (11 characters, ENTER for none)?".

Just press the [Enter] key to indicate no volume label because the volume label is optional. A volume label is simply a name for the disk, partition, or disc storage device you just formatted. After the format process is completed, the amount of data available on the disk is displayed. A command prompt window similar to the following will appear with an accumulation of all information gathered during the steps formatting the USB Flash drive.

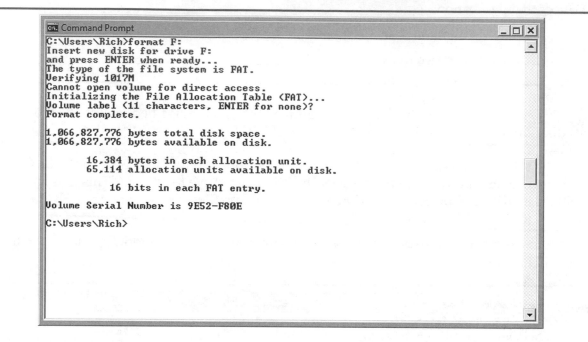

The storage space on a disk is divided into small areas called allocation units. The smallest possible size of allocation unit is 512 bytes. When data or files are saved to a small storage device such as a floppy disk, they are saved in complete allocation units of 512 bytes. As storage device size increases, the smallest file allocation unit also grows in size. In this example, the 1 GB USB Flash drive uses 16,384 bytes for each allocation unit. When formatting a device such as a floppy disk, the following message will appear:

The last screen prompt asks if you wish to format another disk. You must respond with a [Y] for "yes" or [N] for "no," followed by [Enter].

Format another (Y/N)?

When formatting the USB Flash device, no such message will appear.

12. _____ Use the **dir** command to look at the data on the USB Flash drive. Simply enter **dir f:** at the command prompt. You should only see that the drive has no label and that there is a volume serial number such as 9EBA-E70A. Each volume serial number created is unique for each volume or drive. This is a way the Windows operating system keeps track of all drives in a computer or network system.

Record the total available disk space here for comparison later in the laboratory activity.

Total bytes free:_____

Copyright by Goodheart-Willcox Co., Inc.

Name_____

13. ____ Using the **Start** menu, open Notepad, located at **Start I Programs I Accessories I Notepad**.

14. ____ Type four short memos using the following text. Save them as independent files named memo1, memo2, memo3, and memo4. The content of each memo is displayed below.

memo1 = This is memo 1.

memo2 = This is memo 2.

memo3 = This is memo 3.

memo4 = This is memo 4.

Save each memo file to the USB Flash drive.

15. ____ Use the **dir** command to look at the file structure of the USB Flash drive by typing the **dir f:** command. Remember to leave the space between **dir** and **f:**. The four memos you saved to the disk in drive A should be displayed.

Look at the total amount of space available for storage now and compare it to the original space available after saving the four small files. Take into account the size of each file being stored. You will see a vast discrepancy. This is because of the file size saved in the number of bytes used for each file. The amount of space for each of these files is equal to one complete file allocation unit. In other words, if you used only 60 bytes to store the short text file, an entire allocation unit is used to store the file. If only the letter *A* was saved in the text file, an entire allocation unit would be used to store the letter *A*. There will be a lot of unused space on the storage media.

16. ____ The contents of text files can be displayed by using the **type** command. The **type** command is followed by the name of the file and the file extension. For example, **type f:memo1.txt**.

When this command is entered, the ASCII text contents of the file memo1.txt should be displayed on the screen. Be sure to use the file extension .txt or an error will be generated, such as "The system cannot find the file specified."

17. ____ Use the **type** command to display the contents of the other three memos.

18. ____ The **md** or **mkdir** command is used to make a directory. The **rd** or **rmdir** commands are used to remove a directory. It must be followed by the name of the directory that you wish to make or remove. Use the following command to create a directory named level1a: **md level1a**.

19. ____ Use the **dir** command to display the contents of the USB Flash drive. A directory structure similar to the one below should appear.

MEMO1.TXT 16 05-26-00a 10:35a memo1.txt

MEMO2.TXT 16 05-26-00a 10:36a memo2.txt

MEMO3.TXT 16 05-26-00a 10:38a memo3.txt

MEMO4.TXT 16 05-26-00a 10:39a memo4.txt

LEVEL1A <DIR> 05-26-00a 10:45a level1a

4 File(s) 60 bytes

1 Dir(s) 1,066,745,856 bytes free

Note:
The exact file sizes may vary depending on the text-editing program used, whether returns are included in the message body, and the size of storage media being used.

The names, sizes, and creation dates and times are displayed for the files, including the directory. The amount of free space on the disk is also displayed. You will notice that although the four memo files are only 60 bytes in size, the amount of free space on the hard drive has diminished by one allocation unit per file.

Note:
You can learn more about file allocation cluster sizes at the following Microsoft support Web site. http://support.microsoft.com/kb/140365.

---

20. ____ Now use the **md** or **mkdir** command to create a second directory called level1b.

21. ____ Use the **dir f:** command to verify you have made a second directory called level1b. If it does not exist, call your instructor.

22. ____ Now create a second-level directory by typing the following command: **md F:\level1a\ level2a**. This will create a directory inside another directory.

23. ____ Use the **tree** command to verify that you have created two levels. The **tree** command will display all levels of the directory structure. Simply type the **free f:** command, and you should see a command prompt window similar to the following.

```
Command Prompt
C:\Users\Rich>tree F:
Folder PATH listing
Volume serial number is 9EBA-E70A
F:\
    ├───level1a
    │   └───level2a
    └───level1b

C:\Users\Rich>
```

Notice how the level2a directory is indicated as inside the level1a directory. You have created one directory inside another directory. If your screen does not appear similar to the one in the example, call your instructor for assistance.

24. ____ Now, create a third-level directory inside the level2a directory. Use the following command: **md F:level1a\level2a\level3a**.

25. ____ Verify you have created a third-level directory structure by using the **tree** command.

26. ____ Change the default location for the command prompt by accessing drive F. Simply type **f:** at the command prompt and you should see a command prompt with a string of characters similar to the following: F:\>. This indicates you are at the USB Flash drive F.

27. ____ You can move up and down a directory listing. To move down a directory listing, use the **cd** command followed by the next level directory. For example, **cd F:level1a\level2a**. This command changes the default directory from F:\ to F:\LEVEL1A\LEVEL2A. The command prompt should change indicating the new location. If not, call your instructor for assistance.

28. ____ Now you can move down one more directory level to level3a by using the command **cd level3a** at the command prompt. Your command prompt should display your new location as F:\level1a\level2a\level3a>.

29. ____ To move up the directory structure, you can use the command **cd..**, which will move you up one level. Try it now.

Copyright by Goodheart-Willcox Co., Inc.

30. ____ To move completely to the top of the directory structure for the volume, simply type **cd** followed by a space and then the backward slash (\\). For example, **cd **. Now, the prompt should appear as F:\\>.

31. ____ Practice moving up and down the directory structure until you feel comfortable with the **cd** or **chdir** commands. Also, be sure you practice the **tree** command.

32. ____ Type **help rmdir** and read the information about the **rmdir** and **rd** commands. Notice that the **s** switch will remove all contents of the directory to include files and other directions. This is a replacement for the earlier DOS version command **deltree**, which accomplished the same task. Try using the **rmdir** command to remove only directory level2a. For example, **rmdir /s F: level1a\\level2a**. When issued correctly, you will be prompted with an "Are you sure (Y/N)?". You will respond with the letter Y. Using the **tree** command, verify the directory level2a and level3a have been removed.

33. ____ Build the directory structure once more with three levels of directories consisting of level1a, level2a, and level3a.

34. ____ Copy memo1.txt into the level1a directory, memo2.txt into the level2a directory, and memo3 and memo4 into the level3a directory.

35. ____ Use the **tree** command with the **/f** switch to expose the files inside each directory level. Call your instructor to check your directory structure with the memo files included in the directory structure.

36. ____ Use the Windows Explorer to view the directory structure you created on the USB Flash drive.

37. ____ After your instructor has inspected your lab activity, you can go on to answer the review questions. Return the computer to its original condition when you are finished.

Review Questions

1. What is the smallest unit allocation size expressed in bytes? _____

2. What command is the same as **md**? _____

3. When would the command prompt display the word *WINDOWS* as part of the prompt? _____
   _____

4. The command prompt displayed on the screen is always the _____ directory. _____
   _____

5. What will the command **cd..** do? _____
   _____

6. What command is equal to **md**? _____

7. What is the maximum number of characters that can be used for a volume label? _____
   _____

8. To change from the default directory of drive C to the default directory of drive F, which command would you use? _____

9. What is the purpose of the **tree** command? _____
   _____

10. What does the **tree /f** command accomplish? _____

11. Is the following command and example of changing to an absolute or a relative location?
    cd f:level1a\level2a\level3a _____

12. Is the following command an example of a relative or absolute directory location?
    cd level2a _____

13. What switch used with **rd** command will remove all subdirectories and files included in the directory to be removed? _____

Copyright by Goodheart-Willcox Co., Inc.

Name _____ Date _____

Class/Instructor _____

Help File

After completing this laboratory activity, you will be able to:

■ Access the command prompt help files.

■ Use command prompt help files to learn more about common commands and their related switches.

Introduction

The command prompt commands are based on the earlier DOS operating system and have evolved over the years. The command prompt help files are an extremely helpful set of files, especially if you need to know more about commands or command switches. You can access help for a command by going to the command prompt and entering the name of the command followed by the forward slash (/) and the question mark (?). Look at the following examples that will reveal information about the **format** command.

format /?

help format

Be sure to leave a space between the command and the forward slash when using the question mark switch. To see a complete list of commands simply type the command **help** at the command prompt and then scroll through the commands using the scroll bar on the right side of the command prompt screen.

To limit the amount of information displayed on the screen at one time, use the pipe symbol (|) followed by **more** after the **help** command. For example, **help |more**.

In the following example, the **xcopy** command used with the **/?** switch provides too much information to display at one time. The addition of the **|more** flag allows the viewer to scroll one screen at a time by pressing [Enter]. Pressing the spacebar will take you to the end of the help information.

xcopy /?

xcopy /? |more

Copyright by Goodheart-Willcox Co., Inc.

Equipment and Materials

■ Computer with Windows XP or Windows Vista, or both, installed.

Procedure

1. ____ Report to your assigned workstation.

2. ____ Boot the computer and verify it is in working order.

3. ____ Access the command prompt. Enter the commands referred to in the review questions. Add the **/?** switch to access information about the commands and answer the questions.

4. ____ After you have answered all the review questions, close the command prompt and shut down the PC. Remember to use the help files to answer the review questions.

Review Questions

1. What command is equal in function to **del**?_____

2. What switches may be used with the **attrib** command? _____

3. What does the **/F:** switch do when used in conjunction with the **format** command? _____

_____

4. What is the **find** command used for?_____

_____

5. What other command is equal to **md**?_____

6. What does the **/FS:** switch do when used with the **format** command? _____

_____

7. What is the purpose of **xcopy**? _____

_____

8. What is the purpose of the **prompt** command? _____

_____

9. When using the **prompt** command, what does **$Q** mean? _____

_____

10. When using the **prompt** command, what does **$V** mean? _____

_____

Copyright by Goodheart-Willcox Co., Inc.

Name _____ Date _____

Class/Instructor _____

File Attributes

After completing this laboratory activity, you will be able to:
- Use the command prompt to set a hidden file attribute.
- Use the command prompt to remove a hidden file attribute.
- Use the command prompt to set a read-only file attribute.
- Use the command prompt to remove the read-only file attribute.

Introduction

In this lab activity, you will change file attributes to see how a memo file is affected. The two most common file attributes you will be using are hidden and read only.

```
Command Prompt                                          _ □ X

C:\Users\Richard>help attrib
Displays or changes file attributes.

ATTRIB [+R | -R] [+A | -A ] [+S | -S] [+H | -H] [+I | -I]
       [drive:][path][filename] [/S [/D] [/L]]

    +   Sets an attribute.
    -   Clears an attribute.
    R   Read-only file attribute.
    A   Archive file attribute.
    S   System file attribute.
    H   Hidden file attribute.
    I   Not content indexed file attribute.
  [drive:][path][filename]
        Specifies a file or files for attrib to process.
    /S  Processes matching files in the current folder
        and all subfolders.
    /D  Processes folders as well.
    /L  Work on the attributes of the Symbolic Link versus
        the target of the Symbolic Link
```

The following is a list of the various switches that can be used with the **attrib** command.
- The (+) plus sign sets the file attribute that follows it.
- The (–) minus sign removes the file attribute that follows it.
- The **R** switch designates a read-only file attribute.
- The **H** switch designates a hidden file attribute.
- The **S** switch designates a system file attribute.
- The **A** switch designates an archive file attribute.
- The **/S** switch follows the pathname and causes all of the files in all of the directories in the specified path to be assigned the file attribute.
- The **/I** switch designates the "not content indexed" file attribute.

Copyright by Goodheart-Willcox Co., Inc.

A new attribute represented by the letter *I* represents "not content indexed," which means the content of the file will not be listed in the operating system's content index. This feature is new for desktop operating systems and will not be used in this laboratory activity.

The typical format for using the **attrib** command is as follows: **attrib +h C:memo1.txt** followed by [Enter]. This example sets the file named memo1 on volume or drive C with a hidden file attribute. This means that the file cannot be seen by the command **dir**. It is hidden to the viewer and cannot be accessed. The hidden attribute is commonly used to protect certain files from accidental removal or modification.

Equipment and Materials

■ Computer with Windows XP or Windows Vista, or both, installed.

■ The USB Flash drive containing the memo files created in previous laboratory activities.

Procedure

1. ____ Boot the PC and wait for the Windows desktop to appear.

2. ____ Access the command prompt.

3. ____ Look at the memo1 file on the USB Flash drive. Change the file attribute to hidden. You may need to access the command prompt help file to review the procedures for changing a file attribute.

4. ____ View the directory of the USB Flash drive using the **dir** command to see if the memo1 file is still listed.

5. ____ Now, reverse the operation by removing the hidden attribute from the memo1 file. If it was done correctly, the memo1 file should appear again when the **dir** command is issued. Check the USB Flash drive by using the **dir** command. The file name memo1 should reappear.

6. ____ Set the file attribute for memo1 to read only.

7. ____ Open the file memo1 in a text editor and try to alter its contents. What happens?

_____

_____

8. ____ You can display the attributes of files in the current directory by typing the **attrib** command at the DOS prompt. To see the attributes of files in a different directory, you must first make that directory the default directory using the **cd** command, and then issue the **attrib** command. As an alternative, you may type the entire path following the **attrib** command. You must include the names of files you wish to see the attributes of, or you can use wildcards. The following are examples of the two methods.

C:\> **a:**

A:\> **cd\homework**

A:\HOMEWORK>**attrib**

or

C:\> **attrib a:\homework*.***

9. ____ After answering the review questions, return the PC to its original settings and then shut the PC down.

Copyright by Goodheart-Willcox Co., Inc.

Review Questions

1. How can the hidden-file attribute be used for security? _____
_____

2. Why would you give a file a read-only attribute? _____
_____

3. How can the attributes of files in a directory be displayed? _____
_____

Copyright by Goodheart-Willcox Co., Inc.

Notes

Computer Service and Repair Lab Manual

Copyright by Goodheart-Willcox Co., Inc.

Name _____ Date _____

Class/Instructor _____

Help and Support Center

After completing this laboratory activity, you will be able to:

■ Use the Help and Support Center to learn about common tasks.

■ Describe the effects of using incorrect spelling in a Help and Support Center search.

■ Describe how search results can change by using a plural or closely-related word in a Help and Support Center search.

Introduction

In this laboratory activity, you will become familiar with the Help and Support Center features of Windows XP and Windows Vista. Both operating systems provide help and support information about the most common computer tasks. Microsoft expanded the Windows Vista Help and Support Center by providing more support features and more help on common tasks.

The Help and Support Center is accessed directly from the **Start** menu in both Windows XP and Windows Vista. You can also directly access Windows Help and Support Center by pressing the Windows logo key and [F1] simultaneously.

The Help and Support Center provides local support with information resources stored directly on the computer. In addition, you will also have an option to perform a more in-depth search for help and support online or request support using the Remote Assistance feature. Remote Assistance is covered in-depth in another laboratory activity. You can also access the Microsoft Web site to expand your search by using their Knowledge Base. The Microsoft Knowledge Base is a vast collection of information.

Look at the following screen captures of the Help and Support Center home page for Windows XP and Windows Vista. Notice that the areas inside the Help and Support Center window for Windows XP and Windows Vista are organized in similar manner. They both provide a list of common help topics. In Windows XP, the common help topics are listed under **Pick a Help topic**. In Windows Vista, they are listed under **Find an answer**. Both versions of Windows provide a way to obtain more assistance. For example, in Windows XP, a user can obtain more assistance through the **Ask for Assistance** section and in Windows Vista, through the **Ask someone** section. Both versions of Windows also provide a **Search** box that allows you to search for help on a specific topic. The results of a search vary according to the key word(s) you use to begin the search.

Copyright by Goodheart-Willcox Co., Inc.

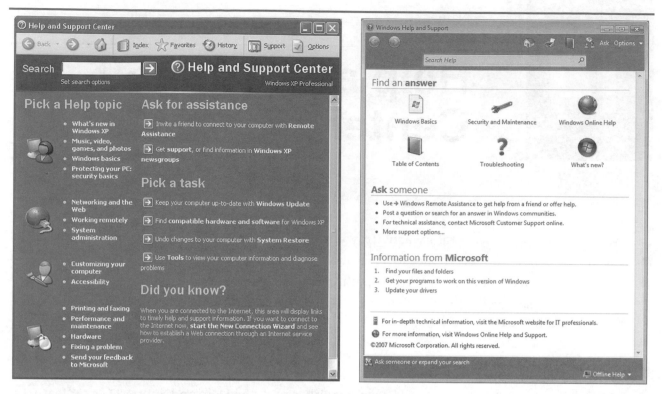

Windows XP Help and Support Center   Windows Vista Help and Support Center

Notice that Windows Vista provides a link to the Microsoft TechNet Web site. This is indicated by <u>For in-depth technical information, visit the Microsoft website of IT professionals</u> at the bottom of the screen. This link will take you directly to the following Web site: http://technet.microsoft.com/en-us/windowsvista/default.aspx.

This Web site is designed for computer and network professionals and is not intended for common everyday uses and for those with limited technical knowledge. The TechNet Web site provides a vast amount of information, but many of the articles assume you have technical experience. The TechNet Web site does not provide information in layman terms. There is also a TechNet subscription service that you can sign up for that will provide you with copies of all the latest software programs, applications, patches, and drivers as they are developed by Microsoft. All software is in beta form and is not the actual finished product.

The last link, <u>For more information, visit Windows Online Help and Support</u>, provides much more information than the local help and support information that is stored directly on the computer. This is the same link as the <u>Windows Online Help</u>, which is located under the **Find an answer** section.

Microsoft Support provides both free support and pay support. At the time of this writing, the fee for pay support was $59.00 per call. The fee is waived for special members of Microsoft, such as Microsoft preferred customers and TechNet subscribers. The members are people who sell Microsoft products and services or who join the TechNet subscription service, which provides the very latest software patches and updates and Microsoft application software in beta form.

Both Windows XP and Windows Vista provide a link in the Help and Support Center to allow the user to ask a friend for help using Remote Assistance. Remote Assistance is a special feature that allows a user to send an e-mail or an instant message to another person and allows that person to connect to the user's computer to help solve the problem. There will be more about Remote Assistance in a later laboratory activity.

Copyright by Goodheart-Willcox Co., Inc.

Free support is usually self-help support. You are given access to the extensive Microsoft Knowledge Base which contains thousands of articles about known problems encountered. The following is a screen capture of the Microsoft TechNet Web page.

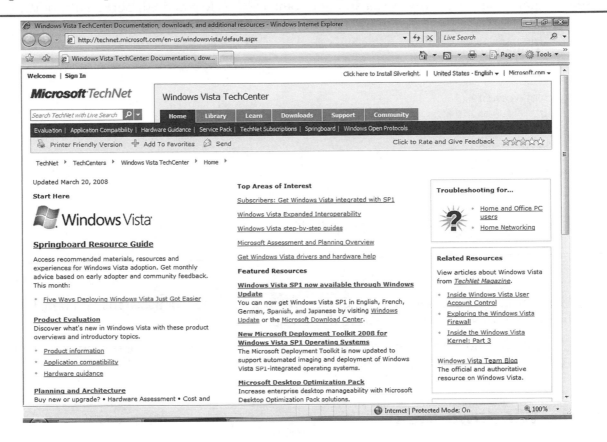

The Microsoft TechNet home page is free, but the level of information provided is typically set at a technician level and is not for the casual user. There are more appropriate help pages available to someone with less than a technician's level of knowledge, such as the Microsoft Windows Vista home page.

Equipment and Materials

■ Computer with Windows XP or Windows Vista, or both, installed.
■ An Internet connection is recommended but not required.

Part I—Windows XP

Procedure

1. ____ Report to your assigned workstation.

2. ____ Boot the computer and verify it is in working order.

3. ____ Locate the **Help and Support** option located off the **Start** menu and then open it. Close the Help and Support Center and open it once by pressing Windows logo and [F1] key simultaneously.

4. ____ Conduct a search in the Help and Support Center on the topics listed below and then quickly review the material presented. Do not read the topics in depth. Simply learn to appreciate the vast amount and quality of the help provided in this manner. You will conduct this search again using Windows Vista and will compare the Help and Support results of the two operating systems.

_____ Printer

_____ Security

_____ Networking

_____ Files

_____ File

_____ Folder

_____ Folders

_____ Folderss (Yes, the subject is misspelled by adding an extra s!)

_____ Password

_____ [Ctrl] [Alt] [Del]

5. ____ Look at the Help and Support Center and locate the **Ask for assistance** section. Click each option in this section and explore the results.

6. ____ This concludes Part I of the laboratory activity. Do not answer the review questions until you complete Part II—Windows Vista.

Part II—Windows Vista

Procedure

1. ____ Report to your assigned workstation.

2. ____ Boot the computer and verify it is in working order.

3. ____ Select the **Help and Support** option located off the **Start** menu.

4. ____ Conduct a search in the Help and Support Center on the topics listed below and then quickly review the material presented. Do not read the topics in depth. Simply learn to appreciate the vast amount and quality of the help provided in this manner. You will conduct this search again using Windows Vista and will compare the Help and Support results of the two operating systems.

_____ Printer

_____ Security

_____ Networking

The next four search terms are closely related but have different results.

_____ File

_____ Files

_____ Folder

Copyright by Goodheart-Willcox Co., Inc.

_____ Folders

_____ Folderss (Yes, the subject is misspelled by adding an extra s!)

The next three terms all can have basically the same meaning but produce very different results.

_____ Display

_____ Monitor

_____ CRT

Run a search for the two items below. This will produce different results when compared to Windows XP.

_____ Password

_____ [Ctrl] [Alt] [Del]

5. ____ Explore the options located in the **Ask someone** section.

6. ____ Explore the links at the bottom of the Help and Support Center screen: <u>For in-depth technical information, visit the Microsoft website of IT professionals</u> and <u>For more information, visit Windows Online Help and Support</u>. These will not work without an Internet connection. At the Microsoft TechNet Web site, notice the type and level of information available to technicians.

6. ____ Complete the review questions. When you are finished answering the review questions, return the computer to its original configuration and shut down the computer.

Review Questions

1. What is the path to Help and Support in Windows XP and Windows Vista?_____
   _____

2. What is Microsoft TechNet? _____
   _____
   _____

3. What key combination will automatically open the Help and Support Center?_____
   _____

4. True *or* False? Using a very similar word in the **Search** box of the Help and Support Center will provide the exact same results._____

5. True *or* False? It makes no difference in the search results if you use the plural form of the search word? _____

6. What is Remote Assistance? _____
   _____
   _____
   _____
   _____

Copyright by Goodheart-Willcox Co., Inc.

Name _____ Date _____

Class/Instructor _____

File Management with Windows Explorer

After completing this laboratory activity, you will be able to:

- Open and navigate Windows Explorer.
- Interpret the symbols and structures used in Windows Explorer.
- Display hidden and system files in Windows Explorer.
- Reconfigure the details view of files and directories to reveal enhanced properties.
- Sort files by characteristics, such as date created, size, and alphabetical order.
- Modify Windows Explorer to view additional file details.

Introduction

This laboratory activity will enhance your skills for using Windows Explorer and navigating directory structures. The Windows XP file structure is revealed in two common ways from the desktop. The first method is to click **My Computer** located on the **Start** menu. This action reveals all of the storage device icons. The display should be similar to that shown in the following screen capture.

Notice that system tasks are listed in the left pane of Windows Explorer. The appearance of the left pane display can be changed by clicking the **Folders** button in the toolbar located at the top of Windows Explorer. Each time the **Folders** button is clicked, the left pane will change to either the common tasks view or the directory tree view.

Copyright by Goodheart-Willcox Co., Inc.

The second method for revealing the directory structure in Windows XP is to open the **Start** menu, right-click **My Computer**, and then select **Explore** from the shortcut menu. When this method is used, the left pane will display the directory structure by default rather than the common tasks view. Look at the following screen capture to see what a typical directory tree view using the right-click method would reveal.

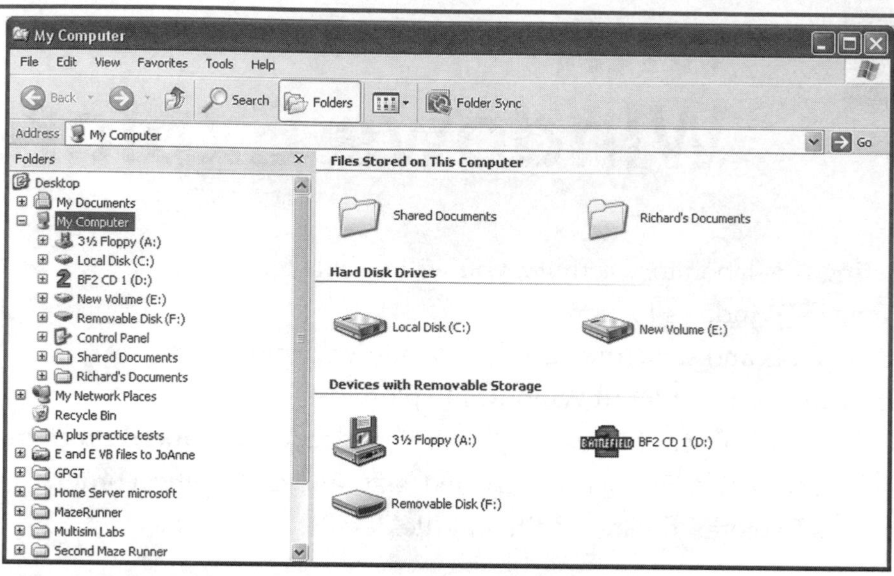

In the first level of the directory structure, you can see icons for all available storage devices, including the floppy drives, hard drives, and CD drives. Double-clicking a drive or directory icon reveals the next level of folders and files for that drive or directory. For example, double-clicking a drive icon reveals a detailed view of the directory structure of the drive. In the following screen capture, you can see a typical directory structure of a C drive for a Windows XP computer. This view was created by double-clicking the **Local Disk (C:)** icon.

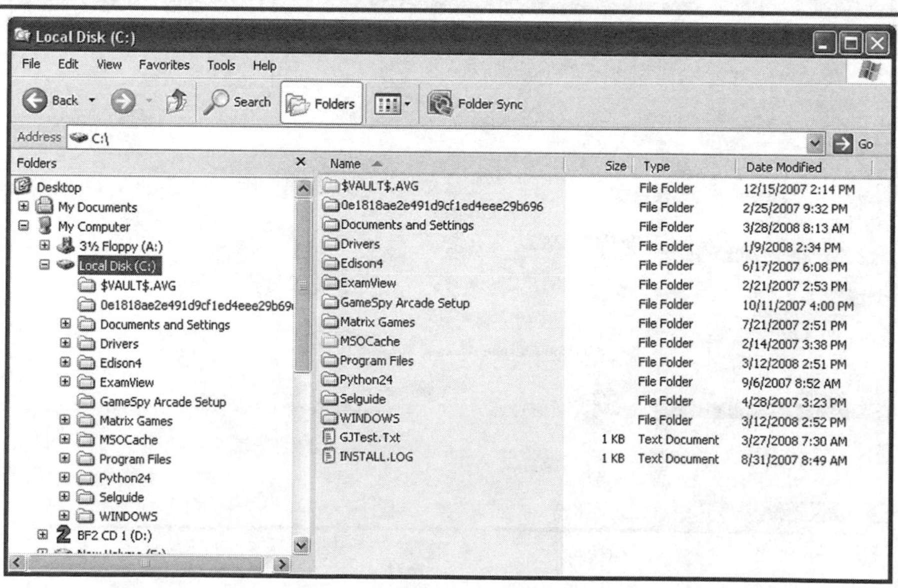

In the screen capture you can see the files and folders found under drive C for Windows XP. (This is a typical drive C directory structure; however, it may not necessarily match the one on the computer you are using.) This is the preferred view of the directory structure for technicians

Copyright by Goodheart-Willcox Co., Inc.

because it displays the hierarchy of the file system structure. This means that the Explorer window allows you to see a detailed display of files, directories (folders), and paths all at one time. You can change back and forth by clicking the **Folders** button located in the toolbar.

Note that Windows Explorer displays information about the files and their structure in two panes. The pane on the left displays the path structure (the available drives, directories, and subdirectories) as an expandable and a collapsible tree. The pane on the right displays the contents of the directory or subdirectory selected on the left. To select a new directory, click the directory's icon. To expand or collapse a branch in the directory tree, double-click the directory's icon or click the box to the left of the folder icon. In the previous screen capture, drive C is highlighted on the left. The files and directories contained in the drive's root directory are displayed on the right.

The directory structure for Windows Vista is very similar to Windows XP. Look at the screen capture of a typical Windows Vista drive C directory structure.

Windows Vista Explorer is similar in many ways to that of Windows XP, but there are also many differences. For example, the commonly accessed tasks are not displayed in the left pane the way they are in Windows XP.

Both Windows XP and Windows Vista Explorer use drive C as the default directory or root directory. The term *root directory* refers to the first directory created on a drive when the operating system is first installed and where the files required to boot the computer operating system are installed.

Take special notice of the plus (+) and minus (–) signs in the small boxes to the left of the directory structure in Windows XP. A directory that contains unexpanded subdirectories is indicated by a plus sign (+) in front of the directory name. Clicking the box expands, or reveals, the subdirectories in the directory tree. When the subdirectories are expanded, a minus sign replaces the plus sign in the box. Directories that contain no subdirectories have no box to the left of their folder icon. Windows Vista dropped the use of the plus and minus sign in a box and simply uses a folder to indicate a directory.

Certain files and folders (directories) are hidden by default. For example, the files required to boot the computer system are hidden to prevent accidentally moving or deleting the files. Hidden files and folders can be revealed by the system administrator or a user with security equal to the system administrator. To display hidden and system files in Windows XP Explorer, select **Tools** from the menu and then select **Folder Options** as indicated in the following screen capture.

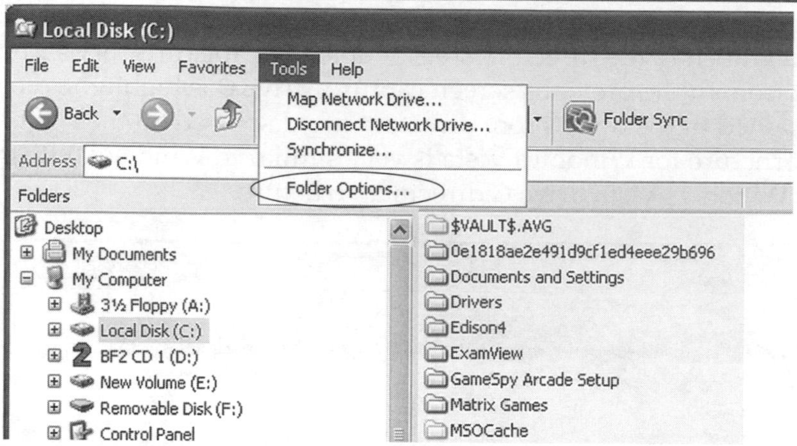

A **Folder Options** dialog box similar to the following will be revealed. Select the **View** tab to reveal a list of viewing options that can be selected using a simple mouse click. Look at a partial list of options below.

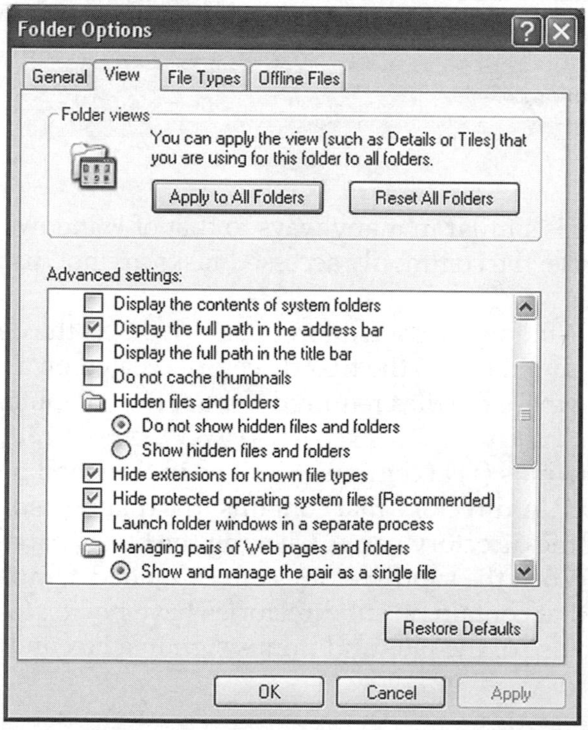

Pay particular attention to the **Do not show hidden files and folders, Show hidden files and folders**, and **Hide protected operating system files (Recommended)** options. By default, the **Do not show hidden files and folders** and **Hide protected operating system files (Recommended)** is selected. You select the appropriate option to view hidden and system files in Windows Explorer. Also, note that

    Copyright by Goodheart-Willcox Co., Inc.

there is a button in the lower-right corner labeled **Restore Defaults**, which is used to return the settings to their original condition.

Compare the following screen captures to see what happens when the hidden and system files are revealed in the directory structure. The one on the left has the default values used to hide critical system files. On the right, you can see the critical files displayed in the root directory.

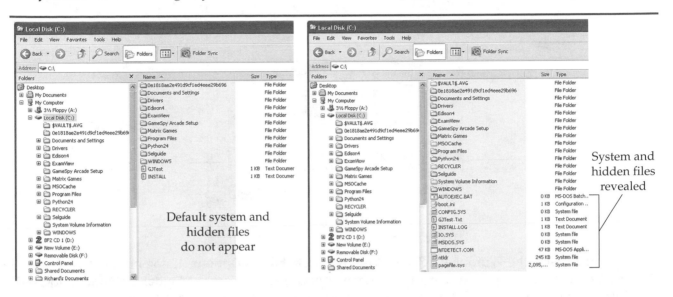

The hidden and system files are displayed lightly rather than sharp and crisp. This is so they can be easily distinguished from regular files. The appearance is very similar in Windows Vista.

In Windows Vista, the way Windows Explorer is organized has changed. To display the hidden and system files, you must first select **Folders and Search Options** listed under **Organize**.

A dialog box very similar to the Windows XP **Folders Option** dialog box will appear. Look at the following screen capture of the **Folder Options** dialog box in Windows Vista and compare it to the Windows XP version shown earlier.

Copyright by Goodheart-Willcox Co., Inc.

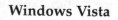

As you can see, the Windows XP and Windows Vista **Folder Options** dialog boxes are very similar. The real difference is how to access them. You can also access the **Folder Options** dialog box through the Control Panel. For Windows XP, select **Start | Control Panel | Appearance and Themes | Folder Options | View**. For Windows Vista, select **Start | Control Panel | Appearance and Personalization | Folder Options | View**.

The details view of files and folders in both Windows Vista and Windows XP is the preferred method of technicians to view the directory structure. In addition to the default details view, you can modify the view to include many different file options. For example, you can include much more file information in the Windows Explorer detail view. You can add additional information columns for such things as file extensions, author, URL, product version and much more.

Windows XP

Windows Vista

Copyright by Goodheart-Willcox Co., Inc.

The number of details about files have been greatly increased in Windows Vista. Many of the details include Web page information and information that is typically stored in Microsoft Office application documents.

You access the **Choose Details** dialog box in the same way for Windows Vista and Windows XP. Simply right-click the top row of any column in the detail view of Windows Explorer to reveal the **More** option. Clicking the **More** option reveals a complete list of available details as shown in the following screen capture.

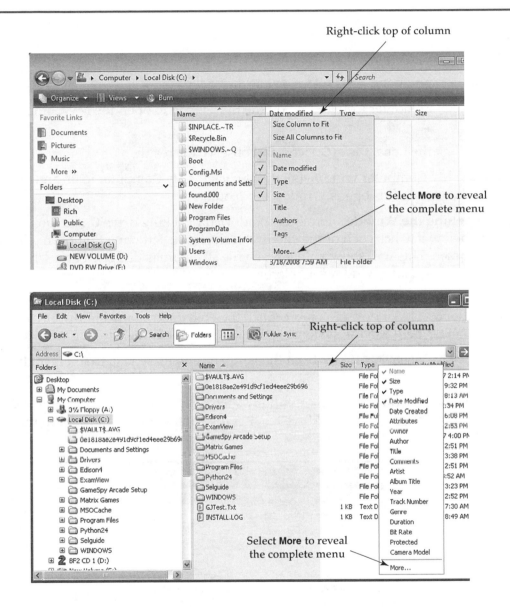

After the detail is selected, a new column is automatically generated to the right side of the existing columns. If the column is empty, it means that there are no such file details available for the file. Since many of the file details depend on the proper configuration of application software, the details selected may not appear in the column. For example, if you do not enter information into the **Author** textbox in a **Properties** dialog box for a Microsoft Office document, then the **Author** column detail will be blank.

You can sort the files by double-clicking the top of anyone of the detail view column headings. For example, double-clicking the file name rearranges the file name list in alphabetical order; double-clicking the size of the file automatically rearranges the column list by file size; double-clicking the file type reorganizes the files by file types, such as documents, or images.

Copyright by Goodheart-Willcox Co., Inc.

Equipment and Materials

- Computer with Windows XP or Windows Vista, or both, installed.
- USB Flash drive with memo1 file (optional).

Part I—Windows XP

Procedure

1. ____ Report to your assigned workstation.

2. ____ Boot the computer and verify it is in working order.

3. ____ Click the **My Computer** icon located on the **Start** menu to open the My Computer window.

4. ____ Double-click the **Local Disk (C:)** icon and observe the result.

5. ____ Close the My Computer window(s). Right-click the **My Computer** icon, and select **Explore** from the shortcut menu. This opens Windows Explorer.

6. ____ After opening the Windows Explorer window, try clicking drive C to expose the directory structure below it. Click each of the subdirectories in the left pane that have plus signs in front of their names. This will show you how the file structure is designed and what files are inside the directories. Close Windows Explorer.

7. ____ Right-click the **My Computer** icon and select **Explore** from the shortcut menu. Locate the **Folder** icon at the top of Windows Explorer. Click the **Folders** icon repeatedly and watch how the left pane changes between the systems tasks view and the directory tree view.

8. ____ Select the My Documents folder from the left pane and leave it so that it is highlighted in blue.

9. ____ Select the **View** menu at the top of Windows Explorer and then select **Choose Details** from the drop-down menu. You should see a list of file details similar to those in the following screen capture.

Copyright by Goodheart-Willcox Co., Inc.

Select the following file details: **Attributes**, **Owner**, and **Date Created**. To do this, simply click the square box in front of the file detail.

10. ____ Now, look at the My Documents directory using Windows Explorer to see the changes in the appearance of file details. Three additional columns should have been added with information about the additional file details requested.

11. ____ Deselect the file details for **Attributes**, **Owner**, and **Date Created** to return the Windows Explorer view to its default state. To deselect the file details, simply click the box in front of the detail you wish to deselect.

12. ____ Now, click the titles at the top of each column to see the effect on the column listing. For example, clicking the **Date Modified** title at the top of the column will automatically reorganize the contents of My Documents in ascending or descending order by the date the file or directory was modified. Repeat for the columns labeled **Size**, **Type**, and **Name**. Experiment for a few minutes before moving to the next step.

13. ____ Now, you will reveal the hidden files and folders. Select **Start | Control Panel | Appearance and Themes | Folder Options | View**. Select the **Show hidden files and folders** option and deselect the **Hide protected operating system files** option.

14. ____ View drive C using Windows Explorer and see if you can identify the hidden and system files. See if the following files can be seen: **ntdlr**, **autoexec.bat**, **io.sys**, **pagefile.sys**, **msdos.sys**, and **boot.ini**. These system files should appear in the directory structure. They are normally hidden.

15. ____ Return the **Folder Options** dialog box back to default settings, by opening the **Folder Options** dialog box, clicking the **View** tab, and then clicking the **Restore Defaults** button. Be sure the **View** tab has been selected and not the **General** tab. Each tab has a **Restore Defaults** button, but the button will only affect the options appearing in that particular tab when selected.

16. ____ This concludes Part I of the laboratory activity. Do not answer the review questions until you complete Part II—Windows Vista. You can take a few minutes to review Part I before moving on to Part II.

Part II—Windows Vista

Procedure

1. ____ Report to your assigned workstation.

2. ____ Boot the computer and verify it is in working order.

3. Click the **Computer** icon in the **Start** menu to open the Computer folder in the system tasks view.

4. ____ Double-click the **Local Disk (C:)** icon and observe the result.

5. ____ Close the Explorer program. From the **Start** menu, right-click the **Computer** icon, and select **Explore** from the shortcut menu. This opens Windows Explorer in the directory tree view.

6. ____ After opening Windows Explorer, click drive C to expose the directory structure. Click several of the drive C subdirectories in the left pane to expand the contents. This will show you how the file structure is designed and what files are inside the directories. Close Windows Explorer.

7. ____ In the **Start** menu right-click the **Computer** icon and select **Explore** from the shortcut menu. Locate and click the **Folders** label in the left pane. Notice how it jumps to the bottom of the left pane when closed. Click the **Folders** label repeatedly and watch how the left pane changes between the directory tree view and no view.

8. ____ In the left pane, click the user account name you are using and then click **Documents**.

9. ____ Select **Views** from the menu at the top of Windows Explorer and then select **Choose Details** from the drop down menu.

10. ____ Now, right-click the top of the column labeled **Name**. A shortcut menu should appear. Select **More** from the bottom of the down menu. The **Choose Details** dialog box should appear. Select the following file details: **Attributes**, **Owner**, and **Date Created**. To do this, simply click the square box in front of the file detail. The list of file details available in Windows Vista is quite long. You will need to use the scroll bar to view the entire list.

11. ____ Look at Documents directory using Windows Explorer to see the changes in the appearance of file details. Three additional columns should have been added with information about the additional files details requested.

12. ____ Deselect the file details for **Attributes**, **Owner**, and **Date Created** to return the Windows Explorer view to its default state. To deselect the file details, simply click the box in front of the detail you wish to deselect.

13. ____ Click the titles at the top of each column to see the effect on sorting the contents of the listing. For example, clicking the **Date Modified** title at the top of the column will automatically reorganize the contents of the Documents directory in ascending or descending order by the date the file or directory was modified. Repeat for the columns labeled **Size**, **Type**, and **Name**. Experiment for a few minutes before moving to the next step.

14. ____ Now, you will reveal the hidden files and folders. Select **Start | Control Panel | Appearance and Personalization | Folder Options | View**. Select the **Show hidden files and folders** option and deselect the **Hide protected operating system files** option.

15. ____ View drive C using Windows Explorer and see if you can identify the hidden and system files. See if the following files can be seen: **bootmgr**, **pagefile.sys**, **autoexec**, **ntldr**, **io.sys**, **msdos.sys**. These system files should appear in the directory structure. They are normally hidden.

16. ____ Return the **Folder Options** dialog box back to default settings, by opening the **Folder Options** dialog box, clicking the **View** tab, and then clicking the **Restore Defaults** button. Be sure the **View** tab has been selected and not the **General** tab. Each tab has a **Restore Defaults** button, but the button will only affect the options appearing in that particular tab when selected.

17. ____ Take a few minutes to review the laboratory activity. Practice accessing the **Folder Options** dialog box without the aid of your lab manual.

18. ____ Complete the review questions. When you are finished answering the review question, return the computer to its original configuration and shut down the computer.

Copyright by Goodheart-Willcox Co., Inc.

Review Questions

1. Which Windows Explorer view allows you to sort files by type?_____

2. Why are system files hidden by default? _____

   _____

   _____

3. What does a plus sign in front of a folder in Windows XP directory tree mean?_____

   _____

4. What is the path in Windows XP to the **Folder Options** dialog box starting from the **Start** menu?

   _____

5. What is the path in Windows Vista to the **Folder Options** dialog box starting from the **Start** menu?_____

   _____

6. How can you rearrange the detailed list of files in descending order by file size when viewed in Windows Explorer? _____

   _____

Copyright by Goodheart-Willcox Co., Inc.

Copyright by Goodheart-Willcox Co., Inc.

Name _____ Date _____

Class/Instructor _____

Recycle Bin

After completing this laboratory activity, you will be able to:

■ Locate the **Recycle Bin Properties** dialog box.

■ Adjust the size of the Recycle Bin.

■ Recover items from the Recycle Bin.

■ Empty the Recycle Bin.

Introduction

The Recycle Bin is located on the Windows desktop and is often referred to as the "trash can" or "trash." The Recycle Bin stores files or folders that the user has deleted. It saves the file or folder until the Recycle Bin has been emptied. Early DOS versions of the Windows operating systems did not have the Recycle Bin feature. Many times users accidentally deleted files or folders and then had no way to retrieve them. The Recycle Bin acts as a safety net that allows users to recover accidentally deleted items. The Recycle Bin operates in similar fashion in Windows XP and Windows Vista. The Recycle Bin is typically displayed on the desktop as a trash can icon. Right-clicking the **Recycle Bin** icon produces a shortcut menu similar to that in the following screen captures.

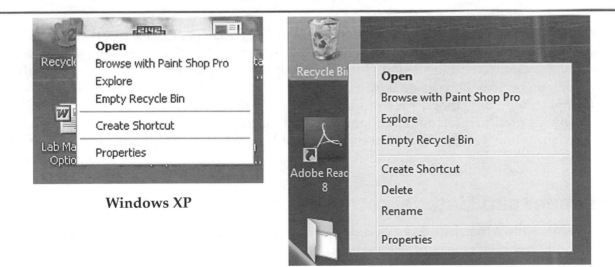

Windows XP

Windows Vista

Copyright by Goodheart-Willcox Co., Inc.

The Recycle Bin in Windows Vista has taken advantage of the more powerful graphics. The **Recycle Bin** icon appears empty when it contains no items and appears full when it contains items. On your computer, you should see the **Open**, **Explore**, **Empty Recycle Bin**, and **Properties** shortcut menu options. Your shortcut menu items will not include the **Browse with Paint Shop Pro** option unless this program is installed on your computer. Often, software applications such as image management applications will install automatically in the Windows menu selections. The following is a screen capture of the **Recycle Bin Properties** dialog boxes for Windows XP and Windows Vista.

Windows XP

Windows Vista

Notice that Windows Vista has eliminated the use of tabs that identify each of the hard drive partitions. It now displays the partition in one viewable window. The size of the Recycle Bin can be changed by the user. You can also modify the Recycle Bin to immediately remove files rather than display a delete confirmation dialog box.

It is important to note that if a file or folder is larger than the size of the recycle bin, it will be automatically deleted without going into the Recycle Bin. To permanently delete a file without needing to empty the Recycle Bin, hold down the [Shift] key while dragging a file or folder to the Recycle Bin.

Equipment and Materials

- Computer with Windows XP or Windows Vista, or both, installed.
- USB Flash drive with memo1 file (optional).

Copyright by Goodheart-Willcox Co., Inc.

Name_____

Part I—Windows XP

Procedure

1. ____ Report to your assigned workstation.

2. ____ Boot the computer and verify it is in working order.

3. ____ Locate and then right-click the **Recycle Bin** icon. Select **Properties** from the shortcut menu. The **Recycle Bin Properties** dialog box will appear. Look over the available options. Be sure to look at and select various tabs available if more than one partition exists.

4. ____ Use the slider to adjust the size of the Recycle Bin. Return it to the default 10% when finished. Take note of the **Use one setting for all drives option**, indicting that one setting can be used for all drives in the computer.

5. ____ Close the **Recycle Bin Properties** dialog box and then right-click the Recycle Bin and select the **Explore** option from the shortcut menu. You should see previously deleted files located in the Recycle Bin. If the Recycle Bin is empty, create a memo file using Notepad or WordPad as in previous laboratory activities. After saving the memo, delete it so that the Recycle Bin contains at least one file.

6. ____ To recover the memo file from the Recycle Bin, simply right-click the file and then select **Restore** from the shortcut menu. The file selected will be automatically restored. Restore the memo file now.

7. ____ Delete the memo file again to resend it to the Recycle Bin.

8. ____ Now, you will permanently delete the memo file by emptying the Recycle Bin. To empty the Recycle Bin, right-click the **Recycle Bin** icon and then select the **Empty Recycle Bin** option from the shortcut menu. You can also empty the Recycle Bin from the Windows Explorer view. Empty the Recycle Bin now.

9. ____ This concludes Part I of the laboratory activity. Do not answer the review questions until you complete Part II—Windows Vista. You can repeat Part I of the lab activity until you feel comfortable using the Recycle Bin in Windows XP.

Part II—Windows Vista

Procedure

1. ____ Report to your assigned workstation.

2. ____ Boot the computer and verify it is in working order.

3. ____ Locate and then right-click the Recycle Bin. Select **Properties** from the shortcut menu. You should see the **Recycle Bin Properties** dialog box. Look over the available options.

4. ____ Note the default size of the Recycle Bin. Windows Vista no longer uses the 10% default size except for hard disk drives of less than 40 GB. Windows Vista uses approximately 4 GB for the first 40 GB and then approximately 5% for the remaining size of the drive. You should write down the size before making any adjustments to the size of the Recycle Bin. Enter a new size for the Recycle Bin. After making a change to the size of the Recycle Bin, return the Recycle Bin to its original size.

5. ____ Now, right-click the Recycle Bin and select the **Explore** option from the shortcut menu. You should see previously deleted files located in the Recycle Bin. If the Recycle Bin is empty, create a memo file using Notepad or WordPad as in previous laboratory activities. After saving the memo, delete it so that the Recycle Bin contains at least one file.

6. ____ To recover the memo file from the Recycle Bin, right-click the file and then select **Restore** from the shortcut menu. The item selected will be automatically restored. Restore the memo file now.

7. ____ Delete the memo file again to resend it to the Recycle Bin. Note the appearance of the **Recycle Bin** icon in Windows Vista. It should appear full of trash. In the next step, you will empty the Recycle Bin, thus changing the appearance of the icon.

8. ____ Now, you will permanently delete the memo file by emptying the Recycle Bin. To empty the Recycle Bin, right-click the **Recycle Bin** icon and then select the **Empty Recycle Bin** option from the shortcut menu. You can also empty the Recycle Bin from the Windows Explorer view. Empty the Recycle Bin now. Note the change in the **Recycle Bin** icon. It should appear empty.

9. ____ You can repeat the Part II of the lab until you feel comfortable using the Recycle Bin in Windows Vista.

10. ____ Complete the review questions. When you are finished answering the review questions, return the computer to its original configuration and shut down the computer.

Review Questions

1. How can you access the **Recycle Bin Properties** dialog box?_____

_____

_____

2. What happens when you delete a file or folder larger than the size of the Recycle Bin?_____

_____

3. How do you delete items in the Recycle Bin?_____

_____

4. What is the default size of the Windows XP Recycle Bin? _____

_____

5. What is the default size of the Windows Vista Recycle Bin? _____

_____

_____

6. When are files and folders permanently deleted? _____

_____

7. How does the appearance of the Windows Vista Recycle Bin change when the Recycle Bin is emptied?_____

_____

8. How can you permanently delete a file as you move it to the Recycle Bin? _____

_____

_____

                    Copyright by Goodheart-Willcox Co., Inc.

Laboratory
Activity
17

Search

After completing this laboratory activity, you will be able to:

- Access the Search feature of Windows XP and Windows Vista.
- Identify configuration options for conducting searches.
- Explain the relationship between the Search feature and hidden and system files.

Introduction

One of the most common problems encountered by computer users is lost files. Everyone loses track of a file saved by an application, copied from an e-mail attachment, downloaded from the Internet, or transferred from some type of media. The main problem is a user's lack of sufficient knowledge of how to navigate the directory tree structure and how items are stored in that structure. All too often a software application will choose to store a file in a location other than the Windows default locations. Many software applications create their own default file location. For example, editing a photo using a software application from a camera manufacturer will most likely create a default directory for that camera. All photos will transfer directly to the default directly created by the camera photo application software rather than the Windows default Pictures folder. A user would most likely open his or her default Windows Pictures directory and would not be able to find the photo they are looking for because it has been saved to a different location.

In this laboratory activity, you will briefly explore some of the features used to locate missing files. The Search feature is located directly off the **Start** menu in both Windows XP and Windows Vista. In Windows Vista, the **Search** box automatically appears when you select the **Start** menu with the mouse. You can also use the Windows logo key and [F] key combination to automatically open the search feature's dialog box, or you can simply press the [F3] key. The shortcut keys work for both Windows XP and Windows Vista.

The Search feature can be modified by file type, location, or type of file by file extension, such as .jpg, .doc, .xml, and .zip. Additional filters were added in Windows Vista for tags and author. A file can be located by size, date modified, or even by a phrase from the document you are looking for. Look at the following screen captures of the **Search Results** window in Windows XP.

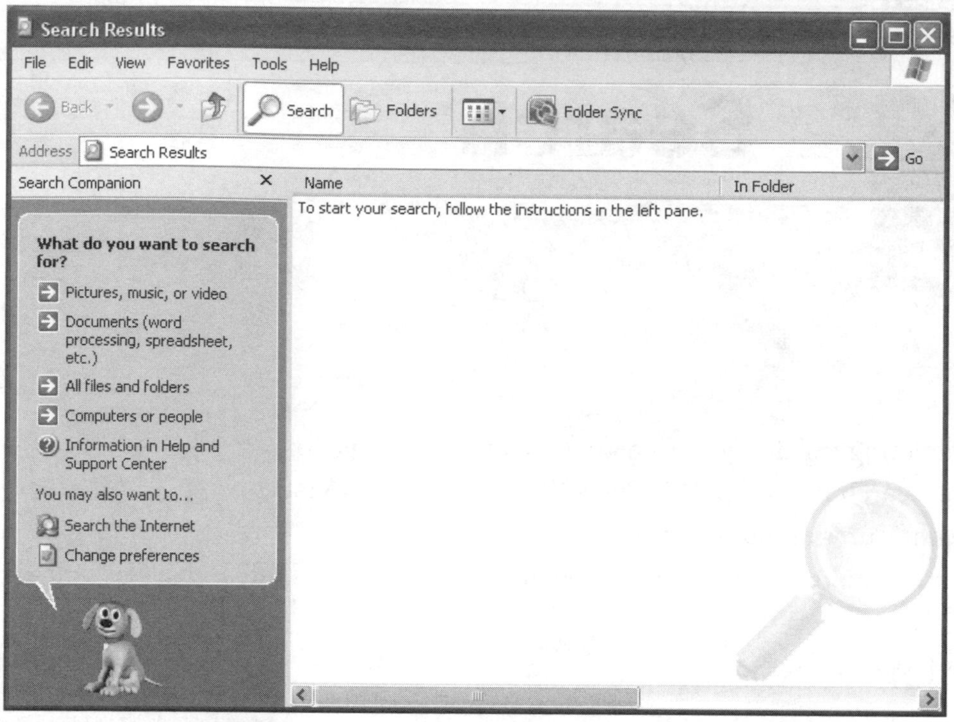

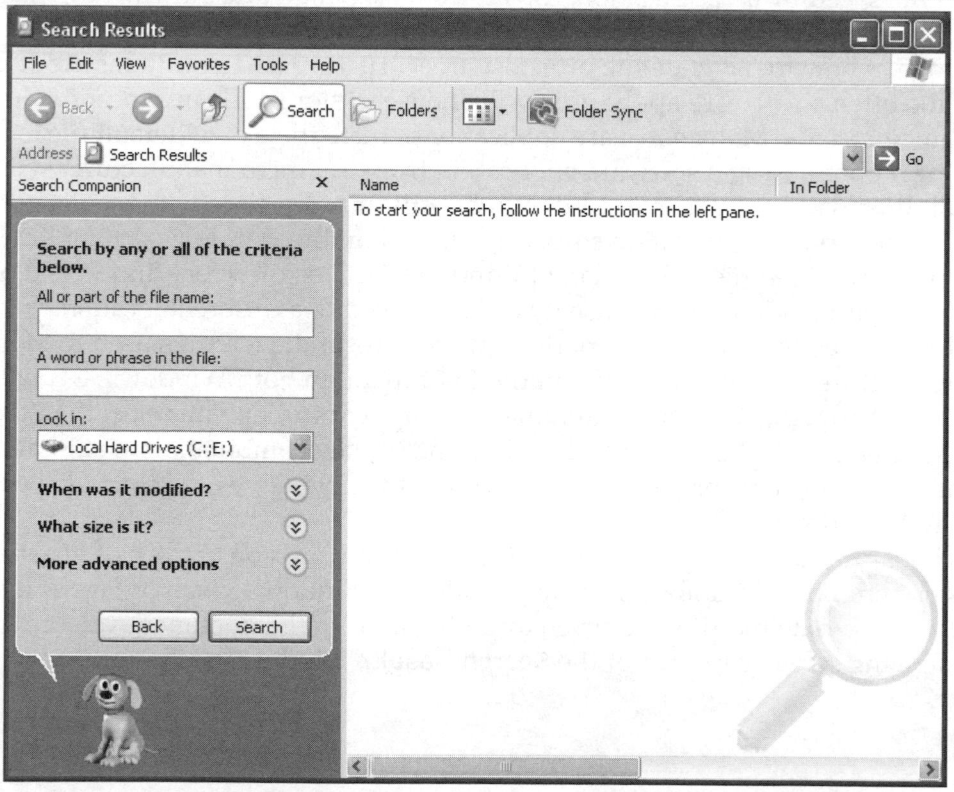

Looking at the screen captures you can see that Windows XP offers many different options to modify your search. You can restrict your search to a specific drive partition(s), directory, or folder; date; file size; and more.

The Windows Vista Search feature is much more robust when compared to Windows XP. There are more features available for modifying the search. As you can see in the following screen capture, its user interface has been changed a great deal.

    Copyright by Goodheart-Willcox Co., Inc.

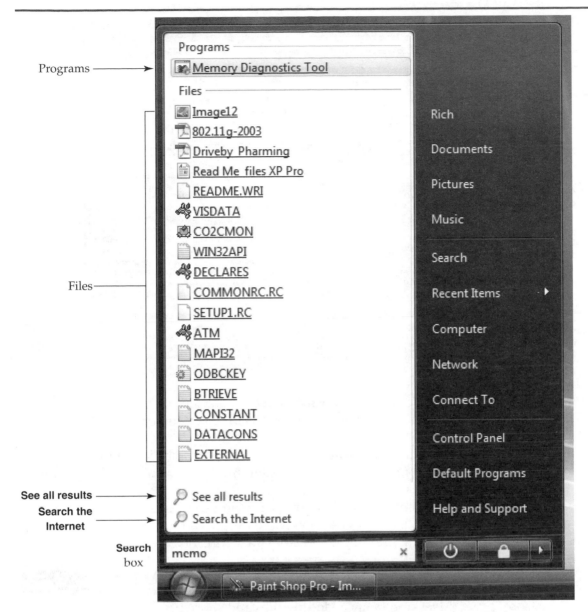

Windows Vista

Windows Vista will start displaying search results directly above the **Search** box while you are typing the name of the file to locate. Notice in the screen capture that not only are files located but programs too. Programs can be executed directly from the **Search** box in the same way programs are run in Windows XP from the **Run** dialog box. You can select the **See all results** option, which displays all the results of the search. A larger dialog box will appear similar to the one in the following screen capture.

The search result has been acquired with the **Advanced Search** option selected in the upper-right corner. The **Advanced Search** option provides more options to select, such as **Include non-indexed, hidden, and system files**.

Be aware that Windows XP and Windows Vista do not look for system or hidden files by default. You must modify the search to reveal hidden and system files, such as drivers or operating system files.

Some common folder names have changed in Windows Vista and some are new. The following table contains a short list of Windows Vista and Windows XP folders and their description. This information may help you when locating files in the directory structure.

Vista	XP	Description
Desktop	Desktop	Desktop items including files and shortcuts.
Documents	My Documents	Default location for all user-created documents.
Pictures	My Pictures	Default location of pictures.
Videos	My Videos	Default location of videos.
Music	My Music	Default location of music.
Downloads	Not Applicable	New folder in Windows Vista where user downloads are temporarily stored.
AppData	NA	Default location for users' application data and binaries.
Links	NA	New folder in Windows Vista that contains Windows Explorer Favorite Links.
Saved Games	NA	New folder in Windows Vista, which is the default location for saved games.
Searches	NA	New folder in Windows Vista, which is the default location for saved searches.

Copyright by Goodheart-Willcox Co., Inc.

Prior to Windows Vista, the Windows operating system saved user profiles in the root folder called Documents and Settings. Windows Vista now uses the Users folder in place of Documents and Settings. The Windows Vista application data folder called AppData can be used for the local profile, low profile, and roaming profile of the user. This is why you will see multiple results for what you might think should be a single existence of a file. For example, the search for the autoexec file will produce multiple results in Windows Vista.

Be aware that when conducting a search using Windows Vista, there will be times when you will need to change the Windows Explorer file properties to allow you to view critical system files. You must do this even when using the Windows Vista advanced search feature.

Equipment and Materials

■ Computer with Windows XP or Windows Vista, or both, installed.

Part I—Windows XP

Procedure

1. ____ Report to your assigned workstation.

2. ____ Boot the computer and verify it is in working order.

3. ____ Access **Start | Search** to open the **Search Results** window.

4. ____ Close the **Search Results** window and reopen it using the Windows logo key and [F] key combination.

5. ____ Open Notepad or WordPad and make a file called Memo1ForSearch. Save it to the My Documents folder.

6. ____ Locate with the Search feature the Memo1ForSearch file you created in the previous step. When the search is complete, record the complete path to the Memo1ForSearch file as indicated below.

Example File   **Example Path**

MemoForSearch1.doc   C:\Users\Rich\My Documents\Memo1ForSearch.doc

MemoForSearch1 path = _____

Save the Memo1ForSearch file on the USB Flash drive. You will need it for the Part II—Windows Vista.

7. ____ Conduct the search again using some of the other search features such as file type and date.

8. ____ Now, conduct a search looking for the batch file called AUTOEXEC.NT. Use uppercase letters. Record the path in the space provided.

AUTOEXEC.NT path = _____

9. ____ Look for the sample picture file called Winter and then record the path. If the result view is an icon you can select the detail view from the **Views** menu in the **Search Results** window toolbar.

Winter path = _____

10. ____ You can use the wildcard symbol asterisk (*) when you conduct a search. For example, you can locate all Dynamic Link Library (DLL) files by using ***.dll** (without the quotation marks) in your search. There should be many files listed in the search results.

11. ____ Now, locate all executable files on the computer. Again, use the wildcard asterisk with the .exe extension. The results should be numerous.

12. ____ Use the Help and Support program located off the **Start** menu to conduct a search for the term *search*. Locate the article titled "Searching for files and folders" and review the contents.

13. This concludes Part I of the laboratory activity. Do not answer the review questions until you complete Part II—Windows Vista. You can take a few minutes to review Part I before moving on to Part II.

Part II—Windows Vista

Procedure

1. ____ Report to your assigned workstation.

2. ____ Boot the computer and verify it is in working order.

3. ____ Access the Search feature located directly off the **Start** menu.

4. ____ Close the Search feature and reopen it using the key combination Windows logo and [F] key.

5. ____ Open Notepad or WordPad and make a file called Memo1ForSearch. Save it to Documents folder and then locate it with the Search feature. You may use the file you made for the Windows XP portion of the laboratory activity.

6. ____ Slowly type the word *memo* into the **Search** box. Watch closely as the results appear and change as you type each letter.

7. ____ Now, complete the name of the file Memo1ForSearch and watch the results. Record the path to the file.

MemoForSearch1 path = _____

8. ____ Conduct a search for the AUTOEXEC file without using the **Advanced Search** option. You should not find the file. Repeat the search for AUTOEXEC again using the **Advanced Search** option. You will also need to select the **Include non-indexed, hidden, and system files** option in the **Advanced Search** dialog box to be successful.

9. ____ Conduct a search looking for the picture file called Forest. Record the path to the file.

Forest path = _____

10. ____ Conduct a search for the file called chimes.wav and then record what type of file it is. You will need to use the **Advanced Search** option and again select the **Include non-indexed, hidden, and system files** option. The type of file will be indicated under the column labeled **type**.

_____

11. ____ Now let's see how many DLL files are located on the Windows Vista computer. Conduct a search using the wildcard symbol asterisk for the file name and the extension .dll. (Example: *.dll). Record the approximate number of files found.

_____

Copyright by Goodheart-Willcox Co., Inc.

Name_____

12. ____ The **Search** box can also be used to start a program. Type the word *calculator* into the **Search** box. The calculator application should appear.

13. ____ Use the Windows Help and Support to conduct a search for the topic "find files." Review the results titled "Tips for finding files," and "Find files and folders on other computers on a network." Some of the information in these two articles will be needed to answer the review questions.

14. ____ Take a few minutes to explore the various Search feature options available in Windows Vista. Look at the ways a search area can be selected, such as drive letters, network locations, and Public folder. You can also search through e-mail for the Microsoft Office Outlook e-mail service.

15. ____ Complete the review questions. When you are finished answering the review questions, return the computer to its original configuration and shut down the computer.

Review Questions

1. What keyboard combination will automatically open the advanced search features in Windows XP and Windows Vista? _____

2. True *or* False? You can locate a file by its creation date. _____

3. What does entering ***.doc** in the **Search** dialog box produce? _____

_____

_____

4. Can the Windows Vista Search feature locate a file on a network? _____

5. By default, will the Search feature produce a result for a hidden or system file?_____

6. How can you locate a system or hidden file using the Search feature? _____

_____

_____

_____

7. What does the term *mapped drive* mean? (You should have read about it when you conducted the search on Windows Vista in step 13.) _____

_____

8. How is a mapped drive identified? _____

_____

Notes

Computer Service and Repair Lab Manual

Copyright by Goodheart-Willcox Co., Inc.

Name _____ Date _____

Class/Instructor _____

Stopping a System Lockup

After completing this laboratory activity, you will be able to:

■ Access the Task Manager several different ways.

■ Identify and end the program that is causing a system lockup or freeze.

■ Unload a problem program from RAM.

Introduction

When a PC appears to lock up, or freeze, many times the program causing the system lockup can be shut down without interrupting other programs that are running. The standard method to attempt a recovery is to press the [Ctrl] [Alt] [Delete] keys simultaneously. When the key combination is pressed, a special dialog box is displayed. This dialog box contains such options as **End Task**, **Switch To**, and **New Task**. A list of programs currently running is also displayed. This list can help you to identify the program that is causing a system lockup or any such program-generated problem. To demonstrate a system lockup, a program called EndlessLoop.exe will be available from your instructor. Obtain the program from the instructor and run it from the floppy drive. You may copy the file to your MyDocuments or Documents folder with the instructor's permission. You must obtain his or her permission first. You may run the program from a USB Flash drive as well without the need to run it from the MyDocuments or Documents folder. To run the program, double-click the file named EndlessLoop.exe in Windows Explorer.

Note:

In some network configuration, using the key combination [Ctrl] [Alt] [Delete] activates the system logon screen as well.

To become familiar with the way the **Task Manager** dialog box works, press the key combination [Ctrl] [Alt] [Delete] one time only. In Windows XP, it will automatically start the Task Manager. In Windows Vista, it will present a window with the following options: **Lock this computer**; **Switch user**; **Log off**; **Change a password**, **Start Task Manager**. You then select the **Start Task Manager** option.

After the **Task Manager** dialog box opens, you can open several programs, such as WordPad, Paint, Calculator, and Notepad. As you start each program, observe the effect on the **Task Manager** dialog box. Pay particular attention to the order the programs appear in the list. Their positions in the list are directly related to the order in which the programs are executed.

Copyright by Goodheart-Willcox Co., Inc.

The following is a screen capture of both the Windows Vista and Windows XP **Task Manager** dialog boxes.

Windows XP   Windows Vista

As you can see, the **Task Manager** dialog box in both operating systems are very similar. The only distinct difference is the new **Services** tab provided in Windows Vista. It presents a view of all services running on the computer. In both Windows Vista and Windows XP, you can see the programs that are currently running on the computer. To stop a program that you suspect is causing a problem, you simply select the suspect program from the list and then click the **End Task** button. The program will end automatically. The program is so similar that you need only use Windows XP or Windows Vista for this laboratory activity unless your instructor wishes you to perform the lab on both operating systems.

There are several other ways to access the Task Manager that you should be aware of to be better prepared for the CompTIA A+ Certification exams. While the key combination [Ctrl] [Alt] [Delete] is the most commonly known key combination to use for opening the **Task Manager** dialog box, pressing [Ctrl] [Shift] [Esc] will work also. In fact, pressing [Ctrl] [Shift] [Esc] will produce **Task Manager** dialog box directly in Windows Vista. You can also access the Task Manager by right-clicking the taskbar and selecting **Task Manager** from the shortcut menu in either Windows Vista or Windows XP. Another way to access Task Manager is to use the **Run** dialog box in Windows XP. Simply type and enter **taskmgr**. In Windows Vista enter **taskmgr** into the **Search** dialog box.

Equipment and Materials

- Computer with Windows XP or Windows Vista, or both, installed.
- Copy of the EndlessLoop.exe program.

Copyright by Goodheart-Willcox Co., Inc.

Procedure

1. ____ Report to your assigned workstation.

2. ____ Boot the computer and verify it is in working order.

3. ____ Press the [Ctrl] [Alt] [Delete] keys simultaneously one time only. This allows you to see all the programs that are currently running. In Windows Vista you will need to select **Start Task Manager** from the list of options displayed on the screen. Keep the **Task Manager** dialog box open while you perform the following steps in the laboratory activity.

4. ____ In the space provided, list the names of the program applications in the order that they appear in **Task Manager** dialog box starting from top to bottom. The top is the first to open and the bottom is the most recent to open.

_____

_____

_____

_____

_____

_____

_____

5. ____ Open the WordPad, Notepad, Calculator, and Paint programs one-by-one while observing the **Task Manager** dialog box. Observe the order of the list of active programs. Repeat this portion of the lab activity, opening the applications in different orders, until you can correlate the opening of a program to its effect on the list of programs.

6. ____ Close all of the programs including Task Manager.

7. ____ Copy the EndlessLoop.exe program file into the My Documents or Documents folder or run it from a USB Flash drive. To run the program, double-click the filename in Windows Explorer.

8. ____ Before you press the **Start Endless Loop** button, try to minimize the window by clicking the **Minimize** button at the top right of the screen. It should reduce the program to a taskbar program icon.

9. ____ Return the program window to full-size by clicking the taskbar icon.

10. ____ Now, press the **Start Endless Loop** button and try to minimize the program window again. This time the program should not respond. The program window should remain full-sized.

11. ____ Press [Ctrl] [Alt] [Delete] to display the **Task Manager** dialog box. Inside the **Task Manager** dialog box, you will see the list of the programs currently running. Verify that the program called EndlessLoop is listed. Close the EndlessLoop program by selecting it and then clicking the **End Task** button located at the bottom of **Task Manager** dialog box.

12. ____ Start the EndlessLoop program again and then press the **Start Endless Loop** button.

13. ____ Press the [Ctrl] [Alt] [Delete] key combination to display the **Task Manager** dialog box. Select the **Process** tab at the top of **Task Manager** dialog box. You will see a list of processes that are running on the computer. Scroll down if necessary until you locate the EndlessLoop program. Look under the **CPU** column and you will see how much of the CPU performance is used by the EndlessLoop program. You can now end the EndlessLoop program by selecting it with the mouse and then clicking the **End Process** button at the bottom of **Task Manager** dialog box. The program should end.

Copyright by Goodheart-Willcox Co., Inc.

14. ____ Now, practice the other options for starting Task Manager. Use [Ctrl] [Shift] [Esc], right-click the taskbar; and enter **taskmgr** into the **Run** dialog box or **Search** dialog box depending on which operating system you are using.

15. ____ If you are using Windows Vista to perform this lab, select the **Services** tab in the **Task Manager** dialog box and look at the various services that are currently running on the computer. You can stop a service by right-clicking the selected service and then clicking **Stop** from the shortcut menu. There is also a button labeled **Services** that will open the services view in the Microsoft Manager Console (MMC) if you have equal to administrative privileges. In the MMC you can view detailed information about services that are running on the computer. There will be much more about MMC in later laboratory activities. Close the MMC at this time.

16. ____ You may now take a few minutes to experiment with the Task Manager and the EndlessLoop program. After you are confident that you know how to stop an application using Task Manager you can shut down the system and return the EndlessLoop program disk to your instructor.

Review Questions

1. True *or* False? The last program activated will appear at the top of the list. _____

2. True *or* False? There are three options to choose from in the **Task Manager** dialog box: **End Task**, **Switch To**, and **New Task**._____

3. What options will appear in Windows Vista when [Ctrl] [Alt] [Delete] is pressed? _____

   _____

   _____

4. What other methods can be used to access the Task Manager program besides the [Ctrl] [Alt] [Delete] key combination? _____

   _____

   _____

5. What new Task Manager tab is provided in Windows Vista? _____

Copyright by Goodheart-Willcox Co., Inc.

Name _____ Date _____

Class/Instructor _____

File Properties

After completing this laboratory activity, you will be able to:

- View a file's properties.
- Change the default program associated with a file.
- Configure the compatibility mode of an executable file.
- Explain the Shadow Copy feature in Windows Vista.
- Identify which versions of Windows Vista provide the Shadow Copy feature.

Introduction

In this laboratory activity, you will explore, at an introductory level, the general properties associated with a file. The **Properties** dialog box will be revisited in later laboratory activities, such as those related to security and network sharing. For now, you will simply look at some of the most common features. Look at the following screen captures comparing the file properties of a typical file in Windows XP and Windows Vista.

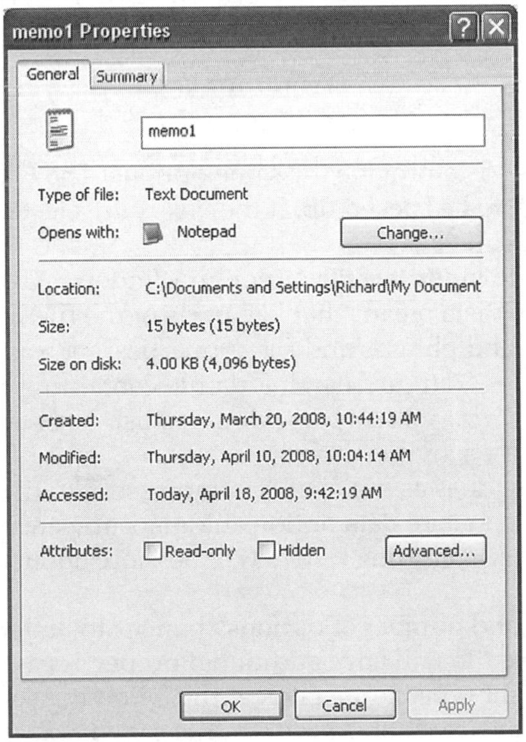

Windows XP

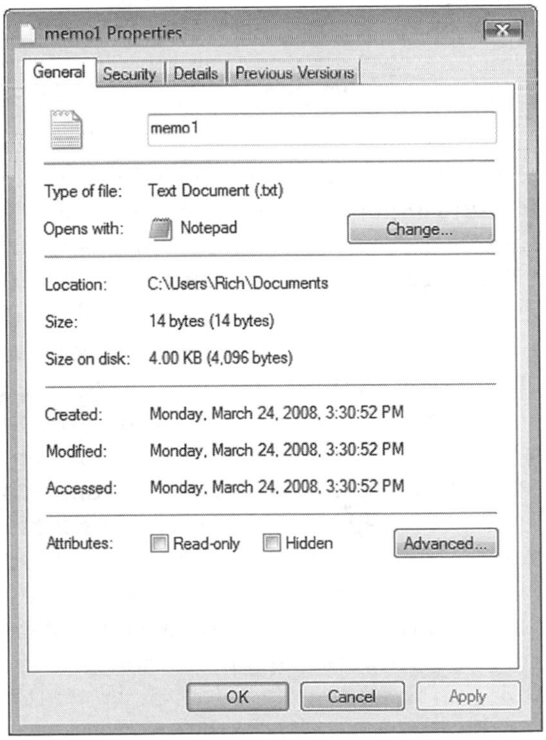

memo1 Properties

General | Summary

memo1

Type of file: Text Document

Opens with: Notepad   Change...

Location: C:\Documents and Settings\Richard\My Document

Size: 15 bytes (15 bytes)

Size on disk: 4.00 KB (4,096 bytes)

Created: Thursday, March 20, 2008, 10:44:19 AM

Modified: Thursday, April 10, 2008, 10:04:14 AM

Accessed: Today, April 18, 2008, 9:42:19 AM

Attributes: ☐ Read-only ☐ Hidden   Advanced...

OK | Cancel | Apply

Windows Vista

memo1 Properties

General | Security | Details | Previous Versions

memo1

Type of file: Text Document (.txt)

Opens with: Notepad   Change...

Location: C:\Users\Rich\Documents

Size: 14 bytes (14 bytes)

Size on disk: 4.00 KB (4,096 bytes)

Created: Monday, March 24, 2008, 3:30:52 PM

Modified: Monday, March 24, 2008, 3:30:52 PM

Accessed: Monday, March 24, 2008, 3:30:52 PM

Attributes: ☐ Read-only ☐ Hidden   Advanced...

OK | Cancel | Apply

Copyright by Goodheart-Willcox Co., Inc.

Notice that the two dialog boxes are very similar and contain the same type of information. The type of file is identified as a "Text Document," and the software application which opens the file by default is indicated. You can see that the default program is Notepad. A button has been provided which allows you to change the default program associated with this file.

The location or path of the file is displayed as well as the size of the file and the amount of space it takes up on disk. As you can see, the file is approximately 14 to 15 bytes but actually uses 4,096 bytes of disk space. This is because the storage space on a hard disk drive is incremental. The size required to store the file is based on the size of the allocation unit established when the disk is first installed. In this example, the file allocation unit is 4,096 bytes, and the entire allocation unit is used to store the small file.

Important dates directly related to the file are also displayed, such as when the file was created, last accessed, and last modified. This is the same information that can be used in a search.

You can change the attribute of the file to either read-only and or hidden. The **Advanced** button provides options to change some other more advanced file attributes, such as file encryption and compression. Look at the following screen capture of the **Advanced Attributes** dialog box for the properties of the memo1 file.

Windows XP   **Windows Vista**

As you can see, both Windows XP and Windows Vista provide the same options. The **File is ready for archiving** option means that the file is ready to be backed up. If the box is unselected, the file will not be copied as part of a regular system backup.

The **For faster searching, allow Indexing Service to index this file** option in Windows XP and the **Index this file for faster searching** option in Windows Vista means that key parts of the file will be stored to assist a fast search. For example, key words and phrases and file properties, such as dates, will be stored in an index that is used to search for files. You can search for a file containing the word *format* and all documents containing the word *format* will be presented in a list. You saw how indexing worked when you did the "Search" laboratory activity.

The **Compress contents to save disk space** option does as indicted. It compresses the file contents to use less storage space. The **Encrypt contents to secure data** option automatically encrypts the contents of a file making it secure from unauthorized viewing. There will be more about compressed and encrypted files in later lab activities.

The appearance of the file **Properties** dialog box and number of options changes to better match the file type. For example, an application or executable file will have additional properties associated with it that would not be necessary for a document type of file. Look at the following screen capture of the **Properties** dialog box associated with the executable program file called *EndlessLoop* and notice the additional tabs, **Version** and **Compatibility**.

Copyright by Goodheart-Willcox Co., Inc.

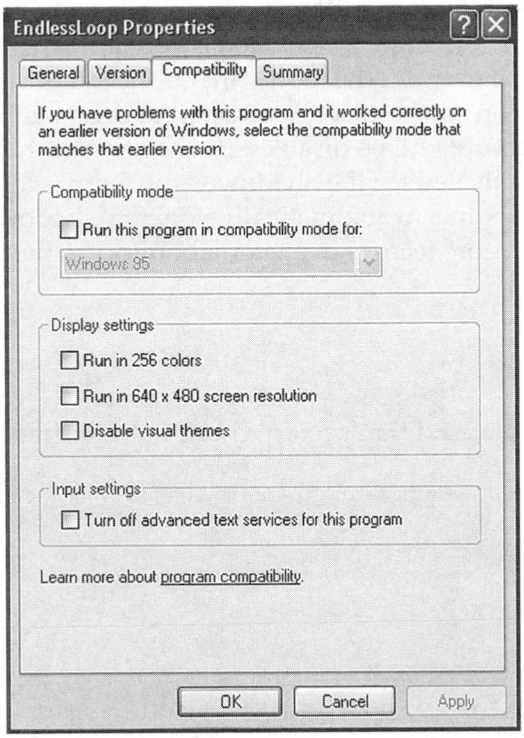

Name_____

Windows XP

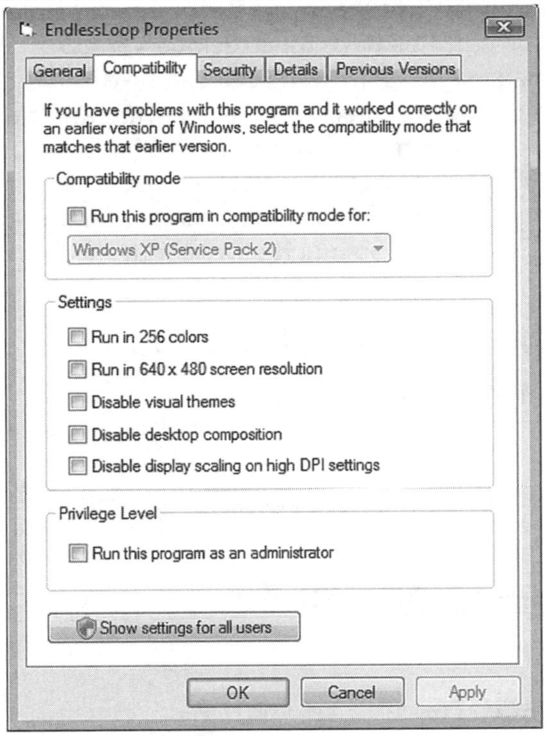

Windows Vista

The options listed under the **Compatibility** tab allow you to select a compatibility mode in which to run the executable program, such as in Windows 95 mode or Windows 2000 mode. You can also see that the display settings can be changed to limit the number of colors or the screen resolution. Pay particular attention to the **Run this program as an administrator** option located in the **Privilege Level** section in Windows Vista. This is a new feature in Windows Vista that allows you full control over the executable file, which you would not normally have as a typical user.

A new feature in Windows Vista is Shadow Copy which is accessed under the **Previous Versions** tab. The **Previous Versions** tab allows the user to select a previous version of a file that was automatically saved at an earlier time. Look at the following screen capture to view the previous versions of a file called folder1 generated by the Shadow Copy feature.

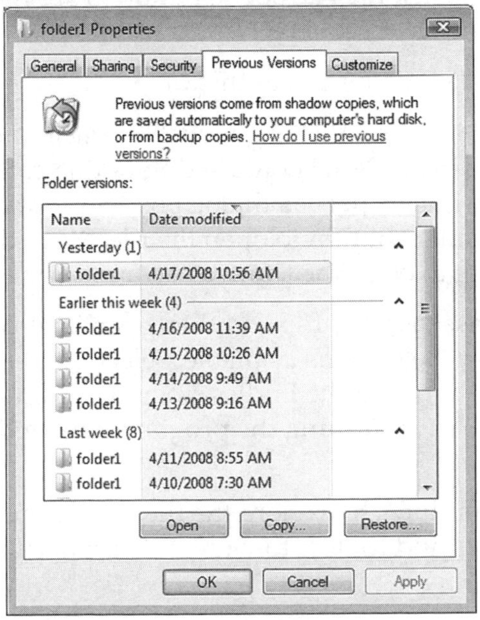

Copyright by Goodheart-Willcox Co., Inc.

Windows Vista Business, Ultimate, and Enterprise editions use the Shadow Copy feature; thus, only these editions have the **Previous Versions** tab. Shadow Copy is activated by default when the operating system is installed but can be disabled by the user or other software applications, such as some third-party system restore software and protection suites. Also, be aware that even without a third-party software application, the Shadow Copy feature will be disabled if you turn off the System Restore feature. The System Restore feature must be activated for the Shadow Copy feature to work. The computer must be able to generate system restore points to automatically generate shadow copies of a file. There will be much more about the System Restore feature in a later laboratory activity.

Equipment and Materials

- Computer with Windows XP.
- Computer with Windows Vista (Business or Ultimate Edition preferred but not required).
- Memo1 file
- Copy of the EndlessLoop.exe program.

Part I—Windows XP

Procedure

1. _____ Report to your assigned workstation.

2. _____ Boot the computer and verify it is in working order.

3. _____ Locate the memo1 file using Windows Explorer and then right-click the file to bring up a shortcut menu. Click the **Properties** option.

4. _____ Look at the properties displayed under the **General** tab for the memo1 file.

5. _____ Click the **Change** button located beside **Opens with** which identifies the default program that opens the file. See what other program(s) will open the document, but do not select any at this time. Take special notice of the **Browse** button which will automatically open Windows Explorer and allow you to select another software application to open the file. Click the **Cancel** button to return to the **General** tab view.

6. _____ From the **General** tab, click the **Advanced** button to see the **Advanced Attributes** dialog box. Study it for a minute and then cancel it.

7. _____ Close the file **Properties** dialog box at this time.

8. _____ Open Windows Explorer, and then right-click the memo1 file to look at some of the various shortcut menu items available. You should see an option called **Open With** that performs the same function as that in the file **Properties** dialog box. This option allows you to choose another program in place of the default program to open the file. Move the mouse curser to a blank area on the display and click once to close the shortcut menu.

9. _____ Now, locate the EndlessLoop.exe file and then open its **Properties** dialog box. Select the **Compatibility** tab and look at the options available. Select the **Run in 640 × 480 screen resolution** and then click the **Apply** button. Run the EndlessLoop program and see the effect the selected option has on the program. After running the program, return the **Compatibility** tab to its original configuration.

10. _____ You may take a few minutes to explore the file **Properties** dialog box at this time. Try selecting some other files and folders to view their properties before going on to Part II—Windows Vista.

Copyright by Goodheart-Willcox Co., Inc.

Part II—Windows Vista

Procedure

1. ____ Report to your assigned workstation.

2. ____ Boot the computer and verify it is in working order.

3. ____ Locate the memo1 file using Windows Explorer and then right-click the file to bring up a shortcut menu. Click the **Properties** option.

4. ____ Under the **General** tab, look at the properties displayed for the memo1 file. They should look very similar to the Windows XP version.

5. ____ Click the **Change** button located beside **Opens with** which identifies the default program that opens the file. See what other program(s) will open the document, but do not select any at this time. Take special notice of the **Browse** button which automatically opens Windows Explorer and allows you to select another software application with which to open the file. Click the **Cancel** button to return to the **General** tab view.

6. ____ Click the **Advanced** button to see the **Advanced Attributes** dialog box. Study it for a minute and then click **Cancel** to return to the **General** tab.

7. ____ Close the file **Properties** dialog box at this time.

8. ____ Open Windows Explorer and then right-click the memo1 file to look at some of the various shortcut menu items available. You should see an option called **Open With** that performs the same function as that in the file **Properties** dialog box. This option allows you to choose another program in place of the default program with which to open the file. Move the mouse curser to a blank area on the display and click once to close the shortcut menu.

9. ____ Open the **Properties** dialog box for memo1 and then select the **Previous Versions** tab. See if there are any previous versions of memo1 available and then close the dialog box.

10. ____ Right-click the Documents folder in the Windows Explorer directory tree and then select **Properties** from the shortcut menu. Then, select the **Previous Versions** tab if available. You should see many different versions available.

11. ____ Close the file **Properties** dialog box at this time.

12. ____ Now, locate the EndlessLoop.exe file and then open its **Properties** dialog box. Select the **Compatibility** tab and look at the options available. Select the **Run in 640 × 480 screen resolution** and then click the **Apply** button. Run the EndlessLoop program and see the effect the selected option has on the program. After running the program, return the **Compatibility** tab to its original configuration.

13. ____ Right-click the EndlessLoop.exe file again. This time, look at the shortcut menu **Run as administrator** option. This option appears for executable files if you have privileges equal to the system administrator. Close the shortcut menu by moving the mouse curser to a blank area on the display and clicking once.

14. ____ You may take a few minutes to explore the Windows Vista file **Properties** dialog box at this time. Try selecting some other files and folders to view their properties before going on to complete the review questions.

Review Questions

1. How do you access a file's **Properties** dialog box in Windows Explorer? _____
   _____

2. Which two file attributes are shown in the **Properties** dialog box under the **General** tab? _____
   _____

3. What file attributes are available in the **Advanced Attributes** dialog box? _____
   _____

4. What file date information is displayed under the **General** tab of a file's **Properties** dialog box?
   _____

5. Why would a small file that is actually only 100 bytes use approximately 4 kB of disk space
   when stored? _____
   _____

6. A customer calls the help desk and complains that the college term paper they were writing
   only opens in Notepad. The file was originally written in Microsoft Word. Tell the customer
   how to correct this problem. _____
   _____
   _____
   _____

7. What two attributes are selected by default in the Windows Vista **Advanced Attributes** dialog
   box?_____
   _____

8. A Windows Vista Business user calls the help desk and says he lost a great deal of the contents
   of his term paper. Somehow, some of the file contents were accidentally deleted. He basically
   lost three months of work. He asks if there is any way he can restore his work. What would you
   tell him? _____
   _____
   _____
   _____
   _____

Copyright by Goodheart-Willcox Co., Inc.

Laboratory Activity
20

Name _____ Date _____

Class/Instructor _____

Create, Copy, Delete, and Move a File or Folder

After completing this laboratory activity, you will be able to:

■ Create a file or folder.

■ Delete a file or folder.

■ Move a file or folder.

■ Copy a file or folder.

Introduction

In this laboratory activity, you will perform some basic folder operations. You will also view the contents of Help and Support presenting basic file and folder concepts. In the Windows XP Windows Explorer, you can create a folder by accessing the **File | New** menu and clicking the **Folder** command. Look at the following capture to see the **File | New** menu and the **Folder** command.

My Documents

| File | Edit | View | Favorites | Tools | Help |

Groove Folder Synchronization ▶   Search   Folders   ▦ ▾   Folder Sync

New ▶

    ☐ Folder

    Shortcut

Create Shortcut

Delete   Microsoft Office Access 2007 Database

Rename   Briefcase

Properties   Microsoft Office Word Document

    Multisim Project File

Close   Multisim Design File

Share this folder   Microsoft Office PowerPoint Presentation

Copyright by Goodheart-Willcox Co., Inc.

If a folder is first selected and then you open the **File** menu, the **Delete** command will become available, allowing you to delete the folder selected. The **Cut**, **Copy**, **Copy To Folder**, and **Move To Folder** commands are available from the **Edit** menu as shown in the following screen capture.

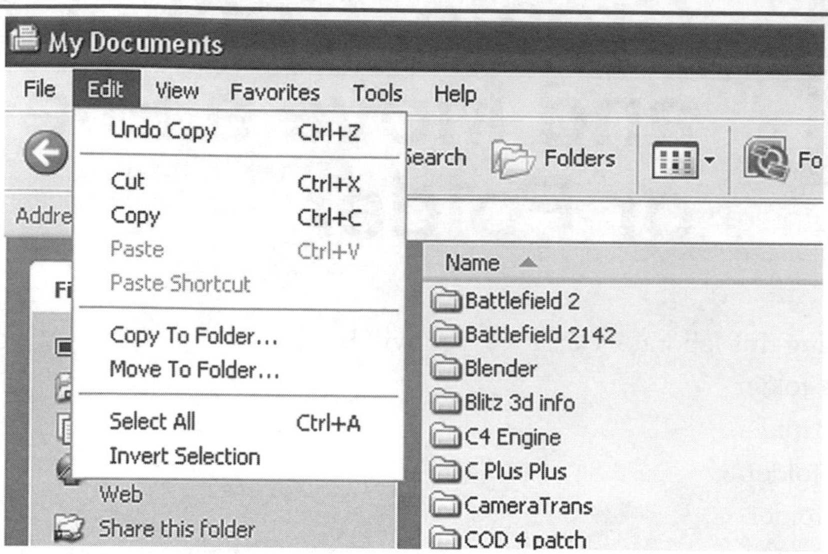

These same options are available in Windows Vista but are presented differently since Windows Vista reorganized the menu items. Look at the following screen capture to see that **New Folder**, **Copy**, and **Delete** commands are located in the **Organize** menu of the Windows Vista Windows Explorer. There is no **File** or **Edit** menu items in Windows Vista.

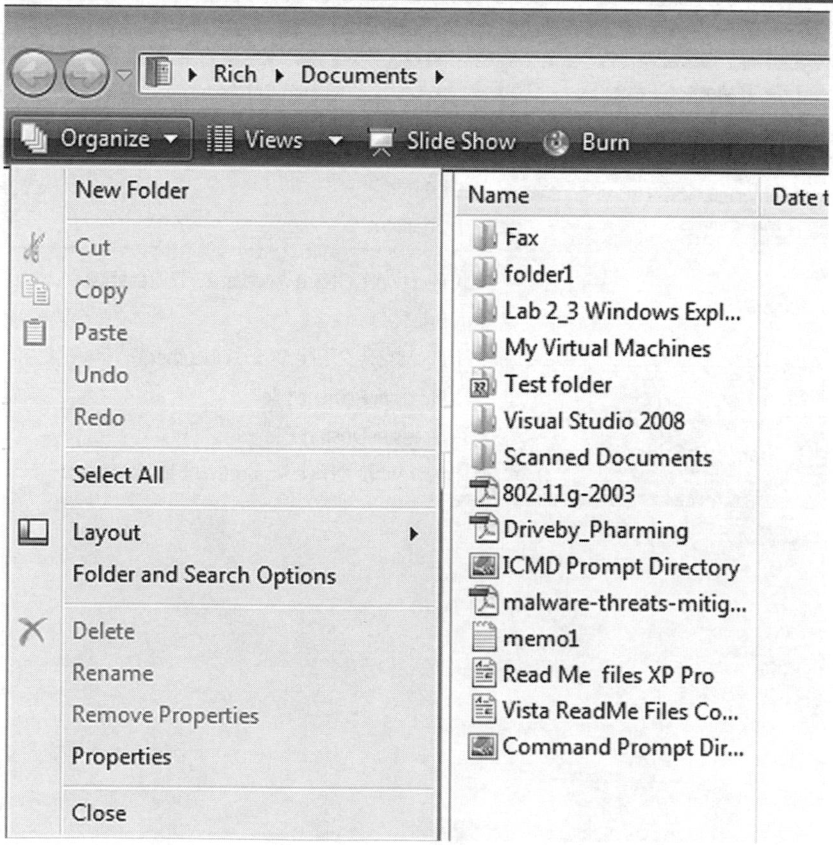

Copyright by Goodheart-Willcox Co., Inc.

Note:

Microsoft has a history of making changes to many of the common tasks and functions of the operating system. While Microsoft believes the changes will make the common tasks better organized, it has proven to be very frustrating to technicians as well as users when they first use the newer systems. As a technician, it is imperative that you learn to be proficient in both operating systems. This is especially true for those of you who will work in a help desk or online support scenario.

You can also access the most commonly used feature of file and folder manipulation by simply right-clicking the file or folder or the blank space contained inside Windows Explorer right pane. This feature is available in both Windows XP and Windows Vista.

Be aware that you can use a very descriptive name for a file to make the contents easy to identify. For example, you could name a file My summer vacation in Western Pennsylvania the summer of 2008. The only limit to the descriptive name is that you can only use a maximum of 255 characters in the name.

Equipment and Materials

- Computer with Windows XP or Windows Vista, or both, installed.
- USB Flash drive with memo1 file. (If you do not have a copy of memo1, make an original before starting the laboratory activity and save it to the USB Flash drive.

Part I—Windows XP

Procedure

1. ____ Report to your assigned workstation.

2. ____ Boot the computer and verify it is in working order.

3. ____ Open Windows Explorer to view the contents of the USB Flash drive.

4. ____ Access the **File I New** menu and then click the **New Folder** command. A new folder will be created with the default name New Folder. You can type a new name for the folder while it is first created.

5. ____ Open Windows XP Help and Support. Type the word *file* into the **Search** text box. You should see several results in the left pane under **Pick a task**. Select each of the following five tasks.

   ____ Copy a file or folder.

   ____ Move a file or folder.

   ____ Create a file or folder.

   ____ Delete a file or folder.

   ____ Save a file.

In the space provided, write a short summary of how to perform each of the five tasks.

_____

_____

_____

_____

_____

_____

_____

_____

_____

_____

_____

_____

_____

_____

_____

6. ____ Create a folder called New Folder 1 on the USB Flash drive. Simply right-click in an open area of the USB drive directory and select **New | Folder** from the shortcut menu.

7. ____ Copy Memo1 to the USB Flash drive. Simply right-click the memo1 file and select **Copy** from the shortcut menu. Right-click the New Folder 1 folder and select **Paste** from the shortcut menu.

8. ____ View the contents of the memo1 file to verify it is the same as the original file.

9. ____ Open the copy of the memo1 file located in the New Folder 1 folder and change the contents. Simply add a word or two using WordPad or Notepad.

10. ____ Compare the contents of the original memo1 file and the copy of the memo1 file. The files should be different.

11. ____ Now, delete the copy of memo1 from the New Folder 1 directory. Simply right-click the file and select **Delete** from the shortcut menu.

12. ____ Move the memo1 file to the New Folder 1 directory by selecting memo1 and dragging it to New Folder 1. Verify the memo1 file is contained in the New Folder 1 folder.

13. ____ Move the memo1 file back to the root of the USB Flash drive by dragging the memo1 to the USB Flash drive in the left pane of Windows Explorer. To drag a file, click the file with the left mouse button and hold down the left mouse button as you drag the file to the new location. The New Folder 1 directory should be empty now and memo1 should appear in the root directory of the USB Flash drive.

14. ____ Double-click the memo1 file. It should open in the default text editor it was last viewed in, either Notepad or WordPad. Use the **Save As** command in the editor to save the file with a new name. The new name for memo1 will be New Name Memo1. Close the text editor.

Copyright by Goodheart-Willcox Co., Inc.

15. ____ View the contents of New Name Memo1 file to verify it contains the same text as the original memo1. Simply double-click the New Name Memo1 file. It should reopen automatically in the text editor. After verifying the text contents, close the text editor.

16. ____ Now, rename the New Name Memo1 file to Same Old Memo1. Simply right-click the New Name Memo1 file and select **Rename** from the shortcut menu. Then, rename the file to Same Old Memo1.

17. ____ Create three levels of folders on the USB Flash drive. Simply create a folder called Level1. Then, select Level1 and create a folder called Level2 inside the Level1 folder. Select the Level2 folder and create a Level3 folder. Copy (do *not* move) memo1 to folder Level3. When you have finished creating the three folders and have made a copy of memo1 in the Level2 folder, call your instructor to inspect your work.

18. ____ Delete the folders Level1, Level2, and Level3 after your instructor has inspected your work. Also, remove all copies of memo1 except for the original memo1 file.

19. ____ Proceed to Part II—Windows Vista.

Part II—Windows Vista

Procedure

1. ____ Report to your assigned workstation.

2. ____ Boot the computer and verify it is in working order.

3. ____ Open Windows Explorer to view the contents of the USB Flash drive.

4. ____ Click **Organize** and then click the **New Folder** command. Create a new folder called New Folder 1.

5. ____ Open Windows Vista Help and Support. Type the word *file* in the **Search** text box. The results should appear with the topic "Working with files and folders" at the top of the list. Select this topic and review its contents. The topic contains all the basic information required for this laboratory activity. Review all the material before proceeding.

6. ____ Create a copy of the memo1 file and place it in New Folder 1. Verify that the content of both the original and the copy is exactly the same.

7. ____ Change the contents of memo1 contained inside the New Folder 1 folder by adding a word or two. Compare the contents of the original memo1 to the copy of memo1. They should be different.

8. ____ Delete the copy of memo1 contained in New Folder 1.

9. ____ Move memo1 to New Folder 1 by dragging the file with the mouse. Simply click memo1 and drag it, with the left mouse held down, to New folder 1.

10. ____ Verify that memo1 is now contained in New Folder 1.

11. ____ Move memo1 back to the root of the USB Flash drive. The New Folder 1 folder should be empty and the memo1 file should appear in the USB Flash drive directory at an equal level to New Folder 1.

13. ____ Double-click memo1 to open it in the default text editor.

14. ____ Select the **Save As** option in the text editor to save memo1 as New Name Memo 1 on the USB Flash drive. Close the text editor.

15. ____ Verify that the contents of memo1 and New Name Memo 1 contain the same exact text.

16. ____ Now, create three levels of folders on the USB Flash drive. Simply create a folder called Level1. Then, click Level1 and create a folder called Level2 inside the Level1 folder. Select the Level2 folder and create a Level3 folder. Copy (do *not* move) memo1 to folder Level3. When you have finished creating the three folders and have made a copy of memo1 in Level2 folder, call your instructor to inspect your work.

17. ____ Delete the folders Level1, Level2, and Level3 after your instructor has inspected your work. Also, remove all copies of memo1 except for the original memo1 file.

18. ____ Take a few minutes to experiment with the creation and deletion of folders and files on the USB Flash drive. Practice right-clicking to see the options available when a folder or file is selected. Also, drag files and the contents of folders to other folders. Right-click the blank white space inside the Windows Explorer and view the shortcut menu options.

19. ____ Go on to answer the review questions. You may use Help and Support to assist you with answering the review questions.

Review Questions

1. True *or* False? When you rename a file, the contents of the file changes. _____

2. True *or* False? When you copy a file and then make changes in the copied file's contents, the contents of the original file are also changed. _____

3. True *or* False? When you use the **Save As** command in a text editor, the contents of the new file is exactly the same as the original file. _____

4. True *or* False? You can move a file to a folder by simply selecting the file, holding down the left mouse key, and dragging the file to the folder. _____

5. What is the maximum number of characters that can be used in a file name? _____

Copyright by Goodheart-Willcox Co., Inc.

Laboratory Activity

21

Identifying PC BIOS and Operating Systems

After completing this laboratory activity, you will be able to:

■ Identify the BIOS manufacturer and version.

■ Identify the Windows operating system.

■ Access and modify the BIOS CMOS settings.

■ Check the browser setup and version.

Introduction

In this activity, you will learn to identify the manufacturer and version of the BIOS, Windows operating system, and browser information.

The BIOS (Basic Input/Output Operating System) translates commands given to it by the operating system into actions carried out by the system hardware. The type of hardware that makes up the PC system must be identified before the BIOS program can carry out commands that affect the system hardware. When the hardware is identified, the BIOS program stores the data in a CMOS (Complimentary Metal-Oxide Semiconductor). The CMOS must use a small battery to retain the settings after power to the computer is turned off.

The PC's hardware is usually identified automatically though Plug and Play technology. The Plug and Play technology automatically detects the hardware and assigns settings to the CMOS data collection. For the Plug and Play technology to work properly, three things must be Plug and Play compliant: the hardware being installed, the BIOS, and the operating system. For example, you may attach a Plug and Play device to a PC that is using a Plug and Play operating system, such as Windows 98. However, if the BIOS is not Plug and Play, the device will need to be installed manually. You may also upgrade the BIOS to a Plug and Play BIOS.

Typically, when the PC first boots, BIOS information is flashed across the screen. For example, a message similar to the one below may appear in the upper-left quadrant of the screen.

AMIBIOS 1992 C American Megatrends, Inc.

BIOS Version 1.00.07

0032 KB memory

Press Fl to enter setup

The above information displays the BIOS manufacturer and version. The amount of RAM is displayed, and then instructions are given for accessing the CMOS Setup program. The exact method of accessing the CMOS Setup program is not standard and is not always displayed on the screen. You may need to consult the PC or BIOS manufacturer through its Web site to identify the exact steps necessary to access the CMOS Setup program.

Copyright by Goodheart-Willcox Co., Inc.

Equipment and Materials

■ Typical PC with Windows 95, or later, operating system.

Procedure

1. _____ Turn on the PC and closely watch for instructions for accessing the CMOS Setup program. If the information is not displayed, you may need to ask the instructor. In the space provided, write down the instructions for accessing the CMOS Setup program. _____

_____

2. _____ After accessing the CMOS Setup program, find and record in the space provided the answers to the questions in the following list. You will not be familiar with much of the information recorded. This is normal. The information displayed in the BIOS settings will become clear to you as you progress through the course. What is important for you to understand is the type of information contained in the BIOS settings and what can be changed. There are many different BIOS Setup programs available and not all will exactly match the information being requested below. Answer all questions to the best of your ability.

Is the system date and time displayed?_____

Can the system time and date be changed? _____

Is the BIOS version displayed? _____

Is the amount of extended memory displayed and if so, how much memory does the PC have?

_____

What information can be viewed about the floppy drives?_____

_____

What information about the hard drive is present? _____

_____

Are there any security features present and if so, describe them. _____

_____

_____

What information about the monitor is displayed?_____

_____

What are the "Boot Options?" _____

What information is provided about the serial ports? _____

Is there any information about the CPU? _____

3. _____ Now that you have found the listed information, make special note of how the BIOS settings program is exited. You usually must exit by choosing an option such as: **Use default settings, Save changes**, or **Do not retain changes to settings**. It is important to realize that changes are not automatically retained by the CMOS.

4. _____ If time permits and you have instructor approval, change the system time indicated in the CMOS Setup program as well as the date. Again, make sure you have instructor approval first.

5. _____ Return the system time and date settings to the correct settings and then shut down the PC.

Copyright by Goodheart-Willcox Co., Inc.

Name_____

Review Questions

1. How did you access the CMOS Setup program?_____
   _____

2. Why aren't the CMOS settings lost after the power is turned off to the PC? _____
   _____
   _____

3. Where is the manufacturer of the BIOS and the version displayed? _____
   _____

4. If instructions for accessing the CMOS Setup program are not displayed on the screen, how could you find the information needed to determine the proper keystroke sequence for accessing the CMOS Setup program? _____
   _____
   _____

Notes

Computer Service and Repair Lab Manual

Copyright by Goodheart-Willcox Co., Inc.

Name _____ Date _____

Class/Instructor _____

System Information (MSINFO32)

After completing this laboratory activity, you will be able to:

- Display the System Information utility by running msinfo32.exe.
- Describe how information is organized in the System Information utility.
- Identify information about the hardware and software installed on your workstation computer system.
- Explain how the System Information utility might be helpful to a technician.

Introduction

The System Information (msinfo32.exe) utility contains general information about the computer system. This utility is used by technicians to identify hardware components without having to physically open the computer. A summary of software components is also available for viewing. Look at the following screen capture of a typical summary viewed in the System Information utility.

The summary provides information about the operating system, BIOS version, CPU, RAM, and much more. In addition to a summary, there are three major categories listed in the left-hand pane: **Hardware Resources**, **Components**, and **Software Environment**. Each major category can be expanded to provide much more detailed information. Look at the following screen capture of the

Components category which has been expanded to provide information about the display. As you can see, a lot of information about hardware devices can be found without the need to open the computer case and read the hardware device labels.

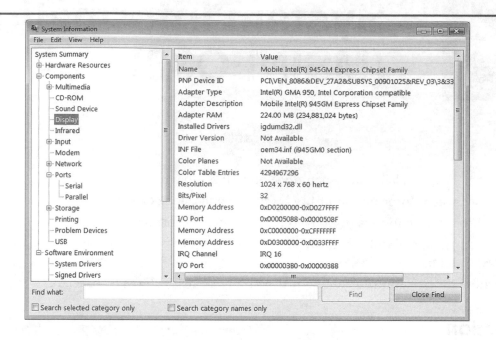

You can print a copy of the summary from the **Print** command in the **File** menu. A printed system summary is often kept on file for each computer that a shop might custom build. The printout of the custom built computer can be filed and later viewed when a customer calls for support. You will have a handy printout of everything installed and configured when the computer is first built. It also provides a means of identifying warranty information.

You can also access summary information about another computer on the network if you have the proper permissions. You simply select **Remote Computer** from the **View** menu. The **Remote Computer** dialog box will display. You can also access the **Remote Computer** dialog box by pressing

[Ctrl] [R] when the System Information utility is open. Look at the following screen capture of the **Remote Computer** dialog box.

You simply select the **Remote Computer on the Network** option and then enter the computer name or IP address. An IP address is a unique number that identifies the computer on the network.

Copyright by Goodheart-Willcox Co., Inc.

The major difference between Windows XP and Windows Vista System Information is the absence of the **Tools** menu in Windows Vista. Windows Vista has relocated these items into other utilities which will be covered in later laboratory activities. Look at the following screen capture of Windows XP **Tools** menu.

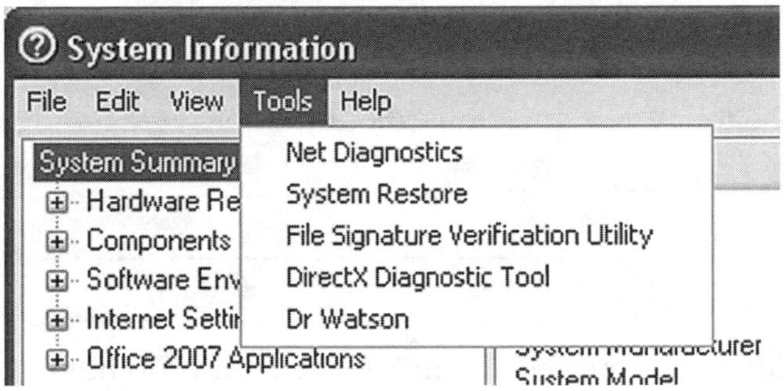

Equipment and Materials

■ Computer with Windows XP or Windows Vista, or both, installed.

Procedure

1. ____ Report to your assigned workstation.

2. ____ Boot the computer and verify it is in working order.

3. ____ Run the msinfo32.exe program from the **Run** dialog box for Windows XP or the **Search** dialog box in Windows Vista. The System Information utility should appear.

4. ____ Answer the following questions about the workstation you are using. Record your answers in the space provided.

What operating system is the system using? _____

What version/service pack is installed? _____

What BIOS version is installed on the computer? _____

What is the system default boot device? _____

What type processor is installed? _____

What is the user name? _____

How much physical RAM is installed? _____

What is the total virtual memory? _____

5. ____ Now, answer the following questions about the hardware resources.

What two IRQs are assigned to the IDE channels also known as the PATA? _____

Are there any hardware items sharing resources, or are there any conflicts? _____

6. ____ Answer the following questions about the components installed.

What brand of CD or DVD drive is installed? _____

What brand or information is provided about the video adapter? _____

_____

What resolution is assigned to the display? _____

7. ____ Now answer the following questions about the software environment.

Are all system drivers currently running? _____

Are all system drivers signed? _____

Are the startup programs listed? _____

8. ____ Look at the **Print** command located in the **File** menu. Do not print a summary without explicit permission from your instructor.

9. ____ Locate the **Remote Computer** command listed in the **View** menu. You can also use the key combination [Ctrl] [R] to access the **Remote Computer** dialog box while viewing the System Information.

Review Questions

1. What is the executable file name used to access the System Information in Windows XP and Windows Vista? _____

2. What are the three broad categories of information displayed in System Information in addition to the summary? _____

_____

_____

3. Which broad category will allow you to view hardware conflicts? _____

_____

4. Which category will allow you to view information about a device such as a DVD drive?

_____

5. Which category will allow you to see information about startup programs? _____

_____

Copyright by Goodheart-Willcox Co., Inc.

Laboratory Activity

23

Device Manager

After completing this laboratory activity, you will be able to:

- Access Device Manager.
- Identify hardware installed on a PC.
- Identify system resources assigned to system hardware.
- Locate **Update Driver** and **Roll Back Driver** options.
- Enable and disable devices.
- Print a summary of hardware devices.
- Configure power management for a device.

Introduction

Device Manager is one of the dialog boxes most frequently used by PC technicians. It contains information about the type of hardware installed, the general condition of the hardware device, and the assignment of system resources such as IRQ, DMA, I/O address, and memory address assignments. The devices, or hardware, installed in the PC can be viewed in Device Manager in one of two ways: by type or by connection.

In Windows XP, the Device Manager can be opened by right-clicking **My Computer**, selecting **Properties** from the shortcut menu, selecting the **Hardware** tab, and then clicking the **Device Manager** button. The Device Manager can also be accessed through **Start | Control Panel | Performance and Maintenance | System | Hardware tab** and then clicking the **Device Manager** button. One of the most common ways to access Device Manager in Windows XP is right-clicking **My Computer**, selecting **Manage** from the shortcut menu, and selecting **Device Manager** from the **Computer Management** utility.

Windows Vista access to Device Manager is somewhat different than Windows XP. You can open Device Manager by right-clicking **Computer**, selecting **Properties** from the shortcut menu, and selecting **Device Manager** from the **Tasks** list. You can also access Device Manager through the Control Panel: **Start | Control Panel |System and Maintenance | Device Manager**. A method similar to Windows Vista is to simply right-click **Computer**, select **Manage** from the shortcut menu, and then select **Device Manager** in the **Computer Management** utility. No matter which way you choose to access Device Manager in Windows Vista, you will need administrative level privileges. Device Manager is very similar in Windows XP and Windows Vista.

Copyright by Goodheart-Willcox Co., Inc.

Look at the following screen capture to see a screen capture of Windows XP Device Manager. (Windows Vista contains the same elements as the Windows XP version of Device Manager.)

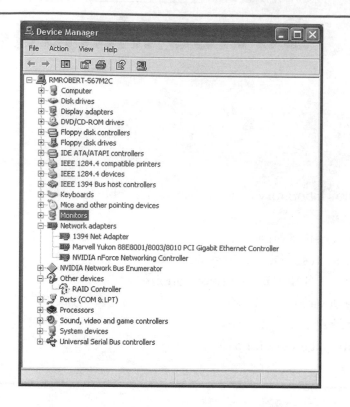

Problems with hardware devices are indicated with special symbols such as a question mark (?) indicating that a compatible driver is installed, but a problem still exists such as the device is in conflict with another hardware device.

A bright red X is used to indicate that a hardware device has been disabled. An exclamation mark (!) is used to indicate that the device has a problem and is not configured properly but may still be functional.

The letter *i* is used to indicate that the system resources were manually selected and that the Automatic Settings feature of Plug and Play was not used to configure the device.

Early computer systems before Plug and Play technology often had conflicting system resources. For example, two hardware devices might be configured manually to share the same IRQ, memory assignment, or DMA channel. Today, system conflicts are rarely experienced. The most commonly encountered problem with hardware devices are problems with the device driver. Often device drivers must be upgraded because of problems discovered after they were released to the public or to correct a compatibility problem when a new operating system or some software application is released. For example, when Microsoft Vista was first released, there were many device driver problems because Windows Vista was designed as a very secure system and added many new features. Hardware and software manufacturers had to write new software drivers to make their existing and future hardware compatible with Windows Vista.

Device Manager has a function built in that will automatically let you upgrade the system driver. Also, be aware that problems can occur after a new device driver is installed. The device might fail to operate properly when the newest driver is installed. If a newly installed device driver has caused a system problem, there is an option called **Roll Back Driver**, which automatically removes the latest driver version and reinstalls the last driver used.

You should note that you can also revert to an earlier driver by selecting a restore point that was created with the **System Restore** feature. A restore point will convert the computer system back to an earlier point in time. The problem with using a restore point to remove a driver is that it

Copyright by Goodheart-Willcox Co., Inc.

Name_____

may remove all updated drivers installed since the restore point was created as well as any system updates and software applications. This could cause even more problems than removing the single driver using the **Roll Back Driver** option. There will be much more about the System Restore feature in a later laboratory activity.

Device Manager also has a Power Management feature that allows the computer to turn off the device when it is not being used in order to save energy. The Power Management feature is not present for all devices.

System resources can be viewed in Device Manager but may not appear for all devices when the hardware devices are configured for Plug and Play. When the system resources do not appear in Device Manager, you may need to disable the Plug and Play feature in the BIOS before the system resources assigned to the hardware device can be viewed. Students are confused at times when viewing the I/O address and memory address information displayed in the Device Manager. System I/O port addresses are expressed in hexadecimal form similar to memory addresses. The I/O port is used in communications between devices and software programs. Devices and software programs must know where to send and receive information. The I/O port address is the location of the device's communication doorway and is used to find the location of the device on the bus.

The memory address is the location of the RAM that the device uses to store information for transmitting and receiving. It can span a single range of one byte or span a very large range of memory addresses, depending on the function of a device. Not every device requires both an I/O port assignment and a range of memory. For example, some simple keyboards have only an I/O port assignment, not memory. Keyboards usually have their own buffer that serves as a memory area. On the other hand, a more sophisticated keyboard with many options such as automatic Internet access, e-mail, volume controls, and more will most likely have some RAM assigned to it. It will also require a drive to be installed from disc.

A chip used as a bus bridge will have both an I/O port address and a range of memory used to store data until it is transmitted across the bus.

System conflicts may arise when two devices share the same IRQ. However, some devices are compatible when using the same IRQ. For example, chipsets that control the bus communications commonly share an IRQ with devices assigned to that bus. In this case, the two devices work well together. Other devices may not function properly when sharing an IRQ assignment.

When two devices share the same IRQ assignment and one of the devices has a problem communicating with the CPU, it is referred to as an IRQ conflict. For example, when a scanner and a sound card are assigned the same IRQ setting, the system may lock up when the user attempts to use the scanner. When an IRQ conflict exists, one of the two devices must be reassigned to a different IRQ.

With Plug and Play, most system resource assignments are managed automatically. Occasionally a conflict still arises. In these cases, you may need to disable the Plug and Play option in the system BIOS settings and manually set a new IRQ for the effected hardware.

USB and FireWire (IEEE 1394) devices are configured very different when compared to earlier technologies. Both USB and FireWire devices are designed to share the same physical bus and they are both managed by the bus controller. The bus controller controls the communications of all devices connected to the bus thus preventing two or more devices from trying to use the bus at the same time. Since devices share the same physical bus, they will also share the same IRQ. The USB and FireWire devices are designed to take turns using the bus. Thus, they do not create system conflicts with each other. For example, all devices connected to a USB may share IRQ 22. USB will support up to 127 devices, and FireWire will support up to 63 devices.

Equipment and Materials

- Computer with Windows XP or Windows Vista, or both, installed.
- USB Flash drive.
- Local printer (optional).

Part I—Windows XP

Procedure

1. ____ Report to your assigned workstation.

2. ____ Boot the computer and verify it is in working order.

3. ____ Right-click **My Computer** and then select **Properties** from the shortcut menu. The **System Properties** dialog box should display.

4. ____ Select the **Hardware** tab, and then click the **Device Manager** button. This will reveal a dialog box similar to the following.

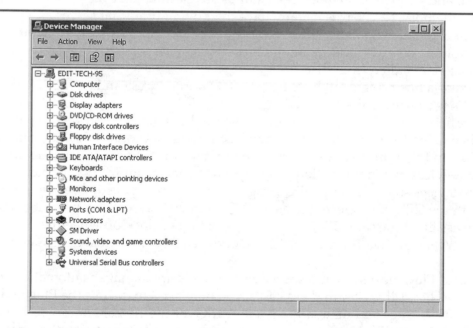

5. ____ Close the **Device Manager** and **System Properties** dialog boxes.

6. ____ Open Device Manager through Control Panel. Use **Start I Control Panel I Performance and Maintenance I System**. Select the **Hardware** tab, and then click the **Device Manager** button.

7. ____ Devices can be viewed in two ways in Device Manager: by device and by connection. Change the view several times by accessing the **View** menu and alternately clicking the **Devices by type** and **Devices by connection**. Pay particular attention to how the devices are arranged in each view. Notice how the structure is similar in design to the Windows Explorer directory structure. Now, with **Devices by type** selected, click the plus sign to the left of **Disk drives**. This expands the device tree and reveals the disk installed in the PC. (There may be more disks depending on the PC used for the lab.)

Copyright by Goodheart-Willcox Co., Inc.

8. ____ Now, click the plus sign left of **Keyboards** to expand the device tree. Right-click the keyboard model that is identified, and then select **Properties** from the shortcut menu. This opens a dialog box that displays general information about the keyboard, the driver, and system resources used. Remember, the term *system resources* refers to I/O, IRQ, memory, and DMA assignments.

9. ____ Fill in the blanks in the following table. Information for the table can be found using Device Manager. Not every table cell will be used. For example, if the device does not use a DMA channel, write "NA" (not applicable) inside the table cell.

Device	IRQ	I/O range	DMA channel
Mouse			
Keyboard			
Floppy drive			
Display adapter			
Monitor			
System timer			
CMOS real-time clock			
Hard drive			
Modem			
USB			

10. ____ With the Device Manager open, locate the resources of the mouse. Attempt to reassign the mouse to interrupt request (IRQ) 11. In the space provided, write a brief explanation of what happens. _____

_____

_____

11. ____ Select **Keyboards** from the Device Manager list to view the exact identification of the keyboard. (Click the plus sign to the left of **Keyboards** in the Device Manager list.) In the space provided, write the type of keyboard identified. _____

_____

12. ____ After you have revealed the type of keyboard, right-click the keyboard device and select **Properties** from the shortcut menu. Then, select the **Driver** tab. This tab identifies the name and location of the driver file for that particular device. It also allows you to update the driver for the device.

13. ____ Now, expand **Universal Serial Bus controllers**.

Copyright by Goodheart-Willcox Co., Inc.

14. ____ Plug in the USB Flash drive while viewing Device Manager. You should see the **USB Mass Storage Device** automatically appear in the list of hardware devices similar to that shown in the following screen capture.

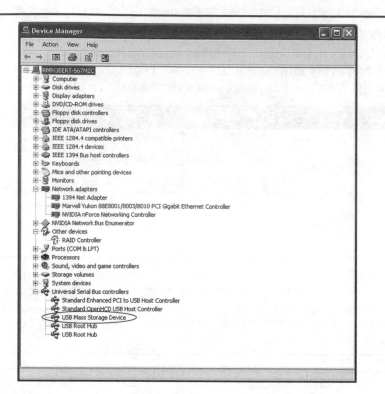

Remove the USB Flash drive while observing the **Universal Serial Bus controllers** section. It should return to its original listing of devices. The change should appear as in the following screen capture.

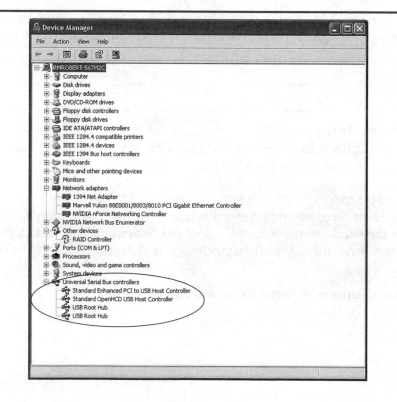

Copyright by Goodheart-Willcox Co., Inc.

15. ____ If you do not have a printer available, skip this step and go on to step 16. If you have a printer, you can print a copy of the Device Manager display. Simply select the **Action** menu and click the **Print** command. If no printer is available, the command may not appear.

16. ____ You may take a few minutes to explore Device Manager at this time before going on to Part II—Windows Vista.

Part II—Windows Vista

Procedure

1. ____ Report to your assigned workstation.

2. ____ Boot the computer and verify it is in working order.

3. ____ Right-click the **Computer** icon located off the **Start** menu and then select the **Properties** option from the shortcut menu. Select **Device Manager** from under the **Tasks** list in the left-hand pane. The Device Manager should automatically appear on the screen.

4. ____ Close Device Manager.

5. ____ Open the **Device Manager** through Control Panel. Use **Start | Control Panel |System and Maintenance | Device Manager**.

6. ____ Devices can be viewed in two ways in Device Manager: by device and by connection. Select the **View** menu. Change the view several times by alternately clicking the **Devices by type** and **Devices by connection**. Pay particular attention to how the devices are arranged in each view. Now, return the default view to **Devices by type** and then select the plus sign to the left of **Disk drives**. This expands the device tree and reveals the disk drive installed on the PC. (There may be more devices depending on the PC used for the lab.)

7. ____ Now, click the plus sign left of **Keyboards** to expand the device tree. Right-click the keyboard model that is identified, and then select **Properties** from the shortcut menu. This opens a dialog box that displays general information about the keyboard, the driver, and system resources used. Remember, the term *system resource* refers to I/O, IRQ, memory, and DMA assignments.

8. _____ Fill in the blanks in the following table. Information for the table can be found using Device Manager. Not every table cell will be used. For example, if the device does not use a DMA channel, write "NA" (not applicable) inside the table cell, or if the device does not exist, fill the entire row with "NA."

Device	IRQ	I/O range	DMA channel
Mouse			
Keyboard			
Floppy drive			
Display adapter			
Monitor			
System timer			
CMOS real-time clock			
Hard drive			
Modem			
USB			

9. _____ With the Device Manager open, locate the resources of the mouse. Attempt to reassign the mouse to interrupt request (IRQ) 11. Write a brief explanation of what happens in the space provided. _____

_____

_____

10. _____ Select **Keyboards** from the Device Manager list to view the exact identification of the keyboard. (Click the plus sign to the left of **Keyboards** in the Device Manager list.) Write the type of keyboard identified in the space provided._____

_____

11. _____ After you have revealed the type of keyboard, select the **Driver** tab. The **Driver** tab identifies the name and location of the driver file for that particular device. It also allows you to update the driver for the device, disable or enable the device, and uninstall the driver. If an option is not available, it will appear shaded or as a ghost rather than bold. You will not be able to select an unavailable option even though it appears in the dialog box.

13. _____ Open Device Manager and expand the **Universal Serial Bus controllers** section.

14. _____ Plug in the USB Flash drive while viewing Device Manager. You should see the **USB Mass Storage Device** automatically appear in the list of hardware devices. Remove the USB Flash drive while observing the **Universal Serial Bus controllers** section. It should return to its original listing of devices.

15. _____ If you do not have a printer available, skip this step and go on to step 16. If you have a printer, you can print a copy of the Device Manager display. Simply select the **Action** menu and click the **Print** command. If no printer is available, the command may not appear.

16. _____ Go on to answer the review questions.

Copyright by Goodheart-Willcox Co., Inc.

Review Questions

1. What are the four system resources?_____

_____

2. Describe two ways of accessing Device Manager in Windows XP._____

_____

3. Describe two ways of accessing Device Manager in Windows Vista. _____

_____

4. How does Plug and Play affect system resources? _____

_____

_____

5. How can the device driver files and location of the driver files be viewed? _____

_____

6. What does a bright red X located beside a hardware device in Device Manager indicate?

_____

7. What does a bright yellow exclamation mark beside a hardware device in Device Manager indicate? _____

_____

8. What does the letter *i* indicate in Device Manager? _____

_____

_____

9. Can two or more devices share the same IRQ? _____

10. Why is the Driver Rollback feature preferred over using a restore point? _____

_____

11. How do you disable the Plug and Play feature so that you might manually assign system resources? _____

_____

12. How many USB devices can be connected to a USB bus? _____

13. How many FireWire devices can be connected to a FireWire bus?_____

14. True *or* False? All USB devices share the same IRQ assignment? _____

Copyright by Goodheart-Willcox Co., Inc.

Notes

Copyright by Goodheart-Willcox Co., Inc.

Name _____ Date _____

Class/Instructor _____

Computer Management Utility

After completing this laboratory activity, you will be able to:

- Access the Computer Management Utility.
- Identify the major Computer Management tool categories.
- Access the major Computer Management tools.

Introduction

In this laboratory activity, you will be introduced to the Windows Computer Management utility. The Computer Management utility provides a centralized location to access important system tools, services, and storage management. The Computer Management utility is also referred to as Microsoft Management Console (MMC) which is an empty version of the Computer Management utility that can be customized with a collection of tools. The two names are often used interchangeably in technical articles.

You will use Computer Management in future laboratory activities where a more in-depth presentation of the common features will be provided as they apply. For example, when the laboratory activity concerns storage devices, the Computer Management Disk Management tool will be covered in detail. For this laboratory activity, you will simply be exposed to the general features of the Computer Management utility.

The Computer Management utility is very similar in Windows XP and Windows Vista. In Windows XP, it is accessed through **Start | Control Panel | Performance and Maintenance | Administrative Tools | Computer Management**. It can also be accessed by right-clicking **My Computer** and selecting **Manage** from the shortcut menu.

In Windows Vista, it is accessed through **Start | Control Panel | System and Maintenance | Administrative Tools | Computer Management**. It can also be accessed by right-clicking **Computer** and selecting **Manage** from the shortcut menu.

When Computer Management opens, you will see the left pane referred to as the Console Tree. This is shown in the following screen capture of the Windows Vista Computer Management utility.

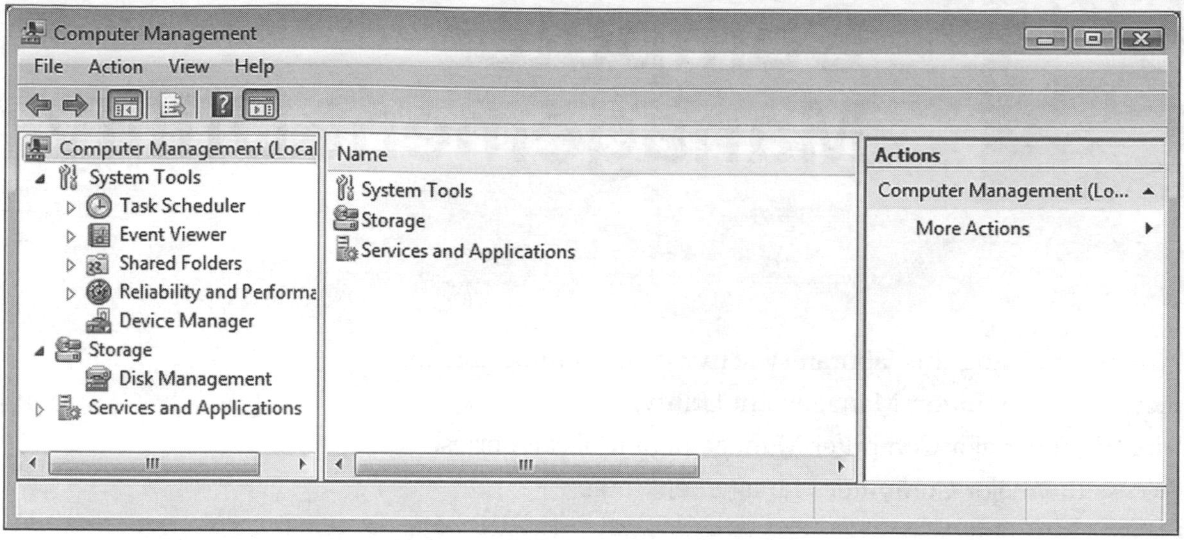

The Console Tree contains a list of all tools associated with Computer Management. It consists of broad categories such as **System Tools**, **Storage**, and **Services and Applications**. Each major category contains tools directly related to the major category. For example, under **Storage** you would see tools such as **Disk Defragmenter**, **Disk Management**, and **Removable Storage**. When a category is selected from the Console Tree view, information will appear in the center pane.

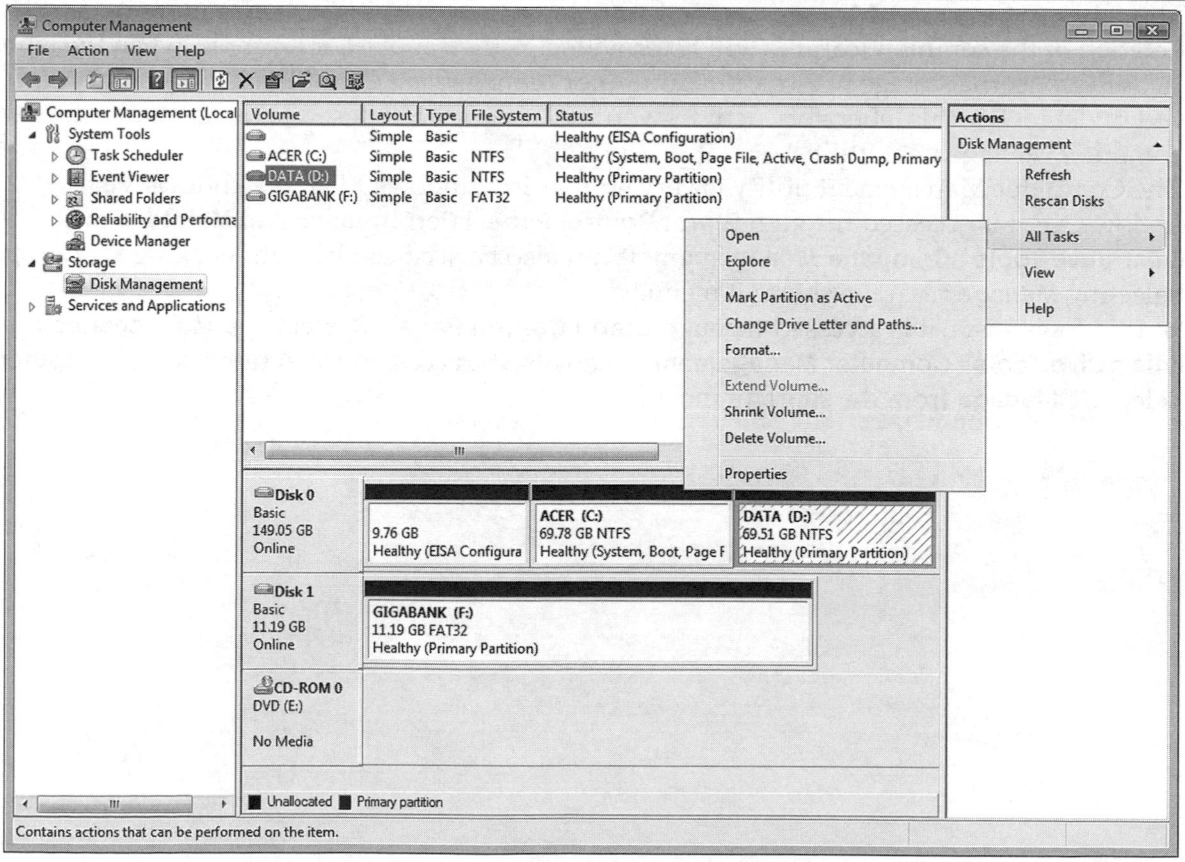

Copyright by Goodheart-Willcox Co., Inc.

The center pane displays information about the tool selected in the left pane. The right-hand pane is new in Windows Vista and is called the **Actions** pane. It provides most of the same options as the **Action** menu item listed at the top of the Computer Management utility. The **Actions** pane provides a list of the most commonly related tools that correspond to the items selected in the center pane and Console Tree. As you can see in the previous screen capture, when the drive D is selected in the center pane, the **Actions** pane can be selected to reveal a cascading menu list of related tools.

The Disk Management feature will be covered in great depth in a later laboratory activity. For now, just be aware of how the three panes in Computer Management relate to each other. Again, the **Actions** pane is new in Windows Vista and does not exist in Windows XP or earlier versions of the Windows operating system. The Windows XP version does have an **Action** menu option listed at the top of the Windows XP Computer Management utility.

The tools that appear in the Computer Management utility are referred to as snap-ins. You can actually create your own custom Computer Management console by running MMC.exe from the **Run** dialog box in Windows XP or the **Search** box in Windows Vista. This feature will not be covered in this laboratory activity, but you can read about it in Help and Support .

Note:
Some features may not match this laboratory activity if the workstation is connected to a network that has limited the access to some specific features. Also, some computer manufacturers may have added their own custom snap-in for Computer Management.

Additional information about Computer Management can be obtained from the Help and Support program located off the **Start** menu. Simply open Help and Support and conduct a search for MMC.

Equipment and Materials

■ Computer with Windows XP or Windows Vista, or both, installed.

Part I—Windows XP

Procedure

1. ____ Report to your assigned workstation.

2. ____ Boot the computer and verify it is in working order.

3. ____ Open Computer Management by right-clicking **My Computer** and selecting **Manage** from the shortcut menu.

4. ____ Close Computer Management and reopen it using the following path: **Start | Control Panel | Performance and Maintenance |Administrative Tools |Computer Management**.

5. ____ Identify the three major categories listed in the left pane of the console in the Console Tree. List the three categories in the space provided.

_____

_____

_____

6. ____ List the subcategories of the major category **System Tools** in the space provided.

_____

_____

_____

_____

_____

Note:
    Subcategories may vary according to the system configuration and network restrictions if the workstation is part of a network system.

---

7. ____ List the subcategories listed under major category **Storage** in the space provided.

_____

_____

_____

8. ____ List the subcategories listed under the major category **Services and Applications** in the space provided.

_____

_____

_____

9. ____ Select **Device Manager** located under the **System Tools** category and observe the information provided in the right pane. This is the same information that is provided in the Device Manager utility.

10. ____ Now, select the **Action** menu. The contents of the **Action** menu changes according to which tool and feature in the left and right panes has been selected. Try selecting various items in the left and right pane and then viewing the contents of the **Action** menu. See how it changes according to the tool and feature selected.

11. ____ Close Computer Management.

12. ____ Access Help and Support located off the **Start** menu of Windows XP. Conduct a search of the topic Computer Management. Explore some of the overviews, articles, and tutorials that appear in the results. Pay particular attention to the overview titled "MMC Overview." Close Help and Support after reviewing some of the overviews.

13. ____ Go on to the Part II—Windows Vista before answering the review questions.

Copyright by Goodheart-Willcox Co., Inc.

Part II—Windows Vista

Procedure

1. ____ Report to your assigned workstation.

2. ____ Boot the computer and verify it is in working order.

3. ____ Open Computer Management right-clicking **Computer** and selecting **Manage** from the shortcut menu.

4. ____ Close Computer Management and reopen it using the following path: **Start | Control Panel | System and Maintenance |Administrative Tools | Computer Management**.

5. ____ Identify the three major categories listed in the left pane of the Console Tree view. List the three categories in the space provided.

   _____

   _____

   _____

6. ____ List the subcategories of the major category **System Tools** in the space provided.

   _____

   _____

   _____

   _____

   _____

   _____

Note:
   Subcategories may vary according to the system configuration and network restrictions if the workstation is part of a network system.

---

7. ____ List the subcategories listed under major category **Storage** in the space provided.

   _____

8. ____ List the subcategories listed under the major category **Services and Applications** in the space provided.

   _____

   _____

9. ____ Select the Device Manager located under the **System Tools** and observe the information provided in the right pane. This is the same information that is provided in Device Manager.

10. ____ Now, select the **Action** menu located at the top of the Computer Management console. The contents of the **Action** menu will change according to which tool and feature in the left and center panes have been selected. Try selecting various items in the left and center pane and then viewing the contents of the **Action** menu. See how it changes according to the tool and feature selected.

Copyright by Goodheart-Willcox Co., Inc.

11. ____ Close Computer Management.

12. ____ Access Help and Support located off the **Start** menu. Conduct a search of the topic "Computer Management." Locate and open "What Is the Microsoft Management Console (MMC)." After you read the article, select the "What Are Administrative Tools" listed under **See also** at the end of the "What Is the Microsoft Management Console (MMC)" article.

13. ____ Go on to answer the review questions. You may use Help and Support to assist you with the review questions.

Review Questions

1. Write the path to Computer Management in Windows XP.

_____

_____

_____

_____

_____

2. Write the path to Computer Management in Windows Vista.

_____

_____

_____

_____

_____

3. What are the three major categories located in the left pane of Computer Management? _____

_____

_____

4. What is an MMC snap-in? _____

_____

Copyright by Goodheart-Willcox Co., Inc.

Name _____ Date _____

Class/Instructor _____

Installing a Pentium 4 Processor

After completing this laboratory activity, you will be able to:

■ Identify the required socket used for an Intel Pentium 4 processor.

■ Explain the key steps to installing an Intel Pentium 4 processor.

■ Explain the importance of properly applying the thermo compound.

Introduction

In this laboratory activity, you will install a Pentium 4 processor and fan and heat sink assembly. The Pentium 4 is designed by Intel and installs into a 478-pin micro Pin Grid Array (μPGA). The symbol for micro (μ) is often used in the acronym. The micro PGA uses less space on the motherboard for the socket because the pins are placed closer together than in any other previous socket design.

The installation of the Pentium 4 processor can be quite complex compared to earlier processor installations. One of the most critical aspects of installing the processor is the installation of the fan and heat sink assembly. The fan and heat sink assembly requires electrical power to operate properly. Electrical power is provided by a three-pin connection located on the motherboard in close proximity to the processor.

Note:

You may need additional instructional sheets if the fan and heat sink assembly does not match the one in this laboratory activity.

Heat exchange between the cooling unit and the processor is also critical. Simply mounting the fan and heat sink assembly on the processor is not sufficient. A thermo compound must be installed between the processor and fan and heat sink assembly to ensure heat will dissipate in the most efficient manner. Without the thermo compound, the heat conduction between the processor and the fan and heat sink assembly is significantly reduced and can cause the processor to overheat. Excessive heat can damage the processor.

The thermo compound looks like a cream-colored, grease-type material. The thermo compound may come in a separate container or be already spread on the processor and protected by a clear plastic cover. If it is already spread on the processor, the protective plastic cover must be removed before installing the fan and heat sink assembly.

Sometimes thermo compound is supplied in a tube. When in a tube, simply open the tube and squeeze the compound onto the base of the heat sink or onto the surface of the processor. Rather than using your finger, you may use a small piece of plastic that comes with the packaging to smear the thermo compound evenly across the surface area.

Note:

When replacing a defective processor, some of the thermo compound may be removed and should be replaced.

Some key points to remember while installing a processor include the following:

■ Always wear a ground strap when handling static-sensitive devices such as a processor.
■ Always place the static-sensitive materials (processor and motherboard) on an anti-static mat or inside the original plastic package. Never lay them on a workbench unless the workbench has been designed to handle static-sensitive devices.
■ The fan and heat sink assembly must be designed specifically for the Pentium 4 processor model you are installing.
■ Thermo compound must be installed between the processor and the fan and heat sink assembly.
■ If the thermo compound is already spread on the fan and heat sink assembly and protected by a clear plastic cover, the protective plastic cover must be removed before installation.
■ A Pentium 4 processor requires a special motherboard with a 478-pin micro Pin Grid Array (µPGA) and a power supply with a rating sufficient to support the processor. The power supply should indicate that it is designed for a Pentium 4 processor.

For more information on Pentium 4 installation procedures, visit Intel's technical support Web site at www.support.intel.com/support.

Equipment and Materials

■ Pentium 4 processor (model determined by instructor) and fan and heat sink assembly.
■ Motherboard with a 478-pin µPGA socket and retention frame.
■ Anti-static mat or packaging for processor and motherboard.
■ Additional instruction sheets may be required for this lab activity, especially if the fan and heat sink assembly do not match the one in this activity.

Procedure

1. ____ Gather all materials required for this laboratory activity and report to your assigned lab location.

Note:

When handling the motherboard or the Pentium 4 processor, be sure to take the proper electrostatic discharge (ESD) precautions.

---

2. ____ If available, read the motherboard manual prior to installing the processor. Read the section specific to processor installation.

Copyright by Goodheart-Willcox Co., Inc.

3. ____ If the retention frame is not already installed on the motherboard, remove the four white pushpins from the black fasteners in each corner of the frame. The four black fasteners should remain fully seated in the retention frame.

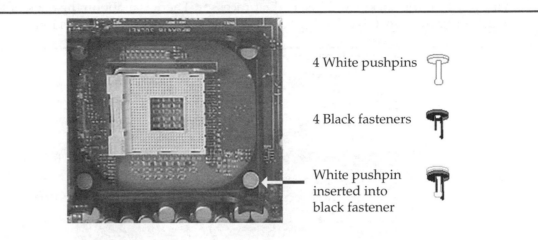

4 White pushpins

4 Black fasteners

White pushpin inserted into black fastener

4. ____ If the retention frame is already installed, skip to step 8.

5. ____ Place the retention frame on the motherboard, aligning it with the four corner holes that surround the processor socket.

6. ____ Secure the retention frame to the motherboard by gently pressing the black fasteners until they snap into place.

7. ____ Insert the four white pushpins into the black fasteners, one at each corner of the retention frame.

8. ____ Carefully remove the processor from its box. Do *not* handle or touch the processor pin area.

9. ____ Place the socket ZIF lever in the fully released position. The fully released position is when the lever is in the upright position.

ZIF lever

Copyright by Goodheart-Willcox Co., Inc.

10. ____ Look closely at the processor pin grid pattern to ensure the pin pattern on the processor matches the pin pattern of the socket. The socket has one corner pin hole missing near the hinge area of the ZIF socket lever. This is where pin 1 is located. Align pin 1 on the processor with pin 1 on the socket and insert the processor. There is a dot on the back of the processor, which indicates pin 1. No force is required to insert the processor pins into the socket.

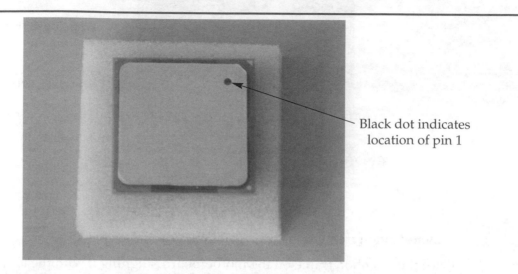

Black dot indicates location of pin 1

11. ____ After the processor has been inserted into the socket, close the ZIF socket lever by pushing the lever down to its lowest position.

12. ____ If the processor fan and heat sink assembly already have thermo compound applied, remove the plastic cover. Do *not* touch the white patch containing the thermo compound.

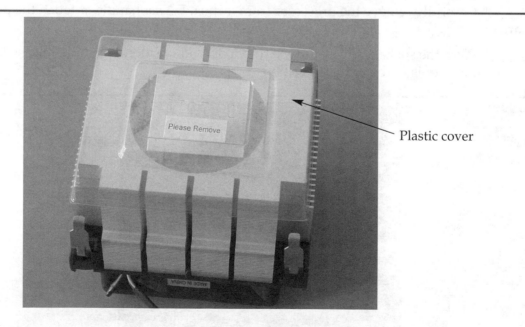

Please Remove

Plastic cover

13. ____ If the thermo compound is included in an applicator with the processor, apply the entire thermal compound material to the center of the processor's surface.

14. ____ Make sure the lever of the fan and heat sink assembly is in the unlocked position. (See the following illustration.)

Copyright by Goodheart-Willcox Co., Inc.

15. ____ Align the fan and heat sink assembly with the retention frame (the fan and heat sink assembly is symmetrical with the retention frame) and place it on the processor. The retaining clips on the fan and heat sink assembly should align with the holes in the retention frame. Make sure the fan and heat sink assembly cable is not trapped between the assembly and retention frame. Allow the heat sink base to compress (without rotating or twisting) the thermal compound material.

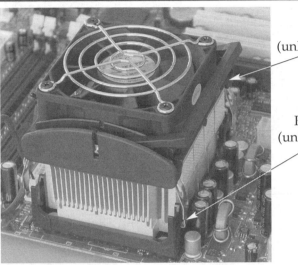

Lever
(unlocked position)

Retaining clip
(unlocked position)

16. ____ Move the lever of the fan and heat sink assembly to the locked position. The lever action will insert all four retaining clips into the holes of the retention frame. It is important to *not* allow the heat sink assembly to rotate or twist on the processor's surface. Securing the fan and heat sink assembly while closing the lever ensures the thermal interface material is not damaged and the processor will operate correctly.

Lever
(locked position)

Retaining clip
(locked position)

17. ____ Once the lever is locked, verify that the fan and heat sink assembly is securely retained and that the retaining clips are properly engaged with the retention frame.

18. ____ Connect the fan and heat sink assembly fan cable to the motherboard fan power header. Consult the motherboard manual to determine the correct fan header to use.

19. ____ Call your instructor to have your project inspected. Do *not* energize your project until the instructor has inspected and approved it.

Review Questions

1. Why should a ground strap be worn during installation or removal of a processor? _____
_____

2. How do you properly install the Pentium 4 processor? _____
_____
_____
_____

3. What does the acronym µPGA represent? _____

4. How many socket pins are used with a Pentium 4 processor? _____

5. What is the purpose of the thermo compound? _____
_____

6. Where would you look to find more specific information about the Pentium 4 processor? _____
_____

7. Any power supply can be used with Pentium 4 processor. True *or* False? _____

Copyright by Goodheart-Willcox Co., Inc.

Name _____ Date _____

Class/Instructor _____

Installing and Uninstalling an Intel Core 2 Processor

After completing this laboratory activity, you will be able to:

■ Explain proper handling and installation procedures of an Intel Core 2 processor.

■ Explain proper handling and installation of the heat sink and cooling fan assembly.

■ Explain the proper removal of the heat sink and cooling fan assembly.

■ Explain the proper removal of the Intel Core 2 processor.

Introduction

In this laboratory activity, you will install an Intel Core 2 processor or equivalent into a motherboard socket 775. The procedures outlined here apply to many of the Intel processors, such as the Intel Core 2 Duo, Intel Core 2 Extreme, and the Intel Core 2 Extreme Quad. The cooling assembly used in this laboratory activity can be used for any of the mentioned Core 2 processors at the time of this writing. As processor speeds increase, the cooling assembly design can change to accommodate the increase in temperature produced by the processor.

Always research the manufacturer's recommended procedures for installing a specific processor and cooling assembly. Always read all manuals and installation information provided with the processor, motherboard, and cooling assembly. There may have been problems encountered in the field after the release of a new processor. Installation instructions are, therefore, updated to correct and or avoid these discovered problems.

The processor in the laboratory activity is a 775-LAND package which means it is designed to fit into a Land Grid Array (LGA) 775 socket that connects using an array of lands rather than pins. Lands are short, raised electrical contacts arranged in a grid pattern rather than traditional Pin Grid Array (PGA) or micro Pin Grid Array (μPGA) used in earlier processor designs. The socket is designed with an array of very short, curved pin connections that match the lands on the processor. Look at the following illustration to see what the design looks like.

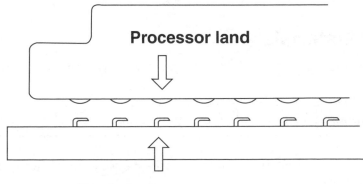

Processor land

Socket pins

You must use extreme caution when placing a 775-LAND package processor into a 775 socket. The processor must be lowered in a vertical motion into the socket. Dropping the processor into the socket or placing the socket at an angle can damage the socket pin grid. In the following figure, you can see the raised electronic components known as capacitors in the middle of the land area grid. The raised capacitors can distort or damage the delicate pins inside the socket if the processor is misaligned when inserted into the socket.

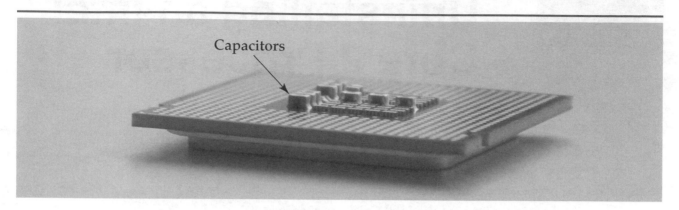

Capacitors

Be aware that when purchasing parts to build or repair a computer system, that the heat sink and fan assembly are not usually provided with the processor. There are numerous cooler assemblies available for specific processors. You must match the cooling assembly to the processor by researching the processor or cooling assembly manufacturer Web site. Most Web sites offer several different cooling assemblies that will match a specific processor. The processor warranty will be void if proper cooling is not provided for the processor.

Note:
You may need additional information sheets if the cooling assembly does not match the one in this laboratory activity.

For a more detailed description of the installation and removal of a Core 2 processor, visit the Intel technical support Web site: http://support.intel.com/support/index.htm. To see a video of how to install the Core 2 Extreme processor and cooling assembly visit the following Intel Web page: www.intel.com/cd/channel/reseller/asmo-na/eng/100617.htm. Keep the following key points in mind when installing and removing any type of processor:

■ Follow ESD procedures.
■ Never touch the socket or processor electrical contact areas, such as the pins and lands.
■ Avoid using a screwdriver to install a cooling system, as the screwdriver may slip and accidentally damage the motherboard.
■ Always check the manufacturer's Web site for the latest information about installation procedures.

Equipment and Materials

■ Intel Core 2 Quad processor. (Most Intel Core 2 processors will work for this laboratory activity.)
■ Heat sink fan assembly for above Intel Core 2 processor.
■ Compressed air. (Optional for removal of foreign objects.)

Note:
Read through all the instructional steps at least once before attempting the installation procedure.

Copyright by Goodheart-Willcox Co., Inc.

Name_____

Part I—Installing an Intel Core 2 Processor

Procedure

1. ____ Gather all materials required for the laboratory activity, and then report to your assigned work area.

2. ____ Motherboards are mounted on a foam anti-static mat or bubble wrap and shipped inside an ESD bag. Remove the motherboard from the ESD bag and save the bag for future use. Use the foam anti-static or bubble wrap under the motherboard.

3. ____ Look at the following images that identify the major parts of the 775 socket assembly.

Load lever locking tab

Load plate

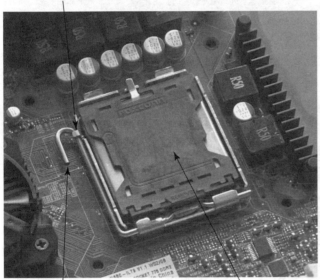

Load lever closed   Protective cover   Load lever open

The new motherboard would have the load lever in the locked position and a protective cover over the socket contact. You can remove the protective cover before or after opening the load plate. Release the load lever from the closed position by pressing down on the lever and then pushing it out to release it from the load lever locking tab. Store the protective socket cover for future use. The load plate must be raised before installing the processor.

4. ____ Inspect the socket for physical damage. Look along the rows of pins for any misaligned or damaged pins. Also, inspect it for any foreign objects or debris. Use compressed air to remove debris. Never use your finger, cloth, or brush to remove debris from the socket area. The pins can be damaged very easily. Rotate the motherboard or change your position around the socket by approximately 90° and inspect the rows once more. Again look for any misalignment, damage, or debris.

5. ____ Remove the processor from its protective package. The processor will have a protective cover over the land area on the back of the processor as shown in the following images.

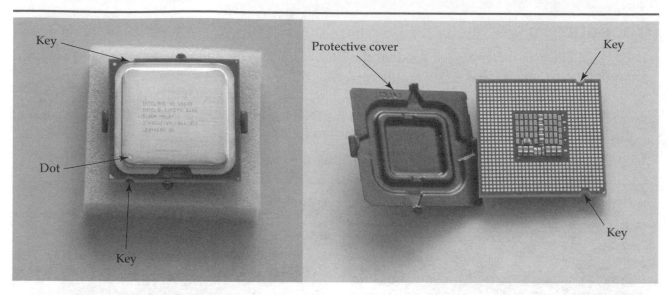

Intel Core 2 Extreme top view   **Intel Core 2 Extreme bottom view**

Handle the processor by its edges. Never touch the lands on the bottom of the processor. Carefully remove the processor protective cover from the bottom of the processor. Visually inspect the processor land area for damage.

6. ____ The processor can only be inserted into the socket in one particular way. The processor and the socket both have a pair of orientation keys that are used to ensure proper installation of the processor. Place the socket orientation keys directly over the socket orientation keys and lower the socket in a direct vertical motion. Do *not* drop the socket into place and do *not* tilt the socket or drag the processor across the socket. Any motion other than direct vertical could damage the socket pin array.

7. ____ After you have inserted the processor into the socket, lower the load plate over the processor. Hold it in position while lowering the load lever and securing the lever under the locking tab. Look at the following image to see what the properly installed processor will look like after the load plate and locked lever are in position.

    Copyright by Goodheart-Willcox Co., Inc.

8. ____ Now you will install the cooling assembly consisting of the heat sink and fan. First remove the protective plastic cover from the bottom of the assembly. Be careful not to touch the thermal compound, or as Intel refers to it, the "Thermal Interface Material (TIM)," on the bottom of the heat sink.

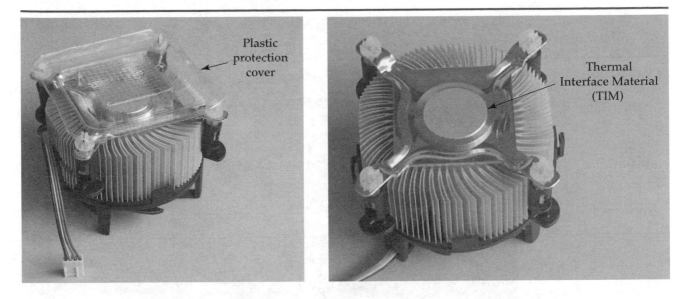

The protective cover also is designed to protect the plastic prongs at the end of the assembly mounting legs.

9. ____ Position the fan over the processor, aligning each of the four mounting legs with the holes in the motherboard. Be sure to position the fan cable close to the fan connection on the motherboard.

10. ____ The cooling assembly is attached to the motherboard by pressing each of the four mounts down into the motherboard. The plastic tip on each mount will slip through the hole in the motherboard and then snap into a locked position. You will need to hold the fan in position while pressing the top of each mounting leg down with your finger or thumb.

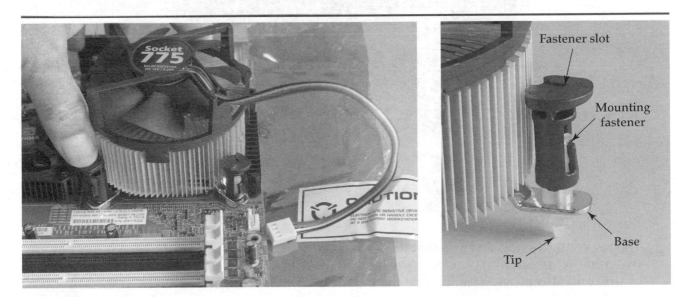

Copyright by Goodheart-Willcox Co., Inc.

When properly installed, the base of each mounting fastener will rest snuggly against the motherboard and the slot at the top of each fastener will align perpendicular to the heat sink. The slot will point directly at the heat sink. For difficult-to-reach mounting fasteners during installation or removal, Intel recommends using a number 2 pencil as shown in the following image.

Simply place the eraser end on top of the mounting fastener and then push down. A pencil is used in place of a screwdriver or other tool that could damage the motherboard if it slipped off the fastener.

11. _____ Connect the fan electrical cable to the motherboard fan connection.

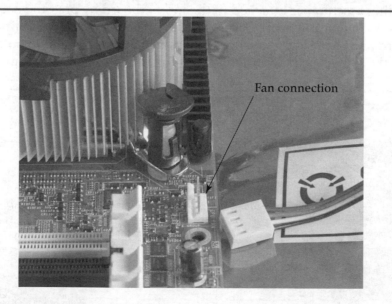

The fan connection is keyed so that the fan connector can only be inserted in one way. Only two pins are required to provide power to the fan. The extra two pins provide a means of speed control and also provide feedback to the system BIOS concerning speed.

    Copyright by Goodheart-Willcox Co., Inc.

12. ____ To complete the processor installation, you will need to connect power to the motherboard processor electrical connection connector. Today's high-performance processors require a separate electrical connection from the power supply.

CPU power connection

Even though the power connection is eight-pin, a four-pin power connecter can be used to provide power to the processor; although, it is not recommended.

13. ____ The installation procedure is complete at this time. As you can see, this would be only a portion of building a computer system. The next section is the procedure for uninstalling the processor and cooling assembly. Do not perform Part II without explicit instructions from your instructor. The instructor may designate that you do not remove the processor at this time.

14. ____ If completing the laboratory activity at this time, return all materials to their proper storage area and go on to answer the review questions. If you are not completing this laboratory activity at this time, go on to Part II—Uninstalling an Intel Core 2 Processor.

Part II—Uninstalling an Intel Core 2 Processor

Procedure

Note:
You will need the protective covers used for the cooling assembly, socket, and processor before proceeding through this portion of the laboratory activity.

1. ____ To uninstall the processor and cooling assembly, you simply reverse the installation procedure. First, make sure all power is off from the computer and that you follow anti-static procedures as outlined by your instructor.

2. ____ Unplug the electrical connections, which include the electrical power to the motherboard processor and the fan cable.

3. ____ Release each of the four cooling assembly mounting mechanisms by rotating the top of the fasteners 90° in the direction indicated on top of each fastener. Do *not* assume a counterclockwise rotation. Hold the cooling assembly in place while releasing the fasteners. When a fastener is properly released, the alignment line on top will be parallel to the cooling assembly. You may need to use a flat tip screwdriver to rotate the fastener caps. Be very careful not to let the screwdriver slip off the top of the fasteners.

4. ____ Pull the fasteners upward gently, but firmly, to unsnap each point from the motherboard.

5. ____ Place the plastic protective cover over the bottom of the cooling assembly to protect the fastener tips and the Thermal Interface Material.

Note:
The material typically cannot be reused and new material will most likely be needed to reinstall the cooling assembly.

---

6. ____ Disengage the locking lever from the locking lever tab while holding the load plate in position. Slowly release the load plate while you move the load lever into the full, open position.

7. ____ Remove the processor using a straight up vertical direction. Do *not* tilt or slide the processor.

8. ____ Place the processor back into the protective cover.

9. ____ Close the processor load plate, lock the locking lever, and replace the socket protective cover. Excess Thermal Interface Material can be removed with a soft, lint-free cloth.

10. ____ Return all materials to their proper storage area as indicated by your instructor, and then answer the review questions.

Review Questions

1. How do you hold a Core 2 processor? _____

_____

2. How do you remove debris and foreign objects such as lint from a motherboard socket? _____

_____

3. What does Intel recommend to use for difficult-to-reach mounting fasteners? _____

_____

4. What compound is used between the cooling assembly heat sink and the processor? _____

_____

5. What is the purpose of the four pins used to connect the cooling fan to the motherboard? _____

_____

_____

_____

6. How is electrical power provided to the Core 2 processor? _____

_____

Copyright by Goodheart-Willcox Co., Inc.

Name _____ Date _____

Class/Instructor _____

Using a Meter to Check Continuity

After completing this laboratory activity, you will be able to:

■ Define the term *continuity*.

■ Explain how to test conductors for continuity.

■ Explain the meaning of the term *ohms*.

■ Explain the difference between infinity and zero ohms.

Introduction

In this laboratory activity, you will use a multimeter to measure resistance in a conductor. Checking resistance in a conductor is also referred to as a continuity test. *Continuity* is the term for a continuous path for the flow of electricity. A good fuse has continuity. A typical fuse found in most electronic equipment is nothing more than a small wire enclosed in a glass tube. The wire is designed to melt when the electrical energy reaches a specific current level. When the current level is exceeded, the wire melts, thus opening the electrical path. When the electrical path is opened, there is said to be no electrical continuity.

During the last part of the laboratory activity, you will take voltage readings of various batteries. This is not a check to determine if the battery is good or bad, but rather a simple exercise to learn how to properly take voltage readings. To check if a battery is good or bad, the voltage level must be checked while the battery is installed in the equipment and the equipment is turned on. A bad battery can produce sufficient levels of voltage to appear as a good battery once it is removed from the equipment.

Equipment and Materials

■ Digital multimeter.

■ 9-volt battery.

■ 6-volt battery.

■ 1 1/2-volt battery (common "D" or "C" cell).

■ 12" of CAT-5 cable (any multiple conductor cable will do).

■ Good fuse (any available size and style).

Copyright by Goodheart-Willcox Co., Inc.

Procedure

1. ____ First, familiarize yourself with the digital multimeter you are provided with for this series of experiments. Look at the available selections, such as voltage, resistance, and current. Look at the various places on the meter where the test leads may be attached.

2. ____ Set the meter dial(s) and install the test leads into the correct input sockets to take a resistance reading. When you think the meter is set up properly to take a resistance reading, call the instructor or raise your hand. Do not continue until the instructor has given approval.

3. ____ Once the meter settings have been approved by the instructor, hold the test leads together and look at the meter display. The following illustration should assist you.

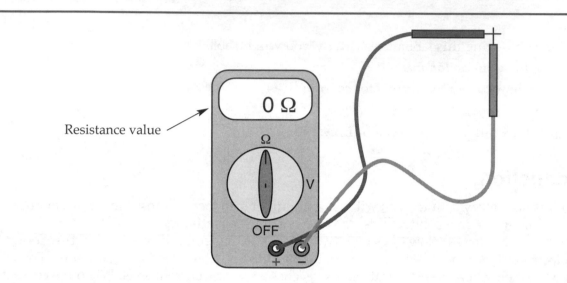

Resistance value

4. ____ Record the amount of resistance indicated on the display in the area provided.

_____

5. ____ Now, hold the leads apart and look at the meter display. Record the amount of resistance indicated on the display. _____

6. ____ Take the good fuse that you have been issued and take a resistance reading of the fuse. The following illustration may be used as a reference.

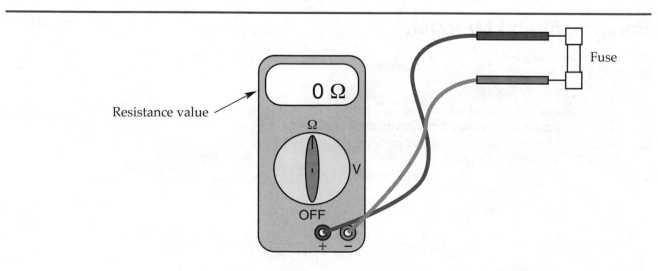

Resistance value

Fuse

Copyright by Goodheart-Willcox Co., Inc.

7. ____ Write the amount of resistance in the good fuse._____

8. ____ Take the segment of wire that you have been issued. Connect the leads to each end of the wire and check the amount of resistance as shown in the following illustration.

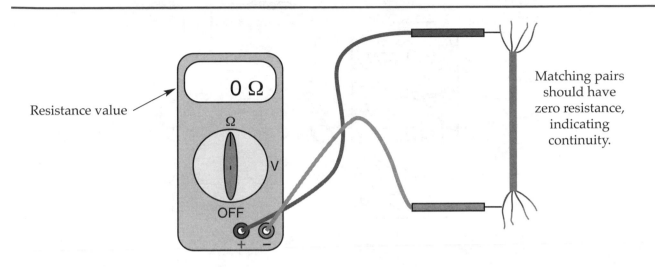

Resistance value

Matching pairs should have zero resistance, indicating continuity.

This type of check is often referred to as a continuity check. An indication of little resistance from one end to the other means the conductor has continuity. A reading of extremely high resistance or infinity means there is no continuity. No continuity is caused by a break in a conductor path. Take readings from one end of the conductor to the other end. There should be continuity between the ends of the wires with matching color. There will not be continuity between ends of the wire with different colors. Test all possible combinations of the wire strands and record your observations in the space provided. _____

_____

_____

_____

_____

_____

_____

_____

9. ____ Now, set the meter to read dc voltage. Once you have set the selector switch and are sure the leads are plugged into the appropriate jacks, call the instructor to check the meter settings before you test the batteries. Be absolutely sure the meter is set to read voltage. If a meter is set to read resistance and is connected to an electrical source, such as a battery, the meter can be permanently damaged. Remember, never connect a meter to an electrical source when the selector switch is set to take a resistance reading.

Copyright by Goodheart-Willcox Co., Inc.

10. _____ You will now read the voltage level of the three batteries provided. The following illustration may be used to assist you. Indicate the voltage of the batteries in the spaces provided.

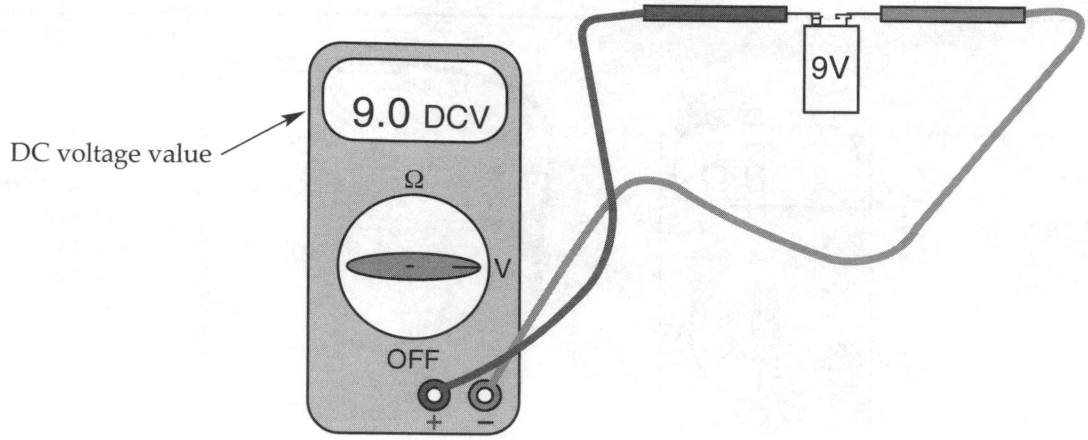

DC voltage value

Battery 1 _____

Battery 2 _____

Battery 3 _____

11. _____ Turn off the power on the multimeter and return the meter and the supplies.

Review Questions

1. When the test leads of the meter are touched together and the meter is set to measure resistance, what should the resistance reading be? _____

2. A good fuse will have how much resistance? _____

3. A blown fuse will have how much resistance? _____

4. A good continuous conductor will have how much resistance? _____

5. A conductor that is broken in two will produce what resistance value? _____

6. When checking a multi-conductor wire, how much resistance should there be between wires of different coloring? _____

7. Define *continuity*. _____

_____

8. What can happen if a meter is set up to read resistance and is then connected to electrical energy? _____

_____

_____

Copyright by Goodheart-Willcox Co., Inc.

Name _____ Date _____

Class/Instructor _____

Exploring and Replacing the Power Supply

After completing this laboratory activity, you will be able to:

■ Replace a PC power supply unit.
■ Determine if a power supply is defective.
■ Check the voltage input and output of a power supply unit.

Introduction

One of the most common PC problems encountered is a defective power supply. The power supply is considered a field replacement unit. A field replacement unit is any module in a PC system that is commonly changed in the field and does not need to be brought back to the repair shop to be replaced or upgraded. The power supply is used to convert 120-volt ac input into 12-, 5-, and 3.3-volt dc outputs. It supplies the correct dc voltage to the PC's modules and devices, such as the motherboard, hard disk drive, and CD-ROM drive. Some of the dc voltages are positive while others are negative. Some of the connections will have no voltage indicated at all. These usually indicate a ground used by system components. Power supplies come in a variety of styles and arrangements. Their physical appearance depends on the motherboard and case style.

Power supplies are classified by their wattage ratings. The wattage rating is an indication of how much electrical energy can be safely supplied to the PC's devices. In general, a higher wattage rating means that more devices can be connected to the power supply. In a typical repair scenario, you would replace a power supply with one that has the same wattage rating. However, if additional devices have been added to the computer, then the power supply may need to be upgraded to a higher wattage rating.

In this laboratory activity, you will remove the existing power supply and then reinstall it in the same PC. After reinstalling the same power supply, you will record the voltage output of the connectors. Note that not all power supplies provide the same voltage levels.

Equipment and Materials

■ Typical PC with an Intel Pentium 4 or later processor.
■ Digital multimeter to take voltage readings.

Procedure

1. ____ Power up the assigned PC and make sure it is working properly. If all is well, properly shut down the unit.

2. ____ Remove the cover from the PC's case.

Copyright by Goodheart-Willcox Co., Inc.

3. ____ Before removing any of the wiring or attempting to physically remove the power supply unit, *unplug the power cord* that runs from the power supply to the 120-volt outlet.

4. ____ Once the power cord has been removed, make a drawing of the power cables, noting their orientation to the various components. For example, draw the position of the red wires running from the power supply to the CD-ROM drive. The connector's orientation can be recorded by the color of the wiring as well as the connector identification marks.

5. ____ Carefully remove each of the power cables from the various devices. As you remove the cables, be careful not to loosen any other connections or adapter cards installed in the PC.

6. ____ After all of the wiring from the power supply has been disconnected, locate the screws that connect the power supply to the case. Carefully remove the screws, being careful not to confuse the power supply mounting screws with the screws used to mount the fan to the power supply. You should not need to remove the power supply fan. Also, do not remove any screws used to fasten the cover to the power supply.

7. ____ After the power supply has been completely removed, call your instructor to inspect your work.

8. ____ Reverse the process to reinstall the power supply. Reconnect all the devices according to your drawing. Do not plug the power cord into the power supply or the outlet until your instructor has inspected your work.

9. ____ After the instructor has approved your reinstallation of the power supply, connect the power cord and power on the PC.

10. ____ Check all devices to make sure they have power. If they do not, call your instructor.

11. ____ Now, take voltage readings at each of the different connectors running from the power supply. You need to turn the power off, sketch the connectors and wiring, disconnect the power cables to the devices, and then reapply power to the power supply. Finally, measure the voltages at each terminal in the various connectors. Use the following illustration as a guide when creating your own sketches. *Be aware that the example given is not intended to match your unit but simply to serve as a model.*

3.3 V+	O	O	3.3 V+
12 V-	O	O	3.3 V+
0	O	O	0
0	O	O	5 V+
0	O	O	0
0	O	O	5 V+
0	O	O	0
5 V-	O	O	0
5 V+	O	O	5 V+
5 V+	O	O	12 V+

Warning:
Disconnecting a power connector from any device while the device is energized could result in permanent damage to the device. This is especially true for the motherboard.

12. ____ After recording all voltages at each power connection, return the PC to its original condition.

Copyright by Goodheart-Willcox Co., Inc.

Name_____

Review Questions

1. What other components of the PC affect the power supply's appearance? _____

_____

_____

2. Do all power supplies supply the same voltages? _____

3. What is the power supply function in the PC?_____

_____

4. What is the wattage rating of the power supply in your test unit? _____

5. What is the rated input voltage and frequency? (Look on the power supply.) _____

_____

Copyright by Goodheart-Willcox Co., Inc.

Notes

Copyright by Goodheart-Willcox Co., Inc.

Name _____ Date _____

Class/Instructor _____

Viewing RAM and Virtual Memory Information

After completing this laboratory activity, you will be able to:

■ Identify the amount of RAM installed in the PC.

■ Identify the amount of virtual memory.

■ Access the Resource Monitor utility.

Introduction

There are several different ways to identify the amount of memory installed in a typical PC. The amount of memory is revealed to the user during the power-on-self-test (POST). The RAM is tested and the results are displayed on the screen during the POST. On many computers, the POST is hidden from view because a splash screen is displayed during the POST. To see the POST, you may need to access the BIOS Setup program and select the BIOS option that will allow the POST to be viewed.

In Windows XP, you can view the amount of RAM installed by accessing **Control Panel | System**. The **System Properties** dialog box will display and reveal the amount of physical RAM installed as well as the type of processor.

In Windows Vista, you can view the amount of RAM installed by accessing **Control Panel | System**. The Windows Vista **System Properties** dialog box reveals similar information as Windows XP.

The quickest way to access System Properties is to right-click **My Computer** in Windows XP or right-click **Computer** in Windows Vista and then select **Properties** from the shortcut menu.

You can also view part of the RAM information for the first 1 MB by entering **mem** at the command prompt. To access the command prompt in Windows XP, type **cmd** in the **Run** dialog box located off the **Start** menu. To access the command prompt in Windows Vista, type **cmd** in the **Search** box located off the **Start** menu.

You can also view more detailed information about the RAM by typing **msinfo32** into the **Start Search** box in Windows Vista or **msinfo32** in the **Run** dialog box in Windows XP. This will bring up the System Information program. This program reveals the physical amount of RAM installed in the system, the total amount of virtual memory, the amount of virtual memory available, and the size of the page file.

Virtual memory is actually a portion of the hard disk drive that is assigned to function as RAM when the entire available RAM has been committed to software programs. Some programs are memory intense, which means they require a lot of memory to perform. Some examples of memory-intense software programs are programs designed to edit pictures, images, music, and videos. These types of data collections require large blocks of memory.

Virtual memory can fill these requirements when all available RAM has been used. Virtual RAM is not as fast as physical RAM, but it will allow you to run software programs that would not

Copyright by Goodheart-Willcox Co., Inc.

be available to you if the entire RAM was used. Check the Help and Support files located on the Windows operating system to learn more about virtual memory.

If you are using Windows Vista for this laboratory activity, you will also access the Resource Monitor to view information about system memory.

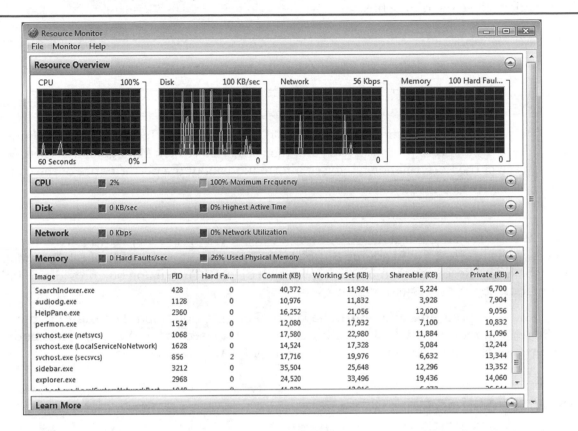

Resource Monitor contains very detailed and extensive information concerning the system memory, CPU, disk drives, and network system. There will be more about the Resource Monitor program in later laboratory activities.

Equipment and Materials

■ Typical PC with 500 MB RAM and Windows XP or Windows Vista, or both installed.

Procedure

1. ____ Report to your assigned workstation.

2. ____ Boot the PC and watch the display closely for the RAM information displayed during the POST. If a splash screen is used to hide the POST results, you may change the BIOS configuration if you have your instructor's permission to do so. Once the BIOS is changed to reveal the POST results, restart the computer and observe the RAM information.

3. ____ Access the **System Properties** dialog box by right-clicking **My Computer** (Windows XP) or **Computer** (Windows Vista) and then selecting **Properties** from the shortcut menu.

4. ____ Record in the space provided the amount of RAM revealed by the **System Properties** dialog box and then close the dialog box.

5. _____ Now, use the System Information (**msinfo32**) program to view information about RAM. In Windows XP, enter **msinfo32** into the **Run** dialog box. In Windows Vista, enter **msinfo32** into the **Search** box. Record, in the space provided, the total amount of physical memory, total amount of virtual memory, available virtual memory, and page file space. After recording the information, close the dialog box.

_____

_____

_____

_____

6. _____ Now, press the key combination [Ctrl] [Alt] [Del] to start the Task Manager in Windows XP. In Windows Vista, press [Ctrl] [Alt] [Del] and then select **Start Task Manager**. After Task Manager appears, select the **Performance** tab to see information about the performance of the computer. In the space provided, record the amount of memory available.

_____

7. _____ If you are using Windows XP for this lab activity, skip this step. If you are using Windows Vista, select the **Resource Button** located at the bottom left side of the **Task Manager** dialog box. The Resource Monitor dialog box will display. This dialog box provides detailed information about the system memory.

8. _____ Close all programs and return the PC to its original condition. Then, answer the review questions. You may leave the PC running so that you can access the Windows Help and Support files to assist you with answering some of the review questions.

Review Questions

1. Where is virtual memory located? _____

2. What is the purpose of virtual memory? _____

_____

3. Approximately how much memory is revealed when you run **mem** at the command prompt?

_____

4. Explain how to use the **msinfo32** command to view system information in Windows XP and in Windows Vista. _____

_____

5. How do you access Task Manager in Windows XP and Windows Vista? _____

_____

Copyright by Goodheart-Willcox Co., Inc.

Name _____ Date _____

Class/Instructor _____

Installing and Upgrading Memory

After completing this laboratory activity, you will be able to:

- Install DDR RAM.
- Describe the symptoms of a defective memory module.
- Describe computer systems that indicate a need for more RAM.
- Determine the technical characteristics of the memory installed on the PC.

Introduction

One of the most common jobs of a PC technician is upgrading memory or installing new memory when building a computer system. The identification and selection of the correct type of memory can often be the most challenging part of an upgrade. Before additional memory can be added, the current memory must be identified. Additional memory should match the existing memory in the PC. The following is a list from the textbook describing the concerns that need to be addressed when upgrading memory:

- **Physical Shape:** What type of memory will be upgraded or replaced? Are you adding DDR, DDR2, or DDR3? Is the computer a laptop requiring a small outline SO-DIMM memory package?
- **Quantity:** What is the total amount of RAM desired? Are you adding to existing RAM or replacing it?
- **Parity or Non-parity:** Does the existing memory have parity checking? Does the existing system support parity checking?
- **Voltage:** At what voltage do the memory chips operate (5 volts, 3.3 volts, or less)?
- **Type:** What type of memory chip will be installed—DDR, DDR2, DDR3?
- **Speed:** Will the existing chip speed be matched or exceeded?

To answer these questions correctly, you must cover all the material in the textbook and correctly identify the type of memory installed in the PC. The physical design of the memory can be misleading. For example, DIMMs may all appear identical, but some proprietary memory modules have non-standard keys. In such cases, attempting to add additional memory or replace existing memory with a nonproprietary memory module could be disastrous. Also, be aware that the three most commonly encountered DIMM RAM is DDR, DDR2, and DDR3, and that they are not compatible. You cannot replace any of the three types of RAM with an older or newer version. Each of the three types of DDR use a key notch in a different location, preventing them from being used in a motherboard designed for one of the three specific types of DDR. In the last laboratory activity, you were taught how to view RAM performance. Some signs of a need to upgrade or add additional RAM are as follows:

- Constant hard drive activity caused by the system using part of the hard drive as virtual RAM.
- Slow screen updates, especially ones with intensive graphics.
- Slow program performance, especially when opening new programs or switching between programs.

Copyright by Goodheart-Willcox Co., Inc.

DIMM can be installed as a single unit or in pairs. When installed in pairs, the DIMM take advantage of dual-channel technology. Motherboards capable of supporting dual-channel technology typically identify the pairs of matched DIMM sockets with color coding. For example, motherboard with four DIMM sockets may have one pair in black and the other pair in white. Any color can be used because the color of the socket has no meaning by itself. The color is used only to identify socket pairs. Look at the following image.

Notice that there are four DIMM sockets: two black and two white. You would install the DDR in one of the two pair indicated by color. Always consult the motherboard manual if available as to which pair of sockets to use for a single pair. In most instances, either pair can be used, but some motherboards recommend a specific pair to be used first.

After the DDR module is inserted in a direct downward motion, the locking levers will automatically close, thus holding the RAM in the socket.

Locking lever in open position

Locking lever in closed position

Be sure to match the memory module notch key with the memory socket position to ensure the memory is installed correctly as shown in the following illustration.

Copyright by Goodheart-Willcox Co., Inc.

Name _____

Equipment and Materials

- A typical PC with DDR, DDR2, or DDR3 installed.
- Anti-static bag, or other type of anti-static container, for temporary storage of a memory module.
- Internet access is also required for assistance in memory identification.

Procedure

1. ____ Boot the PC to be sure it is in working order before you begin the laboratory activity. If the PC is in working order, properly shut it down and prepare to remove the case. Be sure to follow all anti-static procedures as outlined by your instructor.

2. ____ With the electrical power shut off to the PC, remove the PC case.

3. ____ Locate the RAM on the motherboard.

4. ____ Remove all RAM memory from the PC. To remove a DIMM, simply locate the release levers on each end of the memory socket and move them into an outward direction as shown in the following illustration. DIMMs are inserted and removed vertically. Place the memory unit on an anti-static surface.

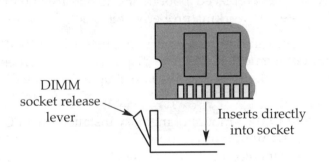

DIMM socket release lever

Inserts directly into socket

5. ____ Look closely at the memory module for identification marks and a manufacturer's name. Record any information found on the memory module. All numbers are important. Go to the Internet and attempt to find the manufacturer of the memory unit. If the exact manufacturer cannot be determined, look up information on the PC at the PC manufacturer's Web site. You may also identify the motherboard, and then go to the motherboard manufacturer's Web site for memory information. List the information about the memory, such as speed, type, and parity issues, in the space provided.

_____

_____

_____

_____

_____

_____

_____

_____

Copyright by Goodheart-Willcox Co., Inc.

6. ____ Before replacing the memory unit, apply power to the PC and boot the system. Observe the sequence of messages on the screen. Write down, in general terms, what is observed and any error messages that may appear.

_____

_____

_____

_____

_____

7. ____ Power down the PC and then replace the RAM memory module(s). Be sure to properly align the notches at the bottom of the memory module with the key notches in the memory socket on the motherboard. This will ensure that you do not install the memory modules backward.

To insert a DIMM, align the memory module with its socket. When the module and socket are perfectly aligned, gently push straight down on the module. When the module is as far down in the socket as it will go, locate the levers on each end of the socket. Move each lever into the upright position. This should seat the memory module at the bottom of the socket and lock it in place.

8. ____ After the memory has been replaced, boot the PC to be sure you have properly installed the memory and that the system is working properly. If it is not, call your instructor.

9. ____ After removing and reinstalling the memory module(s), boot the PC and watch the screen to see if the amount of memory installed is displayed on the screen during the POST. The memory should be displayed, unless the BIOS is set up to hide the display during a system boot.

Another way to quickly identify the amount of memory installed on a PC is to right-click **My Computer** in Windows XP or **Computer** in Windows Vista and then select **Properties**. The amount of RAM installed is displayed under the **General** tab in the **System Properties** dialog box.

11. ____ Close the **System Properties** dialog box, and return the PC to its original condition before leaving the lab area.

Copyright by Goodheart-Willcox Co., Inc.

Review Questions

1. DIMM is installed in pairs to take advantage of _____. _____

2. Where can you find specific technical information about the memory modules installed in the PC? _____

   _____

   _____

   _____

3. What precautions should be taken when removing and replacing memory? _____

   _____

   _____

4. What are three signs that a PC needs more memory? _____

   _____

   _____

   _____

5. What is the fastest way to check how much memory is installed? _____

   _____

   _____

   _____

   _____

Copyright by Goodheart-Willcox Co., Inc.

Copyright by Goodheart-Willcox Co., Inc.

Name _____ Date _____

Class/Instructor _____

Windows XP Performance Tool

After completing this laboratory activity, you will be able to:

- Identify several ways to access Windows XP Performance tool.
- Determine the acceptable performance levels of CPU and page file usage.

Introduction

The only real objective way to judge the performance of a system's CPU and RAM to determine upgrading or replacement needs is through the Windows XP Performance tool. The Performance tool allows you to view a graphic analysis of processor, memory, and hard disk drive activity. There are several ways to access Performance. One way is through the Microsoft Management Console. The other way is to enter **perfmon** or **perfmon.msc** in the **Run** dialog box. A screen similar to the following will display with default monitoring of three objects: memory, physical disk, and processor.

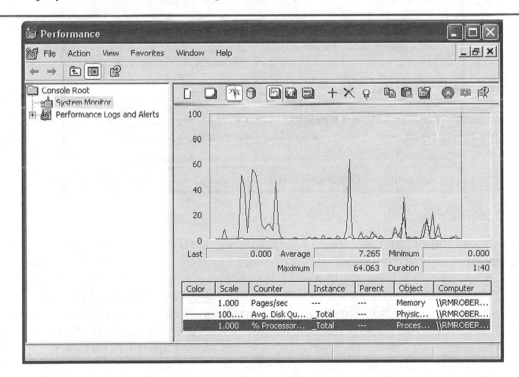

The Performance tool provides a graphic analysis of factors affecting the computer. Some of the items that can be monitored and displayed are memory, cache, page file, physical disk, CPU, and network interface. In general, you can tell if there is a performance problem by viewing the graph. A

Copyright by Goodheart-Willcox Co., Inc.

very high graph reading typically indicates a problem with the associated object being monitored. The screen capture is printed in black and white and shades of gray. The actual Performance tool display is in full color. A unique color is used for each object graphed.

In the previous screen capture, the top line in the graph represents pages per second (pages/sec). It is showing a good indication that more memory is needed. Adding more memory is the most common way to improve a computer's performance.

Another way to access the Performance tool is through the Task Manager. Simply open Task Manager and select the **Performance** tab. Look at the following screen capture to see the **Performance** tab of the **Task Manager** dialog box.

Two of the most important indicators of performance are shown: CPU usage and page file usage. The page file is the virtual memory. CPU usage in excess of 80% to 85 % and page file usage (PF Usage) in excess of 600 MB for Windows XP is considered unacceptable by Microsoft standards.

A high CPU rate indicates that the CPU cannot process data at a rate that provides the best software application performance. For example, a very intensive software application such as Adobe GoLive, AutoCAD, and 3D gaming programs can cause a CPU to register a performance of 100%, which makes the computer system appear as though it is locked up. If CPU usage is high, you can correct this condition by replacing the CPU with one that has more cache or performs at a higher clock rate, or both. However, this is not always an option because a better processor may also require a new motherboard.

Another indicator of performance is the page file usage (PF Usage). The page is created from available space on the hard disk drive. It is used to augment the RAM. When the memory is over-burdened, the page file area of the hard disk drive is used to supplement the RAM. Too much page

Copyright by Goodheart-Willcox Co., Inc.

file activity typically is an indication that there is insufficient RAM available for the system. Page file usage in excess of 600 MB is considered excessive and is unacceptable.

The performance monitoring tools should be used when the computer is under normal usage. A computer that simply has Performance running will have very low readings because no application software is running. This principle will be illustrated in this laboratory activity.

You should concentrate on how to access Performance and be able to interpret the screen display to determine when more RAM or a higher-performance CPU is needed. Also, be aware that some motherboards are designed to accommodate more than one CPU.

Equipment and Materials

- Computer with Windows XP installed.
- Internet connection (optional).

Procedure

1. ____ Report to your assigned workstation.

2. ____ Boot the computer and verify it is in working order.

3. ____ In the **Run** dialog box located off the **Start** menu, enter **perfmon** or **perfmon.msc**. The Performance tool should appear on the screen.

4. ____ While Performance is running, open several applications as though you were working. Open Notepad, WordPad, Paint, and Windows Explorer, and then connect to an Internet site.

5. ____ Look at the Performance tool and see how data was collected and graphed.

6. ____ Now, click the **Add** button from the **Performance** toolbar. The **Add** button is represented by the plus sign (+).

After clicking the **Add** button, the **Add Counters** dialog box will appear similar to the one in the following screen capture.

Select objects such as processor, physical disk, and page file

Explain objects selected

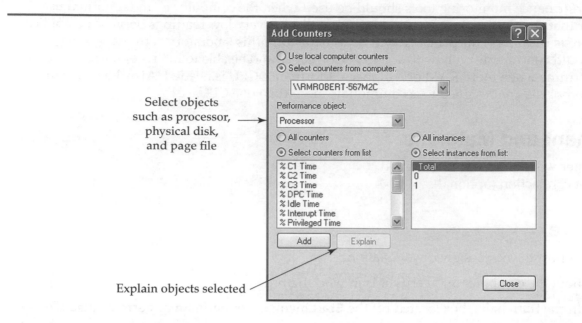

Most of the counter functions are well beyond the needs of the computer technician. Most are geared for software programmers and system engineers. Take a few minutes to look at several Performance objects and counters. Use the **Explain** button to see a brief explanation of the counter.

7. ____ Close Performance and then press [Ctrl] [Alt] [Del] to open the Task Manager.

8. ____ After Task Manager appears, select the **Performance** tab. You should see the CPU usage/ history and page file (PF) usage/history. This is the area you would use as a technician to check the CPU's performance and to determine if sufficient RAM is installed. Excessive page file usage indicates more RAM is needed.

9. ____ With the Task Manager opened and the **Performance** tab selected, open several programs and watch the effect on the CPU and page file. Suggested programs to open are Notepad, WordPad, Paint, and Windows Explorer. Also, connect to an Internet site if Internet access is available. If you have a more system-intensive application such as Adobe GoLive or some graphics application installed, you may use it simply for demonstration purposes.

10. ____ After running step 9 for a few minutes, close Task Manager and all open applications. Then, go on to answer the review questions.

    Copyright by Goodheart-Willcox Co., Inc.

Name_____

Review Questions

1. What command can be entered in the **Run** dialog box to start the Performance tool? _____
   _____

2. What are the three default objects monitored by Performance? _____
   _____

3. What are the two objects monitored and displayed graphically in Task Manager under the
   Performance tab? _____

4. Above what percentage is the CPU considered overloaded? _____

5. What is the most common way to improve computer performance? _____
   _____

Copyright by Goodheart-Willcox Co., Inc.

Name _____ Date _____

Class/Instructor _____

Windows Vista Reliability and Performance Monitor

After completing this laboratory activity, you will be able to:

■ Access the Windows Vista Reliability and Performance Monitor using several different methods.

■ Define *computer performance.*

■ Define *computer reliability.*

■ Describe the purpose of Reliability Monitor.

■ Describe the purpose of Performance Monitor.

■ Describe the purpose of the System Diagnostics utility.

■ Identify command prompt commands associated with the Windows Vista Reliability and Performance Monitor.

Introduction

Windows Vista made dramatic changes for monitoring computer performance by introducing the Reliability and Performance Monitor. This utility is actually a centralized collection of previous performance monitoring applications. Other features have been added as well. Some aspects of the Reliability and Performance Monitor are very sophisticated and well beyond the needs of the computer technician. Many features require a much higher level of understanding computer science and are geared for software engineers, system analysts, hardware designers, and network analysts. This laboratory activity emphasizes the aspects important to a computer technician. It also provides references or those interested in more detailed information.

Computer performance is a measure of how quickly a computer completes software application and system hardware tasks. Computer performance is based on four components: CPU, memory, hard disk drive, and network throughput.

A computer's reliability is a measure of how well the computer system, both hardware and software, meet the expectations of the configuration. It is measured by how often a computer software application, driver, or service fails to start, stop, restart, and initialize.

There are many different ways to access the Reliability and Performance Monitor. It can be accessed through the Task Manager by selecting the **Performance** tab and clicking the **Resource Monitor** button or by entering "Reliability and Performance" in the **Search** dialog box located off the **Start** menu. The **Reliability and Performance** option will appear in the list under **Programs** immediately after the letter *R* is typed.

The Reliability and Performance Monitor can also be accessed through the Computer Management console by right-clicking **Computer**, selecting **Manage** from the shortcut menu, and then clicking **Reliability and Performance**, which is located in the left pane. From Control Panel, it is accessed through **System and Maintenance | Administrative Tools | Reliability and Performance Monitor**.

You can also start the Reliability and Performance Monitor from the command prompt when the command prompt is run with the **Run as Administrator** option. At the command prompt, simply enter **perfmon**.

Copyright by Goodheart-Willcox Co., Inc.

The Reliability and Performance Monitor is actually three tools: Resource Overview, Performance Monitor, and System Monitor. The Resource Overview is opened by default when you select Reliability and Performance from the Computer Management console or when you run **perfmon** from the command line. Look at the results in the following screen capture of the Resource Overview. You will see a graphical display of the four main resources: CPU, disk, network, and memory.

The display is in "real time," which means as it actually is happening. You can see accumulation

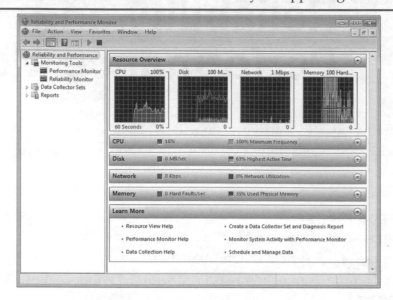

of 60 seconds of data in each of the four displays. The **Learn More** section is provided as a resource for how to use the Reliability and Performance Monitor and is directly connected to the Help and Support files located on the local computer. You will want to review these files during the laboratory activity.

A more common method to access performance information is through the Task Manager, which has been improved over previous versions. Simply use the familiar [Ctrl] [Alt] [Del] key combination and then click **Start Task Manager**. When Task Manager appears, select the **Performance** tab. You will first see a dialog box similar to the following.

Copyright by Goodheart-Willcox Co., Inc.

Task Manager is the most commonly used performance monitor used by technicians. It provides a quick analysis of computer performance. On the **Performance** page, you can see the two main computer components that directly affect computer performance: CPU and memory.

Notice how the number of process, CPU usage, and physical memory percentage is listed at the bottom of the **Task Manager** dialog box. When the CPU usage runs consistently above 80% or the physical memory runs consistently over 80%, a problem is indicated. It is not unusual to encounter a computer system that flat lines CPU usage or memory at the top of the graph, indicating a severe problem with performance.

Most computers perform very well when no software applications are opened or being used. This is referred to as *idle condition*. To test the computer system performance, you need to open and use software applications. Graphically-intense applications such as drawing programs, Web page making programs, computer-aided drafting programs, and games will produce intense conditions. These types of programs can be used to test the system. Also, rely on an interview with the computer users. They can tell you when they are experiencing slow or locked-up conditions. Ask them what programs they were using at the time the problem occurred.

A new utility first introduced in Windows Vista is the Reliability Monitor. The Reliability Monitor measures the reliability of the computer system based on the number and type of incidents and then scores the system with an index from 1.0 to 10.0, with 10 being the best score and 1 being the worst. Look at the following screen capture of the Reliability Monitor.

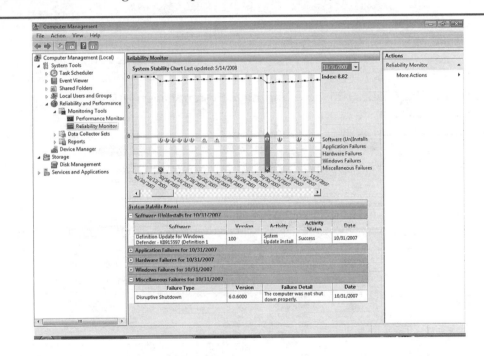

The Reliability Monitor data is gathered every hour from event logs and is then processed once every twenty-four hours to generate a report of events that have occurred. Events are those that have affected the computer system correlated to software applications, software drivers, hardware failures, or Windows operating system failures. The information is then presented in chart form with corresponding dates and which part of the system generated the problem. Events are indicated with symbols such as "i" indicating information of an event, such as the successful update of an antivirus program. The exclamation mark (!) on a yellow background is used to indicate a warning of an event, such as a driver software update failure. An X on a red background indicates a critical event or error, such as a complete improper system shutdown. The icons make it easy to spot a type of event that has occurred over a period of time. The Reliability Monitor makes a great resource for troubleshooting a customer's computer when they report occurrences of a problem over a period of time such as a week or longer.

Copyright by Goodheart-Willcox Co., Inc.

System Diagnostics is a special tool that diagnoses the system when a problem is suspected. To start System Diagnostics, select **Start | Control Panel | System and Maintenance | Performance Information and Tools**. From the left pane under **Advanced Tools**, click **Generate a system health report**. Once started, it runs for approximately sixty seconds. Look at the following screen capture to see what System Diagnostics looks like while it is running.

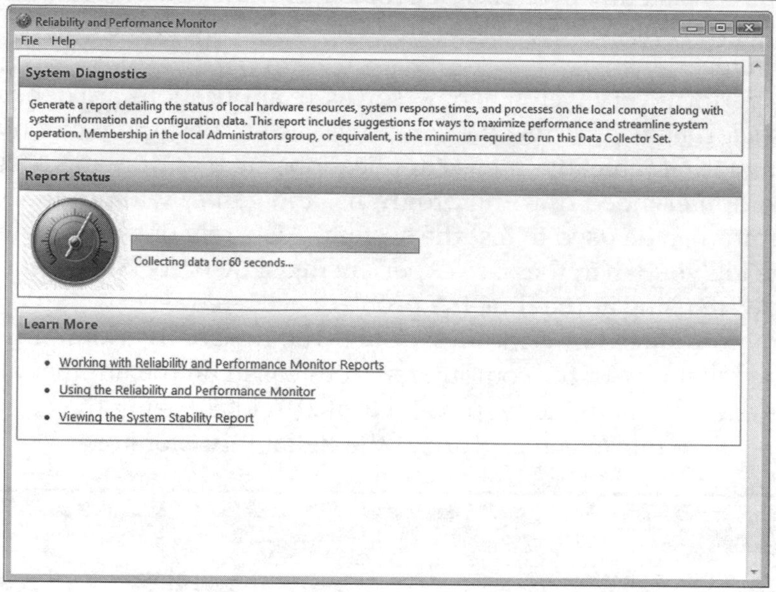

After the System Diagnostics finishes running, a System Diagnostics report is generated similar to the one in the following screen capture.

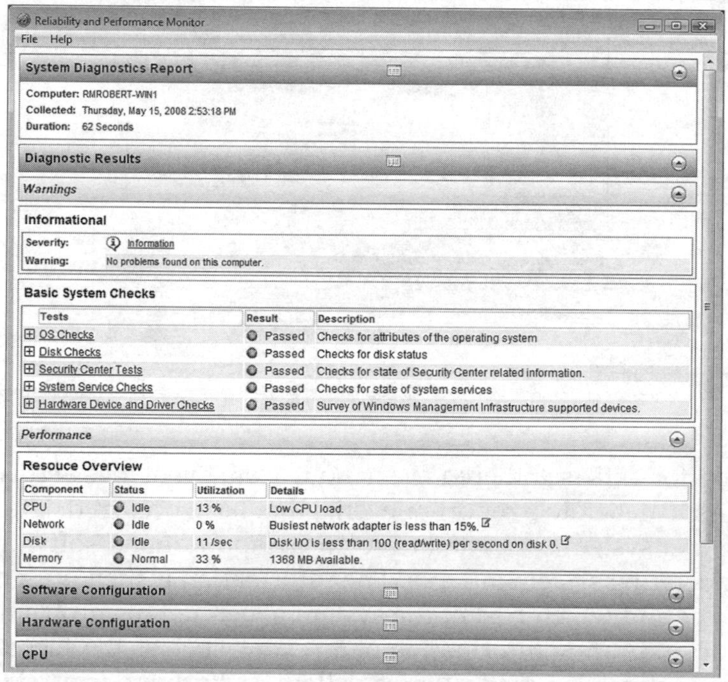

The diagnostic report generates information about the system for the four basic resources: CPU, network, disk, and memory. This information does not need to be generated only when a problem is suspected. A System Diagnostics report can be generated when the computer system is first built to establish a performance baseline. The baseline can be used for comparison at a later date and time.

Copyright by Goodheart-Willcox Co., Inc.

Performance Monitor is used to capture and display computer system performance using counters. Look at the following screen capture of Performance Monitor.

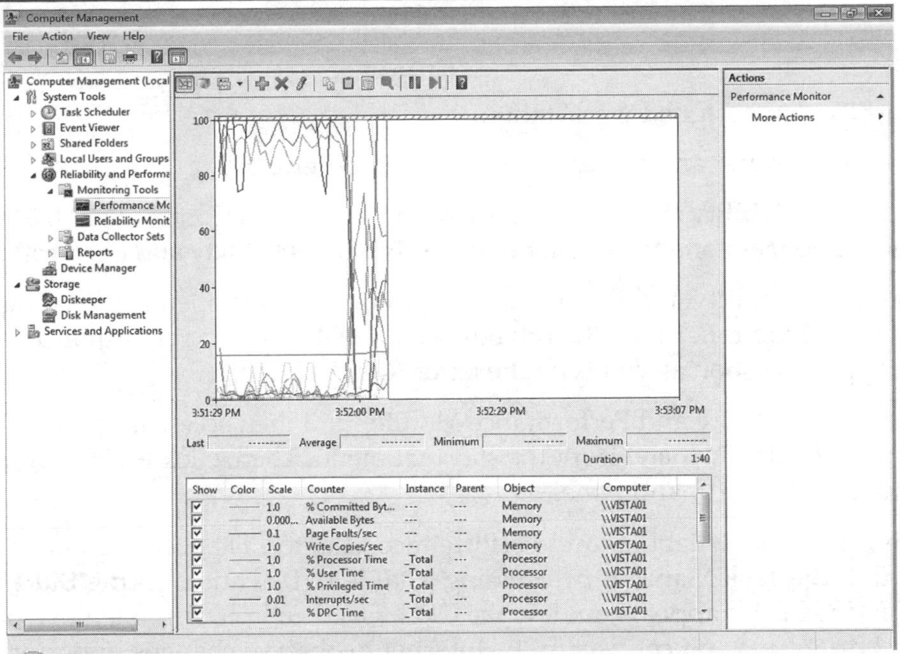

There are many different counters available to choose from, such as number of page faults per second, available bytes, and cache bytes peak. Most of the counters are well beyond the scope of a typical PC technician. The counters are more appropriately applied by software engineers and hardware designers for sophisticated analysis. For entry-level computer technicians, you need only be aware that Performance Monitor exists and how to configure a simple counter.

You should be aware that you can also launch Reliability and Performance Monitor from the command line. First, right-click the **Command Prompt** menu item in the **Start** menu and select **Run as Administrator** from the shortcut menu. Then enter **perfmon** with one of the following four command switches: **sys**, **report**, **rel**, and **res**. The following is a summary of four common command entries used to access Performance and Reliability Monitor:

Command and Switch	Description
perfmon/sys	Launches Reliability and Performance Monitor.
perfmon/report	Generates a status report from the System Diagnostics utility.
perfmon/rel	Launches Reliability Monitor in standalone mode.
perfmon/res	Launches Resource Overview in standalone mode.

For more detailed information about Reliability and Performance Monitor, use the Windows Vista Help and Support feature located off the **Start** menu. You can also conduct an Internet search using the key words "Microsoft Vista Performance and Reliability Monitoring." You will generate a vast amount of information.

Copyright by Goodheart-Willcox Co., Inc.

Equipment and Materials

■ Computer with Windows Vista installed.

Procedure

1. ____ Report to your assigned workstation.

2. ____ Boot the computer and verify it is in working order.

3. ____ Open the Reliability and Performance Monitor through Control Panel: **Start | Control Panel | System and Maintenance | Administrative Tools | Reliability and Performance Monitor**.

4. ____ Close the Reliability and Performance Monitor and then open it by typing "Reliability and Performance Monitor" in the **Search** box. The Reliability and Performance Monitor application should appear as soon as you type the letter *R*.

5. ____ Close the Reliability and Performance Monitor and then access it by right-clicking **Computer** and selecting **Manage** from the shortcut menu. Then, click **Reliability and Performance** from the left-hand pane.

6. ____ Again, close the Reliability and Performance Monitor. Then, access performance information through the Task Manager by pressing [Ctrl] [Alt] [Del] and clicking **Start Task Manager**. When the Task Manager appears, review the CPU usage and physical memory percentages. Open several programs and connect to the Internet to observe changes in performance as presented on the Task Manager **Performance** tab.

7. ____ Close Task Manager and open the Computer Management console by right-clicking **Computer** and selecting **Manage** from the shortcut menu. Select the **Reliability and Performance** option. The **Resource Overview** screen should appear and the four resource charts should start displaying real time data.

8. ____ Click each of the four charts once to open and then once to close the detailed information about the resource. Look at the detailed information in each of the four resource categories. Much of the detailed information will appear very cryptic. This information is more appropriate for an advanced technician. For now, just be aware that detailed information does exist and can be viewed through this tool.

9. ____ In the left-hand pane, click the arrow left of the Reliability and Performance entry to expand the tree. You should see Monitoring Tools subfolder with **Performance Monitor** and **Reliability Monitor** listed beneath it like that in the following screen capture.

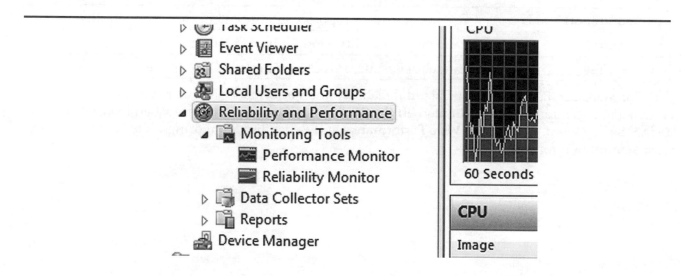

Copyright by Goodheart-Willcox Co., Inc.

10. ____ Click **Reliability Monitor**. You should see the System Stability Chart. Use the scroll bar below the chart to view the dates and see if any events have occurred.

11. ____ Select different dates along the chart and observe how the index rating changes. The index rating is in the upper-right corner of the chart and appears as the following partial screen capture.

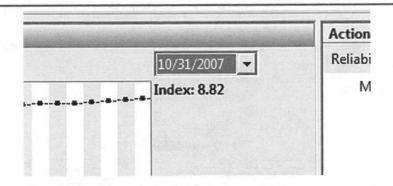

12. ____ Click the drop-down arrow of the box above the index rating. You will see options to select a specific date and to show all dates. Choose the option to select a date and a calendar of events will appear. Dates on the calendar in bold are dates that events occurred. Select a bolded date and view the contents for that date.

13. ____ Now, open Performance Monitor by clicking **Performance Monitor**, which is located in the left-hand pane within the Monitoring Tools subfolder.

14. ____ Click the **Add** button (green plus sign) located in the toolbar. The **Add Counters** dialog box will appear, enabling you to view the various counters available to monitor.

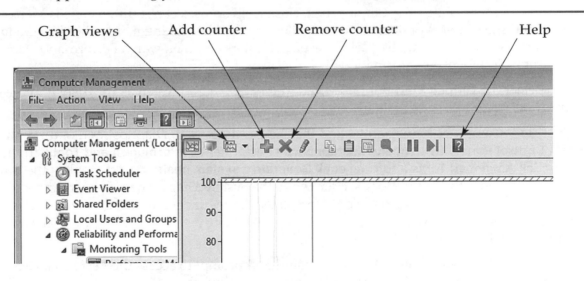

Select the counter or counters you desire and then click the **Add** button to add the counter to the monitor. At the bottom of the dialog box, a description is provided for each counter if the **Show description** option is enabled. After selecting one or more counters, click **OK**. The monitor automatically starts gathering information based on the counters you selected.

15. ____ Now, click the **Help** button (question mark in a blue square) located in the toolbar to view the help files available for Performance Monitor. Take a few minutes to review the contents of the "Add Counters Dialog Box" topic. Then, close Help and select a counter such as Memory and expand the contents of memory counter item by double-clicking it. You should see a long list of various counters available. Select several counters and then watch Performance Monitor as it gathers and displays information.

16. ____ Select the **Graphs View** button located in the toolbar and watch as the display changes from a line graph to a bar graph and then finally to a text-based report.

17. ____ Close Computer Management and then access the System Diagnostics tool through **Start | Control Panel | System and Maintenance | Performance Information and Tools**. In the left pane, click **Advanced Tools** and then click **Generate a system health report**. Look at the three topics listed under the **Learn More** section while the System Diagnostics is generating a report. After a minute or two, the diagnostics is completed. You will need to use the scroll bar on the right side to view all parts of the report. The report is quite detailed and lengthy. Take a few minutes to review the contents of the report.

18. ____ Now, take a few minutes to use the command prompt to access the Performance and Reliability Monitor using the following commands and switches.

- **perfmon/sys** to launch the Reliability and Performance Monitor.
- **perfmon/report** to generate a status report from the System Diagnostics utility.
- **perfmon/rel** to launch Reliability Monitor in standalone mode.
- **perfmon/res** to launch Resource Overview in standalone mode.

19. ____ Close all open tools, and then go on to answer the review questions. You may use the Help and Support option to assist you with the questions.

Copyright by Goodheart-Willcox Co., Inc.

Review Questions

1. Which version of Microsoft operating system first introduced Reliability Monitor?_____
_____

2. Define *reliability*. _____
_____
_____

3. Define *performance*. _____
_____

4. What four resources are viewed by default in the Resource View of Reliability and Performance Monitor?_____

5. What two major computer components directly affect computer performance the most? _____
_____

6. Which major computer component is typically replaced or augmented to improve performance?
_____

7. What is the range of the System Stability Chart?_____

8. What symbol is used by Reliability Monitor to indicate a critical condition or error?_____
_____

9. What symbol is used by Reliability Monitor to indicate an event such as a successful update of an anti-virus program? _____

10. What symbol is used by Reliability Monitor to indicate an event such as failure to properly load a driver, but the event is not critical? _____
_____

11. What is the path for running a system health report? _____
_____
_____

12. Which command line command and switch is used to start the Reliability Monitor only? _____
_____

13. Which command line command is used to launch Resource Overview? _____
_____

14. Which command line command is used to launch Reliability and Performance Monitor together?_____
_____

15. Which command line command is used to launch System Diagnostics and generate a report on the status of the computer? _____

Copyright by Goodheart-Willcox Co., Inc.

Copyright by Goodheart-Willcox Co., Inc.

Name _____ Date _____

Class/Instructor _____

Windows Vista Memory Diagnostics Tool

After completing this laboratory activity, you will be able to:

■ Start and run the Windows Memory Diagnostics Tool.

■ Apply advanced options for the Windows Memory Diagnostics Tool.

Introduction

In this laboratory activity, you will run the Windows Memory Diagnostics Tool to determine if there is a problem with computer memory. The executable file name for the Windows Memory Diagnostics Tool is mdsched.exe.

Computer RAM is composed of millions of microscopic transistors and capacitors at an unbelievably small scale. Anyone of these millions of locations could cause a problem with computer operation. The type of problem can vary. Each memory cell represents a binary one or a zero. The memory may fail to retain the binary value, or it may never change the value. The memory may fail to retain the value after a certain length of time or after a certain temperature is reached. Memory contents may be used to store data or store a vital part of a software application program, driver, or required file for booting the computer. As a result of the critical role of memory in the proper operation of a computer system, Microsoft has incorporated a diagnostic tool into Windows Vista to test the memory.

The Windows Memory Diagnostics Tool writes and stores a series of one's into all memory locations and then checks the sum total through addition. The tool then stores a series of zeros in memory locations and checks the sum total by adding all the memory cell values together. The Windows Memory Diagnostics Tool makes several passes. The term *passes* as related to the Windows Memory Diagnostics Tool means that the series of ones and zeros is repeated several times. Each time is referred to as a *pass*. This is a simple explanation of how memory is tested. There are several different ways to start the Windows Memory Diagnostics Tool. You can use the **Search** box located on the **Start** menu. Simply start typing "Memory" and the Windows Memory Diagnostics Tool will appear in the search list.

You can access the Windows Memory Diagnostics Tool through Control Panel. Simply follow the path **Start I Control Panel I System and Maintenance I Administrative Tools I Memory Diagnostics Tool**.

You can also start the Windows Memory Diagnostics Tool from the command prompt when using the elevated privilege "Run as Administrator." Simply type and enter **mdsched** or the complete file name **mdsched.exe** at the command prompt.

A dialog box will appear, prompting to either restart the computer now or check the computer memory the next time the computer is started. The following screen capture shows the exact options you will be presented with.

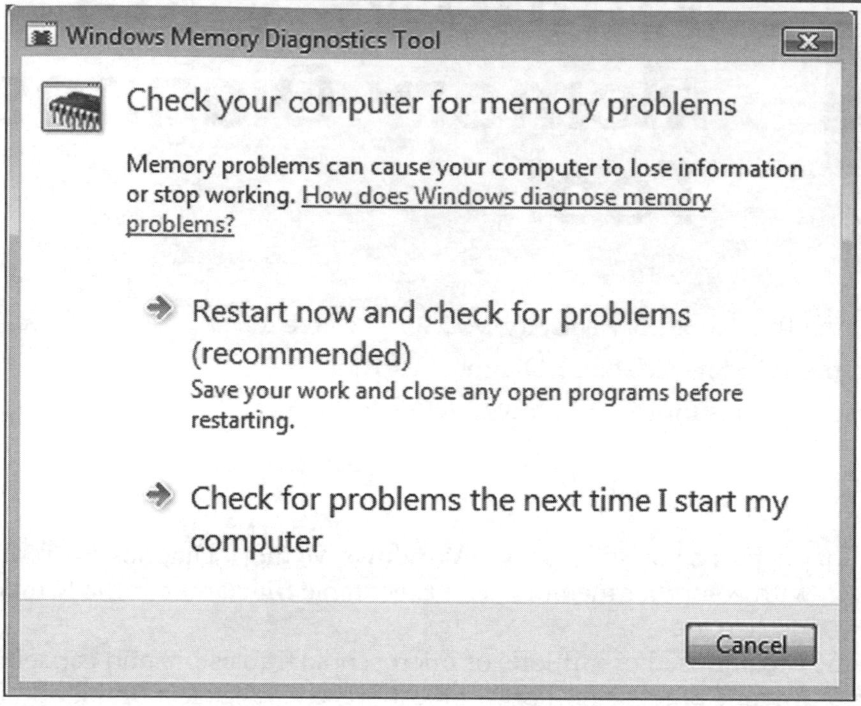

Windows Memory Diagnostics Tool

Check your computer for memory problems

Memory problems can cause your computer to lose information or stop working. How does Windows diagnose memory problems?

→ **Restart now and check for problems (recommended)**
Save your work and close any open programs before restarting.

→ **Check for problems the next time I start my computer**

Cancel

While the diagnostic program is running, a text-based display will appear, providing information about the testing as it proceeds. The following drawing of the Windows Memory Diagnostics Tool shows how the progress of the test is displayed in percentage and as a horizontal bar graph.

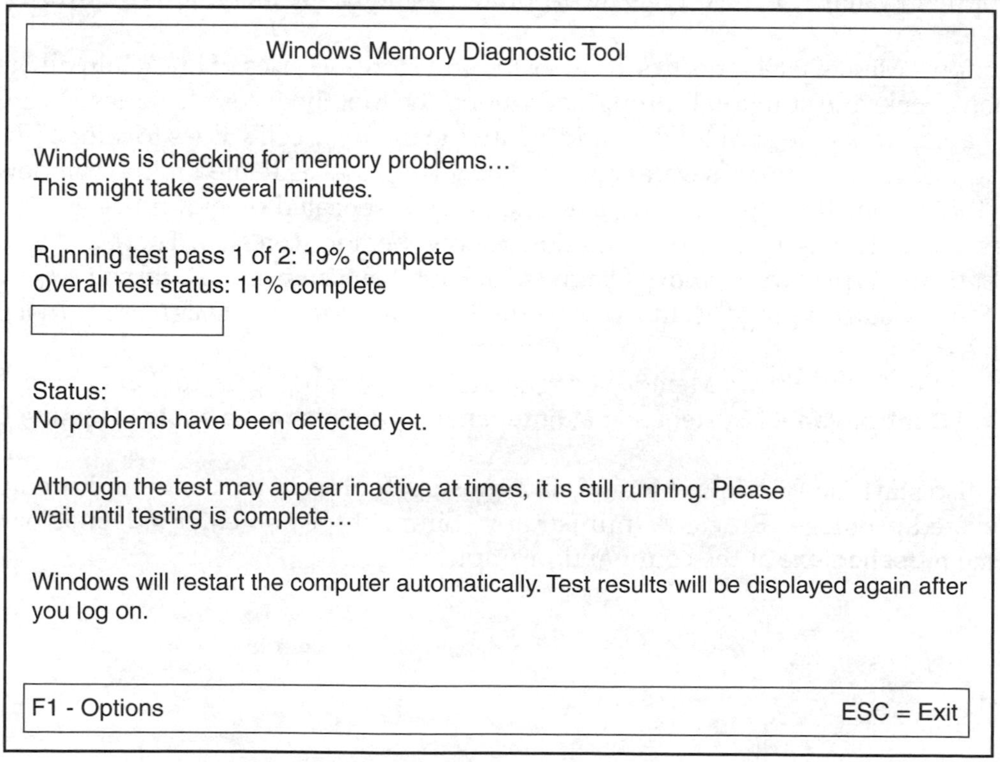

Windows Memory Diagnostic Tool

Windows is checking for memory problems...
This might take several minutes.

Running test pass 1 of 2: 19% complete
Overall test status: 11% complete

Status:
No problems have been detected yet.

Although the test may appear inactive at times, it is still running. Please wait until testing is complete...

Windows will restart the computer automatically. Test results will be displayed again after you log on.

F1 - Options   ESC = Exit

---

254 Computer Service and Repair Lab Manual

Copyright by Goodheart-Willcox Co., Inc.

Name_____

Other test options are displayed by pressing the [F1] key. Also, notice that you can exit the test at any time by pressing the [ESC] key. The options available after pressing the [F1] key are **Basic**, **Standard**, and **Extended**. Look at the following drawing of the **Windows Memory Diagnostics Tool—Options** screen.

```
┌─────────────────────────────────────────────────────┐
│  ┌────────────────────────────────────────────────┐ │
│  │      Windows Memory Diagnostics Tool - Options   │ │
│  └────────────────────────────────────────────────┘ │
│                                                       │
│   Test Mix:                                           │
│           Basic                                       │
│          │Standard│                                   │
│           Extended                                    │
│                                                       │
│   Description: The Standard tests include all the     │
│   Basic tests, plus LRAND, Stride6, (cache enabled),  │
│   CHCKR3, WMATS+, and WINVC.                           │
│                                                       │
│   Cache:                                              │
│           Default                                     │
│           On                                          │
│           Off                                         │
│                                                       │
│   Description: Use the default cache setting of each  │
│   test.                                               │
│                                                       │
│   Pass count (0-99): 2                                │
│                                                       │
│   Description: Set the total number of times the      │
│            entire test mix will                       │
│            repeat (0-infinite).                       │
│                                                       │
│                                                       │
│  ┌────────────────────────────────────────────────┐ │
│  │ TAB = Next        F10 = Apply      ESC = Cancel  │ │
│  └────────────────────────────────────────────────┘ │
└─────────────────────────────────────────────────────┘
```

The Standard test is the default test performed by the Windows Memory Diagnostics Tool. A quicker and less intense test is performed in Basic mode and a much longer and more intense test is performed in Extended mode. Notice that you can select the number of passes to perform during the test.

To navigate the screen, you will need to use the keyboard. Using the mouse is not an option. You navigate the screen by using the arrow keys to move through the choices in each section such as **Test Mix**, **Cache**, and **Pass Count**. Inside each section you use the [Tab] key to highlight a featured option. To select the featured option, highlight it and press the [F10] key.

The more intense additional memory tests involve binary math computations, cache data flow to and from memory, and more. Most are well beyond the scope of understanding necessary for a computer technician to identify a RAM problem. The most frustrating RAM problem is one that occurs intermittently. Because the problem randomly occurs at different times while running different applications, it is hard to identify as a memory-generated problem. All you can do is run the most thorough memory check, which is the Extended option, and the maximum number of passes. The memory may pass the most thorough check and still produce an intermittent problem. If the Windows Memory Diagnostics Tool does indicate a problem with the memory, all you can do is replace the memory module. If you are using a pair of memory modules, you can replace the modules one at a time to determine which one is defective. Always match the existing memory type of module when testing to identify which is defective.

Note:

The Windows Memory Diagnostics Tool was new in the Windows Vista edition, but a Windows XP version is now available from Microsoft. You can download a version of the Windows Memory Diagnostics Tool from the Microsoft Web site and install it in a Windows XP operating system.

To learn more about the Windows Memory Diagnostics Tool , visit the http://oca.microsoft.com/en/windiag.asp and http://oca.microsoft.com/en/windiag.asp#quick_Web sites. You may also locate Windows Memory Diagnostics Tool at the memory manufacturer's Web site, such as Kingston Technology or Crucial Technology.

Equipment and Materials

■   Computer with Windows Vista installed.

Procedure

1. ____   Report to your assigned workstation.

2. ____   Boot the computer and verify it is in working order.

3. ____   Access the Windows Memory Diagnostics Tool by typing **mdsched** into the **Search** box located off the **Start** menu.

4. ____   Close the Windows Memory Diagnostics Tool and access the tool using the path **Start | Control Panel | System Maintenance | Administrative Tools | Memory Diagnostics Tool**.

5. ____   Close the Windows Memory Diagnostics Tool and open the command prompt. Type and enter the command **mdsched.exe**. When the Windows Memory Diagnostics Tool dialog box appears, click the How does Windows diagnose memory problems? link. Briefly look over the information provided and then close the Windows Help and Support dialog box.

6. ____   Select the **Restart now and check for problems (recommended)** option to start the Windows Memory Diagnostics Tool. The system will shut down and then reboot.

7. ____   When the text-mode Windows Memory Diagnostics Tool appears, press [F1] to view the various options available. Leave the test mix at its default setting, Standard. Press [F10] to apply the selection.

8. ____   The test will take several minutes to complete. You may start on the review questions while waiting for the test to complete.

9. ____   Answer all the review questions if you have not yet completed them.

Copyright by Goodheart-Willcox Co., Inc.

Review Questions

1. What is the executable file name of the Windows Memory Diagnostics Tool? _____

   _____

2. What path is used to access the Windows Memory Diagnostics Tool when going through the Control Panel? _____

   _____

3. Which operating system first introduced the Windows Memory Diagnostics Tool? _____

   _____

4. Is there a version of the Windows Memory Diagnostics Tool available for Windows XP? _____

   _____

5. What are the three **Test Mix** options available in the **Windows Memory Diagnostics Tool—Options** screen? _____

6. What does the term *pass* mean in relation to the Windows Memory Diagnostics Tool? _____

   _____

7. What do you do when a memory module is found to be defective? _____

   _____

Copyright by Goodheart-Willcox Co., Inc.

Copyright by Goodheart-Willcox Co., Inc.

Laboratory Activity 34

Keyboard Properties

Name _____ Date _____

Class/Instructor _____

After completing this laboratory activity, you will be able to:

- Adjust typing characteristics of a typical keyboard.
- Explain the purpose of the **Roll Back Driver** option.
- Explain the purpose of the **Update Driver** option.
- Explain the purpose of a digital signature as related to hardware drivers.

Introduction

As a PC technician, you may be called to make certain adjustments to the keyboard. Many people, especially professional secretaries, are sensitive to keyboard characteristics such as the repeat rate of a pressed key. In this laboratory activity, you will make adjustments to the keyboard typing rate characteristics. You will select a set of language characters other than English to be output by the keyboard.

You will also see where the software driver options are located. You will be able to install a new version of a driver, and you will see the location of where to reverse the installation of a software driver.

This laboratory activity will also introduce you to some of the software driver options available to you in both Windows XP and Windows Vista. The following is a screen capture of one of the **Keyboard Properties** dialog boxes of Windows Vista. It looks very similar to that in Windows XP.

There are several driver option buttons you need to be aware of. These choices are available for all hardware devices.

- **Driver Details:** Displays details about the software drivers such as the manufacturer, version, copyright, and if the file is digitally signed. A digitally signed driver ensures that this driver is the real software driver from the stated manufacturer and not malware.
- **Update Driver:** Allows you to install a newer version of the software driver.
- **Roll Back Driver:** Removes the latest software driver version installed and replaces it with the previously installed driver.
- **Disable:** Disables the device.
- **Uninstall:** Removes the installed driver.

These buttons may be shaded and not available as an option if no previous version of the driver exists. These options are available for all types of hardware devices. This is also the preferred method of removing a driver. Never attempt to delete the driver file manually or use some other method to replace or remove the driver. There will be more about driver replacement in other lab activities.

Note:

When some software driver features are not available through the **Keyboard Properties** dialog box, they may be available through Device Manager. The Device Manager is intended for technicians, while the simple **Keyboard Properties** dialog box is typically used by common users.

Equipment and Materials

- Computer with Windows XP or Windows Vista, or both, installed.

Procedure

1. ____ Report to your assigned workstation.

2. ____ Boot the computer and verify it is in working order.

3. ____ Access the **Keyboard Properties** dialog box. For Windows XP, use **Control Panel | Printers and Other Hardware | Keyboard**. For Windows Vista, use **Control Panel | Hardware and Sound | Keyboard**. You should see a dialog box similar to the following.

Copyright by Goodheart-Willcox Co., Inc.

The *repeat delay* is the adjustment for the amount of delay before the first keyboard character will appear after the key is pressed.

The *repeat rate* is the delay between each character appearance on the display or how rapidly the characters appear.

3. ____ Adjust both the repeat delay and the repeat rate, and then test the new rates by typing into the test text box. Experiment to see the effects of each.

4. ____ Adjust the cursor blink rate. The rate should change immediately after changing the position of the **Cursor blink rate** slider.

5. ____ Select the **Hardware** tab located at the top of the dialog box. You will see a dialog box similar to the following.

The **Hardware** tab reveals information such as the manufacturer, port used, and most importantly, the device status.

6. ____ Now, click the **Properties** button located in the lower right-hand corner. You will see a dialog box similar to the following.

The **Device status** text box provides a general condition of the hardware device. In the screen capture, you see that the device is working properly. When the device is not working properly, a possible explanation and related information will be presented in the text box. The same detailed information is revealed under the **Details** tab.

7. _____ Select the **Driver** tab. You will see information about the software drivers installed for the keyboard. Pay particular attention to the **Update Driver** and the **Roll Back Driver** buttons. The **Roll Back Driver** option is very handy and is the preferred method to undo a software driver that was incorrectly installed. For example, a hardware manufacturer offers a newer version of a software driver for your keyboard. After installing the newer driver, the keyboard does not function properly. There are several options to repair this situation. You could install a complete system backup, which would take a lot of time. You could do a system restore. A system restore is a Microsoft operating system feature that allows the system to replace the current operating system configuration with an earlier version. The problem with this approach is that it may change other hardware configuration besides the keyboard. It will also convert to earlier software applications as well. The most sensible and effective way is to use the Roll Back Driver feature. Later in this course, you will perform lab activities explaining this feature and system backups.

The **Driver Details** option reveals information about the provider, file version, copyright, and digital signature. If the **Driver Details** option does not appear, try selecting one of the files listed in the text box by clicking it with the mouse. No detail information will appear unless a file is selected.

Also, be aware that the exact location or path of the driver file is indicated in the text box. In the example, the kbdclass.sys file is located in the Windows\system32\drivers directory. This is where all the 32-bit software drivers are generally located for Windows XP and Windows Vista.

Try using Windows Explorer to locate the file. You must have administrative rights to access system files.

The **Disable** option allows you to temporarily disable a hardware device while troubleshooting or for some other reason. For example, suppose you are using a laptop that has a built-in keyboard and you wish to use a USB full-size keyboard instead. Most of the time, the operating system will identify the USB keyboard and make it the default, but there are times when the two might conflict with each other. You could temporarily disable the default keyboard by clicking the **Disable** button after opening the corresponding **Properties** dialog box.

Copyright by Goodheart-Willcox Co., Inc.

8. ____ Take a few minute to practice accessing the **Keyboard Properties** dialog box starting from the **Start** menu.

9. ____ Answer the review questions.

Review Questions

1. What is the path to access the **Keyboard Properties** in Windows XP? _____
   _____

2. What is the path to access the **Keyboard Properties** in Windows Vista? _____
   _____

3. Why would you use the system **Roll Back Driver** option rather than a system backup or system restore? _____

4. Where are the Windows 32-bit drivers located?_____
   _____

5. A customer calls you in tech support and says that they cannot roll back the driver for a hardware device. The button is there, but nothing happens when they click on it. What is *most likely* the reason? _____
   _____
   _____

6. Why does a software driver indicate a digital signature? _____
   _____
   _____

Notes

Copyright by Goodheart-Willcox Co., Inc.

Name _____ Date _____

Class/Instructor _____

Mouse Properties

After completing this laboratory activity, you will be able to:

■ Adjust the double-click speed of the mouse.

■ Change the mouse pointer icon.

■ Adjust the speed of the mouse pointer.

■ Change the appearance of the mouse pointer trail.

■ Set the mouse for right-handed or left-handed use.

Introduction

In this laboratory activity, you will learn to adjust mouse properties. Mouse properties are the characteristics associated with the mouse, such as pointer movement speed, click speed, and the overall appearance of the mouse pointer. These properties are set in the **Mouse Properties** dialog box. The path for opening the **Mouse Properties** dialog box in Windows XP is **Start | Control Panel | Printers and Other Hardware | Mouse**. For Windows Vista, it is **Start | Control Panel | Hardware and Sound | Mouse**.

The **Mouse Properties** dialog boxes in Windows XP and Windows Vista are so similar, only the dialog boxes from Windows Vista will be presented in this laboratory activity.

Equipment and Materials

■ Computer with Windows XP or Windows Vista, or both, installed.

■ Two-button or three-button mouse. (Various mouse devices may not exactly match the lab content.)

Procedure

1. ____ Report to your assigned workstation.

2. ____ Boot the computer and verify it is in working order.

3. ____ Click the **Start** button and maneuver along the following path: **Start | Control Panel | Hardware and Sound | Mouse**. This will open the **Mouse Properties** dialog box.

The Windows Vista **Buttons** tab allows you to switch the function of the left and right mouse button. Switching the function of the button is an option for left-handed people. You can also adjust the double-click speed of the mouse. Some people have difficulty performing at the default double-click speed. You can increase or decrease the speed here. There is also a "Click Lock" adjustment, which allows you to adjust the time required to hold the mouse button down before dragging an object.

Copyright by Goodheart-Willcox Co., Inc.

The **Pointers** tab allows you to customize the look of the mouse pointer. Windows Vista offers schemes that you can choose from, such as Windows Aero. Earlier versions of Windows did not provide the **Scheme** option.

More mouse modifications are available under the **Pointer Options** tab. Many of the options available here are a matter of user taste or are used to avoid certain annoyances users may encounter.

Copyright by Goodheart-Willcox Co., Inc.

The **Wheel** tab provides a means of configuring the number of lines of text the mouse pointer will cover while scrolling with the mouse wheel.

The **Hardware** tab allows you to view hardware information about the mouse. Clicking the **Properties** button allows you to view information about the mouse hardware drivers and more. Depending on the type of mouse you have installed on your computer, your **Mouse Properties** dialog box may appear considerably different. However, the tools and basic layout should be similar in all cases.

Mouse Properties

Buttons | Pointers | Pointer Options | Wheel | **Hardware**

Devices:

Name	Type
PS/2 Compatible Mouse	Mice and ot...

Device Properties

Manufacturer: Microsoft

Location: plugged into PS/2 mouse port

Device Status: This device is working properly.

Properties

OK | Cancel | Apply

4. _____ There are many mouse properties that can be modified. Practice changing the following properties. Always return the mouse to its default settings before making additional changes.

_____ Change the function of the right and left mouse buttons.

_____ Change the double-click speed.

_____ Display a pointer tail.

_____ Change the mouse scroll to 5 lines per notch.

_____ View the **Hardware** tab and then click the **Properties** button to see what information is available.

5. _____ Take a few minutes to experiment with other mouse properties and functions you might like to modify.

6. _____ Return the mouse to its default settings and then shut down the computer.

Review Questions

1. Which tab allows you to change the appearance of the mouse pointer? _____
   _____

2. Which tab allows you to change the function of the right and left mouse buttons? _____
   _____

3. Which tab allows you to change the double-click speed? _____

4. Which tab would you use to identify the mouse manufacturer? _____

Copyright by Goodheart-Willcox Co., Inc.

Name _____ Date _____

Class/Instructor _____

Display Properties

After completing this laboratory activity, you will be able to:

- Modify the appearance of the desktop area.
- Change the screen saver.
- Adjust the screen resolution.
- Change a monitor's refresh rate.

Introduction

This laboratory activity will familiarize you with the many setting options available for a standard display. You will change many of the display settings and then restore the original settings. Throughout the laboratory activity, you will be prompted to write down the settings before you change or experiment with them. This will assist you when attempting to restore the system to its original configuration.

In Windows XP, the **Display Properties** dialog box can be used to change the appearance of the desktop, screen saver, windows, and dialog boxes. The more advanced settings in the **Display Properties** dialog box affect the technical performance of the monitor, such as refresh rate and energy management. The variety and effect of display setting options depends on the display manufacturer's hardware and drivers. For example, not all monitors allow you to change the refresh rate. For some monitors, refresh rate is determined entirely by the hardware and the driver software.

In Windows Vista, the various display adjustments are made through several dialog boxes accessed through **Control Panel | Appearance and Personalization | Personalization**. The following screen capture shows the locations for changing the color and appearance of the windows and dialog boxes, desktop background, screen saver, refresh rate, and resolution.

Copyright by Goodheart-Willcox Co., Inc.

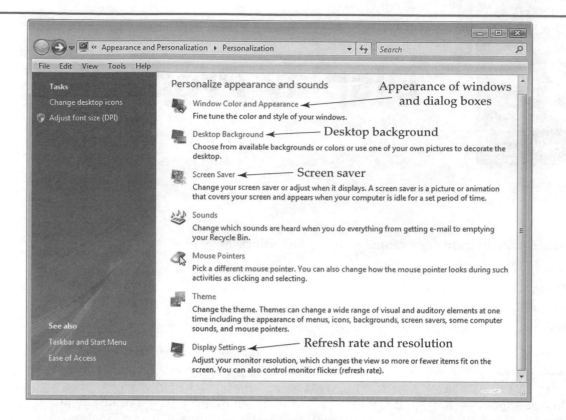

Some of the settings will be viewed but not used in this lab activity. Do not make any permanent changes to the desktop area. If you follow the information in the lab activity, you will not permanently change any of the settings. The settings you change will only be temporary.

Equipment and Materials

- Typical PC with an SVGA monitor and Windows XP or Windows Vista, or both, installed. (A VGA monitor may be substituted.)

Note:
This laboratory activity is divided into two parts. The first part provides procedures for adjusting the display setting in Windows XP, and the second part provides procedures for adjusting properties in Windows Vista. If you have access to both operating systems and ample lab time, perform both parts of the lab activity. This will give you the opportunity to compare the display settings of both operating systems.

Part I (Windows XP)

Procedure

1. ____ Report to your assigned workstation.

2. ____ Boot the computer and verify it is in working order.

Copyright by Goodheart-Willcox Co., Inc.

Name _____

3. ____ Access the **Display Properties** dialog box through **Control Panel | Appearance and Themes | Display**. You can also access **Display Properties** by right-clicking the desktop and selecting **Properties** from the shortcut menu. The **Display Properties** dialog box should appear similar to the one that follows.

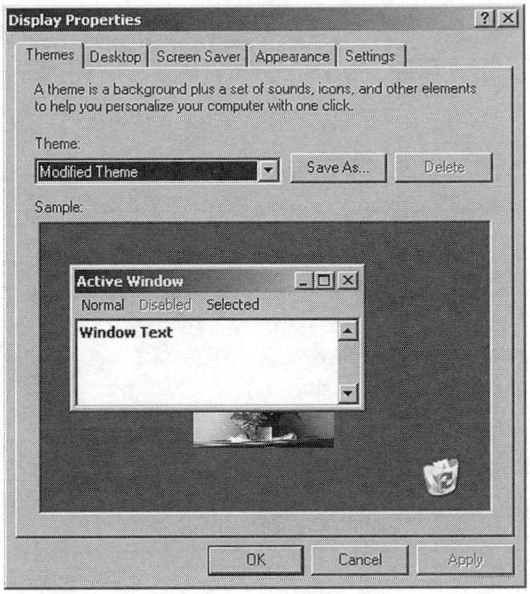

4 ____ In the space provided, list the tabs found in the **Display Properties** dialog box. For example, the first tab is **Themes**.

_____

_____

_____

_____

5. ____ Select the **Settings** tab. A dialog box similar to the following will display.

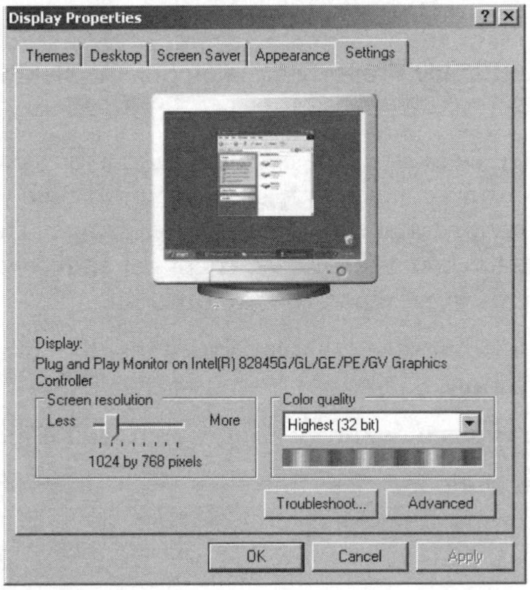

6. Next, click the **Advanced** button. This opens a dialog box that incorporates your video card name in its title bar. In the space provided, list the names of the tabs available in this dialog box.

_____

_____

_____

_____

_____

_____

Plug and Play Monitor and Intel(R) 82845G/GL/GE/PE/GV Grap... [?] [X]

| Color Management | | Intel(R) Extreme Graphics |
| General | Adapter | Monitor | Troubleshoot |

Monitor type

Plug and Play Monitor

Properties

Monitor settings

Screen refresh rate:

70 Hertz ▼

☑ Hide modes that this monitor cannot display

Clearing this check box allows you to select display modes that this monitor cannot display correctly. This may lead to an unusable display and/or damaged hardware.

OK   Cancel   Apply

---

7. ____ Compare the sets of tabs available in this dialog box and the **Display Properties** dialog box. Can you tell which set is used for cosmetic purposes and which set is used for the display's technical settings?

8. ____ Now go back to the **Display Properties** dialog box by clicking the **Cancel** button in the new dialog box.

9. ____ Select the tab marked **Desktop**. This is where the screen's background can be changed. Another name for background is *wallpaper*. A list box beneath the word **Background** lists all of the files in the selected directory that can be used as wallpaper. The currently selected wallpaper is highlighted in the list. On a separate sheet of paper, record the name of the current wallpaper so that you can restore it when you are finished.

10. ____ Scroll through the list and select **Ripple**. Notice that the image of the monitor in this dialog box previews your selection.

11. ____ Select several other types of wallpaper and watch their effect.

12. ____ Restore the original wallpaper selection.

Copyright by Goodheart-Willcox Co., Inc.

13. ____ Next, select the **Screen Saver** tab at the top of the **Display Properties** dialog box. This is where different screen savers can be selected and installed. Write down the name of the screen saver that is displayed in the **Screen Saver** list box so you can restore it after your experiment.

_____

14. ____ Try selecting some different screen savers, and then clicking the **Preview** button to see their effect on the display.

15. ____ Next, select the **Appearance** tab at the top of the **Display Properties** dialog box. Look at the list box labeled **Color Scheme**. This is the title of the screen appearance now selected. Record it in the space provided.

_____

16. ____ Experiment by selecting different schemes.

17. ____ Next, restore the original scheme.

18. Select the **Settings** tab. This tab allows you to change the technical properties of the display, such as refresh rate. Click the button labeled **Advanced** to open a video card **Properties** dialog box. This dialog box is where you can select or identify your video card (also referred to as video adapter) and your monitor. From this dialog box you can also change your refresh rate and accelerate the graphic display.

Note:
   The refresh rate can be changed to a higher setting to help relieve eyestrain. The optimal setting is usually fine, but at times it may need to be faster to relieve eyestrain. The eye can perceive the raster moving across the screen even though the brain allows us to see only the image presented. Nevertheless, the action of the raster can cause eyestrain and headaches after a long period. A screen that has an apparent flicker usually needs a higher refresh rate.

---

19. ____ Take the rest of the time allocated for this lab activity to experiment with the settings available in the **Display Properties** dialog box. If you intend to do the second part of this lab activity, spend only a few minutes and then go on to part two.

Before changing any settings, write down the current setting. After you have experimented with a new setting, immediately restore the original setting before changing the next. Change only one setting at a time. Changing several settings at the same time can lead to confusion when trying to return the display to its original state. For your first experiment, change the **Screen resolution** setting, which is listed under the **Settings** tab. See how this affects the screen display area.

20. ____ You may leave the PC on and the **Display Properties** dialog box open while answering the review questions. After you have answered all the questions, return all display properties to their original settings and properly shut down the PC.

Review Questions (Windows XP)

1. Name two ways of accessing the **Display Properties** dialog box in Windows XP. _____

_____

2. What tab would you select in the **Display Properties** dialog box to change the desktop background? _____

Copyright by Goodheart-Willcox Co., Inc.

3. What other name does Microsoft use for desktop background?_____

4. What tab in the **Display Properties** dialog box would you select to change the color scheme of Windows dialog boxes and screens? _____

5. What tab in the **Display Properties** dialog box would you select to adjust the resolution of the screen display? _____

6. What happens to the size of the screen icons when you select a higher resolution on the **Screen resolution** slider?_____

7. Where would you change the monitor's refresh rate?_____

Part II (Windows Vista)

Procedure

1. ____ Report to your assigned workstation.

2. ____ Boot the computer and verify it is in working order.

3. ____ Access the **Personalization** window through **Control Panel | Appearance and Personalization**. You can also access **Personalization** by right-clicking the desktop and selecting **Personalize** from the shortcut menu. In the space provided, list the options found in the **Personalization** window. For example, the first option is **Window Color and Appearance**.

_____

_____

_____

_____

_____

_____

_____

4. ____ Select the **Display Settings** option and then click the **Advanced Settings** button. This opens a dialog box that incorporates your video card name in its title bar. In the space provided, list the names of the tabs available in this dialog box.

_____

_____

_____

_____

5. ____ Compare the sets of tabs available in this dialog box and the options listed in the **Personalization** window. Can you tell which set is used for cosmetic purposes and which set is used for the display's technical settings?

6. ____ Now, go back to the **Personalization** window by clicking the **Cancel** buttons in the opened dialog boxes.

                    Copyright by Goodheart-Willcox Co., Inc.

7. ____ Select the **Desktop Background** option. A dialog box similar to the following will display. This is where the screen's background can be changed. A list box labeled **Picture Location** lists all of the types of backgrounds that can be used. The pictures for the backgrounds types are listed as a thumbnail in the center window. The currently selected background (thumbnail) is highlighted. In the space provided, note the current background so that you can restore it if you need to.

_____

8. ____ Select the different types of backgrounds and look at the available backgrounds for each type.

9. ____ Click **Cancel** to return to the **Personalization** window.

10. ____ Next, select the **Screen Saver** option. This screen is where different screen savers can be selected and installed. Write down the name of the screen saver that is displayed in the **Screen Saver** list box so you can restore it after your experiment.

_____

11. ____ Try selecting some different screen savers. Watch the effect on the monitor image in the dialog box. To see the effect on your display, click **Preview**.

12. ____ Click **Cancel** to return to the **Personalization** window.

13. ____ Select the **Window Color and Appearance** option. Look at the list box labeled **Color Scheme**. The title of the current screen appearance is highlighted. Record it in the space provided.

_____

14. ____ Experiment by selecting different color schemes.

Copyright by Goodheart-Willcox Co., Inc.

Note:

> To take advantage of Windows Aero features, a computer must meet the recommended requirements or be Premium Ready.

15. _____ Next, restore the original color scheme and then return to the **Personalization** window.

16. _____ Select the **Display Settings** option. This option allows you to change the technical properties of the display, such as refresh rate. Click the button labeled **Advanced Settings** to open a video card properties dialog box. This dialog box is where you can select or identify your video card (also referred to as video adapter) and your monitor. From this dialog box you can also change your refresh rate and accelerate the graphic display.

17. _____ Take the rest of the time allocated for this lab activity to experiment with the settings available in the **Personalization** windows. Before changing any settings, write down the current setting. After you have experimented with a new setting, immediately restore the original setting before changing the next. Change only one setting at a time. Changing several settings at the same time can lead to confusion when trying to return the display to its original state. For your first experiment, change the **Resolution** setting, which is listed under the **Display Settings** option. See how this affects the screen display area.

18. _____ You may leave the PC on and the **Personalization** window open while answering the review questions. After you have answered all the questions, return all display properties to their original settings and properly shut down the PC.

Review Questions (Windows Vista)

1. Name two ways of accessing the **Personalization** window in Windows Vista._____

   _____

2. What option would you select in the **Personalization** window to change the desktop background? _____

3. What option would you select in the **Personalization** window to change the color scheme of Windows dialog boxes and screens? _____

4. What option would you select in the **Personalization** window to adjust the resolution of the screen display? _____

5. Where would you change the monitor's refresh rate?_____

Copyright by Goodheart-Willcox Co., Inc.

Name _____ Date _____

Class/Instructor _____

Typical ATA (EIDE) Hard Drive Installation

After completing this laboratory activity, you will be able to:

■ Replace a hard drive on a typical PC.
■ Add a second hard drive to a PC.

Introduction

The replacement of a hard disk drive is a common PC repair. Fortunately, the mechanics of the replacement are very simple. Before beginning this activity, back up any important data. When replacing a hard drive or adding an additional hard drive to a PC, you should *always* back up important files. The original hard drive can be inadvertently damaged during the installation process. For example, confusion or distraction could result in executing commands such as **fdisk** or **format** to the wrong drive.

This laboratory activity, with slight alterations, can be used to add an additional hard drive to a computer. If your instructor has you add an additional hard drive, skip the removal portion of the activity (steps 2 through 7).

Equipment and Materials

■ Computer with Windows XP or Windows Vista, or both, installed.
■ Additional hard drive.

Procedure

1. ____ Back up your data!

2. ____ Be sure the power is off to the PC. Remove the cover of the PC. Follow all anti-static procedures.

3. ____ Inspect the position of the hard drive and cables. Make a drawing of all cable positions if necessary.

4. ____ Remove the cables (power and data) from the existing hard drive. Do *not* forcibly pull on the cables. Make sure you remove the cables by pulling on the connector and not the cable. Some cable assemblies are poorly made, and the cable can be pulled apart from the connector.

5. ____ Hard drives mount in various ways. Inspect the mounting carefully before removing any of the screws. Unscrew the hard drive mounting screws. Place the screws in a safe location so they will not be lost. A paper cup or small container will prove very handy.

Copyright by Goodheart-Willcox Co., Inc.

6. ____ Slide the drive out of the mounting. The drive should remove easily. If there is a lot of resistance when trying to remove the drive, check for an additional screw.

7. ____ If there is more than one hard drive on the computer you are working with, check the jumper positions on the hard drive you have removed for slave or master identification.

8. ____ Check the jumper settings on the hard drive you are about to add. Make sure the master/slave jumper on the new drive is set to match the removed drive. If there will be only one hard drive in the computer, the jumper should be set to master or single (no setting).

If you are installing an additional hard drive, the jumper setting will be determined by where you install the drive and what is already installed in your computer. If you are adding the drive to an empty cable, the drive can be set as master or single. If you are adding the device to a cable that already has an EIDE device attached, the settings of the preinstalled and new device must be checked. One device must be set as a master and one device must be set as a slave. (Note that the hard drive you will be booting from must be set as a master.)

9. ____ Insert the new drive. Mount it into position using the mounting screws.

10. ____ Attach the power and data cables. When attaching the flat ribbon data cable, be sure to align pin 1 on the hard drive to the colored stripe on the cable assembly. Pin 1 on the hard drive should be identified by a number stamped on the drive. It is usually the pin closest to the power connection. The stripe on the cable is most often red, though it can be blue. Some cables will have the number *1* printed on the proper conductor. See the illustration.

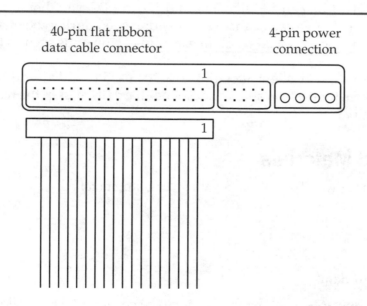

40-pin flat ribbon
data cable connector

4-pin power
connection

11. ____ Before reinstalling the PC cover, power on the PC and boot the system.

12. ____ The new drive should be automatically detected by the Windows operating system. If the drive is not detected, you may have to adjust the CMOS settings. Some drive manufacturers supply a disk with software for their hard drives should a problem arise.

13. ____ When everything is normal, power down the system and reinstall the PC case.

    Copyright by Goodheart-Willcox Co., Inc.

14. ____ After the new hard drive has been installed, you need to use the **fdisk** command or DiskPart to set up partitions on the new drive, even if it will only have one partition. After you partition the drive, proceed to format each partition.

If the computer will not boot up, check that all cables are connected properly. Cables can come loose when installing a new component inside the PC. Also, check if the BIOS supports the drive you are installing. You may need to upgrade the BIOS. Check the Web site of the drive manufacturer for the latest information. Many manufacturers provide free downloads of diagnostic software for their drives.

Tech Tip:
In the field, before you replace a suspected bad hard drive, you will want to verify that the hard drive is actually bad. Try installing the suspect drive in another PC to verify it is indeed bad. There are many items, such as the data cable, the EIDE on the motherboard, or a boot sector virus, that would make the hard drive appear to be defective.

Review Questions

1. What is the first thing you should do before you install a new hard drive? Why? _____

_____

_____

_____

2. What are the possible jumper settings if your PC has only one hard drive? What are your jumper options with two hard drives? _____

_____

_____

3. How is proper data cable alignment assured to prevent connecting the cable backward to the hard drive or motherboard? _____

_____

_____

Copyright by Goodheart-Willcox Co., Inc.

Name _____ Date _____

Class/Instructor _____

Disk Management Tool

After completing this laboratory activity, you will be able to:

■ Access the Disk Management tool.

■ Explain the various options available in the Disk Management tool.

■ Explain how physical disks are identified.

■ Explain the differences between basic disk and dynamic disk.

■ Identify the file format options for a volume or partition.

Introduction

In this laboratory activity, you will explore the features associated with the Disk Management tool located in Computer Management. The Disk Management tool is used to manage computer storage devices, such as hard disk drives, removable storage devices, CD-ROM drives, and DVD drives. The Disk Management tool is very similar for Windows XP and Windows Vista.

Disk Management is available as a Computer Management snap-in. In Windows XP, Computer Management can be accessed by right-clicking **My Computer** and selecting **Manage** from the shortcut menu. In Windows Vista, it is accessed by right-clicking **Computer** and selecting **Manage** from the shortcut menu. You can also access the Disk Management tool by typing and entering **diskmgmt.msc** in the Windows XP **Run** dialog box or the Windows Vista **Search** box. You must include the .msc extension. The following screen captures show the Windows XP and Windows Vista Disk Management tools.

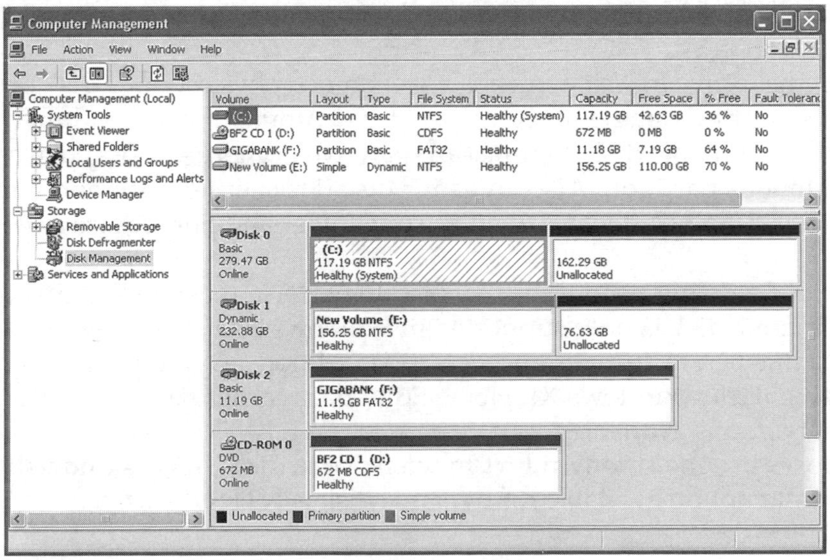

Windows XP

Windows Vista

As you can see, the versions are quite similar in appearance. A lot of disk information is available, such as the type of partition/volume, the size, file system, capacity, free space, and more.

Disk Management is a centralized tool that allows you to carry out all of the most common disk drive tasks such as creating and formatting a partition, deleting a partition, and extending a partition. It automatically provides the status of a disk, such as healthy, or identifies any major problems associated with a partition.

Notice that the first physical disk is identified as Disk 0 and the second is identified as Disk 1 and so on. When you attempt to use a command line utility such as DiskPart, the utility will want you to use disk 0 to identify the first physical disk. The Disk Management tool uses colors to identify various disk parts such as the primary partition, simple volume, and unallocated space.

To use Disk Management, you need to be familiar with some terminology related to disk structuring. These terms are *basic disk, dynamic disk, partition, volume, simple volume*, and *spanned volume*. *Basic disk* uses older disk technology based on the original DOS disk structure in which hard disk drives can be partitioned as a primary partition, extended partition, or logical partition (also referred to as a logical drive). *Dynamic disk* was first introduced in Windows 2000. Dynamic disk uses the term *volume* in place of the term *partition*. A volume on a single disk is referred to as a *simple volume*. A volume that covers two or more hard disk drives is called a *spanned volume*. The main difference between basic disk and dynamic disk is a dynamic disk can span more than one physical disk and basic disk cannot.

Basic disk uses the term *partition*, which is a section of a physical hard disk drive and is limited to the area contained within a single physical disk drive. A dynamic disk volume is not limited to a single physical disk. A dynamic disk volume can span two or more physical drives and identify the volume as one continuous partition. Also, dynamic disk does not need to represent a volume with a drive letter. The volume can be attached to an existing folder and not require a drive letter the way a partition does.

Most dynamic disks do not need to be rebooted to perform most disk maintenance tasks. Basic disk does. Dynamic disk is only supported in Windows 2000, Windows XP Professional, and Windows Vista Business, Ultimate, and Enterprise editions. Dynamic disk is not an option in Windows Vista Home Basic, Windows XP Home Edition, or earlier versions of Windows.

The only format options available for basic disk are FAT, FAT32, and NTFS. When Microsoft articles or dialog boxes use the acronym FAT in reference to disks, FAT is understood to represent FAT16. The only format option available for dynamic disk is NTFS.

Computer Service and Repair Lab Manual

Computer Service and Repair Lab Manual

Copyright by Goodheart-Willcox Co., Inc.

Note:
> You cannot access data stored on a dynamic disk from a computer running a legacy operating system such as Windows XP Home Edition or earlier operating systems such as NT 4.0, Windows Millennium Edition, Windows 98 second edition, or earlier. Windows XP Professional can access data stored on a dynamic volume.

To learn more about disk management visit the Microsoft Support Web site at the following link: http://support.microsoft.com/kb/308424/. You can also use the key words "Microsoft Support 308424" to locate the article. To read an article by Microsoft contrasting basic disk and dynamic disk, use the following link: http://support.microsoft.com/kb/314343.

Equipment and Materials

■ Computer with Windows XP or Windows Vista, or both, installed.

Note:
> The workstation should have a hard drive with at least one volume and one partition. Using a workstation that has only one partition or one volume will only provide limited features of the laboratory activity.

Note:
> You may also use an external hard drive connected by USB for this laboratory activity.

Part I (Windows XP)

Procedure

1. ____ Report to your assigned workstation.

2. ____ Boot the computer and verify it is in working order.

3. ____ Open Disk Management by right-clicking **My Computer** | **Manage** | **Disk Management**.

4. ____ Now, close the Disk Management tool and open it using the Disk Management executable file name **diskmgmt.msc**. You must include the file extension .msc.

5. ____ Look carefully at the first physical disk installed on the system labeled Disk 0. Answer the following questions.

Is Disk 0 basic or dynamic?_____

What drive letter is assigned to the first partition or volume? _____

What type of file format is used on the first partition? _____

_____

Is the first partition a primary, extended, or logical partition? _____

How large is Disk 0? _____

What is the capacity of the first partition or volume?_____

How much free space is available on the first partition or volume?_____

6. ____ Right-click the partition identified as C and look at the available options in the shortcut menu. Notice that some options are in dark bold lettering and others are in light gray lettering. The light gray options are not available to be performed at this time. For example, a partition that contains data and files will not be available to be formatted at this time. This is a safety feature built in to prevent a user from destroying data by performing a format operation on an existing partition or volume. Make a list of the shortcut menu items available in the space provided.

_____

_____

_____

_____

_____

7. ____ Right-click any available partition or volume and then select the **Help** option from the shortcut menu. Explore the available information that pertains to disks, partitions, and volumes.

8. ____ Close Disk Management and Computer Management.

9. ____ This concludes Part I of the laboratory activity. Do not answer the review questions until you complete Part II—Windows Vista.

Part II (Windows Vista)

Procedure

1. ____ Report to your assigned workstation.

2. ____ Boot the computer and verify it is in working order.

3. ____ Open Disk Management by right-clicking **Computer | Manage | Disk Management**.

4. ____ Look carefully at the first physical disk installed on the system labeled Disk 0. Answer the following questions.

Is Disk 0 basic or dynamic? _____

What drive letter is assigned to the first partition or volume? _____

What type of file format is used on the first partition? _____

_____

Is the first partition a primary, extended, or logical partition? _____

How large is Disk 0? _____

What is the capacity of the first partition or volume? _____

How much free space is available on the first partition or volume? _____

5. ____ Look at the colors used to identify various partitions and volumes. The legend is located at the bottom of Disk Management. Not all colors discussed earlier may be present.

                        Copyright by Goodheart-Willcox Co., Inc.

6. ____ Right-click the partition identified as C and look at the available options in the shortcut menu. Notice that some options are in dark bold lettering and others are in light gray lettering. The light gray options are not available to be performed at this time. For example, a partition that contains data and files will not be available to be formatted at this time. This is a safety feature built in to prevent a user from destroying data by performing a format operation on an existing partition or volume. Make a list of the shortcut menu items available in the space provided.

_____

_____

_____

_____

_____

7. ____ Right-click any available partition or volume and then select the **Help** option from the shortcut menu. Explore the available information that pertains to disks, partitions, and volumes.

8. ____ Close Disk Management and Computer Management.

9. ____ Answer the review questions. You may use Help and Support to assist you in answering the questions.

Review Questions

1. Does a dynamic disk contain volumes or partitions? _____

2. Does a basic disk contain volumes or partitions? _____

3. What is the physical disk number of the first hard disk drive?_____

4. What type of file format(s) can be contained on a basic disk?_____

   _____

5. What type of file format(s) can be contained on a dynamic disk? _____

   _____

6. You right-click a partition and look at the shortcut menu options. Some appear in bold dark letters and other options appear in light gray letters. What does it mean when the shortcut menu item is light gray? _____

   _____

Copyright by Goodheart-Willcox Co., Inc.

Name _____ Date _____

Class/Instructor _____

Adding
a Second Hard Drive

After completing this laboratory activity, you will be able to:

- Add an additional hard disk drive to computer.
- Create a partition and volume on a hard disk drive.
- Format a partition as FAT16
- Format a partition as FAT32.
- Format a partition as NTFS.
- Convert a basic disk to a dynamic disk.
- Remove a partition and volume.
- Extend a partition and volume.
- Shrink a partition and volume.

Introduction

In this laboratory activity, you will become familiar with the basic disk operations, such as adding a new physical disk to an existing system. After the disk is added, it is automatically detected by the BIOS and operating system. Disk properties can be viewed and modified using Disk Management as introduced in the previous laboratory activity. In this laboratory activity, you will partition a disk, format the partition, extend a partition, shrink a partition, and remove the partition.

Both Windows XP and Windows Vista use wizards to accomplish tasks designated in Disk Management. For example, when creating a partition, the partition wizard will start and prompt you for information. The partition wizard will partition the disk and format the disk. You can format the partition with FAT16, FAT32 or NTFS. FAT16 is only available for partitions of 2 GB or less.

Windows Vista Disk Management introduced two new options not available in Windows XP: **Extend a partition** and **Shrink a partition**. Prior to Windows Vista, you would need to use third-party software to shrink or extend a partition. You can only extend or shrink an NTFS volume located on a dynamic disk, not a basic disk. A basic disk will be automatically converted to a dynamic type disk when you extend or shrink the NTFS volume. Also, be aware that you cannot extend the active primary partition. The active primary partition contains the files required to boot the computer operating system. Extending the size of the active primary partition is not an option because the action can render the computer operating system as unbootable. You can, however, shrink the active primary partition.

Some partition options, such as **Extend a partition** and **Shrink a partition**, will not be available for a basic disk. Basic disks can be converted to dynamic disk using Disk Management, and then more options will become available. Also, be aware that dynamic disk is only valid for Windows 2000, Windows XP Professional, and Windows Vista Business, Enterprise, and Ultimate editions. Dynamic disk is not an option for Windows XP Home Edition or Windows Vista Home Basic and

Copyright by Goodheart-Willcox Co., Inc.

Home Premium. Also, be aware that the dynamic disk feature is typically not available for laptop computers because it is assumed that they are designed for a single hard drive, not multiple hard drives.

The basic difference between dynamic disk and basic disk is a dynamic disk volume can span two or more physical disks. Basic disk cannot span physical disks with a partition. The basic disk partition is limited to one physical disk.

Disk Management is only available in an existing computer system. Disk partitioning and formatting is completed by the installation DVD during the operating system installation process. The **fdisk** command is not recognized in Windows XP or Windows Vista.

Note:

This laboratory activity is designed for Windows Vista. However, Disk Management and disk management wizards are similar in Windows XP and Windows Vista.

Equipment and Materials

- Workstation running Windows Vista Business, Ultimate, or Enterprise. (You may use Windows XP Professional, but you will not be able to extend or shrink a partition. Windows Vista Home Basic and Home Premium do not support dynamic disk. You will still be able to complete part of the laboratory activity.)
- ATA or EIDE internal hard disk drive with at least 20 GB of space. (An external USB hard disk drive can be substituted for disk drive in this laboratory activity; however, not all USB hard disk drives are compatible with dynamic disk.)
- Small flat-tip screwdriver.
- Small Phillips screwdriver.

Procedure

1. ____ Report to your assigned workstation.

2. ____ Boot the computer and verify it is in working order.

3. Open Disk Management and write down the existing disk drive identification. For example, a single disk drive will be identified as Disk 0, and a computer with two physical drives will be identified as Disk 0 and Disk 1, respectively. This is extremely important. Failure to correctly identify the existing disk drive could cause confusion during the laboratory activity.

4. ____ Power off the computer and follow all anti-static procedures required by your instructor.

5. ____ Open the case and inspect the hard disk drive that is already installed. Check the slave/master jumper settings. The original hard drive should be configured as master. The additional hard disk drive should be set to slave.

6. ____ Install the additional hard disk drive. Connect the data cable and the power cable.

7. ____ Power on the computer. The additional hard disk drive should be automatically detected. Watch the BIOS screen messages to see if two hard disk drives are identified during the boot process. You can also access the BIOS Setup program to see if the additional hard disk drive has been detected.

8. ____ Open Disk Management by entering **diskmgmt.msc** in the **Search** box.

9. ____ The additional disk should appear in Disk Management. If not, call your instructor for assistance.

Copyright by Goodheart-Willcox Co., Inc.

Name_____

10. ____ Right-click unallocated disk space of the additional disk and select **New Simple Volume** from the shortcut menu. The first dialog box to appear welcomes you to the New Simple Volume Wizard.

11. ____ Click **Next** to continue. (You can cancel the wizard at any time by clicking **Cancel**.) The next stage of the wizard prompts you for the size of the volume to create. The size of the first volume should be 4 GB, or 4000 MB as indicated in the dialog box. Specify the size of the new partition now as 4000 MB. As you will see, the actual size will be 3.91 GB because of the size of the allocation units. Rarely will the requested specified size match the actual size when the wizard completes.

12. ____ Click **Next**. You will be prompted for a drive letter. You can assign a drive letter to the new partition or mount the new partition in an empty NTFS folder. When mounted in a folder, no drive letter is necessary. This is great when you need more disk space for something like pictures. You can assign the new drive to the Pictures folder, and the partition space will become part of the Pictures folder. For this laboratory activity, use the default drive letter.

13. ____ Click **Next** to continue. Now you are prompted to select a format for the partition or volume.

The default format for a 4 MB partition is NTFS. You can select other file formats such as FAT32 or FAT, which is FAT16. A 4 MB is too large for FAT16, so it is not an option. Also, notice that you can select the allocation unit size at this point. The default is based on the overall size of the new partition. You can select an allocation unit other than default, but it is not recommended. You can look at the possible allocation sizes, but do not select any other except **Default**. For the file format select FAT32.

Copyright by Goodheart-Willcox Co., Inc.

14. ____ Click **Next** again. A summary of the changes will appear. The summary provides you with an opportunity to view the changes and provides you with a chance to go back and make changes or finish the partition creation process. You may also cancel the wizard at this time. Go ahead and click **Finish**.

After clicking **Finish**, Disk Management reappears. You can watch as the partition is formatted. The percentage complete will appear in the new partition space while the volume is being formatted.

15. ____ Now, repeat the process to create a 2 GB FAT16 partition and an 8 GB NTFS partition. When you finish creating the additional partitions, call your instructor to inspect your work.

16. ____ Right-click the various partitions you created and view the possible options in the short-cut menu. Answer the following questions:

Can you extend or shrink a FAT16 partition?_____

Can you extend or shrink an NTFS partition? _____

17. ____ Convert the additional drive to dynamic disk. Simply right-click the physical drive and select **Convert to Dynamic Disk** from the shortcut menu. The physical disk is represented by the gray box, not the partition area to the right of the physical drive box. *Be sure you select the additional hard disk drive, not the original hard disk drive.*

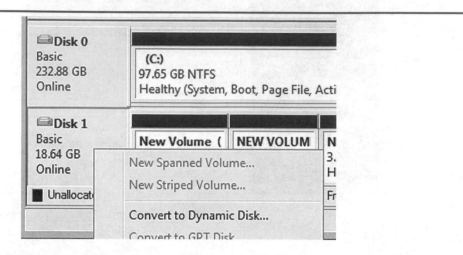

During the conversion process you will see a warning message similar to the one in the following screen capture. Ignore the message and proceed by clicking **Yes**. The wizard will continue, and it will take several minutes to convert the basic disk to dynamic disk. After the Dynamic Disk Conversion Wizard completes, the disk drive will be identified as dynamic disk.

18. ____ Right-click each of the partitions and see if an option to extend or shrink the partition exists. Extend the NTFS partition an additional 4 GB or 4000 MB.

19. ____ Look closely at the new extension of the NTFS partition. When viewed, it will appear as a separate partition, but it will have the same drive letter as the original NTFS partition.

Copyright by Goodheart-Willcox Co., Inc.

20. ____ Now, delete each of the new partitions you created by right-clicking the partition and then selecting **Delete Volume** from the shortcut menu. A warning message will appear telling you that all data will be erased and that you should back up the data before deleting the partition. After all partitions are deleted, the dynamic disk should automatically convert back to basic disk.

21. ____ Take a few minutes to practice creating and formatting partitions and volumes. When you finish experimenting, remove all partitions from the additional hard disk drive. Call your instructor to inspect the drive after all partitions have been removed.

22. ____ Power off the computer and remove the additional hard disk drive from the computer. Replace the computer cover.

23. ____ Reboot the computer to ensure it is in working order. If the system fails to boot, call your instructor for assistance.

24. ____ Go on to answer the review questions and return all tools and material to their proper storage area. You may use the Help and Support feature to assist you answering the questions.

Review Questions

1. What is the name used to identify the space on the drive that is not partitioned?_____
   _____

2. What file system type can be extended or shrunk?_____

3. Can you extend a partition on a basic disk? _____

4. Can you extend a partition on a dynamic disk? _____

5. Which partition contains the operating system files required for booting the operating system?
   _____

6. Can you extend a Windows XP partition? _____

7. What are the three file formats available for a partition?_____

8. How do you convert a dynamic disk back to a basic disk? _____

9. Which operating systems can use dynamic a disk? _____
   _____

10. Can a dynamic disk create a volume that spans two physical disks?_____

11. Can a basic disk create a volume or partition that spans two physical disks? _____

12. How do you convert a basic disk to dynamic disk? _____
    _____

13. What is the main difference between basic disk and dynamic disk?_____
    _____
    _____
    _____
    _____

Notes

Copyright by Goodheart-Willcox Co., Inc.

Laboratory Activity

40

Setting Up a Page File

After completing this laboratory activity, you will be able to:

■ Explain the purpose of the page file.

■ Configure the size of the page file manually or automatically.

■ Determine the size of the page file.

Introduction

In this laboratory activity, you will explore the **Virtual Memory** dialog box associated with the page file. The *page file* is a dedicated area of the hard disk drive storage used to supplement the computer system RAM during times of excessive RAM use. Microsoft recommends using a page file of approximately 1.5 times the size of the actual RAM. For example, a page file of 3 GB would be used to compliment a 2 GB RAM. The term *swap file* is also used for *page file*. The term *swap file* originates from UNIX systems and is also associated with Linux operating systems.

You can access the **Virtual Memory** dialog box in several ways. In Windows XP, access **Start | Control Panel | Performance and Maintenance | System**. The **System Properties** dialog box will display. Click the **Advanced** tab and then the **Settings** button located under the **Performance** section. The **Performance Options** dialog box will display. Click the **Advanced** tab and then click the **Change** button located in the **Virtual Memory** section.

In Windows Vista, access **Start | Control Panel |System and Maintenance | System | Advanced System Settings**. The **System Properties** dialog box will display. Click the **Advanced** tab and then the **Settings** button from the **Performance** section. The **Performance Options** dialog box will display. Click the **Advanced** tab and then the **Change** button from the **Virtual Memory** section.

The path through Control Panel of both operating systems is quite long. An easier way is to access the **System Properties** dialog box through the Windows XP **Run** dialog box or Windows Vista **Search** box and enter **sysdm.cpl**. You must use the .cpl extension. Using this command, you will automatically access the **System Properties** dialog box. From there in Windows Vista, click the **Advanced** tab and then the **Settings** button from the **Performance** section. When the **Performance Options** dialog box displays, click the **Advanced** tab and then the **Change** button from the **Virtual Memory** section.

Copyright by Goodheart-Willcox Co., Inc.

After entering **sysdm.cpl** into the Windows XP **Run** dialog box, the **System Properties** dialog box will display. Click the **Advanced** tab and then the **Settings** button located under the **Performance** section. When the **Performance Options** dialog box displays, click the **Advanced** tab and then click the **Change** button located in the **Virtual Memory** section. Again the path is quite long, but not as long as it is when going through Control Panel.

Windows XP

Windows Vista

After you access the **Virtual Memory** dialog box in Windows XP or Windows Vista, you will see that the configuration options are very similar. The default virtual memory settings are controlled by the operating system. The operating system automatically makes the necessary changes to the amount of page file size needed to support the computer system. The default setting in Windows XP for the system to automatically adjust the page file size in Windows XP is **System managed size**. In Windows Vista, the **Automatically manage page file size for all drives** is enabled. You can also manually adjust the page file size, but this is not usually done. In this laboratory activity, you will simply explore the **Virtual Memory** dialog box and view the various settings.

While most computer systems have only one disk drive, you can configure a computer for better performance by using two hard disk drives and then configuring the page file on the drive that does not contain the operating system files. Do not put multiple page files on multiple partitions on the same physical disk. Also, do not place the page file on a fault tolerant type of RAID disk system such as RAID 1 and RAID 5. Placing the page file on a fault tolerant disk system will cause the disk storage action to slow down.

Copyright by Goodheart-Willcox Co., Inc.

Equipment and Materials

■ Computer with Windows XP or Windows Vista, or both, installed.

Procedure

1. ____ Report to your assigned workstation.

2. ____ Boot the computer and verify it is in working order.

3. ____ Access the **Virtual Memory** dialog box by using one of the methods outlined in the introduction.

4. ____ Look at the various options for making changes to the page file size and location. Do not make changes in the page file.

5. ____ Close the **Virtual Memory** dialog box.

6. ____ Open Help and Support and enter the words "virtual memory" and view the results.

7. ____ Close all open dialog boxes and go on to answer the review questions.

Review Questions

1. What is another name used for page file?_____

2. What is the *page file*?_____

   _____

   _____

   _____

3. What is the default setting for the page file in Windows XP and Windows Vista? _____

   _____

   _____

4. What command is entered into the Windows XP **Run** dialog box or Windows Vista **Search** box to open the **System Properties** dialog box? _____

5. Where should the page file be located on a computer system that uses two hard disk drives?

   _____

6. What is the recommended size for a page file? _____

   _____

Copyright by Goodheart-Willcox Co., Inc.

Computer Service and Repair Lab Manual

Copyright by Goodheart-Willcox Co., Inc.

Name _____ Date _____

Class/Instructor _____

Disk Cleanup

After completing this laboratory activity, you will be able to:

■ Identify the types of files that can be deleted with the Disk Cleanup utility.

■ Identify the Disk Cleanup configuration options.

■ Identify differences between the Windows XP and Windows Vista Disk Cleanup utility.

Introduction

In this laboratory activity, you will become familiar with the Disk Cleanup utility. Disk Cleanup is used to remove unnecessary files from the disk drive(s), thus providing more available disk space. The Disk Cleanup executable file name is cleanmgr.exe.

The Disk Cleanup utility is used to free up disk space on the hard disk drive by searching all files and identifying files that are safe to delete. The following are some of the general file types that are searched:

■ Recycle Bin contents.

■ Temporary Internet files.

■ Downloaded program files such as ActiveX and Java applets.

■ Windows temporary files.

■ Windows optional components that are not being used.

■ Installed programs that are not being used.

There are a number of different ways to access the Disk Cleanup utility. In both Windows XP and Windows Vista, you access the Disk Cleanup utility the same way from the **Start** menu: **Start | All Programs | Accessories | System Tools | Disk Cleanup**.

You can access the Disk Cleanup utility through the Windows Vista Control Panel: **Start | Control Panel | System and Maintenance | Administrative Tools | Free Up Disk Space**. For Windows XP, the path is **Start | Control Panel | Performance and Maintenance | Free up space on your hard disk**.

In Windows XP you can also type the executable name of the Disk Cleanup utility into the **Run** dialog box. The Disk Cleanup utility executable file name is cleanmgr.exe for both Windows XP and Windows Vista.

For Windows Vista, you can type "Disk Cleanup" into the **Search** box. The Disk Cleanup utility will appear at the top of the **Search** results list after "Disk" is typed. You can also type "cleanmgr" into the **Search** box. The Disk Cleanup utility will appear as soon as the letter c is typed. You can run **cleanmgr.exe** from the command prompt if necessary. The Disk Cleanup utilities are very similar in design for Windows XP and Windows Vista.

Windows XP

Windows XP

Windows Vista

Windows Vista

You can select which files to delete by selecting the corresponding box in front of the file type. The **Description** area displays information about each type of file to help you determine if you really want to delete the files contained in that particular category.

As you compare the Windows XP and Windows Vista versions of Disk Cleanup, notice that the XP version has a **More Options** tab. The **More Options** tab provides three more categories of files or options: **Windows components**, **Installed programs**, and **System Restore**. A brief description of each option is provided.

Windows XP

Windows Vista

Copyright by Goodheart-Willcox Co., Inc.

The **More Options** tab in Windows Vista only appears when you select the **Files from all users on this computer** option after clicking the **Disk Cleanup** button from the drive's **Properties** dialog box. Look at the following screen capture of the dialog box that appears in Windows Vista after clicking the **Disk Cleanup** button from the drive's **Properties** dialog box. Notice that there are two options: **My files only** and **Files from all users on this computer**. This dialog box only appears in Windows Vista and is common on Windows Vista computers that have more than one user account configured. This is a very confusing aspect of the Windows Vista version, which may change in future service packs releases.

The Windows Vista **More Options** tab provides two additional categories: **Programs and Features** and **System Restore and Shadow Copies**. Be aware that the actual listing of options in Windows Vista may change according to the version of Windows Vista you are using. For example, the Shadow Copy feature is not available in the Windows Vista Home editions.

To learn more about the Disk Cleanup utility, conduct an online search using the key words "Microsoft Disk Cleanup."

Equipment and Materials

■ Computer with Windows XP or Windows Vista, or both, installed.

Note:
Do not delete any files using the Disk Cleanup utility if your workstation is shared by other students. If you delete files using the Disk Cleanup utility, the next student to use your computer will not have the same advantage as you when looking at all options. Ask your instructor for permission to delete the files identified by the Disk Cleanup utility.

Copyright by Goodheart-Willcox Co., Inc.

Part I—Windows XP

Procedure

1. ____ Report to your assigned workstation.

2. ____ Boot the computer and verify it is in working order.

3. ____ Open a Command Prompt window and then type and enter **cleanmgr.exe** at the prompt to launch the Disk Cleanup utility.

4. ____ Close the Disk Cleanup utility and then open it using the following path: **Start | All Programs | Accessories | System Tools | Disk Cleanup**. If multiple drives or partitions are installed, the **Select Drive** dialog box will open. Simply select the default drive indicated in the dialog box and then click **OK**. The application will now automatically run to determine how much space can be saved. The program can take several minutes to complete the estimate.

5. ____ When the **Disk Cleanup** dialog box displays, click the **More Options** tab and explore the other files that can be deleted. When you click **Clean up** for one of the three file categories, **Windows components**, **Installed programs**, and **System Restore**, you can see the files that would be removed. When you click **Clean up** for the **System Restore** category, you will see a message stating that only older restore points will be deleted. The most recent restore points will not be deleted.

6. ____ Click the **Disk Cleanup** tab. View files that will be deleted by clicking the **View Files** button. For example, if the **Downloaded Program Files** category is highlighted, selecting the **View Files** button will generate a Windows Explorer view of the files that would be deleted.

7. ____ You can now either click **Cancel** to abort the Disk Cleanup operation or click **OK** to complete the Disk Cleanup operation at this time. Remember, you need your instructor's permission to delete the files identified by the Disk Cleanup utility.

8. ____ This concludes Part I of the laboratory activity. Do not answer the review questions until you complete Part II—Windows Vista.

Part II—Windows Vista

Procedure

1. ____ Report to your assigned workstation.

2. ____ Boot the computer and verify it is in working order.

3. ____ Open a Command Prompt window and then type and enter **cleanmgr.exe** at the prompt to launch the Disk Cleanup utility.

4. ____ Close the Disk Cleanup utility and then open the application using the following path: **Start | All Programs | Accessories | System Tools | Disk Cleanup**. If multiple drives or partitions are installed, the **Select Drive** dialog box will open. If there is more than one user account, you will be prompted to select only your files or all computer users' files. This is new in Windows Vista. Select the default drive indicated in the **Select Drive** dialog box and then click **OK**. Disk Cleanup utility will now automatically run to determine how much space can be saved. The program can take several minutes to complete the estimate. When finished, the **Disk Cleanup** dialog box will appear and allow you to select file categories to delete. You can simply use the files selected by default.

Copyright by Goodheart-Willcox Co., Inc.

5. ____ Click the **More Options** tab (if it appears) and explore the other files that could be deleted. When you select one of the **Clean up** buttons, such as the one associated with **Program and Features**, you can see the files that would be removed. When you select the **Clean up** button associated with **System Restore and Shadow Copies**, you will see a message stating that only older restore points will be deleted. The most recent restore points will not be deleted.

6. ____ Click the **Disk Cleanup** tab. View files that will be deleted by clicking the **View Files** button. For example, if the **Downloaded Program Files** category is highlighted, selecting the **View Files** button will generate a Windows Explorer view of the files that would be deleted.

Note:
There may be no list of files if the computer has not downloaded anything from the Internet or if another student using the workstation has already deleted the files.

---

7. ____ You can now either click **Cancel** to abort the Disk Cleanup operation or click **OK** to complete the Disk Cleanup operation at this time. Remember, you need your instructor's permission to delete the files identified by the Disk Cleanup utility.

8. ____ Answer the review questions.

Review Questions

1. What is the name of the Disk Cleanup utility executable file? _____

2. What is the complete path to the Disk Cleanup utility through **Start | All Programs**? _____

_____

3. Why may the **More Options** tab fail to appear in the Windows Vista Disk Cleanup utility? _____

_____

4. Can you view a comprehensive list of files to be deleted by the Disk Cleanup utility before you delete them?_____

Notes

Copyright by Goodheart-Willcox Co., Inc.

Name _____ Date _____

Class/Instructor _____

Disk Defragmenter

After completing this laboratory activity, you will be able to:

- Run the Disk Defragmenter utility.
- Explain how disk files become fragmented.
- Describe the differences between the Windows XP and Windows Vista Disk Defragmenter.

Introduction

In this laboratory activity, you will run the Disk Defragmenter utility. Files become fragmented over the course of time while using the computer. The term *fragmented* in relation to file disk storage means that the file is not saved in a contiguous series of disk clusters but rather are scattered over the disk storage area. Fragmented files take longer to access from disk storage. You can improve disk storage access time by regularly defragmenting the disk storage space using the defragmenter application. The following is a screen capture of the Windows XP Disk Defragmenter Graphic User Interface (GUI) version.

The screen capture was taken while the defragmenter was performing an analysis of volume C. The Disk Defragmenter GUI allows you to watch the defragmentation take place as represented by a series of color bars. The color bars represent fragmented files, contiguous files, free space, and unmovable files.

Windows Vista modified the Disk Defragmenter utility in several ways. First, Microsoft removed the GUI that illustrated the various segments and clusters on the hard disk drive while performing the defragmentation operation. The GUI actually slowed the defragmentation process. Windows Vista also automatically schedules the defragmenter to run at least once a week. The original Windows Vista version of Disk Defragmenter did not allow the user to select which hard drive to defragment. It automatically defragmented all hard disk drives that it determined needed defragmenting. After Windows Vista Service Pack 1 was released, the user could once more manually select which disk drive to defragment, if they so desired.

It is interesting to note that Microsoft has a history of modifying tools and applications after the initial release of the new operating system. This often results in modification of dialog boxes.

Disk Defragmenter requires a minimum of 15% free volume space to perform the defragmentation. The free space is used to hold files temporarily while they are being rearranged in sequential order. You can force a defragmentation with less space, but it will take a great deal longer to perform.

Before defragmenting a volume, you should disable the antivirus program. Turn the antivirus protection back on after completing the defragmentation process.

You cannot defragment a volume that contains corrupt files. When a volume contains corrupt files, it is marked as "dirty" when viewed in the Computer Management Console view of the hard disk drives. A dirty drive must be cleaned using the Chkdsk application. The Chkdsk application will be covered in the next laboratory activity.

The Windows XP Disk Defragmenter GUI version cannot be scheduled, but the command line version can. By default, Windows Vista is scheduled to run automatically at least once a week.

You can run Disk Defragmenter from the command prompt of either Windows Vista or Windows XP. Entering **defrag help** at the command prompt reveals the command syntax and switches for the **defrag** command, as shown in the following screen captures.

```
Command Prompt                                          _ □ x

C:\Documents and Settings\Richard>defrag help

The volume identifier is not valid. The volume identifier must be a valid local
drive letter or mount point.


Usage:
defrag <volume> [-a] [-f] [-v] [-?]
  volume   drive letter or mount point (d: or d:\vol\mountpoint)
  -a       Analyze only
  -f       Force defragmentation even if free space is low
  -v       Verbose output
  -?       Display this help text

C:\Documents and Settings\Richard>
```

Copyright by Goodheart-Willcox Co., Inc.

```
Administrator: Command Prompt                                          _ |□| x|

C:\Windows\system32>defrag help

The volume identifier is not valid. The volume identifier must be a valid local
drive letter or mount point.

Description:  Locates and consolidates fragmented files on local volumes to
              improve system performance.

Syntax:  defrag <volume> -a [-v]
         defrag <volume> [{-r | -w}] [-f] [-v]
         defrag        -c [{-r | -w}] [-f] [-v]

Parameters:

Value          Description

<volume>       Specifies the drive letter or mount point path of the volume to
               be defragmented or analyzed.

-c             Defragments all volumes on this computer.

-a             Performs fragmentation analysis only.

-r             Performs partial defragmentation (default). Attempts to
               consolidate only fragments smaller than 64 megabytes (MB).

-w             Performs full defragmentation. Attempts to consolidate all file
               fragments, regardless of their size.

-f             Forces defragmentation of the volume when free space is low.

-v             Specifies verbose mode. The defragmentation and analysis output
               is more detailed.

-?             Displays this help information.

Examples:

defrag d:
defrag d:\vol\mountpoint -w -f
defrag d: -a -v
defrag -c -v
```

Equipment and Materials

■ Computer with Windows XP or Windows Vista, or both, installed.

Part I (Windows XP)

Procedure

1. ____ Report to your assigned workstation.

2. ____ Boot the computer and verify it is in working order.

3. ____ Open the command prompt and enter **defrag help**. View the contents of the display.

4. ____ Type and enter at the command prompt **defrag c: -a** assuming that drive C is the default drive. Disk Defragmenter will take several minutes to analyze the drive. It will then display the results. If it takes too long, you can exit the command prompt by clicking the **Close** button (X in the upper-right corner of the dialog box) or by right-clicking the title bar and then selecting **Close** from the shortcut menu.

5. ____ After completing step 4, close the dialog box and open Disk Defragmenter using the following path: **Start | All Programs | Accessories | System Tools | Disk Defragmenter**.

6. ____ Close Disk Defragmenter and then access it through the following path: **Start | Control Panel | Performance and Maintenance | Rearrange items on your hard disk to make programs run faster**. The Disk Defragmenter GUI should appear.

7. From the **Help** menu, select **Help Topics**.

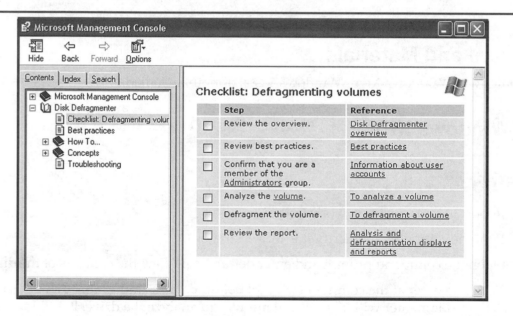

8. _____ The Microsoft Management Console help will appear. In the left-hand pane, navigate to the topic identified as "Checklist: Defragmenting volumes." Take a few minutes to read the information contained in this topic.

9. _____ Close Microsoft Management Console help.

10. _____ Access the Disk Defragmenter using the following path: **Start I All Programs I Accessories I System Tools I Disk Defragmenter**. Select the default volume C to perform an analysis. Wait and watch the results. When complete, a report should appear similar to the one in the following screen capture. Notice that the report can be saved or printed.

Copyright by Goodheart-Willcox Co., Inc.

Analysis Report   [?][X]

Analysis is complete for: (C:)
You do not need to defragment this volume.

Volume information:

Volume (C:)
    Volume size   =   117 GB
    Cluster size   =   4 KB
    Used space   =   76.53 GB
    Free space   =   40.66 GB
    Percent free space   =   34 %
Volume fragmentation

Most fragmented files:

Fragments	File Size	File Name
244	15 MB	\Program Files\Activision\Call of Duty 2\hye\..
212	15 MB	\Program Files\Call of Duty\uo\bismarck_ge_.
156	10 MB	\Documents and Settings\Richard\My Docum.
140	16 MB	\WINDOWS\Cache\Adobe Reader 6.0.1\EN..
120	7 MB	\Documents and Settings\Richard\My Docum.
109	436 KB	\Documents and Settings\Richard\My Docum.
107	13 MB	\Program Files\Microsoft Visual Studio 9.0\VB.
103	50 MB	\Program Files\Microsoft Visual Studio 9.0\Mi.

[Print...]   [Save As...]   [Defragment]   [Close]

11. ____ This concludes Part I of the laboratory activity. Do not answer the review questions until you complete Part II—Windows Vista.

Part II (Windows Vista)

Procedure

1. ____ Report to your assigned workstation.

2. ____ Boot the computer and verify it is in working order.

3. ____ Open the command prompt using the **Run as administrator** option.

4. ____ Type and enter **defrag help** at the command prompt. Take a minute to review the information on the display.

5. ____ Type and enter **defrag c: -a** at the command prompt. Wait a few minutes for the analysis report to be generated and then review it.

6. ____ Close the command prompt.

Copyright by Goodheart-Willcox Co., Inc.

7. _____ Access the Disk Defragmenter by typing **defrag** into the **Search** box located off the **Start** menu. Disk Defragmenter should appear at the top of the search list after only a few letters are typed into the **Search** box . Select the Disk Defragmenter from the search list. A dialog box similar to the one in the following screen capture should appear. The Vista Disk Defragmenter dialog box is very simple in design as compared to the Windows XP design. Notice that the scheduled date and time to run is displayed. Also, the last date and time the operation was performed is displayed as well.

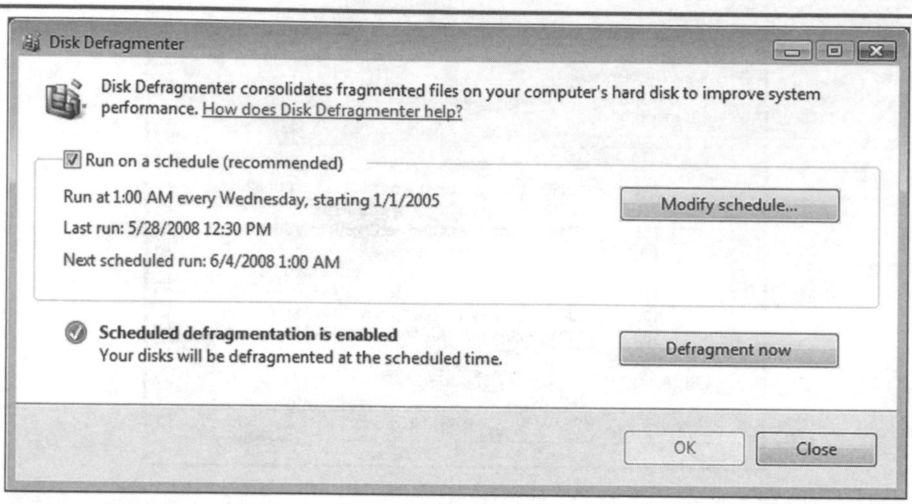

8. _____ Close Disk Defragmenter and then access it through **Start | All Programs | Accessories System Tools | Disk Defragmenter**.

9. _____ Close the Disk Defragmenter again, and then open it through **Start | Control Panel | System and Maintenance | Defragment your hard drive** (located under **Administrative Tools**).

10. _____ Click the **Modify schedule** button and a dialog box similar to the one in the following screen capture should appear.

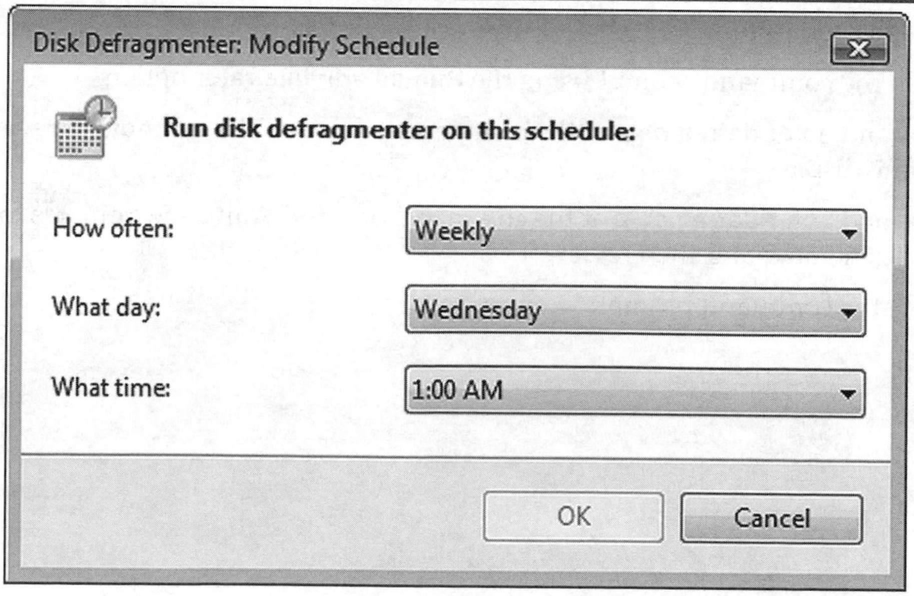

Copyright by Goodheart-Willcox Co., Inc.

Name_____

11. ____ Close the **Disk Defragmenter: Modify Schedule** dialog box and the **Disk Defragmenter** and **System and Maintenance** dialog boxes.

12. ____ Access the Disk Defragmenter using any of the methods encountered thus far. With your instructor's permission, run Disk Defragmenter at this time. Observe the change in the dialog box. The Disk Defragmenter dialog box simply states that it is defragmenting the hard disk drive and that it may take from a few minutes to a few hours. You can cancel the operation any time by clicking the **Close** button.

13. ____ After the Disk Defragmenter finishes or after you cancel the operation, go on to answer the review questions.

Review Questions

1. How much disk free space is required to defragment a disk with the Disk Defragmenter? _____

_____

2. Which file types (FAT16, FAT32, and NTFS) can you defragment?_____

_____

3. Can you defragment a volume containing a corrupt file? _____

4. What program should be disabled before performing a defragmentation? _____

5. True *or* False. Both Windows XP and Windows Vista have a GUI that shows the areas of the disk drive being defragmented as the program runs._____

6. True *or* False. Windows Vista does not allow the user to select which partition or drive to defragment. _____

_____

7. How are volumes or partitions identified that contain corrupt files? _____

_____

8. When running Windows Vista Disk Defragmenter from the command prompt, which switch will perform a full defragmentation and attempt to consolidate all file fragments regardless of size? _____

_____

9. When running Windows Vista Disk Defragmenter from the command prompt, which switch will defragment all volumes on the computer? _____

10. True *or* False. Disk Defragmenter must be manually started in both Windows XP and Windows Vista versions. _____

_____

_____

Computer Service and Repair Lab Manual

Copyright by Goodheart-Willcox Co., Inc.

Name _____ Date _____

Class/Instructor _____

Chkdsk

After completing this laboratory activity, you will be able to:

■ Use Chkdsk to verify the integrity of disks.

■ Identify the available switches associated with the **chkdsk** command.

■ Describe the disk repairs associated with Chkdsk.

Introduction

In this laboratory activity, you will learn to use the Chkdsk tool to check the integrity of a disk and correct many different common disk file errors. Chkdsk will exam FAT16, FAT32, or NTFS file systems, locate the error, and then fix many of the most common file errors such as cross-linked files. The Chkdsk tool cannot repair corrupt data stored in the files, only the file structure.

To understand how Chkdsk makes repairs, you must first look at the way files and directories are stored on disk. The disk is divided into sectors. The sectors are grouped together to form clusters. The clusters are assigned to volumes/partitions. A database is used to identify the location of each and every cluster on a disk. The way the clusters are identified and linked to specific files or directories is determined by the file system that is used such as FAT32 or NTFS. Each partition or volume formatted as FAT16 or FAT32 systems use a file allocation table (FAT). The file allocation table contains the information that relates the location of data files and directories to clusters. NTFS uses a master file table (MFT) that serves the same purpose as FAT.

As you can see, both FAT and MFT are responsible for locating the storage area of all data files on a disk structure. The file table information used to identify each directory or file consists of a series of bits. If a single bit in the FAT or MFT becomes corrupted, then the exact location of the file or directory is altered and will generate an error related to the file. For example, an error can be generated indicating that no such file or directory exists, even when the file does exist on the disk. The corrupt bit can also create an error indicating the wrong location of the first cluster used to store the beginning of the file.

When repairs are made to the files structure, the recovered file may be identified with a new name such as File0000.chk and saved to a folder called Found.000. Both the folder and the file names of the recovered clusters are sequentially named. For example, the second folder created will be called Found.001 and the second file would be called File0001.chk. You can try opening the recovered files by guessing which type of file it is, such as text, graphic, or spreadsheet data. There is no real way of knowing for sure which software application created the recovered file. There are many third-party software tools that claim they can identify the software application that created it.

When viewing the Chkdsk report, you will see the term *volume bitmap*. Microsoft NTFS technology refers to the entire structure of the volume clusters and sectors as a volume bitmap. Do not confuse the term *bitmap* used to describe the disk file system structure with the term *bitmap* used to describe a type of graphics file.

Chkdsk can be run either in text mode from the command prompt or by a graphical user interface (GUI). To run the command prompt version in either Windows Vista or Windows XP and earlier systems, you simply enter the command **chkdsk**. The executable file name for Chkdsk is chkdsk.exe.

Running the **chkdsk** command without any switches is called *read mode*. In this mode, Chkdsk inspects the disk and does no repairs. To run Chkdsk from the command line and make repairs requires the use of command line switches. The most commonly used switches are **/f** and **/r**. They can be used together, for example **chkdsk /f/r**. The **/f** switch repairs errors without scanning for bad sectors. The **/r** switch repairs errors, locates bad sectors, and recovers readable data. When the two command switches are used together, both types of repair functions will be performed.

Be aware that you cannot run Chkdsk when the volume is in use by another program. When Chkdsk displays a message stating that the volume is in use, it also provides you with an option to run Chkdsk the next time the system boots. The following screen captures shows a completed Chkdsk operation run from the command line in Windows XP and Windows Vista. Notice that the screens for each are very similar.

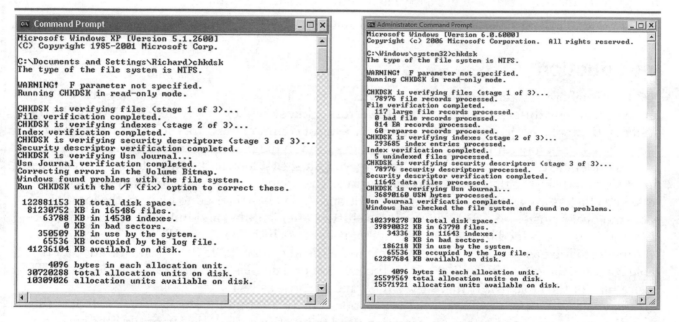

Windows XP　　　　　**Windows Vista**

Look closely at the Windows XP screen captures and you will see how Chkdsk identified a problem and recommended that **chkdsk /f** be run to correct the problem. This message is approximately in the middle of the screen capture.

Copyright by Goodheart-Willcox Co., Inc.

Name____

Chkdsk can also run in a GUI format. To run the GUI version of Chkdsk, open **My Computer** (Windows XP) or **Computer** (Windows Vista) and right-click the drive you wish to check. Select **Properties** from the shortcut menu. The **Properties** dialog box for that drive will display. Select the **Tools** tab. A dialog box similar to those in the following screen captures will display.

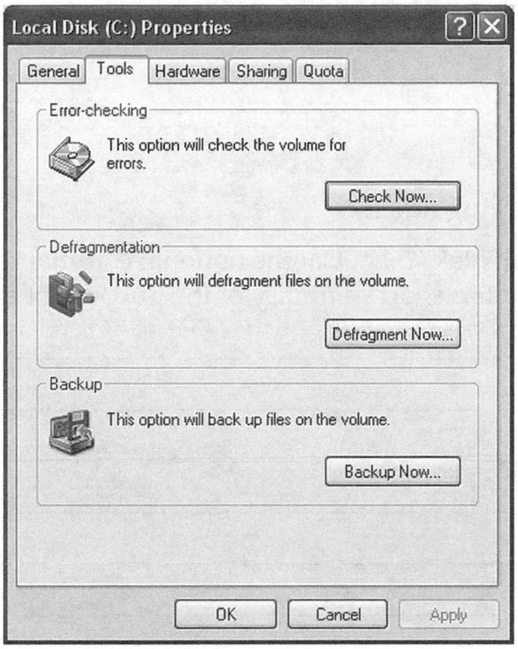

Windows XP

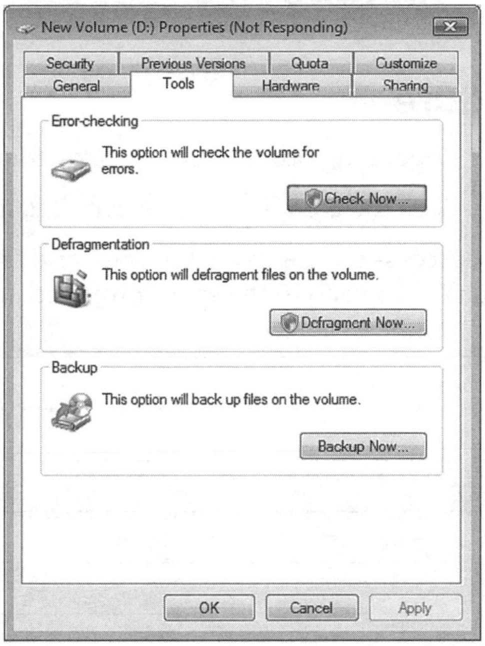

Windows Vista

Click the **Check Now** button located in the **Error-checking** section. A dialog box similar to those in the following screen captures will display, allowing you to select the options to repair errors.

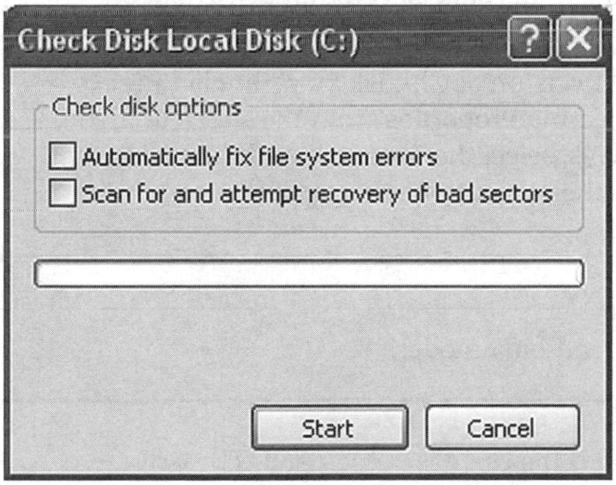

Windows XP

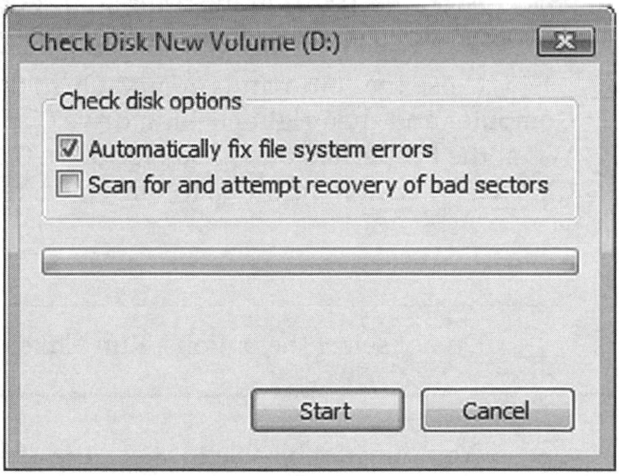

Windows Vista

The options allow you to perform the same functions as the command line Chkdsk switches **/f** and **/r**. The **/f** switch matches the **Automatically fix file system errors** option and the **/r** switch matches the **Scan for and attempt recovery of bad sectors** option.

Copyright by Goodheart-Willcox Co., Inc.

Equipment and Materials

■ Computer with Windows XP or Windows Vista, or both, installed.

Part I (Windows XP)

Procedure

1. _____ Report to your assigned workstation.

2. _____ Boot the computer and verify it is in working order.

3. _____ Access the command prompt and enter **chkdsk /?**. Look at the optional command switches available. List each in the space provided and write a short summary of the purpose of each.

_____

_____

_____

_____

_____

_____

_____

_____

_____

_____

4. _____ Run Chkdsk from the command prompt using the **chkdsk** command without any switches. Observe the process.

5. _____ Close the command prompt. Open the GUI version of Chkdsk by right-clicking **My Computer** and then right-clicking drive C and selecting **Properties** from the shortcut menu. When the **Properties** dialog box for drive C displays, select the **Tools** tab and then click the **Check Now** button. In the space provided, record the two options that appear.

_____

_____

6. _____ Do not select the options. Run Chkdsk in read-only mode.

> **Note:**
> You may not be able to check the disk now if the drive is being used. The drive will be checked when the computer reboots. If this is the case, reboot the computer now.

7. _____ After the results, close Chkdsk and the **Properties** dialog box for drive C.

8. _____ This concludes Part I of the laboratory activity. Do not answer the review questions until you complete Part II—Windows Vista.

    Copyright by Goodheart-Willcox Co., Inc.

Part II (Windows Vista)

Procedure

1. ____ Report to your assigned workstation.

2. ____ Boot the computer and verify it is in working order.

3. ____ Access the command prompt using the **Run as administrator** option. Then, enter **chkdsk /?**. Look at the optional command switches available. Record each in the space provided and write a short summary of the purpose of each.

_____

_____

_____

_____

_____

_____

_____

_____

4. ____ Run Chkdsk from the command prompt using the **chkdsk** command without any switches. Observe the process.

5. ____ Close the command prompt. Open the GUI version of Chkdsk by right-clicking **Computer** and then right-clicking drive C and selecting **Properties** from the shortcut menu. When the **Properties** dialog box for drive C displays, select the **Tools** tab and then click the **Check Now** button. In the space provided, record the two options that appear.

_____

_____

6. ____ Do not select the options. Run Chkdsk in read-only mode.

Note:
     You may not be able to check the disk now if the drive is being used. The drive will be checked when the computer reboots. If this is the case, reboot the computer now.

---

7. ____ After the results, close Chkdsk and the **Properties** dialog box for drive C.

8. ____ Answer the review questions.

Review Questions

1. What is the executable file name for the Chkdsk tool? _____

2. True *or* False. Chkdsk is used to repair corrupt data stored on the disk. _____

   _____

   _____

3. Which Chkdsk command switch is used to repair bad sectors and recover readable information?

   _____

4. Which Chkdsk command switch is used to fix errors on the disk? _____

5. What is the name of the first folder that contains recovered files? _____

6. What is the name of the first recovered file? _____

Copyright by Goodheart-Willcox Co., Inc.

Name _____ Date _____

Class/Instructor _____

Windows Encrypted File System (EFS)

After completing this laboratory activity, you will be able to:

■ Encrypt the contents of a file or folder.

■ Determine when it is appropriate to encrypt a file.

■ Identify which file type is required for file encryption.

■ Explain the results of copying and pasting an encrypted file or folder.

Introduction

In this lab activity, you will learn how to encrypt a file or folder using the Windows XP or Windows Vista operating system. File encryption is used to prevent unauthorized persons from accessing file or folder content. File encryption is a very simple process. The difficulty lies in understanding what happens to encrypted files and folders under working conditions. For example, what happens when you move an encrypted file? Can other users access an encrypted file? Do the contents of an encrypted file look different to the user? By performing the activities in this lab, you will learn the answers to these questions and more.

File encryption is an important aspect of data security. A computer can be easily compromised by unauthorized personnel. A computer may be accessed either directly or over a network. Files could be copied or opened by an intruder and the contents revealed. A notebook computer containing customer lists, corporate information, sensitive e-mail information, bank account information, and many other forms of sensitive information could be lost or stolen. A person might possibly open the files on the computer and reveal the contents. One way to protect files and folder content is to encrypt the contents.

Data encryption is usually based on an encryption key. The key is a secret set of characters applied by a mathematical function to change the contents of the file. For example, a file is represented as a series of ASCII characters. Each letter or number is represented by its equivalent ASCII decimal number. The word *cat* equals the ASCII decimal number series 43, 41, and 54. By adding the number 5 to each of the ASCII decimal numbers, the series would become 48, 46, and 59. The word *cat* would therefore be represented as "hfy."

The encryption key of 5 was only an example. In reality, encryption keys are very long strings of data. Some are 128 characters long. The longer the string of characters in the encryption key, the harder it is to solve the key. The downside of using long encryption keys is it takes longer to encrypt and decrypt the contents of the file.

The Windows Encrypted File System (EFS) requires NTFS to be installed on the partition where the file or folder is to be encrypted. EFS will not work on a FAT partition. Only Windows XP Professional, Windows 2000 Desktop, Windows Vista Business, and Windows Vista Ultimate support EFS. Windows XP Home Edition, Windows Vista Home Basic, and Windows Vista Home Premium do not.

Certain types of files, such as system files and compressed files, cannot be encrypted. You do not want to encrypt files such as .exe, .dll, .com, or system files and compressed files that are critical to other programs. You should only apply encryption to data files.

It is important to note that an encrypted file appears transparent to the user. A typical user cannot tell if a file is encrypted, unless they notice the color of the file name. For more information on Windows XP file encryption, see the Microsoft article Q223316: Best Practices for the Encrypting File System. For more information about Windows Vista file encryption conduct a Help and Support search using the term *EFS*. The search will reveal a great deal of related information. Some important features about EFS are as follows:

- You can either encrypt or compress a file or folder but not both.
- The original creator of the encrypted file has control over who has access.
- When an encrypted file is moved, it remains encrypted.
- Ordinary files become encrypted when placed inside an encrypted folder.
- Files in an encrypted folder remain encrypted when removed from the folder.

Equipment and Materials

- Typical PC with Windows XP Professional, Windows Vista Business, or Windows Vista Ultimate installed. (Do *not* use Windows XP Home Edition, Windows Vista Home Basic, or Windows Vista Home Premium. The file system must be NTFS.)

Note:
Windows Vista Home Basic and Windows Vista Home Premium can be modified to decrypt files but cannot create encrypted files.

Procedure

1. ____ Report to your assigned workstation. Boot the computer and make sure it is in working order.

2. ____ There must be at least two additional user accounts for this exercise: one account with computer administrator access and the other account with limited access. You may wish to use the account names as follows: AdminEqual and LimitedUser. This will help you determine which account is which.

3. ____ Create a new folder in your My Documents (Windows XP) or Documents (Windows Vista) directory and name it "Secret Folder."

4. ____ Right-click Secret Folder and select **Properties** from the shortcut menu. The **Properties** dialog box for Secret Folder will display.

    Copyright by Goodheart-Willcox Co., Inc.

5. _____ Click the **Advanced** button. The **Advanced Attributes** dialog box will display.

6. _____ In the **Compress or Encrypt attributes** section, select the **Encrypt contents to secure data** option.

7. _____ Click **OK** to exit the **Advanced Attributes** dialog box and then click **OK** to exit the **Properties** dialog box.

8. _____ Create a text file that reads "I have many secrets." Name the text file "Secret Memo," and save it to the folder named "Secret Folder."

9. _____ Answer each of the following questions by experimenting with file encryption. If using Windows XP, use the two accounts you created and the Simple File Sharing mode. Record the results after each question.

What color characters represent the encrypted folder? _____

_____

Can another computer administrator-type account send the document to the Recycle Bin? _____

_____

Can another computer administrator-type account view the contents of the encrypted file? _____

_____

What happens when you compress an encrypted file? _____

_____

What happens when you drag or copy the contents of the encrypted file into a different folder that is not encrypted? For example, into the Shared Documents folder? _____

_____

10. _____ If you are using a multi-boot system, copy the encrypted folder and paste it into the C partition. Make sure there is an encrypted file inside the folder before you copy and paste the folder. The C partition should be FAT. Record what happens.

_____

11. _____ When you have finished experimenting with the encrypted files, go on to answer the review questions. Then, remove the user accounts created for this lab and the test folder and file. Return all materials to their proper storage area and restore the computer to its original condition.

Review Questions

1. What does the acronym EFS represent? _____

_____

2. What color is a file or folder name when it is encrypted? _____

_____

3. How can security of critical files be enhanced? _____

_____

4. What happens when you move or copy an encrypted file to a folder that is not encrypted?

_____

5. What happens when a limited user attempts to access an encrypted file or folder? _____

_____

6. What happens when a user with a computer administrator-type account attempts to access the encrypted file or folder of another user with a computer administrator-type account? _____

_____

                          Copyright by Goodheart-Willcox Co., Inc.

7. Can a user with a computer administrator-type account remove or delete another user's encrypted file? _____

8. Who can restore the file from the Recycle Bin? _____

_____

9. What types of files can you *not* encrypt? _____

_____

10. What text command can be used to encrypt files? _____

_____

Copyright by Goodheart-Willcox Co., Inc.

Copyright by Goodheart-Willcox Co., Inc.

Name _____ Date _____

Class/Instructor _____

CD/DVD Drive Installation

After completing this laboratory activity, you will be able to:

■ Install any type of IDE CD-ROM or DVD drive.

■ Identify common problems associated with CD-ROM or DVD drive installation.

■ Identify the major parts required for CD-ROM or DVD drive installation.

Introduction

In this laboratory activity, you will install a new CD-ROM or DVD drive in a PC that didn't previously have one, or you will replace or upgrade an existing CD-ROM or DVD drive. The exact type of procedure will be assigned by your instructor. The installation process is similar for both types of installation.

Installing a CD/DVD drive is a simple task. The installation can be more complicated when a sound card is used in combination with the CD/DVD drive. When a sound card is incorporated with the CD/DVD drive for enhanced audio, some problems may develop. Usually the sound card and CD/DVD drive will share the same IRQ assignment.

The original Plug and Play technology often failed to correctly identify a new CD/DVD drive. This is rarely a problem today, but it still occurs occasionally. When Plug and Play fails to correctly identify the new drive, you will need to use the installation CD that accompanies it. Follow the instructions in the drive's installation manual. When an installation manual is not available, you can usually obtain the information from the manufacturer's Web site as well as the required software drivers or the latest updated driver.

Loading the proper driver can be another problem when installing a CD drive. When the new drive is installed and the computer is booted, the operating system should automatically detect the CD/DVD drive and load the appropriate driver. For example, in Windows XP, Plug and Play identifies the new device and then automatically extracts the driver files from the cab files and installs them. Cab files are located on the hard drive as part of the Windows XP installation. They are compressed files supplied by the manufacturer and are included in the Windows XP installation disc.

New drives are placed on the market daily. The operating system you are using may not contain the very latest drivers needed for the installation. In this case, you will need to find the latest driver and install it manually. A driver is usually included when the CD drive is purchased, but it may not be the latest. It is, therefore, a good idea to check the manufacturer's Web site for the latest driver for the device as well as information about known problems. Checking the Web site can save many frustrating hours during an installation.

Keep in mind that Windows Vista has changed the way driver files are handled by using two distinct steps: staging and installation. During staging, the driver is added to what Microsoft refers to as the driver store. The driver store is the collection of drivers used for all the hardware installed on the computer. A driver can be added to the driver store before the physical hardware is actually installed. Microsoft has a list of "bad drivers" which Windows Vista will not allow to be installed. The bad drivers have been identified by Microsoft and can cause the operating system to lock up or fail. During the installation step, Windows Vista automatically detects the new hardware item and then automatically installs the correct driver from the driver store. The changes to Windows Vista are part of Microsoft's efforts to prevent the installation of software that can harm the operating system.

To manually install a hardware device in Windows XP or Windows Vista, you will need to open **Control Panel** and then select **Classic View** option. The **Add New Hardware** icon is no longer part of the Windows XP or Windows Vista default Control Panel listing of services. Running Windows XP or Windows Vista Control Panel in classic view will provide you with the **Add Hardware** icon, thus allowing you to perform a manual installation of a hardware device.

Proper connection of the CD drive can be another troublesome area during the installation. When installing a CD drive, avoid sharing the IDE connection with the hard drive. Sharing the same IDE connection can create compatibility problems between the CD drive and the hard drive. One problem is resolving the master/slave issue between the two devices. The other is the data transfer speed. An older hard drive will most likely have a much slower data transfer rate than the newer CD drive. This condition will cause the CD drive to transfer data at the lower rate, matching the hard disk drive and thus hurting the performance of the CD drive.

The mechanics of installing a CD drive are quite simple. The only real concern is the possibility of loosening a connection to one of the other drives while installing the CD drive cables. The following illustration of a typical CD drive shows the connection points on the end of the drive.

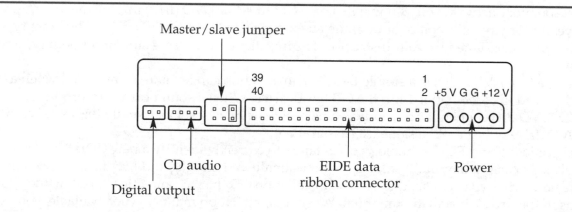

Note the master/slave jumper selection area. The master/slave jumper setup is similar to that found on hard drives. When more than one device is connected to an IDE or EIDE connection, one device must be designated the master and the other as the slave.

Equipment and Materials

- Computer with Windows XP or Windows Vista, or both, installed.
- CD-ROM or DVD drive.

Procedure

1. ＿＿＿ Boot the PC to be sure it is in working order before you begin the installation procedure.

2. ＿＿＿ Once you have verified that the assigned PC is in working order, properly shut it down and turn off the power.

Copyright by Goodheart-Willcox Co., Inc.

3. ____ Remove the PC cover and select the bay in which the new CD/DVD drive will be installed. If you are replacing an existing drive, sketch the drive and its cable connections. Take care to mark the proper orientation of the cables, as you will most likely have to reinstall the original drive at the end of the lab. Once you have sketched the drive setup, disconnect the cables and remove the mounting screws from the mounting rails. Slide the CD/DVD drive out of its bay. This procedure will vary based on the make and model of the drive and the case.

4. ____ If you are performing a new installation, install the mounting rails to the bay now. For a unit replacement, check the existing mounting rails for compatibility with the new drive. You may need to remove the existing mounting rails and replace them with a set of rails compatible with the new drive. Before securing the CD/DVD drive into the case, check the master/slave jumper settings. Be sure to choose the correct setting for the installation. Check the drive's documentation or look on the side of the drive for a chart of jumper settings.

5. ____ Mount the CD/DVD drive into the bay using the mounting rails. Be careful not to over-tighten the mounting screws. Use only the mounting screws that were provided with the drive. Screws that did not come with the drive may be too long and may damage the CD/DVD drive during installation.

6. ____ Attach the power cable to the CD/DVD drive.

7. ____ Attach the ribbon cable between the CD/DVD drive and the IDE controller port on the motherboard.

8. ____ Next, attach the audio cable to the sound card, if the computer is equipped with one. You may need to read the sound card documentation to locate the correct connection for the audio cable. The audio cable may connect to the motherboard if the sound system is integrated into the motherboard.

9. ____ Have the instructor inspect your installation now.

10. ____ After the instructor has checked your installation, you may power up and boot the PC. Watch the screen for the detection of the new CD/DVD drive. If the new drive is not correctly identified, you may need to manually install the driver software. The manual installation begins by accessing the **Add New Hardware** icon in **Control Panel**. The **Add New Hardware** icon is located at **Start | Settings | Control Panel | Add New Hardware**. You will need to change the view for Windows XP or Windows Vista Control Panel to Classic View to access the **Add Hardware** icon.

After accessing the **Add New Hardware** program, simply follow the instructions prompted on the display. You will need to have the disc containing the driver for the CD/DVD drive, because the drive probably will not work with the generic drivers provided by the operating system.

11. ____ After the CD/DVD drive installation is complete, test the drive to be sure it is functioning properly. Either access a disc or burn a disc, depending on the type of drive installed.

12. ____ Open **Device Manager** and record the resource assignment for the CD/DVD drive. The exact resource assignments will vary. You may need to open the sound card assignments to obtain the drive's assignments. Look in both places if a sound card is installed.

13. ____ Have the instructor once more check your project to verify it is working properly. Once inspected, the instructor will advise you to either leave the existing drive mounted in the PC, or reverse the operation and place the original device back into the PC.

14. ____ If you removed the newer drive and reinstalled the original unit, test the system to be sure it is working properly.

15. ____ Answer the review questions.

Copyright by Goodheart-Willcox Co., Inc.

Review Questions

1. What problems might arise during a CD/DVD drive installation? _____

   _____

   _____

   _____

   _____

2. Why should you avoid connecting the CD/DVD drive on the same IDE controller on the motherboard? _____

   _____

3. What are the two stages used by Microsoft Vista for driver installation? _____

   _____

4. Since Windows Vista no longer has the **Add Hardware** icon available in the default view of **Control Panel**, how can you install hardware manually in Windows Vista? _____

   _____

   _____

   _____

5. What does the stripe running along the ribbon cable indicate? _____

   _____

   _____

6. Where could you locate the latest driver for the CD/DVD drive you are installing? _____

   _____

7. Why should you use only the screws designed for the mounting of the drive? _____

   _____

   _____

Copyright by Goodheart-Willcox Co., Inc.

Name _____ Date _____

Class/Instructor _____

Windows XP Printer Installation

After completing this laboratory activity, you will be able to:

■ Install and set up a typical printer.

■ Explain the various printer options available.

Introduction

The installation of a new printer is a common procedure. During the early years of personal computers, printer installation could be quite difficult. Now, in the era of Plug and Play and wizard programs, printer installation is much easier. In this laboratory activity, you will install a printer driver. For the purpose of lab instruction, an HP laser printer is used, although the exact model will not be specified. You should substitute the manufacturer and model of your own printer in its place.

A printer driver is necessary for communications between the software that uses a printer and the printer hardware. The driver translates the communications between processor and printer. The processor communicates in hexadecimal or binary codes. The printer driver translates those and reissues them as commands that the printer can understand. In turn, the printer starts a new page, changes font size or style, copies an image from RAM, or prints a line.

If the correct driver is not selected, many things go wrong. An endless stream of paper may be ejected from the printer, completely blank or filled with unintelligible symbols. The printer may simply sit there and appear dead.

To install a printer in Windows XP, access the printer installation program either through Control Panel or from **Start I Printers and Faxes**. Once the **Printers and Faxes** dialog box is open, click **Add a Printer**, which is listed under **Printer Tasks**.

Equipment and Materials

■ Typical PC with Windows XP installed.

■ Windows XP Installation CD.

■ HP laser printer or equivalent.

> ***Note:***
> The lab is compatible with most printers. Simply substitute the brand and model you are using in place of references made to the HP laser printer.

Procedure

1. ____ Boot the PC and wait for the Windows desktop to appear.

2. ____ Access **Printer and Faxes** located off the **Start** menu. The **Printer and Faxes** dialog box will appear similar to the following.

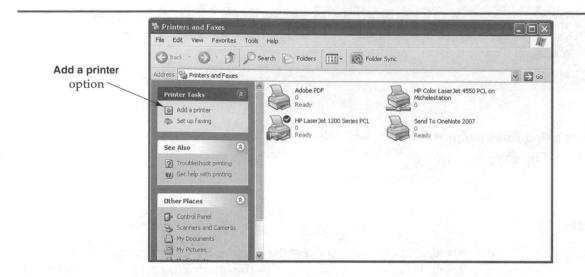

3. ____ Select the **Add a printer** option located under **Printer Tasks** on the left side of the window. The Add Printer wizard should start automatically and will look similar to the following.

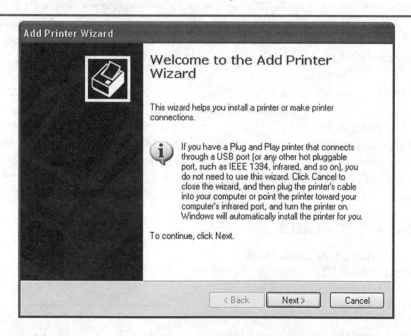

Copyright by Goodheart-Willcox Co., Inc.

4. ____ Click the **Next** button. The **Add Printer** wizard dialog box should look similar to the following. You must make a choice of printer connection by selecting either the **Local printer attached to this computer** or **A network printer, or a printer attached to another computer** option.

Add Printer Wizard

Local or Network Printer
The wizard needs to know which type of printer to set up.

Select the option that describes the printer you want to use:

⦿ Local printer attached to this computer
    ☑ Automatically detect and install my Plug and Play printer
◯ A network printer, or a printer attached to another computer

ⓘ To set up a network printer that is not attached to a print server, use the "Local printer" option.

[< Back] [Next >] [Cancel]

A local printer is one that is directly connected to the PC, while a network printer is one that is accessed via a network. In this lab activity, you should select **Local printer attached to this computer**.

When installing a local printer, the Windows XP operating system usually correctly detects and identifies the correct printer and will automatically configure the correct drivers. For this lab activity, unselect the check box indicating **Automatically detect and install my Plug and Play printer**. This will allow you to see the screens provided for a manual installation.

5. ____ Click **Next**. A dialog box similar to the following will appear, prompting you to select a port. Select the default LPT1 port so that you can see the options available.

Add Printer Wizard

Select a Printer Port
Computers communicate with printers through ports.

Select the port you want your printer to use. If the port is not listed, you can create a new port.

⦿ Use the following port: [LPT1: (Recommended Printer Port) ▼]

             LPT1: (Recommended Printer Port)
Note: Most computers u| LPT2: (Printer Port)
The connector for this p| LPT3: (Printer Port)
             COM1: (Serial Port)
             COM2: (Serial Port)
             COM3: (Serial Port)
             COM4: (Serial Port)
             FILE: (Print to File)
             \\MICHELESTATION\Printer (Local Port)
             Desktop*.pdf (Adobe PDF Port)
◯ Create a new port: DOT4_001 (HP LaserJet 1200 Printer)
   Type of port: My Documents*.pdf (Adobe PDF Port)
             Send To Microsoft OneNote Port: (Local Port)

[< Back] [Next >] [Cancel]

---

6. ____ Click **Next** again. A dialog box similar to the following will appear. This dialog box allows you to manually select the printer manufacturer and printer. There is also an option to use a driver that came on a disc with the printer. This option allows you to install a printer not identified in the list.

7. ____ Cancel out of the manual installation by clicking **Cancel**, unless your instructor wants you to continue with a manual installation.

If you continue with the manual installation, you will be prompted to enter a printer name. The name you choose should be designed to assist you in identifying the printer at a later date. This is especially true of a network shared printer. For example, the printer name might be "LaserJet Room 114."

Before you finish the installation, a screen will appear similar to the following giving you an option to print a test page. Always test the printer configuration by printing a test page.

8. ____ Answer the review questions, and then return the workstation to its original configuration.

Copyright by Goodheart-Willcox Co., Inc.

Name_____

Review Questions

1. Which two physical ports are typically used to connect to an older model printer? _____
   _____

2. What does the printer driver do? _____
   _____
   _____

3. What is the difference between a COM port and an LPT port? _____
   _____
   _____

4. If a printer prints unintelligible characters or symbols when first installed, what is most likely
   the problem? _____
   _____
   _____

Copyright by Goodheart-Willcox Co., Inc.

Copyright by Goodheart-Willcox Co., Inc.

Name _____ Date _____

Class/Instructor _____

Windows Vista
Local Printer
Installation

After completing this laboratory activity, you will be able to:

- Install a local printer using Windows Vista.
- Print a test page.
- Define the term *local printer*.
- Locate information concerning common printer problems.

Introduction

In this laboratory activity, you will explore the Windows Vista printer options. The two broad categories of printer types defined by Microsoft Vista are local printer and network printer. A *local printer* connects directly to a computer port using a cable. All others printer connections are considered a *network printer*, even if they connect wirelessly.

Both Windows XP and Windows Vista have made it extremely easy to install a local printer, especially if the printer is connected by a USB cable. USB is the most common cable type used for connecting printers.

A printer may also be equipped with a network adapter. Beginning with Windows Vista, Microsoft has incorporated new software which automatically locates a printer on a local network. Connecting to a network printer will be covered in the next lab activity.

Some of the most common problems you need to be familiar with when working with printers are very simple, but the solution to these problems are often overlooked by new technicians. The following are some things to check.

- Check that the printer is "on line." This means that the printer is ready to start printing. Most printers have a button or menu selection that has the ability to turn the printer on or off.
- Check that the power cord is plugged in. People can accidentally unplug the electrical power to a printer. Also, a cleaning crew can unplug the power cord from the outlet to use a vacuum cleaner and then forget to plug it back in.
- Check that the printer cable is properly inserted. Cables can work lose or become accidentally unplugged.

When installing a printer for the first time, you may need to supply the print drivers if Windows does not automatically install the print driver. This is especially true if you are installing a printer that was released after the latest Windows operating system was released. A copy of the new printer driver is located on the disc that comes with the printer. Another way to locate the latest print driver is to visit the printer manufacturer's Web site and download the latest printer driver that corresponds to the operating system.

Copyright by Goodheart-Willcox Co., Inc.

Equipment and Materials

- Typical PC with Windows Vista installed.
- Local printer (optional).

Note:
A local printer is not necessary for this lab activity. Also, be aware that the exact steps presented in the lab activity will change if another student has already installed the printer identified in the lab activity. The series of screen captures will not exactly match your lab activity if the other student did not remove the printer as directed.

Procedure

1. ____ Report to your assigned workstation. Do not connect a local printer to the computer at this time.

2. ____ Boot the computer and verify it is in working order.

3. ____ Access **Start | Control Panel | Hardware and Sound** and look at the four options available for the **Printers** option: **Add a printer, Change default printer, Remove a printer**, and **Send a fax**. These are the four most common printer tasks.

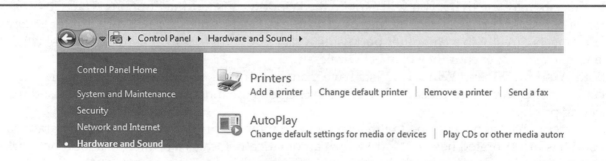

4. ____ Select the **Add a printer** option. The **Add Printer** wizard will appear. You will have two choices: **Add a local printer** and **Add a network, wireless or Bluetooth printer**. Notice that for the **Add a local printer** option, Windows Vista excludes a USB printer. This is because Windows automatically detects USB printers when they are plugged in to the USB port.

Copyright by Goodheart-Willcox Co., Inc.

Name_____

5. ____ Select the **Add a local printer** option. A screen will display allowing you to select the type of port you are connecting to, such as LPT1 or COM1. These ports are seldom used today.

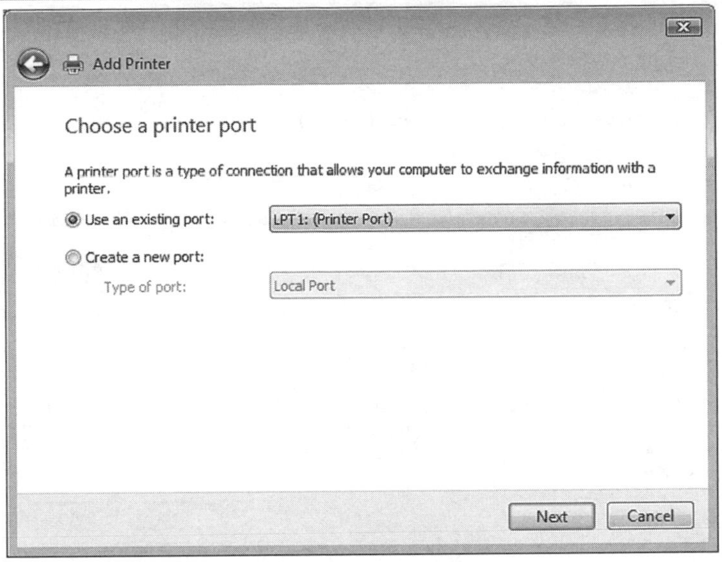

There are two options: **Use an existing port** and **Create a new port**. The **Use an existing port** option is selected by default. Click the drop-down arrow to reveal the list of standard ports that can be used to connect the printer. Scan the list to become familiar with the ports available. Then, choose the default LPT1 port.

6. ____ Click **Next**. The **Install the printer driver** dialog box should appear similar to the one in the following screen capture.

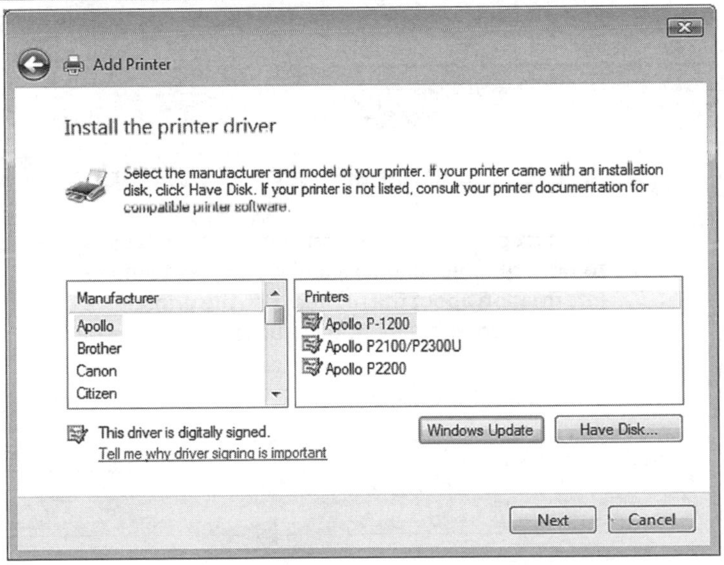

The list of printer manufacturers appears on the left, and the various printers associated with the printer manufacturer are listed on the right. Notice that there is a **Have Disk** button. This button is used to install printer drivers from the CD that comes with the printer. There is also a **Windows Update** button, which looks for the very latest Windows driver available for the selected printer. Before moving on in the lab activity, click the Tell me why driver signing is important link and view the information.

Copyright by Goodheart-Willcox Co., Inc.

7. ____ Choose the default or the Apollo P-1200 printer. A dialog box will appear similar to the following.

The Apollo P-1200 printer has been added. You now have an opportunity to print a test page. Printing a test page is an industry standard practice and ensures that the printer is working correctly.

8. ____ Click the **Print a test page** button. A message box similar to the following will appear.

The test page is sent to the printer queue. The printer queue contains a list of files waiting to be printed.

     Copyright by Goodheart-Willcox Co., Inc.

9. ____ Click the <u>Troubleshoot printer problems</u> link to see information from Windows Help and Support on troubleshooting printer problems. Take a few minutes to explore the information associated with the most common printer problems.

10. ____ After viewing the information, close the **Windows Help and Support** dialog box and the message box. You will be returned to the **Add Printer** dialog box.

11. ____ Click **Finish**.

12. ____ You sent a test page to the printer but you never really installed a physical printer. This will create an error. Open the printer queue to view the pending print jobs. You open the printer queue by following the same path as presented earlier in the lab activity: **Start | Control Panel | Hardware and Sound | Printers**. A dialog box with a collection of available printers will appear similar to the one in the following screen capture.

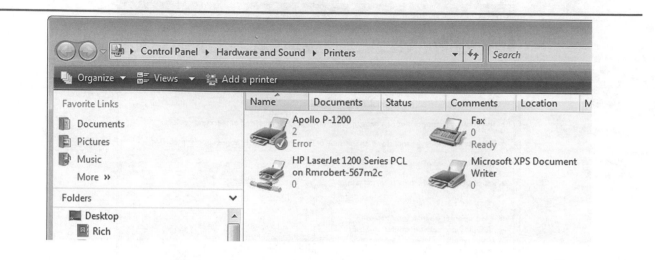

Notice the Apollo P-1200 printer is listed and shows two errors. The errors were generated when two test pages were sent to the printer. Since the physical printer does not exist, errors were generated. Also, notice the check mark on the Apollo P-1200 printer. The check mark is used to indicate the default printer where print jobs are sent. This is important when two or more printers are installed. A common error is to send a print job to the wrong printer.

13. ____ Double-click the Apollo P-1200 printer or right-click the printer and select **Open** from the shortcut menu to view the printer queue.

Document Name	Status	Owner	Pages	Size	Submitted	Port
Test Page	Error - Printing	Rich	1	88.4 KB/192 KB	10:40:04 AM 6/12/2008	LPT1:
Test Page		Rich	1	88.4 KB	10:40:23 AM 6/12/2008	

2 document(s) in queue

When the printer queue opens, you will see a list of all print jobs currently in the printer queue. In the screen capture, you can see two print jobs in the queue. The first one indicates an error. You can now either right-click the document listed in the queue and click **Cancel** from the shortcut menu, or you can access the **Printer** menu and select **Cancel All Documents**. The **Cancel All Documents** command will delete all pending print jobs. Right-clicking a single item in the print queue will only delete the selected item. Delete all pending print jobs from the printer queue now.

Copyright by Goodheart-Willcox Co., Inc.

14. ____ Select the Apollo P-1200 printer and then right-click the printer. From the shortcut menu, select **Properties**. The **Properties** dialog box for that printer will display and will look similar to the following screen capture.

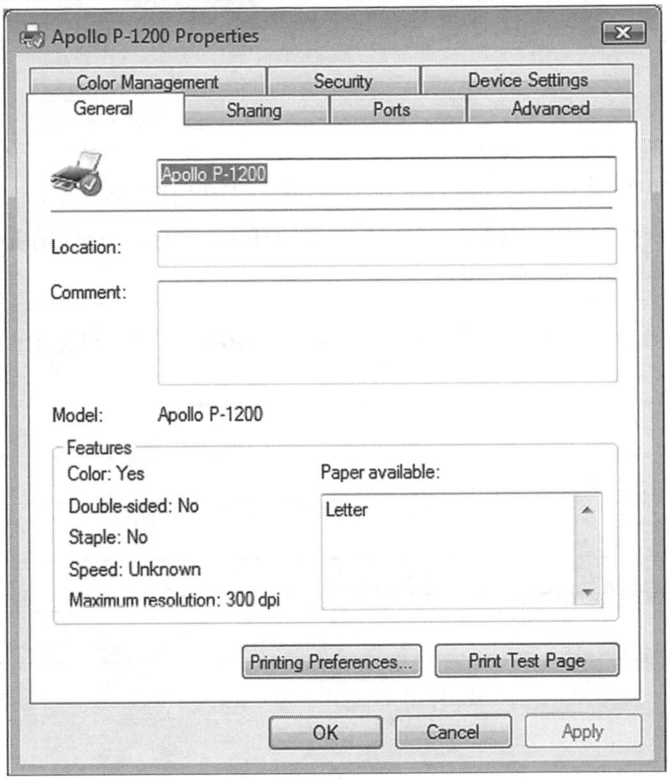

Notice that you can print a test page from the printer **Properties** dialog box. The printer **Properties** dialog box presents many different configuration features for the printer. Take a few minutes to explore the various tabs associated with the **Properties** dialog box. After you have finished exploring the features, close the **Properties** dialog box.

15. ____ Repeat the lab activity, but this time install a different printer and print a test page once more. Delete the test page and then remove both printers. To remove a printer, simply right-click the printer icon in the **Printers** dialog box and then select **Delete** from the shortcut menu.

Note:

At times, Microsoft Vista will not completely remove a selected printer. If you have difficulties removing the printers, call your instructor for assistance. Your instructor can coach you on how to use the System Restore feature to remove the printer.

---

16. ____ Complete the review questions.

Copyright by Goodheart-Willcox Co., Inc.

Review Questions

1. What are the two broad categories of printer types as defined by Microsoft Vista? _____

   _____

2. Define the term *local printer*. _____

   _____

   _____

3. What is the most common cable type used for connecting printers? _____

4. In which Windows Vista Control Panel category is the **Printers** option located? _____

   _____

5. What are the four common tasks associated with Windows Vista Control Panel **Printers** option?

   _____

   _____

6. What is the printer queue? _____

   _____

7. Where would you find the latest version of a printer driver? _____

   _____

Copyright by Goodheart-Willcox Co., Inc.

Name _____ Date _____

Class/Instructor _____

Windows Vista Network Printer Installation

After completing this laboratory activity, you will be able to:

- Create a connection between a computer and a networked printer.
- Identify the UNC printer name format.
- Identify the URL printer name format.

Introduction

One of the major improvements in the Microsoft Windows operating system is how Windows Vista was modified to easily locate other devices on a local network, such as printers. Microsoft Vista incorporates new networking technology based on the Link Layer Discovery Protocol. This protocol will be covered in more detail during the networking lab activities. Simply stated, the Microsoft Vista operating system can automatically detect printers located in the local area network, making it very easy to connect to any networked printer.

Windows Vista also has options that allow you to conduct a search by the assigned printer name. The naming formats can vary. For example, the Universal Naming Convention (UNC) (also known as the *Uniform Naming Convention*) is the original naming convention used for many years by network operating systems to identify device locations in a network. The UNC format consists of two forward slashes followed by the name of the computer the printer is connected to or controlled by, followed by a single forward slash and the name assigned to the printer. For example, a printer called *Laser1* connected to a computer called *HomePC* will appear in UNC format as \\HomePC\Laser1. This naming convention is also used to identify network shares. Remember the format for UNC is \\ServerName\PrinterName.

Another format is the familiar Internet format you are most likely familiar with, known as the Uniform Resource Locator (URL) naming convention. It consists of the computer name and printer name: http://ServerName/Printers/ComputerName.Printer. Notice the URL name ends with ".printer" rather than the familiar ".com" domain name.

Another way Windows Vista can locate a printer is by the TCP/IP address. The TCP/IP addresses consist of a series of unique numbers separated by periods assigned to the printer. For example, 192.168.0.111 is a familiar TCP/IP–assigned local area network printer address. There will be much more about network identification names and TCP/IP addresses much later in the textbook and the lab activity manual. For now, please be patient with the content presented.

For you to be able to connect and use a local area printer, the printer administrator must give permission to other users to connect to the printer. In a home environment, the printer owner must give permission to connect to the local printer. The printer connected to a network must be configured as a network share. A *network share* means that the printer can be shared with other users on the local network once identified by the network administrator and given permission to connect to the printer. Again, information about network shares and permissions will be presented in much more detail later in the networking lab activities.

In this lab activity, you will simply run the wizard and establish a connection to a printer already configured as a network share by your instructor or an advanced student.

Equipment and Materials

■ Typical PC with Windows Vista installed.

Note:

    To be able to perform this lab activity, a printer must be connected to another computer on a local network or connected directly to the local network through a network cable or wireless technology, such as Bluetooth.

Procedure

1. ____ Report to your assigned workstation.

2. ____ Boot the computer and verify it is in working order.

3. ____ Start the Add Printer Wizard by accessing **Start | Control Panel | Hardware and Sound | Printers | Add a Printer**. The **Add Printer** dialog box will display and look similar to the following.

Add Printer

Choose a local or network printer

➜ **Add a local printer**
Use this option only if you don't have a USB printer. (Windows automatically installs USB printers when you plug them in.)

➜ **Add a network, wireless or Bluetooth printer**
Make sure that your computer is connected to the network, or that your Bluetooth or wireless printer is turned on.

Next   Cancel

Copyright by Goodheart-Willcox Co., Inc.

4. ____ Select the **Add a network, wireless or Bluetooth printer** option, and then click **Next**. The Add Printer Wizard will automatically search the local network for all possible printer devices. When the printing devices are found, they will appear in the dialog box similar to that in the following screen capture.

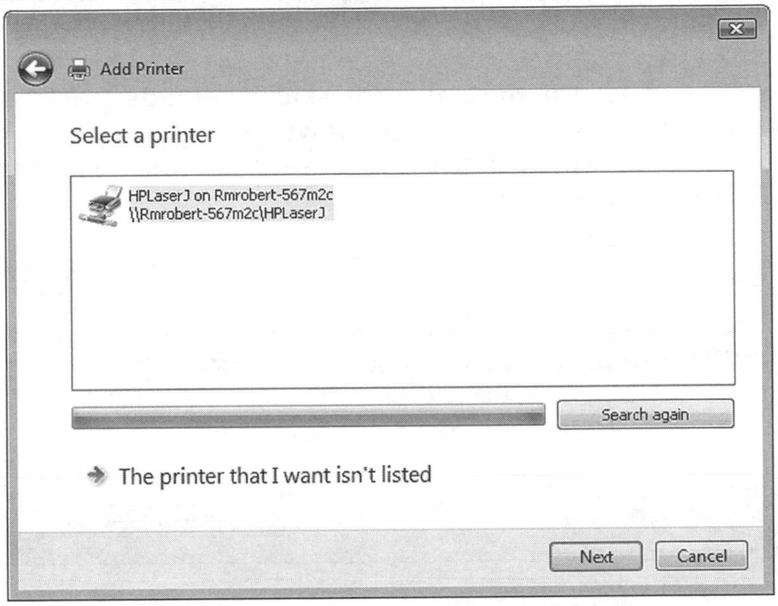

If you do not locate the printer, click **The printer that I want isn't listed**. A new dialog box will appear requesting an additional search for the printer and an option for you to input the assigned printer name. The dialog box is similar to the one in the following screen capture.

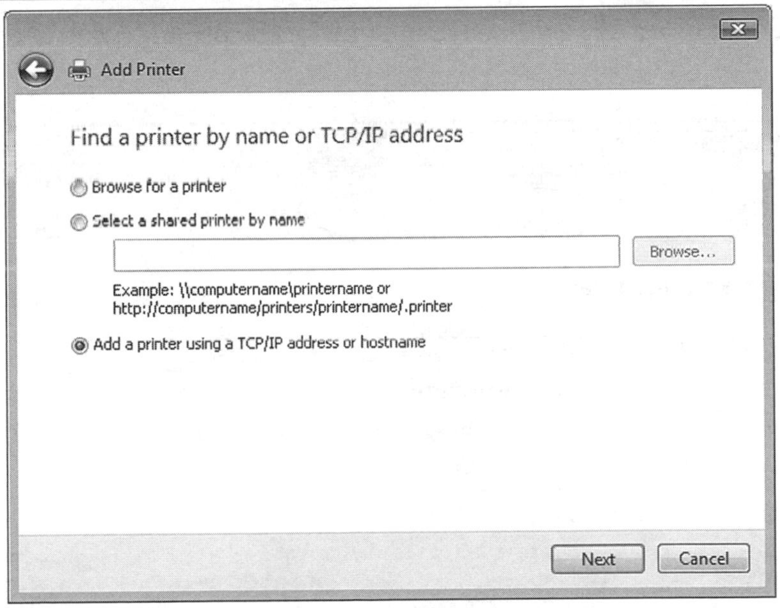

Notice the two formats for printer names. The first example is the original share name, UNC, format, which consists of the computer or print server name followed by the name of the printer: \\ServerName\PrinterName. The other format is the URL, or Internet naming, format, which is written as //ServerName/Printers/ComputerName.Printer. A similar naming format is used to locate Web pages.

Copyright by Goodheart-Willcox Co., Inc.

There is also a third option that allows you to search for the printer by the network TCP/IP address or host name. The TCP/IP address looks like a series of four number groups separated by periods. For example, 192.168.0.111. There will be much more about network properties in later lab activities.

The printer should have appeared in the first dialog box without the need for the additional search procedures.

5. ____ After the printer appears in the dialog box, simply select the printer using the mouse and then click **Next**. The next dialog box to appear will configure the print driver necessary for communicating to the network printer. You will see a notice similar to that in the following screen capture. Click **Install driver**.

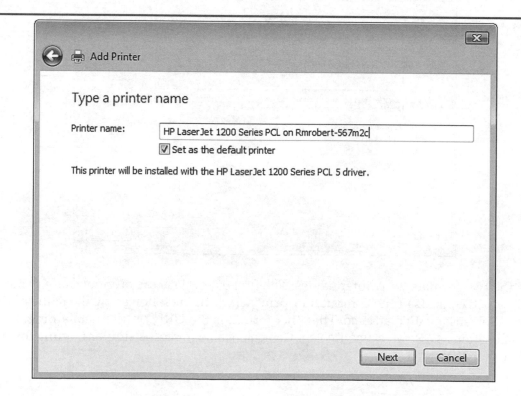

If the printer has already been configured by a previous student, you will see a different dialog box informing you that Windows detected a print driver for this particular printer. It will also request that you use the currently installed print driver or install a different one. If this occurs, simply use the currently installed driver and proceed to the next step.

6. ____ Next, you will be prompted to enter a name for the printer. Look at the following screen capture.

Copyright by Goodheart-Willcox Co., Inc.

There will be a default name already inserted into the text box as a suggestion. You can change the name if you wish. The important thing is to use a name that is very descriptive so that you can easily identify the printer when viewing it over the network. You may want to incorporate a room or building name or a combination of both to better identify the printer. For example, if there are five different HP LaserJet 1200 Series printers in the same building, it will be difficult to tell which is which without additional information being added to the name.

Also, notice that the printer has automatically been selected as the default printer. This means all print jobs will run through this printer. If you connect more than one network printer to a computer, only one can be the default printer. A user can select a different printer in the printer application program software.

7. ____ After the printer has been properly or even improperly configured, a dialog box will appear with the option to print a test page. Always print a test page to ensure the printer is operating correctly.

8. ____ Uninstall the printer by accessing **Start | Control Panel | Hardware and Sound | Printers**. Select the printer and remove the printer as you did in the previous lab activity. Simply right-click the printer and select **Delete** from the shortcut menu. After you have removed the printer, answer the review questions.

Review Questions

1. Write an example of the UNC naming convention for a printer named Printer1 connected directly to a computer named BobsPC. _____

2. What does the acronym UNC represent? _____

   _____

3. Write the URL for a printer named BigPrinter connected to a print server named PrintServer3.

   _____

4. What is a common reason for a person to not be able to connect to an existing network printer?

   _____

5. Who provides permission to connect to a network printer? _____

   _____

Copyright by Goodheart-Willcox Co., Inc.

Name _____ Date _____

Class/Instructor _____

Printer Properties

After completing this laboratory activity, you will be able to:

■ Identify common printer properties.

■ Explain how to change common printer properties.

■ Print a test page.

Introduction

This laboratory activity will familiarize you with the most common printer properties. Windows XP and Windows Vista have very similar **Properties** dialog boxes for printers. Selecting or changing printer properties in most cases is as easy as using the mouse button to select or unselect options.

In Windows XP, the printer **Properties** dialog box is accessed through **Start | Control Panel | Printers and Other Hardware | Printers and Faxes** and then by right-clicking the selected printer and choosing **Properties** from the shortcut menu.

In Windows Vista, the printer **Properties** dialog box is accessed through **Start | Control Panel | Hardware and Sound | Printers** and then by right-clicking the selected printer and choosing **Properties** from the shortcut menu.

Be aware that when a printer is connected locally to a computer, **Printers and Faxes** will appear directly off the **Start** menu and can be accessed directly without going through the Control Panel.

The printer **Properties** dialog box opens with the **General** tab selected by default. Look at the following screen capture of Windows XP and Windows Vista versions of the **HP LaserJet 1200 Series PCL Properties** dialog box.

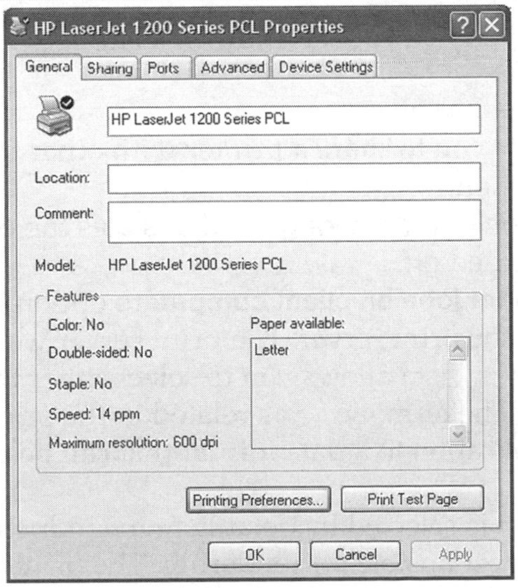

Windows XP 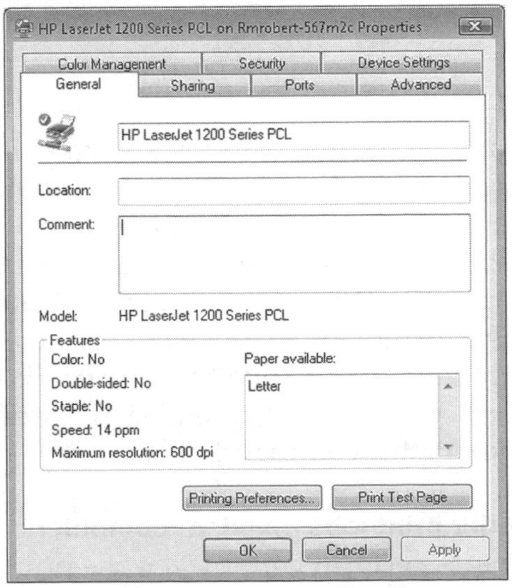   Windows Vista

Copyright by Goodheart-Willcox Co., Inc.

As you can see, the options under the **General** tab are very similar in Windows XP and Windows Vista. The name of the printer "HP LaserJet 1200 Series PCL" was configured automatically during the installation of the print driver software. The user need not supply this information. There is additional text box input options that will allow you to add information about the printer, such as the location of the printer and any comments pertaining to the printer. For example, the location might prove to be important when attempting to locate the exact physical location of a network printer, such as third floor building A. The comments might be used to add additional information such as "black and white printer located in art department workroom. Contact person is Mr. Smith."

Notice how additional features are displayed concerning color, double-sided printing, stapler, printer speed, and resolution. The paper size is also indicated as "Letter".

One of the most important features of the **General** tab printer **Properties** dialog box is the option to print a test page. You will use this many times in the future to verify changes to a client's printer setup.

Another important property is sharing. Look at the following screen capture to see the Windows XP and Windows Vista printer properties **Sharing** tab features.

Windows XP   **Windows Vista**

Both Windows XP and Windows Vista will allow you to share a printer with other users. It is simply a matter of selecting the **Share this printer** option.

Notice the warning on the Windows Vista version of the **Sharing** tab that states the printer will not be available when the computer is sleeping or turned off.

A new option in Windows Vista is the **Render print jobs on client computers** option. Before Windows Vista, print jobs were always managed by the print server. The print server was the designated computer that controlled the printer. Windows Vista allows you to select either the print server or the client computer to render the print job. The term *render* as related to the printer means to convert the graphic commands of the graphic application to a data format that can be understood by the printer.

The **Render print jobs on client computers** option is selected by default. Some industrial-grade network printers perform better when the printer is responsible for rendering. The printer setup documentation typically supplies information about the rendering option when applicable.

                Copyright by Goodheart-Willcox Co., Inc.

An important aspect of the **Printers** dialog box is the automatic connection to the print manu-facturer's Web site. Look at the following two screen captures and compare the Windows XP and Windows Vista **Go to manufacturer's Web site** option.

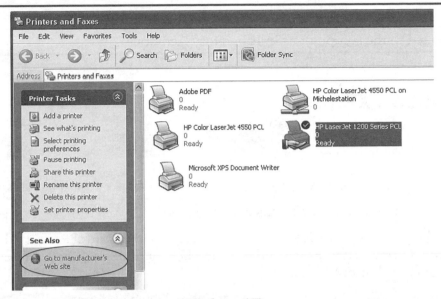

Windows XP

Windows Vista

After selecting the printer in Windows XP, the **Go to manufacturer's Web site** option will appear in the dialog box at the bottom of the left pane. For Windows Vista, you must also select the printer first. However, after selecting the printer, you need to expand the tool bar at the top of the dialog box to reveal the options available for the printer. Listed in the additional options you will see the **Go to manufacturer's Web site**. Once the option is selected, you will automatically connect directly to the printer manufacturer's Web site if you have an Internet connection.

The **Go to manufacturer's Web site** option is very handy when you need to locate such things as supplies, troubleshooting information, or information about the latest driver for that specific printer.

Conduct a Google search using the keyword "Microsoft kb870622" and you should find a Microsoft Help and Support article titled "How to troubleshoot problems that you may experience when you try to print to a local printer by using Office programs in Windows XP." This is a very extensive article that covers all the basics of troubleshooting common Windows XP printer prob-lems. Much of the information will apply to Windows Vista as well.

Copyright by Goodheart-Willcox Co., Inc.

Equipment and Materials

- Computer with Windows XP or Windows Vista and a local printer installed.

Note:

An actual printer is preferred, but you can configure a printer even when one is not connected to the computer as in Laboratory Activity 47.

Part I—Windows XP

Procedure

1. ____ Report to your assigned workstation.

2. ____ Boot the computer and verify it is in working order.

3. ____ Open the printer **Properties** dialog box through **Start | Control Panel | Printers and Other Hardware | Printers and Faxes** and by right-clicking on the selected printer and choosing **Properties** from the shortcut menu.

4. ____ Select the various tabs and view the options available under each.

5. ____ Look at and answer the first three review questions before finishing the Windows XP printer lab.

6. ____ Open Help and Support. You can access Help and Support from off the **Start** menu. Search for the term *printer*. View the results.

7. ____ Print a test page before finishing the Windows XP portion of the lab activity.

8. Go on to Part II of this laboratory activity.

Part II—Windows Vista

Procedure

1. ____ Report to your assigned workstation.

2. ____ Boot the computer and verify it is in working order.

3. ____ Open the printer **Properties** dialog box through **Start | Control Panel | Hardware and Sound | Printers** and by right-clicking on the selected printer and choosing **Properties** from the shortcut menu.

4. ____ Select the various tabs and view the options available under each.

5. ____ Look at and answer the review questions pertaining to Windows Vista before finishing the Windows Vista portion of the lab.

6. ____ Open Help and Support. You can access Help and Support from off the **Start** menu. Search for the term *printer*. View the results.

Copyright by Goodheart-Willcox Co., Inc.

Note:
Some of the review questions may not match the option to the specific printer property tab. For example, the option for changing the amount of printer memory may only show the amount of memory and not allow you to change the amount of memory. This is typically due to you not having the proper permissions or the feature not being available for that particular printer.

Review Questions

1. Which Windows XP printer **Properties** dialog box tab will allow you to change the amount of available printer memory? _____

2. Which Windows XP printer **Properties** dialog box tab will allow you to share the printer with other computers? _____

3. Which Windows XP printer **Properties** dialog box tab will allow you to print a test page? _____

_____

4. Which Windows Vista printer **Properties** dialog box tab will allow you to change the amount of available printer memory? _____

5. Which Windows Vista printer **Properties** dialog box tab will allow you to share the printer? ___

_____

6. Which Windows Vista printer **Properties** dialog box tab allows you to print a test page? _____

_____

Copyright by Goodheart-Willcox Co., Inc.

Lab
50

Portable PCs

Name _____ Date _____

Class/Instructor _____

Windows XP Wireless Connection and Configuration

After completing this laboratory activity, you will be able to:

- Install a typical ad-hoc network.
- Identify key elements associated with an ad-hoc network.
- Identify common causes of problems with an ad-hoc network.
- Define and describe an Independent Basic Service Set (IBSS).
- Define WPAN.

Introduction

In this lab activity, you will install and configure an ad-hoc network using two computers. The ad-hoc network is mostly encountered in a small peer-to-peer network or to form a direct connection between a notebook computer and a full-size PC.

Note:
Microsoft technical information refers to an ad-hoc arrangement as an Independent Basic Service Set (IBSS), while most wireless device manufacturers use the term *ad-hoc*.

Two configuration modes are used for wireless computer communications: ad-hoc and infrastructure. In ad-hoc mode, two or more computers communicate directly with each other. In infrastructure mode, a wireless access point is required to coordinate communications between wireless devices and devices in a LAN consisting of network cabling. The wireless access point controls communications between all wireless devices within its range. It also controls communications between any wireless device and a device on the wired LAN.

Note:
A small wireless network, such as a home-office network, is referred to as a Wireless Personal Area Network (WPAN).

In this lab activity, you will be using wireless devices based on the IEEE 802.11b standard. The 802.11b standard is assigned the 2.4 GHz frequency band as specified by the FCC for radio wave communications. The data rates specified in 802.11b are 1 Mbps, 2 Mbps, 5.5 Mbps, and 11 Mbps. The highest rating of 11 Mbps can only be achieved when the two devices are in close proximity. As the distance increases between two wireless devices, the data rate drops. The typical range for an 802.11b wireless ad-hoc network is 100 meters maximum. This distance may vary because of conditions and building structure materials. For example, a wireless system installed inside a building and transmitting through walls of concrete block will not achieve the 100-meter through 150-meter distance.

Copyright by Goodheart-Willcox Co., Inc.

Note:

Some wireless card manufacturers advertise rates of 22 Mbps for their cards, but these rates are not specified by the 802.11b standard. They are compatible but are not a recognized standard data rate.

The 802.11a standard is assigned the 5 GHz frequency band and supports data rates as high as 54 Mbps. The 802.11a standard is preferred for applications such as video and conferencing. While the 802.11a standard provides a higher throughput, it does not support the same distances as 802.11b. The expected range is approximately half the range of the 802.11b device.

A third standard, 802.11g, combines the 802.11a and 802.11b characteristics. The 802.11g standard uses the higher data rate, 54 Mbps, for shorter distances and the lower frequency, 2.4 GHz, for longer distances. This is a relatively new standard, and at the time of this writing, the cost of the 802.11g devices is more than the 802.11b devices.

All wireless networks require a service set identifier (SSID), which is the name used to identify the network. Both wireless modes of operation, ad-hoc and infrastructure, require the use of an SSID. For devices to communicate with each other on a wireless network, all devices must be identified by the same SSID. Wireless devices usually have a default SSID already assigned by the manufacturer. For example, Dell uses "wireless" and Linksys uses "linksys."

Note:

One reason wireless networking devices from the same manufacturer seem to work automatically when first installed is that the default settings match. When devices from different manufacturers are installed on an ad-hoc network, the SSID must be changed to match the other device(s).

The 802.11b assigned frequency of 2.4 GHz shares the Industrial Science and Medical (ISM) radio frequency band. This means equipment that falls into these categories and uses radio waves for communication may interfere with a wireless 802.11b system. For example, microwave ovens and portable telephones assigned to the 2.4 GHz band will disrupt the wireless communication between the computers.

The placement of the antenna also influences the distance and quality of the radio transmission and reception. For example, the antenna on the back of a PC should be oriented in a vertical position and placed where metal filing cabinets or metal furniture, such as room partitions, will not block the path of the radio signal. A separate antenna can be connected to the wireless card by flexible coaxial cable. This will allow the antenna to be placed in a spot that will support better transmission and reception.

Although setting up a wireless network is simple, there may be times you will experience problems. The following is a list of items to check:

- Check Device Manager to be sure the wireless device is installed and the device driver is loaded.
- Check that all wireless devices are in the same mode of operation: ad-hoc or infrastructure.
- Check that encryption has been enabled, and if so, that the passphrase matches on each device.
- Check for sources of radio interference from microwave ovens, portable telephones, medical devices, industrial devices, garage door openers, wireless PA systems, portable microphones, and any other form of equipment that may transmit radio waves.
- Check that the SSID matches on all devices. Matching the SSID is mandatory in the ad-hoc mode. This is especially true for matching devices from different manufacturers. In infrastructure mode, the matching SSID can be automatically overwritten when an access point is scanned and then selected.
- Check that the same channel is assigned.

Copyright by Goodheart-Willcox Co., Inc.

Name_____

This lab activity is written specifically for Windows XP operating system. You may substitute a Windows Vista operating system computer but only as a last resort. Windows XP is much more difficult to configure than Windows Vista. If you can configure the more difficult Windows XP ad-hoc network, you will have very little problem configuring a Windows Vista system.

Many wireless device manufacturers produce wireless devices that exceed the IEEE wireless standard. For example, the IEEE 802.11g standard states that the highest data rate for the standard is 54 Mbps. Many manufacturers exceed this standard and produce IEEE 802.11g compatible devices with a maximum data rate of 108 Mbps or double the standard rate.

The very latest proposed wireless standard IEEE 802.11n promises data rates as high as 248 Mbps using the existing radio frequencies used by 802.11 g. The range is expected to double that of 802.11g. It is proposed to be backward compatible with existing wireless standards and can operate at the 2.4 GHz and 5 GHz frequencies.

Note:
The 802.11n is a proposed standard at the time of this writing. You may wish to verify that the information is accurate after the release of the official standard by checking the IEEE Web site or other respected Internet sources.

Equipment and Materials

- PC with Windows XP and an 802.11b wireless device installed. The wireless device may be a USB, PCI, or PCIe type.
- Notebook computer with Windows XP and an 802.11b PCMCIA wireless card. (You may use a laptop that is already wireless enabled in this lab activity if approved by your instructor.)
- You will also need the product guide for the 802.11b PCMCIA wireless card. If you do not have the product guide on hand, you can download the product guide from the manufacturer's Web site. Familiarize yourself with the PCMCIA card before beginning this lab activity.

Note:
While this lab activity is designed for a notebook computer and a PC, you may substitute a second PC for the notebook and achieve similar results.

Procedure

1. ____ Gather all materials and report to your assigned workstation. Boot the computers and check that they are in working order.

2. ____ Install the wireless card into the notebook computer. You may need to install the device drivers and software for the PCMCIA card before actually installing the card. While Microsoft Windows XP is designed to automatically detect and configure wireless cards, some manufacturers prefer that you use their software in place of the Windows XP software and drivers. Problems with the wireless card could result from using the Windows XP automatic detection and configuration. Check the PCMCIA wireless card's documentation and take appropriate action before moving on.

3. ____ After installing and configuring the wireless card, you may need to reboot the system for proper setup.

4. ____ If both wireless devices are configured for ad-hoc mode, they should automatically start communicating with each other, especially if they are made by the same manufacturer. When the wireless devices connect automatically, it is referred to as *zero configuration*. Zero configuration means that no configuration is necessary. The wireless devices automatically configure for any wireless connection they find. Not all network devices offer zero configuration.

To check if the wireless devices are communicating, you can simply open **My Network Places** to see if the other wireless computer is listed.

5. ____ Open **Start | Control Panel | Network and Internet Connections | Network Connections** and then right-click the identified wireless connection. A shortcut menu similar to the following will display.

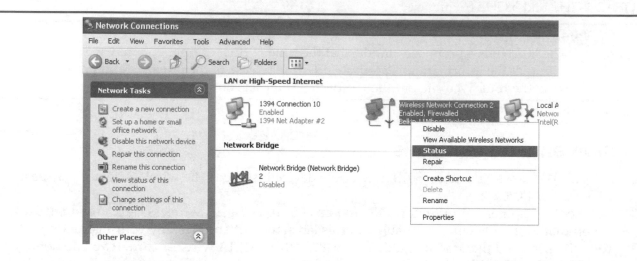

You are given a range of commands: **Disable, View Available Wireless Networks, Status, Repair, Create Shortcut, Delete, Rename,** and **Properties**.

6. ____ Select **Status**. A dialog box similar to the following will display.

The **Wireless Network Status** dialog box displays the signal strength of the wireless device. In the screen capture, a strong signal is indicated by the bar graph showing all five bars. Also, notice that the connection speed indicated is 11 Mbps. The combination of the speed and signal strength is an indication of an excellent wireless communication condition.

 Copyright by Goodheart-Willcox Co., Inc.

Wireless devices send and receive data in the form of packets in the same way wired networks communicates data. The number of packets sent and received is indicated in the dialog box and can help diagnose a problem with the connection. For example, if there are a number of packets sent but none have been received, this would indicate that a connection has not been established.

7. ____ Select the **Support** tab. You should see a dialog box similar to the following. The support tab reveals the TCP/IP properties assigned to this particular wireless card.

8. ____ Click the **Details** button. Look at the information revealed, such as the physical address (MAC address), DNS server address, and the WINS server address. After viewing the contents, click **Close**.

9. ____ Select the **General** tab, and then click the **Properties** button. A dialog box similar to the following should appear.

In the **Wireless Network Connection Properties** dialog box, you see the list of familiar settings associated with a typical network card. You can choose to add or remove clients, TCP/IP settings, and protocols and to set up file and print sharing.

Copyright by Goodheart-Willcox Co., Inc.

10. ____ Select the **Wireless Networks** tab. A dialog box similar to the following should appear.

Pay particular attention to the option **Use Windows to configure my wireless network settings**. When this option is selected, Windows XP configures the network device, not the software provided by the network wireless card manufacturer. This is critical for proper operation of the wireless device.

11. ____ Select the **Use Windows to configure my wireless network settings** option. The button labeled **Advanced** becomes available.

12. ____ Click the **Advanced** button. The **Advanced** dialog box will display. This is where you configure the wireless device for use in ad-hoc or infrastructure mode. The mode of all devices must match for proper operation. Pay particular attention to the option **Automatically connect to non-preferred networks**. When this option is selected, the wireless device is capable of connecting to any wireless device within its range, even if the SSID does not match. If it is unchecked, you may be able to see the other wireless devices when surveyed by the software, but not be able to communicate with the other device because of the configuration values that are set. Be sure the **Computer-computer (ad-hoc) networks only** option is selected, and then close the dialog box. You should return to the **Wireless Network Connection Properties** dialog box.

13. ____ Now select the **Advanced** tab. A dialog box similar to the following should appear.

Copyright by Goodheart-Willcox Co., Inc.

The **Advanced** tab reveals options for enabling the Internet Connection Firewall and also for setting up Internet Connection Sharing. These options are used when a wireless infrastructure mode is configured. They are also used if the computer is using a direct wireless satellite connection. When using a direct satellite connection, you will want to enable the firewall to protect the computer from unauthorized intruders.

14. ____ Now, feel free to experiment with the various settings and options available in the **Wireless Network Connection Properties** dialog boxes. Try changing the mode of operation as well as the SSID to see the effects on the ad-hoc system. Set up a share on one of the two computers and attempt to copy and transfer the contents of the share. Do not experiment with the encryption settings at this time. You will experiment with the encryption in the next lab activity. Use Help and Support to learn more about wireless ad-hoc networks.

15. ____ Return all materials to their proper storage area and then go on to answer the review questions.

Review Questions

1. What are the two modes of wireless operation? _____

2. Which mode does not require an access point? _____

3. What does Microsoft call an ad-hoc wireless configuration? _____

4. An ad-hoc network is most similar to which type of network, a peer-to-peer or a client/server?

5. What are the four typical data rates for an 802.11b standard wireless device? _____

_____

_____

6. What is the assigned FCC frequency for an 802.11b wireless device? _____

7. What is the frequency assigned to an 802.11a device? _____

8. What is the maximum throughput of an 802.11a wireless device? _____

9. What is the expected maximum range of an 802.11b wireless ad-hoc network? _____

10. What two common items found in homes will disrupt wireless communications between computers? _____

_____

11. What is a small wireless network referred to as? _____

12. Is the SSID optional or mandatory for an ad-hoc wireless network? _____

_____

13. At what frequencies does 802.11n operate? _____

14. What is the expected data rate of 802.11n? _____

Copyright by Goodheart-Willcox Co., Inc.

Name _____ Date _____

Class/Instructor _____

Windows Vista Wireless Connection and Configuration

After completing this laboratory activity, you will be able to:

- Explain how to use the Connect to a Network wizard to create an ad-hoc connection.
- Configure an ad-hoc wireless connection.
- Explain the difference between Public, Private, and Domain network connections.
- Explain the most common wireless connection failures.

Introduction

Microsoft Windows XP first introduced tools to automate wireless network configurations. Since Windows XP, Windows Vista has made significant improvements in wireless networking. Some security concepts are introduced in this laboratory activity. Security concepts will be covered in much more detail in later lab activities.

Ad hoc is a temporary wireless connection between two or more computers without the use of a router or other major network device. The most typical ad-hoc connection is a laptop temporarily connected directly to another PC to transfer data. Ad-hoc connections may be configured as secure connections or as unsecure connections. This lab will present both secure and unsecure connections

Windows Vista introduced the Network Discovery feature as part of its operating system. The Network Discovery feature will be covered in more depth in later laboratory activities concerning networking. For now, just understand the Network Discovery feature allows the computer to locate other network devices automatically. All devices that have Network Discovery enabled broadcast information to all other network devices. The Network Discovery feature can be disabled to increase security.

Another feature first introduced in Windows XP is the Windows Firewall feature. A firewall controls the flow of data to and from the computer. A firewall can stop unsolicited connections from other network devices. The firewall can also make exceptions to allow specific devices to accept information from other devices. There will be more about Windows Firewall in future labs. Together, the Network Discovery feature and the Windows Firewall are automatically configured by the operating system depending on the type of network connection you are configuring.

Windows Vista classifies network security settings as Public, Private, and Domain. Each of the three classifications can be connected wirelessly or by cable.

Public networks are the most vulnerable type of networks. They are typically wireless "hot spots." Wireless hot spots typically provide free Internet access and are found in locations such as airports, hotels, coffee shops, and some educational institutions. Windows Vista automatically configures the Windows Firewall to block all unsolicited incoming transmissions. Network Discovery is also disabled by default.

Private networks are typically home networks or small office networks. The small networks allow users to share resources with other users such as printers or certain files. Network Discovery is enabled by default and the Windows Firewall allows the exchange of data on the local network.

Copyright by Goodheart-Willcox Co., Inc.

Domain networks require the users to have a user account configured on a network server. The network account is configured by a network administrator and typically requires a unique network user name and a password. Domain networks are found most often in large business organizations, education settings, and government operations. Network Discovery is enabled by default, but it is often disabled by the network administrator. The Windows Firewall is automatically configured by default to allow the exchange of data on the network, but it is also often reconfigured by the network administrator.

Often, the failure to automatically connect to a network is the result of the Windows Vista security feature. For example, the first time a laptop attempts to connect to a wireless public network, a connection error will occur. Public networks are not secure, so Windows Vista considers them to be a security threat and handles them as such by default. Wireless security is provided by several different techniques.

Equipment and Materials

■ Two Windows Vista workstations (or one Windows Vista workstation and one Windows Vista laptop) both equipped with a wireless adapter.

Note:

You may also elect to perform this lab activity with another student, each of you with a workstation or laptop equipped with a wireless adapter. Your instructor may also set up one or more wireless workstations in the lab to be used as a public network access.

■ The following information provided by instructor. (You will not need the information for an unsecure connection.)

Network name: _____

Security type: _____

Security key or passphrase: _____

Note:

The *network name* is used to identify the wireless network connection. This is especially important if you have more than one wireless network configuration. *Security type* is the type of wireless security being used if any. *Security key* or *passphrase* is a set of letters and numbers used as a seed for the encryption. Each computer must use the same security key or passphrase; otherwise, they will not exchange data.

Copyright by Goodheart-Willcox Co., Inc.

Procedure

1. _____ Report to your assigned workstation.

2. _____ Boot the computer and verify it is in working order.

3. _____ To begin the process of connecting to a network, click the **Connect To** command located off the **Start** menu.

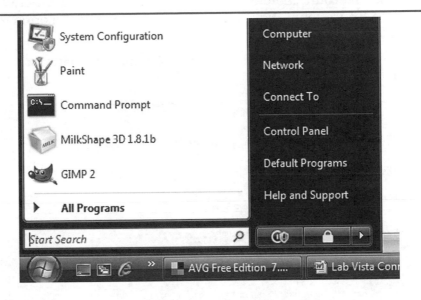

A dialog box similar to the following will appear, prompting you to select the network you wish to connect to. If you are using a laptop already configured with a wireless adapter, the wireless adapter will automatically search for available wireless connections.

The first time you attempt to establish a connection to a wireless hot spot (public network), the **Connect to a network** dialog box will display all broadcasting wireless networks in the area. The strength of each wireless network is displayed by a series of green bars. The more green bars, the stronger the wireless network signal. The security of the wireless network is also displayed.

Copyright by Goodheart-Willcox Co., Inc.

Notice how the network called "default" is not secure and that the network called "linksys2" is secure. You can automatically connect to any unsecure network simply by selecting it with the mouse. To connect to the secure network you must know the type of security encryption being used and configure your wireless adapter with the security key or passphrase.

When connecting to an unsecure network, Windows Vista will warn you with a message stating that the wireless connection is not secure. You simply select to connect anyway. After you have established the first connection to the unsecure hot spot, or public network, the connection can be retained for a future connection. You will be presented with an option to make it a preferred connection.

Look at the following screen capture to see what the **Connect to a network** dialog box looks like after a connection has been established.

After a connection has been established with the public network, the name of the network will be displayed in bold letters. In the previous screen capture, you can see that the wireless network named "default" is in bold followed by the word "Connected." This is how the wireless network that the laptop is connected to is identified. Normally you would be done at this point. A connection has been established to the unsecure network. This means you are connected to the public network and should now have Internet access. If your instructor has configured the lab hot spot for Internet access, go ahead and establish a connection to the Internet at this time. After a connection to the Internet has been established, close the Internet Explorer and go on to step 4.

Copyright by Goodheart-Willcox Co., Inc.

4. ____ Repeat the lab up to step 3 once more, but this time notice the two links in the lower-left corner of the dialog box: **Set up a connection or network** and **Open Network and Sharing Center**. Choose the **Set up a connection or network** option. A dialog box similar to the following will appear.

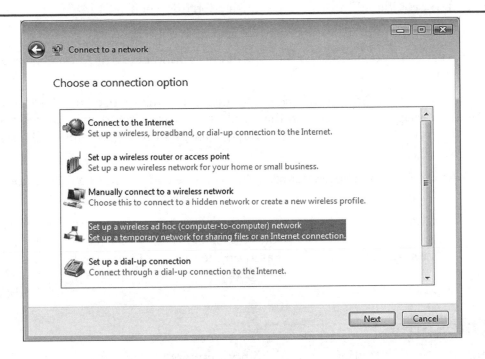

As you can see, the dialog box provides a set of wizards for configuring network connections using a variety of technologies. For this exercise, select the fourth option, **Set up a wireless ad hoc (computer-to-computer) network**. A dialog box similar to the following will appear.

You will provide a name for the network connection, select the security type, and provide a security key or passphrase. You also have an option to save the network connection. This is a means for saving the configuration if you expect to connect to this network often. You will not need to reconfigure the connection each time. To establish a secure ad-hoc network connection, you will need to provide all information requested: name, security type, and security key.

The wireless network name is the security set identifier (SSID).

The network security type identifies the type of encryption being used for the secure communications.

The security key or passphrase is a series of letters and numbers used as a seed to encrypt the contents of all messages exchanged on the wireless network. The security key is similar to a password. The exact name, security key or passphrase, will be dependent on the wireless device manufacturer.

5. _____ Click **Next** to complete the wizard. You should be connected to a secure ad-hoc network at this time.

6. _____ After completing the ad-hoc portion of the laboratory activity, go on to answer the review questions. To answer the review questions, use Windows Vista Help and Support and conduct a search using the term *ad hoc*. Based on the results of the search, answer the review questions.

Review Questions

1. What is the Microsoft Vista definition of "ad hoc network"? _____

_____

_____

_____

_____

_____

2. What is the maximum distance for computers in an ad-hoc network according to "What is a computer-to-computer (ad hoc) network?" _____

3. Using the results from "Wireless networking frequently asked questions," complete the following chart.

Wireless Technology	Speed	Frequency
802.11a		
802.11b		
802.11g		

Copyright by Goodheart-Willcox Co., Inc.

4. What Windows Vista feature allows a computer to automatically locate other devices on a network? _____

5. What are the three Windows Vista network security setting classifications? _____
_____

6. A coffee shop provides free wireless Internet access to all customers. The network does not require a password, which poses a security threat. Which Windows Vista network security setting classification would this *most likely* represent? _____

7. Which Windows Vista network security setting classification automatically disables Network Discovery and enables Windows Firewall to block unwanted connections? _____

8. Which Windows Vista network security setting classification typically requires a user account and password and uses a company network server? _____

9. Which Windows Vista network security setting classification would *most likely* be represented by a home network that allows sharing of resources such as a printer and files? _____

10. What three items are required to establish a secure wireless network connection? _____
_____

11. What does the acronym SSID represent? _____

12. What is the SSID? _____
_____

13. What are the three major types of wireless network security recognized by Microsoft Vista Help and Support? _____
_____

14. What is another name for a passphrase? _____

15. What is a passphrase? _____
_____
_____

Computer Service and Repair Lab Manual

Copyright by Goodheart-Willcox Co., Inc.

Name _____ Date _____

Class/Instructor _____

Windows Vista Mobile PC

After completing this laboratory activity, you will be able to:

■ Access the Mobile PC folder.
■ Access the Windows Mobility Center.
■ Identify the Windows Mobility Center options.
■ Explain the purpose of the three Mobile PC power options.
■ Explain the purpose of Sync Center.

Introduction

This laboratory activity explores the many different configuration options in Windows Mobile PC and Windows Mobility Center. Windows Mobile PC provides a centralized location for modifying the configuration for all common mobile devices, such as laptops and tablet PCs. Mobile PC was first introduced in the Windows Vista operating system.

Look at the following screen capture. Notice that the Mobile PC folder provides quick access to many different mobile device and configuration tools, such as Windows Mobility Center, Power Options, and Sync Center. Take special notice of the Sync Center, which is used to synchronize files between two different locations such as a laptop and a desktop. It can even synchronize files between a local folder and a network folder. The Sync Center ensures the latest version of a file can be accessed. The ability to synchronize a folder on a network is not available in Windows Home Basic or Windows Home Premium.

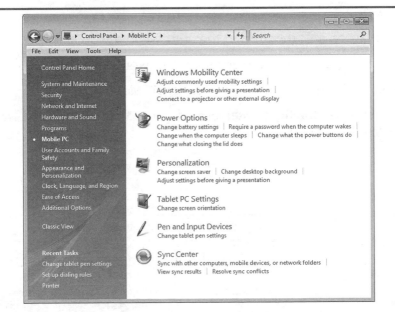

The Windows Mobility Center is designed as a central location for the most commonly used laptop configurations. It is not available in desktop versions of the operating system. The following screen capture is of the Windows Mobility Center of an Acer laptop.

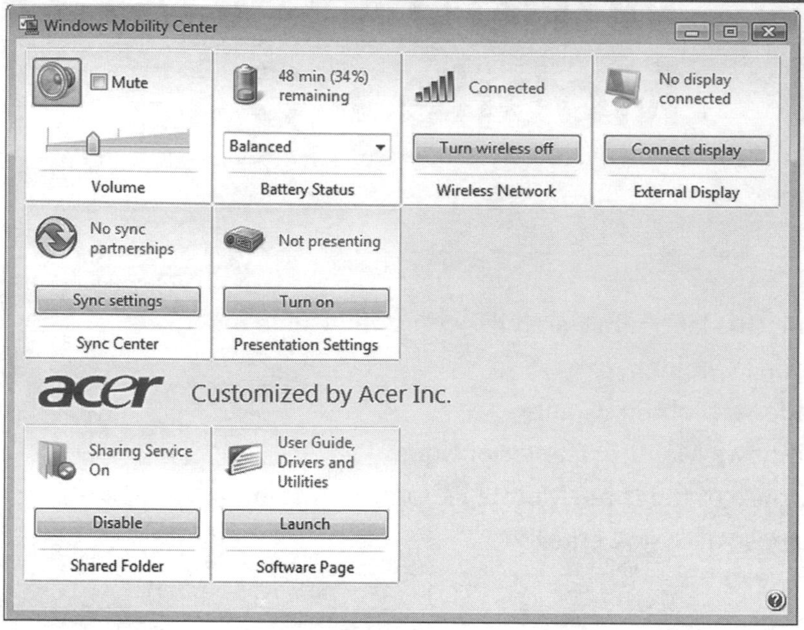

Notice that the Windows Mobility Center contains a collection of the most commonly accessed options in relation to a laptop computer, for example, **Battery Status**, **Wireless Network**, **External Display**, and **Presentation Settings**. Notice the two optional features designed by Acer Inc.: **Shared Folder** and **Software Page**. Many computer laptop manufacturers and distributors modify or customize the Microsoft Mobility Center.

Equipment and Materials

■ Laptop running Windows Vista.

Procedure

1. _____ Check out a laptop and then report to your assigned workstation.

2. _____ Boot the laptop and inspect it to ensure it is in working order.

3. _____ Access Mobil PC through **Start I Control Panel I Mobil PC**.

4. _____ Open the **Windows Mobility Center** located in the **Mobil PC** folder. List the major options available in the Windows Mobility Center.

_____

_____

_____

_____

_____

Copyright by Goodheart-Willcox Co., Inc.

Name_____

5. ____ Open the **Battery Status** option. You should see a dialog box similar to the following.

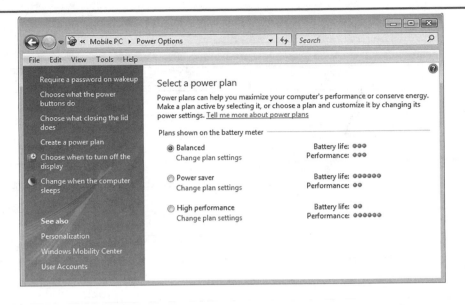

6. ____ Click the <u>Tell me more about power plans </u>link.

7. ____ Go to the review questions and answer the first five questions.

8. ____ Take a few minutes to explore the other options available in the Windows Mobility Center.

9. ____ Conduct a search in Help and Support using the term *Mobility Center*. Take a few minutes to review the results.

10. ____ Finish the review questions, and then return the laptop to its proper storage area.

Review Questions

1. What are the three available power plans for the laptop? _____

_____

2. What is the Power Saver power plan? _____

_____

3. What is the High Performance power plan? _____

_____

4. What is the Balanced power plan? _____

_____

_____

5. Which setting might adversely affect Windows Aero? _____

6. What is the purpose of the Sync Center? _____

_____

_____

7. Which versions of Windows Vista will not synchronize with a folder located on a network?

_____

Notes

Copyright by Goodheart-Willcox Co., Inc.

Name _____ Date _____

Class/Instructor _____

Modem Installation

After completing this laboratory activity, you will be able to:

- Install and configure a typical dial-up modem.
- Explain the options available under the various modem properties tabs.
- Explain how to test a modem.

Introduction

In this lab activity, you will explore how to install and manually configure a telephone modem. It will not be necessary to physically install a modem. Most student labs do not have dial-up available for each workstation.

The term *modem* is a contraction of the two electronics terms *modulation* and *demodulation*. Modulation is the process of modifying an electrical signal or waveform by encoding data into the electrical signal. Demodulation means to extract information from the electrical signal or waveform. A telephone modem encodes the computer digital signal information into the analog signal used on plain old telephone system (POTS) designed for voice communications. In essence, the modem converts the digital signal from the computer into an analog signal and then transmits it over conventional telephone lines. At the destination modem, the analog signal is converted back to a digital signal that can be used by the computer.

The main electronic component inside a telephone modem is the universal asynchronous receiver transmitter (UART). The UART converts the parallel digital signal into a serial analog signal.

Modems can be integrated into the motherboard (onboard modem), installed as a separate unit outside the computer (external modem), or installed inside the computer as an adapter card.

The exact software installation and configuration requirements and steps are similar for Windows XP and Windows Vista. Basically, the modem you first set up as a hardware device and then configure it for a dial-up connection. A telephone modem is typically automatically detected by the operating system and requires very little technician intervention, except for the actual entering of the telephone number, area code, and other information used to identify the telephone connection. The following is a list of troubleshooting tips to help you in case you have problems with the installation.

- Check the telephone line to and from the computer to be sure it is connected. This is the first thing you should check. Telephone lines often become loose or disconnected.
- Dial-up modems only work with analog telephone lines. If the phone line is DSL, you must use a DSL modem, not a dial-up modem.
- Check and verify that the telephone modem is configured for dialing an outside line when required. For example, the telephone modem may require "9" to be dialed to access an outside line.

Copyright by Goodheart-Willcox Co., Inc.

- You can plug a working, analog-type phone into the telephone modem line and listen for a dial tone. This will verify that the line to the telephone company is intact.
- Open Device Manager and locate the telephone modem. See if a problem is indicated.
- Consult the telephone modem installation manual or manufacturer's Web site for information, especially for error code messages relating to the modem and for troubleshooting tips.
- As a last resort, call the telephone provider to verify the line is OK.

Equipment and Materials

- Computer with Windows XP or Windows Vista, or both installed.
- A 56 k modem as an external device, adapter card, or integrated into the motherboard. This will be determined by your instructor. You may also need a device driver for the modem.
- Telephone number provided by the instructor of the line to be used.

Note:
   You may need a number to access an outside line, especially in a school or office building setting.

Procedure

1. ____ Boot the PC and wait for the Windows desktop. This verifies the system is working properly.

2. ____ If you are simulating the installation, go on to step 3. If you are going to physically install an internal telephone modem, shut the computer down. Read the installation manual for additional information required to complete the modem installation.

   If you are installing an external modem, be sure the computer is powered down before connecting the modem cable to the PC.

3. ____ In Windows XP, access **Control Panel | Printers and Other Hardware | Phone and Modem Options**. You should see a dialog box similar to the following.

If you are using Windows Vista computer, access **Control Panel | Hardware and Sound | Phone and Modem Options**. The dialog box will be very similar to the previous Windows XP screen capture.

Copyright by Goodheart-Willcox Co., Inc.

4. ____ Click the **New** button to set up a new phone connection. The dialog box **New Location** will display and look similar to the following for Windows XP or Windows Vista.

This dialog box is used to configure essential information about the telephone connection. You would put in the location name, area code, and other information required as needed. The **Dial using** option at the bottom of the dialog box has **Tone** selected by default. Most telephones in the United States are tone-type. In some rural areas and areas outside the United States, you may encounter pulse-type telephones. Pulse-type telephones use a rotary dial. Tone telephones use push buttons.

5. ____ Select the **Area Code Rules** tab and look at the options in the new dialog box, which is similar to the following. There will most likely be no area code rules defined at this time.

6. _____ Click **New**. The **New Area Code Rule** dialog box will display.

This is where you configure additional information required to dial certain area codes and prefixes. Close this dialog box by clicking **Cancel**.

7. _____ Select the **Calling Card** tab on the **New Location** dialog box. You should see a dialog box similar to the following.

This dialog box allows you to select a calling card to be used when placing a call from the modem. All major calling card companies are identified in the **Card Types** list. You can add an additional calling card company if needed. You would also configure the account number of the calling card as well as the personal identification number (PIN). Clicking the **New** button reveals another dialog box, which allows you to configure a calling card company not included in the list. Look at the information contained there briefly and then close all dialog boxes.

Copyright by Goodheart-Willcox Co., Inc.

Name_____

8. ____ Now, open **Control Panel** and select **Phone and Modem Options** as you did in step 3.

9. Select the **Modems** tab in the **Phone and Modem Options** dialog box. You should see a dialog box similar to the following. If not repeat the steps again.

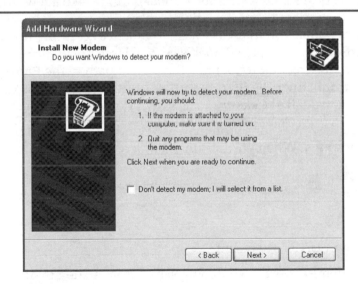

10. ____ Click the **Add** button. A dialog box similar to the following will display.

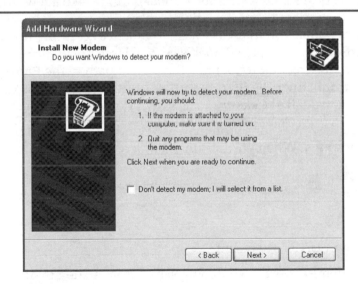

You have now started the Add Hardware Wizard. You would use this wizard to add a new physical modem to the existing computer. Select the **Don't detect my modem; I will select it from a list** option, and then click **Next**. A dialog box similar to the following will display.

Copyright by Goodheart-Willcox Co., Inc.

The Add Hardware Wizard will provide you with a list of modem types and corresponding models. You would now scroll through the list to select the correct model. Go ahead and scroll down the list to view the models, but do not select one at this time.

After you explore the list of models look at the button labeled **Have Disk**. This button would be used if you have a disc supplied with the telephone modem you are installing and the modem is not identified in the list. You would insert the disc into the drive and then click **Have Disk**. The disk would be detected by the operating system and the correct drivers would be automatically installed.

11. _____ Close all dialog boxes by clicking the **Cancel** button. Take a few minutes to practice opening the telephone modem properties dialog boxes. Be sure you know how to access them after opening **Control Panel**. You may also wish to practice accessing the telephone modem properties dialog boxes when Control Panel is set to Classic View. The A+ Certification exams often ask questions requiring you to identify the correct path to the **Phone and Modem Options** dialog box, starting from either the **Start** button or from **Control Panel**. You will be responsible for both the default view (called *Category View* in Windows XP) and the Classic View.

12. _____ Answer the review questions. You may use Windows Help and Support to assist you with some of the questions. When you are finished, return all materials to their proper storage area.

Review Questions

1. What does the acronym UART represent? _____

2. Does a telephone modem convert the outgoing signal from analog to digital or digital to analog?

   _____

3. What does the acronym POTS represent? _____

4. What does the acronym PIN represent? _____

Copyright by Goodheart-Willcox Co., Inc.

Name _____ Date _____

Class/Instructor _____

Dial-Up Modem Configuration

After completing this laboratory activity, you will be able to:

- Configure a dialing location.
- Explain the purpose of a UART.
- Explain how a modem operates.
- Identify various modem configuration options.
- Explain the difference between pulse and tone dialing.
- Explain how to test a modem.

Introduction

In this laboratory activity, you will install and configure a telephone modem. The term *modem* is a contraction of the two electronics terms, *modulation* and *demodulation*. Modulation is the process of modifying an electrical signal or electronic waveform. A modem allows a PC to access the Internet and to connect to an office network or to another PC.

A PC outputs information as a digital signal. A modem converts that high-speed digital signal into an analog waveform that can be carried over a typical telephone line. A typical telephone line is not designed to transport a high-speed digital signal. Therefore, the signal generated by a computer must be converted into an analog signal before it can be transmitted over the phone lines. When the signal reaches the destination, such as another PC, the modem on the receiving end converts the signal from analog back to digital. The signal can then be processed by the receiving PC system.

The main electronic component of a modem is a chip called a *universal asynchronous receiver-transmitter (UART)*. The UART converts the parallel digital signal into a serial digital signal. The digital signal is then converted into an analog signal that is a series of waves of varying height and width. See the following illustration.

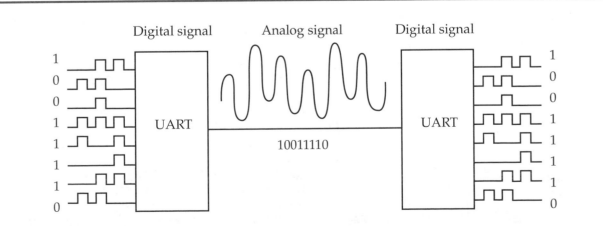

Copyright by Goodheart-Willcox Co., Inc.

There are two basic modem categories: broadband and dial-up. A broadband modem is used for high-speed DSL lines or cable connections. Dial-up modems, also referred to as "voice modems," are designed to use low-speed conventional phone lines, not high-speed DSL. The conventional telephone lines are also referred to as "plain old telephone system," or POTS.

The modem can be integrated into the motherboard (onboard modem), installed as a separate unit outside the PC (external modem), or installed inside the PC as an adapter card (internal modem). Your instructor will determine the type of modem to be used for the installation portion of the lab activity. Modern modems are very easy to install and require practically no intervention by the installer. This type of modem is Plug and Play. It is automatically detected and its system resources are automatically configured by the computer. The most difficult installations will require you to assist the Plug and Play installation by providing the modem software drivers.

The Windows operating system uses the Telephone Application Programming Interface (TAPI) protocol to support modem communications. The TAPI protocol is a set of standards used as a design guide for electronic engineers and software programmers to follow when designing telephone communication devices intended to work with the Microsoft operating system.

Dial-up telephone modems share the same telephone line as the regular land line telephone system that is wired into the home or office. When a person placed a call over the conventional phone line to the place where a telephone modem is used, a busy signal would be produced. This is because the telephone modem and the regular phone system shared the same telephone line to the residence. Today, modern telephone modems use modem on hold (MOH) technology. Modem on hold is a modem feature that allows a modem to be used with the call waiting feature associated with telephone service. Since telephone modems share the same line as the normal voice telephone service, the MOH feature will allow the modem to automatically switch to hold while a telephone call is being received on a telephone. The modem will switch back to the ISP after the call is terminated.

If a problem occurs, open Device Manager and locate the modem. A question mark or an exclamation mark is used to indicate a problem with the modem or any hardware device. The most common modem installation problem is usually driver related. You should check the manufacturer's Web site for known problems related to the operating system or hardware-related items. Also, check for and install the very latest driver. This will typically clear the problem.

If the Device Manager indicates no problem with the modem, you most likely have a configuration problem involving the dialing rules. For example, some locations such as schools or offices require a special number to be inserted before the telephone number of the switchboard can be bypassed. A number such as 9 is typically used but not always. It depends on the phone system equipment being used at the location.

Before installing the modem for this lab, review the modem installation procedures on the CD or the booklet that accompanied the modem, or view the modem installation procedures at the manufacturer's Web site. This lab can be completed without installing a physical modem. If your instructor chooses not to use a real modem, then ignore references made in the lab activity to the installation and removal of the physical modem.

                Copyright by Goodheart-Willcox Co., Inc.

Equipment and Materials

- Computer with Windows XP or Windows Vista, or both, installed.
- 56 k modem (optional).
- Access to an active telephone line (optional).
- Telephone number to be used by your PC modem is _____. (Provided by instructor.)

Note:

The dialog boxes that appear on your computer may not match the ones in this lab activity. Microsoft shares its programming software utilities, referred to as Application Program Interfaces (API). It is common for companies to create their own versions of dialog boxes, which open in the Windows operating system. To match this lab activity, use a computer that has no modem installed.

Procedure

1. ____ Report to your assigned workstation.

2. ____ Boot the computer and verify it is in working order.

3. ____ If installing an internal modem, turn the power off to the PC and remove the cover. Be sure to follow all anti-static precautions outlined by your instructor. Insert the modem into the appropriate expansion slot. If installing an external modem using a USB cable, simply plug the modem cable into the computer USB port or serial port, depending on the design.

4. ____ Power on the PC and watch as the modem is automatically detected and installed by the Plug and Play system. If it is not automatically detected or if a system resource conflict should appear, contact your instructor.

5. ____ Next, access **Control Panel** and select **Hardware and Sound**. Then select **Phone and Modem Options**. The **Phone and Modem Options** dialog box will appear similar to the following and open to the **Dialing Rules** tab by default.

The location from which you are dialing is indicated and the area code and dialing rules are accessed here. You can have more than one originating location when using a laptop computer and will thus need to configure a different set of dialing rules for each location.

---

6. ____ Click the **New** button. The **New Location** dialog box should appear and look similar to that in the following screen capture. The **Edit** button in the **Phone and Modem Options** dialog box will also open a similar series of dialog boxes, allowing you to edit an existing set of dialing rules.

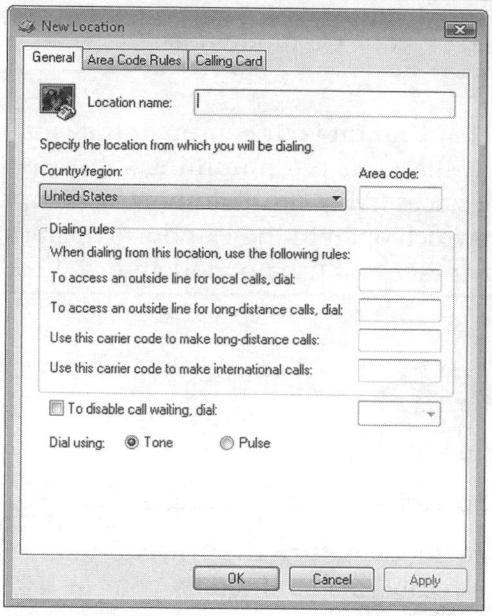

The **New Location** dialog box will allow you to configure information required to place a call from the new location. You identify the location with a descriptive name such as home, office, or regional office. Provide the area code and the country or region.

The dialing rules are entered also, such as any number needed to access an outside line from a business location.

Notice the option to disable call waiting and the options for tone or pulse dialing. Modern phones use tone dialing, which is set by default. Some areas of the world require pulse dialing, which is associated with the old rotary dial phones. Push button phones are tone dialing phones.

7. ____ Click the **Area Code Rules** tab and then click the **New** button. You will see a dialog box similar to the following.

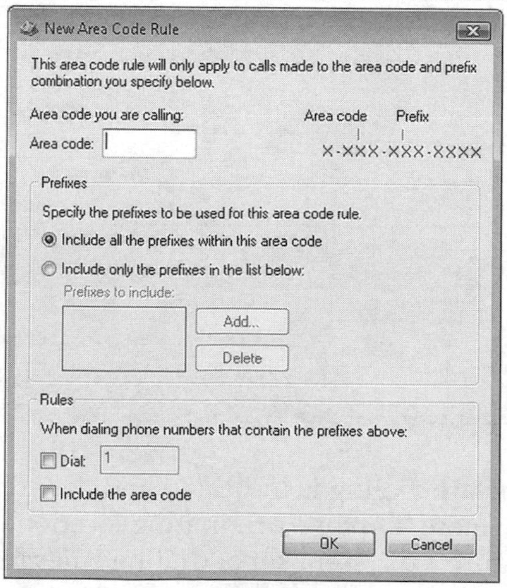

Copyright by Goodheart-Willcox Co., Inc.

As you can see, this is where you configure rules for dialing area codes. Since businesses commonly require worldwide travel, using a telephone modem may require very different configurations for access than used in the United States. Close the **New Area Code Rule** dialog box.

8. _____ Click the **Calling Card** tab. You should see a dialog box similar to the following.

As you can see, under this tab you can select a calling card to use to pay for phone services. You would input the account number and personal ID number (PIN) that corresponds to the type of card you are using. Close the **New Location** dialog box. You should return to the **Phone and Modem Options** dialog box.

9. _____ Click the **Modems** tab. You should see a dialog box similar to the following.

Any modems installed on your computer will be identified here. You can also start the Add Hardware Wizard by clicking the **Add** button. The wizard will prompt you through a series of dialog boxes, which will result in the manual installation and configuration of a modem.

Copyright by Goodheart-Willcox Co., Inc.

10. ____ Click the **Advanced** tab. A set of currently installed telephony providers will display.

11. ____ Now close all dialog boxes.

12. ____ You will now simulate the manual installation and configuration of a modem for the PC. Open **Control Panel** and then select **Phone and Modem Options**.

13. ____ Click the **Modems** tab and then click the **Add** button. Add Hardware Wizard should appear.

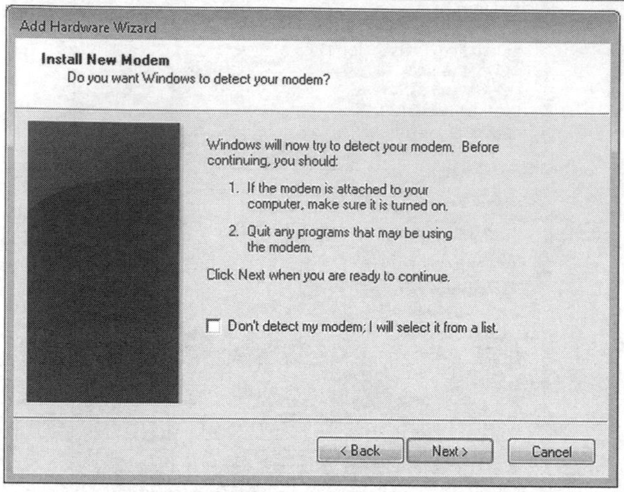

If you do not see the Add Hardware Wizard, it might be located under one of the other open dialog boxes. The wizard will ask you if you want Windows to detect your modem. Select the **Don't detect my modem; I will select it from a list** option. Then, click **Next**. This will start the manual configuration.

14. ____ The next dialog box will appear similar to the one in the following screen capture.

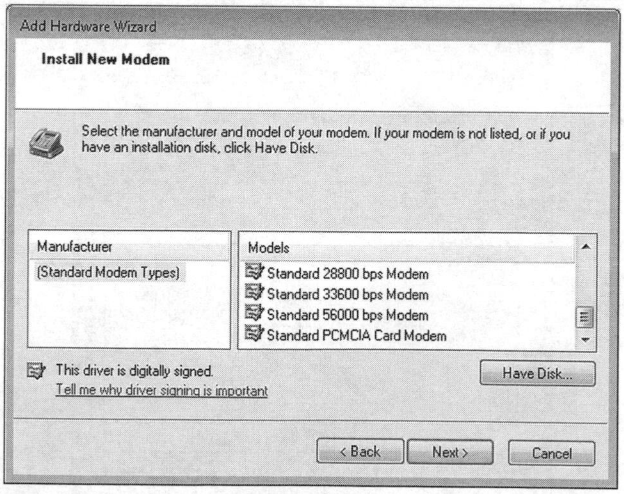

Notice the **Have Disk** button. If your modem is not listed, then you have the option to install the drivers for the modem by using the **Have Disk** button. You would insert the disk or disc that came with the modem and then follow the screen prompts. For this lab activity, you do not have a disk, so you will simply scroll down and select the **Standard 56000 bps Modem** from the list and then click **Next**. The new dialog box to appear identifies the port for the modem.

Copyright by Goodheart-Willcox Co., Inc.

15. ____ Select the modem port "COM1" and then click **Next**. Windows will now simulate install-ing the modem as directed, followed by a dialog box stating the wizard is now finished. Click **Finish** to complete the installation.

16. ____ Open **Control Panel | Phone and Modem Options** and then click the **Modems** tab. The Standard 56000 bps Modem should be listed. If not, call your instructor for assistance.

17. ____ Click the **Properties** button. A dialog box similar to the following will appear, providing a means to edit or verify all properties related to the modem hardware.

It is interesting to note that the dialog box will indicate "This device is working properly," even though no such device exists. This is because most hardware devices depend on the software drivers to detect errors and then transmit the errors to the Windows API. Since there is no real device, the software driver does not detect any errors. As you can see, this is a classic example of troubleshooting when no problem is indicated, yet one does exist.

18. ____ Click the **Diagnostics** tab.

The **Diagnostics** tab is as stated, a means to run diagnostics on the installed modem. Since you only simulated installing a modem and no real modem was installed, the diagnostics will indicate a problem with the modem. Run the diagnostic test now by clicking the **Query Modem** button and view the results. An error should report, informing you that the modem is not working

Copyright by Goodheart-Willcox Co., Inc.

properly. After viewing the results, close all open dialog boxes. When a real modem is queried, a set of standard modem commands are transmitted to the modem to test it. A list of commands as well as the response for each will appear in a text box. You can also select the **Append to Log** option, which will generate a list of all the commands and responses so that they can be viewed later. This is the standard way to test a modem.

19. ____ Now, remove the simulated modem by going through **Control Panel | Phone and Modem Options**. Remove the new location listed under the **Dialing Rules** tab and then remove the simulated modem located under the **Modems** tab.

20. ____ If your instructor has provided you with a real modem, go ahead and install it now. Use the information obtained through the simulated lab and the information provided by the modem booklet to assist you with the modem installation and removal. Before you physically install the modem, be sure to turn off the computer power switch. Then, follow antistatic procedures while installing the physical modem. Use the phone number and dialing rules supplied by your instructor to configure the telephone modem. Call your instructor to inspect your project when complete.

21. ____ After your instructor has inspected your project, remove the telephone modem and the configuration from the computer. Before physically removing the modem, be sure to turn off the power to the computer. Follow antistatic procedures when handling the modem.

22. ____ Open **Help and Support** and conduct a search using the term *modem*. Briefly review the results. You will find extensive information about modems, modem configuration, and troubleshooting.

23. ____ Answer the review questions and then return all materials to their proper storage area. You may use Windows Help and Support to answer the review questions.

Review Questions

1. The term *modem* is a contraction of what two electrical terms? _____
_____

2. Does a transmitting voice modem convert analog signals to digital or digital signals to analog?
_____

3. What is TAPI? _____
_____
_____
_____
_____

4. What are the two categories of modems? _____
_____

5. What is the difference between a broadband and a dial-up modem? _____
_____
_____

6. What does the acronym MOH represent? _____

7. Which is the default setting for the modern push button phone: pulse or tone dialing? _____
_____

8. How do you test a telephone modem? _____
_____
_____

Copyright by Goodheart-Willcox Co., Inc.

Name _____ Date _____

Class/Instructor _____

Remote Desktop

After completing this laboratory activity, you will be able to:

■ Configure a client and a remote computer for use with Remote Desktop.

■ Access a remote computer using Remote Desktop Connection.

■ Describe the various options available in the **Remote Desktop Connection** dialog boxes.

■ Identify some common issues that might prevent establishing a Remote Desktop connection.

■ Identify the type of connection media that will support Remote Desktop.

Introduction

In this laboratory activity, you will become familiar with the Remote Desktop feature in Windows XP and Windows Vista. Remote Desktop allows a user to access and run programs on a remote computer just as if the user were sitting at the remote computer. The Remote Desktop feature is only available in Windows XP Professional, Windows Vista Ultimate, and Windows Vista Business. You can, however, connect to a remote computer using Windows 95 or later.

Note:

The computer that is used to access a remote computer is called the *client*.

Remote Desktop is designed to work on a persistent connection such as a LAN, MAN, WAN, DSL, ISDN, cable, and wireless. The remote computer must use a persistent connection with a persistent IP address. If not, the client will not be able to find the remote computer. The remote desktop connection will not work correctly when the remote computer is connected to an ISP that issues temporary IP addresses.

The connection between the client and remote computer can also be completed using a local area network or a dial-up connection. The client can use a Web browser to access the remote computer instead of using the Remote Desktop Connection utility. Connecting through a Web browser will not be covered in this lab activity, but you can visit Microsoft's Web site to learn more about it.

Note:

When using Remote Desktop, the remote PC must use Windows XP Professional, Windows Vista Ultimate, or Windows Vista Business. The client computers may use any Windows operating system starting with Windows 95.

Copyright by Goodheart-Willcox Co., Inc.

This laboratory activity can be confusing because of all the options available in the Windows XP properties dialog boxes. The following abbreviated instructions for setting up and using Remote Desktop will give you an overview of the procedure that follows.

1. Connect the computers as a peer-to-peer network.

2. Start Remote Desktop on the remote computer.

3. Identify the users who may access the remote computer.

4. Leave the remote computer running.

5. If the client is using Windows XP, start Remote Desktop Connection on the client computer, set necessary options, and connect to the remote computer.

6. If the client is using Windows XP, install Remote Desktop using the Windows XP installation CD. You can then start Remote Desktop Connection on the client computer, set the necessary options, and connect to the remote computer.

There are many things that can cause a remote connection to fail. If you experience problems connecting to the remote computer, proceed through the following troubleshooting list:

■ Check all cable connections.

■ Ping the localhost and the remote host.

■ Make sure TCP port 3389 is not blocked by a firewall. Port 3389 is used to establish the remote connection.

■ Make sure the desired shared folder is shared.

■ Check if static IP addresses have been assigned to the computers.

■ Check if the correct subnet mask has been assigned to the computers.

■ If one of the computers in your Remote Desktop setup is not running Windows XP, the WINS service needs to be started on the computer that is not running Windows XP. The WINS server should then be identified in the **Advanced TCP/IP Settings** dialog box of the Windows XP computer. Note that the WINS service is only needed if you are using the computer name to connect to the host computer.

■ Check the media type setting in the **Choose your connection speed to optimize performance** textbox located under the **Experience** tab of the **Remote Desktop Connection** dialog box. If you are performing this activity on a LAN, it must be identified as such.

■ Check the Microsoft Management Console (MMC) to see if the services that support Remote Desktop are running.

■ You may need to add "Administrator" to the list of users allowed to access the remote computer.

■ You must log on to the remote computer using a password, or you will not be able to establish a remote connection.

Note:
As a matter of security, only accounts that require a password for logging on can configure a remote desktop session and use it. If the computer you are using for this lab activity does not have a password-enabled login, you will need to open Users Accounts and change the requirement by forcing the user to use a password to log on to the computer. Setting up a password requires that you must be a member of the Administrators group on the computer. You are most likely already a member of the Administrators group but may need to modify the user account to use a logon password.

Windows Vista Remote Desktop is very similar in design but is much simpler to configure than the Windows XP version. Remote Desktop is installed by default in Windows Vista, but you may need to make some configuration changes to make it work. For example, if a connection fails, it can be caused by a firewall, a switch, or router that is configured to prevent the remote connection.

    Copyright by Goodheart-Willcox Co., Inc.

After a Remote Desktop connection is established, it will show up in the **Start** menu as **Remote Desktop Connection**. You can access the Remote Desktop Connection the first time by going through **Start | All Programs | Accessories | Remote Desktop Connection**. When you access **Remote Desktop Connection**, the **Remote** page of the **System Properties** dialog box will display and will look like the following.

There are three options for Windows Vista Remote Desktop: **Don't allow connections to this computer, Allow connections from computers running any version of Remote Desktop (less secure)**, and **Allow connections only from computers running Remote Desktop with Network Level Authentication (more secure)**. Once the computer is configured to accept connections, you should have no real problems with remote desktop in the lab activity.

Equipment and Materials

- Two PCs connected in a peer-to-peer network. At least one PC must have Windows XP Professional installed. For the Windows Vista section, at least one PC must have Windows Vista Ultimate or Vista Business installed.
- Two 3 × 5 cards or equal. The cards will be used to label the two computer stations in the lab activity as either client or remote. While performing this activity, you can become easily confused reading the instructions for the client and remote computer and forget which computer you are working at.

Copyright by Goodheart-Willcox Co., Inc.

Windows XP—Part I

Procedure

1. ____ Report to your assigned workstation or workstations.

2. ____ Boot the computers and verify they are in working order.

3. ____ Identify each computer by its name and assign it as either a client or remote PC. Remember that the remote computer must be running Windows XP Professional. The client computer can run Windows XP Professional, Windows XP Home Edition, Windows 2000, Windows 98, Windows Me, or Windows 95. In addition, you must set up a user account on both the host and client computers and set the account to require a password for logging on.

Client PC name: _____

Remote PC name: _____

User account name: _____

Logon password: _____

4. ____ On the remote computer, open the **Start** menu, right-click **My Computer**, and select **Properties** from the shortcut menu. Select the **Remote** tab. A dialog box similar to the following should appear.

> **Note:**
> You can also access the **System Properties** dialog box if the keyboard is equipped with a key displaying the Windows logo. Simply press the Windows logo key and hold it while pressing the [Break] key.

Copyright by Goodheart-Willcox Co., Inc.

5. ____ Note that you can select either Remote Assistance or Remote Access. There are also two links that allow you to directly access the Help and Support feature to learn more about these two subjects. You may view the contents of both if you wish. After viewing the file contents, close the window and move on to the next step.

6. ____ Click the **Select Users** button. The **Remote Desktop Users** dialog box will display. This dialog box allows you to create a list of users who may access the computer remotely.

Remote Desktop Users [?][X]

The users listed below can connect to this computer, and any members of the Administrators group can connect even if they are not listed.

Richard already has access.

[Add...] [Remove]

To create new user accounts or add users to other groups, go to Control Panel and open User Accounts.

[OK] [Cancel]

---

7. ____ Click **Add**. The **Select Users** dialog box will display. The **Select Users** dialog box is used to search for users you wish to give remote access to and to create a Remote Desktop user list. Note that Microsoft refers to a user as an object type.

Select Users [?][X]

Select this object type:

Users   [Object Types...]

From this location:

INFINITY-WINXP   [Locations...]

Enter the object names to select (examples):

| [Check Names]

[Advanced...]   [OK] [Cancel]

---

8. ____ Search for the user you wish to add. You may simply search by object type and location, or you may narrow your search by entering the name of the user. To see examples of the search format, select the <u>examples</u> link. You can refine your search by clicking the **Advanced** button. A dialog box similar to the following will display. Note that you can conduct a search for other object types such as computers.

9. ____ Click **OK** to add the user to the Remote Desktop user list.

10. ____ After creating the authorized user list, close all dialog boxes and then move on to Windows XP—Part II to configure the client computer.

Windows XP—Part II

Procedure

1. ____ If the client is not running Windows XP Professional Edition, use the Windows XP Professional Setup CD to install the Remote Desktop client program, Remote Desktop Connection. When the Windows XP Setup CD starts, select the **Perform Additional Tasks** option. Next, select **Set up Remote Desktop Connection** from the lists of tasks in the **What do you want to do menu list**. The next image you will see is the flying folder transferring the necessary files for setting up Remote Desktop. The Install Shield Wizard appears and starts the installation process for the Remote Desktop. It is a very simple process with only a few prompts.

2. ____ When the Remote Desktop Connection installation has completed, you will be returned to the Welcome to Windows XP screen. Click **Exit** and then remove the CD.

3. ____ Check if the utility has indeed been installed. You can do this by opening the **Start** menu and then selecting **Program I Accessories I Communications**. Remote Desktop Connection should be listed as a choice. If you do not see Remote Desktop Connection, call your instructor.

Copyright by Goodheart-Willcox Co., Inc.

4. ____ At the client computer, open Remote Desktop Connection by selecting **Start | Programs | Accessories | Communications | Remote Desktop Connection**.

5. ____ Enter the name or the IP address of the computer you wish to connect to and then click **Connect**.

6. ____ Click the **Options** button. A dialog box similar to the following will appear. You will see several tabs for setting the Remote Desktop Connection properties. Remote Desktop Connection automatically opens to the **General** page.

The **General** page is used to configure the connection properties, such as the computer name, user name, password, and domain or workgroup. You can save these settings once they are created. You can also create more than one account to access more than one location.

7. ____ Click the **Display** tab. In the **Display** page, you can configure the display to be compatible with the remote computer. Using the default computer screen configuration could cause a problem if the client does not support the same configuration settings.

Note the check box labeled **Display the connection bar when in full screen mode**. If the check box is selected, a thin bar will appear across the top of the desktop, which indicates that a remote session has been established. The connection bar can be used to distinguish between the client and remote display when the displays are similar.

8. ____ Click the **Local Resources** tab. The **Local Resources** page is used to configure remote computer sound, Windows key combination use, and to select which local devices the user will be able to control when logged on to the remote computer.

9. ____ Click the **Programs** tab. The **Programs** page allows you to configure a specific program to start on the remote computer. For example, you could configure the dialog box to automatically start a Microsoft Office program when a connection is established.

10. ____ Click the **Experience** tab. The **Experience** page allows you to configure the type of media that the connection will use and the general display properties. This property window is critical in this lab activity. You must set the connection speed as LAN (10 Mbps or higher) since you are connected as a peer-to-peer connection in the lab. Select this option now by clicking in the drop-down box and selecting **LAN (10 Mbps or higher)**.

11. _____ After setting the needed options, make the connection to the remote computer by clicking the **Connect** button. If the client fails to establish a connection with the remote computer, enter the IP address of the remote computer in the **Computer** field on the **General** page.

12. _____ Now, open a document or image file on the remote computer, copy the contents, and paste the contents into a folder on the client computer.

13. _____ Try accessing the remote computer's Device Manager and looking at the resources of one of the devices.

14. _____ You may take some additional time to explore the remote desktop feature. When you are finished, go on to answer the review questions.

15. _____ After answering the review questions, terminate your connection to the remote server. Be aware that there are two ways to terminate a remote session. You can log off to terminate a session, or you can simply disconnect from a session. When you have ended your session, shut down the computers and return all materials to their proper storage area.

Windows Vista Part I—Procedure

1. _____ Report to your assigned workstation or workstations.

2. _____ Boot the computers and verify they are in working order.

3. _____ You do not need the installation DVD to install Windows Vista Remote Desktop as you do when using Windows XP. Windows Vista Remote Desktop is installed by default. Simply log on and then write down the computer name and IP address of the computer that will serve as the remote computer. To locate the computer name, right-click **Computer** and then select **Properties** from the shortcut menu. For the IP address, enter **cmd** into the **Search** box. Next enter **ipconfig** at the command prompt. Also, record the account information for this computer. You must use the Remote Desktop computer local user account information when establishing the remote connection.

Computer name: _____

IP address: _____

User name: _____

Password: _____

Now you have all the information you need to establish a connection for the lab activity.

4. _____ Open the **System Properties** dialog box. You can open this dialog box by right-clicking **Computer** and selecting **Properties** from the shortcut menu. Click **Advanced system settings** and select the **Remote** tab. Then, enable the **Allow connections from computers running any version of Remote Desktop (less secure)** option.

5. _____ Close **System Properties** dialog box and then proceed to Windows Vista—Part II. Be sure to leave the computer running.

Copyright by Goodheart-Willcox Co., Inc.

Windows Vista—Part II

Procedure

1. ____ Again, you do not need to install Remote Desktop in Windows Vista. It is installed by default. You are now at the Remote Desktop client computer. You simply select **Start | All Programs | Accessories | Remote Desktop Connection** and the initial dialog box will appear, prompting you for the computer name of the Remote Desktop computer. You can use the Remote Desktop computer name or its IP address. You can use either the computer name or IP address to identify the computer. Use the IP address.

2. ____ You are now prompted for the user name and password in a dialog box similar to the following.

Make note of the **Remember my credentials** option. When checked, your user name and password are remembered and do not need to be entered again. Input the local user account name and password of the other computer and then click **OK**.

3. ____ Now, you should be connected to the remote computer. The screen should appear similar to that in the following screen capture.

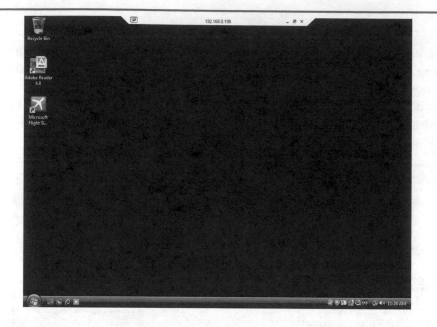

The desktop will appear black and you will see the Remote Desktop bar at the top of the window. The computer name and IP address will appear in the toolbar as well as the familiar **Minimize**, **Restore**, and **Close** icons.

4. ____ Try opening the remote computer's Windows Explorer. You can access Windows Explorer through **Start | All Programs | Accessories | Windows Explorer**. You should see the Windows Explorer program open and be able to navigate the file system on the remote computer. If not, call your instructor for assistance.

5. ____ Close Windows Explorer and then close the remote desktop using the **Close** (X) icon at the top of the screen. A **Disconnect Terminal Services Session** message box will appear. Click **OK** to end the Remote Desktop session.

6. ____ Now, reestablish the Remote Desktop connection, but this time click the **Options** button in the **Remote Desktop Connection** dialog box.

Copyright by Goodheart-Willcox Co., Inc.

After clicking the **Options** button, a dialog box similar to the one in the screen capture below will appear.

As you can see, there are many different tabs to choose from that control the configuration of remote computer's desktop. Take a few minutes to explore the various tabs to see what changes can be made to the Remote Desktop configuration.

7. ____ Close the Remote Desktop connection and then type "Remote desktop" into the Search textbox and take a few minutes to view the information available.

8. ____ Go on to answer the review questions.

Review Questions

1. In a typical scenario using remote access, the computer that is being controlled is called the _____ computer and the computer used to control the other computer is called the _____

   _____

2. What operating systems can be used on the client computer when using Remote Desktop?

   _____

3. What operating system must be installed on the remote computer when using Remote Desktop?

   _____

4. What key pressed after the Windows logo key will open the **System Properties** dialog box?

   _____

5. JoAnne has her notebook computer with her while traveling for her company. She needs to connect to her home computer to look at some files. Which will her notebook computer *most likely* be in this scenario, the client or the remote computer? _____

   _____

6. Which TCP port must be opened for Remote Desktop to work?_____

7. Why will using a connection that is not persistent cause a problem with Remote Desktop?

   _____

   _____

8. When the remote and client computers have identical screen displays, what can you do to distinguish them when displaying the remote desktop in full-screen mode? _____

   _____

9. List several items that might interfere with establishing a Remote Desktop connection. _____

   _____

   _____

   _____

   _____

   _____

Copyright by Goodheart-Willcox Co., Inc.

Name _____ Date _____

Class/Instructor _____

Remote Assistance

After completing this laboratory activity, you will be able to:

- Configure a computer for Remote Assistance.
- Identify operating systems that support Remote Assistance.
- Identify media that support Remote Assistance connections.
- Describe the variables that must be configured by the person requesting help.
- Describe the roles of the expert and novice.
- Compare and contrast Remote Desktop with Remote Assistance.
- Compare and contrast Windows XP and Windows Vista versions of Remote Assistance.

Introduction

This laboratory activity introduces you to the Remote Assistance feature first introduced with Windows XP. Remote Assistance can make the technician at the help desk more efficient because the technician can actually see the computer desktop of and chat or send text messages to the user who needs assistance.

The person who needs assistance is referred to as the *novice*, and the person providing the assistance is referred to as the *expert* or *helper*. The novice begins the request for assistance by starting Remote Assistance and then following the screen prompts. The novice then chooses to use either e-mail or Microsoft Instant Messenger as a way to send the request to the expert. The request is referred to as an *invitation*.

The expert receives the invitation and opens the attachment. The expert must use a password to start the connection process. The password should have been already provided by telephone or through a separate, secure e-mail. When the connection is established, the expert can chat with the novice, and at the same time, view the computer desktop. The expert cannot take control of the other computer unless the novice gives permission. The novice can terminate the session at any time by pressing the [Esc] key.

Note:

Both computers must be using Windows Instant Messenger, an e-mail client that is Messenger Application Programming Interface (MAPI) compliant, Outlook, or Outlook Express. "MAPI compliant" means that the third-party e-mail software has applications designed by Microsoft incorporated into it.

Copyright by Goodheart-Willcox Co., Inc.

Both Remote Assistance and Remote Desktop are based on the same Microsoft technology, but they are very different. Look at the following table that compares Remote Assistance with Remote Desktop.

Remote Assistance	Remote Desktop
Two persons must be present: one who needs assistance (novice) and the other who provides assistance (expert).	One person (the same person) accesses the remote computer from the client computer.
The expert or helper must receive an invitation via e-mail or instant messaging to access the novice's computer.	The client connects directly to the remote computer. No invitation is necessary.
The expert can be given full or partial control over the novice's computer.	The client has full control over the remote computer.
Uses a temporary connection such as one provided by an ISP issuing a temporary IP address.	Relies on a persistent connection such as DSL, ISDN, Cable, wireless, or network connection.
Both computers must be running Windows XP or Windows Vista, or a combination of the two.	Only the remote computer requires Windows XP or Windows Vista. Both are compatible with earlier operating systems such as Windows 2000 and Windows 98.
An e-mail is used to identify the expert.	Uses a computer name or IP address to establish a connection.
Available in Windows XP Home and Professional editions as well as in Windows Vista Home Basic, Home Professional, Business, and Ultimate editions.	Available in only Windows XP Professional and Windows Vista Business and Ultimate editions.
Provides limited control over the remote computer.	Provides complete control over the remote computer.
Located in Help and Support in Windows XP. In Windows Vista it is located in Help and Support as well as under **All Programs I Maintenance**.	Located under **Start I All Programs I Accessories I Communications** in Windows XP and under **Start I All Programs I Accessories** in Windows Vista.

Note:

Windows Vista allows connection by IP address if the computers are in an Active Directory domain setting which is quite helpful for help desk situations in large corporate, government, or educational settings. No e-mail is then required to initiate the session.

Copyright by Goodheart-Willcox Co., Inc.

Name_____

The following are some changes that have taken place in the Windows Vista version of Remote Assistance:

■ Remote Assistance works through a firewall.
■ You will not lose your Remote Assistance connection if the novice computer must be rebooted as part of the fix.
■ Windows Vista Remote Assistance no longer supports voice sessions the way Windows XP does. You now have to use a separate voice application or a telephone. Windows Vista with the Aero interface and combined voice session used too much bandwidth. Therefore, the Windows Vista implementation of Remote Assistance no longer incorporates voice session.
■ Windows Vista also has another new feature that allows not only for you to request help, but also to initiate a support session by sending an e-mail to offer help. This feature is extremely valuable for people working a help desk. They can initiate a session after someone calls the help desk for help.
■ Allows for Web-based mail. When Web-based mail is used, the invitation ticket is saved to the default location C:\Users\UserName\Desktop\Invitation.msrcincident. As indicated in the file path, the invitation is saved to the user's desktop. Later, the invitation is attached to the Web mail and sent to the expert for help.

The problems associated with Remote Assistance are similar to the problems associated with Remote Desktop. If you are experiencing problems with your Remote Assistance connection, review the troubleshooting list in Laboratory Activity 55. Also, check the following:

■ The e-mail client on both computers is MAPI compliant. (Windows Vista allows Web-based e-mail.)
■ Port 3389 is opened and not blocked by a firewall.
■ Antivirus and Internet security third-party software, such as Norton, are not interfering with the connection.

Additional Remote Assistance references are available at the Microsoft Support Web site. The following is a list of articles that can be found at that site.

■ Q300546: Overview of Remote Assistance in Windows XP.
■ Q306791: How To: Provide Remote Assistance in Response to an E-mail Invitation in Windows XP.
■ Q306800: How To: Provide Remote Assistance in Response to Windows Messenger Invitation in Windows XP.
■ Q300692: Description of the Remote Assistance Connection Process.

Equipment and Materials

■ Two PCs each running Windows XP or Windows Vista and each with separate Internet access. (This lab activity can also be performed between two students' home computers.)
■ Each PC must have either Instant Messenger, or a MAPI compatible e-mail client, such as Outlook, Outlook Express, or Windows Mail. Web mail may also be used on the Windows Vista PCs to support Remote Assistance.

Part I—Windows XP

Procedure

1. ____ Report to your assigned workstation.

2. ____ Boot the computers and verify they are in working order.

3. ____ On the computer that will be sending an invitation, access the **System Properties** dialog box. Select the **Remote** tab and select the **Allow Remote Assistance invitations to be sent from this computer** option. Close the dialog box and move on to the next step.

4. ____ Open Remote Assistance by clicking **Start | Help and Support** and selecting **Remote Assistance** from the Help and Support Resources list. A dialog box similar to the following will appear.

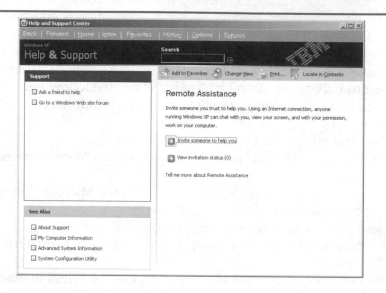

5. ____ You will see two options: **Invite someone to help you** and **View invitation status**. Select **Invite someone to help you**. A dialog box similar to the following will appear.

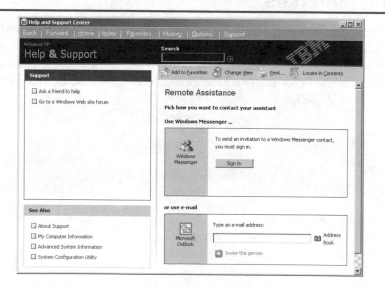

Copyright by Goodheart-Willcox Co., Inc.

6. ____ Next, you may select either the Windows Messenger or e-mail option to contact the person for help. Notice that e-mail also has an option to access the address book. Select to use e-mail by typing the e-mail address of the expert in the **Type an e-mail address** text box.

7. ____ Click **Invite this person**. The following screen will display.

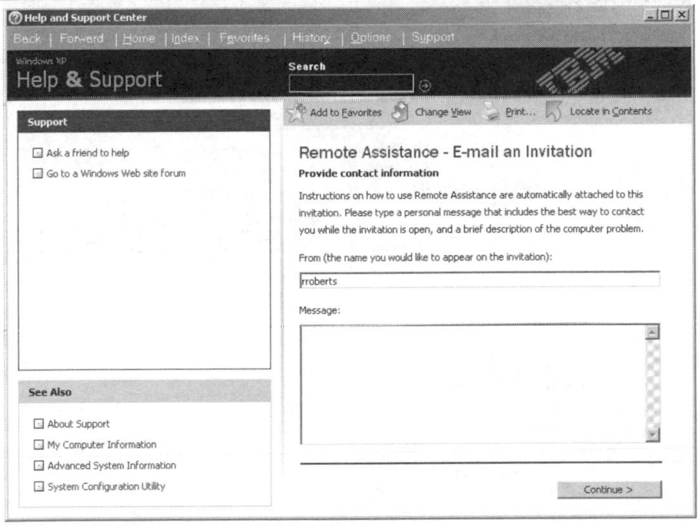

8. ____ In the **Message** text box, type a note requesting help or a brief description of the problem.

9. ____ Click **Continue**. A screen similar to the following will appear.

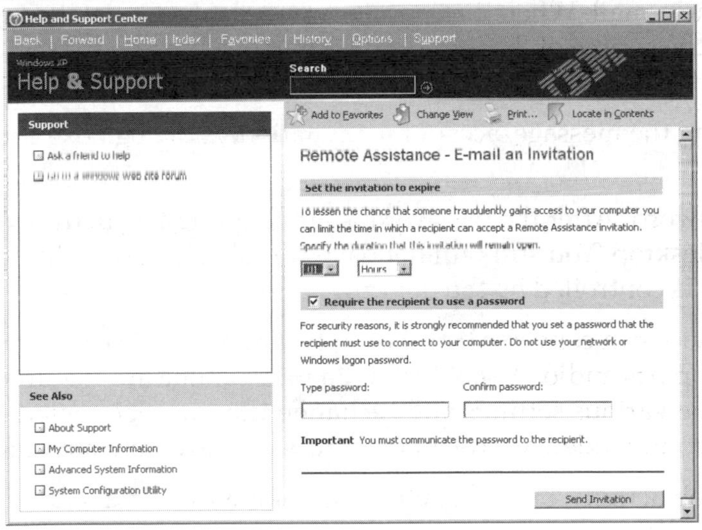

10. ____ Select a password to use to establish a connection from the expert. You can also select the duration of the connection from a few minutes to 30 days. After setting the duration for 3 hours, type a password to be used for the session. You must convey the password to the expert by a different means such as a separate e-mail or telephone call.

11. ____ Click the **Send Invitation** button. The request for assistance will be sent to the expert for help. The expert need not be at their computer at this time. The expert could be away from their computer and can answer the request at a later time.

Copyright by Goodheart-Willcox Co., Inc.

12. _____ You can check the status of the request by opening the Remote Assistance utility and then selecting **View invitation status**. In the status screen, the invitation can be reviewed, resent, or deleted.

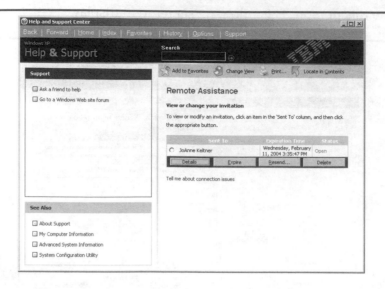

The resend feature is handy in case you sent a request and the expert did not receive the request or the computer settings at the expert location would not allow the request to be accepted. This happens often when the expert location is protected by a firewall. The novice user simply resends the request for assistance after the expert either disables the firewall or opens port 3389.

13. _____ At the destination computer where the expert resides, an e-mail will arrive with the invitation. Open the e-mail. When the e-mail is opened, a more detailed description is revealed. Also included are the source of the e-mail and a personal message. Pay particular attention to the attachment in the e-mail. This is the Remote Assistance invitation.

14. _____ After reading the message, accept the invitation. A dialog box requesting a password will appear.

15. _____ Enter a password. After the password is authenticated, you, the expert, will be able to view the novice's desktop. You still will not have complete control. The amount of control over the novice desktop is controlled by the novice.

The expert and novice can converse by sending text messages to each other or talk in real time if the computer supports audio. A speaker and a microphone are required for conversation. Experiment with the various settings and exchange text messages between the novice and expert. Visit the recommended Microsoft resources to learn more about Remote Assistance.

16. _____ Repeat the lab activity, but switch the roles of novice and expert.

17. _____ Restore the system to its original configuration and then go on to Part II—Windows Vista.

Copyright by Goodheart-Willcox Co., Inc.

Part II—Windows Vista

Procedure

1. ____ Report to your assigned workstation.

2. ____ Boot the computers and verify they are in working order.

3. ____ On the computer that will be sending an invitation, access the computer **System Properties** dialog box and then click **Advanced System Settings**. Select the **Remote** tab and then select the **Allow Remote Assistance invitations to be sent from this computer** option. Close the dialog box and move on to the next step.

4. ____ Open Remote Assistance by clicking **Start | All Programs | Maintenance | Windows Remote Assistance**. You can also access Remote Assistance through the Help and Support feature or by typing **msra.exe** in the **Search** box. The first dialog box to appear is similar to the following.

You are presented with two options: **Invite someone you trust to help you** and **Offer to help someone**. The second choice is very valuable for persons working a help desk. When they receive a phone call from someone requesting help, the help desk technician can initiate the Remote Assistance session. This feature was not available in Windows XP.

Copyright by Goodheart-Willcox Co., Inc.

5. _____ Select the **Invite someone to help you** option. A dialog box similar to the following will appear.

Windows Remote Assistance

How do you want to invite someone to help you?

With Remote Assistance, you can invite someone you trust to connect to your computer and help you with a computer problem. How does this work?

Use e-mail to send an invitation
If your e-mail program is not configured yet, choosing this option will start the configuration process.

Save this invitation as a file
If you use web-based e-mail, choose this option.

Cancel

Select the **Use e-mail to send an invitation** option if you have an e-mail account configured on the workstation such as in Outlook or Microsoft Mail. If you are using a Web-based e-mail account, select **Save this invitation as a file** option. You will then be able to attach the invitation to the Web-based mail. The invitation is located on the desktop by default and looks similar to the one in the following partial screen capture.

Invitation

---

6. _____ If you selected the **Use e-mail to send an invitation** option, the next dialog box to appear will prompt you for an e-mail address and a password to use for the session. Enter the e-mail address of the Remote Assistance expert and a password. The suggested password for this activity is "password."

Copyright by Goodheart-Willcox Co., Inc.

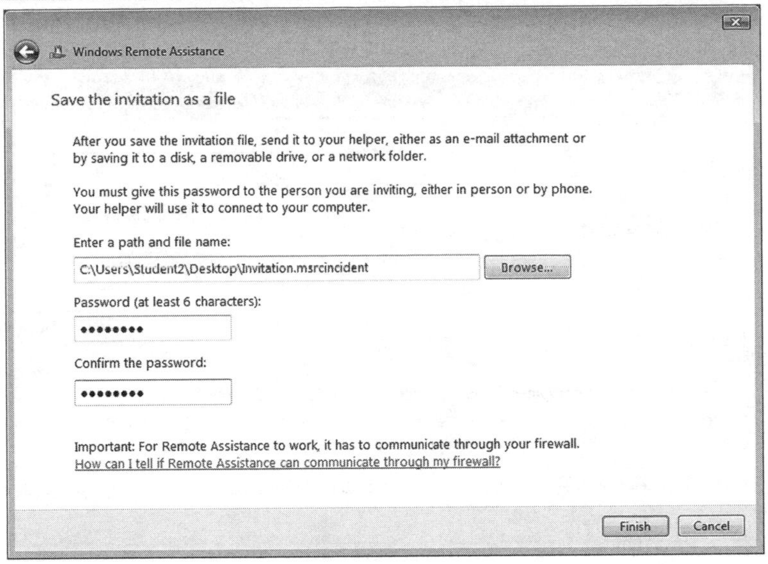

If you selected the **Save this invitation as a file** option, you will be prompted for a password for the session but not an e-mail address. The invitation is saved to the user desktop. When you start your Web mail session, you will attach the invitation to the Web mail and send it to the expert. The following screen capture shows what a Web mail dialog box might look like with the invitation attached.

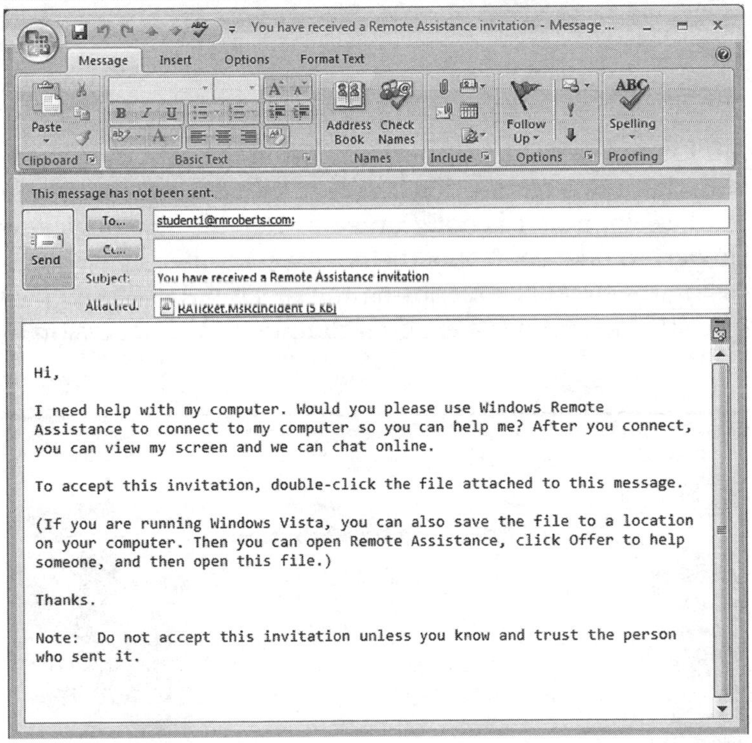

The text body message is automatically created by the Remote Assistance program. You can see the invitation "RATicket.MsRcIncident" in the **Attached** text box. When the invitation is opened, the connection process will automatically begin. The following screen capture shows what the expert might see when receiving Web-based mail from the novice.

Copyright by Goodheart-Willcox Co., Inc.   Laboratory Activity 56   411

7. _____ After the e-mail is sent, you will see a Windows Remote Assistance dialog box on the novice computer similar to the one in the following screen capture.

The novice will wait for an incoming connection. When the expert opens the e-mail and then opens the attached invitation, a connection between the two computers will be established. Full control of the novice computer is not granted by default. The novice computer must give permission to the expert to take control of the novice computer. The novice may end the session at any time by pressing the [Esc] key or closing the session dialog box. The following is a screen capture of Remote Assistance from the expert's computer. A chat session has been established with the novice.

Copyright by Goodheart-Willcox Co., Inc.

Name_____

8. ____ Now that the connection has been established between the two computers, experiment with the session. See if you can access System Tools located at **Start | All Programs | Accessories | Tools** and see if you can run some of the tools that have capabilities to repair the novice computer.

9. ____ Close both the novice and expert controls.

10. ____ Repeat the lab activity, but switch the roles of novice and expert.

11. ____ Restore the system to its original configuration and then go on to answer the review questions. Be sure to visit the recommended Microsoft resources to learn more about Remote Assistance.

Review Questions

1. List several differences between Remote Assistance and Remote Desktop. _____

_____

_____

_____

2. What is the person who is requesting the assistance referred to as? _____

3. What is the person who is providing the assistance referred to as?_____

4. What are the e-mail requirements for Remote Assistance on a Windows Vista computer? _____

_____

_____

5. What key is used to instantly terminate the Remote Assistance connection?_____

_____

6. What does the acronym MAPI represent? _____

_____

7. Which TCP port is used by Remote Assistance? ____ _____

_____

8. How can the expert and novice exchange information?_____

_____

_____

9. What are the five primary changes in Windows Vista Remote Assistance as compared to Windows XP Remote Assistance? _____

_____

_____

_____

_____

_____

_____

10. List three ways to access Remote Assistance in Windows Vista? _____

_____

_____

_____

11. Where is the default location for storing a Remote Assistance ticket in Windows Vista? _____

_____

12. What is the file name used to identify the Remote Assistance ticket for Windows Vista? _____

_____

Copyright by Goodheart-Willcox Co., Inc.

Name _____ Date _____

Class/Instructor _____

Virus Test Software

After completing this laboratory activity, you will be able to:

■ Test a typical antivirus program to ensure it is installed correctly.

■ Build the EICAR virus test program.

Introduction

In this lab activity, you will access the EICAR Web site at www.eicar.org and download a copy of the EICAR utility. The utility is designed to test an installed version of any antivirus software.

EICAR (European Institute for Computer Antivirus Research) has developed a virus test program that checks if an antivirus program has been installed correctly and is working. The EICAR test file is a simple text file that contains the following symbols:

X5O!P%@AP[4\PZX54(P^)7CC)7}$EICAR-STANDARD-ANTIVIRUS-TEST-FILE!$H+H*

You can copy the line of text above using Notepad or WordPad and save it as a plain ASCII text file named EICAR with the file extension of .com, .dll, or .exe. When typing the line of text, be sure to enter the third letter symbol as the capital letter *O* and not as a zero. All the letters should be entered as uppercase letters.

The antivirus program installed on your computer should prevent you from saving the EICAR antivirus file. When the EICAR file is activated, you should see a window similar to the McAfee dialog box that follows. The look of the dialog box will vary according to the brand of antivirus software you are using.

Seeing a window similar to this window means that the software is working. However, it does not ensure that all options for the antivirus utility are correctly configured. It just lets you know that the general antivirus program is installed and working. For example, it does not mean the antivirus program you are using is up-to-date and contains the latest virus definitions or that the program is scanning e-mail automatically.

Copyright by Goodheart-Willcox Co., Inc.

The following screen captures are another sample of dialog boxes triggered by the EICAR.COM program.

These two images are windows created by the F-Secure Anti-Virus software utility. If your computer is not equipped with an antivirus utility package, you can download an evaluation package from www.fsecure.com. After downloading the evaluation package, install the antivirus utility following the screen prompts. You can either create the EICAR file or download the test file from most antivirus Web sites. The file is free to download and use to test antivirus programs.

Equipment and Materials

■ Typical PC with Windows XP or later operating system, Internet access, and an antivirus program installed. (If you do not have an antivirus program installed, you can download a 30-day antivirus trial version from many different sites including www.symetec.com, www.mcaffee.com, and www.fsecure.com.

■ Floppy disk or USB Flash drive for saving the EICAR file.

Procedure

1. ____ Boot the computer and open Notepad (not Microsoft Word or any other high-end word processor). The file must be a plain ASCII text file.

2. ____ Type the following list of symbols exactly as they appear and save as a file called eicar.txt to the floppy disk or Flash drive. The string of characters must appear exactly like the list that follows. You may also download this file from www.eicar.org/anti_virus_test_file.htm.

X5O!P%@AP[4\PZX54(P^)7CC)7}$EICAR-STANDARD-ANTIVIRUS-TEST-FILE!$H+H*

If you have trouble activating the EICAR file by typing the string of symbols, try a downloaded copy. Note that the file should be saved as a .txt file not as a .com, .dll, or .exe. If you attempt to save this file as any of these three file extensions, it may trigger any antivirus program installed on your computer. When you wish to use the file for testing antivirus software, you change the file extension to .com, .dll, or .exe. You can name the file anything you wish. It does not have to be named EICAR. You can name it VirusTestProg.exe for example.

Copyright by Goodheart-Willcox Co., Inc.

3. ____ Test the antivirus program by attempting to save the eicar.com file to the hard disk drive from the floppy drive or Flash drive. (Note that any attempt to save the EICAR file to the floppy drive or Flash drive may activate any existing antivirus software already loaded on the computer.) The exact reactions to the EICAR program vary from one antivirus utility to another.

4. ____ Experiment with the EICAR file by changing the type of file extension and by changing your antivirus software settings. You should also try changing one or two characters in the character string inside the EICAR file. Try installing the file in different directories. See what happens.

5. ____ After you are done with your laboratory experiments, remove the EICAR test program from the computer and return the computer to its original condition.

Review Questions

1. What types of file extensions are used with the EICAR virus test program? _____

_____

2. What does the acronym EICAR represent? _____

Computer Service and Repair Lab Manual

Copyright by Goodheart-Willcox Co., Inc.

Name _____ Date _____

Class/Instructor _____

Windows Defender

After completing this laboratory activity, you will be able to:

- Configure Windows Defender.
- Identify the symptoms of a computer infected with spyware.
- Identify Windows Defender alter levels and appropriate corrective actions.

Introduction

In this laboratory activity, you will explore Windows Defender application. Windows Defender scans the computer to identify and remove spyware and some forms of malware. Spyware is designed to collect information about the user, generate pop-up ads, and in some cases, change computer settings without user permission. Besides being annoying, spyware can also slow the performance of the computer. Some spyware symptoms are as follows:

- Pop-up advertisements appear, even when not connected to the Internet.
- The default home page or the search program changes.
- The computer suddenly starts to perform slowly.
- You are automatically taken to a Web site other than the one requested.

Note that these symptoms may also indicate certain other malware classifications. The two most common symptoms of a large number of spyware programs running on a computer are pop-up ads and slow performance. Windows Defender is designed to identify spyware and also some malware software applications. The following is a screen capture of the Windows Defender screen.

Windows Defender is accessed through **Start | All Programs | Windows Defender**. You can also access Windows Defender through the Control Panel default view, **Start | Control Panel | Security | Windows Defender**, or the classic view, **Start | Control Panel | Windows Defender**. The executable file name for Windows Defender is MSASCui.exe and can be run through the **Search** dialog box.

Defender Tools and Settings screen, located through the **Tools** menu of Windows Defender provides access to Windows Defender configuration options. Look at the following screen capture to see the various options under **Tools and Settings**.

The following table lists and describes the **Tools and Settings** screen items.

Item	Description
Options	Allows you to turn Windows Defender on or off, schedule times to perform scans, and configure the action to take when spyware or threats are detected.
Microsoft SpyNet	An online community that keeps the user up-to-date on threats. You can send a copy of suspicious software to this site. SpyNet membership is optional.
Quarantined Items	At-risk items are stored as quarantined items. You can remove or restore items listed in the quarantine folder.
Software Explorer	Allows you to view and monitor all software.
Allowed Items	Allows you to view software that you chose not to monitor because you know it is safe.
Windows Defender Website	Microsoft Web site.

    Copyright by Goodheart-Willcox Co., Inc.

Windows Defender is free and is automatically installed during the Windows Vista installation process. Windows Defender was first available for Windows XP in beta form. Windows Live OneCare is an all-inclusive antivirus and security suite provided by Microsoft at an additional cost. Windows Live OneCare is not installed by default during the Windows Vista operating systems installation process. Windows Live OneCare incorporates all the features that are available in Windows Defender. There will be more about Windows Live OneCare in another lab activity

Spyware is classified by Windows Defender as to how much personal information may be collected, how much the computer configuration can be changed, and other harmful effects. The following table provides information about the Windows Defender alert level and possible problems and actions you should take to prevent harm. For more detailed information about Microsoft Defender, use Help and Support located off the **Start** menu.

Alert Level	Actions
Severe	Malicious program similar in nature to a virus or worm and that can cause harm to your computer. Remove immediately.
High	Most likely collects personal information and may damage your computer or change configurations. Remove immediately.
Medium	May affect your privacy and possibly make changes to your computer configuration. If you are not familiar with or do not trust the publisher, remove the software.
Low	Typically unwanted software that may collect personal information or change computer configuration based on the software license agreement. You will want to view the publisher and then make a decision to remove it or not.
Not yet classified	Usually not harmful. You will want to review the publisher and then decide to remove it or not.

Most spyware collects data through the Internet. There is a direct correlation between the amount of spyware installed on a computer and the number of Web sites visited. As more and more spyware is collected on a computer, the slower the computer will perform even if the spyware has a low alert level. Running defender or another spyware tool and then removing undesirable programs will improve the computer performance. There can be thousands of individual pieces of spyware on a single unprotected computer.

Windows Live OneCare is the Microsoft security suite used to detect and remove viruses and worms as well as spyware. Windows Defender is designed to detect and remove spyware.

Two other very common spyware utilities are Adaware and Spybot. Both are available as free software applications for home use and also as commercial packages. Visit their Web sites for more information.

A computer should always have antivirus and spyware software protection applications installed as routine protection from infections. However, spyware and antivirus applications do not provide 100% protection from malicious software. Every day new spyware and antivirus malware is released on the Internet, so a computer that is running protection can still be infected. An antivirus and antispyware program will prevent most malicious software.

Equipment and Materials

■ Typical PC with Windows Vista and Windows Defender installed. (You can also use a Windows XP PC and a downloaded copy of Windows Defender.)

Procedure

1. ____ Report to your assigned workstation.

2. ____ Boot the computer and verify it is in working order.

3. ____ Open **Control Panel | Security | Windows Defender**. The **Windows Defender** dialog box should appear.

4. ____ Look at the toolbar and locate the **Scan** option. Click the down arrow immediately right of the **Scan** option. Select the **Quick scan** option and then scan your computer. Watch closely as it runs. You will see the various files and directories identified as they are being scanned. Allow Windows Defender to run for a few minutes. If it takes too long because of limited class time, you can end the scan at any time. Typically, the scan takes only a few minutes.

5. ____ After the scan has stopped or after you stop the scan, select the **Tools** option from the toolbar. The **Tools and Settings** dialog box should appear.

6. ____ In the **Settings** section, click **Options**. The **Options** dialog box will display, allowing you to select how Windows Defender should run on the computer.

The **Options** dialog box allows you to configure when to run Windows Defender, what to do with the offensive program as related to the threat category, and more. As you scroll down the dialog box, locate and then select the Understanding real-time protection link and then read the information it contains.

Copyright by Goodheart-Willcox Co., Inc.

7. ____ Select the **Tools** option from the toolbar and then select **Software Explorer**. You should see a dialog box similar to the following.

The **Category** drop-down textbox displays the categories of programs that will automatically load and run in the background when Windows Vista completes the boot process. You can select a particular program listed in the left pane and view detailed information about the program in the right pane. The buttons at the bottom of the dialog box allow you to remove, disable, and enable a program. These features help you to isolate a suspect program.

8. ____ Now, select the **Category** drop-down textbox to see the four choices available. The following is a partial screen capture of the **Software Explorer** dialog box with the **Category** list shown.

The available four options, **Startup Programs**, **Currently Running Programs**, **Network Connected Programs**, and **Winsock Service Providers**, allow you to view programs on the computer listed by related functions. For example, the Winsock Service Providers are services used by network programs to support the exchange of data across a network both locally and via the Internet. You can also see which programs are currently running on the computer and which program applications are supporting a network connection.

9. ____ Click the <u>Using Software Explorer</u> link to learn more about the purpose and function of Software Explorer.

10. ____ If you have an Internet connection, select the **Tools** menu and then select the **Windows Defender website** option. The Windows Defender Web site provided by Microsoft will provide you with even more information about Windows Defender. Spend a few minutes looking at the information available at the Web site. If you do not have an Internet connection, simply skip this step.

11. ____ Take a few minutes to explore Windows Defender and become more familiar with the features. Do not remove any programs or services.

12. ____ Close Windows Defender and then answer the review questions. You may use the Help and Support feature to assist you in answering the review questions.

Review Questions

1. What is spyware? _____

_____

_____

2. What is the difference between Microsoft Windows Defender and Windows Live OneCare? ___

_____

_____

_____

3. What are the two most common symptoms exhibited on a computer with multiple spyware infections? _____

_____

4. What is the executable file name for Windows Defender? _____

_____

5. Does antispyware software provide 100% protection from spyware infections? _____

Copyright by Goodheart-Willcox Co., Inc.

Name _____ Date _____

Class/Instructor _____

Security Center

After completing this laboratory activity, you will be able to:

■ Explain the purpose of Security Center.

■ Access Security Center.

■ Enable and disable Windows Firewall protection.

■ Enable or disable automatic updates.

■ Enable or disable virus protection.

Introduction

Security Center was first introduced in Windows XP and has become a vital part of the Windows Vista security system. It is a centralized location that contains all of the most commonly used tools concerning computer security. Security Center is very similar in Windows XP and Windows Vista as you can see when comparing the following screen captures.

Windows XP   **Windows Vista**

The security status of Window Firewall, automatic updating, and malware protection are indicted in Security Center by the colors red and green and the words *OK* and *OFF*. Red indicates "off" or that a security application is not installed, such as malware protection not installed. You can quickly enable Window Firewall simply by selecting the Firewall drop-down arrow. An option to turn on the firewall will be presented. You will also see a warning that two or more firewalls running can cause system conflicts. You should only run one firewall system on a single computer or only one firewall system in a small local area network, such as a home or small office network.

Copyright by Goodheart-Willcox Co., Inc.

Often, a home or small office network has a firewall incorporated into the network gateway or router. The gateway or router is a device that typically provides a central connection point to the Internet that all the computers in the network use. They either connect to the router or gateway wirelessly or by cables.

Automatic updating allows the operating system to automatically check for new operating system updates and to automatically download and install the updates as they become available. Keeping the operating system up-to-date will help protect the computer from hackers and malicious software as well as help prevent system crashes and problems.

Malware protection will help prevent system infection caused by malware. Malware is commonly known as viruses and worms. Malware also includes spyware. Windows Vista comes with Windows Defender, an antispyware program. Microsoft does not include an antivirus package by default. Microsoft does offer an antivirus program called Windows Live OneCare. Windows Live OneCare is not free at the time of this writing.

The last major option in the Windows Vista Security Center is **Other security settings**. The other security settings refer to the User Account Control (UAC) and Internet security settings. The UAC is new in Windows Vista and is designed to prevent unauthorized configuration changes to the computer system. The UAC requires standard users to use a password to access certain computer configuration options. Users that are equal to a computer administrator will receive a warning before they change a critical system configuration. There will be more about the UAC in later laboratory activities.

The Internet security settings are a collection of various options that affect the way a user accesses and interacts with Internet locations and Web pages. The Internet security options will be covered in more detail in a later laboratory activity.

Equipment and Materials

- Typical PC running Windows XP with Service Pack 2 installed or Windows Vista, or both, installed.

Part I—Windows XP

Procedure

1. ____ Report to your assigned workstation.

2. ____ Boot the computer and verify it is in working order.

3. ____ Access the Security Center through **Start | Control Panel | Security Center**.

4. ____ Open the **Firewall** section and select the How does a firewall protect my computer link and read the information.

5. ____ Open the **Automatic Updates** section and then select the How does automatic updates help protect my computer link. Read the information contained within.

6. ____ Open the **Virus Protection** section and then select the How does antivirus software help protect my computer link. Read the information contained within.

7. ____ Close the Windows XP Security Center and go on to Part II—Windows Vista.

Copyright by Goodheart-Willcox Co., Inc.

Part II—Windows Vista

Procedure

1. ____ Report to your assigned workstation.

2. ____ Boot the computer and verify it is in working order.

3. ____ Access Security Center through **Start | Control Panel | Security | Security Center**. You can also access Security Center by entering **Security Center** into the **Search** text box.

4. ____ Open the **Firewall** section and select the <u>How does a firewall protect my computer</u> link and read the information.

5. ____ Open the **Automatic Update** section and then select the <u>How does automatic updates help protect my computer</u> link. Read the information contained within.

6. ____ Open the **Malware protection** section and then select <u>How does anti-malware software help protect my computer</u> link. Read the information contained within.

7. ____ Open the **Other security settings** section. Select the <u>How does User Account Control help protect my computer</u> link and read the information provided.

8. ____ Close Security Center and go on to answer the review questions. You may use Help and Support to help you with your answers.

Review Questions

1. What is the name of the Microsoft Windows antispyware application? _____

2. What is the name of the Microsoft antivirus program? _____

3. How can you access the Windows Vista Security Center? _____

4. What is UAC? _____

5. How does the UAC help protect the computer? _____

6. When would you turn Windows Firewall off? _____

7. How does automatic updating protect the computer? _____

8. Which operating system, Windows XP or Windows Vista, uses UAC to enhance system security? _____

9. Does Windows XP install Windows Defender by default to protect against spyware? _____

Copyright by Goodheart-Willcox Co., Inc.

Computer Service and Repair Lab Manual

Copyright by Goodheart-Willcox Co., Inc.

Name _____ Date _____

Class/Instructor _____

System Boot Sequence

After completing this laboratory activity, you will be able to:

■ Describe the three stages of computer operation.

■ Identify each boot sequence stage when viewing the screen display.

■ Explain in general terms what has taken place during the boot sequence.

Introduction

Troubleshooting is very difficult for the inexperienced technician. This laboratory activity is designed to help you understand what is most likely causing the system failure or problem. After completing this laboratory activity, you should be able to isolate the computer problem area by observing the boot sequence of the computer.

There are three stages of computer operation: POST or EFI, loading and initializing the operating system files and drivers, and after logon. The after logon period involves loading the startup programs and running applications.

Stage	Visuals Queue	Description
POST or EFI	BIOS name, key combination to enter for the BIOS Setup program, memory count	Performs basic hardware detection; checks the RAM, hard disk drive, and video card; and loads a set of generic drivers for basic input and output. Searches for the hard disk drive active partition and MBR.
OS Loading and Initialization	Progress bar	At this point, critical operating system files and drivers have been successfully loaded. Loads and initializes operating system files and drivers.
After Logon	User logon	Logon means most critical operating system files have been successfully loaded as well as drivers. After logon, services and startup programs are loaded.

Copyright by Goodheart-Willcox Co., Inc.

After the power switch is used to start the computer, the power-on self-test (POST) or Extensible Firmware Interface (EFI) will begin. The POST or EFI performs basic hardware detection; checks the RAM, hard disk drive, and video card; and loads a set of generic drivers. The POST is run from the BIOS and uses the values stored in CMOS by the BIOS Setup program. A routine similar to POST is run by EFI. The EFI stores values in a database. You will see a series of text information on a black background during the POST. Look at the following illustration to see an example of a POST display.

Phoenix - Award BIOS V6.00GP; An Energy Star Ally
Copyright (©) 1984 - 2003, Phoenix Technologies, LTD

Main Processor: Intel (R) Pentium (R) D CPU 3.00 GHz (200 x 15.02 CPUs)
Memory Testing: 1048576 k OK
CPU Brand Name: Intel (R) Pentium (R) D CPU 3.00 GHz
EM64T

DDR DIMM Speed: 533
IDE Channel 0 Master: None
IDE Channel 0 Slave: None
IDE Channel 1 Master: Memorex DVD + - RAM 525GV1 G.01

Detecting IDE Drives...

Press F9 to Select Booting Device after POST
Press Del to enter SETUP
10/23/2006 - PHM 800P - 823

Not all computers are configured to display the BIOS text messages. Some computers mask over the text messages by displaying a graphic during the POST. For example, Dell computers display a Dell logo during the POST, and some Intel motherboards display an Intel logo during the POST. You can enable or disable the graphic with the BIOS Setup program.

You can typically pause the BIOS text display by pressing the [Pause] key. The POST will resume when you press [Enter]. The BIOS will display information about the hardware detected as well as RAM memory test results.

When the POST is successfully completed, it loads the bootstrap program located on the active partition. The bootstrap program will start the loading of the operating system. A failure during POST will produce a beep code or error message that is used to indicate which hardware item is at fault. You can view information on POST errors at the BIOS or EFI software designer's Web site or at the motherboard manufacturer's Web site. Sometimes the computer manufacturer's Web site posts this information as well.

Failure of the POST to locate the hard disk drive active partition will typically generate an error message such as "Non system disk," "Reboot and select proper boot device," and "No boot device found." Failure to locate the active partition or a corrupt master boot record (MBR) will generate errors such as "Invalid partition table," "Error loading operating system," and "Missing operating system."

If the POST successfully locates the disk drive, active partition, the MBR, and the bootstrap program, the system initiates detecting hardware and configuring the hardware devices and loads critical operating system files as well as drivers for the various hardware items detected. Look at the following screen capture of the Windows Vista ntblog.txt file. This text file shows the sequence of drivers being loaded.

Copyright by Goodheart-Willcox Co., Inc.

```
ntbtlog.txt - Notepad                                              ─  □  ✕
File  Edit  Format  View  Help
  Service Pack 1 7 16 2008 11:08:07.484
Loaded driver \SystemRoot\system32\ntoskrnl.exe
Loaded driver \SystemRoot\system32\hal.dll
Loaded driver \SystemRoot\system32\kdcom.dll
Loaded driver \SystemRoot\system32\mcupdate_GenuineIntel.dll
Loaded driver \SystemRoot\system32\PSHED.dll
Loaded driver \SystemRoot\system32\BOOTVID.dll
Loaded driver \SystemRoot\system32\CLFS.SYS
Loaded driver \SystemRoot\system32\CI.dll
Loaded driver \SystemRoot\system32\drivers\wdf01000.sys
Loaded driver \SystemRoot\system32\drivers\WDFLDR.SYS
Loaded driver \SystemRoot\system32\drivers\acpi.sys
Loaded driver \SystemRoot\system32\drivers\WMILID.SYS
Loaded driver \SystemRoot\system32\drivers\msisadrv.sys
Loaded driver \SystemRoot\system32\drivers\pci.sys
Loaded driver \SystemRoot\system32\drivers\partmgr.sys
Loaded driver \SystemRoot\system32\drivers\volmgr.sys
Loaded driver \SystemRoot\system32\drivers\volmgrx.sys
Loaded driver \SystemRoot\system32\drivers\intelide.sys
Loaded driver \SystemRoot\system32\drivers\PCIIDEX.SYS
Loaded driver \SystemRoot\system32\drivers\mountmgr.sys
Loaded driver \SystemRoot\system32\drivers\atapi.sys
Loaded driver \SystemRoot\system32\drivers\ataport.SYS
Loaded driver \SystemRoot\system32\drivers\fltmgr.sys
Loaded driver \SystemRoot\system32\drivers\fileinfo.sys
Loaded driver \SystemRoot\system32\Drivers\ksecdd.sys
Loaded driver \SystemRoot\system32\drivers\ndis.sys
Loaded driver \SystemRoot\system32\drivers\msrpc.sys
Loaded driver \SystemRoot\system32\drivers\NETIO.SYS
Loaded driver \SystemRoot\system32\drivers\tcpip.sys
Loaded driver \SystemRoot\system32\drivers\fwpkclnt.sys
Loaded driver \SystemRoot\system32\Drivers\Ntfs.sys
Loaded driver \SystemRoot\system32\drivers\volsnap.sys
Loaded driver \SystemRoot\System32\Drivers\spldr.sys
```

It is not unusual to load several hundred drivers during this part of the boot sequence. Drivers are required not only for obvious hardware devices such as video cards, keyboards, mouse, modems, and disk drivers, but also for less obvious devices such as motherboard chipsets, ports, and buses. The operating system essential programs are also loaded and initialized one by one.

Some of the more familiar error messages that can be generated typically relate to missing critical startup files such as "Ntloader not found," "Missing Operating System," or "Invalid partition table." Other errors generated during this time may be produced by the hardware manufacturer driver and display messages related to the hardware device. The most common error is to have the hardware driver simply stop the boot process. A stop during the boot process is typically caused by a memory issue or discrepancy between the installed physical RAM and the software driver program. For example, a software driver trying to install program code or a numeric value in an occupied area of RAM that is already in use. Drivers that are certified for use with a specific operating system typically do not cause this type of problem.

After the POST is completed, the next visual queue that you will see is the Windows progress bar on the display. Look at the following example.

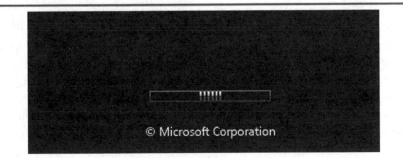

Seeing the Windows Vista or Windows XP progress bar means that the operating system kernel has been successfully loaded. It also means that almost all of the required operating system files and hardware drivers have been loaded. If you do not get this far in the boot sequence, then you most likely have a corrupt system file, corrupt driver, or registry problem. The system could simply

Copyright by Goodheart-Willcox Co., Inc.

stop responding without displaying an error message. You can try pressing the [F8] key to only load a minimal set of drivers and operating system files. Pressing the [F8] key will display the Advanced Menu Options, also known as safe mode.

After the operating system is loaded and initialized, the next item to appear on the display is the user logon. The following is a screen capture of the logon screen.

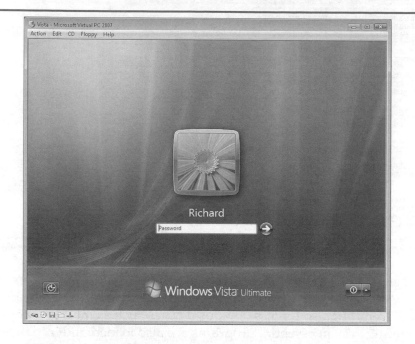

After a successful logon, the operating system loads and runs services and startup programs. After the successful loading and running of services and startup programs, the user can start software applications, such as Microsoft Office, Microsoft Outlook, Internet Explorer, and game applications. You can prevent the loading of startup files by holding down the [Shift] key during logon.

If the system fails during or immediately after the logon, you most likely have a problem with a service or a startup program. You can temporarily disable startup applications and services using the System Configuration Utility, which is covered in a later lab activity. Windows Defender will also allow you to view, disable, or remove startup files.

Failures during POST are typically hardware related, such as to memory and adapter cards. POST typically has a set of diagnostic beep codes and text-based error messages that provide a possible indication of the problem. Normally, there is one beep at the end of the POST to indicate that the POST has completed. Any other combinations of beeps indicate a problem. You can also use a POST diagnostic card to diagnose POST problems. The card, inserted into a PCI slot, produces a diagnostic code to indicate the problem. You can also simply replace hardware devices until the problem is resolved. Start by removing all noncritical components, such as the modem and network card. You can then proceed to replace suspect hardware such as RAM with known good parts.

Failure during the operating system initialization and loading is usually caused by a corrupt operating system file or driver. The best solution is to do a repair. To run a repair, use the installation DVD to start the installation process and then select the **Repair** option. Check the Microsoft article for repairing Windows XP at the following link: http://support.microsoft.com/kb/315341. Also, another great link for troubleshooting startup problems is http://support.microsoft.com/kb/308041.

Failure after the system logon is usually caused by a service or a startup application. The best tool for repairing a system that is suspected of having a driver or service error is to run the System Configuration Utility (Msconfig) and then do a diagnostic startup followed by deleting specific services and startup applications. You can access the System Configuration Utility after pressing the [F8] key and selecting Safe Mode from the Boot Options or Advanced Boot Options menu.

Copyright by Goodheart-Willcox Co., Inc.

Name_____

Using the System Configuration Utility will help you to identify the source of the problem 95% of the time. However, it does not take into account problems generated by viruses or heat. Viruses can cause many problems that appear to be hardware or software related. The problem may even change during the infection period. Heat-related problems can occur at different times, depending on the temperature of the environment and the amount of heat generated by the computer components, such as the CPU and memory.

CPU throttling allows the CPU to run at different frequencies, thus adjusting to the actual processing load. This means that during periods of low processing performance, such as during word processing, the CPU will generate very limited amount of heat because it is running at a low frequency to save energy. During periods that require high processor performance, such as running intense graphics for gaming, video editing, and computer-aided drafting, the CPU will generate much more heat. More repair options will be explored in later laboratory activities.

Equipment and Materials

■ Computer with Windows XP or Windows Vista, or both, installed.

Procedure

1. ____ Report to your assigned workstation.

2. ____ Boot the computer and verify it is in working order.

3. ____ Reboot the computer and watch the boot sequence closely. See if you can identify the first two stages of the boot sequence: POST and loading and initiating the operating system. If your computer uses a splash screen during boot process to mask over the text messages during the POST, access the BIOS and see if you can locate the option to disable the splash screen during boot up. You may need to consult the BIOS manufacturer's Web site for information about disabling the splash screen. If you successfully disable the splash screen, restart the computer and observe the text messages displayed during the POST.

4. ____ Shut down the computer and then disconnect the hard disk drive. Follow antistatic procedures while disconnecting the drive.

5. ____ Restart the computer and observe the startup sequence. What error message is displayed when the hard disk drive could not be found?

_____

6. ____ Shut down the computer and then reconnect the hard disk drive. Be sure to follow all antistatic procedures.

7. ____ Reboot the computer and observe the boot sequence. Repeat booting the computer until you can clearly identify the stages of computer boot sequence.

8. ____ Visit the Phoenix Web site, www.Phoenix.com, and view information about Phoenix and Award BIOS error codes and beep codes.

9. ____ Visit the AMI Web site, www.AMI.com, and view error and beep code information.

10. ____ Locate the Microsoft article about Windows XP installation repair: http://support.microsoft.com/kb/315341. Save a copy of the article and then look at the links to many other closely-related troubleshooting articles provided by Microsoft.

11. ____ Locate the Microsoft article about advanced troubleshooting for startup problems in Windows XP: http://support.microsoft.com/kb/308041. Again, save a copy of the article for your use.

12. ____ Shut down the computer and answer the review questions

Review Questions

1. What part of the boot process starts immediately after the power switch is turned on? _____
   _____

2. What does seeing the Windows progress bar indicate? _____
   _____

3. What generally causes a failure during the POST? _____

4. When are services and startup applications loaded? _____

5. When are most operating system critical files loaded and run? _____
   _____

6. When would an error such as "Ntloader is missing" occur? _____
   _____

7. What tool should be used when startup programs or services are suspected of having errors?
   _____

8. Which key is used to stop the loading of startup files? _____

9. Name two programs that will allow you to view startup programs. _____
   _____

Copyright by Goodheart-Willcox Co., Inc.

Name _____ Date _____

Class/Instructor _____

Advanced
Boot Options

After completing this laboratory activity, you will be able to:

- Access the Advanced Boot Options menu.
- Explain the purpose of each Advanced Boot Options menu option.
- Explain the purpose of the ntbtlog.txt file.
- Explain why the Advanced Boot Options menu may not be available to a technician.

Introduction

One of the most important steps in troubleshooting a PC system is accessing the Windows **Advanced Boot Options** menu. This menu is accessible only after a successful POST has been completed. If you cannot access the **Advanced Boot Options** menu, you most likely have a hardware problem and the computer did not successfully complete POST. Another reason you will not be able to access the **Advanced Boot Options** menu is because required system startup files are corrupted. If system files are corrupted, you will need to reinstall the system files.

The most common option in the **Advanced Boot Options** menu is **Safe mode**. This option allows the computer to finish the complete boot sequence, but with a minimal number of drivers and services. Drivers and services are often the cause of a computer system failing to complete the boot process. By loading only a minimal number of drivers and services, a failed computer system can be often started in safe mode and repaired.

The **Advanced Boot Options** menu is accessed at startup by pressing the [F8] key after POST and before loading the operating system. The following table describes each menu option. Similar options are available in Windows XP.

Advanced Boot Option	Description
Safe Mode	Starts the operating system with only the minimal drivers and services required to operate the system.
Safe Mode with Networking	Includes the necessary network adapter drivers and services needed to establish a network connection.
Safe Mode with Command Prompt	Starts with the command prompt rather than the GUI. Requires fewer drivers this way.
Enable Boot Logging	Creates a log file called ntbtlog.txt, which lists all the drivers installed during the startup sequence.
Enable low-resolution video (640x480)	Uses the lowest possible video resolution and a low refresh rate for minimal impact of system resources.
Last Known Good Configuration (advanced)	Starts Windows using the last set of successful registry and configuration settings.
Directory Services Restore Mode	Used for starting a domain controller for directory support.
Debugging Mode	Used for advanced troubleshooting, usually by programmers. Sends information to another computer via a serial connection.
Disable Automatic Restart on System Failure	Will not let the system automatically restart on a boot failure.
Disable Driver Signature Enforcement	Does not require drivers to have a driver signature.
Start Windows Normally	Starts Windows normally, not with any reduced drivers, services, or configuration.

As a computer repair technician, your main interest will be the following four boot options: **Safe Mode**, **Safe Mode with Networking**, **Safe Mode with Command Prompt**, and **Last Known Good Configuration**.

Safe Mode is the most commonly accessed option when troubleshooting a computer using the **Advanced Boot Options** menu. It loads only the bare minimum drivers required to run the system. Once the computer is started in safe mode, you can access other utilities such as System Restore, System Configuration Utility, Backup, and other troubleshooting tools.

By selecting the **Enable Boot Logging** option, the ntbtlog.txt will be created during the system boot. The ntbtlog.txt file contains a list of all drivers loaded and not loaded during the boot. This information can help you determine what driver file the computer is having problems loading. The ntbtlog.txt file can be read using Notepad or a similar software application. The following screen capture shows an example of the ntbtlog.txt file contents. As you can see, all drivers are clearly identified as either "Loaded driver" or as "Did not load driver."

Copyright by Goodheart-Willcox Co., Inc.

```
ntbtlog - Notepad                                              [ □ ][ ▭ ][ ✕ ]
File  Edit  Format  View  Help
Did not load driver @netrasa.inf,%mp-ipv6-dispname%;WAN Miniport (IPv6)
Did not load driver @netrasa.inf,%mp-pppoe-dispname%;WAN Miniport (PPPOE)
Did not load driver @netrasa.inf,%mp-pptp-dispname%;WAN Miniport (PPTP)
Did not load driver AFD.SYS
Did not load driver AFD.SYS
Did not load driver AFD.SYS
Did not load driver AFD.SYS
Did not load driver AFD.SYS
Loaded driver \SystemRoot\system32\DRIVERS\cdfs.sys
Did not load driver AFD.SYS
Did not load driver AFD.SYS
Did not load driver AFD.SYS
Did not load driver AFD.SYS
Microsoft (R) Windows (R) Version 6.0 (Build 6000)
12  4 2007 07:43:30.484
Loaded driver \SystemRoot\system32\ntkrnlpa.exe
Loaded driver \SystemRoot\system32\hal.dll
Loaded driver \SystemRoot\system32\kdcom.dll
Loaded driver \SystemRoot\system32\mcupdate_GenuineIntel.dll
Loaded driver \SystemRoot\system32\PSHED.dll
Loaded driver \SystemRoot\system32\BOOTVID.dll
Loaded driver \SystemRoot\system32\CLFS.SYS
Loaded driver \SystemRoot\system32\CI.dll
Loaded driver \SystemRoot\system32\drivers\wdf01000.sys
Loaded driver \SystemRoot\system32\drivers\WDFLDR.SYS
Loaded driver \SystemRoot\system32\drivers\acpi.sys
Loaded driver \SystemRoot\system32\drivers\WMILIB.SYS
```

The computer will automatically start up in a modified boot menu called **Windows Error Recovery** if the computer did not shut down properly—for example, if you shut the computer down with the power switch rather than use the option from the **Start** menu. There will be only four choices to choose from: **Safe Mode**, **Safe Mode with Networking**, **Safe mode with Command Prompt**, **Start Windows Normally**. If no selection is made in approximately 30 seconds, the computer will automatically select the **Start Windows Normally** option.

Equipment and Materials

■ PC with the Windows Vista operating system installed. (You may substitute a Windows XP system for this lab activity.)

Procedure

1. ____ Boot the computer and wait for the desktop to be displayed. This step is to ensure your system is working properly.

2. ____ Restart the PC and press [F8] during the boot sequence to access the **Advanced Boot Options** menu. At times, it is very difficult to catch the exact moment when POST ends and the loading of the operating system begins. You can try tapping the [F8] key repeatedly after the computer starts and continue until the **Advanced Boot Options** menu appears on the screen. If you cannot access the **Advanced Boot Options** menu, call your instructor for assistance.

3. ____ After the **Advanced Boot Options** menu appears, select the **Safe Mode** option.

4. ____ When the computer starts in safe mode, the words "Safe Mode" will appear in all four corners of the display. The desktop background will be black. Also, the screen resolution is reduced.

5. ____ In the space provided, list all **Advanced Boot Options** menu options.

_____

_____

_____

_____

_____

_____

_____

_____

_____

6. ____ Indicate with a "yes" or "no" if each of the following can be accessed during a safe mode operation.

Backup and Restore _____

Windows Remote Assistance _____

Command Prompt _____

System Tools _____

System Restore _____

Access the Internet _____

Event Viewer _____

Task Manager _____

Control Panel _____

7. ____ Now, reboot the computer and let the computer start normally. Do not press the [F8] key.

8. ____ Shut down the computer using the power button. Restart the computer and see which boot options are available to you. List the available options in the space provided.

_____

_____

_____

9. ____ Now, reboot the computer and select **Safe Mode with Command Prompt** from the **Advanced Boot Options** menu. Answer the following question.

Is the user interface text mode only or graphic user interface? _____

_____

10. ____ Type and enter the **dir** command at the command prompt and observe the action.

Note:

To stop the directory command, press [Ctrl] [Pause Break].

Copyright by Goodheart-Willcox Co., Inc.

11. _____ Type and enter **exit** at the command prompt. Then, press [Ctrl] [Alt] [Del] and click the **Shut down** button in the lower-right corner of the display. This will shut down the computer.

12. _____ Restart the computer and then use [F8] to open the **Advanced Boot Options** menu.

13. _____ Select the **Enable Boot Logging** option to create a driver status log.

14. _____ Look in the root directory and under the Windows folder to see if the ntbtlog.txt file exists. The file is a hidden system file, so you will need to change the folder options to show hidden files. You can do this by opening an Explorer window and selecting **Tools | Folder Options | Show hidden files and folders**. You can use the **Start** menu **Search** box to assist you in locating the file. After the file is opened, look at its contents. Close the file and shut down the computer.

15. _____ Now, restart the computer and select **Safe Mode** from the **Advanced Boot Options** menu.

16. _____ After the computer enters safe mode, type **msconfig** into the **Search** box to start the System Configuration Utility. After the **System Configuration Utility** dialog box opens, select the **Services** tab to observe which services were loaded. All services should be marked "Stopped" under the "Status" column.

17. _____ Close the System Configuration Utility and then shut down the computer.

18. _____ You may spend a few minutes exploring the **Advanced Boot Options** menu at this time. If you are having difficulty opening the **Advanced Boot Options** menu, take some time to practice.

19. _____ Return the workstation to its original condition and then go on to answer the review questions.

Review Questions

1. Which function key is used to access the **Advanced Boot Options** menu? _____

2. Which options are available when restarting a computer after turning off the computer using the power switch? _____
   _____
   _____
   _____

3. Can you access Control Panel while in safe mode? _____

4. Can you run **msconfig** from the **Search** box while in safe mode? _____

5. What is contained in the ntbtlog.txt file? _____
   _____
   _____

6. Where is the ntbtlog.txt file located? _____

7. Can you run the System Configuration Utility while in safe mode? _____

8. What services are shown running in the System Configuration Utility during safe mode? _____

   _____

9. What words appear in the four corners of the display during safe mode? _____

10. What would cause the **Advanced Boot Options** menu or safe mode not to be available? _____
    _____
    _____

Copyright by Goodheart-Willcox Co., Inc.

Name _____ Date _____

Class/Instructor _____

Windows XP Recovery Console

After completing this laboratory activity, you will be able to:

■ Install and use the Recovery Console utility.

■ Explain how to find help for commands used in the Recovery Console.

■ Give examples of when the Recovery Console is an appropriate method of system recovery.

Introduction

This lab activity will familiarize you with the powerful troubleshooting utility known as the Recovery Console. Recovery Console is not installed by default, but you will learn how to install it.

The Recovery Console allows you to recover from a startup problem that cannot be solved by other methods, such as by using the System Restore feature or safe mode. There are three ways to access and start the Recovery Console:

1. Using the Setup CD and then selecting the **R** option when prompted.

2. Using the 6-disk set of Setup boot disks and again selecting the **R** option. (See the Microsoft article Q310994: Obtaining Windows XP Setup Boot Disks.)

3. Installing the Recovery Console on the hard disk drive and selecting Recovery Console from the list of installed operating systems.

The first method of accessing the Recovery Console involves booting the problem computer with the Setup CD inserted into the CD-ROM drive. If the CD fails to start, you may need to open the BIOS Setup program and make the CD-ROM your first boot device.

After "Welcome to Setup" appears on the screen, press the [R] key to start the Recovery Console. You will be prompted for the administrator password before you can use the Recovery Console. If there is only one person who uses the computer, they are the administrator. On a networked computer, the systems administrator may need to provide the password.

To see a list of Recovery Console commands, type **recovery console commands** at the command prompt or **help,** followed by the command name you desire information about. When you are finished using the Recovery Console, type **exit** at the command prompt.

Copyright by Goodheart-Willcox Co., Inc.

Below is a partial listing of commands associated with the Recovery Console. Many of the listed commands are not internal or external commands, but are available only through the Recovery Console command prompt.

Command	Description
attrib	Expose or change the file attributes.
batch	Execute batch file commands.
bootcfg	Manipulate boot file configuration and recovery.
cd (chdir)	Change current directory.
cls	Clear the screen area.
copy	Copy one file.
del (delete)	Delete one file.
dir	Display the contents of a directory.
disable	Disable a particular service.
diskpart	Manage disk partitions.
enable	Enable a particular service.
exit	Terminate the recovery console and then restart the computer.
expand	Expand a compressed file.
fixboot	Repair the boot sector on the system partition.
fixmbr	Repair the master boot record of the boot partition.
format	Format a partition.
help	List all available commands or reveal information about a particular command.
listsvc	List all available services and drivers.
logon	Log on to a different location or subdirectory.
map	Expose current device mappings.
md (mkdir)	Make a directory.
more	Display the contents of a text file one screen at a time.
net use	Connect to a remote share.
rd (rmdir)	Remove a directory.
ren (rename)	Rename a file or directory.
set	Sets and displays system environment variables.
setroot	Sets the current directory as the system root.
type	Display the contents of a text file.

Many times when repairing a computer, you will require the skills taught in this lab activity to complete the instructions presented by the Microsoft support Web site. Microsoft typically provides a list of step-by-step instructions to assist in recovery from a known or identified problem.

Copyright by Goodheart-Willcox Co., Inc.

Name_____

Equipment and Materials

■ Typical PC with the Windows XP installed.
■ Windows XP Setup CD or a set of Windows XP Setup boot disks.

Procedure

1. ____ Gather necessary materials and report to your assigned workstation.

2. ____ Boot your PC to verify it is in working order before you begin. If there is a problem, notify your instructor.

3. ____ Reboot the system and access the system BIOS Setup program to verify the first boot device. Before changing the sequence of the boot devices, list the existing sequence below so that you can return the system to its original state when you are finished with the lab activity.

   Boot Device Order:

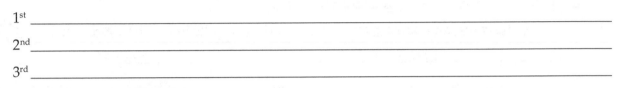

   1st _____

   2nd _____

   3rd _____

4. ____ Now, insert the Setup CD into the CD-ROM drive and reboot the system.

5. ____ When the "Welcome to Setup" screen appears and the various options are offered, choose the Recovery Console by pressing the [R] key. On a multiboot system, you will need to identify which partition or system you wish to access with the Recovery Console utility.

Note:
You do not have to boot the PC with the Setup CD. You can access the Recovery Console on a system that is booted to Windows XP. Insert the Setup CD in the CD-ROM drive. Open the **Start** menu and click **Run**. Type **D:\i386\winnt32.exe** in the **Open** text box and click **OK**.

---

6. ____ When you are prompted for the administrator password, enter the password.

Note:
No password is required for Windows XP Home Edition.

---

7. ____ At the command prompt, type and enter **help**. Describe what is displayed when the **help** command is entered. Use the space provided. _____

_____

_____

Note:
Do not try commands you are not familiar with. Using commands at the command prompt you are not familiar with can result in an unrecoverable system failure.

---

8. ____ Now type and enter **help diskpart** and record in the space provided what is displayed.

_____

Copyright by Goodheart-Willcox Co., Inc.

9. _____ At the command prompt, type and enter **diskpart** and record in the space provided what is displayed. _____

_____

_____

10. _____ Press the [Esc] key to cancel the **diskpart** command.

11. _____ Type and enter the command **enable**. Write a brief summary in the space provided of what is displayed. _____

_____

_____

12. _____ Type and enter the command **bootcfg** and observe what information is revealed.

13. _____ Now type and enter **bootcfg /scan** and then observe the action taken and the results. Be sure to leave a space between **bootcfg** and **/scan**.

14. _____ Try the command **bootcfg /lists** and record the results in the space provided. _____

_____

_____

15. _____ Now type and enter the **chkdsk** command and observe what happens.

16. _____ Use the **help** command with **chkdsk** to learn more about the command. Write in the space provided what the **chkdsk** command is used for. _____

_____

_____

17. _____ If you have your instructor's permission and there is ample lab activity time left, you can use the **help** command with the remaining commands to find out more about them.

18. _____ When finished, reboot the system to be sure it is in working order. Be sure to remove the Windows XP Setup CD from the drive. Return the BIOS setup program to its original state.

19. _____ Go on to answer the review questions and then return all materials to the appropriate area.

If the Recovery Console has been installed on the drive and becomes part of the boot system, your instructor may wish you to remove it from the computer. To remove Recovery Console from the computer's hard drive, follow these steps:

1. Boot the computer to the Windows XP desktop.

2. Open Windows Explorer.

3. Access **Tools | Folder Options** and then select the **View** tab.

4. In the **Advanced Settings** text box, select the **Show hidden files and folders** option and then clear the **Hide protected operating system files** check box.

5. Apply the changes and click **OK**.

6. Locate the boot.ini file.

7. Right-click the boot.ini file and click **Properties**.

8. From the **Properties** dialog box, remove the read-only attribute by clearing the read-only check box.

Copyright by Goodheart-Willcox Co., Inc.

Name_____

9. Use Notepad to open the boot.ini file and then delete the line from the boot.ini file that references the Recovery Console. Delete only that particular line. Removing other lines from the file will result in a boot failure. This is especially true for multiboot systems.

10. When you have saved your changes and closed the boot.ini file, restore the boot.ini file and the **View** options to their previous settings.

Review Questions

1. Explain how to install or start the Recovery Console. _____

_____

_____

2. What should you do if the computer fails to boot to the Setup CD? _____

_____

_____

3. What command reveals the Recovery Console list of commands?_____

4. How do you get information about a specific command? _____

_____

5. What command is used to quit the Recovery Console and start the computer?_____

_____

6. Which command reveals information about the partition structure? _____

_____

7. Which command will repair the disk boot sector? _____

_____

8. Which command will repair the master boot record? _____

_____

9. Which command can be used to check the condition of the hard disk drive and repair or locate bad disk sectors?_____

_____

10. What information is revealed by the **bootcfg /list** command?_____

_____

Copyright by Goodheart-Willcox Co., Inc.

Name _____ Date _____

Class/Instructor _____

Windows Recovery Environment (WinRE)

After completing this laboratory activity, you will be able to:

■ Reinstall required Windows Vista system files.

■ Recover a Windows Vista operating system from a catastrophic failure.

■ Explain the various repair options in the **System Recovery Options** dialog box.

Introduction

This laboratory activity is designed to familiarize you with the Windows Vista system recovery procedures. The Windows Recovery Environment (WinRE) is a most appropriate tool to use when a system failure happens before the startup progress bar appears. Usually, the system hangs or an error appears, identifying a critical file failure or driver. When you cannot start the Windows Vista computer in safe mode using the [F8] key, your next option is to use the Windows Recovery Environment. You simply insert the Windows Vista installation disc into the appropriate drive and then reboot the system. After a couple of screens, the **System Recovery Options** dialog box will appear providing five options:

■ **Startup Repair**.

■ **System Restore**.

■ **Windows Complete PC Restore**.

■ **Windows Memory Diagnostic Tool**.

■ **Command Prompt**.

Some proprietary systems offer six options, which redirect you to their own proprietary fix that is usually located on another partition.

If the **Startup Repair** option and other options such as writing a new master boot record or a new boot sector fail to fix the computer, then you most likely will need to reformat the existing partition and then reinstall the operating system. Formatting the partition and then reinstalling the operating system will wipe out any existing files, thus causing the loss of all data, documents, pictures, music, e-mail, and user settings.

Be aware that many proprietary computer models such as Dell and Acer have their own system recovery procedure. For example, Acer has a separate partition containing the operating system recovery files. The system can be completely reinstalled from the separate partition. In a typical recovery operation, the user simply presses [Alt] [F10] simultaneously. The user is then prompted to perform a system recovery. You must be careful because some recovery operations are designed to format the partition before installing the system files, thus destroying all existing data. Always check the manufacturer's Web site for the correct recovery procedures and if the procedure will cause the loss of data.

Copyright by Goodheart-Willcox Co., Inc.

Computer users are constantly reminded to perform regular backups of important data. Users seldom actually perform a system backup. As a result, valuable data is often lost. You can actually recover important data from a failed system by simply installing a second hard disk drive, loading the operating system on the second disk drive, and then recovering the data stored on the original disk drive from the new hard disk drive.

Equipment and Materials

- Typical computer with Windows Vista installed.
- Windows Vista installation DVD.

Procedure

1. ____ Report to your assigned workstation.

2. ____ Boot the computer and verify it is in working order.

3. ____ Insert the Windows Vista installation DVD into the appropriate drive and reboot the computer. When you are prompted, press any key to boot from the DVD. If you do not press a key, the computer will attempt to boot from the hard disk drive instead of from the installation DVD. After a few minutes, you will see the **Install Windows** dialog box, which will look similar to the following:

Copyright by Goodheart-Willcox Co., Inc.

4. ____ Select the appropriate regional preferences and then click **Next**. A dialog box similar to the following will appear presenting two repair options: **Install now** and **Repair your computer**.

The **Install now** option will reinstall the Windows Vista operating system. You will be prompted for the 25-character installation key and required to accept the familiar licensing agreement. This option should only be chosen if the **Repair your computer** option fails to recover the system. The **Install now** option allows the partition to be reformatted, which will cause the loss of important data such as documents, music, pictures, and e-mail. The **Repair your computer** option does not format the partition and does not cause a loss of data.

5. ____ Select the **Repair your computer** option to launch the Windows Recovery Environment (RecEnv.exe). A dialog box similar to the following will display. The Windows Recovery Environment will automatically scan all partitions to locate any existing operating systems.

After searching all partitions for operating systems, a list of all operating systems will be listed similar to that in the following screen capture.

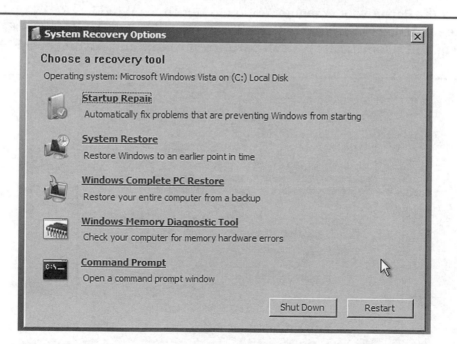

If the hard disk drive containing the operating system does not appear, it could be caused by a corrupt hard disk drive driver. In this case, you should then use the **Load Drivers** button to load the hard disk drive driver. The **Next** button will take you to the **System Recovery Options** dialog box, which provides a list of recovery tools and options. Click **Next** now. The **System Recovery Options** dialog box will display and look similar to the following.

Copyright by Goodheart-Willcox Co., Inc.

The **System Recovery Options** dialog box will present five different options. The available options are as follows:

Startup Repair: This option replaces all required startup files and drivers associated with a boot failure. This option preserves files such as documents, data files, pictures, multimedia, e-mails, and other noncritical files.

System Restore: This option reconfigures the computer system based on an earlier time when the system registry was automatically backed up. It does not reinstall system boot files and drivers. This option also preserves all documents, data files, pictures, multimedia, e-mail and other non critical files. Any application software installed since the restore point was created will not run if a restore point is selected that is earlier than when the application software was installed. Also, be aware that many security suite software applications prevent system restore points from being created, thus rendering this option useless.

Windows Complete PC Restore: This option requires that a complete system backup was performed at an earlier date. Most users do not have a complete backup of their system.

Windows Memory Diagnostic Tool: This tool checks for memory hardware errors. A failure indicated by this tool means that the system memory must be replaced. Ironically, passing the memory test does not mean that the memory is good. The memory can still be bad and require replacement.

Command Prompt: The command prompt is often used to replace a specific file or files or even start an executable program.

Two of the most common commands issued from the command prompt in an effort to repair a system startup problem are listed in the following table. Notice that Windows Vista uses the **BootRec** command with either the **FixBoot** or **FixMBR** switch.

Win XP Recovery Console	Windows Vista System Recovery	Description
FixBoot	**BootRec/FixBoot**	Write a new boot sector on the system partition.
FixMBR	**BootRec/FixMBR**	Write a Master Boot Record (MBR) to the system partition.

6. ____ With your instructor's permission, you may select and run the **Startup Repair** option.

7. ____ Remove the Windows Vista installation disc and then complete the review questions. Be sure to return the Windows Vista installation disc to your instructor.

Review Questions

1. When is it appropriate to run the Windows Recovery Environment? _____
   _____

2. What files are replaced when the **Startup Repair** option is selected from the **System Recovery Options** dialog box? _____

3. What repair activities would wipe out any existing files on a computer, thus causing the loss of all data, documents, pictures, music, e-mail, and user settings? _____
   _____

4. What is the executable file name of the Windows Recovery Environment? _____

5. Which **System Recovery Option** dialog box option requires an earlier backup of the system? ___
   _____

6. What Windows Vista command is equal to the Windows XP **FixBoot** command? _____
   _____

7. What Windows Recovery Environment command would you use to write a new master boot record? _____
   _____

Copyright by Goodheart-Willcox Co., Inc.

Name _____ Date _____

Class/Instructor _____

Windows XP Automatic System Recovery

After completing this laboratory activity, you will be able to:

■ Create an Automatic System Recovery disk.

■ Use an ASR disk to recover from a system failure.

■ Explain when an ASR disk should be created.

■ Identify when a system recovery should be attempted using the ASR disk.

■ Identify the danger to user data when using an ASR disk.

Introduction

In this lab activity, you will make an Automatic System Recovery (ASR) disk for a Windows XP system. Automatic System Recovery is new to Windows XP. It is an advanced feature of the Backup utility and replaces the Emergency Repair Disk technology used in Windows 2000 and Windows NT. ASR is designed to recover systems after extreme system failure. You would use ASR as a last resort. Microsoft recommends that you format the hard drive and reinstall the Windows XP operating system if the system cannot be restored using ASR.

ASR is designed to restore system critical files on the system and boot partitions. It is to be used when the computer will not start in normal, safe, or with Recovery Console mode. That's why it is referred to as the "last ditch" effort. If you cannot boot the PC in Recovery Console mode, then this is the last repair effort that Microsoft has designed for Windows XP.

The main reason the ASR is a last resort recovery method is because it formats the system partition, which can destroy all vital data unless a backup has been made. The proper way to create an ASR disk is to also make a complete data backup at the same time. Because this is a lab only, you will simply make an ASR floppy disk and not a complete backup, unless otherwise instructed by your instructor. There are several important things to consider before using the ASR feature to restore the system:

■ The ASR feature will format the system drive partition as part of the recovery process. If user data is saved on the same partition, data can be lost.

■ ASR restores only the operating system files determined to be defective or corrupt.

■ ASR does not automatically restore system data; the System Restore feature should be used before attempting to use ASR.

To use the ASR disk, you would start the Recovery Console using the Windows XP Professional Setup CD. After the system restarts, you are prompted for the ASR disk. Simply respond with the [F2] key and insert the ASR disk. You will also indicate the location of the mass storage device that contains all the backup files in addition to the ASR files.

The Backup utility and ASR feature is only available in the Windows XP Professional version, not the Home Edition. Since the ASR is part of the Backup utility, you should make an ASR disk as part of a regular backup routine.

Equipment and Materials

- Typical PC with Windows XP Professional installed, not the Home Edition.
- Floppy disk to be used to store ASR data.
- Your instructor may also require a CD-RW or tape drive to also make a backup of selected files, designated by the instructor.

Procedure

1. ____ Report to your assigned workstation. Boot the computer and ensure that it is in working order.

2. ____ Open the Backup utility located at **Start | Programs | Accessories | System Tools | Backup**. A dialog box similar to the following will appear.

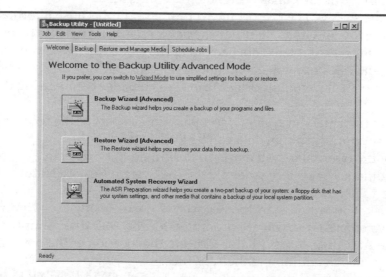

3. ____ Select the **Advanced Mode** option. The Backup utility will appear on the screen similar to that in the following figure.

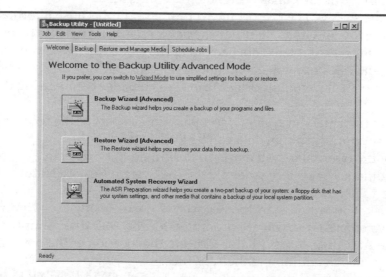

Three main options are provided by the Backup utility: **Backup Wizard (Advanced)**, **Restore Wizard (Advanced)**, and **Automated System Recovery Wizard**.

Copyright by Goodheart-Willcox Co., Inc.

4. ____ Select the **Backup** tab at the top of the Backup utility. The **Backup** tab reveals the complete directory structure of the disk(s) in the computer. You can select various parts of the directory to back up as part of the Automated System Recovery. If no data is selected, then only the system files necessary to make a recovery will be backed up. When performing a system recovery, the ASR will reformat the system drive and reinstall necessary files for booting and running the system. Without a backup of important data, the data can be lost. Normally, you would make a backup of important data and select the areas by clicking the appropriate check boxes. For this lab activity, it is not necessary to make a backup of all data, unless your instructor has told you to do so.

5. ____ Select the **Welcome** tab and then select the **Automated System Recovery Wizard** icon. A dialog box should appear similar to the following.

6. ____ Click **Next**. A dialog box similar to the following will appear.

Look closely at the default name of the backup file indicated in the text box. In the example, A:\Backup.bkf is the default name. You can accept this as the name of the file to be created on the floppy disk or use the **Browse** button to locate other places to create a backup and rename the file. For example, you may wish to use a CD-RW, a recordable DVD, or a tape drive. For this exercise, use the default as indicated and a floppy disk.

Copyright by Goodheart-Willcox Co., Inc.

7. ____ Click **Next** and then, **Finish**. The wizard starts the process and will display a progress screen. This screen provides a way to view the progress of the system backup. Because the floppy disk will not hold all of the data requested for the backup, the system will prompt you for another location or disk. Simply abort the entire operation.

8. ____ The ASR creates a log of each backup and it is possible to view the contents of the log. Look at the following figure to see a sample of backup log contents.

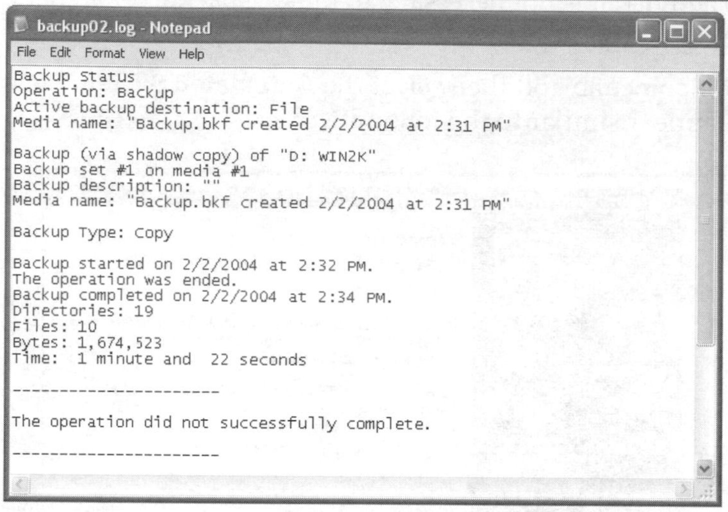

Important information about the backup is recorded in the log such as date, time, media name, and if the operation was successful. In this example, you can see that the backup was not successful as indicated in the last line of the log.

9. ____ Now, start the Backup program once more, but this time, select the **Wizard Mode** option.

10. ____ When the Welcome to the Backup or Restore Wizard screen displays, click **Next**.

11. ____ Select the **Backup Files and Settings** option and then click **Next**. A dialog box similar to the following figure will appear.

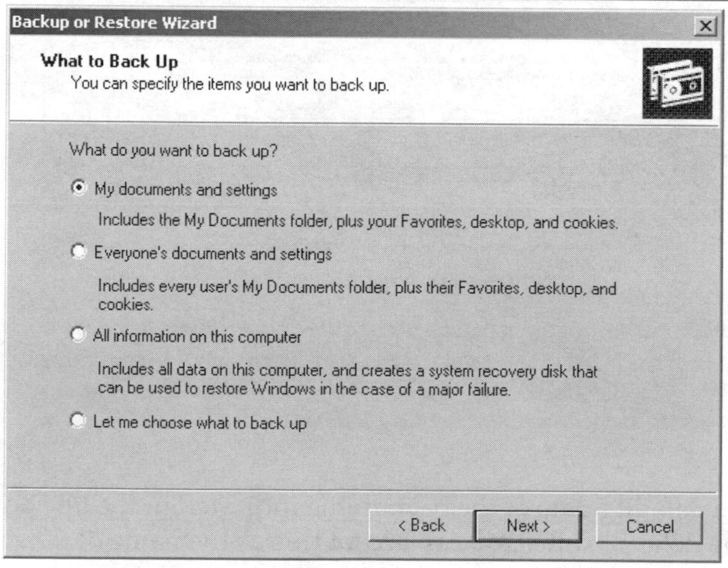

Copyright by Goodheart-Willcox Co., Inc.

You are given five options of what to back up: **My documents and settings, Everyone's documents and settings, All information on this computer,** and **Let me choose what to backup.**

If you have a mass storage device such as a CD-RW, DVD, or tape system, you may perform a system backup with your instructor's permission. If not, click **Cancel** to abort the wizard.

12. ____ Return all materials to their proper storage area and then go on to answer the review questions.

Review Questions

1. Why is the ASR considered a last resort recovery utility? _____
   _____
   _____

2. When should an ASR disk be made? _____
   _____

3. What is the default name of the ASR disk? _____
   _____

4. Why would you perform a system backup when creating an ASR disk? _____
   _____

Copyright by Goodheart-Willcox Co., Inc.

Name _____ Date _____

Class/Instructor _____

System Configuration Utility (MSCONFIG)

After completing this laboratory activity, you will be able to:

- Start the System Configuration Utility.
- Use the System Configuration Utility to diagnose and modify the system startup.
- Explain the difference between Windows XP and Windows Vista versions of the System Configuration Utility.
- Explain how to use the various startup options to diagnose a startup problem.

Introduction

In this laboratory activity, you will simulate a system startup repair by using the System Configuration Utility to perform a diagnostic startup and modify system services and other files. The System Configuration Utility can be used to solve operating system startup problems, such as when a computer abruptly stops during the boot process after a successful POST or when the computer progress bar has appeared or after logon. The System Configuration Utility allows you to disable startup program applications and services that may be preventing the computer system from completing the startup process. This System Configuration Utility is an essential troubleshooting tool used by technicians and skilled novices.

If you can start a problematic computer using the [F8] key to access the Advance Boot Options menu and run the computer in safe mode, then you can also access the System Configuration Utility. Look at the following screen captures to compare the Windows XP and Windows Vista System Configuration Utility.

Windows XP   **Windows Vista**

Copyright by Goodheart-Willcox Co., Inc.

The Windows XP and Windows Vista System Configuration Utility are very similar, but there are some differences. Both versions have **Normal startup**, **Diagnostic startup**, and **Selective startup** options. The **Normal startup** option is used to start the operating system normally. The **Diagnostic startup** option is used to load only basic devices and services. The **Selective startup** option allows you to choose which services and startup items not to load.

Something new in the Windows Vista System Configuration Utility is the **Tools** tab, which contains a list and access to common tools used to assist in troubleshooting startup problems. For example, it includes System Restore, Remote Assistance, and Event Viewer.

The System Configuration Utility is accessed by entering **msconfig.exe** in the **Run** dialog box in Windows XP or the **Search** box in Windows Vista. The System Configuration Utility opens to the **General** tab by default.

The **Diagnostic startup** option will start the computer with only necessary files and drivers, thus eliminating required Windows operating files as the cause of the problem. If the system still fails after selecting the **Diagnostic startup** option, then a required system file or a hardware driver is most likely causing the problem. To correct a problem caused by a driver or required system file, you would need to replace the basic system files and drivers. This is accomplished by starting the computer with the Windows Installation CD/DVD and then selecting the **Startup Repair** listed under the **System Recovery Options**. There will be more about recovery in later laboratory activities.

Another option is to press [F8] while the computer is booting, after the POST and before the logon screen appears. You then select the **Repair your computer** option in the **Advanced Boot Options** screen. This option is only available from the **Advanced Boot Options** menu if repair tools have been installed on the hard disk drive and the drive is accessible.

Note:

Be aware that many computers have their own proprietary software installed on the computer to recover from a disaster.

The **Selective startup** option allows you to start the computer with basic files and services and to disable system service, and startup files which may be causing the problem. If the computer problem does not occur after disabling startup services and applications, then you can assume one of the software programs in the two categories is the probable cause of the problem. Now you can enable either services or startup applications to determine which category is causing the problem. Then, you can disable the software programs and then enable them once more until you determine which specific program is causing the problem.

When there are many programs in a category, it is a recommended procedure that you disable one-half of the programs to determine which half of the programs are causing the problem. Continue with the divide in half approach until you have narrowed it down to the specific program. You could also disable all programs and then enable them one by one until the problem program is identified. For more information on using the System Configuration Utility, read the Microsoft article located at the following link: http://support.microsoft.com/kb/950093.

Equipment and Materials

■ Computer with Windows XP or Windows Vista, or both, installed.

Copyright by Goodheart-Willcox Co., Inc.

Part I—Windows XP

Procedure

1. ____ Report to your assigned workstation.

2. ____ Boot the computer and verify it is in working order.

3. ____ Click the **Start** button and select the **Run** option. In the **Run** dialog box, enter **msconfig** in the **Open** text box. Take special notice of the three options in the **Startup Selection** area of the dialog box. These options are **Normal Startup**, **Diagnostic Startup**, and **Selective Startup**. Selecting the **Normal Startup** option causes the PC to start normally. This option should be selected when you are done testing the system.

4. ____ Select each of the tabs at the top of the System Configuration Utility one by one to view the contents of each.

5. ____ While the System Configuration Utility is still open, access the System Configuration Editor by running **sysedit** in the **Run** dialog box. The System Configuration Editor utility was used to view and change the contents of the win.ini and system.ini files. The contents could be altered by typing the word *rem* in front of an entry and then saving the file. The system.ini and win.ini files are used to support legacy software applications and are seldom encountered. Windows Vista does still provide the System Configuration Editor, but it is seldom used.

Note:

Read these directions carefully. Notice that the names of the programs are very similar. The program activated by running **sysedit.exe** is named System Configuration Editor. The program activated by running **msconfig.exe** is named System Configuration Utility.

---

6. ____ Select the **System.ini** tab in both the System Configuration Utility and the System Configuration Editor. Compare the contents in each. Both should be the same.

7. ____ Select the **Win.ini** tab in the System Configuration Utility and the System Configuration Editor and compare the contents of each. The contents of each should be the same.

8. ____ Close the System Configuration Editor and leave the System Configuration Utility running.

9. ____ Select the **Diagnostic Startup** option and then click the **Apply** button and then the **OK** button. The system will prompt you for a system reboot on exit. Select the reboot option and then observe closely.

10. ____ Now, select the **Selective Startup** option and again reboot the computer and observe closely.

11. ____ Close the System Configuration Utility and then shut down the Windows XP computer. Move on to Part II—Windows Vista. A more detailed laboratory activity is presented. The purpose of Part I—Windows XP was just to familiarize you with the Windows XP version of System Configuration Utility.

Copyright by Goodheart-Willcox Co., Inc.

Part II—Windows Vista

Procedure

1. _____ Report to your assigned workstation.

2. _____ Boot the computer and verify it is in working order.

3. _____ Type **msconfig** into the **Search** box located at the **Start** menu. "Msconfig" will appear at the top of the search list under **Programs**. You simply press the [Enter] key to start the System Configuration Utility.

4. _____ Locate the three major startup selection options: **Normal startup**, **Diagnostic startup**, and **Selective startup**.

5. _____ Select the **Diagnostic startup** option and then click the **Apply** button and then **OK**. After a minute or so, you will be prompted to restart or exit without restart. Choose the restart option. Windows Vista will reboot and automatically run the diagnostic mode of System Configuration Utility.

6. _____ With the computer running in diagnostic mode, open the Task Manager. Press [Crtl] [Alt] [Del] to access Task Manager. With Task Manager running, select the **Services** tab and then count the number of services running. Enter the number of services in the space provided and then close the Task Manager.

   Number of services running in diagnostic mode = _____.

7. _____ Start the System Configuration Utility once more and then select the **Normal startup** option. Restart the computer and then open the Task Manager. Count the number of services and enter that number in the space provided.

   Number of services running in normal mode = _____.

   Compare the number of services in the two modes. There should be a significant increase in the number of services running in normal mode as compared to diagnostic mode.

8. _____ Close the Task Manager.

9. _____ Start the System Configuration Utility. This time, select the **Selective startup** option. Deselect the **Load system services** option and the **Load startup items** option and then click **Apply**. The system will prompt you for the restart option once again. Restart the computer once more to see the effect on the system. There is no need to open the Task Manager at this time.

10. _____ Open the System Configuration Utility. Select the **Boot**, **Services**, and **Startup** tab to see what features and options are available.

Copyright by Goodheart-Willcox Co., Inc.

11. ____ Now, select the **Tools** tab and look at all the related tools that are available for your use. A short description of each tool appears after the name of the tool. Also, notice that when you select a tool with the mouse, the executable name and location of the file is indicated at the bottom of the dialog box. Fill in the table below using the information provided under the **Tools** tab of System Configuration Utility.

Tool Name	Executable File Name
Example: About Windows	*Winver.exe*
System Information	
Remote Assistance	
System Restore	
Computer Management	
Event Viewer	
Programs	
Security Center	
System Properties	
Internet Options	
Internet Protocol Configuration	
Performance Monitor	
Task Manager	
Command Prompt	
Registry Editor	

You can use the table as a reference for starting the tools from the command prompt or the Search box. This table may prove to be a handy reference for preparing for the CompTIA A+ exam. The executable file names are often asked for on the test.

12. ____ Take a few minutes to launch several of the tools by selecting the tool and clicking the **Launch** button. Do *not* select or launch **Disable UAC** or **Enable UAC** during this laboratory activity.

13. ____ Select the **Normal startup** option before closing the System Configuration Utility.

14. ____ Answer the review questions.

Review Questions

1. What is the executable file name for the System Configuration Utility? _____

2. What are the three main options featured in the **General** tab view of System Configuration Utility? _____

    _____

3. What happens when the **Diagnostic startup** option is selected? _____

4. Which tab will allow you to stop specific software applications from starting up automatically at the end of the boot sequence? _____

5. Which tab will allow you to stop specific services from running during the boot operation?

    _____

Copyright by Goodheart-Willcox Co., Inc.

Name _____ Date _____

Class/Instructor _____

System Restore

After completing this laboratory activity, you will be able to:

- Create a restore point.
- Reconfigure a computer using System Restore.
- Explain when a restore point should be created.
- Change the amount of disk space used by System Restore.
- Identify the type of data restored and not restored with a restore point.

Introduction

This laboratory activity is designed to familiarize you with the System Restore feature found in Windows XP and Windows Vista. System Restore was first introduced in the release of Windows Millennium Edition. The System Restore feature is designed to take a snapshot of the system configuration and of certain files and have them available for restoration at a later time. The copy of vital system files, called a *restore point*, is saved on the hard disk drive.

Prior to System Restore, the only way to restore the computer system was by reinstalling a complete backup of system files. That was only possible if there was a complete backup made. Another way of restoring the system configuration and vital information was by reinstalling a copy of the system registry.

System Restore creates restore points automatically when major system events occur, such as installing a new driver. The System Restore wizard can also be run manually. It is recommended that the System Restore be run manually when major events are going to occur because the System Restore feature could be turned off at the time of a major event. Running the System Restore manually will ensure that an actual restore point has been created.

System Restore does not affect the contents of application data files such as the My Documents folder, e-mail contents, browser history, favorites, music, pictures, and similar files. If you have created a document after the last system restore point, and then roll back the system to the previous restore point, the document data will not be affected. System Restore does not perform a complete backup of the system to include file contents. It only includes critical files.

The System Restore process does affect file types like .exe and .dll, which have been changed by installing software packages. System Restore will return disk partitions to their previous state if they have been altered.

Note:
Microsoft warns that encrypted files may become unencrypted after applying the System Restore. To avoid encrypted files being affected by the System Restore, you should disable the System Restore feature before encrypting files and then reactivate System Restore after encrypting the files. If you forget to reactivate the System Restore feature, restore points will not be automatically made each day or after significant events.

You should use the System Restore wizard before making any changes that might negatively affect the system, such as installing a patch, a service pack, a new software application, a game, a new hardware device, or anything that might change system settings. The following is a list of files restored by System Restore and a list of files not affected by System Restore.

Files Affected by System Restore:
- User profiles.
- DLL files.
- COM files.
- Device drivers.
- Critical system files.

Files Not Affected by System Restore:
- Security password.
- Authentication for network logon.
- User-created files, documents, music, pictures, games, and applications.

System Restore is enabled by default when the operating system is installed. Windows XP requires a minimum of 200 MB of storage space on the system partition and Windows Vista requires 300 MB. If there is not sufficient space, the system automatically disables itself. The System Restore wizard does not replace the need to perform regularly scheduled system backups to protect user-created files.

Be aware that when inspecting a user's computer, you may not find any system restore points created. This is often caused by security suites. Security software packages often disable the system restore feature and provide their own proprietary feature. Proprietary security software claim that System Restore makes backup copies of files that might contain viruses or other malware. Rolling back a computer system to a previous restore point could reinstall a malware program.

Equipment and Materials

- Computer with Windows XP, Windows Vista, or both, installed.

Part I—Windows XP

Procedure

1. ____ Report to your assigned workstation.

2. ____ Boot the computer and verify it is in working order.

Copyright by Goodheart-Willcox Co., Inc.

Name_____

3. ____ Open System Restore by using the following path: **Start | All Programs | Accessories | System Tools | System Restore**. A screen similar to the following should appear. Note the three options on the right side of the System Restore wizard.

4. ____ Select the **Create a restore point** option and then click **Next**. A screen similar to the following will appear.

5. _____ In the **Restore point description** text box, enter short description that will help you identify the restore point. This will help you when looking for the cause of a system problem. A problem created by installing an application or hardware item may not become apparent for some time. For example, you could install a new modem and the system seems to work perfectly fine. A few days or even weeks later after installing the new modem, you attempt to use your scanner only to find it causes the system to lock up. By entering a short description, you will be able to identify prior changes in the system through the System Restore feature. For this laboratory activity, describe the restoration point as follows: Lab activity to create a system restore point.

6. _____ Click **Create**. A confirmation of the restore point with the date, time, and the short description or reason for the creation will be displayed. The amount of time it takes to create the restore point will vary according to the amount of data being stored and the individual computer performance characteristics. It should only take a few seconds to create the restore point on a new computer.

7. _____ When the restore point has been created, you will have two possible options: **Home** and **Close**. Click the **Close** button now.

8. _____ Now, you will roll back the system to the restore point you created earlier. Start the System Restore wizard. You may need to look at step 3 to see the path to System Restore.

Copyright by Goodheart-Willcox Co., Inc.

9. _____ Select **Restore my computer to an earlier time**. A few seconds will pass before a screen similar to the following appears. Manually created system restore points will appear in bold numbers. If you select a restoration point, the description about that particular point will appear in the right panel of the display window.

10. _____ Click the restore point you just created and then click **Next**. What warning message is displayed in red letters on the **Confirm Restore Point Selection** screen? Write the warning in the space provided.

_____

_____

11. _____ Click **Next** and watch the screen display area. A message will appear confirming the restore process. This can take a while, from 30 seconds to a few minutes. The system will reboot automatically when it is finished. Then another period of waiting will take place while the system reinitializes. The screen will display a desktop with no taskbar or icons. After a period of time, the taskbar and desktop icons will appear. This can take a few minutes. When completed, a System Restore confirmation window will appear. Simply click **OK** and your normal desktop should appear.

12. ____ Now, select System Restore again. This time when the System Restore wizard appears, select the **System Restore Settings** option located on the left side of the screen. After selecting the **System Restore Settings** option, the **System Properties** dialog box similar to the following should appear.

Note the many drives displayed in the text box. To change the System Restore settings of a drive, select the desired drive and then click the **Settings** button. You can also deactivate System Restore for a drive by selecting the **Turn off System Restore on this drive** option. You may need to deselect this option when encrypting files or when correcting a virus problem.

13. ____ Close the System Restore wizard and related dialog boxes. Go on to Part II—Windows Vista.

Part II—Windows Vista

Procedure

1. ____ Report to your assigned workstation.

2. ____ Boot the computer and verify it is in working order.

Copyright by Goodheart-Willcox Co., Inc.

3. _____ Open System Restore by using the following path: **Start | All Programs | Accessories | System Tools | System Restore**. A screen similar to the following should appear. Notice the options available.

5. _____ Select the **To create a restore point, open System Protection** option located at the bottom of the screen to create a restore point. A screen similar to the following will appear.

6. _____ Click the **Create** button to create a restore point. In a few seconds, you should see a dialog box similar to the following:

7. _____ Enter a short description that will help you identify the restore point. By entering a short description, you will be able to identify prior changes in the system through the System Restore feature. For this lab activity, describe the restoration point as follows: Lab activity to create a system restore point.

8. _____ Click **Create**. A confirmation of the restore point will be displayed. The amount of time it takes to create the restore point will vary according to the amount of data being stored and the individual computer performance characteristics. It should only take a few seconds to create the restore point on a new computer.

9. _____ After the system restore point is created, you will be returned to the **System Properties** dialog box with the **System Protection** tab selected.

10. _____ Now, you will roll back the system to the restore point you created earlier.

11. _____ Click the **System Restore** button in the **System Properties** dialog box under the **System Protection** tab. A few seconds will pass before a screen similar to the following appears.

Copyright by Goodheart-Willcox Co., Inc.

12. _____ Select the **Choose a different restore point** option to view a list of available system restore points. A screen similar to the following will appear.

13. _____ Click **Cancel** to return to the **System Properties** dialog box. The **System Protection** tab is selected by default.

14. _____ Click the **System Restore** button and then accept the default option **Recommended restore**. This option selects the latest restore point. After a few minutes, the system will roll back to the earlier system restore point.

15. _____ Close System Restore and then go on to answer the review questions. When you have finished answering the review questions, shut down the system and return all materials to their proper storage area.

Copyright by Goodheart-Willcox Co., Inc.

Review Questions

1. Write the file path beginning at the **Start** menu for accessing and running the System Restore wizard of either Windows XP or Windows Vista. _____

   _____

2. When should you use the System Restore wizard? _____

   _____

   _____

   _____

   _____

3. How are the documents in the My Documents folder affected by a system configuration rollback using System Restore? _____

4. When are restore points automatically created? _____

   _____

   _____

5. What are the two ways system restore points are created? _____

   _____

6. What is the minimum disk space required for the storage of restore points? _____

   _____

7. What types of files are not affected by System Restore? _____

   _____

8. What might be the reason for no system restore points on a given computer? _____

   _____

Copyright by Goodheart-Willcox Co., Inc.

Name _____ Date _____

Class/Instructor _____

Roll Back Driver

After completing this laboratory activity, you will be able to:

- Execute the Roll Back Driver feature.
- Explain when using the Roll Back Driver feature is appropriate.
- Explain other options available for managing device drivers.

Introduction

This laboratory activity is designed to familiarize you with the Roll Back Driver feature. This feature was first introduced in Windows XP.

As a regular part of routine maintenance of a PC, you may wish to upgrade drivers for devices. Upgrading drivers is routinely recommended before installing certain software packages. Upgrading device drivers is an easy task, but at times, installing a new device driver can cause problems with the existing system components or software. For example, a new device driver could be downloaded and installed for a game control joystick. After installing the new driver, the system slows and eventually locks up. You determine it is a problem with the device driver. The device driver may have been corrupted during the download process. Now you must remove the last device driver installed.

With earlier version of Windows, when you installed a new device driver, the original driver was replaced. If you needed to switch to the original driver, you would need to locate the driver disk and reinstall it. With Windows XP and Windows Vista, you can remove the new driver and reinstall the original driver automatically. Windows XP and Windows Vista do not completely remove the original driver. The original driver is stored on the system and is available if needed. The Roll Back Driver feature removes the newest driver and "rolls back" to the previous version.

Copyright by Goodheart-Willcox Co., Inc.

While performing the Roll Back Driver lab activity, take time to become familiar with the other options located under the **Driver** tab of a hardware device's **Properties** dialog box. Examine the options displayed in the following screen capture.

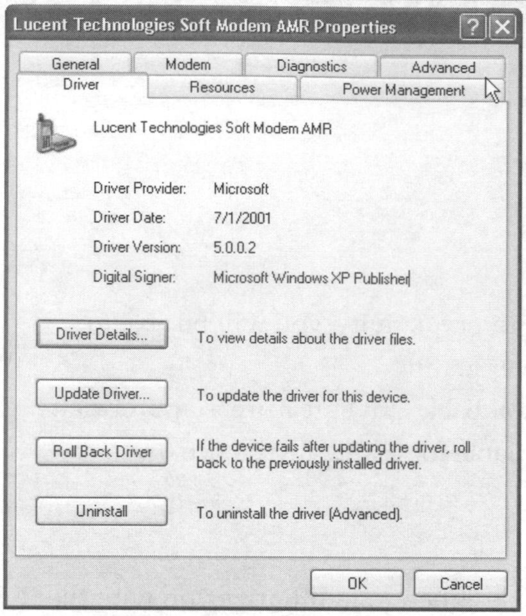

The **Driver Details** option opens the **Driver Files Details** dialog box. This dialog box displays the complete path and name of the currently installed driver. The **Update Driver** option starts a wizard that assists in installing the latest driver for the device. The **Roll Back Driver** option installs a previous driver, and the **Uninstall** option uninstalls the present driver.

New in Windows Vista is a button that allows you to disable the hardware device. To disable a device in Windows XP, you must right-click the device in Device Manager and then select the **Disable** option from the shortcut menu.

Note:

The System Restore feature may not have a restore point created when the last hardware driver was updated. Remember that many security software applications disable the System Restore feature. Also, be aware that the Roll Back Driver option is preferred over using the System Restore feature. This is because the Roll Back Driver option only replaces the driver for that particular hardware device and does not affect any other hardware device. Using System Restore will possibly change more than that particular device driver. Using System Restore can uninstall the latest software patches and may also uninstall any other critical system files or even other hardware driver updates.

Equipment and Materials

■ Computer with Windows XP, Windows Vista, or both, installed.
■ A driver disk matching the hardware device as identified by your instructor. (The device driver disk is optional and not a requirement for performing this lab activity, unless indicated by your instructor).

Copyright by Goodheart-Willcox Co., Inc.

Name_____

Part I—Windows XP

Procedure

1. ____ Report to your assigned workstation.

2. ____ Boot the computer and verify it is in working order.

3. ____ Access **Device Manager** by first opening **System Properties**. You can access **System Properties** by clicking **Start** and then right-clicking **My Computer** and selecting **Properties** from the shortcut menu. You can also access **System Properties** through **Start | Control Panel | System**.

4. ____ From the **System Properties** dialog box, select the **Hardware** tab. The **Hardware** page reveals several buttons that allow quick access to hardware-related utilities and the Add Hardware Wizard.

5. ____ Click the **Device Manager** button. The Device Manager screen will display.

6. ____ In **Device Manager,** right-click the modem and then select **Properties** from the shortcut menu. (You may need to expand the device driver category first to see the individual driver.) A dialog box similar to the following should appear.

7. ____ The modem **Properties** dialog box has several tabs. Choose the **Driver** tab. A dialog box similar to the following should appear. On the **Driver** page, there are four options to choose from: **Driver Details, Update Driver, Roll Back Driver,** and **Uninstall.** Select the **Roll Back Driver** option.

Copyright by Goodheart-Willcox Co., Inc.

Note:

　　If no previous driver was ever installed, you will get a message stating, "No driver files have been backed up for this device." Your lab activity computer will most likely display this message. If there has been a previous driver installed, abort the operation. You do not want to install the previous driver unless specifically told to do so by your instructor.

8. ____ Click the **Driver Details** button. You should see a list of paths with the name of each installed driver at the end of each path. This is very valuable information when you are trying to determine which driver is installed.

9. ____ If you have your instructor's permission, explore the other options on the **Driver** page. Do *not* uninstall the driver unless your instructor has given you permission. Do *not* uninstall the driver unless you have the original driver on disk or are certain the correct driver will be installed automatically through Windows.

10. ____ Go on to Part II—Windows Vista.

Part II—Windows Vista

Procedure

1. ____ Report to your assigned workstation.

2. ____ Boot the computer and verify it is in working order.

3. ____ Access Device Manager by selecting **Start | Control Panel | Hardware and Sound | Device Manager**. You should see a dialog box similar to the following.

You can also access Device Manager by right-clicking **Computer**, selecting **Properties** from the shortcut menu, and then clicking the **Device Manager** button. Another way is to type **Device Manager** into the **Search** box. Device Manager will appear under the **Programs** section. Click the **Device Manager** entry to open it.

4. ____ Now, access a hardware device **Properties** dialog box by double-clicking a hardware device, such as the DVD drive. The hardware device **Properties** dialog box will appear. Select the **Driver** tab. Look at the screen capture of the NEC DVD device **Properties** dialog box.

Any button that is shown as a ghost image, lighter in color, is disabled and therefore cannot be activated. For example, if there is no earlier driver for the device, then the **Roll Back Driver** button will be shown as a ghost image. To update a driver, you simply click the **Update Driver** button. Windows Vista will search for the new device driver or you will have an option to locate the new driver manually.

5. ____ Click the **Update Driver** and watch while Windows Vista attempts to locate a new driver. Also, select the manual option to see how it works.

6. ____ Try to access the **Properties** dialog box of several more devices, such as the keyboard, mouse, and hard disk drive. Notice that each device may have different buttons disabled and a different number of tabs to select from. Take a few minutes to view the tabs of each device.

7. ____ Close all open device **Properties** dialog boxes and then go on to answer the review questions.

Review Questions

1. Why would you use the Roll Back Driver feature rather than the System Restore to install a previous driver? _____

_____

_____

2. What new button was added under the **Driver** page in Windows Vista device **Properties** dialog box? _____

Copyright by Goodheart-Willcox Co., Inc.

Name _____ Date _____

Class/Instructor _____

Event Viewer

After completing this laboratory activity, you will be able to:

■ Access the Event Viewer.

■ Describe the contents of the Event Viewer's logged events.

■ Modify each of the major event log's properties.

■ Describe the types of events recorded by the major logs.

■ Explain how the event log can be used in a troubleshooting situation.

Introduction

This laboratory activity will familiarize you with the Windows Event Viewer located in the Microsoft Management Console (MMC). The Event Viewer is a sophisticated tool that records, into a log, events as they occur. The three major logs are security, system, and application.

The application log records events that are generated by software applications. Software programmers write routines that generate error messages based on anticipated problems that might occur while the software is running. The routine generates error messages that are displayed on the screen and written to the application log. These messages are similar to the error messages recorded by the Dr. Watson utility. Users often encounter errors, but are unable to describe them accurately to technicians. The log is an excellent source of errors encountered by the user that can be shared with the technician.

The security log records all activities related to system security, such as unauthorized attempts to log on to the system or attempts to access shares. If you think there have been attempts to access the system by unauthorized persons, this log can be reviewed.

The system log records activities relating to the operating system. Examples are DVD failures, failure of a device driver to load, or failure of any activity controlled by the operating system.

Copyright by Goodheart-Willcox Co., Inc.

When you open the Windows XP Microsoft Management Console, you will see the three logs listed under the Event Viewer folder in the left pane of the console window. The type of event, date, time, source, category, ID number, user at the time of the event, and more can be seen in the log. The following figure shows a typical event of a Windows XP security log.

This Windows XP event indicates that an unknown user or bad password was used in an attempt to access the computer. You can readily see the importance of recording such events as it relates to security.

Within the three types of logs, there are five event types that could possibly be recorded:

- **Error:** A serious event has occurred, such as the failure of a service to load.
- **Warning:** A noncritical event, such as a low disk space warning.
- **Information:** A strictly informational event, such as when a service starts.
- **Success Audit:** A monitored routine event, such as when a user successfully logs on to the computer.
- **Failure Audit:** Opposite of a success audit, such as a failed attempt to log on to the computer.

Windows Vista introduced a new event type called Critical events. Windows Vista Event Viewer logs differ from those in Windows XP. Windows Vista introduced two more Windows logs: setup and forward events. The setup log is used to record events that take place during application setup. The forward events log is used to store events collected from remote computers.

The log size default for Windows XP is 512 kB. The default for Windows Vista logs varies according to the hard disk drive size, but will range from approximately 1 GB to 4 GB maximum. The log file sizes for Windows Vista are much larger than that for Windows XP because hard disk drive storage is much larger than when Windows XP was introduced as an operating system.

Equipment and Materials

- Computer with Windows XP, Windows Vista, or both, installed.

Note:

The Event Viewer logs will not have events recorded if you use a newly installed system. If the system has been in use in the lab for a few days of lab activities, it will most likely have ample events recorded for this lab activity.

Copyright by Goodheart-Willcox Co., Inc.

Part I—Windows XP

Procedure

1. ____ Report to your assigned workstation.

2. ____ Boot the computer and verify it is in working order.

3. ____ Access the Microsoft Management Console by opening the **Start** menu, right-clicking **My Computer**, and selecting **Manage** from the shortcut menu. The Event Viewer can also be accessed by clicking **Start** and then **Run**, and entering **eventvwr** in the **Open** text box.

4. ____ Once the Microsoft Management Console is open, expand the Event Viewer folder to see the three types of logs.

5. ____ Select the **Security** log and view the list of events recorded in the log.

6. ____ Double-click any of the events to view details about the event. You can also view details by right-clicking the event and selecting **Properties** from the shortcut menu. After reviewing the details of the event, close the dialog box and move to the next step.

7. ____ Right-click the **Security** log listed under the Event Viewer folder and then select **Properties** from the shortcut menu. You should see a properties dialog box similar to the one in the following figure.

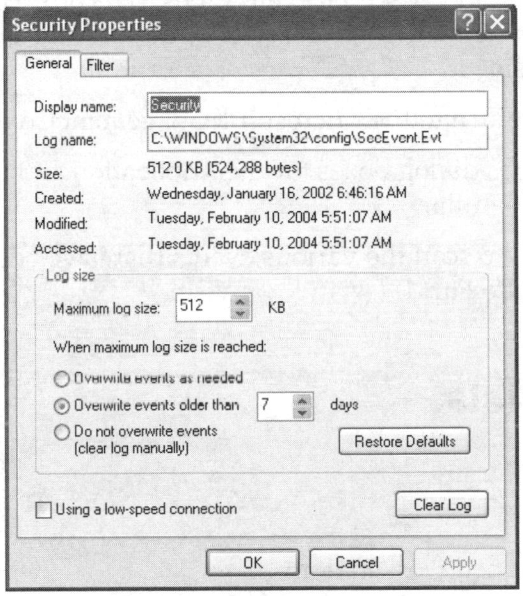

In this dialog box, you can rename the log, configure the size of the log, and select options of how to handle events after the log has reached its maximum storage size. The three options listed are: **Overwrite events as needed**, **Overwrite events older than (x) number of days**, and **Do not overwrite events**.

8. _____ Select the **Filter** tab at the top of the **Security Properties** dialog box. A dialog box similar to the following should appear.

On the Filter page you can modify which event types to record. The five event types are recorded automatically by default. You can select or deselect the event types to record by simply clicking the check box beside it.

9. _____ Click **Cancel** and return to the Microsoft Management Console view.

10. _____ Access the properties dialog boxes for the **Application** and the **System** logs and see if the property dialog boxes are similar.

11. _____ Take a few minutes to scan the various events that have been recorded in each of the three logs, and then go on to Part II—Windows Vista.

Part II—Windows Vista

Procedure

1. _____ Report to your assigned workstation.

2. _____ Boot the computer and verify it is in working order.

3. _____ Access the Windows Vista Event Viewer by typing **Event** into the **Search** dialog box located off the **Start** menu and pressing [Enter].

4. _____ Close the Event Viewer and then open a command prompt. Enter the executable file name **eventvwr** and watch as Event Viewer appears on the screen.

Copyright by Goodheart-Willcox Co., Inc.

Name____

5. ____ Close the Event Viewer and the command prompt, and then access the Event Viewer by opening Computer Management. Expand the left panel so that you can see the various sections of the Event Viewer similar to that in the following screen capture.

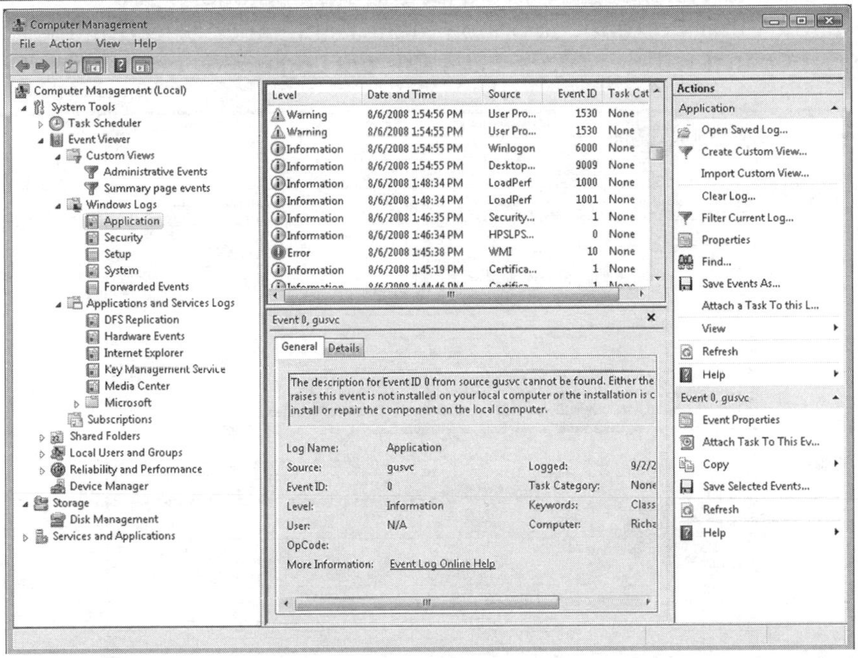

6. ____ Right-click the **Application** log listed under the **Event Viewer | Windows Logs** folder and then select **Properties** from the shortcut menu. You should see a properties dialog box similar to the one in the following screen capture.

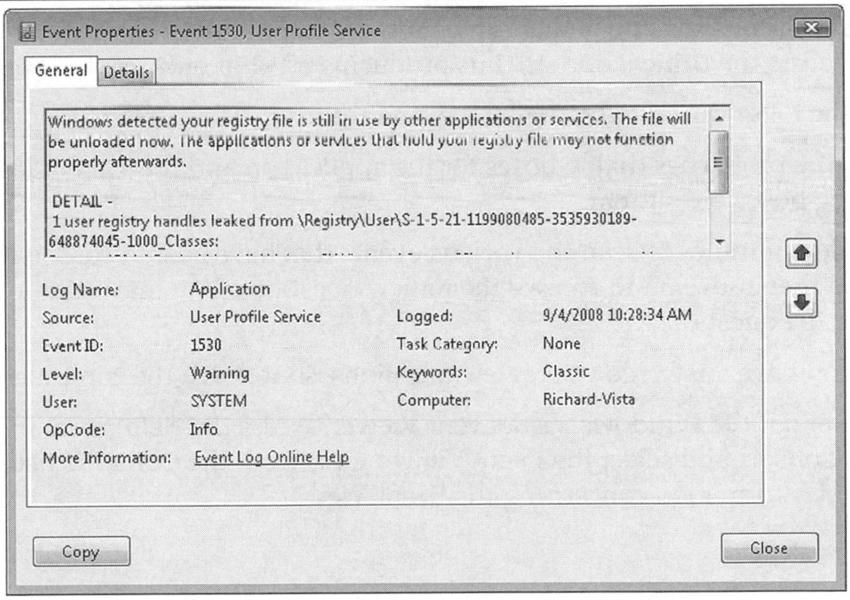

Facts about the event are displayed, such as the time, date, computer name, and more. There is also an option to view details about the event.

Copyright by Goodheart-Willcox Co., Inc.

7. ____ Close the **Event Properties** dialog box. You should be viewing Computer Management once more. If not, open Computer Management.

8. ____ You can filter events by double-clicking the top of the columns of the event categories such as **Level, Date and Time, Source, Event ID,** and **Task Category.** You can also filter the event log by selecting the **Filter Current Log** option in the right panel. Selecting the **Filter Current Log** option in the right panel will produce a **Filter Current Log** dialog box similar to the following.

You can see the various selections that can be used to filter events. For example, you can filter the log by selecting the **Critical** option, thus producing a list of only critical events.

9. ____ Close the **Filter Current Log** dialog box and return to Microsoft Management view.

10. ____ Access the properties dialog boxes for the application and the system logs and see if the property dialog boxes are similar.

11. ____ Take a few minutes to scan the various events that have been recorded in each of the three logs, and then move on to answer the review questions. You may refer to the Event Viewer as you answer the questions.

12. ____ After you have answered the review questions, shut down the computer.

To learn more about the Windows Vista Event Viewer, access the **Help** menu in the Computer Management Console and select the Event Viewer topic from the **Contents** listing. There is a large volume of information concerning the Event Viewer.

Copyright by Goodheart-Willcox Co., Inc.

Review Questions

1. What are the three logs recorded by the Windows XP Event Viewer? _____

_____

_____

_____

2. Where would you find an unauthorized attempt to access the system by password guessing?

_____

3. What is the default size of a Windows XP event log? _____

4. Where would you look for a recorded event that concerned a failure by a piece of system hardware? _____

_____

5. Does the security log contain who has logged on to the computer?_____

6. Does the security log record the event by day or by time of the event?_____

7. What command can be used from the Windows XP **Run** dialog box or the Windows Vista command prompt to launch the Event Viewer? _____

_____

8. What five event types are related to filtering? _____

_____

_____

_____

9. What are the three options available for handling a Windows XP log that has reached its maximum size? _____

_____

_____

10. What two new event logs are introduced in Windows Vista? _____

11. What new event type was added by Windows Vista? _____

_____

Computer Service and Repair Lab Manual

Copyright by Goodheart-Willcox Co., Inc.

Name _____ Date _____

Class/Instructor _____

Windows XP Registry

After completing this laboratory activity, you will be able to:

■ Describe the registry structure and its contents.

■ Identify the major folders associated with the registry.

■ Explain the difference between the regedit and regedt32 utilities.

■ Access the system registry and then view or modify its settings.

■ Determine when it is appropriate to directly edit the registry.

Introduction

This lab activity introduces you to the Windows XP registry. It is important to note that Microsoft posts warnings about how changing the registry can render the computer system inoperable. The warnings are posted throughout their Support Web site as well as throughout their reference materials. Despite these warnings, there will be times when a technician must access and modify the system registry. One of the most common reasons to modify the system registry is to recover from registry changes made by malicious software, such as viruses and worms.

The registry is a hierarchical database used to configure the operating system and hardware. The registry database contains information about the users, hardware, and software installed on the computer. Microsoft used text-based files referred to as "ini" (pronounced "I and I") before the registry was used. Config.sys and autoexec.bat files were also used to store software and hardware configuration information. The config.sys and autoexec.bat files are rarely encountered and are not required. They are only used when legacy software or legacy hardware is installed on a computer. Look at the following figure to see what a typical registry looks like.

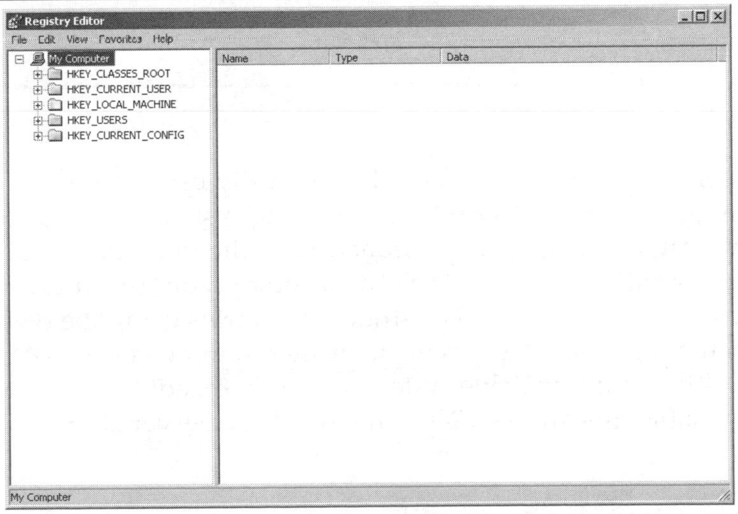

Note the five major folders associated with the registry system. The following chart lists and defines each of these major folders.

Folder Title	Description
HKEY_CURRENT_USER	Configuration information for the current user logged on to the computer.
HKEY_USERS	Root of all users on the computer.
HKEY_LOCAL_MACHINE	Configuration information for the computer for all users.
HKEY_CLASSES_ROOT	Contains information that is the product of both the users and the computer.
HKEY_CURRENT_CONFIG	Contains the information used by the local computer during startup.

Microsoft uses the terms *hive*, *key*, and *subkey* when describing the registry. A key is another name for the folders that appear in the Registry Editor on the left side of the panel. A subkey is a key that is beneath a major key. A hive is a collection of keys and subkeys that are closely related. For a more concise set of definitions of these terms, consult Help and Support.

Folders, or keys, can be expanded to show the contents of the database that relates to the specific keys. In the following figure, the Adobe software folder has been expanded to view its contents.

Regedt32 is the 32-bit version of the Registry Editor utility used in Windows XP. The original Registry Editor was designed for 16-bit Windows operating systems and was called *regedit*.

To run the registry editor, you simply type **regedt32** in the **Run** dialog box off the **Start** menu. Pay close attention to the spelling of regedt32. Students often type "regedit32." The misspelling automatically generates an error message. The student then tries using the regedit command, and they successfully open the registry. Changes made using the 16-bit version of regedit will cause problems, possibly resulting in an unstable system. Use only regedt32 to view or modify the registry. Regedt32 is also available in Windows 2000 and Windows Server 2003.

Copyright by Goodheart-Willcox Co., Inc.

Note:

It is not necessary to obtain an in-depth knowledge of the registry. But it is essential to be familiar with the basic aspects of the registry for future work as a technician. A technician may be required to make system registry changes to correct effects caused by software. The technician typically researches a problem using the Microsoft Support site and makes the recommended changes as directed. The Microsoft Support site provides detailed, step-by-step information for modifying the registry.

Changes made directly to the registry using regedt32 utility should be a last resort attempt to fix a problem. Changes to the system configuration should be made using Control Panel or other software programs designed by the manufacturer to configure the system.

Microsoft recommends making a backup of the registry before making any changes to the registry. In Windows XP, the registry is backed up by making an Automatic System Recovery disk (ASR). The ASR method is new in Windows XP. Prior to the release of Windows XP, the registry backup method was accomplished in various ways depending on the versions of the operating system. For example, in Windows 98 and Windows Me, the registry contents are backed up by running **scanregw**. The utility automatically makes a backup of the entire registry contents. In Windows 2000, making an Emergency Repair Disk (ERD) backs up the entire registry.

Note:

Always make a backup of the registry before modification. Never use a copy of the registry from another computer to restore the registry contents. Make changes directly to the registry as a last resort.

To learn more about the registry, visit Microsoft's Support Web site and view the following articles:

■ Q256419: How to back up the registry in Windows 98 and Windows Millenium Edition.
■ Q322756: How to back up, edit, and restore the registry in Windows XP and Windows Server 2003.
■ Q322754: How to back up, edit, and restore the registry in Windows 95, Windows 98, and Windows Me.
■ Q141377: Differences between regedit.exe and regedt32.exe.

Equipment and Materials

■ Typical PC with Windows XP installed.

Note:

Make notes to identify the original screen saver settings of the PC before performing this lab activity.

Procedures

1. ____ Report to your assigned workstation. Boot the PC and make sure it is in working order.

2. ____ Enter **regedt32** in the **Run** dialog box located off the **Start** menu. The system Registry Editor utility should open.

3. ____ Close the Registry Editor (regedt32) and then try opening the Registry Editor by running **regedit** from the **Run** dialog box. The Registry Editor (regedit) utility should open and look similar to the last editor.

4. ____ Close the Registry Editor (regedit) utility and then misspell the utility by entering **regedit32** in the **Run** dialog box. An error message should appear. Write the error message in the space provided. _____

_____

5. ____ In this part of the lab activity, you will make system changes and view their effect on the registry contents. You will modify the screen saver properties. First open the **Display Properties** dialog box by right-clicking the desktop and then selecting **Properties** from the shortcut menu. Next, select the **Screen Saver** tab.

6. ____ Select the **Marquee** screen saver from the **Screen saver** text box.

7. ____ Click the **Settings** button. A dialog box similar to the following should appear. Notice the default text in the text box "Your text goes here."

8. ____ Change the default text to "This is the place to enter the text," and then click **OK**.

9. ____ Next, click the **Preview** button in the **Display Properties** dialog box. The text you just entered should appear as a Marquee message moving across the screen. If not, call your instructor for assistance.

10. ____ Click anywhere on the screen to return to the **Display Properties** dialog box. Close the **Display Properties** dialog box.

Copyright by Goodheart-Willcox Co., Inc.

Name_____

11. ____ Start the Registry Editor using the **regedt32** command from the **Run** dialog box. The Registry Editor should appear on the screen.

12. ____ Select the **HKEY_CURRENT_USER | Control Panel | Screen Saver.Marquee** path in the Registry Editor by clicking the plus signs in front of each key name. Look at the right side of the Registry Editor to see the values for the Screen Saver.Marquee. (You must click the **Screen Saver.Marquee** folder to view its contents.) Pay particular attention to the "Text" value on the right. Any changes you make in the **Display Properties** dialog box will be stored in the registry. Also take note of the registry path indicated in the lower-left corner of the Registry Editor.

13. ____ Next, double-click the **Text** value. A dialog box similar to the following should appear. You can use the **Edit String** dialog box to change the characters in the Marquee message.

Edit String   ? X

Value name:

[Text]

Value data:

[This is the place to enter text.]

                              OK   Cancel

---

14. ____ Change the Marquee's text value to "The Marquee text value has been changed, using the String Editor." Click **OK** and then close the Registry Editor.

15. ____ Open the **Display Properties** dialog box and test the Marquee screen saver to see if the change took effect. If the Marquee message did not change, call your instructor for assistance.

16. ____ Close the **Display Properties** dialog box and run the Registry Editor using the **regedt32** command.

17. ____ Record the default values of background color, font, size, speed, and text color values in the space below. You will use these values as a reference.

Background color: _____

Font: _____

Size: _____

Text color: _____

18. ____ Close the Registry Editor and open the **Display Properties** dialog box and then change Marquee Screen Saver properties to the following values:

Background color = Red

Font = Times New Roman

Size = 72

Text color = White

19. ____ Test the new settings to see if they have taken effect.

20. ____ Close the **Display Properties** dialog box and reopen the Registry Editor.

21. ____ Compare the values in the right panel to the original values you wrote in step 17. Do you see the changes reflected in the registry data? If not, call your instructor for assistance.

Copyright by Goodheart-Willcox Co., Inc.

22. _____ Now, make the following changes to the values in the system registry to see how they affect the Marquee screen saver.

Background color value = 255 255 255. (Leave one space between each of the 255 values.)

Size = 24

Text = The registry values are now changed.

Text color = 128 128 128

23. _____ Close the Registry Editor. Open the **Display Properties** dialog box and test the new Marquee values.

24. _____ You may experiment with the Marquee settings using the Registry Editor, but *do not* change values of any other registry contents. Do not enter any value higher than 255 for the color values. Changes to other values in the registry may cause the system to crash.

25. _____ Return the screen saver values to their original settings before moving on to answer the review questions.

Review Questions

1. What is a registry key similar to when compared to a directory of folders and files?_____
   _____

2. What is a subkey similar to when compared to a directory of folders and files? _____
   _____

3. What is a hive? _____
   _____
   _____

4. What is the registry? _____
   _____
   _____

5. How do you access the Registry Editor in Windows XP?_____
   _____
   _____

6. What is the difference between regedit and regedt32? _____
   _____
   _____

7. When should the system registry be directly altered using the regedt32 utility? _____
   _____
   _____

Copyright by Goodheart-Willcox Co., Inc.

Name_____

8. Which is the preferred command to start the Windows XP Registry Editor? Read each answer carefully.

   A. regedit
   B. regedt32
   C. regedit32
   D. modifyreg

9. How do you make a backup of the registry contents for Windows XP? _____

   _____

   _____

10. How do you make a backup of the registry contents for Windows 2000? _____

   _____

   _____

Copyright by Goodheart-Willcox Co., Inc.

Copyright by Goodheart-Willcox Co., Inc.

Name _____ Date _____

Class/Instructor _____

Windows Vista Backup and Restore Center

After completing this laboratory activity, you will be able to:

- Back up selected files and then restore them.
- Perform a complete system backup and restore.
- Identify which Windows Vista editions support disk imaging.
- Explain the difference between the **Back up files** and **Back up computer** options.
- Identify alternative methods to repair a system other than performing a restore from a backup.

Introduction

In this laboratory activity, you will perform a backup using the Windows Vista Backup and Restore Center. There are two options for completing backup operations: **Back up files** and **Back up computer**. The **Back up files** option lets you select which files to backup. It is available in all versions of Windows Vista. The **Back up computer** option makes a complete backup of the entire disk/partition, including the boot sector and all critical operating system files. The **Back up computer** option creates an exact copy of the disk bit by bit. This type of copy is often referred to as a disk image. The **Back up computer** option is only available in Windows Vista Business, Ultimate, and Enterprise editions and is referred to as the Complete PC Backup feature. Windows Vista is the first Microsoft operating system that provides a backup of the disk image. Prior to Windows Vista, you had to use a third-party software application, such as Norton Ghost, to make an image of the disk.

Once the complete backup is made, you can restore the computer to the captured state at any time. Even if there is a complete system failure caused by missing required system files, you can insert the install DVD, and at the appropriate point, recover the system when prompted for the backup image.

The most common method of computer backup is using an external hard drive for the backup. The external hard drive connects to the computer through a USB port. Most external hard disk drive systems have their own proprietary backup software. Windows Vista is compatible with most third-party systems. If Windows Vista can identify the exterior hard drive storage device, then you can use the Complete PC Backup feature.

You can also use other media to perform a backup of files, such as writable CDs, DVDs, Flash drives, and network locations. There are even home servers available that are designed to use for system backups as well as to share files and directories.

The only real protection for data is regular backups. Antivirus and security software only protect the computer from unauthorized access and possible destruction of data and system failure. A backup is the only way to restore data. Thus, it is the best way to protect data.

A complete backup of the entire computer can take hours to perform. The quickest method of backup is to only perform a backup of important data, such as of the Documents folder. After a complete computer failure, you can reinstall the operating system and then install the backup of the Documents folder.

Note:
>   The actual lab you perform may not exactly match the screen presentations in the laboratory activity if the computer has had another student perform a backup on it. The dialog boxes will appear with other options because of the previous backup.

Equipment and Materials

- PC with Windows Vista Business or Ultimate installed.
- Exterior hard drive for backup storage.

Note:
>   You need to familiarize yourself with the exterior hard drive device instructional booklet if available. If a booklet is not available, most manufacturers have information at their Web site concerning the installation procedures for the exterior device.

Procedure

1. ____ Gather the required backup materials, such as the exterior hard disk drive, cables, and power supply. Report to your assigned workstation. To perform a complete backup, the operating system must be Windows Vista Business or Ultimate.

2. ____ Boot the computer and verify it is in working order.

3. ____ Access the Backup and Restore Center through **Start | All Programs | System and Maintenance | Backup and Restore Center**. In a few seconds, the Backup and Restore Center will appear, similar to the one in the following screen capture.

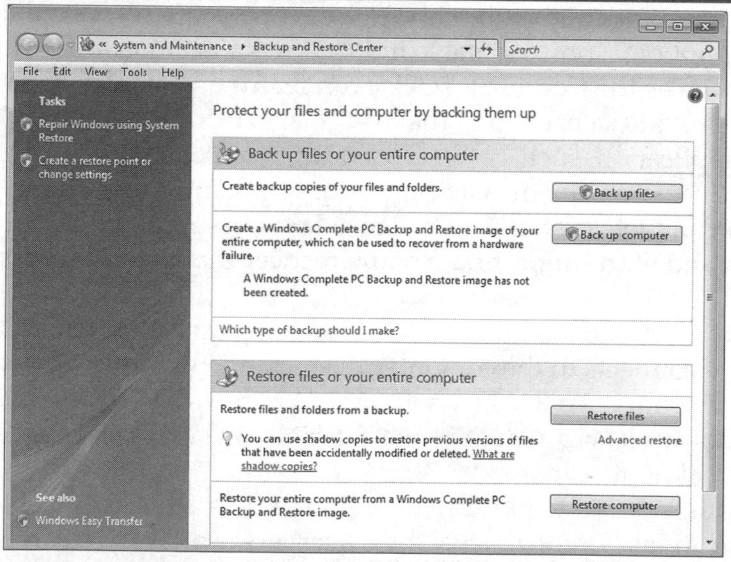

Notice that you have two backup options: **Back up files** and **Back up computer**. The **Back up files** options lets you select specific files to backup. The **Back up computer** option will back up the entire contents of the computer, including the boot sector and all critical operating system files. It makes a complete snapshot of all files residing on the disk.

You also have two similar restore options: **Restore files** and **Restore computer**. These are a reverse of the corresponding backup options.

Copyright by Goodheart-Willcox Co., Inc.

Name_____

4. ____ For this laboratory activity, select **Back up files**. There is not sufficient time in a typical school lab to perform a complete backup.

5. ____ After a short period, the next dialog box to appear will prompt you for a storage location. The dialog box will be similar to the following.

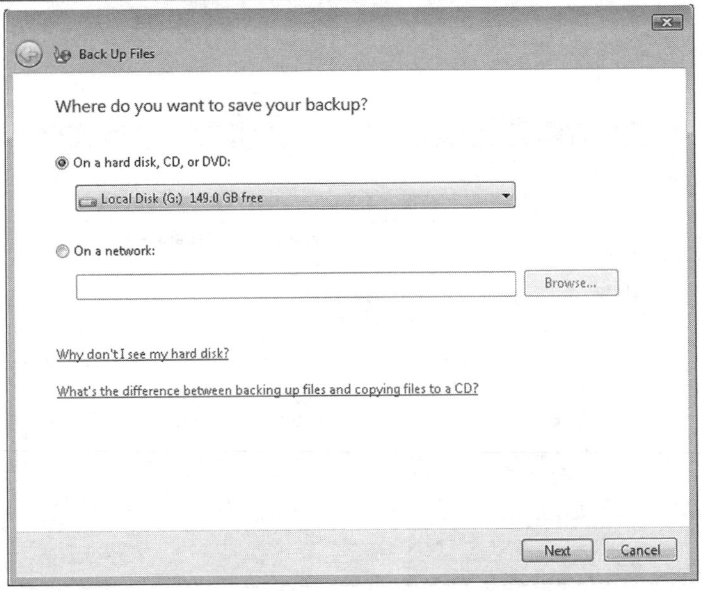

Windows Vista will search for all available backup locations. You must select which location you wish. You may need to open Windows Explorer and verify which drive letter is used for the exterior hard drive. Select the exterior hard drive as the place for the backup. Windows Vista will check and verify that there is sufficient space for the backup. If there is not sufficient space for the backup, Windows Vista will notify you using a yellow triangle with an exclamation mark accompanied by a short message. Also, notice that there is an option to browse the network to locate a storage area or device.

6. ____ After selecting the appropriate drive, click **Next**. The next two dialog boxes will prompt you for which disk to include if you have more than one partition. Each partition is referred to as a *disk* or *volume* as shown in the following screen capture.

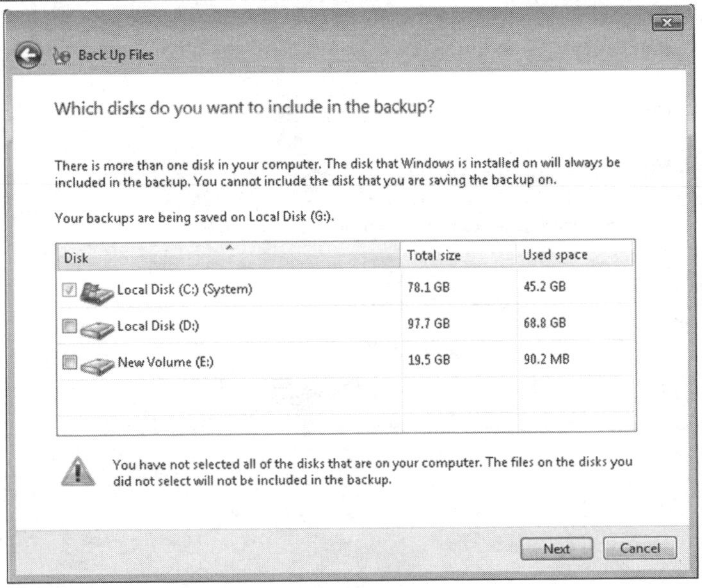

Copyright by Goodheart-Willcox Co., Inc.

7. _____ The next dialog box will prompt you for which files to backup. The exact list will vary according to the version of Windows Vista. For this lab activity, select the Documents folder to back up.

8. _____ The next dialog box will ask you to confirm or configure how often to create a backup. The default settings are Weekly, Sunday at 7:00 PM. Click the **Save settings and start backup** button. The backup procedure will now begin. A message box will appear providing information about the progress of the backup.

Copyright by Goodheart-Willcox Co., Inc.

9. ____ The next dialog box will confirm the backup as a success or failure. You can see in the following screen capture the backup was successfully performed. Notice also the date and time and when the next backup is scheduled to occur.

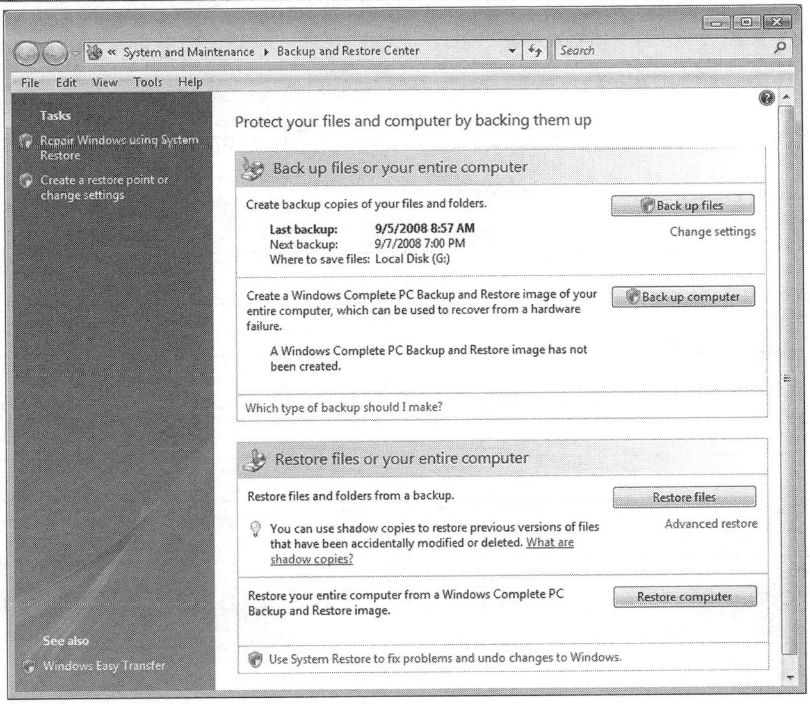

You can modify the automatic backup configuration by clicking **Change settings**. The Which type of backup should I make? link contains information about backup. Also, notice the references to shadow copies and System Restore. These are other options to recover files and computer system files, which may be more appropriate than performing a long computer restore from a large backup copy. A shadow copy is a copy of a data file that is made of a file before its last change. The Shadow Copy feature allows you to select a previous version of a file. System Restore was presented in another laboratory activity and allows restoring a computer system to a previous point in time condition. Both of these are alternatives to performing a restoration from a backup.

9. ____ To restore a backup, simply reverse the operation by selecting the appropriate restore option, and then follow the screen prompts.

10. ____ If time permits, you may perform a restore from the backup copy. Be sure to read each screen message and dialog box closely.

11. ____ Return all materials to their proper storage area and then go on to answer the review questions.

Review Questions

1. Which Windows Vista versions can perform a complete computer backup? _____
   _____

2. Which Windows Vista versions can perform a limited file backup? _____

3. What is the best way to protect data? _____

4. What is the difference between the **Back up files** and **Back up computer** options?
   _____
   _____
   _____
   _____
   _____
   _____
   _____
   _____

5. Which other two features are made available to the user to recover from a failed computer or lost data file? _____

Copyright by Goodheart-Willcox Co., Inc.

Name _____ Date _____

Class/Instructor _____

Windows XP PCI Network Adapter Installation

After completing this laboratory activity, you will be able to:

■ Install and configure a typical PCI Ethernet network adapter.

■ Identify common problems associated with installing a network adapter.

■ Use Device Manager to confirm proper installation of the network adapter.

■ Disable or uninstall a network adapter for troubleshooting purposes.

■ Identify system resources assigned to the network adapter.

Introduction

In this laboratory activity, you will install a typical PCI Ethernet network adapter, commonly referred to as a NIC (network interface card). While most network adapters are automatically configured through Plug and Play technology, many times a technician's intervention is required. This most commonly happens when the network adapter and the operating system are from two different eras. For example, when installing a dated network adapter into a computer with the latest operating system, a driver may need to be manually installed.

You should check the Microsoft Hardware Compatibility List (HCL) prior to purchasing a network adapter. Purchase a network adapter that is on the list. Network adapters not on the HCL may present a problem during installation. When using a network adapter not previously tested and approved by Microsoft, a warning message may appear. The message will inform you that the drivers are not digitally signed and will advise you not to install the card. You may ignore the warning and continue with the installation process. Most times, the network adapter will install properly, but you will most likely need to supply the driver disc during the installation process.

All network adapters require driver software. Typically, when a Plug and Play network adapter is detected by the operating system, the driver is automatically installed and no further intervention is required from the technician. Occasionally, a network adapter driver must be installed manually. When such an instance occurs, the next step in the installation process can vary depending on how much information about the network adapter the operating system identified. For example, a newly installed device may be identified as a network adapter, but the technician must supply the driver. Or, the newly installed device may not be identified by type of device, and the network technician must identify the device as a network adapter and manually install the driver. The operating system may not detect the newly installed device at all. In such a case, the technician must start the installation from **Control Panel I Add Hardware**.

Device Manager can be used to view the status of a hardware device installed in the computer. From Device Manager, the technician can uninstall, disable, scan for property changes, or update the network adapter driver. Device Manager can also be used to view the system resource assignments of hardware devices. Network adapters use three system resources: Interrupt Request (IRQ), I/O port, and RAM memory. Some network adapters also use Direct Memory Access (DMA). Device Manager usually detects conflicts between devices using the same system resource.

Copyright by Goodheart-Willcox Co., Inc.

The Windows XP operating system installs the TCP/IP protocol by default when a network adapter is installed. To verify that the TCP/IP protocol is installed, issue the **ping** command at the command prompt. If TCP/IP is not installed, you will not be able to use the **ping** command.

Note:

When installing a network adapter into a computer that has a network port built into the motherboard, the motherboard network port usually needs to be disabled to prevent a conflict with the additional network adapter. The network port can be disabled through Device Manager.

Equipment and Materials

- Windows XP Professional workstation. (Do not use Windows XP Home Edition for this laboratory activity.)
- Patch cable.
- Windows XP installation CD. (May be required when configuring the network adapter.)
- PCI Ethernet network adapter with driver disc.
- Manufacturer's instructions for installing the network adapter. (Your instructor may have you download the installation instructions and drivers from the manufacturer's Web site.)
- Hub.
- Screwdriver to match expansion slot screw.
- Anti-static wrist strap.

Procedure

1. ____ Gather all required materials and then report to your assigned workstation.

2. ____ Familiarize yourself with the manufacturer's installation instructions.

3. ____ Boot the computer and verify it is in working order.

4. ____ Shut down the computer and then unplug the power cord. Follow anti-static procedures as defined by your instructor.

5. ____ Remove the computer case cover and then check for an available PCI slot. Remove the slot cover associated with the chosen PCI slot. A small screw at the top of the slot cover typically retains the slot cover. Some slot covers do not use a screw to hold it in place. Slot covers without a screw usually must be bent back and forth several times to break free of the metal frame. Some computer cases use a simple latching mechanism to retain the slot cover. If you are in doubt as to how to remove the slot cover, call your instructor.

6. ____ Position the network adapter over the PCI slot and then insert the card by applying firm, even pressure along the top edge of the card. Do not rock the card excessively.

7. ____ After the card has been fully inserted into the PCI slot, use the screw or appropriate mechanism to mount the card.

8. ____ Plug in the power cord and then boot the computer. The network adapter may or may not be automatically detected and configured. If it is not automatically detected and configured, you will need to configure the card manually. You will be prompted to identify the hardware device or to install the driver or both. When prompted for installing the driver, click the **Have Disk** button.

Microsoft Windows may automatically detect the presence of the network adapter, but not be able to automatically configure it. This typically occurs when it does not have a compatible driver for the device.

Copyright by Goodheart-Willcox Co., Inc.

Note:

Be sure to read each screen carefully. Most installation problems are caused by failure to read the information presented.

9. ____ After the driver is installed, open Device Manager to check the status of the network adapter. To access Device Manager, right-click **My Computer** and select **Properties** from the shortcut menu. Select the **Hardware** tab and then click the **Device Manager** button. The Device Manager list will display.

In the Device Manager list, you should see **Network adapters**. Expand **Network adapters** by clicking the plus sign that is next to it. Clicking the plus sign expands the device type **Network adapters** and shows all network adapters installed in the computer. In the following screen capture, two network adapters are identified. Both are in working order. No problems are indicated.

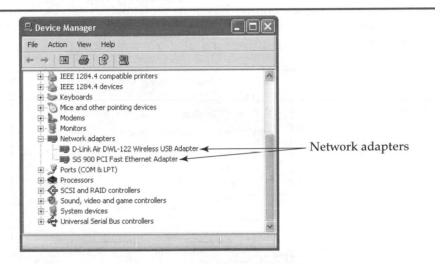

Device Manager indicates a hardware device problem by inserting a symbol over the device name. A red *X* indicates the device is disabled. A black exclamation mark (!) on a yellow field indicates the device is having a problem but may still be working. A blue *i* on a white field indicates that the resources for the device were manually selected.

10. ____ Right-click the network adapter entry. A shortcut menu will appear with the following commands: **Update Driver, Disable, Uninstall, Scan for hardware changes**, and **Properties**.

Copyright by Goodheart-Willcox Co., Inc.

11. ____ Select **Disable** from the shortcut menu. Notice the effect on the appearance of the device. What symbol appeared over the network adapter to indicate that it is disabled?

_____

12. ____ Enable the network adapter by right-clicking the network adapter entry and selecting **Enable** from the shortcut menu. The **Enable** option appears in the shortcut menu after the **Disable** command is selected.

13. ____ Right-click the network adapter entry and select **Uninstall**. After uninstalling the network adapter using the Device Manager, Windows XP will automatically detect the network adapter and install the driver. A message box will appear informing you that the network adapter has been installed and will ask if you want to set up a network. It will give you an option to run the Network Setup Wizard. Do not run the Network Setup Wizard at this time.

14. ____ After the network adapter has been reinstalled, open Device Manager and select the network adapter once more. Right-click the network adapter entry and select **Properties** from the shortcut menu. You should see a dialog box similar to the following.

The **General** dialog box indicates that the network adapter is working properly. You can also enable or disable the device from here and start the automatic troubleshooter if you are having problems with the device.

                    Copyright by Goodheart-Willcox Co., Inc.

Name_______________________________

15. ____ Select the **Advanced** tab. The **Advanced** dialog box allows you to change various properties for the network adapter card, such as the type of media the card is connected to.

Look at the following screen capture. The **Media Type** property is set to auto configure by default. Auto configure allows the card to automatically run a software program to detect the type of media connected to the card. You can also manually select the media type. For a small to medium network, auto configure is fine. For a large network, manually selecting the media type improves the overall performance of a large network. It prevents the card from sending out numerous packets to detect the media type and will thus reduce network traffic.

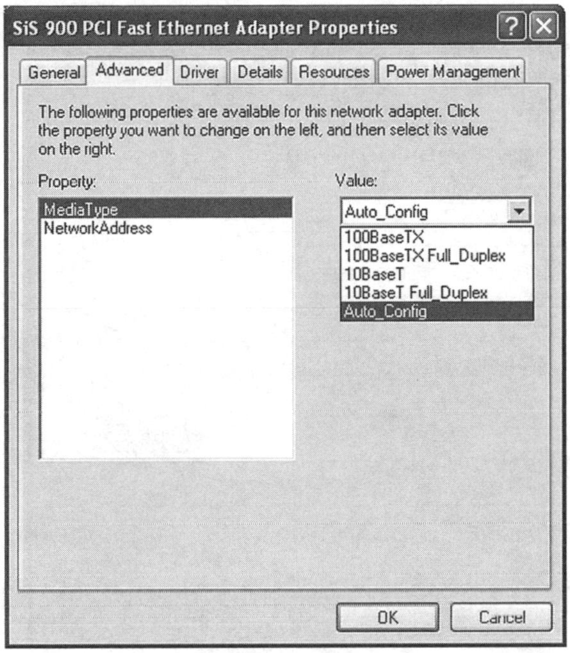

16. ____ Select the **Driver** tab. From the **Driver** dialog box, you can view driver details, update the driver, roll back the driver, and uninstall the driver.

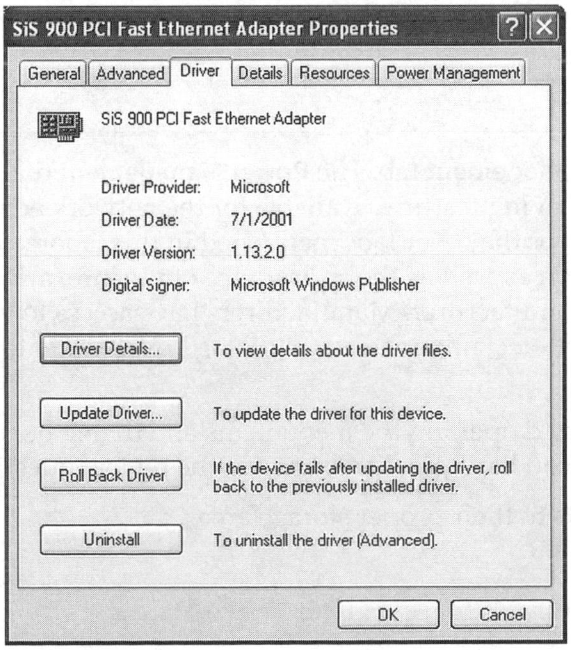

Copyright by Goodheart-Willcox Co., Inc.

The **Driver Details** button reveals information about the manufacturer, where the driver is located, and if the driver was digitally signed. A digitally signed driver means Microsoft has approved the driver. The **Roll Back Driver** option or feature removes the last installed driver for the card. You would normally use this option in place of using the System Restore feature, which rolls back all changes to the computer since the last restore point was created. Rolling back all changes since the last restore point was created can undo many changes that you wish to retain. The Roll Back Driver feature is the best choice for uninstalling a driver.

17. ____ Select the **Resources** tab. A dialog box similar to the following will appear and will display system resources assigned to the network adapter.

18. ____ Record the resources assigned to your network adapter in the spaces provided.

I/O range: _____

Memory range: _____

IRQ: _____

19. ____ Select the **Power Management** tab. The **Power Management** dialog box displays several options related to power-saving features available for the network adapter. Typically, you will not need to access this tab or the other tabs mentioned in this laboratory activity. Also, be aware that the type of information as well as the appearance of the information presented in a dialog box can change by card manufacturer. Manufacturers have access to Windows XP programming information. They often change the way a dialog box appears to match the capabilities of their network adapters.

20. ____ Practice accessing and opening the menu items and dialog boxes presented in this laboratory activity. After you have practiced, answer the review questions.

21. ____ Return all materials to their proper storage area.

Copyright by Goodheart-Willcox Co., Inc.

Name_____

Review Questions

1. What does the acronym NIC represent? _____

2. What does the acronym HCL represent? _____

3. What symbol is used in Device Manager to indicate a device is disabled? _____

4. What symbol is used in Device Manager to indicate there is a problem with a device?

   _____

5. What four options are available from the **Driver** tab? _____

6. Why is the Roll Back Driver feature the preferred way to remove a network adapter driver?

   _____

7. What three system resources are assigned to a network adapter? _____

   _____

Computer Service and Repair Lab Manual

Copyright by Goodheart-Willcox Co., Inc.

Name _____ Date _____

Class/Instructor _____

Introduction to Windows Vista Networking

After completing this laboratory activity, you will be able to:

■ Identify vital parts of the Windows Vista Network and Sharing Center.

■ Explain the function of the Microsoft Link-Layer Topology Discovery (LLTD) protocols.

■ Access the Network and Sharing Center in several different ways.

■ Use the Network and Sharing Center to reveal information about the network or start a network wizard.

■ Identify the connection wizards available in **Set up a connection or network** dialog box.

Introduction

This laboratory activity is designed to familiarize you with the Windows Vista Network and Sharing Center. Networking in Windows Vista has evolved to new level that makes networking easier than in any previous version of the Windows operating system. Windows Vista practically networks itself, especially in a local area network environment. Sharing files and data is automatic as well as configuring printers and other networking devices. Wireless networking is also very easy to configure as compared to configuring it in Windows XP.

The heart of Windows Vista networking is the Network and Sharing Center. All aspects of the local area network can be accessed or controlled from this central location. You can immediately see if you have a connection established to the Internet by looking at the partial map at the top of the dialog box. You are connected to the Internet if you do not see a red "X" between the house icon and the world icon. The house icon represents the local area network, and the world icon represents the Internet.

Copyright by Goodheart-Willcox Co., Inc.

You can access the Network and Sharing Center in several different ways. You can right-click **Network** on the **Start** menu and then select **Properties** from the shortcut menu. You can type **Network** into the **Search** box. The "Network and Sharing Center" entry will appear under **Programs** in the search results before you type the first three letters. You can access the Network and Sharing Center through **Start | Control Panel | Network and Internet | Network and Sharing Center**.

Windows Vista networking is based on the Link-Layer Discovery Protocol (LLDP) specification. The specification describes how network devices can automatically communicate with each other, thus discovering their locations and functions in the local area network topology. Based on the LLDP specification, Windows Vista introduced two new network protocols: Link-Layer Discovery Mapper I/O Driver and Link-Layer Topology Discovery Responder. Together, these two protocols automatically send out messages on the network that are received and replied to from other network devices, thus creating a map of the local area network.

The map contains all Windows Vista network devices as well as network equipment that uses the LLDP specification. In this way, the Network and Sharing Center can create a map of all compatible devices connected to the local area network. Devices identified but not located appropriately in the map do not comply with the LLDP specification. For example, Windows XP and earlier operating systems would not show up in their proper location in the network map because they do not have the Link-Layer Discovery Mapper I/O Driver and Link-Layer Topology Discovery Responder configured with the network adapter.

There is a patch that can be downloaded from the Microsoft Web site that is designed to install on a Windows XP system. This patch serves the same purpose as the LLDP protocols. Once installed, the Windows XP system can be discovered by the Windows Vista system.

In the following screen capture, the local area network and their relative position in the network wireless devices are connected by a dashed line. Wired devices are connected by a solid line. If network devices such as hubs, switches, and routers comply with the LLDP specification, they also will appear in the map. Devices that do not comply with the LLDP specification may be detected and may appear separately, not joined to the network. Notice that at the bottom of the screen capture, a computer called "RMROBERT-567" has been identified but not located in the map structure.

Copyright by Goodheart-Willcox Co., Inc.

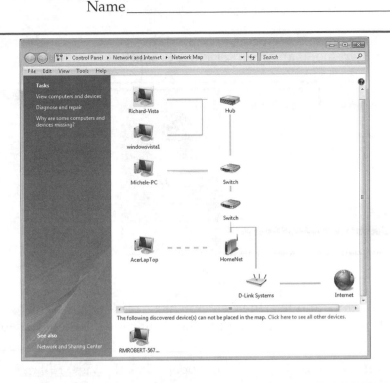

To enable Windows Vista computers to locate Windows XP computers in a local area network (peer-to-peer), you must download and install the Microsoft Link-Layer Topology Discovery Responder for Windows XP. Conduct a Google search using the key term "KB922120" or "WindowsXP-KB922120-v5-x86-ENU.exe," which is the executable file name. You will find the link to the Link-Layer Topology Discovery Responder used to upgrade Windows XP. Also, check the article "KB922120," which explains the importance of the Link-Layer Topology Discovery Responder so that Windows XP can be mapped by Windows Vista. Windows XP SP 3 contains the hot fixes to correct discrepancies between the Windows Vista Link-Layer Discovery Mapper I/O Driver and Windows XP.

Equipment and Materials

■ PC with Windows Vista installed.

Note:
This lab activity can only be completed using Windows Vista in a peer-to-peer network setting. Earlier operating systems will not be appropriate for this lab activity because they do not contain the Network and Sharing Center.

Procedure

1. ____ Report to your assigned workstation.

2. ____ Boot the computer and verify it is in working order.

3. ____ Open the Network and Sharing Center by entering **Network** in the **Search** box.

Copyright by Goodheart-Willcox Co., Inc.

4. ____ Close the Network and Sharing Center and then access it more by right-clicking **Networking** in the **Start** menu and then selecting **Properties** from the shortcut menu.

5. ____ Close the Network and Sharing Center again. This time open the Network and Sharing Center by going through **Start | Control Panel | Network and Internet | Network and Sharing Center**.

6. ____ With the Network and Sharing Center open, click the <u>View full map</u> link. You will see a map of all LLDP-based devices connected as a network map. The appearance of the map will depend on the number of devices connected as a peer-to-peer network in your classroom lab.

7. ____ With the map open, take a look at the tasks listed in the left side panel.

The **View computers and devices** option opens the **Network** dialog box and the network devices appear as they do in previous versions of Windows—as a collection of individual devices rather than mapped.

The **Diagnose and repair** option replaces the Windows XP version of Network Diagnostics. In fact, Windows Vista constantly runs a diagnostic program in the background, checking the network for problems. When the **Diagnose and repair** task is selected, Windows Vista automatically runs a diagnostic program and reveals the results. It performs much faster than Windows XP Network Diagnostics.

The **Why are some computers and devices missing?** option takes you to Windows Help and Support. Select this option now and take a few minutes to view the very important information provided. After viewing the Windows Help and Support information, close the Network Map.

Copyright by Goodheart-Willcox Co., Inc.

8. ____ The Network and Sharing Center should still be open after closing the Network Map. If not, open the Network and Sharing Center. Click the <u>View status</u> link. A dialog box similar to the following will display.

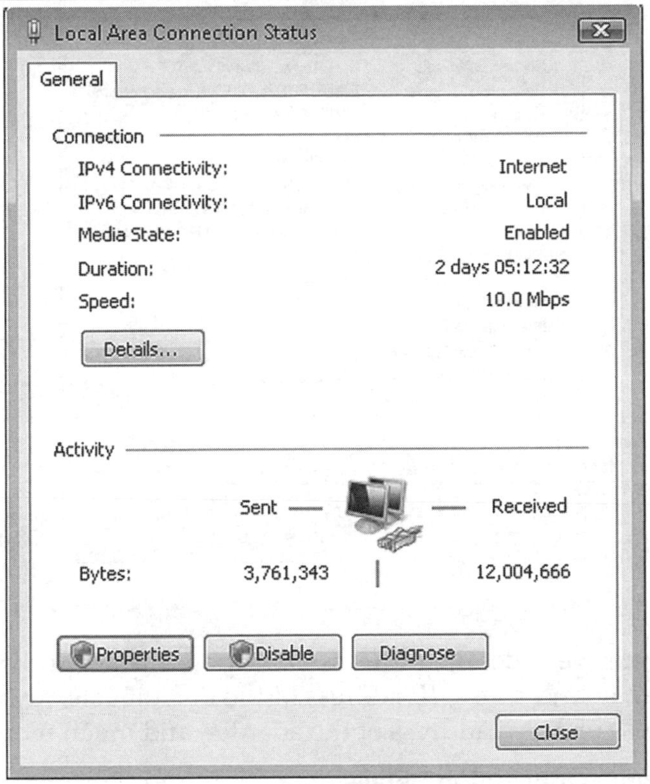

Local Area Connection Status

General

Connection

IPv4 Connectivity:	Internet
IPv6 Connectivity:	Local
Media State:	Enabled
Duration:	2 days 05:12:32
Speed:	10.0 Mbps

Details...

Activity

	Sent —		— Received
Bytes:	3,761,343		12,004,666

Properties   Disable   Diagnose

Close

You will see general information about the computer network connection and the status of the connection. Look at all the information presented in the screen capture and compare it to your **Local Area Connection Status** dialog box. By examining the **Local Area Connection Status** dialog box in the screen capture, you can tell the following:

- The adapter is using both IPv4 and IPv6 protocols: IPv4 for the Internet connection and IPv6 for the local connection.
- Media State is "Enabled," which means it is working and connected.
- The connection was established 2 days, 5 hours, 12 minutes, and 32 seconds ago.
- The speed of the connection is 10 Mbps.
- The number of bytes sent and received by the network adapter.

9. ____ Click the **Details** button to reveal a dialog box similar to the following.

This dialog box provides very detailed information about the network adapter, such as the IP address of the adapter, subnet mask, IP address of the default gateway, IP address of the DNS server, physical address or MAC address of the adapter, and much more.

10. ____ Close the **Network Connection Details** dialog box and the **Local Area Connection Status** dialog box. The Network Sharing and Center should still be on the desktop. If not, open the Network and Sharing Center.

11. ____ Look at the list of tasks located at the left side of Network and Sharing Center.

Two of the options are the same as the ones presented in the Network Map tasks list. These are **View computers and devices** and **Diagnose and repair**. There are three new options to select from in the Network and Sharing Center tasks list: **Connect to a network**, **Set up a connection or network**, and **Manage network connections**.

These tasks will be explored in future lab activities, but for now it is important to open and view the dialog box when **Set up a connection or network** is selected.

Copyright by Goodheart-Willcox Co., Inc.

12. ____ Click **Set up a connection or network**. A dialog box similar to the following will display.

The **Set up a connection or network** dialog box is where you start the wizards that will help you automatically configure network connections. This includes wired, wireless, and Internet connections. Each choice provides a brief explanation of its purpose. You will become more familiar with these choices as you progress through future lab activities.

13. ____ Close the **Set up a connection or network** dialog box. You should be returned to the Network and Sharing Center. If not, open the Network and Sharing Center.

14. ____ Look at the choices available in the **Sharing and Discovery** section of Network and Sharing Center.

Sharing and Discovery		
Network discovery	On	⌄
File sharing	On	⌄
Public folder sharing	On (password required)	⌄
Printer sharing	On (password required)	⌄
Password protected sharing	On	⌄
Media sharing	Off	⌄

Show me all the files and folders I am sharing

In this section, you control the network discovery feature as well as how files, printers, media, and the Public folder are shared from your computer. This area will be explored more in a future lab activity. For now, you may select each of the items and look at the options available. Do not change any of the options at this time.

15. ____ Now, look at the **See also** located at the bottom of the left pane.

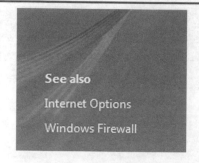

Two areas that are closely associated with networking are **Internet Options** and the **Windows Firewall**. Both of these items will be covered in detail in future lab activities.

16. ____ Close the Network and Sharing Center.

17. ____ Open Windows Help and Support and then type **Networking** in the **Search** box. Look at all the extensive information listed. Take a few minutes to explore some of the topics.

18. ____ Close Windows Help and Support and then go on to answer the review questions.

Copyright by Goodheart-Willcox Co., Inc.

Review Questions

1. How do you access the Network and Sharing Center?

   _____

   _____

   _____

   _____

   _____

   _____

2. What does the acronym LLDP represent? _____

   _____

3. How is a lost Internet connection indicated in the Network and Sharing Center? _____

   _____

4. What type of information is displayed in the Network and Sharing Center <u>View status</u> link?

   _____

   _____

   _____

   _____

5. Which Network and Sharing Center task listed in the left panel would you select to create a new Internet access connection? _____

6. Which Network and Sharing Center task listed in the left panel would you select to create a new dial-up connection? _____

7. Which Network and Sharing task in the left panel would you select to create a connection to your workplace network? _____

8. Which Network and Sharing task in the left panel would you select to create a new wireless connection? _____

Copyright by Goodheart-Willcox Co., Inc.

Copyright by Goodheart-Willcox Co., Inc.

Name _____ Date _____

Class/Instructor _____

Windows Vista NTFS Network Sharing

After completing this laboratory activity, you will be able to:

■ Create or delete an NTFS share on a Windows Vista computer.

■ Change the share permissions of an NTFS folder.

■ Identify and modify user and group access to a share.

■ Use Computer Management to create a share.

■ Use the Computer Management to identify all shares and their status.

Introduction

In this laboratory activity, you will create a standard share for a peer-to-peer network configuration. Windows standard sharing is much more detailed sharing based on either FAT or NTFS file permissions. Since the Windows Vista default file system is NTFS, the lab will only pertain to NTFS file system shares. The NTFS file system allows for very detailed share control as compared to Windows Vista Public folder sharing or Windows XP Simple File Sharing.

You can use both the Public folder sharing and standard file sharing on the same computer at the same time in a peer-to-peer network. In a domain network setting, Public file sharing can still be used but is typically disabled by the domain administrator. The domain administrator usually retains complete control of all network sharing.

To create a standard folder share you simply right-click the desired folder and then select **Share** from the shortcut menu. You can also create a share using Computer Management. This utility has a share wizard that will automatically configure the new shared folder or file through a series of dialog boxes that prompt you for information. In Computer Management, you can also stop sharing.

There have been many reported bugs in Windows Vista when attempting to stop a share. Probably the best way to create a share and stop a share is through Computer Management. Directly accessing the shared folder or file with the right-click method often will not allow the user to stop or delete the share. I expect a hot fix or patch to be issued by the time you are using this lab manual. If you install Windows Vista on a lab computer but did not install the latest service pack, you may experience some difficulties trying to remove a shared folder or file.

Equipment and Materials

■ Two Windows Vista workstations, both configured with an NTFS partition. The computers should be configured in a peer-to-peer network.

Note:
This can be a two-student lab activity, each using his or her assigned workstation.

Copyright by Goodheart-Willcox Co., Inc.

Part I—Right-Click Folder/File Method

Procedure

1. ____ Report to your assigned workstation.

2. ____ Boot the computer and verify it is in working order.

3. ____ Identify one workstation as the host and the other as the client.

4. ____ At the host, create a new folder called NTFS Share by opening the Document folder and then selecting **File | New | Folder**. Then, rename the new folder "NTFS Share."

5. ____ Use Microsoft WordPad to create a document with the following contents, "This is a document of the NTFS share file." Save the document as "NTFS Share Document" into the new folder called NTFS Share.

6. ____ Right-click the NTFS Share folder and then select the **Share** option from the shortcut menu. Look at the following partial screen capture to see an example.

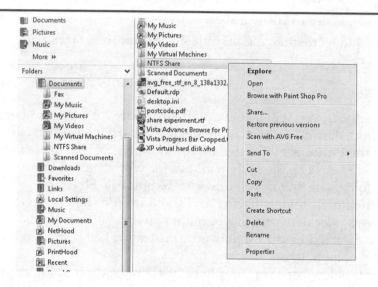

7. ____ The next dialog box to appear will prompt you to select people with whom you wish to share the folder or file.

Name_____

8. _____ You can use the arrow at the end of the text box to expose other eligible users with whom to share the folder. Select a user on your computer to add to the list.

9. _____ You can now assign a permission level to the user. The three permission levels available are Reader, Contributor, and Co-owner.

Leave the default Reader permission level for the added users. Click the **Share** button. The new share can be seen in the Windows Explorer directory structure. Look for the new share to confirm its existence. If the share was not created or cannot be found, call your instructor for assistance.

10. _____ Attempt to access the share from the client. You may need to supply a user name and password the first time you access the share.

11. _____ Remove the NTFS shared folder before proceeding to Part II—Computer Management Method. If you cannot successfully remove the share, rename the share "NTFS Share 2." You will be able to remove the NTFS share using Computer Management in Part II.

Part II—Computer Management Method

Procedure

1. _____ At the host, open the Document folder and then access **File | New | Folder**. Then, rename the new folder "NTFS Share."

2. _____ Use Microsoft WordPad and create a document with the following contents: "This is a document of the NTFS share file." Save the document in the NTFS Share folder, naming the file "NTFS Share Document."

3. _____ Use Computer Management to create the new share. To access Computer Management, open the **Start** menu, right-click **Computer**, and then select **Manage** from the shortcut menu. Computer Management should appear. Navigate the left pane until you have opened a view of all the shares on the computer.

4. _____ Select the **New Share** option from **Actions | More Actions** located in the right pane or from the **Action** menu located at the top of the window. Either method will start the Create A Shared Folder Wizard. When the Create A Shared Folder Wizard starts, you will see a dialog box similar to the following.

Copyright by Goodheart-Willcox Co., Inc.

Notice that Windows Firewall is automatically reconfigured to allow access to the share from other computers. Later, modifying the firewall could affect access to the share. Also, be aware that third-party firewalls could disable access to the share. You should only use one firewall to protect the computers in a peer-to-peer network and to prevent confusion by conflicting firewall configurations. Ideally, the device used to share Internet access should contain a firewall, which will protect all computers.

5. ____ Click **Next** to begin creating a new share.

6. ____ The next dialog box to open will prompt you for the location of the new share. You can navigate to a file or folder using the **Browse** button. Navigate your way to the NTFS Share folder and then click **Next**.

Create A Shared Folder Wizard

Folder Path
Specify the path to the folder you want to share.

Computer name: WINDOWSVISTA1

Type the path to the folder you want to share, or click Browse to pick the folder or add a new folder.

Folder path: |

Example: C:\Docs\Public

[< Back] [Next >] [Cancel]

---

7. ____ The wizard will display the folder path in the **Folder path** text box. Click the **Next** button to confirm the location or click the **Back** button and correct the location.

Create A Shared Folder Wizard

Folder Path
Specify the path to the folder you want to share.

Computer name: WINDOWSVISTA1

Type the path to the folder you want to share, or click Browse to pick the folder or add a new folder.

Folder path: C:\Users\Richard\Documents\NTFS Share

Example: C:\Docs\Public

[< Back] [Next >] [Cancel]

---

8. ____ Now, you are prompted for a share name and description.

The default share name is taken from the existing folder name. You can change it if you wish. The share path is presented using the Universal Naming Convention (UNC) to identify the computer name and the share name. Notice that the entire path is not used in the UNC name, just the computer and the shared folder name.

9. ____ Now you are prompted to choose a permission type. There are four types to choose from. For this lab activity, select the second option: **Administrators have full access; other users have read-only access**.

Copyright by Goodheart-Willcox Co., Inc.

10. _____ The last dialog box to appear confirms all the information you provided. Look closely at the actual directory structure path to the share in the example, C:\Users\Richard\Documents\NTFS Share. Later, you will compare the actual path to the UNC path. You can now click **Finish**.

Create A Shared Folder Wizard

Sharing was Successful

Status:

You have successfully completed the Share a Folder Wizard.

Summary:

You have selected the following share settings on \\WINDOWSVISTA1:
Folder path: C:\Users\Richard\Documents\NTFS Share
Share name: NTFS Share
Share path: \\WINDOWSVISTA1\NTFS Share

☐ When I click Finish, run the wizard again to share another folder

To close this wizard, click Finish.

Finish   Cancel

---

11. _____ Open Computer Management to confirm the creation of the new folder share.

12. _____ Go to the client and open the share that is located on the host. You may need to supply a password. If you cannot access the NTFS Share folder and the document inside, call your instructor for assistance.

13. _____ At the host computer, locate the NTFS Share folder using Windows Explorer, not Computer Management. Right-click the folder and select **Properties** from the shortcut menu. The **Properties** dialog box for the shared folder should appear similar to the following. The exact directory structure location is indicated starting at the root of drive C.

NTFS Share Properties

| General | Sharing | Security | Previous Versions | Customize |

NTFS Share

Type: File Folder

Location: C:\Users\Richard\Documents

Size: 202 bytes (202 bytes)

Size on disk: 4.00 KB (4,096 bytes)

Contains: 1 Files, 0 Folders

Created: Today, August 29, 2008, 6 minutes ago

Attributes: ☑ Read-only   Advanced...
               ☐ Hidden

OK   Cancel   Apply

---

14. ____ Select the **Sharing** tab. You should see a dialog box similar to the following.

Pay particular attention to the network path indicated in UNC format. The UNC does not display the actual directory structure or the full path to the share. The UNC only consists of the computer name and the share name. Also, notice the <u>Network and Sharing Center</u> link. This is new in Windows Vista for a **Share Properties** dialog box.

15. ____ Click the **Share** button. The **Choose people to share with** screen will display, just as it did earlier in the lab activity.

16. ____ Close the **Choose people to share with** screen by clicking **Cancel**. The **NTFS Share Properties** dialog box should still be on the desktop. If it is not, open it again.

Copyright by Goodheart-Willcox Co., Inc.

17. ____ Select the **Securities** tab. You will see a list of user names and groups that are assigned to the share similar to that in the following screen capture.

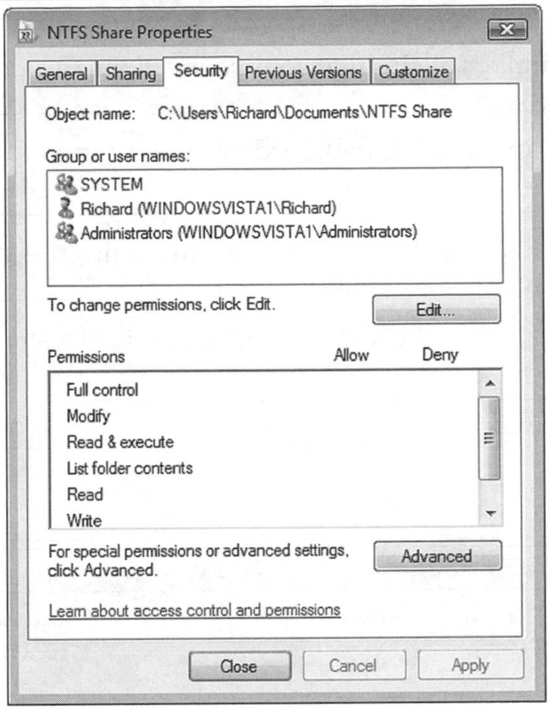

You can view the permissions assigned to each user or add an additional user to the share. Take a good look at the new, additional permissions that can be assigned to a user or group. Clicking the **Advanced** button will reveal another dialog box that allows an even more detailed configuration of user and group permissions.

18. ____ Select the Learn about access control and permissions link to learn more about these topics. There is a lot of information located at the link. Briefly look it over since you cannot possibly review it all during this lab activity. You may wish to review it again at a later date.

19. ____ Close all dialog boxes and then use Computer Management to remove the share. Simply right-click the share in Computer Management and then select **Stop Sharing** from the shortcut menu. The share will disappear from the **Shares** section in the right pane.

20. ____ Open Windows Explorer and delete the document inside the NTFS Share folder and the NTFS Share folder.

21. ____ If time permits and you have your instructor's permission, perform the second part of the lab again. Experiment with some of the permissions and try accessing the file and folder from another computer. When finished, remove the shares you created and the documents. Go on to answer the review questions.

Review Questions.

1. Which method provides the most detailed control over share permissions: Windows Vista Public folder sharing or standard sharing? _____

2. What is the maximum number of simultaneous connections to a peer-to-peer share? _____

3. What two items are used in the UNC path to identify the network share? _____

4. Does the Create A Shared Folder Wizard automatically configure Windows Firewall to allow the share to be accessed by other computers? _____

5. Complete the following sentence: Read-only is an example of a share _____

6. What are the four kinds of shared folder permissions available in the Create A Shared Folder Wizard? _____

_____

_____

_____

_____

Copyright by Goodheart-Willcox Co., Inc.

Name _____ Date _____

Class/Instructor _____

Creating a Network Share in Windows XP

After completing this laboratory activity, you will be able to:

- Create a share on a peer-to-peer network.
- Identify the types of security associated with a peer-to-peer network.
- Enable and disable Simple File Sharing.
- Explain the effects of Simple File Sharing on the share permissions.

Introduction

Sharing files and hardware is the main purpose of a network. In this lab activity, you will set up a network share. You will share a folder with another person in your lab. You will set up a share for a variety of items such as the hard disk drive, CD/DVD drive, and a folder. You will also modify share permissions.

There are two main types of share security commonly used in network systems: share-level and user-level. Share-level security is commonly associated with peer-to-peer networks, while user-level security is associated with centrally administered networks that typically use a centralized network server. A user-level share account is configured by the domain network administrator. A share-level account is administrated by the owner/creator of the share on the local computer.

To see what folders are shared on your computer, you can use the Computer Management console. To open **Computer Management**, right-click **My Computer**, and then select **Manage** from the shortcut menu.

In this lab activity, you will be creating shared folders, files, and devices. Please be sure you return the system to its original configuration before ending this lab activity. This is especially true if other students use the assigned workstation.

Note:

This is a two-workstation lab activity.

Equipment and Materials

- Two PCs each running Windows XP and configured as a peer-to-peer network.

Note:

For the lab activity to work properly, the partition should be formatted as NTFS, not FAT32.

Copyright by Goodheart-Willcox Co., Inc.

Procedure

1. ____ Report to your assigned workstation(s) and power on the PC(s).

2. ____ Open **Windows Explorer** and create a folder named "ShareTestFolder."

3. ____ Right-click ShareTestFolder and then select **Sharing and Security** from the shortcut menu. The **Properties** dialog box for that folder will display and will be open to the **Sharing** page like the following:

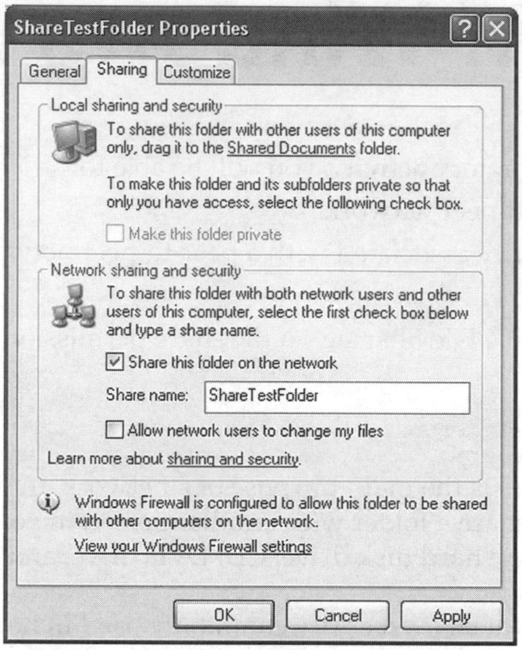

4. ____ Enable the **Share this folder on the network** option, which is located in the **Network sharing and security** section. The default name for the share will be the name already assigned to the folder. Click **Apply**. The folder is now configured as a share on the local network.

5. ____ Open **Computer Management** to view all shares available on the workstation. To open **Computer Management**, right-click **My Computer**, and then select **Manage** from the shortcut menu. In the left-hand pane, click **Shared Folders** and then click **Shares**. The shares on the computer will appear, similar to those in the following screen capture.

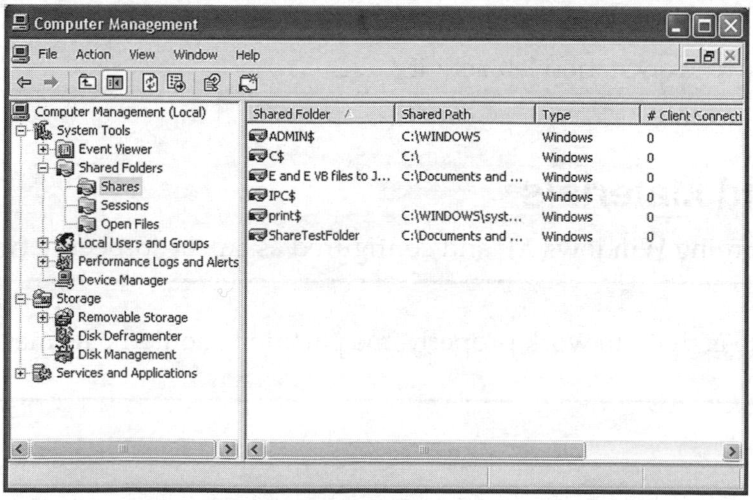

Copyright by Goodheart-Willcox Co., Inc.

Name _____

Notice that all administrative shares have a dollar sign in the folder name. User shares do not have the dollar sign. You should see the folder called ShareTestFolder at the bottom of the list. If not, call your instructor for assistance.

6. ____ Close **Computer Management**.

7. ____ To enable the Simple File Sharing feature, open **My Documents**, select **Tools** from the menu, and then select **Folder Options**. The **Folder Options** dialog box will display. Select the **View** tab. A dialog box similar to the following will display.

Scroll down the list until you see the **Use simple file sharing (Recommended)** option. If you do not find this option, call your instructor for assistance.

8. ____ You will now experiment with the effects of the Simple File Sharing feature on the shared folder you created earlier. Take time now to enable and disable Simple File Sharing. Compare the effects that enabling and disabling Simple File Sharing has on folder permissions. You should see that the complete set of permissions is not available for the folder when Simple File Sharing is enabled. When disabled, you should see options to various configurations of detailed permissions for the folder. Open **Computer Management** and see if you can access the share permissions when Simple File Sharing is enabled. You will be asked about viewing the permissions in the review questions.

9. ____ Before moving on, disable the Simple File Sharing feature.

10. ____ Now, you will create a shared CD/DVD drive. To create a shared CD/DVD drive in Windows XP, simply right-click the drive while in Windows Explorer. You will see a dialog box similar to the following.

Select the **Share this folder** option. The share always has a default name of the existing drive. You can rename the drive or folder when shared. Also, you can control the number of users who can access the share. The maximum number of users is 10 by default. Go ahead and create the shared CD or DVD drive by clicking the **Apply** button.

11. ____ After sharing the CD/DVD drive, open **Windows Explorer** and view the appearance of the drive. Test the access of the drive from the other computer. If you cannot access the shared drive from the other computer, call your instructor for assistance.

12. ____ Now, unshare the CD/DVD by repeating the previous steps. Start by right-clicking the shared CD/DVD drive, and then unselecting the **Do not share this folder** option.

13. ____ Repeat the file sharing exercise for folders and devices until you are sure you can create and disable a share without the assistance of this lab activity sheet.

14. ____ Now, create a shared folder and place a file, such as a short text document, inside the shared folder. You can use Microsoft Word or Notepad to create the document.

Copyright by Goodheart-Willcox Co., Inc.

15. ____ Right-click the folder and look at the available properties and permissions for the folder. The permissions are located under the **Security** tab in the **Properties** dialog box. Look at the following screen captures.

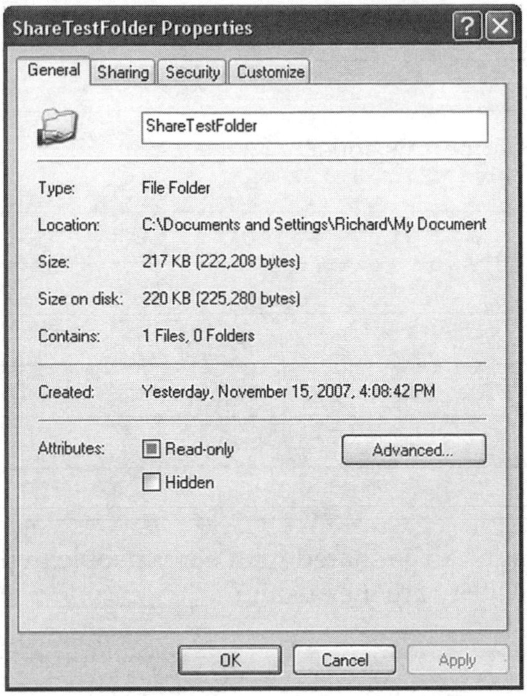

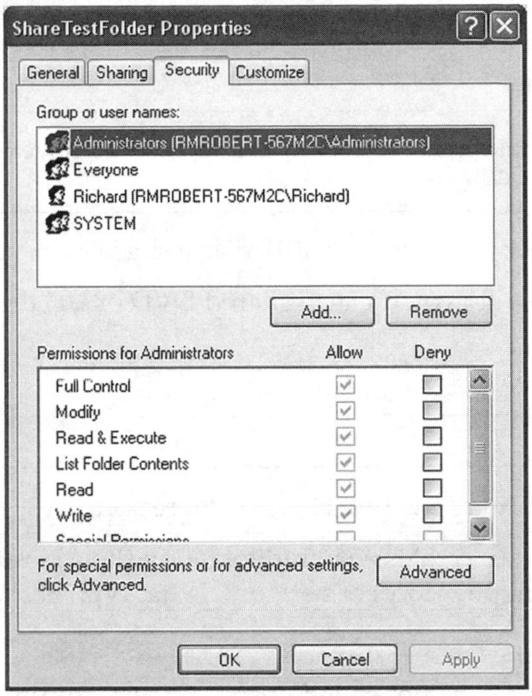

Notice that the folder's **Properties** dialog box provides access to set up a share for the folder and to security features, such as who can access the folder and what permissions are configured for that particular user.

The folder **Security** tab exposes various permissions available for the folder. You can also add or delete users or groups to keep them from accessing the share.

16. ____ Now, right-click the document file inside the folder and view the permissions available to be used with the file. The permissions are located under the **Security** tab.

17. ____ Take a few minutes to repeat the above steps and familiarize yourself with the many different permissions.

18. ____ Be sure to return all shares and folder permissions to their previous condition before completing the lab activity review questions.

Review Questions

1. How do you create a shared folder in Windows XP? _____
_____
_____
_____

2. What effect does Simple File Sharing have on folder permissions? _____
_____

3. How is a folder identified as a share in Windows XP? _____

4. How do you create a shared DVD or CD drive? _____
_____
_____
_____

5. What are the two types of share security? _____

6. A user creates a shared folder on their local computer to be shared with other people in the local peer-to-peer network. What type of share security are they using? _____
_____

7. Who is responsible for creating and administrating user-level security for shares?
_____

8. How do you access Computer Management to view the shares available on a computer?
_____

9. You use Computer Management to view the shares on a local computer; however, you cannot view a shared folder's permissions. What is *most likely* the problem? _____
_____
_____

Copyright by Goodheart-Willcox Co., Inc.

Name _____ Date _____

Class/Instructor _____

Windows XP Network Diagnostics

After completing this laboratory activity, you will be able to:

■ Activate the Windows XP Network Diagnostics utility.

■ Modify the Network Diagnostics scan features.

■ Save the results of a system scan to a file for later reference while troubleshooting.

Introduction

With the introduction of Windows XP came a powerful troubleshooting network diagnostic utility called Network Diagnostics. This lab activity will familiarize you with the various features of Network Diagnostics. Network Diagnostics combines many individual troubleshooting and informational tools into one convenient utility. The utility is designed to check network connectivity, common network services, and network-related programs. Look at the following screen capture.

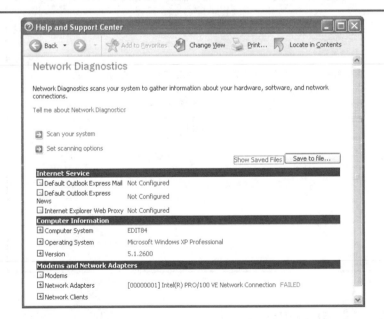

Three major categories of diagnostics are performed: Internet Service, Computer Information, Modems and Network Adapters. At the top-left corner of the window, you see two options: **Scan your system** and **Set scanning options**. As the name implies, when you select **Scan your system**, a system scan is performed. This scan checks all options selected in the three major categories. After the scan is completed, information is displayed immediately to the right of the diagnostic topic. An error is indicated by the word *FAILED* displayed to the right of the tested feature.

Each area with a plus sign in the check box can be further expanded to reveal detailed information. See the following screen capture.

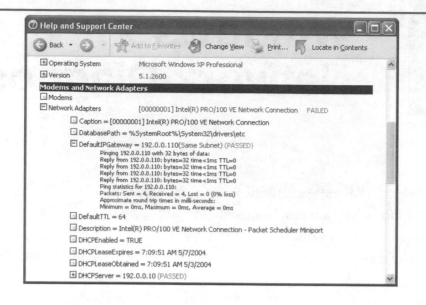

Scanning options can be readily modified as indicated in the following screen capture. You simply select the items you want scanned or clear the items you don't want scanned. The more features selected, the longer the scan will take.

Equipment and Materials

■ Typical PC with a connection to a client/server or peer-to-peer network. Windows XP operating system must be installed.

Note:

A network connection is not essential, but having one will better demonstrate the utility's features.

Copyright by Goodheart-Willcox Co., Inc.

Procedure

1. _____ Report to your assigned workstation and boot the computer. Make sure the computer is in working order.

2. _____ Click **Run** in the **Start** menu, and type **msinfo32** in the **Open** text box. The System Information screen will display.

3. _____ From the **Tools** menu, select **Net Diagnostics**.

---

4. _____ Select the **Scan your system** option to run a diagnostic test of the network system. You can run this test even if the computer is not connected to a network.

5. _____ Look at the results and expand any area containing more information. These areas are noted by the plus sign inside the box to the left of the service or device. When expanded, a detailed report is typically revealed.

6. _____ Now select **Set scanning options**. Look at how the various options are revealed. Select or clear any of the listed options. After changing the scanning options, run the scan once more. Take special note of the **Save Options** button. This button is used to save the modified selection of items to scan. Failure to select this button will cause the scan to apply the default selections, not the newly-made selections.

7. _____ Save your options and run the scan once more. Take special note of the **Save to file** button. Clicking this button saves to a file the results of the scan. The saved file can be referenced at a later date for troubleshooting references.

8. _____ Click the **Save to file** button to save the results of your scan.

9. _____ After the file is saved, select the **Show Saved Files** option. The scan results are saved as an HTML file and are viewable with Internet Explorer.

10. _____ Leave the Network Diagnostics utility open and go on to answer the review questions. You will need to refer to the utility while answering the questions in the review.

11. _____ After answering all the questions to the best of your ability, close all programs and shut down the computer.

Review Questions

1. What are the three major categories that are tested by the Network Diagnostics utility?

   _____

   _____

   _____

2. Can network connections be tested? _____

3. Can a DNS service be verified? _____

4. Can a DHCP service be verified? _____

5. Can a WINS service be verified? _____

6. Can the Media Access Control (MAC) address be determined? _____

7. Can the assigned IP address be determined? _____

8. Can you access the Network Diagnostic utility when the computer is booted in safe mode?

   _____

9. Can you save the results of a system scan? _____

10. What type of file is created when the scan results are saved? _____

Copyright by Goodheart-Willcox Co., Inc.

Name _____ Date _____

Class/Instructor _____

Service Management

After completing this laboratory activity, you will be able to:

- Explain the role of system services.
- Locate and view the services running on a computer system.
- Start, stop, pause, and restart services.
- Configure service startup options.
- Configure services recovery actions.
- Examine service dependencies.

Introduction

In this laboratory activity, you will become familiar with how to view, start, and stop services on a Windows XP and Windows Vista workstation. A service is a special program that enhances the function of the operating system. The kernel is the heart of the operating system. Additional programs, often referred to as services, extend the capability of the kernel. Some services are required to run to support other services. Normally, the required services are started when you configure a workstation using a wizard.

Not all services are loaded when the operating system is started. As the system state changes, services are loaded into RAM and are run automatically. The more services that become incorporated into an operating system, the more RAM the system requires or performance will slow. As RAM space is consumed, some of the services are switched out of RAM to allocated space on the hard drive. When hard drive space is used for programs running in the background, the entire system slows drastically. Transferring the service to and from the hard disk and RAM requires substantially more time then if the service resided entirely in RAM.

Technicians will be required to inspect the state of a service to determine if it is running or not. They may also be required to stop and then restart a service as a recommended solution to a problem suggested by a vendor. This is especially true on mission critical servers or computers that must remain running if possible.

Copyright by Goodheart-Willcox Co., Inc.

The following screen captures show the Windows XP and Windows Vista **Computer Management** screen with **Services** (Service snap-in) selected.

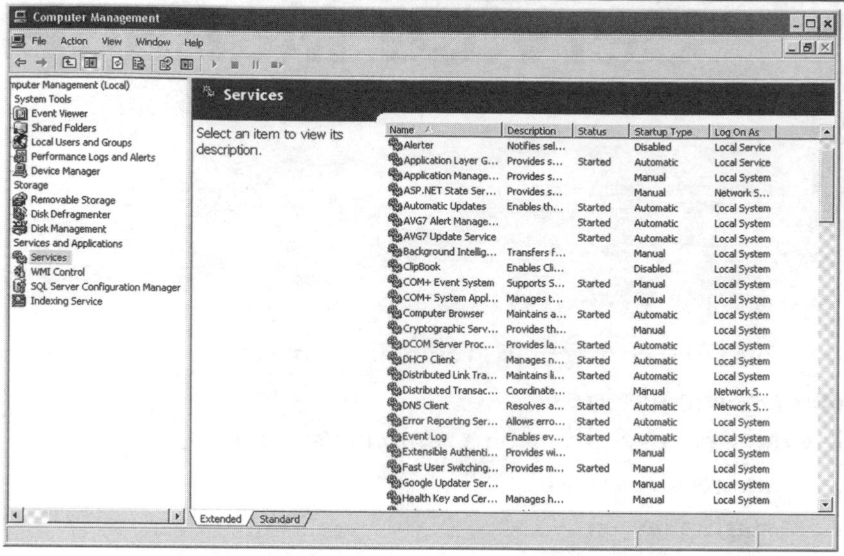

Windows XP

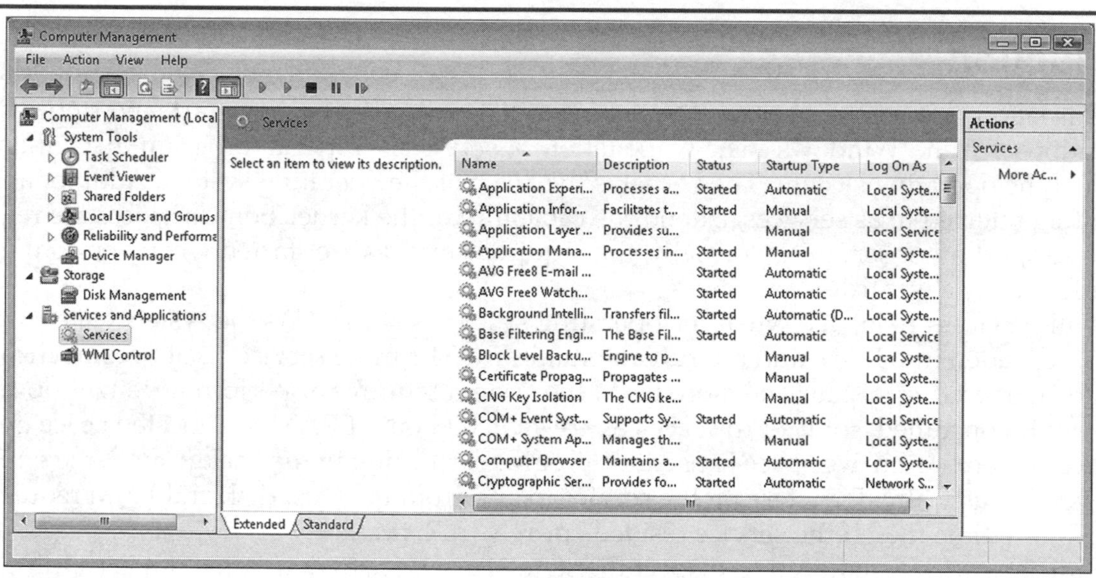

Windows Vista

Notice that in Windows XP, a list of services associated with the operating system are shown in the right pane and in Windows Vista they are shown in the center pane. In the first column, **Name**, the name of the specific service is listed. In the second column, **Description**, a short description of the service is provided. This is very handy for identifying what the service is used for. The third column, **Status**, indicates if the service has been started. The fourth column, **Startup Type**, indicates if the service must be manually started or automatically started when the system boots. The fifth column, **Log On As**, indicates if the service is run locally or requires a network logon connection.

Copyright by Goodheart-Willcox Co., Inc.

You can view more detailed information about each individual service simply by double-clicking a particular service. Doing so displays a dialog box similar to the following.

Windows XP

Windows Vista

In the screen captures, the **DHCP Client Properties (Local Computer)** dialog box is displayed. The actual name displayed for the dialog box of a service may be different. In this example, you can see a much more descriptive name of the service.

There are dozens of services and applications available in Windows that can be monitored, started, and stopped. Some of the services available are HTTP Web service, File Transfer Protocol (FTP), Internet Connection Sharing (ICS), Remote Access, Security Logon, and Remote Desktop. There are too many services available to name them all, but you will view them shortly.

Dependencies are related services and software applications that can be affected by the service. Many services are dependent on one another, and stopping a service can have an adverse effect on another service or program.

It is not necessary for you to memorize all the features related to services. Simply be aware of the features so that you can sufficiently perform the duties associated with an entry-level technician. The Services snap-in generally requires very little attention. You will need to access the Services snap-in occasionally to perform troubleshooting tasks. Do not be intimidated at this time by the list of services.

Copyright by Goodheart-Willcox Co., Inc.

Equipment and Materials

■ Computer with Windows XP, Windows Vista, or both, installed.

Part I—Windows XP

Procedure

1. ____ Report to your assigned workstation.

2. ____ Boot the computer and verify it is in working order.

3. ____ Open Computer Management.

4. ____ Expand the **Services and Applications** directory if needed to reveal **Services**. Then select **Services** to reveal the list of services.

5. ____ Look at the bottom of the Computer Management console at the two tabs labeled **Extended** and **Standard**. Click each several times and observe the changes in the way the information is displayed. Click an individual service once while in extended mode. Information about the service will be displayed.

6. ____ While in the extended mode, select the **Help and Support** service listed in the first column. A short description will appear, providing information about the Help and Support service. Write the description in the space provided. _____

    _____

    _____

7. ____ What startup type is associated with the Help and Support service? _____

    _____

8. ____ Double-click the **Help and Support** service to open the related dialog box. What is the service name of the Help and Support service? _____

    _____

9. ____ Stop the **Help and Support** service and watch closely to see what happens. You should see a small message box indicating the service is being stopped.

10. ____ Now, start the service using the button labeled **Start** and observe the action.

11. ____ Practice stopping and starting this particular service a few times. When you are done practicing, leave the service in the running mode.

12. ____ Click the tab labeled **Log On**. Notice that a dialog box can be used to require a user to log on to this service. Do *not* change any settings in this dialog box; simply study it for a minute.

13. ____ Double-click the **Help and Support** service to open the **Help and Support Properties (Local Computer)** dialog box. Then, click the **Recovery** tab. This is where the actions can be modified as to what to do when the service fails. View the items in the **First failure** list box. Do *not* make any changes; simply observe.

14. ____ Click the **Dependencies** tab and observe the service dependencies listed.

15. ____ Close the **Help and Support Properties (Local Computer)** dialog box by clicking **Cancel**.

Copyright by Goodheart-Willcox Co., Inc.

16. _____ In the following procedures, you will be asked specific questions about services on your computer. Answer all questions to the best of your ability. If the service is not installed, skip that particular question. Do not change any of the service settings or configuration. Use the **Cancel** button to exit the dialog box.

17. _____ Double-click the **Event Log** service and select the **Recovery** tab. What is revealed?

_____

_____

18. _____ Double-click the **Smart Card** service and write the service name in the space provided.

_____

19. _____ What other services does the Smart Card service depend on? _____

_____

20. _____ Double-click the **Remote Access Connection Manager** service and list the service dependencies in the space provided. Be sure you select **Remote Access Connection Manager**. There are other services listed with very similar names. _____

_____

_____

_____

21. _____ Now, double-click **Logical Disk Manager** and record the service dependencies._____

_____

22. _____ Right-click the **DNS** service and observe the shortcut menu. Be sure to right-click the service, not double-click. Notice the various options such as **Start, Stop, Pause, Resume,** and **Restart**. The same options are located under the **Action** menu. Look at the **Action** menu now.

23. _____ Close **Services** and **Computer Management**.

24. _____ Answer the review questions and then return the computer workstation to its original condition.

Part II—Windows Vista

Procedure

1. _____ Report to your assigned workstation.

2. _____ Boot the computer and verify it is in working order.

3. _____ After the Windows desktop appears, open **Computer Management**.

4. _____ Expand the **Services and Applications** directory if needed to reveal the **Services** choice. Then select **Services** to reveal the list of services.

5. _____ Look at the bottom of the Computer Management console at the two tabs labeled **Extended** and **Standard**. Click each several times and observe the changes in the way the information is displayed. Click an individual service once while in the extended mode. Information about the service will be displayed.

6. ____ While in the extended mode, select the **DCHP Client** service. A short description will appear in the **Description** column, providing information about the DCHP service. Write the description in the space provided. _____

_____

_____

_____

_____

7. ____ Stop **DCHP Client** service and watch closely to see what happens. You should see a small message box indicating the service is being stopped.

8. ____ Now, start the service and observe the action.

9. ____ Practice stopping and starting this particular service a few times. When you are done practicing, leave the service in the running mode.

10. ____ Double-click the **DCHP Client** service. The **DCHP Client** Properties (Local Computer) dialog box will display. Then, select the **Log On** tab. Notice that a dialog box can be used to require a user to log on to this service. Do *not* change any settings in this dialog box; simply study it for a minute.

11. ____ Click the **Recovery** tab. This is where the actions can be modified as to what to do when the service fails. View the items in the **First failure** list box. Do *not* make any changes, simply observe.

12. ____ Click the **Dependencies** tab and observe the service dependencies if any are listed.

13. ____ Close the **DHCP Client Properties** dialog box by clicking **Cancel**.

14. ____ Close **Services** and **Computer Management**.

15. ____ Answer the review questions and then return the computer workstation to its original condition.

Review Questions

1. How do you access **Services** snap-in from the **Start** menu? _____

_____

2. How do you start a service? _____

_____

3. Are all services dependent or independent of other services? _____

_____

4. When would a computer technician be required to access the **Services** snap-in? _____

_____

Copyright by Goodheart-Willcox Co., Inc.

Laboratory Activity 77

Name _____ Date _____

Class/Instructor _____

IP Address Verification with IPCONFIG

After completing this laboratory activity, you will be able to:
- Inspect the assigned IP address of a workstation using the **ipconfig** command.
- Explain the purpose of a DHCP server.
- Explain the purpose of APIPA.

Introduction

One of the most commonly used utilities for diagnosing a network problem is ipconfig. Ipconfig is run from the command prompt in Windows 2000, XP, and Vista. It is not supported by Windows Me or Windows 98. When the **ipconfig** command is run, you should see the DNS server connection name, assigned IP address, subnet mask, and default gateway address.

When run with the **/all** switch, you should see additional information such as the host name, MAC or physical address, if Dynamic Host Configuration Protocol (DHCP) is enabled, the default gateway address, the address DHCP server address, and the DNS server. You will also see a lease period if the IP address has been issued dynamically.

An IP address can be configured statically or dynamically. *Statically* means that the IP address is assigned to the computer manually. *Dynamically* means that the computer is issued an IP address automatically by a DHCP server. The Windows XP and Windows Vista operating system is configured by default to receive a dynamic IP address from a DHCP server. A computer must have an IP address to be able to communicate on a network, even on a small local peer-to-peer network. If the DHCP server is not available, the computer is issued an Automatic Private IP Address (APIPA) so that the computer can still communicate with other computers in the network. The computer will generate its own APIPA in the range from 168.254.0.1 to 169.254.255.254 and a subnet mask of 255.255.000.000. If you see an IP address that starts with 169.254, you will know the computer has a problem obtaining an IP address from the DHCP server.

Copyright by Goodheart-Willcox Co., Inc.

The operating system will request an IP address from the DHCP server every few minutes. If the problem with the DHCP server is fixed, the Automatic Private IP Address will be dropped and an IP address will once again be issued from the DHCP server. Look at the following screen capture to see the results of the **ipconfig** command and then of the **ipconfig/all** command.

```
Command Prompt                                                         _ □ ×

Microsoft Windows XP [Version 5.1.2600]
(C) Copyright 1985-2001 Microsoft Corp.

C:\Documents and Settings\Richard>ipconfig

Windows IP Configuration


Ethernet adapter Local Area Connection 2:

        Connection-specific DNS Suffix  . : hsd1.fl.comcast.net.
        IP Address. . . . . . . . . . . . : 192.168.0.102
        Subnet Mask . . . . . . . . . . . : 255.255.255.0
        Default Gateway . . . . . . . . . : 192.168.0.1

C:\Documents and Settings\Richard>ipconfig/all

Windows IP Configuration

        Host Name . . . . . . . . . . . . : rmrobert-567m2c
        Primary Dns Suffix  . . . . . . . :
        Node Type . . . . . . . . . . . . : Unknown
        IP Routing Enabled. . . . . . . . : No
        WINS Proxy Enabled. . . . . . . . : No
        DNS Suffix Search List. . . . . . : hsd1.fl.comcast.net.

Ethernet adapter Local Area Connection 2:

        Connection-specific DNS Suffix  . : hsd1.fl.comcast.net.
        Description . . . . . . . . . . . : NVIDIA nForce Networking Controller
        Physical Address. . . . . . . . . : 00-13-D4-D2-39-8E
        Dhcp Enabled. . . . . . . . . . . : Yes
        Autoconfiguration Enabled . . . . : Yes
        IP Address. . . . . . . . . . . . : 192.168.0.102
        Subnet Mask . . . . . . . . . . . : 255.255.255.0
        Default Gateway . . . . . . . . . : 192.168.0.1
        DHCP Server . . . . . . . . . . . : 192.168.0.1
        DNS Servers . . . . . . . . . . . : 192.168.0.1
        Lease Obtained. . . . . . . . . . : Friday, November 16, 2007 1:14:10 PM

        Lease Expires . . . . . . . . . . : Friday, November 23, 2007 1:14:10 PM

C:\Documents and Settings\Richard>
```

The information in the response of **ipconfig** or **ipconfig/all** will verify the assigned IP address and help you troubleshoot the network problem. The following are some switches commonly used that you should be aware of.

- **ipconfig/release:** Removes the IP address and displays 0.0.0.0 for the IP address.
- **ipconfig/renew:** Issues a new DHCP IP address. It may be the same as the last IP address used by the computer.

Equipment and Materials

- A workstation running Windows 2000, XP, or Vista. (You cannot use Windows 95, 98, or Me for this lab activity.)

Copyright by Goodheart-Willcox Co., Inc.

Procedure

1. ____ Report to your assigned workstation.

2. ____ Boot the computer and verify it is in working order.

3. ____ Access the command prompt and issue the **ipconfig** command.

4. ____ In the space provided, record the assigned IP address, the subnet mask, and the default gateway address.

    IP address: _____

    Subnet mask: _____

    Gateway address: _____

5. ____ Now, issue the **ipconfig/all** command.

6. ____ In the space provided, record the MAC address (physical address), the host name, whether or not the DHCP enabled, the DHCP server IP address, and the lease period.

    MAC address: _____

    Host name: _____

    DHCP enable: Yes ____ or No ____

    DHCP server address: _____

    Lease period: _____

7. ____ Disconnect the network cable and record the message that appears on the screen after running **ipconfig**.

    _____

    _____

    _____

8. ____ Reconnect the network cable and run **ipconfig**. You should see the original IP address listed. If not, check the network cable connector to see that it is properly installed. If you cannot obtain an IP address, call your instructor for assistance.

9. ____ Now, use the **ipconfig/release** command and record the results for the IP address, the subnet mask, and the default gateway address.

    IP address: _____

    Subnet mask: _____

    Gateway address: _____

10. ____ Issue the **ipconfig/renew** command and record the results for the IP address, subnet mask, and default gateway address.

    IP address: _____

    Subnet mask: _____

    Gateway address: _____

11. ____ Now issue the **ipconfig/?** command and review the other available switches.

12. ____ Return the computer to its original configuration and then answer the review questions.

Copyright by Goodheart-Willcox Co., Inc.

Review Questions

1. Which operating systems support the **ipconfig** command? _____

   _____

2. What does the acronym APIPA represent? _____

3. What does the acronym DHCP represent? _____

4. What two ways are IP addresses normally issued to a computer? _____

   _____

5. What is the purpose of a DHCP server? _____

   _____

   _____

6. What IP address will a computer have after issuing the **ipconfig/release** command? _____

   _____

7. What is the range of APIPA IP addresses? _____

8. What message appeared when you ran the **ipconfig** command with the network cable
   disconnected? _____

   _____

9. What does it mean when you see an IP address of 169.254.1.122 assigned to an adapter that is
   configured for DHCP? _____

   _____

   _____

Copyright by Goodheart-Willcox Co., Inc.

Name _____ Date _____

Class/Instructor _____

PING

After completing this laboratory activity, you will be able to:

- Use the **ping** command to verify a network connection.
- Use the **ping** command to verify that the NIC is operating properly.
- Be familiar with the various **ping** command switches.

Introduction

The ping utility is a basic network-troubleshooting tool that verifies a connection between the PC and a remote location. The ping utility is run from the command prompt. It sends out a data packet to a remote location. The remote location sends a return reply if a connection can be established.

Several switches associated with ping are important. Switches added to the **ping** command determine the size of the packet sent, how many times the packet is sent, how long the packet is allowed to circulate on the Internet or network, and whether addresses are resolved to host names.

The time-to-live, or TTL, switch (**-i**) indicates how long the packet will be allowed to travel on the Internet before it is discarded. Without a TTL, the packet would theoretically circulate endlessly. As more and more **ping** commands are issued, the Internet would eventually be slowed to a crawl because of all the endless **ping** command data packets circulating.

Two of the commands you will most frequently issue are **ping 127.0.0.1** and **ping localhost**. These commands are quick and easy tests for the network card. They ensure that the basic setup is correct, but do not guarantee that the NIC will work correctly as part of the network.

Several new switches are available when using the Windows Vista **ping** command. The newest switches were designed to be used with the IPv6 protocol. By default, the **ping** command uses the IPv4 version to carry the **ping** command test packets. Several of the **ping** command switches are designed to work exclusively with IPv4. You can view all of the **ping** switch commands by issuing **ping/?** or **ping/help** from the command prompt. You can force the **ping** command to use only IPv4 or IPv6 packets by using the corresponding switch. For example, ping **192.168.0.1 -4** for IPv4 and ping **192.168.0.1 -6** for IPv6.

If you ping a Windows Vista computer from another Windows Vista computer by name in a peer-to-peer configuration, the reply will be in the IPv6 format such as fe80::c09:3ce8:3f57:3f3a. The format does not matter because all you really want to do is determine that there is a complete path between the local computer and the remote device, such as a computer, server, router, or gateway.

Equipment and Materials

■ PC with Internet access or, at the very least, a small peer-to-peer network set up in a lab.

> **Note:**
> Some network firewalls and some switches, routers, and gateways will prevent the **ping** command from working correctly.

Procedure

1. ____ Report to your assigned workstation.

2. ____ Boot the computer and verify it is in working order. Do not connect to the Internet at this time.

3. ____ Go to the DOS prompt and use Help to identify the switches used with the **ping** command. Help can be accessed from the command prompt by typing **ping/?** or **ping/help**.

4. ____ At the command prompt, type **ping 127.0.0.1** and note the response. The command **ping 127.0.0.1** is used to verify that the NIC is working properly.

5. ____ Now, enter the command **ping localhost** and note the response. Practice the two forms of **ping** commands and compare the results. In the space provided, write the information that is included when the **ping localhost** command is issued, but not included when the **ping 127.0.0.1** command is issued. _____

_____

_____

6. ____ Now attempt to ping a name of a Web site. The instructor can supply you with the name of a Web site to use. *Do not connect to the Internet yet.* You will need to go to the DOS prompt to issue the **ping** command.

7. ____ What is the message received after the **ping** command was sent? _____

_____

> **Note:**
> Some models of PC with updated versions of software will automatically connect to the Internet when the **ping** command is issued.

Copyright by Goodheart-Willcox Co., Inc.

8. ____ Now, connect to the Internet and once again ping the chosen site. What response did you get? Write it below. A typical response would be similar to the following:

Reply from 127.103.010.12: bytes = 32 time<10ms TTL=128

Reply from 127.103.010.12: bytes = 32 time<10ms TTL=128

Reply from 127.103.010.12: bytes = 32 time<10ms TTL=128

Reply from 127.103.010.12: bytes = 32 time<10ms TTL=128

Ping statistics for 127.103.010.12:

Packets: Sent = 4, Received = 4, Lost = 0 (0% loss).

Approximate round trip times in milliseconds:

Minimum = 10ms, Maximum = 10ms, Average = 10ms

_____

_____

_____

_____

_____

_____

_____

_____

9. ____ Try to ping several other sites and compare the statistics. You do not need to write them down. Why do you think that there are differences in the reply from the sites? Hint: think about the way the network is designed and what happens when other users attempt to access the same site._____

_____

_____

10. ____ Go on to answer the review questions. Use the **ping/?** or **ping/help** commands to answer the questions. When you have finished, properly shut down the computer.

Review Questions

1. How can the size of the data packet sent be increased? _____
   _____

2. What do the letters TTL mean? _____

3. What does the packet's TTL determine? _____
   _____

4. How can the TTL be increased? _____
   _____

5. How can the **ping** command be used when troubleshooting a network? _____
   _____

6. What message is generated if the **ping** command does not receive a reply? _____
   _____
   _____

7. Which protocol version is used by default for the Windows XP **ping** command, IPv4 or IPv6?
   _____

8. How can you modify the **ping** command to use only IPv4 or IPv6 packets when testing a connection? _____
   _____
   _____

Copyright by Goodheart-Willcox Co., Inc.

Name _____ Date _____

Class/Instructor _____

TRACERT

After completing this laboratory activity, you will be able to:

■ Determine the route taken by a packet.

■ Explain how the tracert utility can be used to verify network connection paths across multiple devices such as routers and gateways.

Introduction

A very handy TCP/IP utility is tracert, which is a contraction of the two words *trace* and *route*. The tracert utility reveals more than the simple ping. The **tracert** command can be issued with the target's IP address or URL name. In the screen capture shown, a **tracert** command is issued from the command prompt. Yahoo.com is the target of the trace. The IP address, if it is known, can also be used to trace the route.

```
C:\DOCUME~1\JKELTNER>tracert yahoo.com

Tracing route to yahoo.com [206.190.60.37]
over a maximum of 30 hops:

  1    <1 ms   <1 ms    2 ms  172.18.5.1
  2     3 ms    2 ms    4 ms  64-7-105-37.urbancom.net [64.7.105.37]
  3     6 ms    4 ms    4 ms  64-7-96-38.urbancom.net [64.7.96.38]
  4     5 ms    4 ms    5 ms  fa0-19.na01.b006532-1.ord01.atlas.cogentco.com [38.104.99.113]
  5     6 ms    5 ms    7 ms  gi0-7.3519.core01.ord01.atlas.cogentco.com [66.250.8.217]
  6    15 ms     *      8 ms  te7-2.mpd01.ord01.atlas.cogentco.com [154.54.1.98]
  7    20 ms   17 ms   16 ms  te8-1.mpd01.mci01.atlas.cogentco.com [66.28.4.185]
  8    26 ms   28 ms   28 ms  te9-4.mpd01.dfw01.atlas.cogentco.com [154.54.5.125]
  9    30 ms   29 ms   28 ms  te8-3.mpd01.dfw03.atlas.cogentco.com [66.28.4.174]
 10    30 ms   29 ms   30 ms  yahoo.dfw03.atlas.cogentco.com [154.54.10.6]
 11    48 ms   51 ms   47 ms  so-1-0-0.pat2.dcw.yahoo.com [216.115.96.20]
 12    47 ms   50 ms   50 ms  ae2-p141.msr1.re1.yahoo.com [216.115.108.59]
 13    52 ms   50 ms   48 ms  ge-9-3.bas-a2.re4.yahoo.com [216.39.49.7]
 14    48 ms   49 ms   47 ms  w2.rc.vip.re4.yahoo.com [206.190.60.37]

Trace complete.

C:\DOCUME~1\JKELTNER>_
```

The path taken by the data and IP address of the destination are displayed. The amount of time to complete each hop is indicated in milliseconds. The IP address of each network or router along the way is also displayed. The default setting for the tracert utility is 30 hops. A hop is an intermediate connection along the path taken by the tracert packet. Routers are an example of a hop as are the Internet service provider and the final destination. Each hop along the route sends a packet back to the source identifying itself to the source.

This is a handy tool when troubleshooting a large enterprise network. It will verify the route from a PC through the network routers and on through the gateway or firewall. You can quickly determine if the network problem exists on the local network system or in the public system.

The Windows Vista version of tracert introduced several new switches to accommodate IPv6. Until IPv6 Internet communication completely replaces IPv4, IPv6 commands will be limited to only local area networks that exclusively use the IPv6 protocol.

Copyright by Goodheart-Willcox Co., Inc.

Equipment and Materials

■ PC with Windows Vista. (You can use a Windows XP operating system, but you will not see any of the IPv6 switches.)

■ List of Internet addresses to use with the **tracert** command. (Write the addresses provided by your instructor in the following spaces.)

_____

_____

_____

_____

_____

Note:

   Some network firewalls, routers, and gateways will prevent the tracert utility from working correctly.

Procedure

1. ____ Report to your assigned workstation.

2. ____ Boot the computer and verify it is in working order.

3. ____ Test the Internet connection by connecting to any host on the Internet.

4. ____ Access the command prompt and trace the routes to the addresses provided by the instructor. To run the tracert utility from the command prompt, type **tracert** followed by the target address and press [Enter].

5. ____ Take the assigned IP address of another PC station in the lab and attempt to trace the route to the other PC station. Record the final destination IP addresses for each destination.

_____

_____

_____

6. ____ Try using the IP address instead of the URL of the target to trace a route with the tracert utility. Observe the results.

7. ____ Take a few minutes to look at the various switches available for the **tracert** command by using the **/?** or **/help** switch. Simply enter **tracert /?** at the command prompt, and all the various switches will appear on the screen. You will see the IPv6 switches when using a Windows Vista system.

8. ____ Shut down the computer after completing the review questions.

Copyright by Goodheart-Willcox Co., Inc.

Review Questions

1. How can the tracert utility help in a troubleshooting situation? _____

    _____

2. What is the default number of maximum hops? _____

3. What two forms of destination addresses can be used with the tracert utility? _____

    _____

4. How can you specify that the **tracert** command only use IPv6 packets? _____

    _____

Copyright by Goodheart-Willcox Co., Inc.

Copyright by Goodheart-Willcox Co., Inc.

Laboratory Activity

80

Name ______________________________ Date ______________

Class/Instructor ______________________________

PATHPING

Lab 80

WAN

After completing this laboratory activity, you will be able to:

- Use the **pathping** command to test a network route.
- Describe the various commonly used command switches associated with pathping.
- Compare and contrast ping, tracert, and pathping results.

Introduction

This laboratory activity will review the **ping** and **tracert** commands as well as introduce the **pathping** command. The **pathping** command is an enhancement of the combination **ping** and **tracert** commands. The **pathping** command first displays path information in a similar fashion as the **tracert** command but then does an analysis of each hop along the path by sending a series of **ping** commands and performing calculations to display statistics about packet loss at each hop. The statistics can be used to identify problem areas along the path from source to destination. You can identify device failure along the intended path or identify areas of high traffic, causing packet delays. The following screen capture shows the results of the **pathping** command issued to www.comcast.net.

```
Command Prompt
C:\Documents and Settings\Richard>pathping www.comcast.net

Tracing route to a1526.g.akamai.net [96.17.75.89]
over a maximum of 30 hops:
  0  rmrobert-567m2c.hsd1.fl.comcast.net. [192.168.0.101]
  1  73.17.116.1
  2  [illegible]
  3  te-3-2-sr01.arcadia.fl.westfl.comcast.net [68.87.238.105]
  4  te-9-4-ur01.portcharlott.fl.westfl.comcast.net [68.87.238.101]
  5  te-8-2-ur01.northport.fl.westfl.comcast.net [68.87.238.65]
  6  [illegible]
  7  te-8-1-ar01.venice.fl.westfl.comcast.net [68.87.238.13]
  8  te-9-3-ar01.sumter.fl.lakecnty.comcast.net [68.85.229.246]
  9  te-9-4-ar01.leesburg.fl.lakecnty.comcast.net [68.85.210.5]
 10  te-2-4-ar01.augusta.ga.augusta.comcast.net [68.85.229.242]
 11  te-7-1-ar02.northdade.fl.pompano.comcast.net [68.86.91.82]
 12     *      pos-0-7-0-0-cr01.miami.fl.ibone.comcast.net [68.86.85.194]
 13  pos-0-11-0-0-cr01.atlanta.ga.ibone.comcast.net [68.86.85.193]
 14  a96-17-75-89.deploy.akamaitechnologies.com [96.17.75.89]

Computing statistics for 350 seconds...
            Source to Here   This Node/Link
Hop  RTT    Lost/Sent = Pct  Lost/Sent = Pct  Address
  0                                           rmrobert-567m2c.hsd1.fl.comcast.ne
t. [192.168.0.101]
                                9/ 100 =  9%   |
  1    7ms     9/ 100 =  9%     0/ 100 =  0%  73.17.116.1
                                0/ 100 =  0%   |
  2    8ms     9/ 100 =  9%     0/ 100 =  0%  ge-2-2-sr01.sebring.fl.westfl.comc
ast.net [68.86.199.77]
                                0/ 100 =  0%   |
  3    9ms     9/ 100 =  9%     0/ 100 =  0%  te-3-2-sr01.arcadia.fl.westfl.comc
ast.net [68.87.238.105]
                                0/ 100 =  0%   |
  4    9ms     9/ 100 =  9%     0/ 100 =  0%  te-9-4-ur01.portcharlott.fl.westfl
.comcast.net [68.87.238.101]
                                0/ 100 =  0%   |
  5   10ms     9/ 100 =  9%     0/ 100 =  0%  te-8-2-ur01.northport.fl.westfl.co
mcast.net [68.87.238.65]
                                1/ 100 =  1%   |
  6   10ms    10/ 100 = 10%     0/ 100 =  0%  te-8-4-ar02.venice.fl.westfl.comca
st.net [68.87.238.25]
                                0/ 100 =  0%   |
  7   10ms    10/ 100 = 10%     0/ 100 =  0%  te-8-1-ar01.venice.fl.westfl.comca
st.net [68.87.238.13]
                                0/ 100 =  0%   |
  8   16ms    10/ 100 = 10%     0/ 100 =  0%  te-9-3-ar01.sumter.fl.lakecnty.com
cast.net [68.85.229.246]
                                0/ 100 =  0%   |
  9   17ms    10/ 100 = 10%     0/ 100 =  0%  te-9-4-ar01.leesburg.fl.lakecnty.c
omcast.net [68.85.210.5]
                                0/ 100 =  0%   |
 10   27ms    10/ 100 = 10%     0/ 100 =  0%  te-2-4-ar01.augusta.ga.augusta.com
cast.net [68.85.229.242]
                                0/ 100 =  0%   |
 11   50ms    10/ 100 = 10%     0/ 100 =  0%  te-7-1-ar02.northdade.fl.pompano.c
omcast.net [68.86.91.82]
                                0/ 100 =  0%   |
 12   51ms    10/ 100 = 10%     0/ 100 =  0%  pos-0-7-0-0-cr01.miami.fl.ibone.co
mcast.net [68.86.85.194]
                                0/ 100 =  0%   |
 13   65ms    10/ 100 = 10%     0/ 100 =  0%  pos-0-11-0-0-cr01.atlanta.ga.ibone
.comcast.net [68.86.85.193]
                                0/ 100 =  0%   |
 14   65ms    10/ 100 = 10%     0/ 100 =  0%  a96-17-75-89.deploy.akamaitechnolo
gies.com [96.17.75.89]

Trace complete.
```

Copyright by Goodheart-Willcox Co., Inc.

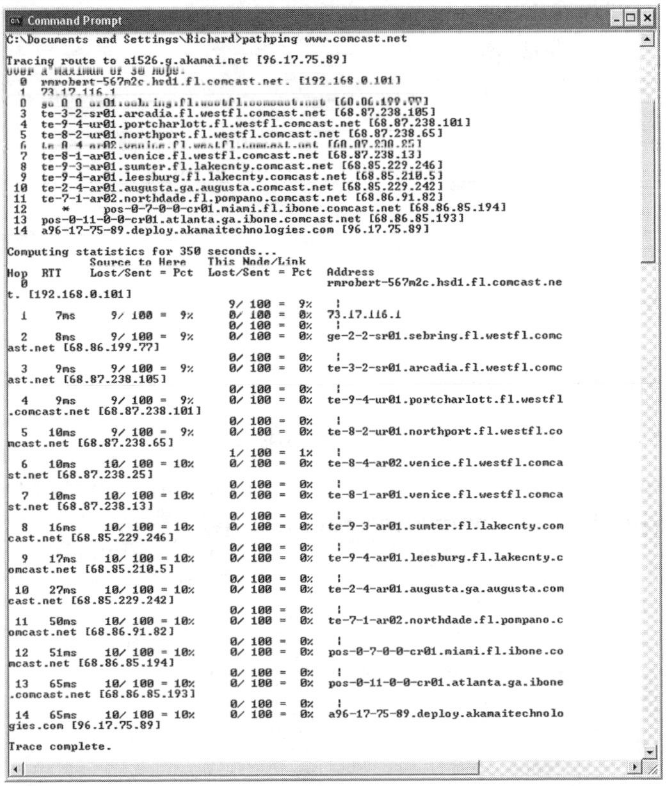

The immediate results in the top portion of the screen capture contain a list of the 14 hops, but it does not provide information about the amount of time to each hop. The information is not yet complete. As indicated in the screen capture, an additional 350 seconds (5–6 minutes) will be needed to perform additional echo requests so that a set of statistics about the route can be completed. The additional time is used to perform tests such as calculating packet loss, which indicates problems along the route.

The computer statistics for the **pathping** command indicate problem areas along the route. Packet loss is an indication of congestion, usually caused by excessive traffic on the network. Some routers in the result have various amounts of packet loss, which means that they are experiencing more traffic than they can handle. Also, be aware that many routers are programmed to reject ICMP packets. ICMP packets carry the basic commands such as **ping**, **tracert**, and **pathping**. These basic network commands are often viewed as network probing, and as a matter of security, have the echo return blocked by a firewall, router, or gateway. This also causes packet loss errors.

Commercial utilities are also available to perform detailed analysis of routes between source and destination points. One such product is called Ping Plotter and is available for free at the time of this writing. You can conduct an Internet search for Ping Plotter and then add a copy to your software tool kit.

Windows XP and Windows Vista have several switches intended for use with IPv6. Use the **pathping/?** command to view all available switches.

Note:
   A firewall, router, or gateway can be configured to block ICMP packets and may be a problem when using any of the TCP/IP utilities.

Equipment and Materials

■ PC with Windows XP or Windows Vista and Internet access. The commands are so similar, there is no need to run this lab on both operating systems.

■ Test sites provided by instructor:

_____

_____

_____

_____

_____

Procedure

1. ____ Report to your assigned workstation.

2. ____ Boot the computer and verify it is in working order.

3. ____ Access the command prompt and test the connection to one of the Internet sites using the **ping** command. For example, **ping www.comcast.net**.

Copyright by Goodheart-Willcox Co., Inc.

Name_____

4. ____ Now use the **tracert** command to view the hops from your workstation to the destination. For example, **tracert www.comcast.net**. Answer the following questions based on the result of the **tracert** command.

How many hops were encountered? _____

How were the hops identified, by IP address or name? _____

_____

_____

5. ____ Use the **pathping** command to the same Internet site used for the **tracert** command. For example, **pathping www.comcast.net**. Answer the following questions based on the result of the **pathping** command?

How many hops were encountered along the route? _____

How long was the delay for calculating statistics of the trace? _____

_____

_____

6. ____ Now use the **/?** switch to look at additional information about the **tracert** command.

Which switch can be used to change the default number of hops? _____

Which switch can be used to change the default wait time of each reply? _____

What is the unit of time used to measure wait time? _____

7. ____ Now use the **/?** switch to answer the following questions about the **pathping** command.

Which switch is used to change the default number of hops? _____

Which switch is used to change the timeout period to wait for a reply? _____

Which switch is used to change the wait period between echo request packets? _____

Which switch is used to increase the total number of queries per hop? _____

Which switch is used to restrict the test to using only IPv6 type packets? _____

8. ____ Answer the review questions.

Copyright by Goodheart-Willcox Co., Inc.

Review Questions

1. The **pathping** command is a combination of which two commands? _____

   _____

2. Which command will provide the quickest check of a network path and verify that a complete connection exists between the source computer and the destination device? _____

3. Which command will produce a detailed analysis of the network path between two devices and includes the most detailed packet analysis? _____

4. Which command takes the greatest amount of time to complete? _____

5. What can cause a failure of the **ping**, **tracert**, and **pathping** commands? _____

   _____

   _____

   _____

6. What is the purpose of ICMP packets? _____

   _____

Copyright by Goodheart-Willcox Co., Inc.

Name _____ Date _____

Class/Instructor _____

Using the Windows XP Network Setup Wizard

After completing this laboratory activity, you will be able to:

■ Set up a SOHO network using the Windows XP Network Setup Wizard.

■ Explain three ways to access the Network Setup Wizard.

■ Explain the various options available through the Network Setup Wizard.

Introduction

One of the many nice features of Windows XP is the different wizards available that make life easier for not only the novice but also the experienced technician. It is very easy to forget something important when performing tasks such as setting up a small network. A wizard is comparable to an automated list of important steps needed to complete a task. While all wizards will not solve every installation problem, they can make installation easier.

Remember, wizards aren't foolproof. Plenty of things do go wrong even when using them on a small network. The advantage of using Windows XP Network Setup Wizard is it is easy to use and requires only a minimum knowledge of networking. The disadvantage is you may leave security holes by relying on the default settings. Security is often left nonexistent, especially by novice users. If you are setting up a share using TCP/IP, keep in mind that not only can all computers in the workgroup see other workgroup computers, computers outside the workgroup can access all the computers in the workgroup. Be sure to put the proper security in place by doing things such as configuring the firewall or incorporating a gateway.

The Network Setup Wizard is designed for small-office/home-office (SOHO) networks. It is not intended to use on large complicated networks because of the IP addresses that are assigned automatically by the wizard. The Network Setup Wizard typically assigns non-registered IP addresses as identified by the Internet authority.

Non-registered IP Address Ranges:
10.0.0.0—10.255.255.255
172.16.0.0—172.16.255.255
192.168.0.0—192.168.255.255

When running the Network Setup Wizard, a series of step-by-step dialog boxes appear on the screen. Be sure to read carefully each screen presentation to avoid missing any important information and making an improper selection. Some installers rapidly go through a wizard clicking **Next** without reading the dialog options or explanations. Default selections do not always work for every possible network configuration. That is why choices are presented in the first place.

Networking wizards are available through a number of operating systems. Most of the wizards generate a disk when you run the wizard for the first time on a network. The disk contains configuration data to be used on other computers in the network. Using the wizard eliminates the need to manually assign IP addresses, the DHCP server location, and WINS server location.

The Network Setup Wizard gives you an option to generate a floppy disk to set up other computers in the SOHO network. The disk generated during the wizard installation contains configuration data identifying the PC with the Internet connection, the workgroup name, and a list of IP addresses that have already been issued. This prevents issuing the same IP address to two or more PCs. Duplicate IP addresses will cause problems in the network. Only one of the PCs among those with the same IP address will be able to communicate on the network.

If all the computers in the peer-to-peer network are using Windows XP, you do not need to use the generated disk. You can use the Network Setup Wizard at these computers. When the Network Setup Wizard is run, it accesses the host PC for the configuration data. Remember that a computer that connects directly to the Internet is referred to as the host and will share the connection with the computers referred to as clients. For the host to provide Internet access, Internet Connection Sharing (ICS) must be established on the host PC. *Always* set up the host first and then configure the clients.

Equipment and Materials

- A minimum of two computers: one with Windows XP and Internet access through a dial-up connection and the other with Windows 98, Me, or XP installed. (Do not use Windows NT, 2000, or Vista for this laboratory activity.)
- 3 1/2″ floppy disk.

Note:

You will need to have administrative privileges on each of the workstations to complete this lab activity.

Note:

A dial-up Internet connection is not an absolute necessity for this lab activity. This activity can be completed without any type of Internet connection or by using another form of Internet connection.

Note:

If your lab has a security software system installed, you may have some problems with the lab activity. In such cases, set up a small peer-to-peer network without a connection to the Internet or the regular network system.

Procedure

1. ____ Report to your assigned workstation.

2. ____ Boot the computer and verify it is in working order.

3. ____ Access the **Network Setup Wizard** by opening **Control Panel** and double-clicking **Network Connections**.

4. ____ From the **Network Tasks** menu on the left side of the screen, select **Set up a home or small office network**.

5. ____ Close the **Network Setup Wizard** and access the wizard by going through **Start I All Programs I Accessories I Communications I Network Setup Wizard**.

6. ____ Close the **Network Setup Wizard** and access the wizard once more by right-clicking **My Network Places** and selecting **Properties**.

Copyright by Goodheart-Willcox Co., Inc.

7. ____ From the **Network Tasks** menu on the left side of the screen, select **Set up a home or small office network**.

8. ____ Repeat the three access methods indicated in steps 3 through 7 as many times as necessary to be able to remember them in the future before going on.

9. ____ Open the **Network Setup Wizard** by using any one of the three methods. The "Welcome to the Network Setup Wizard" screen will display.

Network Setup Wizard

Welcome to the Network Setup Wizard

This wizard will help you set up this computer to run on your network. With a network you can:

* Share an Internet connection
* Set up Internet Connection Firewall
* Share files and folders
* Share a printer

To continue, click Next.

< Back   Next >   Cancel

In the space provided, list the four things that can be accomplished with the Network Setup Wizard.

_____

_____

_____

_____

10. ____ Click the **Next** button. The **Before you continue** dialog box will display.

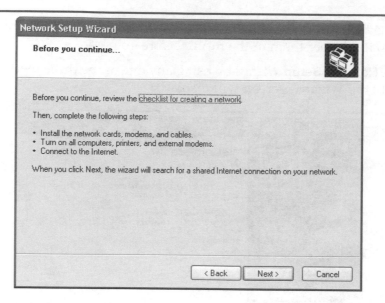

Near the top of the dialog box, you are prompted to review the checklist for creating a network. Do *not* click the <u>checklist for creating a network</u> link at this time. Instead, list the three steps that should be completed in the space provided.

_____

_____

_____

11. ____ Now, click the <u>checklist for creating a network</u> link. An extensive listing will appear in the Help and Support Center similar to the one below. The same information provided here can be also accessed through **Start | Help and Support** at any time.

Copyright by Goodheart-Willcox Co., Inc.

12. ____ Scroll down the listing to see what type of information is available. You may wish to minimize the Help and Support Center before moving on so that it can be referenced at any time during the installation process.

13. ____ Click the **Next** button. The **Select a connection method** dialog box will appear. You are prompted to select the statement that best describes the computer on which you are running the Network Setup Wizard. Write these three statements in the space provided.

_____

_____

_____

_____

14. ____ Select the appropriate statement and click **Next**. The series of screens and selections after the **Select a connection method** dialog box will vary according to the choice made in this step. Follow the series of screen prompts until the host computer and the clients are all configured. Remember, you can use the 3 1/2" floppy to create a disk that will assist in setting up the clients.

15. ____ Test the connection to the Internet from each workstation. Be sure you can connect to the Internet. If you experience problems connecting, be sure of the following:

■ The host is connected to the Internet. No other workstations will be able to access the Internet unless the host is connected.

■ There is no firewall protection activated on any workstation except the one making a direct connection to the Internet.

■ Each workstation uses a unique name.

■ Each workstation is using the same workgroup name.

■ Each workstation is using the same subnet mask.

16. ____ Set up a shared directory on one of the networked computers. Create a short text file and save it in the shared directory. The text file content can be anything. In the space provided, write the complete directory path to the shared file.

_____

17. ____ Set up a shared printer on one of the networked computers. In the space provided, write the complete path for the printer share. Be careful to use the correct slashes (backward, forward) when writing down the path name.

_____

18. ____ Have your instructor inspect your project.

19. ____ After your instructor has checked your project, return all materials to their proper storage area. Your instructor may want you to repeat this lab activity using different Internet connection types as well as a variety of networking materials.

20. ____ Complete the review questions. You may use Help and Support located on a Windows XP computer.

Copyright by Goodheart-Willcox Co., Inc.

Review Questions

1. What are the three ranges of non-registered IP addresses? _____
   _____
   _____

2. What does the acronym SOHO represent? _____

3. List several ways the Network Setup Wizard can be accessed. _____
   _____
   _____
   _____
   _____

4. What does the acronym ICS represent? _____

5. Which computer is identified as the host in an ICS configuration? _____
   _____

6. What is the name of the file that starts the network setup 3 1/2" floppy? _____
   _____

7. What symbols are not allowed as part of the computer name? (See Help and Support.)
   _____

8. What is the maximum number of characters permitted in a computer name? _____

9. Can spaces be left in the name—for example, "Station 12"? _____

10. Is it best to leave the workgroup name the same as the computer name?_____

Copyright by Goodheart-Willcox Co., Inc.

Name _____ Date _____

Class/Instructor _____

Windows Vista Public Folder Sharing

After completing this laboratory activity, you will be able to:

- Explain the differences between Windows XP and Windows Vista file and folder sharing.
- Explain the purpose of the Public folder.
- Change the Public folder permissions using the options available in the Network and Sharing Center.
- View all shared folders on a workstation by using Computer Management.
- Identify common problems associated with Public folder shares.

Introduction

In this laboratory activity, you will experiment with Windows Vista Public folder sharing. Windows Vista uses two network sharing models: Public folder sharing and standard (NTFS) file sharing. Public folder sharing is similar to Windows XP Simple File Sharing model except that Public file sharing can be used on the same computer that is running standard file sharing. Windows XP Simple File Sharing cannot be used on the same computer at the same time standard file sharing is used.

The Network and Sharing Center interface contains the following options for file and folder sharing: **File sharing**, **Public folder sharing**, and **Password protected sharing**. The **File sharing** option allows folders (directories) and individual files to be shared by the host computer and be accessed by client computers on the network.

The **Public folder sharing** option can be configured in three different ways. First, it can allow anyone with network access to access the contents of the Public folder. Second, it can allow anyone with network access to change and create folders in the Public folder. Third, it can deny access to network users but still allow local computer users to access the Public folder. The **Password protected sharing** option allows people who have a password-protected local user account on the host computer to access the shared Public folder or the shared printer. The following screen capture shows each of these options.

Copyright by Goodheart-Willcox Co., Inc.

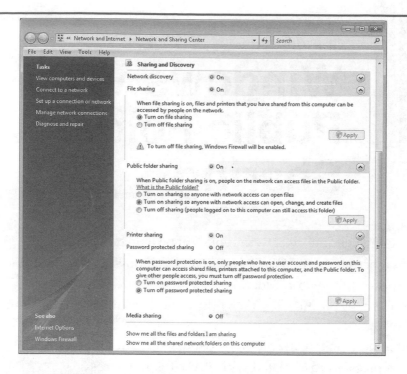

Notice that the Public folder can be automatically reconfigured to accommodate the most common sharing scenarios encountered on a small, home network. Microsoft does not recommend using the Public folder method of sharing for business office purposes. Public folder sharing is basically an all or nothing sharing model that provides one of three share permission: read-only, full control, and no access.

Look once more at the Network and Sharing Center screen capture and locate the two links at the bottom. These two links will allow you to see what files and folders you are sharing and all the shared folders on the computer. These links are very handy because they can help you keep track of the files and folders being shared. You can also see a list of all shared files and folders in Computer Management.

Public folder sharing can be affected by configuring other items on the computer. The following is a list of things that can possibly affect the access of a shared file or folder.

■ Changing the computer location from Public to Private will enable the firewall and may prevent other users from accessing a shared folder, even if it is the Public folder.

■ Third-party firewalls may prevent access to a share. Windows Firewall does automatically change the firewall configuration to allow for shares the first time shares are created, but the firewall configuration can change, especially in a lab setting where more than one student uses a computer workstation.

■ Windows Vista standard users cannot create shares or change share permissions on another network computer. Only an administrator or equal to administrator user can create or modify a share in the network. A standard user can create or modify a share if they know the administrator password.

■ Changing the directory location of a share after configuring the share changes the path to the share. Also, changing the path to the share can make the share inaccessible.

■ Changing the password requirement may cause other users not to be able to access a share. This is especially true if the user does not use a password for logon. They simply select their user icon and then immediately access the desktop without the need of a password.

■ Changing permissions on a file or folder can make the file or folder inaccessible by a particular user or group.

■ Placing a standard share folder inside the Public folder can cause a conflict in folder access permissions.

Copyright by Goodheart-Willcox Co., Inc.

- Moving a share to inside a shared folder can cause a problem with access. For example, if a file with full access is placed inside a folder with read-only access, the file will become read-only.
- Changing an account user name can make a share inaccessible. Also, deleting a user account and then recreating an account using the exact same name will cause share access problems.
- Changing the network location from Private to Public can affect share access.

As you can see, there are many different possibilities that indirectly can change the accessibility of a shared folder or file.

To learn more about Windows Vista sharing, conduct a Google search using the term "File and Print Sharing in Windows Vista bb727037." The article is located on the Microsoft TechNet Web site and provides the latest information about Windows Vista network sharing. Or, use the following link: http://technet.microsoft.com/en-us/library/bb727037.aspx.

Equipment and Materials

- A peer-to-peer network with two Windows Vista workstations. The lab activity can be further enhanced by adding an additional Windows XP workstation. The host computer requires an NTFS partition

> **Note:**
> This lab activity can be performed by two students, one student using the host computer and the other student using the client.

Procedure

1. ____ Identify two Windows Vista workstations connected as a peer-to-peer network. Designate one as the host and the other as the client.

2. ____ Boot both computers and verify they are in working order.

3. ____ On both the host and the client, open the Network and Sharing Center and check if **Network Discovery** is set to **On**.

4. ____ At the host computer, turn on **File sharing** and **Public folder sharing**. Enable the second option under **Public folder sharing**: **Turn on sharing so anyone with network access can open, change, and create files**.

5. ____ At the host, use WordPad to create a short document containing the following text "This is a sample file to share." And then save the file as "Test File 1" to the Public Document folder.

6. ____ From the client computer, try to access and open Test File 1 located in the Public folder on the host computer. You can access it by double-clicking **Network** located off the **Start** menu and then double-clicking the host computer's icon. All available shares should appear. Double-click the Public folder and then double-click the Public Documents folder. If you cannot access the shared folder or file, call your instructor for assistance.

7. ____ Change the contents of Test File 1 by typing the additional word *change* at the end of the sentence and then save the file. The permissions on the folder and file are such that you can change the contents of the file.

8. ____ At the client computer, close the open file and then close all dialog boxes.

9. ____ At the host computer, change the permission of the Public folder to read-only by changing the option in the **Public folder sharing** section to **Turn on sharing so anyone with network access can open files**. Click **Apply**.

Copyright by Goodheart-Willcox Co., Inc.

10. _____ From the client computer, open the Public Documents folder located on the host computer. Change the contents of the Test File1 file by deleting the contents of the file. Then, attempt to save the change. A message should appear on the screen similar to the one below, telling you that the file is read-only.

As you have experienced, you can view the contents of a read-only file, but you cannot change the contents.

11. _____ From the same client computer, try to create a new folder in the Public Documents folder located on the host computer. You will see a message box informing you that you do not have the proper permission to perform this action.

12. _____ From the client computer, try to delete Test File1 on the host computer by right-clicking the file and selecting **Delete** from the shortcut menu. Again, you should be denied permission to delete the file.

13. _____ If two students are performing this lab activity, switch roles now and repeat the lab activity.

14. _____ Now, at the host computer, open Computer Management. You can open Computer Management by accessing the **Start** menu, right-clicking **Computer**, and selecting **Manage** from the shortcut menu. Computer Management will open and look similar to the following.

Copyright by Goodheart-Willcox Co., Inc.

15. ____ Expand the Computer Management **Shared Folders** section by double-clicking **Shared Folders** and then double-clicking **Shares**. The **Shared Folders** will expand and all shares located on the computer will be shown just like that in the following screen capture.

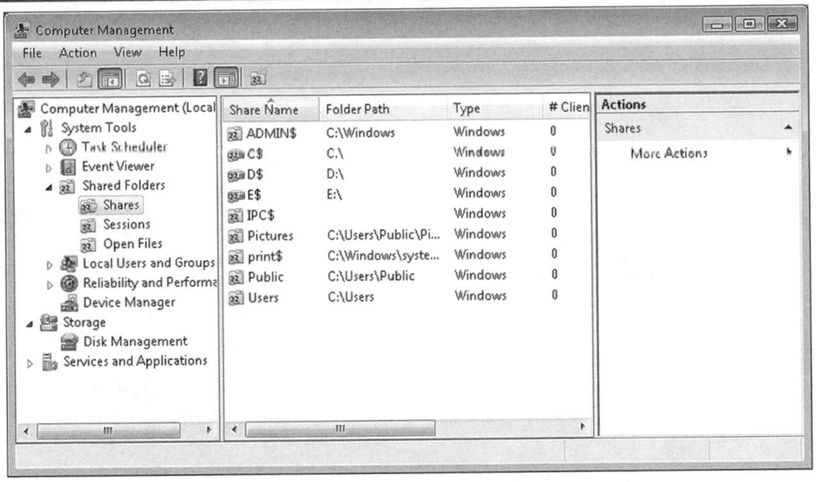

Notice the two other options in the **Shared Folders** section: **Sessions** and **Open Files**. These two options will show you shares being accessed and by who at this moment. It will also allow you to close shares or disconnect users from the share.

In the center pane, notice the special folders that contain a dollar sign ($) at the end of the folder name. The dollar sign indicates administrative folders. These folders are not for user access and are hidden folders that do not appear on the network when viewed from other computers.

16. ____ In the center pane of Computer Management, double-click the Public folder. The **Public Properties** dialog box will appear similar to the one in the following screen capture.

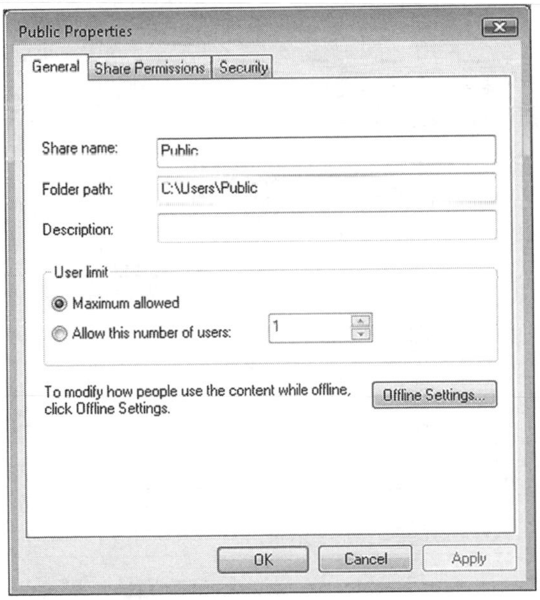

You will see the name of the share, the folder path, and the number of users allowed to simultaneously access the folder. Microsoft uses the term *concurrent users*, which means simultaneous users. The maximum allowed is ten users by default, but you have an option to permit a lesser number than ten.

Copyright by Goodheart-Willcox Co., Inc.

17. ____ Select the **Share Permissions** tab and you will see who has permission to access the folder and what the permission is set to for a user or group.

As you can see in the screen capture, the group Everyone only has the read permission. Select the Administrators group and watch as the permissions change to full control, change, and read. You also have an option to add additional users to the list and assign permissions. The sharing properties under the **Share Permission** tab is based on the Windows Vista Public folder sharing model.

18. ____ Select the **Security** tab and you will see a more detailed set of permissions and users. This set of users and groups permissions is based on the standard (NTFS) model of sharing.

19. ____ If time permits, you may take a few minutes to experiment with the file permissions.

20. ____ Close all dialog boxes at this time and then go on to answer the review questions.

Copyright by Goodheart-Willcox Co., Inc.

Review Questions

1. How does Windows Vista Public folder sharing differ from Windows XP Simple File Sharing?

_____

_____

_____

2. What three major options in Network and Sharing Center affect how shares and the Public folder are shared in the local network? _____

_____

3. What are the three options available for the Public file sharing configuration? _____

_____

_____

_____

4. Which Public file sharing option is the same as the read-only permission? _____

_____

5. What are the three folder permissions associated with the Public folder? _____

_____

6. What does the dollar sign signify behind a share name? _____

_____

_____

7. What affect does the **Password protected sharing** option have on a share? _____

_____

Copyright by Goodheart-Willcox Co., Inc.

Notes

Computer Service and Repair Lab Manual

Copyright by Goodheart-Willcox Co., Inc.

Name _____ Date _____

Class/Instructor _____

Windows Security Center Firewall

After completing this laboratory activity, you will be able to:

■ Enable and disable firewall protection.

■ Explain how a firewall protects the computer system.

Introduction

A firewall is a centerpiece in network security. It is designed to control the flow of inbound and outbound packets from network adapters, such as wireless network adapters, wired network adapters, telephone modems, and Cable modems. The firewall protects against unauthorized access from the Internet and some forms of malicious software. A firewall protects the computer by monitoring such items as the IP address of the source, the port address being used, the software program application name, and the content of packets sent to and from the computer.

Microsoft Windows first introduced the firewall in Windows XP. It referred to the firewall as Internet Connection Firewall (ICF). In Windows Vista, the ICF has evolved into a more enhanced version and is now referred to as the Firewall. The original Windows XP ICF only monitored inbound packets. Later, as part of Windows XP SP 2, the firewall was modified to monitor both inbound and outbound packets. The Windows Vista version monitors both packet types and is composed of a simple user interface and a much more advanced interface. The Windows Vista advanced firewall interface requires a much more in-depth understanding of firewall protection similar to the type of protection found on network servers and network security devices. The advanced configuration options will only be briefly introduced in this lab activity, as there is no need of real mastery of the advanced options.

Note:

There is quite a bit of conflicting information about the configuration of the Windows firewall. Always take into consideration the source of the information. This lab activity and the information within are based on the very latest Microsoft sources. There is a great deal of misinformation from other sources, especially on the Internet, about the firewall and how it should be configured.

The Windows Firewall can protect a computer system from some forms of malicious software, such as worms, but not necessarily if the worm is attached to an e-mail that is opened by the user. The firewall protection is limited to some extent by user interaction. Another example is when the user downloads or runs a program found on the Internet. The firewall produces a dialog box informing the user that a program is attempting to connect to the computer. The user has the option to allow or not allow the program to connect to the computer. The firewall warned the user, but the user must make the final decision, directly affecting computer security.

Windows Firewall is integrated into the Windows Internet Explorer and Windows networking. Both can be directly affected by the firewall settings.

Copyright by Goodheart-Willcox Co., Inc.

Note:

Windows Firewall has been known to change in appearance and function when some major service packs or some hot fixes have been installed on the computer. For example, when Windows XP introduced Internet Connection Firewall (ICF), it was disabled by default. When Windows XP SP 2 was installed, the Windows Firewall was enabled by default, thus causing some problems, especially on network systems.

There should be only one firewall running on a network. Two or more firewalls on a single network can cause problems with such things as Internet access and sharing folders and other devices. Today, most small networks found in the home or small office setting contain a device that shares an Internet connection with all the computers in the network, both wired and wireless. The device designed to share the Internet connection is usually referred to as a router or a gateway. The modern routers typically contain a firewall program. When the router contains a firewall program, it is usually best to use the router firewall.

Firewall configuration involves restricting access based on port numbers, IP addresses, and packet contents. Port numbers range from 1 to 65535 and are associated with specific programs and services. When a network connection is made between two computers or devices, the port number tells the packet which software program or services will use the packet information. For example, port 110 is used by the POP3 Post Office Protocol. When a POP3 e-mail is received by the computer, port 110 is part of the packet address. The computer knows to redirect the packet to the e-mail client on the computer. If port 110 is blocked, then the computer can not receive e-mail based on the POP3 specification. If the port number in the packet is 80, the computer knows the packet is a Web page and will redirect the packet to the browser program. If port 80 is blocked, the computer browser will not be able to receive Web pages from Internet.

To learn much more about port numbers, visit www.iana.org/assignments/port-numbers. For more detailed information about Windows Vista Firewall, visit http://technet.microsoft.com/en-us/library/cc748991.aspx. A TechNet magazine article on Windows Vista Firewall is located at http://technet.microsoft.com/en-us/magazine/cc138010.aspx. For information about problems caused by Windows XP Firewall, visit http://support.microsoft.com/kb/298804, or conduct a Google search using key terms "298804 Internet Firewall."

Equipment and Materials

■ Computer with Windows XP, Windows Vista, or both, installed.

Part I—Windows XP

Procedure

1. ____ Report to your assigned workstation.

2. ____ Boot the computer and verify it is in working order.

578   Computer Service and Repair Lab Manual   Copyright by Goodheart-Willcox Co., Inc.

3. _____ Access the Windows XP Firewall through **Start | Control Panel | Security Center**. You should see the familiar **Windows Security Center** dialog box similar to the following.

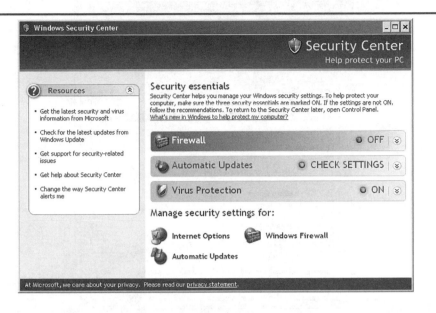

4. _____ Select the **Windows Firewall** option under the **Manage security settings for** section. A dialog box similar to the following will display.

Under the Firewall **General** tab, you can modify the firewall with the options to turn the firewall on or off. The **Don't allow exceptions** option can be selected when the firewall is enabled. When the **Don't allow exceptions** option is not selected, you will see a message dialog box that will prompt you to allow or not allow connections through the firewall. This option is commonly used in public areas, such as airports, coffee shops, and other hot spots.

5. _____ Select the **Exceptions** tab. A dialog box similar to the following will appear.

Your dialog box most likely will not contain as many exceptions as the one in the screen capture. Exceptions can be made for specific software programs. Each software program can be enabled or disabled individually. Also, notice that you have buttons to allow you to configure additional programs, ports, or edit existing exceptions. Notice the **Display a notification when Windows Firewall blocks a program** option located near the bottom of the dialog box.

6. _____ Click the **Add Port** button. The **Add a Port** dialog box will display and look similar to the following.

The **Add a Port** dialog box will allow you to select specific ports to block by the firewall. There are over 64,000 different possible ports. This option is only practical when the Windows operating system fails to correctly identify a software application automatically and a specific port is required to block the software applications. To identify the port number you would research the port number using a Microsoft reference, such as from the TechNet or the software application Web site.

    Copyright by Goodheart-Willcox Co., Inc.

7. ____ Click the **Change scope** button. You will see a dialog box similar to the following.

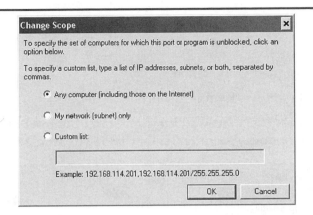

The scope refers to what computers the firewall restriction will affect. You can select specific computers and network devices by IP address or by network address, which is identified by the subnet mask.

8. ____ Close the **Change Scope** dialog box and then select the **Advanced** tab. You will now see a dialog box similar to that in the following screen capture.

Under the Firewall **Advanced** tab, you can select the connection for which to enable or disable the firewall protection. It also provides you with an option to enable security logging. Security logging creates a log file, which can be helpful when troubleshooting suspected problems related to a particular software application and the firewall. Another option is available for configuring aspects of the Internet Control Message Protocol (ICMP). ICMP is commonly used to send and receive error and control messages using the TCP/IP protocol suite. For example, the ICMP settings can be configured to stop the reply from ping requests sent by other computers.

The **Restore Defaults** button does just that, restores the firewall to its default settings. Take a minute and look at the options available for ICMP. Then, close the **Windows Firewall** dialog box.

9. ____ Complete the Windows Vista section before answering the review questions.

Part II—Windows Vista

Procedure

1. _____ Report to your assigned workstation.

2. _____ Boot the computer and verify it is in working order.

3. _____ Access the Windows Vista Firewall through **Start | Control Panel | Security Center**. You should see the familiar **Windows Security Center** dialog box similar to the following.

4. _____ You can also access the Windows Vista Firewall through the Control Panel in a more direct route through **Start | Control Panel | Security | Allow a program through Windows Firewall** or **Start | Control Panel | Security | Windows Firewall**. Try both methods now.

5. _____ Open the Windows Firewall one more time using the following path: **Start | Control Panel | Security | Windows Firewall**. You should see a dialog box similar to the following.

Copyright by Goodheart-Willcox Co., Inc.

6. ____ Click the Change settings link. A dialog box similar to the following will display.

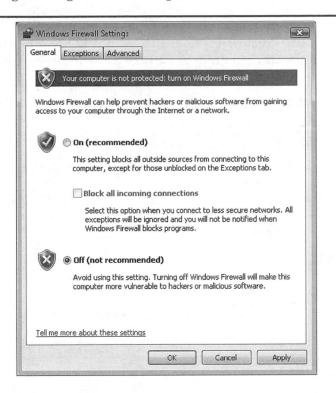

To enable Windows Firewall, simply select the **On** option and to disable the Windows Firewall, select the **Off** option. The **Block all incoming connections** option will not be enabled until the firewall is enabled. Turning the firewall on is the recommended option, but there will be times when you should not enable the firewall. For example, when the computer is connected to a router or gateway that has a firewall incorporated into the device.

7. ____ Select the **Exceptions** tab. A dialog box similar to the following will display.

As software programs are installed on a computer, you are prompted to allow the program to communicate through the Internet or to other devices in a network. When you respond to the prompt by saying the program application is safe, an exception will be created automatically in the firewall. You can also create exceptions manually and identify the program by program name or by the port number the program uses. Take a few minutes to explore the **Add program** and the **Add port** option buttons.

8. ____ Now, select the **Advanced** tab. The following dialog box will display.

The **Advanced** tab will allow you to select a specific network connection and also provide an option to restore defaults. There will be times when working with a firewall you might make so many changes attempting to get a program to work correctly that you may need to reset the computer to the default firewall settings.

One of the big changes between Windows XP and Windows Vista is the relocation of the ICMP and logging settings. Take notice of the <u>Where can I find ICMP and logging settings?</u> link in the lower-left corner of the **Advanced** tab view. This link will take you to Help and Support, but not provide a direct answer to the question. The ICMP and logging options are now considered too advanced for the regular user. There are actually two firewall designs now: Windows Vista Firewall and Windows Vista Firewall with Advanced Security.

Copyright by Goodheart-Willcox Co., Inc.

9. ____ Close any open dialog boxes and then enter "Firewall" into the **Search** box off the **Start** menu. You will see a result similar to that in the partial screen capture below.

The top two results of the Windows Vista search reveals two different programs: Windows Firewall and Windows Firewall with Advanced Security. Select the **Windows Firewall with Advanced Security**. A dialog box similar to the following will display.

The **Windows Firewall with Advanced Security** dialog box provides a user interface with many various options, such as inbound rules, outbound rules, connection security rules, and more. The interface is very extensive and requires an in-depth understanding of firewall technologies. You can learn more by selecting the links at the bottom of the dialog box, provided that you have an Internet connection. Selecting a link topic such as "Getting started" or "Diagnostics and troubleshooting" will automatically connect you to the Microsoft TechNet Web site where the articles are stored. The information in these articles may be well beyond your full comprehension until you have completed a networking fundamentals course. If you have an Internet connection, you may take a few minutes to familiarize yourself with the topics and information available.

Copyright by Goodheart-Willcox Co., Inc.

10. ____ Click **Windows Firewall Properties**, which is located in the middle of the **Windows Firewall and Advanced Security** dialog box. A dialog box similar to the following will display.

The first three tabs correspond to the network locations identified by Windows Vista: Domain, Private, and Public. This advanced feature allows you to change the default settings for a computer configured for Domain, Public, or Private settings, rather than use the default for these locations.

11. ____ Select the **Private Profile** tab and then the **Public Profile** tab to view the options for each location.

Copyright by Goodheart-Willcox Co., Inc.

Notice that each location has similar options and allows you to change the default settings concerning the inbound and outbound packets. Pay particular attention to the default firewall settings (firewall on or off and inbound and outbound blocked or allowed) and the default configuration for each location.

12. _____ Close all dialog boxes and then go on to answer the review questions.

Review Questions

1. How does Windows Firewall provide network security? _____
   _____

2. What does the firewall protect the computer from? _____
   _____

3. When was Windows Firewall first introduced? _____

4. What are ports? _____
   _____
   _____

5. Why has Windows Firewall and Advanced Security not integrated directly into the Windows
   Firewall? _____
   _____
   _____
   _____

6. What is the firewall state for a Public location, on or off? _____

7. What is the outbound and inbound state for a Public location? _____
   _____

8. What is the firewall state for a Private location? _____

Copyright by Goodheart-Willcox Co., Inc.

Name _____ Date _____

Class/Instructor _____

Virtual Private Network Connection

After completing this laboratory activity, you will be able to:

■ Install and configure a virtual private network connection.

■ Describe the characteristics of Point-to-Point Tunneling Protocol.

■ Describe the characteristics of Layer 2 Tunneling Protocol.

Introduction

In this lab activity, you will install a virtual private network (VPN) connection between two computers on a LAN. You will use the New Connection Wizard to configure the VPN connection. The VPN is one of the several options found in the New Connection Wizard.

Virtual private network connections increase security and privacy when two computers are exchanging data. Computer systems exchange data over the Internet and on local area networks using the TCP/IP protocol suite. The TCP/IP specifications and the Internet system are open standards. This means that in this form of public communication, anyone connected to the network (LAN or Internet) is capable of intercepting data packets and viewing the contents.

A VPN is created using either the Point-to-Point Tunneling Protocol (PPTP) or the Layer 2 Tunneling Protocol (L2TP).

PPTP is part of the TCP/IP protocol suite. It allows TCP/IP, IPX/SPX, or NetBEUI packets to be encapsulated inside PPTP frames and transported across an open communication system. The PPTP protocol incorporates authentication, encryption, and compression. Authentication ensures that only authorized persons can view the contents of the frames. Encryption ensures that if the frame is captured, the information inside will remain secure. Compression allows for large collections of data to be compressed and transported in a more efficient manner.

Layer 2 Tunneling Protocol is proprietary and jointly developed by CISCO systems and Microsoft. The characteristics are similar to PPTP, but there are a few differences. The main difference is that L2PT was designed to support data transmission across frame relay, ATM, and X.25 systems in addition to TCP/IP. The Windows XP version only supports TCP/IP. See the following Microsoft articles for more information on setting up and troubleshooting a VPN:

■ 305550: How to Configure a VPN Connection to Your Corporation.

■ 331816: VPN Client in Windows XP Disconnects after 1 Minute.

Note:

Some ISP providers do not permit VPN connections through their access. Also be aware that some routers and switches require special configuration to allow a VPN connection through the device.

Copyright by Goodheart-Willcox Co., Inc.

Equipment and Materials

- Two PCs with any combination of Windows XP and or Windows Vista installed.
- The following information provided by your instructor:

Company name: _____

Client name or IP address: _____

Host name or IP address: _____

Note:

A user name and password must be established on both computers before starting the lab activity. If the user does not have a user account on the computer, a VPN cannot be established because it relies on user authentication to complete the connection between the two computers. You can create a VPN using the New Connection Wizard, but you will not be able to access the host computer.

Part I—Windows XP

Procedure

1. ____ Report to your assigned workstation.

2. ____ Boot both computers and verify they are in working order.

3. ____ Open the **Network Connections** dialog box by right-clicking **My Network Places** located on the **Start** menu and selecting **Properties** from the shortcut menu. Then, select **Create a New Connection** from the **Network Tasks** list.

4. ____ The New Connection Wizard will start. Follow the prompts until you encounter the dialog box similar to the following.

---

5. ____ Select **Connect to the network at my workplace** from the list of options. Pay particular attention to the reference made to "VPN" in the description below it.

Copyright by Goodheart-Willcox Co., Inc.

6. ____ Click **Next**. A dialog box similar to the following will appear.

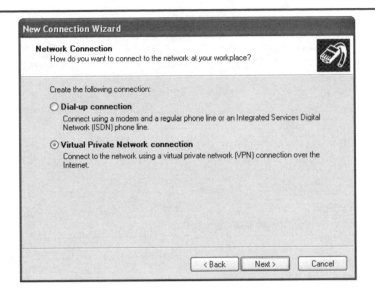

7. ____ Select the **Virtual Private Network connection** option.

8. ____ Click **Next**. A dialog box similar to the following will appear.

9. ____ Type in the company name provided by your instructor. This text box is used to identify the purpose of the VPN connection. It is possible to create more than one VPN connection on a computer.

Copyright by Goodheart-Willcox Co., Inc.

10. ____ Click **Next**. A dialog box similar to the following will appear.

11. ____ Type in the host name or IP address provided by your instructor. Pay particular attention that the host name should be entered in the Fully Qualified Domain Name (FQDN) format. Look at the example that is given in the dialog box.

12. ____ After entering the IP address, click **Next**. A dialog box similar to the following will appear. This dialog box allows you to create a desktop shortcut for the VPN connection. Your instructor must give you permission to create a shortcut.

Copyright by Goodheart-Willcox Co., Inc.

Name_____

13. ____ Click **Finish**. A dialog box similar to the following will appear.

14. ____ Test your VPN connection by entering the user name and password and clicking **Connect**. A connection will be established after the user name and password are authenticated.

15. ____ After accessing the other computer via the VPN, see if you can access any shares on the computer. If you are experiencing problems connecting to the other computer, use the following checklist to resolve the problem.

- Have you created a logon password?
- Have you correctly typed the user name and password? (Check if the [Caps Lock] has been accidentally enabled.)
- Check if the network cable is plugged in.
- Make sure the firewall has been disabled on both computers.
- Check if third-party security and antivirus software is preventing the connection.
- Is Internet Connection Sharing (ICS) installed on one of the network computers? If so, this may cause the VPN connection to fail.

16. ____ Return the computers to their original condition. If you have access to a Windows Vista computer, go on to Part II—Windows Vista. If not, go on to answer the review questions and then return all materials to their proper storage area.

Part II—Windows Vista

> **Note:**
> In this lab activity, you will at first configure a VPN connection without actually establishing a connection. With time permitting and your instructor's approval, you will run the Windows Vista VPN lab a second time using a second computer or a remote server address to actually establish a VPN connection.

Procedure

1. ____ Report to your assigned workstation.

2. ____ Boot both computers and verify they are in working order.

> **Note:**
> If another student used the workstation to create a VPN, some of the dialog boxes may look different. You will need to read carefully and select options to avoid using the already established VPN.

3. ____ Open the Network and Sharing Center and select **Set up a connection or network** from the left pane.

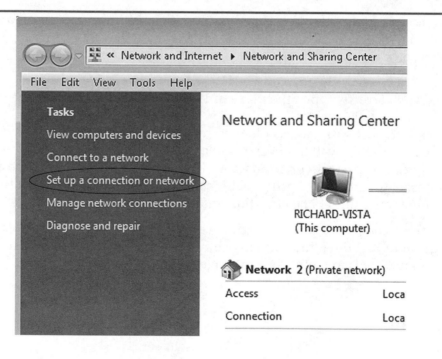

Copyright by Goodheart-Willcox Co., Inc.

4. ____ The Set up a connection or network wizard will appear. Select the **Connect to a work-place** option to start the configuration of a VPN connection.

6. ____ The next dialog box to appear will prompt you to select either a VPN connection through the Internet or to connect using a dial-up modem. Select the **Use my Internet connection (VPN)** option.

7. _____ The next dialog box will prompt you for the Internet address of the destination and a name for the VPN connection.

The Internet address can be an IPv4 or IPv6 IP address or a URL name such as VPN.RMRoberts. com. The destination name is used to identify the connection, which is especially important when you have more than one VPN connection. Also, notice that there are several other configuration options, such as **Use a smart card**, **Allow other people to use this connection**, and **Don't connect now; just set it up so I can connect later**.

For this lab activity, input the IP address of the other computer you are establishing a VPN with. Give it a name such as "VPN test connection." Select the **Don't connect now; just set it up so I can connect later**.

8. _____ The next dialog box to appear informs you that the connection is now ready to use.

If you click **Connect now**, the computer will automatically attempt to establish the VPN connection. Since it does not exist, the diagnostic dialog box will appear. The computer receiving the VPN connection needs to be configured to accept a VPN connection.

Copyright by Goodheart-Willcox Co., Inc.

Name_____

9. ____ Open the Network and Sharing Center and then select the **Manage network connections** option.

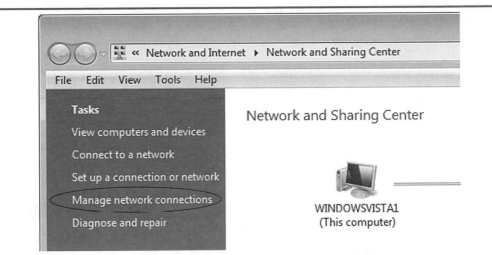

10. ____ Select **New Incoming Connection** from the **File** menu.

11. ____ A dialog box will display prompting you to select the users who can use the VPN connection. Select the users to whom you want to give access.

12. ____ Once the VPN connection is configured, you can start the VPN connection by selecting **Connect To** located off the **Start** menu.

A dialog box similar to the following will display. Select the VPN connection you created and then click **Connect**.

Copyright by Goodheart-Willcox Co., Inc.

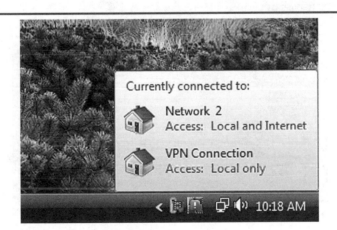

13. ____ When the Vista VPN has been established, you will be able to verify the connection in several ways. First, if the network adapter has been configured to show the network status in the toolbar, you will see the presence of the established VPN connection when the mouse pointer is moved over the network icon as in the following partial screen capture.

You can also open Network and Sharing Center. Notice that in the following screen capture the VPN Connection is listed. You can click the View status link to view the status of the VPN connection.

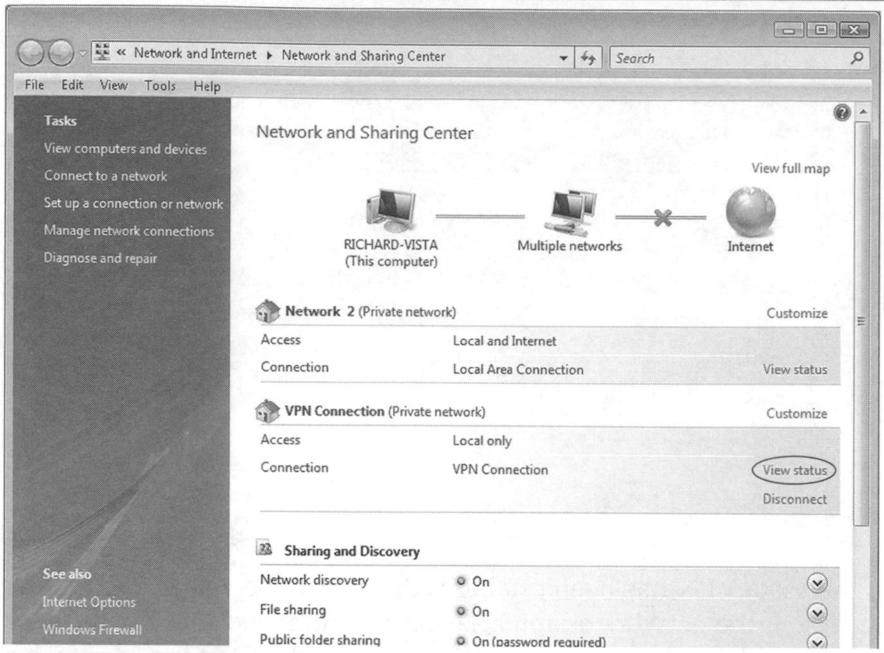

You can also open the **Networking** folder, right-click on the VPN connection icon, and select **Status** from the shortcut menu.

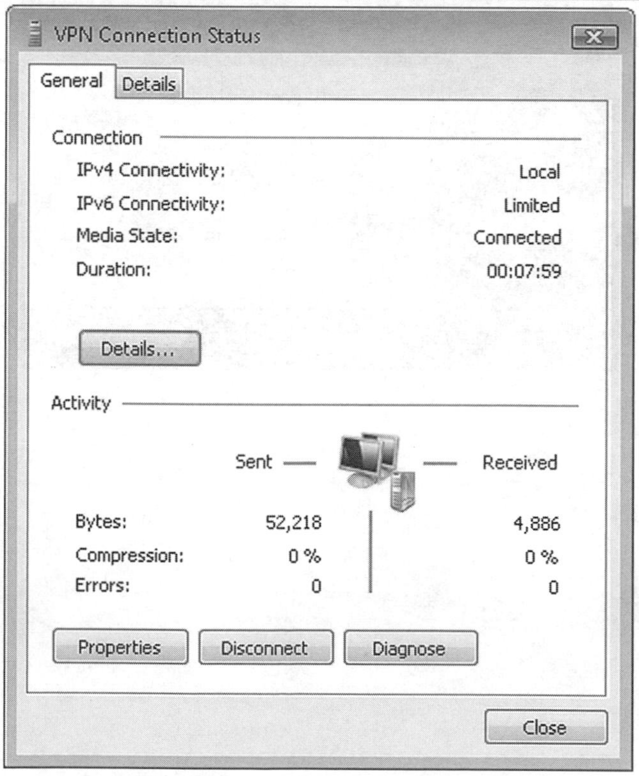

14. ____ Go on to answer the review questions. Then return the computers to their original condition and return all materials to their proper storage area.

Copyright by Goodheart-Willcox Co., Inc.

Name_____

Review Questions

1. Which two tunneling protocols are associated with VPN?_____

2. Which tunneling protocol was jointly developed by CISCO systems and Microsoft?_____

3. Which protocols can be passed through a VPN using PPTP?_____

_____

4. What two methods are used to identify the host computer?_____

_____

5. What must be established on each computer before configuring the VPN?_____

Copyright by Goodheart-Willcox Co., Inc.

Notes

Copyright by Goodheart-Willcox Co., Inc.

Name _____ Date _____

Class/Instructor _____

Internet Connection Sharing

After completing this laboratory activity, you will be able to:

■ Configure Internet Connection Sharing (ICS).

■ Explain the purpose of a default gateway or ICS host.

■ Explain the assignment of IP addresses in an ICS peer-to-peer network.

Introduction

This laboratory activity shows you how a single Internet connection can be shared by multiple PCs. The Windows Internet Connection Sharing (ICS) feature is especially useful for a home office and is available in Windows 98 SE (Second Edition), Windows Me, Windows 2000, Windows XP, and Windows Vista. The ICS program is installed on the host computer only. The host computer connects to the Internet through typical means, such as a modem, ISDN adapter, or Cable modem. The connection is then shared with other computers through a peer-to-peer network.

An IP address is composed of four octets. Each octet represents a range of decimal numbers from 0 to 255. The host is assigned IP address 192.168.0.1. The other PCs are assigned IP addresses such as 192.168.0.2 and 192.168.0.3. In this example, the last octet uniquely identifies the individual PC station, and the first three octets identify the network. Therefore, this network has a subnet mask of 255.255.255.0, which identifies it as a Class C network.

Default gateway is another name for the ICS host. In a large network system, the default gateway is usually the file server. In a smaller ICS network system, the default gateway is an individual computer that connects directly with the Internet and shares the connection with the ICS clients. The default gateway may also be a special device usually referred to as a *router*. The typical small-office/home-office (SOHO) network router consists of several RJ-45 cable ports and a wireless port. The router provides DNS and DHCP services for the network. The default gateway is the only device seen from the Internet, and it has two assigned IP addresses. The first IP address is the IP address assigned to the gateway device by the Internet provider. The second IP address is the ICS host address. Look at the following screen capture.

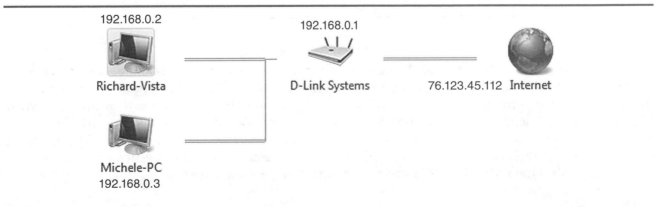

192.168.0.2
Richard-Vista

Michele-PC
192.168.0.3

192.168.0.1
D-Link Systems

76.123.45.112 Internet

Copyright by Goodheart-Willcox Co., Inc.

In the illustration, you can see that the D-Link Systems router is assigned two IP addresses. The first IP address is 192.168.0.1 and identifies the D-link router as the ICS Host. The second IP address 76.123.45.112 is the address assigned by the Internet provider and that is used for the D-Link router Internet connection. The D-link Internet connection is shared with the other local network computers and devices, including printers when applicable.

The gateway or ICS host has several duties to perform. The ICS host provides the DNS service, which resolves the names of the individual computers to their assigned IP addresses. The ICS host is also the default DHCP server, which supplies and keeps track of all assigned IP addresses used by all other computers and devices on the local network.

There are two ways to assign IP addresses to ICS client PCs: manually and automatically. The **Internet Protocol (TCP/IP) Properties** dialog box, accessed through the **Local Area Connection Network Properties** dialog box, is where the manual or automatic method is selected. Look at the following screen capture of a typical Windows XP **Internet Protocol (TCP/IP) Properties** dialog box. To manually assign the IP address, select **Use the following IP address**. To automatically assign the IP address, select **Obtain an IP address automatically**.

When manually assigning IP addresses, you must access the **Local Area Connection Network Properties** dialog box of each client computer and enter a unique IP address. The IP address must be within the proper range. For the example, each computer must have a unique IP address between 192.168.0.2 and 192.168.0.254. You cannot use 192.168.0.0 or 192.168.0.255 for any ICS client. These addresses are reserved addresses used for special network broadcast communications. The subnet mask for each computer must be set to 255.255.255.0. The subnet mask identifies which part of the IP address describes the individual PCs and which part describes the network.

Copyright by Goodheart-Willcox Co., Inc.

When assigning IP addresses automatically, you must access the **Internet Protocol (TCP/IP) Properties** dialog box on each PC and select **Obtain an IP address automatically**. To access the **Internet Protocol (TCP/IP) Properties** dialog box, access the **Local Area Connection Network Properties** dialog box. Next, select **Internet Protocol (TCP/IP)** from the configuration listing. If there is more than one TCP/IP configuration listed, select the one that refers to the network adapter, not the dial-up network. Next, click the **Properties** button to reveal the **Internet Protocol (TCP/IP) Properties** dialog box.

Both Windows XP and Windows Vista automatically locate the ICS host and accept the DHCP assigned IP address. The Network Setup Wizard will automatically prompt you for a storage device, such as a USB Flash drive to save automatic configuration information for client computer IP address assignments.

Equipment and Materials

- Minimum of two PCs with Windows XP or Windows Vista installed, connected as a peer-to-peer network (one PC designated as the ICS host and the other as the client).
- Internet connection for the ICS host. (There is an option available that will allow you to create the ICS host even when an Internet connection is not available at this time.)
- A USB Flash drive may be required to create an automatic configuration file for the network adapter.

Note:

You may also use a router or gateway device as assigned by your instructor since it is the most common way ICS is configured. When using a router or gateway device, be sure to read the manual for the device or visit the manufacturer's Web site to learn how to configure the ICS host device. Most will automatically set up the shared Internet shared connection.

Part I—Windows XP

Procedure

1. ____ Report to your assigned Windows XP host computer. The host device or computer must have an Internet connection.

2. ____ Boot the host computer and verify it is in working order.

3. ____ After booting the host computer, open the Help and Support Center and conduct a search for "ICS." Review the results for the following articles: "Internet Connection Sharing overview," "Internet Connection Sharing settings," and "Choosing Your Internet Connection host computer."

Copyright by Goodheart-Willcox Co., Inc.

4. ____ Close the Help and Support Center and then open the Network Setup Wizard located at **Start | All Programs | Accessories | Communications | Network Setup Wizard**. A dialog box similar to the following will display. As you can see, the Network Setup Wizard can be used to share an Internet connection and more.

5. ____ Click **Next**. The next dialog box to appear provides an opportunity to open the Help and Support Center to learn more about configuring network connections. Select the <u>checklist for creating a network</u> link and take a few minutes to review the information.

6. ____ Close the Help and Support Center and then click **Next**. Follow the rest of the screen prompts until the wizard is completed. Read each dialog and message box completely. There are many different options and one will match your situation perfectly.

Copyright by Goodheart-Willcox Co., Inc.

7. ____ After completing the Network Setup Wizard, test the installation by booting all PCs in the peer-to-peer network and then accessing the Internet. The ICS host must be connected to the Internet before the clients can access the Internet. If the ICS system fails, check the following items:

- All PCs are set to obtain an IP address automatically through DHCP.
- Windows Firewall is enabled only for the ICS host computer for the network adapter assigned to the Internet provider connection. All other network adapters should not have the firewall enabled.
- File sharing is enabled for each network adapter card.

You may use the troubleshooting feature of the Help and Support Center to assist you in further diagnostics.

8. ____ When the lab activity has been completed, check with your instructor to see if the computers need to be returned to their original state.

Part II—Windows Vista

Procedure

1. ____ Report to your assigned Windows Vista host computer. The host device or computer must have an Internet connection.

2. ____ Boot the computer and verify it is in working order.

3. ____ After booting the PC, access Windows Help and Support located off the **Start** menu. Conduct a search using the term "ICS." Review the results for the following articles: "Using ICS (Internet Connection Sharing)," "Set up a shared Internet Connection using ICS (Internet Connection Sharing)," and "Sharing one Internet connection among several computers."

4. ____ Close Help and Support Center and then open the Network Setup Wizard located at **Start | Control Panel | Network and Internet | Network Sharing Center | Set up a connection or network**. You should see the **Set up a connection or network** dialog box similar to that in the following screen capture.

5. ____ Select the **Connect to the Internet** option. The next dialog box to appear will be similar to the following. The exact appearance will depend on which types of physical connections are possible on the computer because Windows Vista will automatically detect the possible connection adapters present.

Notice there is even an option for a connection adapter that was not automatically detected. Choose the appropriate connection for the computer. If you are not sure, call your instructor for assistance.

6. ____ The remaining Network Setup Wizard dialog boxes will prompt you to select options and input information, depending on the specific factors in your computer arrangement. Read each one carefully before proceeding to the next Network Setup Wizard screen.

7. ____ Test the installation by booting all PCs in the peer-to-peer network and then accessing the Internet. The ICS host must be connected to the Internet before the clients can access the Internet. If the ICS system fails, check the following items:

- All PCs are set to obtain an IP address automatically through DHCP.
- Windows Firewall is enabled only for the ICS host computer for the network adapter assigned to the Internet service provider connection. All other network adapters should not have the firewall enabled.
- File sharing is enabled for each network adapter card.

You may use the diagnostic feature built into the Network and Sharing Center to assist you with a failed setup.

8. ____ When the lab activity has been completed, check with your instructor to see if the computers need to be returned to their original state.

Copyright by Goodheart-Willcox Co., Inc.

Review Questions

1. What does the acronym ICS represent? _____
   _____

2. What is the IP address assigned to the peer-to-peer network in this activity? _____
   _____

3. What is the default subnet mask of the IP address 192.168.0.0? _____
   _____

4. What IP address identifies the ICS host in this activity? _____
   _____

Copyright by Goodheart-Willcox Co., Inc.

Copyright by Goodheart-Willcox Co., Inc.

Name _____ Date _____

Class/Instructor _____

SOHO Performance Test

After completing this laboratory activity, you will be able to:

- Demonstrate competence in SOHO network design.
- Demonstrate competence in SOHO network configuration.

Introduction

In this lab activity, you will design and configure a small-office/home-office (SOHO) network based on the type of Internet connection your instructor tells you to use, for example, a DSL or a 56 k modem. The SOHO network should share an Internet connection and a printer. You will make a materials list for this project. The materials list should include any additional hardware that may be required. You will then make a drawing representing the SOHO network based on the information supplied by the instructor. The drawing should include the relative placement of objects in the network and the approximate pathway of any cables required for the network. Have your instructor check the materials list and drawing before you proceed to install and configure the SOHO network.

Both Windows XP and Windows Vista have a great deal of information located in the **Help and Support** option off the **Start** menu. Conduct searches using the key word "network" and view the results. For more information about Microsoft Windows Vista, visit the following link: https://windowshelp.microsoft.com/Windows/en-US/default.mspx. You will see many "How to" articles directly related to this lab activity.

Equipment and Materials

You will create an equipment and materials list similar to the following. Your list will vary depending on the information provided by your instructor.

- Two or more PCs.
- Network adapters.
- Cables.
- Printer.
- One or more of the following: router, hub, switch.
- Modem (56 k dial-up, ISDN, DSL, or Cable).
- Needed drivers and software for network cards, modem, and printer.

Procedure

1. _____ Create a materials list for SOHO network and Internet connection described by your instructor.

Materials List

_____

_____

_____

_____

_____

_____

_____

2. _____ Draw the SOHO network and Internet connection described by your instructor.

Copyright by Goodheart-Willcox Co., Inc.

3. _____ After the instructor has approved your materials list and drawing, gather all required materials and report to your assigned workstation.

4. _____ Install all necessary hardware components and then configure the network as specified by your instructor.

5. _____ Set up and configure network shares as specified by your instructor.

6. _____ Test the network configuration.

7. _____ Have your instructor inspect your project.

8. _____ After the instructor has inspected your project and you have completed any additional instructions from the instructor, return all materials to their original storage area.

Copyright by Goodheart-Willcox Co., Inc.   Laboratory Activity 86   613

Copyright by Goodheart-Willcox Co., Inc.